FRENCH PROPERTY AND INHERIT
PRINCIPLES AND PRACT

FRENCH PROPERTY AND INHERITANCE LAW— PRINCIPLES AND PRACTICE

by

HENRY DYSON

Solicitor

OXFORD

UNIVERSITY PRESS

OXFORD

UNIVERSITY PRESS

Great Clarendon Street, Oxford OX2 6DP

Oxford University Press is a department of the University of Oxford.
It furthers the University's objective of excellence in research, scholarship,
and education by publishing worldwide in

Oxford New York

Auckland Bangkok Buenos Aires Cape Town Chennai
Dar es Salaam Delhi Hong Kong Istanbul Karachi Kolkata
Kuala Lumpur Madrid Melbourne Mexico City Mumbai Nairobi
São Paulo Shanghai Taipei Tokyo Toronto

Oxford is a registered trade mark of Oxford University Press
in the UK and in certain other countries

Published in the United States
by Oxford University Press Inc., New York

British Library Cataloguing in Publication Data
Data available

Library of Congress Cataloging-in-Publication Data
Data available

ISBN 0–19–925475–3

1 3 5 7 9 10 8 6 4 2

Typeset in Times by
Cambrian Typesetters, Frimley, Surrey
Printed in Great Britain
on acid-free paper by
Biddles Ltd,
Guildford and King's Lynn

CONTENTS—SUMMARY

Introduction		xv
Table of Cases		xxi
Table of Statutes		xxix
Abbreviations		xxxvii

1 The legal profession — 1

PART I: LAND LAW

2 Immovable property in French law		13
3 The sale of land		25
4 *Compromis de vente*		39
5 *Promesse de vente*		51
6 Other contracts for sale of land		55
7 Completion		59
8 Sales of land 'on plan'		69
9 Property owning companies		83
10 The Société Civile d'Attribution		95
11 *Pluripropriété*		99
12 Sales *en viager*		105
13 Sales by auction		111
14 Charges on property		119
15 *La copropriété*		129
16 Joint ownership of land		147
17 Residential leases		159
18 Business leases		173
19 Powers of attorney		185
20 The *régime matrimonial*		195
21 *Union libre*		201
22 Land and its taxation		209
23 Capacity		223

PART II: INHERITANCE LAW

24 Inheritance law		233
25 Domicile and residence		241
26 The English trust		247
27 Intestate succession		255

28 *La réserve*   261
29 Avoiding the *réserve*   267
30 The surviving spouse   273
31 Wills   285
32 *Donation-partage* and *donation de biens à venir*   295
33 The *exécuteur testamentaire*   301
34 The beneficiary's election   305
35 *Saisine*   313
36 Legacies   317
37 Administration of an estate   323
38 Gifts *inter vivos*   331
39 Inheritance and gifts tax   339

Appendix—Precedents   353
Glossary   421
Index   443

CONTENTS

Introduction   xv
Table of Cases   xxi
Tables of Statutes   xxix
Abbreviations   xxxvii

1 The legal profession
The notary   1
The *avocat*   9
The *avoué*   9
The *huissier*   10

PART I: LAND LAW

2 Immovable property in French law
Introduction   13
The nature of property   13
Interests in property   16
Rights over land   16
Rights *in rem*   16
Ownership   18
Le patrimoine   19
Types of sales of land   19
Charges   20
The Land Registry system   20
Etat civil   22

3 The sale of land
Introduction   25
Negotiation of sales   26
The estate agent   27
Choice of *notaire*   29
The *notaire*   30
Classes of contracts   30
Statutory protection for the buyer   31
La Loi Scrivener   34
La lésion   34
Matters common to all contracts   35

4 *Compromis de vente*
Introduction   39
Identity of the property sold   40
The sale price   41
Death or incapacity of one party   41
The seller's obligations   42

5 *Promesse de vente*
Introduction   51
Form of the contract   51
Assignment of the contract   52
The option   52

6 Other contracts for sale of land
Pacte de préférence   55
The *vente à réméré*   56
Offre d'achat   57

7 Completion
Introduction   59
For consideration by the buyer   61
For consideration by the seller   63
Completion   64
Failure to complete   65
After completion   66

8 Sales of land 'on plan'
Introduction   69
Vente en l'état futur d'achèvement   70
Vente à terme   78

9 Property owning companies
Introduction   83
Nature of the French *société*   84
The applicable law   85
Formation of a *société civile*   85
The form of the *statuts*   87
The shareholders   88
Contents of the *statuts*   89
Meetings of shareholders   91
Share transfers   91
Management of a *société civile*   92
Liquidation   93
Fiscal considerations   93
The Companies Registry   94

10 The *Société Civile d'Attribution*

Introduction	95
Shareholders' obligations	96
Shareholders' rights	96

11 *Pluripropriété*

Introduction	99
The owning company	100
Share sale offers	100
The *statuts* of the company	100
Management	101
Meetings of the company	101
Disposal of shares	102

12 Sales *en viager*

Introduction	105
Nature of *viager* transactions	106
The consideration	106
The element of chance	107
Viager occupé	107
The *rente viagère*	107
Rights and liabilities of the parties	108
Tax effects	109

13 Sales by auction

Introduction	111
Adjudications volontaires	111
Adjudication judiciaire	114

14 Charges on property

Introduction	119
Types of mortgages	119
Remedies of a mortgagee	120
Hypothèque conventionnelle	120
Property which can be mortgaged	121
Capacity to mortgage property	122
The execution of mortgages	123
The registration of mortgages	123
Privilèges	124
Transfers of mortgages	125
Release	125
Hypothèque légale	125
Hypothèque judiciaire	126
Le tiers déteneur	127

15 *La copropriété*
Introduction   129
Definition of *copropriété*   130
Basis for service charges   131
The *règlement de copropriété*   131
Service charges   133
Meetings of the *copropriété*   136
The *syndic*   141
The *conseil syndical*   145

16 Joint ownership of land
Introduction   147
Ownership *en indivision*   147
Ownership *en tontine*   154

17 Residential leases
Introduction   159
The extent of the *Loi Mermaz*   160

18 Business leases
Introduction   173
Term of the lease   174
The rent   174
The contents of the lease   175
Security of tenure   178
Renewal of lease   179
Compensation   182
Droit de maintien   183
Droit de repentir   183
Le bail dérogatoire   183

19 Powers of attorney
Introduction   185
Remuneration of the attorney   186
Duties of the attorney   186
Determination of power   187
Enduring powers   188
Duration of powers   189
Copies of powers   189
Execution of powers   190
The Hague Convention   190
Form of power   192
Choice of attorneys   192

CONTENTS

20 The *régime matrimonial*
Introduction   195
Le régime de communauté légal   196
Le régime de communauté conventionnelle   197
Le régime de la séparation des biens   198
Variation of a *régime*   199

21 *Union libre*
Introduction   201
Proof of *concubinage*   201
Fiscal effect of *concubinage*   202
The ownership of land   202
Financing a purchase of land   204
The *pacte civile de solidarité et du concubinage*   205
Who may enter into a PACS   206
The PACS contract   207
Determination of a PACS   207
Ownership of assets   207
Fiscal consequences of a PACS   208
Other benefits of a PACS   208

22 Land and its taxation
Introduction   209
Taxes on acquisition   209
Taxe sur la valeur ajoutée   211
Taxes during ownership   212
Tax on disposals   218

23 Capacity
Introduction   223
Infants   224
Adoption   225
Children's capacity to inherit   227
Persons of full age under a disability   227
Capacity in respect of wills   228
Married persons   230

PART II: INHERITANCE LAW

24 Inheritance law
Introduction   233
Source of inheritance law   233
Intestate and testamentary inheritance   235
Executors   236

Types of French wills 236
Agreements to make a will 237
Capacity to inherit 237
Commencement of administration procedure 237
Saisine 238
Acceptance of an estate 238
The *réserve* 239
Winding up an estate 239

25 Domicile and residence
Introduction 241
The significance of domicile 242
Renvoi 243
Droit de prélèvement 244
Residence 245

26 The English trust
Introduction 247
Recognition of trusts 247
Effects of English trusts 248
Proposed French trust law 250
Fiscal considerations 250
French quasi-trusts 252

27 Intestate succession
Introduction 255
Order of succession 255
Représentation 257
Droit de retour 258

28 *La réserve*
Introduction 261
The *réservataires* 261
Calculation of the *réserve* 263
The surviving spouse 265

29 Avoiding the *réserve*
Introduction 267
A company as owner 267
Ownership *en tontine* 269
Sales *en viager* 270
Régime de communauté universelle 270

30 The surviving spouse
Introduction 273
Capacity to inherit 273

The spouse in intestate successions   274
Rights of the surviving spouse in an intestacy   275
Rights of the surviving spouse in testate successions   278
Donation entre époux   282

31 Wills
Introduction   285
Types of will   286
Joint wills   290
Revocation   290
Registration of wills   292
Use of non-French wills   292

32 *Donation-partage* and *donation de biens à venir*
Introduction   295
Donation-partage   295
Donations de biens à venir   298

33 The *exécuteur testamentaire*
Introduction   301
Powers of *exécuteurs testamentaires*   301
The grant of *saisine*   302

34 The beneficiary's election
Introduction   305
The available options   306
The exercise of the option   307
Acceptation pure et simple   307
Acceptation sous bénéfice d'inventaire   309
Renonciation   309
Revocation of exercised options   310
The effects of international law   310

35 *Saisine*
Introduction   313
Proof of right to *saisine*   313
Beneficiaries without *saisine*   314

36 Legacies
Introduction   317
Types of legacies   318
Restriction of alienation   319
Penal clauses   319
Lapse   320

37 Administration of an estate
Introduction   323
Preliminary steps   324

CONTENTS

Sealing the property 325
Inventory of contents 325
Bank accounts 326
Documents in an administration 326
Distribution 328

38 Gifts *inter vivos*
Introduction 331
Donations indirectes 332
Donations simulées 332
Revocation of a gift 333
Gifts between spouses 335
Donations par personne interposée 337
Gifts and marriage 337

39 Inheritance and gifts tax
Introduction 339
Droits de succession 340
Droits de donation 351
Reliefs 351

Appendix—Precedents 353
Glossary 421
Index 443

INTRODUCTION

Whilst for a full appreciation of the contents of this book, it is by no means necessary to have a profound knowledge of the French legal system, considerable benefit will be derived from reading the relevant chapters in Bell, Boyron and Whittaker, *Principles of French Law* (1st edn, OUP, 1998). The law of every country reflects the character of its citizens and if full use is to be made of the contents of this book and pleasure derived from an understanding of the branches of French law which it treats, it is desirable that the reader has some appreciation of how the French function as a people. It must be accepted that French law is formalist and it is necessary to take fully into account what is of such importance to the French lawyer—the written word. It is not without significance that an English transfer of land can be achieved by means of a single printed page whilst the majority of French conveyances are likely to run to over a dozen closely typed pages. Moreover, the French system is tinged with the presumption that trust is not a natural element in dealings between parties and it does not need a very close study of the *Code civil* to see how clearly Napoléon appreciated this and framed his *Code* accordingly.

The English lawyer should also always bear in mind when he is dealing with problems related to land or inheritance to any kind of property in France that, in contrast to the English system, there is no equity jurisdiction, no system of binding judicial precedents and that the trust has no place in French law. The absence of these pillars of the English legal system is very tellingly commented on by Professor Malinvaud in his *Introduction à l'étude du droit* (Editions Litec, 1995). He says, 'It may happen in fact that a rule of law, conceived in the abstract, proves to be unjust, inequitable, when brutally applied to a concrete situation. It is to be hoped that the judge can reach a fair decision. Arbitrators, when so authorized by the parties, can do this. Judges do not have this power. Their judgments may be overturned if they openly apply Equity. Hence, what they cannot do openly, they can do in another way by the expedient of their own interpretation of the law. Judges should not appear to be robots whose task is mechanically to apply the words of a Statute. Often, instead of following previously adopted reasoning, they reverse it, giving to the legal rule an intuitive and equitable solution . . . A Court of first instance is free not to follow even the most established rule of law; the worst that can happen will be that its judgment will be overruled on appeal.'

Whilst one senses here the spirit which gave rise to the Courts of Equity in England, such a parallel jurisdiction has never developed in the same way in France and 'equity' is merely the equivalent of not following the law in order to reach what the individual judge considers to be a fair result in any given case.

Such an attitude makes for the uncertain interpretation of the law in France. A judgment, be it approved by the highest Court in the land, has not the authority of law and is not binding in subsequent cases. It must, nevertheless, be admitted that a conscious effort is made by most Courts to respect decisions of the *Cour de Cassation* as the highest French Court of Appeal. However, whilst the French *notaire*, who is the lawyer with whom readers of this book will come most into contact, will readily cite by heart many relevant articles of the *Code civil*, the author in many years' experience in France has never had a judgment quoted to him.

This book is intended to enlighten the practising English lawyer involved in French property transactions in their widest sense and also in connection with French inheritance matters where the law is so vastly different from that in England. It is hoped that it will assist also the English academic in his studies of those branches of French law. It is essential, when seeking advice on the laws and procedures of countries other than one's own, to obtain that advice from a source which has not only mere theoretical but also a practical knowledge of both systems of laws obtained by regular practice of both in both countries.

The two branches of French law which are treated in this book have been combined since these are the two subjects with which the English lawyer is most likely to be concerned. A detailed study of commercial and tax law is outside the scope of the book save to the extent that these impinge on its main subject matter. Thus, inheritance involves the payment of inheritance tax and the various methods of the ownership of land need reference to tax and company law. It is also necessary for the reader to have at least a rudimentary understanding of the *régime matrimonial* and of one or two other matters of general French law and these are dealt with either in separate chapters or in the chapter which has been considered most appropriate.

The French legal profession differs radically from its English counterpart and in the case of both land and inheritance law, it is the *notaire* who is involved almost to the exclusion of other lawyers. For this reason the opening chapter has been devoted to the workings of the *notariat* with short notes on the *avocat*, the *avoué* and the *huissier*. To ensure anything approaching useful co-operation between solicitor and *notaire* it is essential to appreciate how the latter thinks and works and the differences in relationship between lawyer and client in each of the two countries.

It is fortuitous that the first edition of this book appears shortly after the passage into law of two French enactments which alter fundamentally the laws relating to the sale of land and to testate and intestate succession. The former, relating to contracts for the sale of land, appears to be without real value to the community and to be a piece of what is now curiously known as 'politically correct' legislation. The latter effects long overdue reforms to a number of aspects of the law of inheritance to all kinds of property and will considerably affect the English.

The chapters of this book dealing with real property have been arranged as far as possible to assist readers to follow the sequence of events in typical transactions such as the purchase and sale of land in various circumstances, gifts, mortgages, and lettings. Other chapters deal with family matters connected with the ownership of land. French inheritance law differs so radically from that which is in force in England that it has been thought helpful not always to deal with its impact in the chronological order of the date of death to the winding up of the estate. Certain fundamental concepts and rules must be explained before it is possible to follow through a typical administration of a French estate. These explanations have been given with the events specifically in mind which the English and their families are most likely to encounter in France, whether they are domiciled or resident in England or in that country. It must, however, be admitted that the philosophy behind most aspects of French inheritance law, much of which is founded in Roman law overlaid by Revolutionary concepts, is so different from that to which the English lawyer is accustomed that it requires several generations of French blood flowing through the veins to appreciate some of the rules of this branch of the law. For this reason, it has been thought not helpful to deal with some of these in great depth but to limit references to their effect in practice.

It has, however, been thought useful to include a short chapter on the English trust as seen through the eyes of French civil and fiscal law. It is sometimes necessary to take account of the ways in which French law has tried to comprehend the trust which can pose problems at times. Some years ago, a Bill was laid before the French Parliament designed to introduce the trust into French law. It was much supported by the notarial profession. It was a strange adaptation of English law bearing in mind that equitable interests are unknown in French law. For reasons explained in that chapter, it is unlikely that it will ever see the light of day.

It will be noticed that it is substantially with English law that comparison is made with French law. It is not necessary to remind the English lawyer that Scotland has its own laws but it is worth mentioning that despite the historical link between France and that country, very few French lawyers are aware that Scots law does differ substantially from English law, that domicile in Scotland is not domicile in England and Wales with consequent results in matters of inheritance which pass unnoticed by the average French lawyer. Many are also unaware that there is no such nationality as English.

The author's decision when to use only the original French or when to resort to English translations or to show both is not entirely idiosyncratic, as may seem to be the case. It is based on the assumption that the reader has a reasonable knowledge of French and that it is tedious to see continuously both the original French and its English translation. It must, however, be admitted that French legal jargon often bears as little resemblance to standard French as does its counterpart in English law to English as it is generally spoken.

French terms of law or descriptions are not always followed by their English translation every time they appear and it is for this reason that a Glossary has been included. It has been prepared in the nature of an additional index in the sense that references to pages are given against each term explained and it is hoped that this will both avoid too much cross-referencing and at the same time knit together the same French technical terms where they appear in different chapters. Quotations are usually followed by their English translations at least on their first appearance.

There appear from time to time short quotations in English from the *Code civil* which are not the author's translations and are unattributed. They are those of 'A Barrister of the Inner Temple' whose translation of the *Code Napoléon* into English was published in 1824 by Charles Hunter, Law Bookseller of Bell Yard, Lincoln's Inn. It has been possible through the kindness of the Assistant Librarian of the Inner Temple Library to identify the 'Barrister of the Inner Temple' as George Spence, a member of the Inn who lived from 1787 to 1850. The Dictionary of National Biography says that among other publications he was well known for his book in two volumes *The Equitable Jurisdiction of the Court of Chancery* published in 1846–9 which, since it is said to be 'the standard authority on the abstruse and intricate subject of which it treats', would appear to have been the forerunner of *Snell on Equity*.

The translation is of interest not only because the *Code* was then only twenty years old but also because many of the articles remain unaltered today. The work is one of great skill and serves to remind one of the charm and excellence of the English language then spoken by members of the learned professions.

This book contains precedents of some French documents which are the most likely to be met with by the reader. None is rendered in English in full but only in précis form. In this respect the word 'translation' has deliberately not been used. The Italians rightly say '*Traduttore, traditore*' and this dictum applies with great force to legal documents in any language. The author has done his best to convey the basic meaning of these French documents without attempting to provide literal translations. It is assumed that no reader will make use of these precedents for his own purposes without advice and they are included with the sole purpose of assisting him to understand better the French system. It is strongly recommended that translations of any document when needed should always be made into the language of the translator and by someone versed in the subject matter of the document. A general ability to translate is not sufficient. It is worthwhile adding that the greatest care must be taken in the use of Anglo-French legal dictionaries since, in many cases, English, Canadian and American legal terms may be used quite indiscriminately.

English readers of French law books will not be surprised, in view of what has been said about the lack of the binding effect of judgments in France, that very few have the equivalent of a Table of Cases. Those which do are usually textbooks for higher grade and university studies rather than for everyday use by the legal profession. Reference to cases is usually by way of footnote only. This practice has not been adopted in this book and references are usually given in the text to avoid the irritating diversion of the eye to print smaller than the text. A Table of Cases has been provided in this book and the reader is asked to pay special attention to the Note at its head.

Many French Acts normally find their way sooner or later into the *Code civil* or one of the other *Codes* such as the *Code de Commerce* or the *Code Général des Impôts* as new articles or amendments of existing articles. It is perhaps, therefore, not surprising that few books contain a Table of Statutes and this makes cross-referencing almost impossible. This book attempts to repair that omission by providing such a Table. A note is also provided on some major websites which provide useful information, in some cases in English as well as in French. It remains to add that the French are poor indexers and it is an art in itself to make use of such indexes as appear in French law books.

The author of any book on a technical subject who hopes to have pleasure in writing it and that his efforts will find favour with its readers must rely on three limitless wells of patience. The author of this book has been amply so provided.

Maître Chantal Pasqualini, *notaire* of Nice, her late husband, Maître Guy Rousseau, and members of the staff of their *étude* have with unstinting patience spent many hours teaching me much of the French law I know. My wife, Yve Menzies, has exhibited incredible patience with the difficulties which every author encounters in writing a book and which can only be appreciated by a fellow author, and whose mastery of both English and French is unrivalled, without which I doubt if I would have received the patient sympathy provided to me by Chris Rycroft, the Editor in Chief, Practitioner Law of Oxford University Press, and his admirable editorial staff.

TABLE OF CASES

FRENCH

The hierarchy of the Courts in France consists of the *Tribunal d'Instance*, the *Tribunal de Grande Instance*, the *Cour d'Appel* and the *Cour de Cassation*. Their equivalents in England may be considered to be the County Court, the High Court, the Court of Appeal and the House of Lords. The first has a limited jurisdiction whilst the second has a general jurisdiction, excluding commercial cases which are heard in the Commercial Court, and certain other cases of a specialized nature. Most towns will have a *Tribunal d'Instance*. Every *département* at one time had a *Tribunal de Grande Instance* but now the larger and more populous *départements* may have two or more such Courts. There are 30 Courts of Appeal in France spread over the country, and there is talk of creating more to relieve the current judicial delays. The *Cour de Cassation*, so called because to quash a judgment is to '*casser*' it, is therefore the highest Appeal Court and the equivalent of the House of Lords.

Notwithstanding that the rule of judicial precedents is not known in French law, it may well surprise the English practitioner that of over 180 judgments referred to in this book, more than 140 are those of the *Cour de Cassation*. By way of comparison, a leading textbook on inheritance law quotes 97 decisions of the *Cour de Cassation* and 14 of the two lower jurisdictions so that the proportion of decisions of the highest Court in the land to those lower down the ladder is more or less the same in both books. The noble Law Lords in England might be surprised if their decisions were so often quoted.

The *Cour de Cassation* sits in six divisions or *chambres*: three civil, one criminal, one social and one commercial. It is not wholly clear why the judgments are not known by the names of the parties although it has been suggested that this is to avoid publicity. Be that as it may, a few cases (possibly those of great interest) are quoted by name but this is a rarity compared to the English practice. Civil cases are reported in the *Bulletin des arrêts de la Cour de Cassation* (*Bull. civ*) or *Répertoire du notariat Defrénois* (*Déf*) in date order. Copies of judgments of the *Cour de Cassation* are also available from the Greffe des arrêts, 5, Quai de l'Horloge, TSA 19204, 75005 Paris. When ordering, it is necessary to say whether the case was heard in the civil or commercial division. The cases quoted in this book were all heard in the civil division except those where the indication 'Comm.' appears in the reference. Jugments of the Courts of Appeal and other Courts may be had of the Greffe of the relevant Court.

Copies of any judgments are also available on the Internet at www.legifrance.gouv.fr.

Those who wish for a more profound insight into the reporting of cases in France and other sources of French legal information should refer to Part III 'Studying French Law' of *Principles of French Law* (OUP) mentioned in the Introduction to this book. Not only does it give much information of great value but it is provided in a manner which indicates that the authors have achieved a complete understanding of the problems the French system creates. The degree of appreciation by the reader of a certain humour in the contents is an admirable indication of how well he has understood the French and their judicial way of life.

Cour de Cassation

Date of Judgment   *Page*

18.11.1821 332
19.5.1847 111
27.8.1855 302
18.8.1862 264
12.8.1863 317
26.1.1879 330
19.4.1865 309
27.3.1888 309
10.7.1888 299
5.6.1899 253
2.7.1903 259
13.5.1912 43
30.5.1927 319
13.4.1932 225
4.2.1936 45
4.5.1936 40
23.4.1938 56
12.6.1949 34
31.3.1954 44
18.7.1956 29
4.12.1956 309
14.2.1956 334
14.1.1957 35
12.2.1958 66
15.4.1958 66
12.5.1958 66
21.5.1958 109
25.5.1960 317
14.12.1960 336
9.11.1961 35
25.10.1961 44
30.10.1961 (Comm.) 182

19.2.1962 184
21.3.1962 (Comm.) 182
16.5.1962 43
16.7.1962 177
18.8.1962 264
17.7.1963 242
1.12.1964 263
5.4.1965 6
12.5.1965 291
4.1.1966 66
28.2.1966 184
6.12.1966 37
15.12.1966 130
19.5.1967 36
11.1.1968 138
25.4.1968 182
24.2.1969 299
7. 5.1969 182
10.6.1970 139
5.3.1971 44
16.2.1972 118
8.11.1972 184
21.11.1972 130
2.10.1974 187
6.3.1974 37
27.10.1975 . . . . .70, 160
6.1.1976 200
11.5.1976 36
19.1.1977 130
17.5.1977 308
28.7.1977 71
22.11.1977 335
7.12.1977 179
27.11.1979 40
6.2.1980 88
3.2.1981 97
10.2.1981 186
24.3.1981 183
28.10.1981 76
9.11.1981 . . . . .179, 183
17.11.1981 324
5. 5.1982 105
12.5.1982 205

TABLE OF CASES

9.6.1982 116

16.6.1982 65

7.7.1982 93

11.1.1983 203

18.1.1983 175

29.6.1983 122

2.10.1984 174

13.2.1985 75

18.2.1986 317

11.3.1986 187

8.10.1986 28

11.2.1987 179

11.6.1987 71

14.10.1987 142

11.7.1988 141

26.10.1988 77

13.12.1988 308

21.12.1988 55

28.3.1990 43

6. 3.1991 131

9.10.1991 188

17.12.1991 192

1.4.1992 55

14.5.1992 310

11.6.1992 136

30.6.1992 286

26.5.1993 132

17.11.1993 71

1.6.1993 55

24.11.1993 200

26.1.1994 183

30.3.1994 121

6.4.1994 308

17.5.1994 44

1.6.1994 286

21.9.1994 90

15.10.1994 118

8.11.1994 188

14.12.1994 166

20.12.1994 . . . . 35, 75

2.3.1995 102

15.2.1995 175

11.5.1995 179

21.6.1995 179
21.11.1995 188
4.1.1996 44
31.1.1996 132
12.6.1996 107
8.10.1996 121
14.1.1997 186
17.7.1997 40
27.5.1998 121
1.7.1998 . . . . 32, 53
16.6.1998 186
20.10.1998 (Comm.) 214
2.12.1998 179
9.3.1999 121
23.3.1999 121
16.6.1999 . . . . 55, 160
21.7.1999 166
8.12.1999 166
3.3.2000 244
19.4.2000 167
11.5.2000 136
21.11.2000 134
24.1.2001 139
27.2.2001 121
13.3.2001 4
17.7.2001 (Comm.) 42
28.1.2002 15
23.5.2002 165

Court of Appeal

Date of Judgment   *Page*
Agen 2.5.2000 169
Aix en Provence 13.11.1945 92
Aix en Provence 1.6.1986 169
Aix en Provence 13.12.1988 154
Bourges   1.3.1988 205
Chambéry   7.7.1980 177
Douai   7.7.1998 201
Montpellier   30.4.1997 5
Nancy   2.12 1949 92
Paris   25.2.1982 163
Paris   7.1.1983 76

Paris   27.4.1983 176
Paris   16.6.1988 178
Paris   19.2.1991 166
Paris   16.6.1992 52
Paris   10.2.1994 167
Paris   9.4.1994 92
Paris   14.10.1994 139
Paris   21.6.1995 174
Paris,   21.2.1996 134
Paris   11.10.1996 139
Paris   22.10.1997 132
Paris   30.10.1997 166
Paris   23.1.1998 137
Paris   10.2.1998 166
Paris   24.4.1998 136
Paris   6.5.1998 139
Paris   24.6.1998 133
Paris   25.11.1998 142
Paris   25.9.1999 52
Paris   4.1.2000 132
Paris   4.10.2000 179
Rennes   14.2.1972 319
Rouen   3.2.1981 200
Rouen   14.2.1996 137
Toulouse   16.7.1890 117
Versailles   14.2.1992 74
Versailles   29.10.1990 132
Versailles   9.11.2000 138

Tribunal de Grande Instance

Date of Judgment   *Page*
Beaumes les Dames 27.6.1953 113
Seine 22.4.1953 4
Seine 15.12.1966 37
Paris 10.2.1964 208
Bayonne 12.5.1975 45
Versailles 29.3.1996 8

ENGLISH

The English cases listed below have been quoted in the text since the judgments are of interest in relation to the relevant French law.

Messenger v Andrews [1828] 4 Russ 478 321
Oldfield v Preston [1861] 45 ER 939 155
Gilliat v Gilliat L.R.9 Eq.60 113
Webb v Webb [1994] 3 AER 911 17

TABLE OF STATUTES

FRENCH

Laws and Decrees

One of the practical problems which assails the non-French lawyer (but presumably not his French counterpart) is how the contents of some of the Laws seem partly to amend the *Code civil* or some other *Code* and partly to stand on their own so that one may have to look both at the relevant *Code* and also at the original Law to be completely informed. The simplest manner in which to overcome this difficulty is to have to hand an up-to-date copy of the Dalloz *Code civil* or other appropriate *Code* (of which there are nearly 30) if specialist subjects are involved. If full use is made of the information available in these books in addition to the text itself, much of assistance can be gleaned. A *décret* and an *ordonnance* may be taken from a practical though not constitutional point of view as the equivalent of an English Statutory Instrument.

Care must be taken when referring to the *Code civil* and other *Codes* since subsections of articles are indicated by a number preceded by a dash and not by the use of brackets as in English statutes. Thus article 1000-5 does not indicate articles 1000 to 1005 but subsection 5 of article 1000. Since legislation by means of Laws in many cases becomes embodied in the *Code civil* and it is not possible to renumber the whole *Code* when new legislation is added, on occasions subsections of an article may seem to be somewhat out of place.

Copies of Laws and *décrets* can be obtained from DJO, service information-diffusion, 26, Rue Desaix, 75727 Paris Cedex 15, Tel 01.44.32.50.50, Fax 01.45.79.17.84 and are available also from www.legifrance.gouv.fr. Tax information may be obtained from Affiches Parisiennes, 144, Rue de Rivoli, 75001 Paris, Tel 01.42.60.36.78 and on the Internet at www.minefi.gouv.fr.

	Page
Loi du 17 Nivose An II (8 January 1794) (Inheritance)	234
Loi du 4 Germinal An VIII (25 March 1800) (Inheritance)	234
Loi du 25 Ventose An 11 (16 March 1803) (Notaires)	288
Loi du 14 juillet 1819	244
Décret 53-960 du 30 septembre 1953 (Business leases)	173
Loi 65-557 du 10 juillet 1965 (Copropriété)	129
Loi du 13 juillet 1967 (Companies)	84
Loi 67-1253 du 30 décembre 1967 (Business lettings)	17, 173
Loi 69-1168 du 26 décembre 1969 (Formalité unique)	21
Loi 70-9 du 2 janvier 1970 (Loi Hoguet)	27

Décret 71-941 du 26 novembre 1971 (Notaires) 4
Loi 76-1286 du 31 décembre 1976 (Indivision) 148
Loi 78-9 du 4 janvier 1978 (Companies) 85
Loi 78-573 du 17 juillet 1978 (Companies) 85
Loi 79-596 du 13 juillet 1979 (Loi Scrivener) 34, 47, 114, 120
Loi 89-462 du 6 juillet 1989 (Loi Mermaz) (Leases) . . . . .160 et seq
Loi 89-1008 du 31 décembre 1989 (pre-Loi SRU) 32, 47, 278
Loi 91-650 du 9 juillet 1991 (Execution procedures) 45
Décret 93-819 du 14 mai 1993 (3% tax on land) 216
Loi 94-624 du 21 juillet 1994 (Residential leases) 168
Décret 96-97 du 7 février 1996 (Asbestos) 45
Loi 96-1107 du 18 décembre 1996 (Loi Carrez) (Copropriété) 40
Décret du 26 aôut 1997 (Residential leases) 163
Loi 99-471 du 5 juin 1999 (Termites) 46
Loi 99-944 du 15 novembre 1999 (PACS) . . . . .205 et seq
Loi 2000-1208 du 13 décembre 2000 (La loi SRU) 25, 134, 140
Loi 2001-1135 du 3 décembre 2001 (Inheritance) 205, 235, 243, 255, 273

Code Civil ('C.civ.') *Page*

Art 6 86
   102 241
   205 277
   207-1 278
   267 to 269 333
   304 333
   356 to 358 . . . . .225, 227
   368-1 259
   370-3, -4, -5 226
   490 227
   491-2 227
   501 228
   515-1 to -7 205
   515-8 211
   516 13
   517 . . . . .13, 14
   523 and 524 14
   525 14
   544 18
   546 18
   551 and 552 18
   627 277
   631 277

634 and 635 277
675 to 685-1 16
686 et seq 16
718 228
720 323
724 . . . . 228, 313
725 237
725-1 225
726 to 729 229
730 . . . . .313, 327
732 274
734 to 740 . . . . .255 et seq
741 257
744 257
751-755 . . . . .257, 258
756 227
757 275
758 276
763 276
764 277
767 215
775 305
778 308
784 309
795 309
796 308
798 309
800 309
803 301
804 301
815 to 815-16 . . . . .147, 149, 328
831 329
843 263
866 265
870 305
871 305
883 330
894 331
895 317
900 . . . . .253, 254, 319
904 224
906 274
913 to 932 . . . . .261, 278, 295, 331

947 298
953 254
955 334
956 334
959 335
960 333
968 290
970 to 980 . . . . .286, 287, 289
1000 294
1004 . . . . .250, 315
1008 315
1010 318
1025 301
1031 301
1035 to 1037 . . . . .290, 291, 302
1044 320
1045 328
1046 291
1047 . . . . .291, 335
1048 252
1075 296
1076 297
1078 297
1082 298
1091 to 1100 335
1094-1 278
1095 224
1096 . . . . .282, 335
1099-1 . . . . .205, 333, 336
1128 86
1131 205
1133 205
1134 71
1152 37
1168 46
1179 . . . . .48, 154
1226 52
1231 37
1244 to 1251 . . . . .169, 204
1250-1 and -3 204
1259 125
1325 35
1326 37

1328	.287
1387	.195
1397	.199
1394	.196
1398	.224
1401 to 1440	.196
1483	.326
1527	.198
1582	.25, 26, 39
1583	.25, 32, 40
1589	.40
1593	30
1601-1 to -3	.69
1602	.42
1603	.42
1605	.65
1614	.42
1616 to 1618	.40
1626	.42
1627	.43
1630	.43
1636	.43
1641	.43
1645	.44, 117
1659 to 1673	56, 57
1674	34
1689	.164
1690	.56
1717	.177
1719	.162
1722	.166
1731	.165
1709 to 1778	.159, 170
1792	.77, 78
1832	.84, 88
1835	.87, 89
1844	.88, 89, 93, 102
1848-1	.92
1849	.93
1851	.92
1852	.93
1857	.85
1860	.90

1861 91
1864 92
1869 102
1870 92
1873-1 to -18 . . . . .148, 150
1888 203
1968 to 1983 106-110
1984 to 2010 185-188
2074 41
2092 . . . . .19, 115
2093 19
2118 121
2123 126
2124 121
2125 123
2127 123
2129 122
2130 122
2131 122
2143 123
2159 125
2161 126
2169 115
2185 114
2204 114
2262 18
2265 18
2270 77
2279 330

Code de Commerce ('C.com')

Art 632 . . . . .84, 85
Art L145-1 to 60 173

Code Général des Impots ('CGI')

Art 683 41
    751 . . . . .215, 342
    575-8 343
    794 and 795 342
    768 344
    785 349

990D-G 216, 343
1655 ter 217
1840-A 52, 71

Code de Construction et d'Habitation ('CCH')

Art L121-60 to 76 100
L212-1 95
L231-2 79
L231-1 to -13 70,79
L232-1 and -2 70
L241-1 L261-2 78
L261-10 to-19 69,74
L261-22 69
L271-1 and -2 31
R231-1 to -4 70,79
R231-8 82
R232-1 to -7 70
R261-1 75,76
R261-14 74
R261-21 76
R261-28 to -31 72
R261-33 69

Code des Assurances ('C.assur')

Art 242 . . . . .78, 82
L132-12 343

Code de Procédure Civil ('C.pr.civ.')

Art 697 116
700 116

Code de la Propriété Intellectuelle ('C.prop.intell.')

Art L123-6 278

ENGLISH

The following English Statutes are referred to in the text.

Wills Act 1837 291,320
Married Womens' Property Act 1882 199
Law of Property Act 1925 . . . . .25, 43, 159, 164
Trustee Act 1925 . . . . .225, 294, 301
Administration of Estates Act 1925 .15, 244, 257, 262
Landlord & Tenant Act 1954 Part II 173, 181
Variation of Trusts Act 1958 200
Wills Act 1963 293
Matrimonial Causes Act 1973 291
Inheritance (Provision for Family & Dependants) Act 1975 243
Powers of Attorney Act 1971 . . . . .185, 189
Civil Jurisdiction and Judgments Act 1982 17
Companies Act 1982 93
Recognition of Trusts Act 1987 247
Income amd Corporation Taxes Act 1988 268
Administration of Justice Act 1994 . . . . .289, 301

INTERNATIONAL CONVENTIONS

The following Conventions have been ratified by France and form part of French internal law.

Hague Convention of 5 October 1961 . . . . .190, 293
Anglo-French Double Tax Convention of 21 June 1963 . . . . .216, 246, 340
Brussels Convention of 27 September 1968 17
Basle Convention of 16 May 1972 292
Hague Convention of 2 October 1973 249
Washington Convention of 26 October 1973 .236, 289
Hague Convention of 14 March 1978 . . . . .200, 270
Hague Convention of 1 July 1985 247
Brussels Convention of 25 May 1987 190
Hague Convention of 13 January 2000 . . . . .189, 237

ABBREVIATIONS

AR post	Registered AR post
C.civ	*Code civil*
C.assur	*Code des assurances*
C.com	*Code commercial*
CA	*Cour d'Appel*
Cass.com	*Cour de Cassation*—Commercial Division
Cass	*Cour de Cassation*
CCH	*Code de la construction et de l'habitation*
CGI	*Code Général des Impôts*
CPC	*Code Procédure Civil*
DAT	*déclaration d'achèvement des travaux*
DIA	*déclaration d'intention d'aliéner*
HT	*hors taxe*
IHT	inheritance tax
ISF	See Glossary
Loi SRU	See Glossary
PACS	See Glossary
SAFER	See Glossary
SCI	*société civile immobilière*
SMIC	minimum salary fixed by law
ssp	See Glossary
TGI	*Tribunal de Grande Instance*
TTC	*tous taxes compris*
TVA	See Glossary
VAT	value added tax

THE LEGAL PROFESSION

The notary 1
The *avocat* 9
The *avoué* 9
The *huissier* 10

The notary

There are approximately 7,700 *notaires* in France, of whom some 70 per cent practise in partnerships. Virtually every document connected with dealings in land must be *authentique*, that is executed in the presence of a *notaire* and authenticated by him. In addition, his involvement is obligatory in the administration of all estates of deceased persons which include *immeubles* among their assets. He is charged with the preparation and modification of *contrats de mariage*, most documents involving gifts *inter vivos*, mortgages, releases, certain types of wills and generally documents the solemnity of which requires *authenticité*. He also undertakes certain company work and often advises on tax problems in connection with the ownership of land and the administration of estates. He does not indulge in litigation.

The *notaire* is the French lawyer whose work is most closely comparable to that of the 'family solicitor' engaged exclusively in non-contentious matters. Nevertheless, this comparison must be treated with considerable reserve. The work he undertakes is 'generally little understood if not totally mysterious'. Since that is a comment in a leading French textbook on the notarial profession (Gilles Rouzet, *Précis de Déontologie Notariale* (3rd edn, Presses Universitaires de Bordeaux)), it must be of the greatest importance that the English lawyer who has dealings with the *notaire* has a clear appreciation of the functions of his profession, its rules and the work he undertakes.

The *notaire* is, in the words of the *ordonnance* of 2 November 1945 (which amended the Law of the 25 ventose an XI—16 March 1803), an *officier public* whose task is 'to receive all documents and contracts to which the parties are required to or desire to give that character of authenticity which attaches to documents of a public nature, to confirm their date, to keep the same in safe custody and to provide engrossments and certified copies thereof'. Apart from such documents as are required by law to be *actes authentiques*, other documents may, if the parties so desire, be executed in that form.

The office of a *notaire* is a closed shop. He is appointed by the *Garde des*

Sceaux (which is the French equivalent of the Lord Chancellor) and only in most exceptional circumstances is the current overall number in any one area exceeded. As *officier ministériel* as well as *officier public*, he is the owner of an office (*charge*) which entitles him to the right of presentation of a successor to that office. As from 1986, he may undertake work throughout the country, whereas previously his area of competence was limited to areas by reference to the limits of jurisdiction of certain Courts. Even today, in the case of certain transactions which are considered to be of prime importance, such as the first transfer for valuable consideration of immovable property, his power to authenticate documents is limited on the pre-1986 geographical basis. A *notaire* may negotiate the sale of any property anywhere in the country. *Notaires*, it remains to add, are strictly forbidden to advertise in any form.

Solicitors may be interested to learn that any person who commits or threatens to commit 'an outrage' against a *notaire*, which is described as any act which impugns his dignity or the respect which is due to his office, is liable to a heavy fine. He is also protected against any unqualified person who is not the holder of a public office who carries out 'any function reserved to the office' of a *notaire* and the term of imprisonment for this offence can run to three years.

An *acte notarié* is endowed with a special quality which has no significance in English law in respect of documents prepared in England for use in that country. It is that of *authenticité*. Such a document *fait foi* as between the parties to it and their successors in title providing inherent proof which is in practice virtually irrefutable, as to the authenticity of its date, its execution and its contents based on what the *notaire* has seen and heard. It is the duty of a *notaire* to obtain for himself such information as he requires for the drafting of such a document and to obtain from his client any further facts which he may need. His duty is to check the correctness of such facts.

In addition, an *acte authentique* is *exécutoire*. This means that in many cases such a document has the force of a judgment. Thus an *acte authentique* which records an obligation to pay a debt in a certain sum on a given date can be enforced by the creditor by merely providing a *huissier* with a certified copy of the document which enables that official to enforce payment as though he were executing a judgment debt.

An action, of which there are few and of which even fewer are successful, to question the truth of statements in such a document, lies in an action of a criminal nature. Such a procedure is known as *inscription de faux* and, bearing in mind the significance of *authenticité*, carries severe penalties for the *notaire* who deliberately falsifies or is a party to the falsification of the contents of an *acte authentique*. However, the probative value of a statement in an *acte authentique* attaches only to those statements which flow from the professional competence of a *notaire*. The statement by a *notaire* before whom is made a *testament authentique* that the testator 'is of sound mind' may be questioned without the need to have recourse to the special procedure referred to above since its veracity is not within the competence of a non-medical person (Cass. 25.5.87). An interesting situation may arise in connection with the statement of domicile made in an *acte de notoriété après décès*. The *notaire* taking the *acte* is not normally liable for the truth of such a statement, the information for which is supplied by the witnesses to the document who, for example, are seldom likely to be the persons swearing as to domicile when an application for an English grant is made in the English estate of a person who had also estate in France. It is by no means unknown for one domicile to be sworn to in England and another to appear in this document.

There are, of course, some fine distinctions. For example, if an *acte notarié* relates that one party has in the presence of the *notaire* paid over a given amount, should this not be true, this is a situation in which the professional integrity of the *notaire* is in question. But if a *notaire* merely recounts in an *acte* that he has been told by one of the parties that he has handed over to the other an amount on account of the payment of a sale price and this is untrue, the *notaire* cannot be held responsible for any such inaccuracy appearing in an *acte authentique*.

Documents which are not *authentique* are said to be *sous seing privé* or ssp but it is not satisfactory to describe these as 'under seal' and 'under hand' respectively and the French terms themselves must be used. There is the reverence for the *acte authentique* not accorded to the document ssp as perhaps there is for the English deed (or was when seals, even if in the form of wafers, were affixed) but this has nothing to do with the presence or absence of consideration.

Notarial documents are either *en brevet* or *en minute*. The former are documents the original of which is handed to the person by whom it is made. These are, for example, powers of attorney, life certificates required by annuitants or receipts for rent or other sums. The *minute* is the sole original of a notarial document which is by law required to be retained by the *notaire* before whom it was made. Virtually all documents to be registered at the Land Registry are *en minute* as are gifts *inter vivos* and notarial wills. An *expédition* is a certified copy of a *minute* and it is this which is delivered to the purchaser of property once the registration of the transfer to him has been completed. As will be seen hereafter, an *expédition* of an *acte de vente* does not constitute proof of ownership of a particular property but merely of its purchase on a particular date. Documents both *en minute* and *en brevet* must be recorded daily in special registers by every *notaire* who must supply the Registrar of his local Court with a copy of their contents during the first two months of every year. Failure to do so still incurs a fine of 100 French Pounds as provided for in the Law of 16 floréal an IV (6 May 1796). Ultimately, these records find their way to the archives of each *département*.

The *notaire* also fulfils the functions of the English notary public as to documents executed in one country for use in another. This subject is elaborated in Chapter 19 on Powers of Attorney and all that need now be said is that it is never necessary to have any document, *authentique* or ssp, executed out of France before a French Consul. It is a fairly constant cry of the *notaire* unversed in international work that the services of the French Consul are required and since French Consuls, not all of whom have the powers of a *notaire*, are considerably less thick on the ground than notaries public, such a cry may happily go unheeded.

In France, the apostille is affixed to documents for use in the United Kingdom which under the convention require this formality by the local Court of Appeal. *Notaires* are also empowered by English law in their capacity as *notaires* to take oaths for use in England. They are similarly easier to find than British Consuls and may be used for this purpose.

The professional obligations of the *notaire* fall into three categories.

1. He owes the duty of a *mandataire* or attorney of his client so that, as his 'alter ego', he must ensure that the document which he prepares fully carries into effect the arrangements which he has been instructed to record. It is interesting to note that, as late as 1722, a *notaire* could be sued in negligence only if he provided an *acte* which was void for want of proper form. Although this failure on the part of the *notaire* to comply with certain formalities has as recently as 1971 (art 23 *Décret* 71–941) been repeated as a ground for an action in negligence, the current situation is happily no longer so strictly limited. 'Notaries are not just scribes whose role is simply passive but have the duty to enlighten their client on the consequences and dangers of the documents which they authenticate' (TGI de la Seine 22.4.53).

2. He must provide advice to the parties. He is under the obligation 'to ensure that their interests are safeguarded, to advise them of their respective rights and obligations, to explain the effects of the liabilities which they propose to undertake, to make clear the risks to which they are exposing themselves and to indicate to them the means which the law places at their disposal to ensure the carrying into effect of their wishes' (Yaigre and Pillebout, *Droit Professionnel Notarial*, paras 240 and 269). He must, for example, specifically warn his client of unexpected or unusual risks which he may encounter. Thus, he must explain to a buyer of new property the special French VAT rules which apply to such a purchase (Cass.2.5.90). 'The notaire must give advice to all his clients even those who are themselves lawyers or acknowledged experts in their field' (Gilles Rouzet, *Précis de Déontologie Notariale* (3rd edn, Presses Universitaires de Bordeaux).

A more recent and slightly disturbing view of the liability of the *notaire* in not dissimilar circumstances is provided by the judgment of the *Cour de Cassation* (Cass.13.3.2001), the facts of which were as follows. It is incumbent (usually on the owner of the land) in the case of newly built property to effect cover for a period of ten years in respect of defects arising by reason of defaults on the part of the builders. During that period, details of that insurance must figure in every *acte de vente*. In the instant case, the seller who was the developer had failed to effect such cover and in accordance with the requirements of the *Code des assurances*, the *notaire* mentioned this omission in the *acte* but did not offer any advice on the subject at completion. Subsequently, the house suffered damage which was found to be due to bad workmanship on the part of the builder. The buyer sued the seller and his builder and also the *notaire* for failing to fulfil his duty to advise. It was held that the *notaire*, having mentioned the lack of insurance cover in the *acte*, was not liable to the buyer 'since he was not required specially to call the attention of the parties to the consequences following necessarily from the lack of insurance'.

It is therefore reassuring to find a Court of Appeal decision expressing a somewhat more expected view (CA Montpellier 30.4.97). This was in respect of a case where a non-French seller had sold to a non-French buyer a business specializing in the hire of yachts. The *notaire*, with full knowledge of what were the intentions of the buyer as to the future conduct of the business, failed to tell him that this would involve him in expensive Customs requirements, had he been aware of which would have caused him not to conclude the purchase. The Court in holding against the *notaire* said that 'the *officier ministériel* had in this case a particular duty to advise since his clients were of foreign nationality and on the evidence lacked knowledge of (French) commercial ways and of French legislation'.

3. He must act in the best business interests of his clients by ensuring that their instructions are carried into effect in a manner which is the least expensive and is also the most satisfactory from every aspect including that of taxation.

These basic rules of conduct seem admirable and, without considering the effect of a variety of judgments passed over the years on their interpretation in practice, are easily recognizable by an English lawyer as proper professional rules. However, the comment in Yaigre and Pillebout, *Droit Professionnel Notarial* (paras 240 and 269) merits more than passing consideration in its comparison between the Latin (French) notarial system with the Anglo-Saxon (English) system adopted by solicitors. The former, it is said, is a liberal profession in the form of a public service; the latter is governed by professional bodies but without the intervention of the State. 'Each system has its advantages and disadvantages. There is more liberty in the organization and exercise of the profession in Anglo-Saxon countries but the spirit of the Latin system ensures that the draftsman of a document entered into between parties when they were in agreement shall not be the same person who attacks or defends it when difficulties arise between the parties.' A more telling support for the maintenance in transactions in which the English are involved of the basic English rule of separate representation would be difficult to find.

Happily, what would seem to be a less narrow and one hopes more favoured view of the obligations of the *notaire* at least when dealing with non-French parties is to be found in a paper prepared by Me Hervet and Me Ryssen for the

88th *Congrès des Notaires de France* held in Grenoble: 'Thus the involvement of a lawyer in Anglo-Saxon countries is different which explains the differences in his behaviour . . . His responsibilities are not based on the same criteria. Each party is represented by his own adviser. It is necessary to take into account the difference in the behaviour of foreigners in France who frequently ask for the intervention of their own advisers or a *notaire* of their choice.'

It is not suggested that the French *notaire* does not consider the rules of his profession to be sacred to him and that in circumstances in which it often will be almost impossible for him to succeed, he will do his best to fulfil his professional obligations where conflicts of interest exist. It means that he is forced to view every transaction where he is acting for both parties in a manner which is totally at odds with the English lawyer's attitude. How otherwise is he to fulfil the dictum of the *Cour de Cassation* (Cass.5.4.65) that 'the degree and extent of the duty to advise (of a *notaire*) must take account of the circumstances and particularly whether the *notaire* has played any part in the negotiations relative to the terms of the agreement or has simply been involved in giving a *forme authentique* to already concluded agreements'. Even if this comment is applied only to the sale of land, it may safely be assumed that the majority of these transactions which come into the hands of the *notaire* are those of 'an already concluded agreement' prepared in the majority of cases by the seller's estate agent.

There can, therefore, be only one rule to follow in all cases in which those used to the Anglo-Saxon (English) system are involved. Each party should be separately represented by his or her *notaire* in all cases where there is or may be a conflict of interest. Parties have an absolute right to their choice of *notaire* and nothing can override this right. Such a choice does not make for delay; on the contrary, it frequently ensures that the transaction moves along at a normal pace. Nor in the case of the purchase of land does it increase the costs for the buyer; the *notaires* involved split the fee. However, care must be taken in certain other circumstances (such as the administration of estates) where professional rules dictate who will act for which party and specific enquiries must be made.

Mention must be made of the various *Centres de recherche d'information et de documentation notarial* (CRIDON). There are five such CRIDONS at Lyon, Paris, Bordeaux-Toulouse, Nantes and Lille. They are set up by the local regional Councils and are available to members of the profession in each appropriate region. CRIDON gives opinions and advice in difficult cases to any *notaire* who consults it. It mirrors the English system of solicitors seeking opinions of counsel and the advice which it gives can generally be considered to be of the quality of the opinion of Queen's Counsel.

The work carried out by the *notaire* is charged for either by *émoluments* which are fixed by scale or *honoraires* which may be freely negotiated. The former apply, inter alia, to the majority of transactions involving land and many *actes* necessary in the administration of estates as well as the negotiation of sales. Certain other types of work are charged as *honoraires* according to the value to the client of the work done and the time taken over the transaction such as the formation of companies, the preparation of wills and general advising. Such fees are charged according to article 4 of the Decree of 8 March 1978 which requires prior notification in writing to the client of the proposed fee or method of calculation but the agreement as such of the client in writing is not obligatory. Thus the provision itself by the client of the amount asked for on account of costs is a matter which the taxing official is entitled to take into account when considering if there had been agreement under this article. All costs are subject to taxation at the instance of the client. The *notaire* may agree totally to waive his scale fees but he may not agree to reduce them except with the consent of the local *chambre des notaires*. The object of this sensible rule is to prevent *notaires* indulging in the discreditable practice of 'fee cutting' to attract work.

In the case of the sale of land, the total cost, subject to any agreement to the contrary between the parties, is always paid by the buyer. Such cost is known as *frais de notaire*. This is a misleading term since it implies that it covers only the remuneration of the *notaire*. In fact, it covers all that is involved in the transaction including stamp duties, Land Registry fees and other disbursements in addition to fees proper. It is an absolute rule of the profession that all *frais* incurred in the preparation of any notarial document must be paid to the *notaire* in advance of its preparation. This arises from the duty described above which the *notaire* owes to his client qua *mandataire* in which capacity he incurs personal liability for all disbursements.

Clients' money is required to be held in a separate account at the local *Caisse des Dépôts et Consignations* or rarely in some parts of France with Crédit Agricole. The former is not a clearing bank. It belongs to the State, does not pay interest and is not noted for the speed of dealing with transfers to and from France. The overall rule is that *notaires* may not accept cheques or drafts drawn on non-French banks. An alternative to the use of the *Caisse des Dépôts* is to give the *notaire* a draft in his favour drawn on a French bank. If the sum in question exceeds Euro 40,000 a draft is obligatory. For lesser amounts, a personal French cheque can be used if the seller will accept this but clearing times in France can be much longer than they are in the United Kingdom.

The profession is self-regulating. Each *département* has its own *chambre des notaires* in addition to a regional Council for the area covered by each Court of Appeal. There is also the *conseil supérieur du notariat* in Paris. The *chambre des notaires* has wide disciplinary powers providing annual inspections of the accounts of *notaires* and generally regulating the *notaires* within its area. The regional Council deals mainly with the interests of members of the profession *inter se* in its area. The task of the *Conseil Supérieur* is primarily to represent the profession in its dealings with the government of the day and to advise on questions of significance to the profession generally. It is normally to the local

7

chambre that the public would make any complaints. *Notaires* do not usually attack each other and it may well appear to those more familiar with the workings of the Law Society and the Office for the Supervision of Solicitors (OSS) that the French notarial profession is more zealous in the protection of its members against the public than is its English counterpart.

A *notaire* may be sued in negligence but it would be fair to say that this is not a course of action which is as likely to result in success for the client as often as would a similar action against a solicitor. Certainly, the French public is not encouraged to sue its *notaires*. There are nevertheless a considerable number of such claims every year but the proportion of *actes* giving rise to such claims is small when one considers how many such documents are prepared every year. In 1997, out of nearly 4,500,000 *actes authentiques*, only 4,000 gave rise to negligence claims. In 1998, the Court found in favour of the *notaire* in 60 per cent of these claims (*Rev Gestion & Fortune* May 1999 No. 83).

Much judicial time has been spent upon the question of whether a claim lies in contract or in tort depending on whether the fault is a breach of the duty to provide advice or to act properly as *mandataire*. The significance lies in the procedure to be adopted by the claimant, the choice of Court in which to bring the proceedings and the number of persons who can be made the subject matter of the claim. Failure on the part of the client fully to instruct the *notaire* clearly reduces the latter's liability since 'clients cannot ask the *notaire* to cover their own faults and omissions' (TGI Versailles 29 March 1966).

The *notaire* is required to effect indemnity cover in an amount equal to twice the average gross income of all notarial offices in France for the preceding year. Of the payments due to clients under such cover at least one-tenth must be found by the *notaire* personally with a limit which varies from year to year and was FF50,000 for the year 2000, or currently about Euro 7,625. Certain acts committed by a *notaire* such as those of a fraudulent nature are not covered in this way. There exists also for the profession the equivalent of the Law Society's Compensation Fund. Initially, this Fund covered only loss to clients of money and securities placed with *notaires* but in 1955 this was extended to cover all loss occasioned by *notaires* and their staff arising from negligence or other defaults in the normal course of their business. The authors of *Droit Professionnel Notarial* (paras 318 and 319) speak of the 'uncertainty of the law' as to the application of this Fund. The Fund exists on two levels. There is the *Caisse régionale de garantie* of which there is one for each area covered by a Court of Appeal. There is a *Caisse centrale de garantie* in Paris run by the *Conseil supérieur du notariat*. Contributions from each *notaire* are paid to the *Caisse régionale* which passes them on to the *Caisse centrale*. Its function is to advance to the regional *caisses* moneys required to answer claims made on them which are repayable to the central fund only out of recoveries obtained from defaulting *notaires* and their estates. It also assists and advises regional *caisses* in all aspects of claims made against them.

The *avocat*

This branch of the legal profession deals mainly but not exclusively with contentious matters. Since an excellent rule for the non-French to observe is never to become involved, if it is at all possible, in litigation in France, the *avocat* is not a professional whom the foreigner is likely often to meet. Litigation in France is not particularly expensive but it can be extremely slow and the French have a tendency to appeal any unfavourable decision since this puts off the evil day for a long period. It cannot be without significance that whilst an appellant who has lost in the Court of First Instance need not satisfy the judgment against him as a condition of lodging his appeal, if on losing his appeal he is minded to go higher to the *Cour de Cassation*, he must then comply with the judgment of the Court of Appeal before his case can be heard at that lofty level. Appeals to that Court can take many years to be heard and this rule is a useful protection for the party which has won the appeal in the Court of Appeal.

The services of the *avocat* are, however, required by the non-French client when it is desired to bid at auction or when it is necessary to obtain the *exéquateur* of the French Court to enforce an English judgment if, for example, it is desired to register a mortgage in France based on an English judgment debt.

The profession is organized into a number of Bars based on large towns and not as a countrywide profession with various circuits. The local Bar is administered by a *Conseil de l'Ordre* which has at its head a *Bâtonnier*. The right of audience of local *avocats* is limited to the Courts of the area to which the local Bar is attached. He may, however, prepare pleadings and all other documentation for any Court in the country and, of course, deal with any non-contentious matter which is within his professional competence anywhere in France.

The rules of conduct of an *avocat* are enforced by the local Bar in which reside all the necessary disciplinary powers. He is free to charge whatever fees he agrees with his clients. He is, of course, liable in negligence to his clients, the local Bar covering this under a global indemnity cover. Some *avocats* effect additional cover of this nature. With the exception of those few who specialize (and these are almost always *ex-conseils juridiques* whose speciality was before fusion with the *avocat* mainly in commercial and tax work) the *avocat* has a general practice and there is not the same obligation on him to act for clients needing his services as with the *notaire*. He is not an *officier ministériel*.

The *avoué*

This profession now hardly exists, having been some years ago amalgamated with that of the *avocat*. His role today is limited to work before the Courts of Appeal where his services are obligatory. He is normally instructed by *avocats* and represents the interests of their client before the Court, draws pleadings and deals with other documentation but he does not plead in Court.

9

The *huissier*

The main services provided by the *huissier* can be particularly valuable in relation to transactions in land. He is, like the *notaire*, an *officier ministériel*, whose primary tasks are the service of documents and judgments, the execution of judgments and other work of a nature akin to that of the English bailiff or sheriff's officer. However, he is also available to the public as well as to the courts, as a process server and many private documents are required by law to be served *par voie d'huissier*.

He is also invaluable as the provider of the *constat*. This is a document prepared by a *huissier* at the request of either a private individual or of the court which records a situation as at the date of inspection. Whilst in law it has no special authority and can be contraverted by suitable proof, in practice it is treated with great respect and seldom, if ever, questioned. Its uses are manifold.

Thus, if a dispute arises over a building contract as to whether the builder has kept to his time schedule or has failed to use prescribed materials or is otherwise alleged to be at fault a *constat* is indispensable if proceedings are contemplated. On sales of property, if there are arguments as to what *meubles* have or have not by attachment become *immeubles* and the answer may turn on the method by which such attachment has been effected, a *constat d'huissier* is called for. It is the standard method of preparing Schedules of Condition and Dilapidations or to establish a trespass. It is interesting to note that in accordance with French reverence for such detail, a *constat* is void if it does not show the full names, occupation, address, nationality, and date and place of birth of the person at whose request it was made. This ubiquitous requirement to be found in many other circumstances need deter no one who is forewarned.

In his capacity as process server, the usual procedure is to attend at the address of the person to be served and if that person is absent, to leave notice of his visit indicating that he will deposit the process at the local *mairie*. This will be counted as good service if it is reasonable to expect that it will come to the notice of the person to be served. If that person is known to be abroad, the document to be served will be translated and sent to the country of that person's residence by what are known as *voies diplomatiques*. If this is England, it will be served by the local county court bailiff or arrive via the French Embassy. The delay in this method of service can be astounding. A recent and typical example is of a French writ dated 1 March 2001 with a date for the equivalent of appearance of 21 August 2001 which was served in England in February 2002.

PART I

LAND LAW

2

IMMOVABLE PROPERTY IN FRENCH LAW

Introduction 13
The nature of property 13
   Immeubles 14
   Meubles 15
   The distinction between *immeubles* and *meubles* 15
Interests in property 16
Rights over land 16
Rights *in rem* 16
Ownership 18
Le patrimoine 19
Types of sales of land 19
Charges 20
The Land Registry system 20
Etat civil 22

Introduction

This chapter is intended to provide in general terms a short explanation of many of the facets of the ownership of land in France. Most of these are dealt with in detail in subsequent chapters but it is considered that it would prove helpful if the contents of those chapters can be appreciated in the light of a general understanding of the subject.

The nature of property

The laconic wording of article 516 of the *Code civil* announces that all property (the French all-embracing word used is *biens*) is either *immeuble* or *meuble*. It is not wholly safe to apply the English distinction between realty and personalty to what at first sight seem to be their French counterparts. At the time when the French *Code civil* was promulgated in the early nineteenth century, some 90 per cent of all property in France consisted of land or interests in land and only 10 per cent was accounted for by other kinds of property. Since that time, the situation has much changed so that many types of property of widely varying kinds, then unknown, have come to play an increasingly important part in the national economy of any country. It has, therefore, become necessary to fit property of a nature unknown in 1804 into the wording of article 516. Hence the following article 517 provides some elaboration of what are to be deemed to be and to be treated as *immeubles* and *meubles*.

It is considered more satisfactory when describing the nature of French property to retain the terms used by the *Code civil*, namely, 'immovables' and 'movables', the former meaning in general terms that which can be touched but not moved whilst the latter may conveniently be defined as things which are not immovables. As will be seen from what is said below, it is, when dealing with the nature of *immeubles*, necessary to have also an appreciation of what constitutes *meubles* in French law.

Immeubles

Property is defined as being immovable by article 517 '*ou par leur nature, ou par leur destination ou par l'objet auquel ils s'appliquent*' (by reason of (i) its innate character or (ii) the use to which it is or is intended to be put or (iii) the object to which it is applied). Articles 518 to 524 elaborate this basic definition. It follows from this group of articles that:

1. By reason of its innate character, the soil itself and generally all that is attached to it are *immeubles*. Hence, they include buildings for whatever purposes they have been erected and, specifically by virtue of article 523, pipes conducting water to a house or other building are *immeubles*. Wild or cultivated plant life on land and trees and forests are *immeubles* but harvested crops or fruit or felled trees are *meubles*.

2. By application of the general rule of French law that '*l'accessoire suit le principal*' ('the general includes the particular') *meubles* intended to be used together with the ownership of an *immeuble* are converted into *immeubles*. Hence, all objects which may by themselves be *meubles* placed by the owner on his own land and necessary for its enjoyment or for the enhancement of its value or its use and all things permanently attached to the land or which cannot be removed without damage to that part of the land to which they are attached are treated as *immeubles*. Article 524 contains a charming list of items which are thus converted into *immeubles* which includes 'rabbits in warrens, pigeons belonging to dove-houses, fish in ponds' and items required in the husbandry of land and in viticulture. The list gives one an interesting picture of the use to which land was put at the time when the Code was enacted.

   This list also includes 'all movable effects which an owner has attached to the land so to continue for ever'. This addendum coupled with the effect of article 525 can have a more immediate and significant result. That article dictates that items attached to premises by 'plaster, lime or cement' become part of the *immeuble* as do mirrors when 'their frames form part of the body of the wainscot' and also statues (including those found in gardens) when 'placed in niches formed expressly to receive them even though they may be capable of removal without breaking or damage'. This can cause considerable unhappiness on the part of a seller when faced with an obdurate buyer and surprise on the part of a non-French buyer if he is not conversant with the normal French ways exhibited by a French seller. There has, however, been a recent case (Cass.23.01.02) in which, reversing the judgments of the Courts below, it was held that electric convector heaters hung on walls are *meubles* as opposed to other electrical equipment which has become attached to an *immeuble*. This has led to what appears to be the novel and salutary practice of indicating clearly in sale contracts that the seller may not remove as part of the *immeuble* such things as door handles, light sockets and even fitted carpets which are often stuck with glue to the floor.

3. Property which is treated as *immobilier* by reason of the object to which it is applied are *droits réels* and are strictly artificial rights in the sense that they are not *choses* but rights in respect of *choses*. They differ from *droits personnels*, the number of which are, in the words of a French Professor of Law, limited only by the extent of the ingenuity needed to add to those already in existence, in that *droits réels* are creatures of statute and thus limited in their number by law. Such rights which include easements and life interests are referred to hereafter in this chapter.

Meubles

These include, as would be expected, most of the objects defined as personal chattels by the Administration of Estates Act 1925, section 55(i)(x). Also included in French law as *meubles* is certain property specifically excepted by that definition section and, among other assets, intellectual property and rights of action in respect of movables. As in English law, leasehold interests are *meubles* also in French law, conferring only a contractual right of occupation. There are certain exceptions (with which admittedly few non-French are likely to come into contact) to this rule. Certain leases of this exceptional kind are also referred to below under the heading of 'Rights *in rem*'.

The distinction between immeubles and meubles

The need to distinguish between these two types of property can on occasions give rise in French property transactions to more difficulty than does the need to distinguish in England between what are fixtures and fittings and what does and what does not pass with the property sold. Failure to appreciate these differences even when the parties involved are both French can be a source of acrimony and it is essential to ensure (as it is the undoubted duty of the *notaire(s)* involved so to do) that all contracts precisely indicate what is and what is not included in a sale of an *immeuble*.

There are also a limited number of circumstances when what is ostensibly a movable is treated at least fiscally as an immovable. Thus, the mooring for a boat in a marina may be owned through the ownership of shares in the company which owns the marina itself. The ownership of a flat in a block may be linked to the ownership of shares in a company owning the whole building (Chapter 10). The shares in each case are *meubles* but a sale of these shares is deemed to be a sale of the underlying asset which is an *immeuble* and will attract stamp duty and capital gains tax on that basis. On the other hand, such an asset will pass on the death of the owner as a *meuble* in accordance with the law of his domicile.

Interests in property

The interests in immovables and indeed in all other types of property which can exist in French law are: (i) *pleine propriété* or an absolute interest in possession; (ii) *usufruit* or a life interest; (iii) *nue propriété* or absolute interest in remainder. The division of an absolute interest into a life interest and an interest in remainder is known as the *démembrement de propriété*. The *usufruit* must not be confused with the *droit d'occupation et d'usage* which is often granted for life and has a particular significance in inheritance law. It may safely be compared to a mere personal licence to occupy premises.

Life interests in land and in any kind of property can be created *inter vivos* in addition to those which arise on a death. The reasons for the *inter vivos* creation of life interests among the French are usually fiscal since there is basically no charge to inheritance tax on the cesser of a limited interest on death. However, the French Revenue is wide awake to what can be so achieved in this manner which it is pleased to call on occasions an *abus de droit* or tax evasion and such arrangements if indulged in for tax reasons need skilful advice for both the English and the French.

Rights over land

Easements over and restrictions against property arise by operation of law which may be of a general nature such as rights of eavesdrop, drainage or rights of way of necessity imposed by C.civ.arts.675 to 685-1. Others may be imposed by individual Laws for the benefit of the community, such as planning rules and restrictions or rights of compulsory purchase given to most local authorities and in country areas to SAFER (*Sociétés d'Aménagement Foncier et d'Établissement Rural*) which are local Agricultural Committees whose task is to watch over the market in agricultural property. Easements and rights may also be freely created by agreement *inter partes*. These run with the land and rules (C.civ.arts.686 et seq) apply to the acquisition of and to the extinguishment of such rights by prescription.

Rights *in rem*

Such rights are *droits réels* and are subdivided into two types, namely, *droits principaux* and *droits accessoires*. The former are rights of ownership of various interests in respect of land, easements, certain types of leases and the *concession immobilière*. The latter are rights of the recovery of land under the various types of mortgage which exist in French law. The derogation from the general rule that a lease cannot create a *droit réel* has exceptions which have no statutory foundation but appear to stem from judge-made law based on sociological considerations alone. The types of leases which fall within the exception all contain provisions which are deliberately more attractive to a lessee than are those which normally appear in an ordinary lease at a rack rent and are:

(1) the *bail emphytéotique* which is a lease akin to the English long lease at a ground rent intended to encourage the development of agricultural land but not always granted for that limited purpose;

(2) the *bail à construction* or building lease designed for the building of property available for letting purposes only.

These two kinds of leases must be granted for terms of not less than eighteen nor more than ninety-nine years.

(3) the *bail à réhabilitation* which has no counterpart in English law and which may only be granted for a minimum term of twelve years to a limited type of lessee and is intended to facilitate the provision of housing for occupation by the underprivileged in property known as HLM or *habitations à loyer modéré*.

A further type of lease created by statute (Law of 30 December 1967) considered generally to be a quasi-*droit réel* is the *concession immobilière*. This is grant of the occupancy of business premises for a minimum of twenty years against payment of an annual licence fee which, without conferring all the benefits of a lease of such premises, gives certain useful rights to the occupier without requiring payment of a premium by the tenant.

A conflict between rights *in rem* and *in personam* can arise in what are likely to be not unusual circumstances relating to the purchase of property by the English in France. By Article 16(1) of the Brussels Convention of 27 September 1968 on Jurisdiction and the Enforcement of Judgments in Civil and Commercial Matters which was given the force of law in England by the Civil Jurisdiction and Judgments Act 1982 the exclusive jurisdiction in proceedings which 'have as their object rights *in rem* in immovable property' was awarded to the Courts of the country in which the immovable property is situate. As stated above, a right *in rem* in respect of immovable property is the right to ownership in such property as against the world at large. A right *in personam* in English law can also exist in respect of immovable property but may not qualify for the application of Article 16(1) of the Convention.

It was so held in the case of *Webb v Webb* [1994] 3 All ER 911, the facts of which were as follows. An English parent transferred his own cash in England to his son's account in France with which to buy a flat in that country to be registered in the name of the son. Both parent and son occupied the flat from time to time. Later, the father applied to the Court in England for a declaration that the son held the flat as a bare trustee and that on being called upon to do so, he should vest its ownership in the father. The son challenged the jurisdiction of the English Courts on the grounds that since what was involved was a right *in rem* in immovable property, the French Courts alone had jurisdiction. The son lost his action at first instance and on appeal the case was referred to the European Court. It was there held that it was not enough that the action had a link with immovable property for the Convention to apply. The father had a claim based on a right *in personam* in respect of immovable property, namely that the son held the property in a fiduciary capacity. Hence the right in this and presumably similar cases is not covered by the Convention.

Ownership

C.civ.art.544 says that 'ownership is the right to enjoy and dispose of *choses* in the most unfettered manner but so that they are not used in a manner prohibited by law or regulation'. This right of ownership extends by virtue of article 546 to the 'products (of land) and to all things appertaining to it whether naturally or artificially'. It incorporates (article 551) all that is attached to the land and (article 552) all that is above and below the soil.

Ownership may be acquired in two ways. It may be acquired from a previous owner by purchase for consideration or by way of gift or inheritance. In general terms, since the period of prescription in respect of actions concerning land is thirty years, a thirty-year title is required on a purchase. In any event, as a matter of Land Registry practice, every *acte de vente* must refer to the registration of the vendor. Special rules in this respect apply to sales by donees *inter vivos* or by beneficiaries on a death.

Ownership may also be acquired by adverse possession (*prescription acquisitive* or *usucaption*). Title by adverse possession is based on C.civ.art.2262 which provides a general prescriptive rule which is applicable to land as well as to other property and rights. The use of land by a person as though he was its owner over a period of thirty years (which can in certain circumstances be interrupted or suspended) peacefully, publicly, and in a non-equivocal manner will satisfy the requirements of the article.

Save in the case of the acquisition of easements by prescription, a further method of such acquisition exists under C.civ.art.2265. If a person has reason in good faith to consider that he has acquired property under an *acte* but his seller was not at that time the owner of the property (but not by reason of mere lack of form in respect of that document), he may obtain a title by adverse possession in ten or twenty years depending on whether the true owner lives or does not live within the jurisdiction of the Court of Appeal in which the property is situate. The title so acquired is in either case evidenced by a notarial *acte de notoriété* signed by trustworthy witnesses recounting the relevant facts.

Le patrimoine

There is no English translation in common parlance which precisely explains this French word which describes the totality of all the *droits* or *biens* belonging to a person which are capable of being reduced to terms of money, It is, however, a word which hovers frequently on the lips of the French and describes a situation of which they are very conscious. In law, a *droit* or right expresses the power which a person has over a thing such as the right of absolute or limited ownership or over another person who is his debtor. A *bien* or thing may be *corporéal* such as a house or a machine or may be *incorporéal* such as a chose in action or a debt. To figure in a *patrimoine*, a *droit* or a *bien* must be of a nature capable of being seized in execution since the essence of the *patrimoine* is that its assets must be able to answer for its liabilities. This characteristic, known in French as its *universalité de droit*, results in the application of the *droit de gage générale* available, with few exceptions, to all creditors by virtue of C.civ.arts.2092 and 2093 who are thereby enabled to seize and sell any goods of a debtor in repayment of a debt. The *gage* is not in respect of any one determined asset but on all the assets of the debtor and no creditor has any preference in respect of any asset if that asset is not subject to a specific charge.

Types of sales of land

The French system includes types of sales which either do not exist in England or, if their equivalent is to be found in the English system, are hardly recognizable in their French form to the English practitioner. These include:

1. Sales of property *en copropriété* (Chapter 15) which is the only method which can be used in France for the transfer of the ownership of flats. The English equivalent is what is now referred to as commonhold and it is also known in the United States as condominium ownership. Since a very large proportion of the French live in flats, this type of sale is frequent.
2. Sales of property via a *société civile d'attribution* (Chapter 10). These are effected by the sale of the shares in such a company which give the right to the ownership of a part of the property yet to be built or reconstructed. It will be appreciated that all subsequent sales of such flats will be sales *en copropriété*.
3. Sales *en viager* (Chapter 12), the consideration for which is the payment of an annuity to the seller with or without payment also of a capital sum.
4. Sales *en l'état futur d'achèvement* and sales *à terme* (Chapter 8) which are sales 'on plan' and which can be used for the purchase of a single house or of a flat or part of a property to be constructed and which are much hedged around by statutory rules.
5. Sales *en jouissance à temps partagé* (Chapter 11) which are time-share sales which can only be achieved through the medium of a special type of company

which is much controlled by statute in a manner which obviates many of the doubts which can arise with this type of ownership in other countries.

Charges

There being no distinction made between what English law describes as legal estates and equitable interests, all mortgages in respect of land are the equivalent of the English charge by way of legal mortgage. The standard charge created by agreement between the parties (*hypothèque conventionnelle*) is the case of the ordinary house purchase mortgage. Other charges which arise by operation of law or which are based on the judgment of an appropriate court have perhaps a tinge of the English equitable charge but there exists nothing such as the charge by the deposit of deeds that exists in France. Indeed, as is explained elsewhere, possession by an owner of a certified copy of his document of purchase, the original of which remains in the archives of the appropriate *notaire*, provides proof only of the act of purchase itself and not of continued ownership thereafter by the purchaser. Thus, its deposit with another provides no security at all.

The Land Registry system

Land registration in France is known as *publicité foncière*. The equivalent of the English Land Registry in France is under the control of the Ministry of Finance. It is made up of a number of local *bureaux des hypothèques* each with a *conservateur* or local Land Registrar together with the local offices of the *cadastre*. Land Registry fees are known as the 'salary' of the Registrar. Each *commune* or local authority area has its own cadastral office which holds the local cadastral plan. This indicates by means of numbered *lots* (plots) of land the identity of the owner of each plot. It is an elaborated equivalent of that section of the English Land Registry which maintains the public index map on which are based the filed plans. Copies of the cadastral plans can be obtained on request which it is often desirable to do since many *actes de vente* contain no plans but merely a description of the property sold by reference to its cadastral plot numbers.

From 1930 onwards the *cadastre* has been gradually updated and most (but not all) properties are now described by reference to what is known as the *cadastre renové*.

However, the *cadastre* has an added fiscal significance unknown to the English Land Registry since it was set up in Napoleonic times primarily as an aid to the taxation of the ownership of land. From time to time the taxation element of the *cadastre* makes itself apparent for it is not unknown for the seller of land to be pursued for the payment of *taxe foncière* or land tax long after he has sold his land since the local *cadastre* office has not been told of the transfer of ownership by the *bureau des hypothèques*. An indication of ownership of a piece of land at the local *cadastre* is not proof of its ownership.

There are kept at the relevant *bureaux des hypothèques* (i) *fiches personnelles* (Proprietorship Register) in the name of each owner of land or right affecting land and (ii) *fiches parcellaires* (Property Register) for each *lot* in the *cadastre* and which record all transactions relating to that *lot* and in which are registered all charges and rights over the land. In addition, special *fiches* are kept for properties in towns which can be more easily identified by street numbers. The system is not ineffective but is often very slow in its operation. It is worthy of note that all the registers appear to be kept in handwriting so that the results of all searches are also in (French) handwriting and are frequently difficult for the non-French to read. The registers are open to all and are often a simple way to track down the *notaire* who dealt with the last transaction. Surprisingly but as part of the ubiquitous French system of *état civil*, to make a search, it is necessary to give not only the name and address of the owner but also his place and date of birth and, if the owner is female, details of her maiden name and date of marriage.

Until 1969 documents relating to the transfer of land and to various other transactions related to land were, as in England, subject to the double requirement of stamping and subsequent lodgement for registration at the Land Registry together with the payment of the appropriate Land Registry fees. With certain few exceptions, this system was replaced by the Law of 26 December 1969 with what is known as *la formalité unique* so that stamp duty (*enregistrement*) and Land Registry fees (*salaire du Conservateur*) are now represented by a single payment.

The registration of transactions falls into two groups:

1. Transactions the registration of which is required by law so that failure to register:
   (a) results in the transaction being unenforceable as against third parties to the transaction. Such transactions include:
      (i)   all transfers of land *inter vivos* whether by way of gift, exchange or for any other valuable consideration including the allotment of shares in a company,
      (ii) the creation of life interests, rights of occupation, the grant of easements and the renunciation of certain rights over land,
      (iii) *bail à construction*, and
      (iv) the grant of leases for a term exceeding twelve years.
      Not included among this type of transaction is the abandonment of interests in land by reason of the renunciation by a beneficiary of his interest in the estate of a deceased person (Chapter 34) or certain changes of a *régime matrimonial* (Chapter 20); or
   (b) gives grounds for an action for damages at the suit of any person injured by a failure to register a transaction. Included in this numerous category are documents relating to the rights of inheritance on a death such as an *acte de notoriété*, the fulfilment of a condition, *conventions d'indivision*,

certain administrative decisions relating to land and documents interrupting or renouncing the benefit of a period of prescription.

2. Transactions the registration of which is voluntary but where failure to register renders the transaction unenforceable as against third parties. The most important of these is the mortgage and the *privilège du vendeur* (Chapter 14) where a lender or a seller in an unregistered transaction is left without the protection of his security and is left with only the personal covenant of the borrower or buyer as the case may be.

In this connection, it must be remembered that a *promesse de vente* must for purely fiscal reasons (CGI.art.1840-A) whether made in the form of an *acte authentique* or *sous seing privé* be stamped within one month and registered within two months if in the former form (being not subject to the *formalité unique*) or within ten days if in ssp form after its execution. Failure to do so renders the *promesse de vente* void. On the other hand, this requirement being solely to prevent tax evasion, registration as such confers none of the benefits available to transactions of the kind referred to above.

With the exception of the *promesse de vente*, only documents in the form of an *acte authentique*, *acte administratif* or court judgment can be registered so that a sale evidenced only by a document *sous seing privé* cannot be registered although the document itself may fulfil the requirements as to a binding sale of C.civ.art.1582. Such a document executed *sous seing privé* can, however, be lodged with a *notaire* and provided that all the parties formally recognize the contents and their signatures, that document can be treated as an *acte authentique*.

Registration must be effected within two months of execution of the relevant *acte*. The transfer of the property in question is, as between the parties, perfected by the execution of the *acte de vente* but only registration renders it valid as against third parties. It must also be noted that, unlike the English system, registration does not provide any state guarantee of title.

A particular point arises in connection with searches (*états hypothécaires*). These do not effect a blocking of the register as they do in England. Thus, it is possible for a seller who has contracted to sell to A to sell the same property to B without it necessarily coming to the knowledge of the parties or the *notaire(s)* at completion. It is likewise possible for a seller to mortgage his property between contract and completion and for this not to be known to anyone at completion. This problem is treated at more length in Chapter 7 but would appear to be a serious defect in the system which could be remedied by recourse to that in force in England.

Etat civil

It may appear strange that it should be necessary to make any special reference in this chapter to the *état civil* of persons which, however, it is obligatory to disclose in respect of almost every transaction in France. Its use goes far beyond the mere identification of the person involved. French documentation abounds in personal information and few documents are complete without the date and place of birth of the parties, their dates and places of marriage (if applicable), details of their divorce (if any) and of subsequent remarriage (or not as the case may be), a description of their *régime matrimonial* and of their nationality. Each item plays some role in the ability of a person to acquire, dispose of or deal in property of any kind and in ensuring that he is the person and has the capacity he claims in the document.

The English do not have *régimes matrimoniaux*. By no means all *notaires* are aware of this and many tend to describe English married couples as 'married according to British (sic) law under a marriage contract of the separation of goods'. Nor is it unknown to find a reference to the '*régime* created by' the Married Woman's Property Act 1882. The correct description of the English married couple's property rights *inter se* is '*mariés à défaut de contrat préalable à leur mariage célébré le . . . . . . à . . . . . . sous le régime anglais équivalent au régime français de la séparation de biens*'.

It is important to be aware of the need to supply and check these details on innumerable occasions and also to know that birth, death and marriage certificates must be not more than three months 'old', that is, in the case of such English documents, the certified copy must be obtained not earlier than three months before the date on which it is produced in France. The need for this arises from the French registration system which is interlinked so that the death of a person is noted against his birth certificate and his divorce against his marriage certificate and so on. In addition, the English 'short' birth certificate is not acceptable when it is necessary to show *filiation* (parentage) which is needed more frequently in France than might be supposed.

3

THE SALE OF LAND

Introduction 25
Negotiation of sales 26
The estate agent 27
    Qualification to act 27
    Mandat de vente 28
    Taking of deposits 28
    Agent's commission 29
    Liability of estate agents 29
Choice of *notaire* 29
The *notaire* 30
Classes of contracts 30
Statutory protection for the buyer 31
    La Loi SRU 31
    Contracts *sous seing privé (ssp)* 32
    Notarial contracts 33
La Loi Scrivener 34
La lésion 34
Matters common to all contracts 35

Introduction

Article 1582 which is the opening article of the first chapter of Part VI of the *Code civil* headed 'Of Sale' reads as follows: '*La vente est une convention par laquelle l'un s'oblige à livrer une chose et l'autre à la payer*' (A sale is an agreement by which one party is bound to deliver a thing and another to pay for it). The subsequent article 1583 continues '*Elle est parfaite entre les parties et la propriété est acquise de droit à l'acheteur à l'égard du vendeur, dès qu'on est convenu de la chose et du prix quoique la chose n'ait pas encore été livrée ni le prix payé*' (It (a sale) is complete as between the parties and property passes in law to the purchaser from the seller as soon as both the thing and price have been agreed upon notwithstanding that the thing has not been delivered or the price paid'). It must be assumed that the draftsman of the article has deliberately used the word '*chose*' (thing) to indicate that it applies to both immovable and movable property of every kind. Such a provision which envisages a verbal as well as a written agreement is, of course, a significant departure from the venerable rule of English law in respect of sales of land which is enshrined in section 40 of the Law of Property Act 1925 that contracts for the sale or other disposition of land must be or be evidenced in writing. However, recent very significant changes in the law effected by la Loi SRU, to which reference is made hereafter, relating to contracts for the sale of land by non-professional purchasers have bitten deeply into the previous fundamental concept of *consensuelisme* reflected by article 1582 in respect of what must be a very large proportion of transactions of this nature.

The *Code civil* contains no less than fifty-four articles on the various methods of proof. In many cases, writing is an absolute requirement as evidence of proof but it is necessary to appreciate that compliance with such a requirement does not affect the validity of the agreement in issue. Thus, it is incorrect to say that the *Code civil* contains any rule that a contract for the sale of land must be in writing. It may be necessary to have writing to be able to prove the existence of such a contract but this need not be the contract itself.

Notwithstanding the basic inviolability of an agreement under article 1582, there have clearly been few who wished in practice to rely on the article alone. A naked agreement of the kind which it envisages has evident disadvantages. Modern legislation is of a complex nature and affects the ownership of property in many fundamental ways, so that few would-be buyers have wished to be unconditionally bound to buy without any professional investigation of all the relevant factors involved in such a transaction. Moreover, many would not wish to be bound to complete a purchase without at least a formal date for completion being fixed. In such circumstances, the parties not wishing to be bound by an agreement perfected by article 1582 have for many years made use of one of a number of contracts which govern the progression to completion of the transaction and thus modify in practice the effect of the article.

To avoid much misunderstanding, it must be borne in mind that what in England is known as a contract for the sale of land, in France is called an *avant-contrat* or pre-contract. What in English conveyancing parlance is the conveyance or transfer is in French the *contrat*, the document used being known as an *acte de vente*. To avoid confusion, the French *avant-contrat* is throughout this book called 'the contract' and the transfer an *acte de vente*.

Negotiation of sales

Very few contracts for the sale of land of any kind are entered into by the parties themselves without the intervention of a professional negotiator. Even in the deepest country, such as the Auverne or Corrèze, it is unlikely that the Frenchman will indulge, as still does the Italian peasant, in the *'attino'* or 'little conveyance' which is a void transfer of land under which the 'buyer' is tacitly allowed to retain possession until he has obtained a prescriptive right to the land. It is a simple method, if undetected, of avoiding taxation on both the seller and the buyer and all legal costs. The French have also, however, an ingrained dislike of paying tax incurred in transactions in land—capital gains tax by the seller and stamp duty by the buyer—and 'under the table' sales should always be looked on with grave suspicion. Estate agents notoriously indulge in this practice; *notaires* are supposed to be unaware of it. If this kind of tax evasion is practised, it usually involves the preparation of two contracts by the agent, that at the higher price being retained by him and that at the lower price disclosed to the *notaire* who works on it as the basis of the transaction. That at the higher price is kept as a threat against the failure of the buyer to make the necessary 'under the table' payment. It is a practice never to be indulged in by either buyer or seller. It is neither honest nor safe.

The estate agent

Qualification to act

Although the *notaire* is still involved in negotiating sales of property, his role is very limited and usually in respect of sales of property in estates in the administration of which he has been instructed. By far the most frequent intermediary between seller and buyer is the *agent immobilier* or estate agent. His profession is very strictly controlled by the Loi Hoguet of 2 January 1970, the persons subject to this Law being those who regularly engage on behalf of others in (inter alia) the purchase, sale, letting or exchange of buildings or land or of shares in companies which give the holder the right to the ownership of such buildings or land including time-sharing and also generally in the management of property. The Law applies to all (i) dealings in land in France, (ii) transactions where the client of the agent is French or (iii) cases when the price in question is paid in France but not to *marchands de biens* or property dealers.

No person may carry on the business of an estate agent in France unless he is the holder of a *carte professionnelle*, given by the local *Préfecture*, and indicating that the holder has complied with all the statutory requirements. These include the fact that he has achieved a certain level of proficiency which may vary from a comparatively high knowledge of law to that which does not appear to require much knowledge of the legal and practical aspects of the sale of and other dealings in land. In addition, no one may carry on such a business if he is not covered by a fidelity bond and professional indemnity policy or is under any legal incapacity or has been disqualified from carrying on such a business.

Any citizen of the EU can obtain a *carte professionnelle* if he can produce evidence of a standard of professional ability equivalent to that required of the French (of which he may be asked to sit a test) and also has a sufficient knowledge of the French language. There is, therefore, no reason why an English person working from England cannot, if he fulfils all the requirements, obtain a *carte professionnelle*.

Anyone who acts in any of the transactions referred to above in circumstances which demand a *carte professionnelle* without holding one is liable to a fine of

Euro 4,500 for the first offence and twice that amount and/or imprisonment of not more than six months for any further offence.

Mandat de vente

No estate agent may undertake any of the activities enumerated above unless he has obtained the written authority of his client in a form laid down by the Loi Hoguet and, in the case of the sale of land, called a *mandat de vente*. This is a document which all sellers of land are or should be asked to sign when instructing an agent and which, although it is usually in fairly standard form, requires careful attention as to certain of its contents. It is unlikely that a seller will not be asked to sign such a document since failure to hold one in due form ensures that the agent is not entitled to commission.

A *mandat de vente* must by law contain certain information. It must indicate the price or at least the minimum price at which the agent may sell, what is his commission and how it is calculated, whether it creates an exclusive or non-exclusive agency, how the agency is determined and what limits are placed on the seller if he sells himself or through another agent. The duration of the *mandat* must be stated, irrespective of whether the agency is exclusive or non-exclusive. Failure to provide this information renders the *mandat* void. A *mandat* which provides for automatic renewal in default of notice to determine is valid as to its initial period but becomes thereafter void (Cass.8.10.86). Great care must be taken with the clause which designates the duration of the agency and its renewal and determination and its provisions must be rigorously adhered to. A *mandat* must be signed in two parts and entered in a special register kept by the agent and given a number which must appear in the document itself.

Taking of deposits

Agents who take clients' money must operate a separate clients' bank account. The question may arise whether any deposit paid on the signature of a contract should be paid to the agent or to the *notaire(s)* instructed. It is prudent for a buyer to pay his deposit to his own *notaire* to be held by him until completion but many sellers insist that it be paid to their *notaire* if the parties are separately represented. If the payment is made to the seller's agent, he has no lien on it for his commission or any special entitlement for its recovery other than to sue for it under his *mandat*. It follows, therefore, that it is not lawful for an agent to account at completion for the deposit less his commission; it is, however, not unknown for this to happen and it is often tolerated.

The role of the *agent immobilier* has, since the coming into effect of the Loi SRU, taken on another significant role in respect of the receipt of deposits from purchasers. Such a person being the possessor of a *carte professionnelle* is treated as a professional covered by a fidelity bond who is therefore authorized by that Law to accept such deposits during the period when purchasers may withdraw from contracts into which they have entered.

Agent's commission
The general rule throughout France is that the seller pays the sale commission. It is not unusual for property to be sold at a price which takes into account commission so that the seller has in effect required the buyer to pay the commission. On the other hand, there are a few parts of France where commission is shared between seller and buyer or, of course, a seller can ask a buyer to pay all the commission and not hide it in the price he asks. Whatever is the case, the arrangements made must figure in the *mandat* and are again repeated in whatever kind of contract is eventually signed.

Liability of estate agents
An *agent immobilier* to whom a *mandat* is given is by reason of his right to remuneration a person to whom the obligations of C.civ.art.1992 apply: 'an agent is liable not only in fraud but also for all misconduct he may commit during his agency. The liability of an agent who acts gratuitously is in respect of his misconduct less than that in the case of an agent in receipt of remuneration.' He is therefore liable at the top end of the scale to his clients for any failure properly to execute his duties. It is common practice for contracts to be drawn by the seller's agent, the argument being that this saves much time (but not expense) and the parties can feel that they have a firm bargain much earlier than if one or possibly two *notaires* were involved. Many agents do not have the ability to draw contracts, particularly in the case of country properties, and errors such as the omission of easements or misdescriptions of parts of the property and more serious errors can occur. There can be no hard and fast rule on this score but generally it is safer for a buyer having instructed a *notaire* of his choice to require a contract drawn by the seller's *notaire* and submitted to his own *notaire* for approval so that independence of advice is achieved from the outset and the contract has been prepared by those proficient in the law.

The rates of agents' commission are freely negotiable but are likely to be within the range of 6–7 per cent of the sale price. It must be remembered that French TVA or VAT is 19.6 per cent and care must be taken to discover whether commission is HT (*hors taxe*) or TTC (*tous taxes compris*).

Choice of *notaire*

A buyer should not accept without advice any suggestion that he use a *notaire* who is recommended by the agent. The *notaire* suggested will usually be the person who acts for the vendor or, if not, has some link with the agent. It is desirable when the nationality of one of the parties is not French to obtain prior advice as to the choice of *notaire* from a suitable person acquainted with the laws and procedures of both countries. It is an inviolable rule that the purchaser has the choice of his own *notaire* and it cannot be too often repeated that this right should always be exercised.

The *notaire*

On occasion, negotiations for a sale will be carried out by a *notaire*. This is comparatively rare but there are still a few *notaires* individually or in groups who specialize in this kind of work. Usually the *notaire* has a less parochial outlook than the *agent immobilier* whose geographical range can be surprisingly limited. Those *notaires* who undertake the negotiation of sales and purchases are subject to a series of regulations, some of which are national and some of which are promulgated by their local *chambre des notaires* in addition to the general rules which govern their professional behaviour. It follows from this that when negotiating a land transaction, the *notaire* does not act as the adviser of one party only. He must be impartial, advising both parties and disclosing all the defects as well as the advantages of the property in question. He may not advertise business of this kind generally although he is permitted to do so in specialized journals and in his own office provided that the details are limited to one particular property.

The choice of a *notaire* to negotiate the sale or purchase of a property does not bind the potential buyer or seller to use that *notaire* for the subsequent conveyancing work and if separate *notaires* are instructed, each will be paid the scale fee for the work he has done. A *notaire* instructed to negotiate a sale of or seek a property for a buyer requires a *mandat* but it is not subject to the rules which cover those of the *agent immobilier*. It may create an exclusive or a non-exclusive agency and it is desirable that it should state clearly whether the task of the *notaire* is limited to finding a buyer or a seller or whether he is authorized to prepare and have signed a suitable contract.

The fees of a *notaire* for negotiating a sale are normally paid by the purchaser as forming part of the *frais d'acte* payable by every purchaser (C.civ.art.1593) notwithstanding that the *mandat* was given by the seller. If this rule is to be varied, the *mandat* and the contract must so state. It will be very rare that the fees payable to a *notaire* for negotiating a transaction are not less than those payable to an *agent immobilier*. They are scale fees based on the value of the property as to which, see page 7.

Classes of contracts

There are four principal kinds of contracts for the sale of land. These are:

1. *La promesse unilatérale de vente.* As its name implies, a contract of this kind is not of the nature used in ordinary English transactions. It is, in fact, the grant of an option by the seller to an intending buyer providing a *promesse unilatérale* by the seller to sell at an agreed price if the buyer exercises his option on or before a given date. It is not clear why this type of agreement has come to be used for what is very rarely other than an ordinary sale with no option intended to be involved. Generally, it is used by the *notaires* and other

draftsmen fairly frequently in parts of France north of the Loire but it is rarely used south of that river. It is not the type of contract which is preferred by the majority of *notaires* or estate agents throughout France and since the choice falls on the parties themselves (however infrequently this choice may be offered), it should not be used unless a true option to purchase is sought. It has certain practical disadvantages when used for the straightforward sale for which its use was never intended. It has no advantage for the buyer seeking mortgage finance since his situation is protected by La Loi Scrivener which is discussed below.

2. *La promesse synallagmatique de vente*. This is happily always known shortly as a *compromis de vente*. It comes in two forms. Usually, it is the equivalent of the standard English contract binding the seller to sell and the buyer to buy subject to the fulfilment of such conditions as it may contain. This is the kind of contract always to be preferred. It also sometimes comes in a form *ne valant pas vente* when it creates no contractual relationship but presumably can be of use in enabling the parties to see clearly on paper what each requires as pre-conditions to each signing an *acte de vente*. It is of no practical value and to be avoided.

3. *La pacte de préférence* or agreement giving a right of first refusal and the *vente à réméré*. Such contracts are rare and need special care in their drafting (Chapter 6).

4. *Le contrat préliminaire*. This type of contract is that used only on the sale of property en *l'état futur d'achèvement* or *à terme* (Chapter 8).

The above must not be confused with the *offre d'achat* or the *offre de vente* which are mere offers and remain as such until accepted by the seller or the buyer as the case may be.

Statutory protection for the buyer

La Loi SRU
Virtually all contracts where the buyer is what is designated as a 'non-professional' benefit from the provisions of the Loi SRU the full title of which is a Law *'relative à la Solidarité et au Renouvellement urbains'* but which is known, as is the custom in France, by its ugly and unpronounceable acronym of SRU. In addition to providing wide-ranging amendments to planning and condominium law, it also amends sections L271-1 and 271-2 of the *Code de la construction et de l'habitation* ('CCH') which now applies to all new and old property and property to be built or to be used as private dwellinghouses or in the case of a mixed user, if housing is the primary user. Its terms are for the benefit of all private persons (who are not defined in the Law) and apply to contracts of every kind. It specifically excludes its benefits from buyers who are builders, restorers and developers of property. It catches every seller without exception and every type of contract,

other than the *pacte de préférence* but including the *contrat préliminaire*, is affected. It also applies to contracts for the subscription of shares in *sociétés civiles d'attribution* and *à temps partagé* (Chapters 10 and 11).

Originally, the Law of 31 December 1989 had introduced the sections of the CCH referred to above which had limited application. They then provided that no contract ssp for the purchase or construction 'on plan' of a new private dwelling-house including flats by a 'non-professional' buyer should become binding until the expiration of a seven-day period after receipt by him of a copy of that document. During that period, the buyer had a right of cancellation which, if exercised, resulted in the refund of any deposit which had been paid on the signature of the contract.

It is arguable that a purchaser who makes a decision to buy 'on plan' based solely on a set of drawings and specifications and an empty space in the shape of a muddy plot of land, a half completed concrete block or, if building has progressed far enough, a show flat, may on further reflection have a change of heart. In fact, on the whole, purchasers appear rarely to have resorted to this right to rescind. It may perhaps be said that the opportunities to be less than scrupulous which are available to builders who sell 'on plan' are such that all other considerations apart, the parties to this kind of transaction are not always on an equal footing. No such argument can possibly be advanced in support of the innovations introduced by the Loi SRU in respect of existing property which can be inspected, surveyed, and valued before a decision to buy is made. As may be imagined, this Law has found no favour with the notarial profession or those involved in the property market and it seems difficult to advance any good reasons for its introduction other than those based on political motives. This view is clearly supported by the somewhat limited explanation given in the French Parliament by those presenting the Bill that 'it is fitting to guarantee in every case to the non-professional buyer the possibility to benefit from a "period of reflection" before his obligations become binding even when the contract has been entered into through the offices of a *notaire*'.

It must always be borne in mind that the Loi SRU does not negative the effect of article 1583 which is subject to no restriction whatsoever (Cass.1.7.98) since the article requires no contract between the parties. Indeed, it would seem clear that a contract subject to the Loi SRU must be a binding contract if it can be cancelled by one of the parties. The Law distinguishes between contracts which are notarial and those which are ssp. However, it also provides that if there is no *avant contrat*, it applies to the *contrat* (ie the *acte de vente*) as it would to an *avant contrat*. In this way, the rule about the payment of a deposit is safeguarded since if there is no *avant contrat*, there will be no person authorized to hold a deposit.

Contracts sous seing privé (ssp)

The buyer under such a contract enjoys an unrestricted right of renunciation which can be exercised within the period of seven days commencing on the day following the day of receipt by him of a copy of the signed contract. This copy must be sent to the buyer by registered AR or recorded delivery post or by some other means equally effective to prove the date of delivery. Notice of renunciation must be given by similar means. The right of renunciation is absolute and requires no motive.

The Law places restrictions on the taking of deposits. With the sole exception of deposits taken on the signing of *contrats préliminaires* for sales 'on plan', a deposit may only be taken by a 'professional' who is authorized by the seller to act in connection with the sale and who is covered by a fidelity bond. He will often be an estate agent who is the holder of a *carte professionnelle* entitling him to act in that capacity but *notaires* and *avocats* also qualify. Any deposit so taken must be returned to a buyer within twenty-one days of the day following the day on which he cancels the contract. A deposit taken in contravention of the Law carries a heavy fine which may reach Euro 30,000.

Nothing in the Law prevents the inclusion in such a contract of a provision for the payment of a deposit after the period of cancellation has passed. In such a case, the contract is deemed to be conditional on the payment of that amount on the expiration of that period or on such other day thereafter as may have been agreed. Doubts have been expressed as to the effect of this provision which, until it has been tested in practice and by the Courts, must be considered as 'ambiguous'.

Notarial contracts

In deference to the outcry raised by the *notariat* that it was unthinkable that contracts in *authentique* form could be 'unmade' at the whim of one of the parties, a different rule applies. In such cases, the contract in its final draft form is sent to the buyer by the *notaire* in the same manner as a contract ssp. The buyer has the same right to change his mind within the same time limits as if the contract were ssp but the Law does not provide specifically for the same method of advising the *notaire* of his decision either to sign or not to sign. Clearly it is safe to adopt the same procedure. This is a right out of which a buyer cannot contract and in no event can the contract be executed until the seven-day period has elapsed nor may any payment of any kind in connection with the contract be received. It should be remembered that whilst traditionally many contracts are prepared by the selling agent, the wise purchaser will instruct his own *notaire* to ensure that it is drafted by the seller's *notaire* and then agreed by both. It is not, however, a question of who drafted the contract but whether it is in *authentique* form or not and it is its nature which governs which rule applies. Many contracts drawn and agreed by *notaires* will be executed ssp.

There are certain rules of a similar nature relating to contracts for the purchase of land in a *lotissement* or residential estate.

A further novelty has been introduced by the Loi SRU. Prospective buyers were often asked to sign an *offre d'achat*, a unilateral offer to buy at a stated price which becomes effective when signed by the selling owner of the property. It was frequently accompanied by a payment by the intending buyer of a deposit (usually) of 10 per cent of the offered price 'as a token of good faith'. It must be admitted that when less than scrupulous agents are involved and certainly when the intending buyer is a foreigner, this practice can lead to abuses. The agent alleged that his client, the seller, would more easily agree to accept less than his asking price if he saw a signed offer of this nature particularly if a deposit has also been paid. This practice enabled the agent to collect a number of such documents and deposits and in effect conduct an auction with no buyers present.

Henceforward, all such arrangements are void if they have been entered into by one party 'with the intention of acquiring any property or interest in land in respect of which any payment of whatever nature and for whatever reason is required of or received from the intending purchaser'. This kind of transaction if unaccompanied by the demand or receipt of any payment remains lawful.

No penalties have been provided for being involved in unlawful *promesses d'achat* but in the case of a demand or receipt of any payment or of any undertaking to make a payment in defiance of the rules relating to the right to cancel a contract or to exercise the period of 'reflection', the penalty is Euro 30,000.

La Loi Scrivener

This Law provides all non-professional buyers seeking mortgage finance with the possibility to make contracts for the purchase of non-commercial property subject to the condition that such finance is obtained. It also controls the making and acceptance of loan offers and related subjects. This Law is fully dealt with as to obtaining a mortgage in Chapter 14 and as to the condition of obtaining a loan to be inserted in contracts in Chapter 4.

La lésion

This extraordinary right for which it is difficult, if not impossible, to find an equivalent or even a comparison in English law, is provided by C.civ.art.1674 which says that a vendor of property who has sold it at a price which has deprived him of more than seven-twelfths of its proper value may require the 'unmaking' of the sale. This right is available only to the seller and can be made use of even if he has renounced it in the original sale contract. It applies only to the sale of an *immeuble* and not for example to a transfer of such an asset to a company as the consideration for the allotment of shares (Cass.12.6.49). The right is not available in cases of sales which require an Order of the Court. Nor can it apply in any case of a *vente aléatoire* or a sale where the vendor reserves a life interest since the price paid depends on the element of chance involved.

To succeed in a claim for *lésion*, the seller must prove to the satisfaction of the Court which has an entire discretion in the matter that the price as shown in the *acte de vente* was less than five-twelfths of the value of the property at the moment of sale. No other proof is required and no element of fraud or duress need be invoked. The right becomes statute-barred two years after the date of the sale.

An action to prove *lésion* falls into two parts. The seller must first satisfy the Court that there is a case to answer based on the facts on which he relies and that there is a reasonable presumption that he has been *lésé* (Cass.20.12.94). If the Court finds in favour of the seller, the value of the property at the date of sale must be the unanimous opinion of three experts appointed by the Court unless previously agreed on by the parties. The Court is not bound to follow the opinion of these experts (Cass.9.11.61).

If the Court decides that it will entertain the seller's application, the purchaser has the choice either to revest the property he has purchased in the seller and receive back the price he has paid or to retain the property, paying the price which the Court decides to be the proper price less 10 per cent of the total price. This option may be exercised up to the time of judgment and even thereafter.

Matters common to all contracts

With very few exceptions to which attention is called in the relevant chapter, there are a number of points common to all kinds of contracts which must be borne in mind:

1. Unless it is specifically stated in the contract, the benefit of a *compromis de vente* is freely assignable and without notice to the seller. It is not unusual to find that the buyer is described as contracting '*en s'obligeant et en obligeant solidairement et indivisiblement entre eux ses héritiers et ayant cause à quelque titre que ce soit . . .*' (for himself and for his heirs and successors in title jointly and severally however so entitled). This is a point of significance for the non-French buyer. In many cases, if proper advice is obtained, it may well be that there are fiscal or inheritance advantages if the ultimate buyer is not the person shown as the contracting buyer and it is essential between the signature of contracts and completion to obtain such advice. Special rules apply to the assignment of the option in a *promesse de vente* which are recounted in Chapter 5.

2. It is highly desirable always to ensure that the provisions of C.civ.art.1325 are complied with. This article provides that any contract of which there are not as many executed copies as there are parties is void. This has been held (Cass.14.1.57) to be a necessary measure of security for each party to avoid the possibility that the assignee of a contracting party who does not have a copy would be unaware of any amendments made without his knowledge. However, failure to abide by this rule does not in fact result in the nullity of the contract but only that it cannot be produced as evidence in support of the terms of the contract itself of which extrinsic proof must then be adduced. Part

performance of the contract overcomes such an omission. A method much used to circumvent this rule is for all the parties to agree that there will be only one part to the contract which will be deposited with a named third party for safe custody. This method can only be used with safety if, for example, that third party is the sole *notaire* acting in the transaction who has no special interest in or duty towards one only of the parties (which is hardly possible) for otherwise the requirements of the article should be 'scrupulously respected' (Cass.19.5.67). Since the proper advice is that each party should have his own *notaire* and estate agents are frequent offenders when they themselves draw a contract, this practice should be guarded against carefully.

3. It is not customary for contracts in France to be made 'subject to survey' and few buyers (and not even all mortgagees) ask for surveys. Rarely, a contract may contain a condition that the purchase is subject to an independent valuation.

4. *Moyens de contrainte* as they are known in French, of which three are in current use for the *compromis de vente*, range in severity from the innocuous deposit through the payment of *arrhes* to the genuine penalty clause. It is curious that it is considered that in the case of the *promesse de vente*, which the English lawyer readily recognizes as an option to purchase, the provision of the cost of the option (*indemnité d'immobilisation*) is also considered a 'means of constraint' utilized 'to oblige a contracting party to honour his obligations' (Me Picard, *Technique de la vente de l'immeuble* (Litec, 1984)). These 'means of constraint' are as follows.

   (a) The *dedit*. This payment is close to the English deposit and is usually called an *accompte* or payment on account. It can be and usually is paid for the benefit of one party only, namely the seller. In the event of the buyer failing to complete, the *dedit* does not automatically become payable to the seller since there must first be served on the buyer or on the seller if he is the defaulting party a *mise en demeure* or notice to complete. Even then, the average *notaire* holding a *dedit* is usually not anxious to part with it without an Order of the Court which has the power to disallow such payment if it considers that the party claiming such payment is guilty of a lack of good faith or if his behaviour implies a renunciation of the right to receive it (Cass.11.5.76).

   (b) *Les arrhes.* Such a payment is covered by C.civ.art.1590 which reads: 'A contract providing for the payment of *arrhes* may be avoided by either party when he who has paid them loses them and he who has received them returns twice their value.' Such a provision (which in fact applies to a contract for the sale of anything) is, of course, rarely found in contracts for the sale of land and clearly must be avoided. The payment of *arrhes* in effect makes the contract conditional since either party can revoke it by asking the requisite payment to the other party. However, it has been held that if the amount of such a payment is too large, it will be treated as a *dedit* or payment on account of the sale price (TGI Seine 15.12.66). Similarly, it has held (Cass.6.12.66) that the Court reserves the right to consider if the payment or repayment of *arrhes* would be 'equitable' in all the attendant circumstances.

(c) *La clause pénale*. The object of such a clause is clearly recognizable by English lawyers but in French law is subject to the provisions of the Law of 9 July 1975 which modified the provisions of C.civ.arts.1152 and 1231. As these articles are currently worded, the Court can, by virtue of article 1152, vary upwards or downwards any penalty agreed upon by the parties to a contract if it is manifestly excessively large or derisively small. It is considered that a penalty of 10 per cent of the sale price is reasonable. In addition, article 1231 provides that where there has been part performance of a contract, the Court may vary the penalty payable having regard to the extent of that part performance. Any provision in a contract attempting to oust the effect of these articles is void. It should be noted that the Loi SRU forbids any payment made to guarantee the payment of a penalty in the same manner as it forbids any other payment in respect of a contract ssp not made to a professional who is furnished with the owner's authority to deal with the property in question.

Payments on account of the purchase price to accompany the signature of contracts which will in most cases be by way of *dedit* will normally be by way of cheque.

5. Many are the occasions when the signatory to a French document is asked to add a *mention* to his signature. The usual words in the case of a contract for the sale of land are '*bon pour vente/achat*' or '*lu et approuvé*'. This is wholly unnecessary, stemming from a misapplication of C.civ.art.1326 which concerns only the equivalent of a Deed Poll where one party only binds himself to pay a sum of money or to sell a thing to another (Cass.6.3.74). Contracts, other than those which will very rarely be used for land transactions, will always be bilateral. It has, however, been seriously suggested that the addition of a *mention* is of assistance to a graphologist if the handwriting of a party to a contract is questioned since it makes available to him normal writing other than a signature.

6. It remains to add that a number of estate agents use printed contracts which have English translations. None is ever correct in the sense that either the translation itself is wrong or, more usually, terms of English (but sometimes American) law have been used which create a false impression of the meaning of the original French. Neither party should rely on such translations as indicative of their rights and obligations and should always seek suitable advice.

4

COMPROMIS DE VENTE

Introduction 39
Identity of the property sold 40
The sale price 41
Death or incapacity of one party 41
The seller's obligations 42
    To provide information 42
    To give quiet enjoyment 42
    Vices cachés 43
    Covenants as to health hazards 45
    Standard conditions 46
    Conditions for the benefit of the buyer 47
    Conditions for the benefit of the seller 48
    Other clauses 49

Introduction

This kind of contract, the proper title of which is *promesse synallagmatique de vente*, corresponds to the contract used in England in a land transaction to bind the parties to buy and sell subject to such conditions as may be contained in the contract. Such a contract is said to be one *valant vente* since by the agreement of the parties on the thing sold and the price the requirements of *Code civil* (C.civ. art.1582) as noted in Chapter 3 have been fulfilled. It will normally be (but is not required by law to be) in writing and in the form of a single document but may be for example by an exchange of letters. It may be executed ssp or may be *authentique*. The run of the mill contract is frequently prepared by the seller's estate agent and signed ssp. It can only be said that certainly in the case of a non-French buyer or seller, it is highly desirable when urban properties are involved and essential when they are in the country that the contract is prepared by the *notaire* acting for the seller who preferably should not also be acting for the buyer. The fact that it is prepared by a *notaire* does not mean that it must be in *authentique* form. The advantages of this kind of contract are self-evident to the English compared to the disadvantages of the *promesse de vente* which is dealt with in Chapter 5. The *compromis* does not require registration at the Land Registry as does the *promesse de vente* with the resultant lack of publicity which is by no means an unimportant feature for the French.

    Unlikely to be made use of though it may seem to be, a land transaction may also be dealt with by a contract of this kind *ne valant pas vente*. In such a case, the contract must specifically exclude the effects of C.civ.arts.1583 and 1589 which support the previously mentioned article 1582. The words negativing these articles must be in the clearest possible terms. Thus, to say that a sale will not be concluded until an *acte notarié* has been subsequently drawn is not sufficient to oust the effect of these articles (Cass.4.5.36). On the other hand, the words 'until *réalisation* of the *acte authentique*' have the desired negativing effect (Cass.17.7.97). In the case of a contract of this kind, the parties are only under an obligation to execute the *acte de vente* so that failure by one party to do so cannot lead to an Order for specific performance but only to damages.

Identity of the property sold

C.civ.art.1110 says that mistake is not a reason for the avoidance of a contract unless it is of a fundamental nature. An error resulting from mere negligence is not such a reason (Cass.27.11.79) and the duty of the party who has suffered from an error to make his own enquiries plays its part. It is essential that the description of the property sold should be in accordance with its cadastral description. A contract for the sale of rural property or of building land should always have a plan annexed but often this is lacking.

It is sometimes desirable to include in the description of the property an indication of its area. (As to the need by law to do so in the case of the sale of flats, see below under La Loi Carrez.) This is particularly desirable in the case of country properties. C.civ.arts.1616, 1617 and 1618 say that if an area of property is disclosed it is that area which must be sold on completion but if the seller cannot do so or if the buyer does not demand the full area contracted to be sold the sale price must be reduced. If on the other hand the area turns out to be greater than that contracted for the buyer has the choice to pay an additional price or refuse to complete if the area exceeds by one-twentieth the area disclosed in the contract. This provision can be, and often is, negatived.

There is a special rule applicable to the sale of flats *en copropriété* enacted by la Loi Carrez which came into force in July 1997. This requires that on pain of nullity, every contract for the sale of any *lot* or part of a *lot* (which separately or together will normally form a flat) must mention in the contract the measurements of the flat if they exceed 8 square metres. The method of measurement is laid down by the Law. This is virtually always done by an expert and its results annexed to the contract. A seller is not advised to undertake this himself since a mismeasurement can cause considerable trouble.

It is not necessary to indicate in the contract the root of title but it is desirable if only to indicate that the draftsman of the contract has looked at the title to see, among other things, if the property is subject to rights and easements. Although all property is registered in France, conveyancing itself is more attuned to what was involved in dealing with unregistered land in England and many contracts are drawn by estate agents insufficiently familiar with that art.

The sale price

This must be clearly stated in the contract and be clearly capable of determination. It is frequent that a deposit, usually of 10 per cent, is paid on signature of contract and this should if at all possible be paid to the *notaire* acting for the buyer or if the seller objects to his *notaire*. It should not if it is at all possible to avoid this be paid to the seller's agent. In the event of a dispute arising in respect of the contract as a result of which the deposit might be forfeit to the seller or refundable to the buyer, a *notaire* will not normally part with it to either party without their agreement or an Order of the Court. Agents can be less scrupulous. In the light of the technical requirements of C.civ.art.2074 it is not usual to arrange that this payment acquires the full force of a *gage* which may be taken as the equivalent of the payment being made to the seller's solicitor as agent for the seller. Such a payment in England is rare indeed; it is extraordinarily rare in France. It is customary for the *frais de notaire*, which are normally borne by the buyer, to be shown in the contract as an addition to the sale price to be found on completion.

It is as well that a warning is given as to payment of part of a purchase price 'under the table'. It is part of the French character that if the payment of tax can be avoided, it should be avoided. It is true that when stamp duty on the sales of land in France was unreasonably high, it was common for part of the price to be paid in this way and it must be said that the reduction of that tax to its present level (Chapter 22) has not lessened the occasions on which buyers are tempted to indulge in this tax evasion. It also occurs when the property sold is in the estate of a deceased person and its value for inheritance tax purposes has been deliberately kept low. To sell to a buyer at that low value would be unthinkable but to sell at the proper price would give rise to immediate Revenue enquiries. 'Under the table' transactions must not be indulged in for a variety of reasons almost all of which risk being to the disadvantage of the buyer. Suffice it to say that if such a payment is made, it must be made without the knowledge of the *notaire*: it is then as though it had never been made. If, for example, on completion it is discovered that there is an undisclosed easement affecting the land sold or a defect in the property which, had it been known to the buyer, would have led him not to buy the property or offer a lower price, any money he has paid 'under the table' is irrecoverable. It is naive to rely on the wording of CGI.art.683 which imposes stamp duty on the 'value expressed' in a document since it is implicit that it is the 'true value expressed' and the French Revenue can, of course, substitute and tax that true value.

Death or incapacity of one party

The rules as to capacity to contract are set out in Chapter 23. One of the advantages of a *compromis de vente* as opposed to the *promesse de vente* stems from the fact that in the event of the death of either party, the former provides a binding contract in existence as at that date so that the residuary beneficiaries in the estate of the deceased buyer will normally be obliged to fulfil the contract unless they elect to renounce (Chapter 34) whilst the death of the seller between contract and completion removes the property from his estate and makes unnecessary the delay which may be involved in the preparation of the usual *attestation immobilière*.

The seller's obligations

To provide information

In accordance with C.civ.art.1602, a seller has a duty 'to explain clearly what it is that he binds himself to do' so that 'every obscure or ambiguous bargain is construed against him'. Thus he is bound to disclose to the buyer all that is within his own sole knowledge and which is not known to the world in general. The most commonly disclosed information relates to easements and other matters adverse to country property. There does not fall within the rule, for example, the failure of a seller to advise the buyer of a shop of the intended opening of a supermarket in the neighbourhood since this is knowledge easily available to any ordinary shopkeeper (Cass.com.17.7.2001).

A seller has in addition by C.civ.art.1603 two principal obligations, that of delivering and that of warranting the thing which he sells. Delivery is defined in the following article as 'transferring the thing sold into the power and possession of the purchaser'. C.civ.art.1614 provides that 'the thing must be delivered in the state in which it is at the moment of sale' and according to the Code that will have been in any event not later than the signature of the contract. Indeed, ostensibly this is not an unreasonable provision since the sale price will have been agreed based on the state of the premises at that time. However, since there will be a space of time between the signature of the contract and the date of actual completion, it is usual to provide in derogation of that article that the property will be delivered in that state in which it is at the date of entry into possession by the buyer which will in most cases be the date of completion. In such case the seller is liable for damage suffered by the premises due to his negligence since he is required to look after them during this period *'en bon père de famille'*. Delivery of the property includes all that are *immeubles par destination* for which reason, as has been said in Chapter 2, care must be taken to ensure that all that should be passed over by the seller is in fact delivered by him. Completion of the sale and delivery of the premises are dealt with in Chapter 7.

To give quiet enjoyment

C.civ.art.1626 provides for an implied covenant on the part of the seller for quiet enjoyment for the whole or part of the property sold and freedom from any encumbrances undisclosed at the time of sale. The ambit of this covenant is not unlike that provided for by the Law of Property Act 1925 and enures for the benefit of the successors in title of the buyer. It is not subject to any prescription period (Cass.13.5.12). Excluded from the effect of the covenant are easements which are apparent or which exist by operation of law or which arise from the situation of the property, such as a right of way of necessity, or are in favour of a local or other authority. On the other hand, an easement which cannot be known to a buyer such as a right of underground drainage in favour of a third party is caught by the covenant (Cass.28.3.90).

In the event of a breach of this covenant the remedy of the buyer depends upon who has caused the breach. If it is the seller himself, the buyer may proceed directly against him. If the breach is due to an act of a third party, he may either sue the seller or may first proceed against the offending third party and if unsuccessful against the seller. The buyer may rely on this covenant even after he has disposed of the property if he himself is then subject to a similar covenant.

If the breach results in the need for the buyer wholly to quit the premises he may recover from the seller all amounts laid out by him in connection with his purchase, that is the purchase price and all costs in connection therewith and appropriate damages (C.civ.art.1630). These will include not only any loss in value of the property but will also take into account any increase in its value which must be added to the price paid by the buyer. If the breach relates to part only of the property the buyer may require the avoidance of the sale if, without that part of the property in respect of which the seller is in breach of covenant, he would not have bought it (C.civ.art.1636).

Not surprisingly, C.civ.art.1627 permits the parties to agree to increase or diminish the effect of the covenant for quiet enjoyment or wholly release the seller from its effects and it is not uncommon to see a seller so released in a *compromis de vente*. Thus, the contract will disclose all easements and the like to which the property is, to the knowledge of the seller, subject and will provide that the buyer takes the property only so subject and *à ses risques et périls* without any right of recourse against the seller. It is self-evident that such a clause comes under very careful scrutiny and good faith on the part of the seller is an essential ingredient (Cass.16.5.62).

Vices cachés

According to C.civ.art.1641, 'the seller of property is liable for all latent defects in the thing sold which render it unsuitable for the purpose for which it was sold or diminish such suitability to such an extent that the buyer would not have bought it or would have paid a lower price if he had been aware of them'. This is currently known as the *garantie de vices cachés*. The corollary appears in the following article that a seller is not liable for defects which are apparent and of which a buyer could have taken cognizance himself. Article 1641 does not import the need, as does English law, that the buyer must make known to the seller the use for which the item sold is destined but it has been held that this must be its normal use (Cass.4.1.96). Thus, in the case of a property to be put to an unusual use, the seller is not liable under this article if the buyer cannot show that he informed the seller of such use and that it was within the contemplation of both parties to the contract for the sale of the thing sold (Cass.17.5.94).

A latent defect to be actionable must therefore:

1. Affect in a serious or at least genuine manner one of the essential features of the property sold, in particular when it prevents or limits the use to which the buyer intends to put the property (Cass.25.10.61).
2. Be hidden and not apparent which the buyer can see for himself. The buyer is not expected to seek the advice of an expert so that a defect may be considered latent even though it could have been discovered by an expert. The Court has a total discretion to decide which defect is latent and which is apparent (Cass.5.3.71). Examples of defects judged to be latent are:
   (a) a crack in an exterior wall covered by a vine;
   (b) a crack in a wall of a living room covered by a thick wall covering such as fabric or heavy wallpaper;
   (c) damp caused by lack of a damp proof course which is unobservable without lifting the floor but not damp the results of which are in general visible;
   (d) the validity of a planning consent in respect of which notice has been served on the seller to discontinue permitted works.
3. Have existed prior to the date of sale even if only in an undeveloped state and remained latent up to the completion of sale. If this is not the case the buyer will have bought with knowledge of the defects. The fact that the seller was unaware of them is immaterial.

Liability for latent defects gives rise to an action in damages. If the seller was aware of their existence it involves a lack of good faith and by C.civ.art.1645 the buyer may both claim back the sale price and damages. In other cases, the buyer has the choice of either claiming repayment of the price or retaining the property and claiming such reduction in the price as 'the experts' appointed by the Court may consider appropriate.

In these circumstances and bearing in mind that prior to the signature of the contract, the average buyer is assumed to have had sufficient time to make a thorough inspection of the premises, the majority of contracts provide that the seller gives no guarantee as to the state of the building and also excludes all liability for defects both latent and apparent. Such an exclusion clause is construed strictly and in favour of the buyer. It covers only construction defects (Cass.31.3.54) and does not extend to (say) the presence of termites but this has been overtaken by recent law.

For a seller to benefit from a clause so limiting his liability it is necessary that:

(1) he is not a professional who is presumed as such to be aware of defects in his property. A professional includes a person or a company engaged in selling

or restoring property and a building expert who was involved in the construction of the building which he is selling;

(2) he has acted in good faith ie he was unaware of the latent defects when he himself occupied the premises;

(3) he has committed no act amounting to fraudulent misrepresentation (*dol*) by the failure to disclose such defects.

These limitations are exclusive of one another so that a property developer is always prevented from benefiting from such a protective clause in a contract.

It always remains a source of surprise that the average French buyer does not have a survey made of the property he intends to buy except possibly in the country when he will be more interested in the boundaries and the easements (frequently rights of water and drainage) over and for the benefit of the land than in the state of the property itself. Contracts are never 'subject to survey' and the offer of a loan by a bank or other financial institution is not of itself a guarantee of the good condition of the property.

It is a question of doubt to what extent the average estate agent examines this situation and advises the parties before including or not, as the case may be, a clause exonerating a seller from his liability for latent defects. It is recognized as a serious part of the duty of the *notaire* to make enquiries as to *vices cachés* and to make certain that the parties are well aware of their rights and liabilities. It has been held that in appropriate circumstances a *notaire* who has failed in this duty may find himself jointly and severally liable with a seller to a buyer.

Any action by a buyer based on a seller's liability for *vices cachés* must be instituted 'within a short time' having regard to the nature of the defect and what is customary in the area in which the property is situate. What constitutes 'a short time', which runs from the date of discovery of the defect which is best confirmed by a suitable expert, is a matter for the Court. A buyer who has resold the property may nevertheless pursue such an action if he has suffered loss by reason of the defect. A sub-purchaser may rely on the statutory right if not negatived in the contract and can sue the original seller direct (Cass.4.2.36).

Sales by Order of the Court and of properties 'on plan' are excluded from the ambit of this guarantee; the former on the grounds that it would be unreasonable to apply it to sales almost always conducted as matters of urgency and the latter because the ultimate liability for defects falls on the developer and his architect in any event (TGI Bayonne 12.5.75).

Covenants as to health hazards
Of recent years, a number of enactments have been passed relating to certain health hazards and sellers are obliged in all contracts for the sale of property to which these enactments apply to make certain disclosures.

1. *As to the presence of asbestos*: The rules apply to all buildings with the sole exception of those used for habitation in a single occupation. In the case of all

such buildings built before 1 July 1997, an inspection must be made by a suitable expert for the presence of asbestos. If asbestos is found, a periodic control must be made during three years and such works as are necessary must be carried out. The contract must state if such a search has been made and with what result and a copy of the expert's report must be annexed.

2. *As to the presence of lead*: There are certain zones which by Prefectoral decree are specified as liable to risk from lead poisoning. Buildings constructed after 1948 are not affected. In the case of the sale of an affected building, there must be annexed to the contract a statement not made more than a year previously by a suitable expert describing the risk or its absence. No clause in a contract which negates the seller's liability in respect of *vices cachés* is valid in respect of the existence of lead on the property.

3. *As to the presence of termites and other similar insects*: These rules affect buildings, the occupants of which are under an obligation to inform the local *mairie* if they are aware of the presence of such insects. Failure to make such a report incurs a heavy fine. In such cases, the local authority can require the owner to carry out the necessary eradication and prevention of future infestations. In areas in which by Prefectoral decree these rules apply, the seller of property must obtain a report from a suitable expert setting out the state of the property in this respect. A clause exonerating the seller from liability for *vices cachés* is ineffective in this respect unless such an *état parasitaire*, made not more than three months prior to the date of completion, is annexed to the *acte de vente*.

Standard conditions

Known in French as *Conditions Suspensives* these are not conditions in the English legal sense as being opposed to warranties but are conditions precedent. This is neatly commented on, citing C.civ.art.1168, in Cheshire and Fifoot, *Law of Contract* (Butterworths) (14th edn, Ch. 6 sect. 3) as follows: 'To the lawyer familiar with . . . . . . and trained in modern continental systems, the use of the word "condition" must appear a solecism. By them, a condition is sharply distinguished from the actual term of a contract and is taken to mean not part of the obligation itself but an external fact upon which the existence of the obligation depends.' This is a very precise explanation of the French system since that article says that 'an obligation is conditional when it is made to depend on a future and uncertain event either by suspending it until that event happens or by cancelling it depending upon whether the event occurs or not.'

As may be supposed, it is more frequently the buyer who wishes to ensure that he is not bound to complete his purchase until he has established certain important facts into which it would take too long to enquire before the contract is signed. There are a number of standard conditions for the benefit of both seller and buyer.

Conditions for the benefit of the buyer

1. By virtue of the Loi Scrivener (Chapters 3 and 14), if the buyer is seeking mortgage finance he will be asked to say so in the contract giving details of the intended loan and of the lender and confirming that there are no legal or other reasons why the loan should not be granted and that the intended repayments do not exceed a reasonable proportion. The latter indication may run as far as asking for the extent of the buyer's current loan indebtedness and his monthly income but these go beyond what is required by law and should be resisted. If, on the other hand, the buyer is not seeking a loan, he is required to make a declaration to that effect in the contract thus: *Je, sousigné, déclare que je n'ai l'intention de solliciter aucun prêt pour le financement de cette acquisition et je déclare en outre avoir pris connaissance de l'article 18 de la loi du 13 juillet 1979 et reconnais avoir été informé que si je recours néanmoins à un prêt, je ne pourrais me prévaloir du bénéfice de cette loi et notamment du fait que la présente vente sera alors conclue sous la condition suspensive de l'obtention d'un ou plusieurs prêts.* (I, the undersigned, declare that I do not intend to seek a loan in connection with the financing of this purchase and I further declare that I have been advised of the effect of article 18 of the Law of 13 July 1979 and I understand that if nevertheless I should seek such a loan, I will be unable to benefit from the protection of that Law and in particular that this sale could have been subject to the condition precedent of my obtaining one or more loans.)

2. That enquiry of the planning authorities does not reveal anything adverse to the property by way of planning decisions or limitations on the use of the property, the construction of new roads or their widening, or similar works. It is a close equivalent of an English local authority search and is often obtained for the *notaire* drawing the *acte de vente* by a planning expert. The system is new resulting from the Loi SRU and contains less information than it did prior to 1 April 2001. It is possible to make a more detailed search which will, among other things, show if the property can be built on for the purposes indicated in the search. It will also show what planning taxes, if any, are payable on new buildings, restorations, and so on. It will be appreciated that such searches are of not much significance in the case of town property but are vital in the country. For any buyer whose French is sufficiently good, a visit to the local *mairie* with or without an architect is often useful.

3. That the property, if this be the case, is free from all easements and charges adversely affecting the property other than those disclosed.

4. That the seller can give a thirty-year root of title.

5. That the property is not subject to any mortgage or charge created by the seller or any predecessor in title in an amount which is equal to or exceeds the sale price. This is the equivalent of the English statutory implied covenant for freedom from encumbrances which does not exist in French law.

In addition to these standard conditions it may be thought desirable to add, depending on the situation and ownership of the property, that there exist no rights of pre-emption vested in a local authority or in SAFER or in any other person.

In the case of local authorities, a very large proportion of property in France is in theory subject to rights of compulsory purchase. It is, therefore, in the case of most sales, necessary to give notice of the intended sale to the local authority of the area in which the property is situate and trust that this right will not be exercised. The *notaire* serves on the *mairie* of the *commune* a *déclaration d'intention d'aliéner* (DIA). The *mairie* has two months in which to reply notifying the seller either that it does or does not, as the case may be, intend to purchase. Silence after the two-month period indicates a negative decision but this formality is a well known source of delay in completing purchases.

A right of pre-emption residing in the third party may arise if the property has been let (Chapter 17) or is jointly owned *en indivision* (Chapter 16). This should become evident before the contract is agreed and a suitable condition included if necessary. SAFER (*Sociétés d'Aménagement Foncier et d'Etablissement Rural*) are local agricultural committees whose task is to oversee the agricultural market. They have a right of pre-emption over all agricultural properties within their area and application must be made to them prior to the sale of an affected property. SAFER has two months in which to reply, silence being the equivalent of the non-exercise of its pre-emption right. A sight of the *acte de vente* on the purchase by the seller will indicate if the property is so subject. The hand of a SAFER is not limited to rural areas since it seems that those which have become urbanized sometimes retain a SAFER and parts of so large a conurbation as, for example, Nice are still so subject. Decisions of SAFER sometimes appear to be linked to local politics.

Such conditions and any others upon which a buyer is advised to insist are said to be 'in the sole interest of the buyer', who, in the event of any one remaining unfulfilled, is entitled not to proceed with the sale and obtain a refund of any sum paid on account. The deadline for fulfilment of these conditions is normally just before the date fixed for completion (Chapter 7).

Conditions for the benefit of the seller

The standard condition for the benefit of the seller is that the transfer of the property sold is subject to the signature by the buyer of the *acte de vente* and the payment of the price. This gives rise to the problem of the wording of C.civ.art.1179 which states that the fulfilment of a condition has effect retrospectively to the date of the making of the contract. Thus, the transfer of the property technically takes place before the payment of the price. In order therefore to avoid the effect of this article, the clause is often stated to be in derogation of that article and that the transfer of property remains subject to the execution of the *acte de vente* and the payment of the price. This clause is said not to be a *condition suspensive* but a mere 'stipulation' not affecting the effectiveness of sale as between the parties subject only to the *conditions suspensives* in favour of the buyer.

Other clauses
Among the more usual clauses in a contract the following may also be found.

1. A statement, unless the draftsman is instructed otherwise, that the *notaire* to act shall be Me XYZ. This is in pursuance of the practice that one *notaire* acts for both parties. A condition in this form should never without specific advice be accepted. It is the right of the buyer to choose his own *notaire* and this right should always be exercised. In the unlikely event that the seller wants to use the same *notaire* as that instructed by the buyer, it is a choice which must perforce be accepted but at least the choice of the sole *notaire* is the original choice of the buyer.
2. If the property is a flat in a *copropriété* an indication of the situation regarding works being carried out or intended to be carried out to the block (Chapter 7).
3. A date for completion: this may be linked to the fulfilment of the *conditions suspensives* or may be an independent date chosen by the parties. It is seldom a fixed date and on most occasions is on an 'on or before' basis.
4. The date on which vacant possession will be given which normally is the date of actual completion on payment of the sale price. It is unusual but not unknown for possession to be given before completion on such terms as may have been agreed between the parties.
5. An indication of the payment which will be due to the seller if the buyer fails to complete. This in standard sales will be the amount of the deposit paid by the buyer.
6. A formal agreement by the seller not to sell the property elsewhere or mortgage it prior to completion.
7. A provision permitting assignment of the contract.
8. An undertaking to pay the *frais* ie the notarial costs, stamp duties and all disbursements of the sale.
9. An agreement that the sale was negotiated by a certain estate agent and that his commission will be paid in whole or in part by the seller and/or the buyer.

It is evident that contracts will vary considerably depending on the nature of the property sold. Contracts prepared by a *notaire* tend to be less cumbersome than those prepared by an estate agent and it must be remembered, particularly for the purposes of la Loi SRU, that a contract prepared by the former is not likely to be *authentique* so that the retraction period will be the same in both cases.

5

PROMESSE DE VENTE

Introduction 51
Form of the contract 51
Assignment of the contract 52
The option 52
The exercise of the option 52

Introduction

La promesse unilatérale de vente is 'a contract by which one party undertakes to sell to another but the latter does not bind himself to buy' (J. Picard, *Technique de la vente de l'immeuble* (Litec, 1984)). To the English practitioner it is a straightforward option to buy but, as has been said previously, sales of property in some 50 per cent of France are effected through the medium of this kind of contract. It is only on the rarest occasions that it is intended to or does fulfil its true intention as the grant of an option to buy. In effect, the buyer reserves to himself a 'period of reflection' in addition to that provided by *la Loi SRU* and the protection afforded by *la Loi Scrivener* (Chapter 3) which go beyond the needs of the ordinary buyer of residential property unless possibly he cannot complete such a purchase until he has sold an existing property. Buyers with no such problems must, therefore, look on this kind of contract, if that is all that is offered, as a *compromis de vente* once the date for the exercising of the option has been reached.

However, since prior to the exercise of the option, there are special rules involved which do not apply to the *compromis de vente*, consideration is given to these in this chapter. This type of contract, as indeed in English law, must be distinguished from the *pacte de préférence* which is dealt with in Chapter 6.

Form of the contract

In the case of contracts of this nature, neither seller nor buyer would be initially bound if it were not that the seller undertakes not to sell elsewhere provided that the buyer accepts his offer within a fixed period of time. This results in a blockage of the property entitling the seller to be indemnified for the potential loss he might suffer. Such a sum is called an *indemnité d'immobilisation* and not unexpectedly, it is usually 10 per cent of the offered sale price, as is the standard deposit in the case of the *compromis de vente*.

51

The *Code Général des Impôts*, art.1840A requires that all contracts of this kind for the sale of any *immeuble* or interest in an *immeuble* are whether by *acte authentique* or ssp registered at the Land Registry within ten days of the execution of the contract. Failure so to register them results in their nullity which involves among other things the inability of the estate agent who negotiated the sale to be paid his commission which was provided for in the contract and any money paid by the buyer as option money must be repaid (CA Paris 16.6.92).

Assignment of the contract

In the absence of any relevant provision to the contrary in the contract, either party, who will usually be the buyer, may assign his interest in the contract only with the consent of the other party if that other party has entered into the contract with him on the basis of his 'personality'. This is frequently difficult to substantiate and it is desirable to include in the contract specific rules as to assignment. At all events, the assignment for value by a *professionnel de l'immobilier* of his rights under a *promesse de vente* is forbidden by the Law of 29 January 1993 so that such assignments are void. The definition of a *professionnel de l'immobilier* is very widely drawn and goes well beyond the estate agent and property dealer. The same rules as apply to the registration of the contract apply also to assignments.

The option

The date on which the option must be exercised is a matter for the parties but clearly should not be too far ahead. It is also necessary to link that date to the date on which the conditions in the contract must be fulfilled and there is no reason why the option date should not in fact be the date when those conditions are fulfilled.

Notwithstanding that it is customary that the option money is 10 per cent of the sale price, its amount is entirely within the choice of the parties. It is not considered to be in the nature of a penalty in the sense of C.civ.art.1226 since the buyer does not break any contractual obligation in not exercising his option. Hence, the buyer who does not exercise his option cannot benefit from the power of the Court to vary penalty payments (CA Paris 25.9.99). In the event of the buyer exercising his option but failing to complete, the option money he has paid cannot, in default of any provision in the contract to the contrary, count towards any penalty or other payment he has contracted to make for such failure.

The exercise of the option
Failure to exercise the option on or before the due date results in the termination of the contract. There is no obligation on the seller to advise the buyer of the

approach of such date and once it has passed without being expressly or tacitly extended, unless the buyer gives notice that he exercises the option, the *indemnité d'immobilisation* in theory becomes the property of the seller. However, the Cour de Cassation has held (Cass.1.6.93) that a delay of a few days when the contract had not specifically indicated that failure to exercise the option on a given day would result in the termination of the contract was not sufficiently serious to cause such a result. Such a decision demands careful drafting of the contract. Since it is the duty of the seller to make full disclosure of all that affects the sale, failure on the part of the seller to do so can enable the buyer not to exercise his option without suffering the loss of the amount he has paid for it. Thus failure on the part of a seller to disclose an easement in the form of a wayleave over the land in question entitles the buyer to repayment of his option money if he fails for that reason to pick up the option (Cass.1.7.98).

If the option is exercised, it must be unequivocal and in accordance with the provisions in the contract. Such an exercise results in a definite sale as though the parties had originally signed a *compromis de vente*. The effects of the exercise of the option are that:

(1) the buyer becomes the owner of the property subject to the execution of the *acte de vente* and the payment of the price;
(2) the property is thenceforward at 'the risk and peril' of the buyer;
(3) the buyer becomes entitled to the income of the property (if any);
(4) the existence of *vices cachés* are established at that time;
(5) if an action *en lésion* is envisaged, the two-year period runs from this date;
(6) stamp duties and similar expenses are calculated on the value of the property as at that date.

It must be remembered that if the buyer is seeking mortgage finance for his purchase, the offer of a loan he has received is basically good for only four months (Chapter 14). If the *acte de vente* is signed after that date by reason of the delay in exercising the option, the loan offer must be renewed by the lender. Care must also be taken to include in the period before the option must be exercised the period of at least a month allowed for by the *Loi Scrivener*.

From the date of the exercise of the option, the sale proceeds as though it were based on a *compromis de vente* and all the provisions affecting sales under such a contract are to be found in Chapter 4.

6

OTHER CONTRACTS FOR SALE OF LAND

Pacte de préférence 55
The *vente à réméré* 56
Offre d'achat 57

Pacte de préférence

The grant of a right of first refusal does not, of course, constitute in French law a sale in that it does not bind the current owner of property to sell unless the beneficiary of the offer takes it up. It is also known as a *pacte de préemption*.

It is used, again as in England, in the form of an option for a lessee to purchase his lessor's interest in the land comprised in a lease and perhaps more unusually as an option for the lessor to purchase the leasehold interest if the lessee has in mind disposing of his lease. It arises by operation of law in the form of a pre-emption right in the case of property held *en indivision* as between joint owners in favour of each other (Chapter 16).

Although not itself a sale contract, the *pacte de préférence* must fully describe the property affected. It may be created by *acte authentique* or document executed ssp. It is customary for the price of the property to be sold not to be fixed when the agreement is made but for the price to be agreed at the time when the offer is accepted by the beneficiary. If no period of time before which the offer to sell must be made is mentioned, the offer ceases to be effective after the period of thirty years.

A *pacte de préférence* included in a lease of business premises (Chapter 18) is treated as an agreement separate from the lease but ceases to have effect on the termination of the lease and is not renewed automatically on the renewal of the lease (Cass.21.12.88). However, during the period during which a business lessee may exercise his *droit de maintien*, he may still rely on it (Cass.16.6.99).

If, during the period prior to the owner making his offer to sell to the beneficiary of a *pacte de préférence*, he lets the property to a lessee who obtains, for example, a statutory right of pre-emption (Chapter 17), that right overrides the effect of the *pacte de préférence*. However, an owner having rendered himself incapable of fulfilling his obligations is liable to the beneficiary of the *pacte* in damages (Cass.1.4.92). The burden of the *pacte* falls on the beneficiaries in the estate of a deceased owner unless the document clearly shows that the liability was personal to the deceased owner. In the same way, the donee of a gift of the property is bound by the terms of the *pacte*. The benefit of a *pacte* may also be assigned but is not binding on third parties unless the notice of the assignment is given to the owner of the property in pursuance of the C.civ.art.1690.

A *pacte de préférence* is from a Land Registry point of view not treated as a restriction on the owner of the property's freedom of disposal and is thus not subject to compulsory registration if executed ssp. It may, however, be the subject of voluntary registration for the purpose of giving notice to the world at large. It is therefore desirable that a *pacte de préférence* should be in the form of an *acte authentique* and duly registered at the local *bureau des hypothèques* as is required of documents in that form.

The *vente à réméré*

The *vente à réméré* or *pacte de rachat* as it is also known is an old-fashioned type of sale by virtue of which the parties agree that the seller shall have the option to repurchase the property sold within five years of the date of sale, repaying the price he received together with all the buyer's costs to which should be added the cost of all necessary works carried out by the buyer. The transaction is covered by C.civ.arts.1659 to 1673. Such popularity as it still enjoys is possibly due to the fact that it can be used to provide a developer of land with enough density from a planning point of view to enable him to complete his development and then revest part of the property in the seller to him shorn of its density value.

The rule is that the buyer receives from his seller the price he paid to him on the original sale and not the value of the property on the day of resale. It is, however, open to the parties to agree that the price on repurchase shall be more or less than the original price but care must be taken that the repurchase price is not so different from that original price as to raise a suspicion in the minds of the tax authorities.

The period before which the option must be exercised must not exceed five years. If a longer period has been agreed, it is reduced to that time by C.civ.art.1660 but the parties may initially agree on a shorter period. The exercise of the option binds the original buyer and failure thereafter by him to conclude the resale gives rise to all the normal remedies available to the buyer who is now turned seller (Cass.23.4.38).

A contract for such a sale follows all the usual rules which may be appropriate. In particular, the period of retraction given to the non-professional buyer by the Loi SRU notwithstanding the power of resale and the provisions of the *Loi Scrivener* apply. The contract must be registered at the *bureau des hypothèques*. If the buyer creates any mortgages or charges against the property before such registration has been effected, such encumbrances will be enforceable against the seller on repurchase but otherwise he takes free of their effect. He is, however, bound by any lease created by the buyer.

The right of repurchase is freely assignable unless forbidden by the terms of the original sale. It may be renounced for value or by way of gift and may be deemed to have been renounced tacitly where, for example, it is common knowledge that the seller has not the funds with which to repurchase the property. Such a right of itself cannot be made the subject of a *saisie* (Chapter 14).

The buyer may exercise all the rights of his seller pending the exercise by the seller of the right. Thus he may create *droits réels* subject to the exercise of the option; he may redeem mortgages created by the seller and he may dispose of the property within the limits of his rights. He is required to maintain the property *en bon père de famille* and is liable for damage to it or its destruction arising through any fault on his part.

On the failure by the seller to exercise the option, the buyer 'remains irrevocably the owner' (C.civ.art.1662). The option is exercised by the seller or by his successors in title. Complex rules are made to cover the possibility that the option becomes vested in a number of persons *en indivision* as beneficiaries in an estate and if the undivided shares become ultimately vested in one beneficiary alone.

The option must be exercised by notice in writing to the buyer or to his successors in title before the expiration of the five-year period or earlier if so agreed. The amount to be paid is as indicated above or as may have been agreed. Payment of such an amount completes the sale and gives repossession of the property to the seller. The result is that the situation is as it was before the original sale and, provided the contract has been duly registered, free from any encumbrances with which the buyer may have burdened it.

The exercise of the option produces all the results of a normal sale. Stamp duty is payable on the usual ad valorem basis unless the property is within the TVA regime. The usual Land Registry fees are payable. The transaction is subject to capital gains tax in the perhaps unlikely event that the figures merit this tax.

If the buyer dies before the option to repurchase has been exercised, the property forms part of his estate. If the option is exercised between the date of death and the lodging of the *déclaration de succession*, it is the amount actually paid by the original seller which is chargeable to French inheritance tax. In the case of the death of the seller before he has exercised his option, nothing need be carried in unless the beneficiaries sell the option when *droits de succession* become payable on the sale price. For ISF purposes, the property is treated as the property of the buyer so long as the option has not been exercised.

Offre d'achat

It is obvious that an offer to buy so long as it remains unaccepted is no contract but it was at one time used as a ploy to induce a binding contract for a sale. It is to be hoped that the effect of the *Loi SRU* as described in Chapter 3 in relation to the *offre d'achat* will result in its disappearance. It is in the form of an offer in very short form placed before a possibly interested buyer by an estate agent in the hope that he will sign it with the results described in that chapter. No prospective buyer should sign such a document without the clearest possible independent advice. The giving of a cheque as an earnest of good faith which could be shown to the agent's client, the seller, is now forbidden.

7

COMPLETION

Introduction 59
For consideration by the buyer 61
For consideration by the seller 63
Completion 64
Failure to complete 65
After completion 66

Introduction

Whatever the nature of the contract to purchase or sell a property may be, the sale will be completed by the signature of an *acte de vente* which is required primarily for fiscal reasons to be *authentique*. Its form will vary according to the nature of the premises purchased but in many respects, it follows a recognized pattern. It will be *reçu* by the *notaire* in whose office completion takes place and there may be present also a second *notaire* said to be *en concurrence* if each party has instructed his own *notaire*. If the buyer has contracted a loan, the lender will send the funds to the sole *notaire* acting or to the *notaire* acting for the buyer/borrower and is unlikely to be separately represented. Completion takes place at a *rendez-vous de signature* and the signature of the *acte de vente* is the *réitération de vente par acte authentique* or the 'repetition' of the sale already valid by reason of C.civ.art.1582 previously subject to but now free of all *conditions suspensives*.

Unless a single *notaire* is acting, when obviously completion will take place at his office, completion will usually take place at the office of the *notaire* acting for the buyer but this depends on local rules set by the Court of Appeal for the area in which the property is situate. If it is the first sale of a flat in a new development or of a newly built house, then completion is at the offices of the *notaire* acting for the developer.

The duty of the *notaire* at completion is to read the *acte de vente* to the parties, explain it to them and answer any questions they may raise. His duties in this respect are covered in Chapter 1 but, in considering what is their value to an English client, there are three things to be remembered. In the first place, the *notaire* will probably not speak English and, if he does, it is unlikely to run to legal English. Hence, any explanation he may give of the effect of any provision of the *acte de vente* may not unreasonably be doubtful because he is not using the correct English technical terms. By the same token, unless the parties are proficient in legal French, they will not be able to explain the full nature of their enquiry. In the second place, it is unlikely that a non-French client has seen the draft of the *acte de vente* before completion. There is no tradition of correspondence with the client to explain the effect of the *acte* and whether there are any peculiarities on which the *notaire* needs instruction. A leading book on legal matters, admittedly written for the intelligent layman, advises that two days before completion the buyer ask the *notaire* to send him a copy of the draft *acte de vente* so that he may study it and be able to raise questions at completion. Thirdly and more important, unless there are two *notaires* involved, is that there is no possibility of a second person checking the work of the draftsman of the *acte* and ensuring that it fairly covers the opposing needs of seller and buyer. Indeed, the *acte de vente* presented at completion frequently does not represent a final document and can be and often is varied as completion proceeds. Above all, practitioners for whom possibly a conveyance of unregistered land is not nowadays a common sight must remember that every *acte de vente* presents precisely such an appearance without the benefit of a prior perusal of an Abstract of Title. Custom is that the parties attend and frequently (and particularly in the country) attend with persons not parties to the sale. There is no reason why non-French parties should not attend but it is unwise in the extreme that they should do so unaccompanied by an adviser who understands precisely what is being discussed. Preferably, it should be an adviser who has previously conferred with the *notaire* acting for that party to whom he can give advice before completion.

As has been said in Chapter 4, completions in France are on an 'on or before' basis and very seldom on a fixed date. A journey to France may be totally wasted or needlessly extended whilst the non-French party can appoint his suitable adviser to act as his attorney and behave as would his own solicitor in England.

It must be made clear that these comments are not intended to denigrate the French system. They are intended to show how fundamentally different is the French system from that used in England and the dangers of failing to appreciate this.

The contents of Chapter 29 are intended to give an appreciation of the methods which can be employed to circumvent some of the effects of the French legal system which are not always palatable to the English. It is evident that to decide which of these methods is the best or whether it is desirable to use any of them is something which demands a considerable knowledge of the family and financial backgrounds of the persons involved. This is information already at the fingertips of their solicitor in England. It is wholly absent from the knowledge of the *notaire* in France and probably in any event beyond his appreciation. This means that at least immediately after a contract has been signed, proper advice must be sought and it is suggested that this best comes from a person knowledgeable in both French and English law and procedure and is the person who should be appointed attorney to attend completion of any purchase or sale of land.

Between the signature of a contract and completion of a sale, the *notaire* will undertake enquiries very similar to those undertaken by a solicitor in England. He will make enquiries of local authorities, make Land Registry searches, ensure that all the conditions precedent are fulfilled, consider the title and whether the property is adversely affected by easements and other rights and, if what is being bought is a flat *en copropriété*, peruse the *règlements*, contact the *syndic* but, unless something very serious is revealed, is unlikely of his own volition to carry on any correspondence with his client.

The *notaire* labours under a difficulty which is absent for the solicitor in England. The various parts of the *administration* (which is a comprehensive and slightly contemptuous term for any department or office which is under the control of central or local government) are not known for the speed of their replies to any enquiry and no such thing as a result by fax or e-mail or by telephone exists.

It is essential to have a grasp of a number of matters which impinge on the completion of a French land transaction and which in many cases would also be dealt with by solicitors in England.

For consideration by the buyer

Points to be considered are as follows:

1. If a party is to be represented by an attorney at completion, his identity may be accepted from the contents of the power of attorney but it is always wise to provide a photocopy of the donor of the power's passport or equivalent identity document. The manner in which to deal with a power is covered in Chapter 19 but it is worthwhile repeating that in any event it is not advisable that there should be a sole attorney who is a member of the *notaire*'s staff.
2. Strange as it may seem, there is no rule, except the reluctance of the seller to accept it, which prevents a buyer from paying by means of a personal cheque. Assuming, however, that this is not acceptable to the seller, as will normally be the case, payment may be made by means of a bank draft drawn on a French but never on a foreign bank in favour of the *notaire* and handed over on completion. The most satisfactory method of payment from out of France is by a bank to bank transfer to the appropriate *caisse des dépôts et consignations* of which there are branches in the largest towns and at which *notaires* are required to keep their clients' accounts. It is a state institution which pays no interest on sums it holds and is not a clearing bank. Generally, it falls behind the standard of UK banks when transfers of cash are involved so that the transfer should leave the United Kingdom reasonably well in advance of completion. It is also useful to give whomever in France is concerned to know of the arrival of the cash details of the transmitting bank with its phone number and a name which can be contacted if an unreasonable delay seems to have occurred.

Notaires are not permitted to receive cash payments in excess of Euro 40,000 and are reluctant to receive cash in any quantity.

Since, as is said in Chapter 1, members of the profession are not permitted to prepare documents which would involve them in any liability jointly with their clients without being covered for that liability, failure to include *frais de notaire* in the transfer for completion will hold up the transaction.

3. The completion statement such as it is known in England is unknown in France. The contract will have given an amount for *frais* which will be reasonably accurate and any balance remaining will be refunded to the buyer after completion together with a full and largely incomprehensible statement. The reason why completion statements are unknown will become apparent from the following comments.

4. On completion, with one exception, there are no outgoings to apportion.

   (a) *Taxe d'habitation* is not apportionable and is paid in full by the occupier of the property sold on 1 January in the year of sale.

   (b) *Taxe foncière* is apportionable but since it is payable in arrear and demands do not issue until autumn at the earliest, it is not possible to make any accurate calculation unless completion takes place late in the year. If the calculation can be made, it will be made at completion and one party will give the other a cheque for his apportioned part. Otherwise, it is necessary to await the issue of the demand and for the party receiving it to contact the other and agree the mathematics. The authority which is the recipient of the tax will not itself prepare apportioned demands.

   (c) Insurance premiums are not and should never be apportioned. In any event, policies should never be taken over. The seller's policy should be cancelled and the buyer should effect new cover. This should be specifically provided for in the *acte de vente*. Notaries do not effect cover for their clients.

5. Although not strictly a matter for apportionment between seller and buyer, care must be taken on the purchase of a flat to ascertain whether the *copropriété* intends to vote or has actually voted that works be carried out to the block. There is no rule of law as to whether the costs of such work fall on seller or buyer but the generally accepted principle is that the cost of all works voted before the exchange of contracts whether they have been completed or are in the course of completion or have not yet begun are to be borne by the seller; the cost of all works voted after that date and before completion are for payment by the buyer. The usual arrangement is that if there is a meeting held between contracts and completion, the seller will so advise the buyer and if so requested will give him a proxy to attend that meeting and vote in the place of the seller.

6. The importance of knowing what *meubles* have taken on the character of *immeubles* and passed with the property has been discussed in Chapter 2. It is also essential that any *meubles meublants* are listed and valued and an inventory

annexed to the contract both for stamp duty purposes and to ensure that certain things such as light bulbs and door furniture have not been removed or changed.

For consideration by the seller

Whilst the buyer is rightly concerned to know that he has bought what he bargained to buy and the full extent of his liabilities as new owner, the seller also has concerns which in the case of the non-French need attention since some of them may be unexpected.

1. Prior to completion but, as will be seen, not too soon before that date, the question of capital gains tax must be considered. The liability to that tax, as is explained in Chapter 22, depends basically on whether the seller is or is not resident for tax purposes in France. In the case of a non-resident seller, the necessary return is filed by the *notaire* together with a copy of the draft *acte de vente* so that this very important step cannot be taken until that document is in its intended final form. It is convenient to remind sellers who would like to be treated as tax resident in France for the purposes of this tax (and so probably avoid its payment) that the *acte de vente* must then disclose their local French tax office which if they have not in fact paid French income tax it will not be able to do.

   Prior to 1 January 2003 the return in the form of a request for exemption from the need to appoint a *représentant fiscal accredité* which, if granted, was in effect a clearance for the tax at the figures disclosed. If the *dispense* was not granted a *représentant fiscal* had to be appointed. It is still essential to consider carefully the advice given in Chapter 22 and not to allow this appointment to be made, with possibly a deduction from the sale price by way of deposit to cover the *représentant*'s potential liability, unless the seller feels fully satisfied with the arrangements proposed by the *notaire*.

2. The normal arrangement is that the seller pays his agents' commission although in parts of France this may be split between buyer and seller or rarely as a matter of agreement paid solely by the buyer. The custom is for the agent to attend completion with his account for payment. If the deposit has been paid to him, he may well arrive with the deposit less his commission. This is unlawful and should not be countenanced.

3. Special rules apply if the property sold is a flat in a *copropriété*. In this case, the intention to sell must be made known to the *syndic* since he has a right to require the *notaire* holding the sale price to withhold its payment to the seller if there are outstanding service charges or other sums due to the *copropriété*. It must be realized that this right extends to the totality of the sale price. This is normally dealt with by the *notaire* giving notice well before completion to the *syndic* and obtaining a figure for service charges apportioned to the date

of sale and of any other outstanding amounts. This enables the *notaire* to make the necessary payment out of the proceeds of sale and so release them from this *opposition* for which the *notaire* is personally liable. Unfortunately but infrequently some *notaires* forget to obtain the necessary figure but much more frequently, the *syndic* is at fault and fails to reply to the *notaire* except at the last moment under extreme pressure. It is possible for the flat-owner personally to pay the *syndic* all that is due in advance of completion and obtain a clearance from him which will then satisfy the *notaire* but this is usually best left to the *notaire*.

Completion

It is essential that before completion, a buyer receives competent advice on the manner in which he should buy. In virtually every case, to delay a decision of this nature until after completion will considerably increase the overall costs. Properly to give such advice inevitably requires the co-operation of the buyer's solicitor who should appreciate that comparatively little time is available to reach decisions of a nature with which he reasonably may not be well acquainted.

The *notaire* at whose office completion takes place is said to *recevoir l'acte*. Completion can be a tedious affair, since, as explained above, in theory the *notaire* is required to read out the *acte de vente* which can run into many pages and to make certain that the parties understand its effect. Some *notaires* religiously follow this requirement and some do not. It is undoubtedly part of the duty of the *notaire* who is taking completion to be certain that all parties understand the import of the *acte de vente*. When one of the parties does not speak French, this burden is heavier. Many *notaires* insist on having present at completion an interpreter. A minimal number are conversant with legal niceties and few are able to explain to English parties the significance of the contents of an *acte de vente*. If English parties do not have a sufficient knowledge of French to understand themselves what is involved, they fail at their peril to seek advice of an expert bilingual in both languages and experienced in the laws of both countries. In very many cases, an interpreter present at completion who has not those qualifications is an active danger.

Almost as essential at completion as the completion moneys are details of one's *état civil* and this runs beyond what a passport will provide. There is no tradition in France of accepting the identity of a person on his 'say so', leaving it to him to suffer the consequences if he wrongly describes himself. The *notaire* will require a full *état civil* and in the case of the English, care must be taken to know the significance of the place where they were married and subsequently lived. If this is England, there should be no difficulty but for buyers married in (say) Scotland or the United States or most European countries, the *notaire* must be advised in advance since in some cases one spouse will not be able to buy or sell without the other spouse joining in.

It is normal for additions and corrections to be made during completion. That this can now be done on computer avoids much waste of time but it gives time for the buyer to become more acquainted with the seller and to ask last minute questions such as which keys fit which locks. C.civ.art.1605 says that 'delivery of a property is effected by the seller by the handing over of the keys' and this can become a very important formal part of the ceremony. The significance of this ceremony may be gauged from the judgment (Cass.16.6.82) that the article applies only to cases where the seller hands the keys over himself, the buyer having refused to accept them from a neighbour with whom they had been left.

It may surprise buyers to know that if they have obtained a mortgage, the *acte de vente* will incorporate the mortgage document so that since the *notaire* must be assured that the buyer/borrower fully understands and agrees the loan details in that part of the *acte*, they are read out so that the seller becomes aware of the buyer's financial arrangements.

The *acte de vente* will contain an *élection de domicile* which is on the face of it an address for the service of documents in connection with the transaction. Such an address will also be in every contract. It is sensible to consider which is the most suitable address to give, particularly if it is of a party normally resident out of France. *Notaires* tend to include an *élection de domicile* at the offices of the (or of each) *notaire* involved. Parties should think carefully if they have confidence in the *notaire* concerned to advise them out of the country of any communication he receives since some have seven-day limits for answers. Possibly the best solution is that they choose the address of their adviser in France who, if they have followed the advice given as to his choice, should be in tune with English methods.

Failure to complete

In the event of either party to the transaction refusing to complete, it is open to the other party to institute proceedings to enforce the contract. To this end, the *notaire* who is due to 'receive' the *acte de vente* will prepare a Notice to Complete which should be served on the party in default by a *huissier*. If that party still does not attend to complete, the *notaire* will prepare a *procès-verbal* recounting the facts and based on this, an action can be commenced. It is possible in such circumstances to register at the Land Registry the contract (if it has not in the case of a *promesse de vente* already been registered) together with the *procès-verbal* and in this way ensure, if the defaulting party is the seller, that the property is not sold elsewhere whilst proceedings are in process.

A final judgment of the Court against the seller takes the place of the *acte de vente* once it has been registered at the Land Registry. The plaintiff, who would normally then be the seller, can also ask for damages in lieu of the completion of the contract under a *clause résolutoire* but whatever steps are taken, neither a buyer nor a seller is advised to involve a French court since litigation in France is a tedious and long drawn-out affair.

After completion

The sale completed, the seller wishes to receive his sale price. It will be remembered that in France, Land Registry searches do not block the register which means that a clean search obtained before completion does not ensure that between the receipt of the result and completion, the seller has not sold elsewhere, encumbered the property himself or suffered the registration of some charge by a third party such as a creditor or an unpaid tax collector.

In the light of what is said above, it is useful to be aware of the special difficulty to which the French Land Registry system can give rise in connection with the sale of property. It is clearly the professional duty of the *notaire* to ensure that the buyer acquires that property free from encumbrances. This is not so straightforward a situation as it is in England where a Land Registry search made just before completion of a sale will reveal what charges, if any, are on the Register, and at the same time block the Register for a short but renewable period. Not only is this not the case in France but the Land Registry does not reply swiftly to searches and then only by post. At one time, all *actes de vente* contained a declaration by the vendor that the property sold was free from encumbrances. The sale price was withheld by the *notaire* and if a subsequent search revealed that this was not the case, the outstanding mortgage could be paid off and the seller be given the balance of his sale price. If the result showed an unpaid mortgage the amount of which exceeded the sale price, the buyer could be refunded the price he had paid but was not covered for any loss he might have suffered.

This was a situation which displeased the *notaires* who saw themselves as being forced into the situation of being more than the traditional mere draftsmen of documents to give effect to what had been agreed between the parties. The Court subsequently held (Cass.12.2.58) that the *notaire* was indeed required to undertake all enquiries relating to the property sold and in particular as to encumbrances. 'This decision came to the notarial profession as a veritable judicial bomb' (J. Picard, *Technique de la vente de l'immeuble* (Litec, 1984)). There followed two further judgments (Cass.15.4.58 and 12.5.58) which upheld the view that the *notaires* were constrained as part of their duty to advise rigorously to verify prior to completion whether or not the register revealed any outstanding mortgages. This duty, which must seem evident to the English solicitor, was again upheld (Cass.4.1.66) when the Court added that the *notaire* who could not advise a buyer whether a property was free of encumbrances or not committed an act of professional negligence.

To pay out to a seller the proceeds of sale only to find that there are others who have their hands on it would be an evident breach of duty on the part of the *notaire*. What is the solution? In many country districts, it is considered an inevitable part of the completion of the sale that the seller does not get his money for at least two months and possibly longer. The current ruling of the *Conseil Supérieur du Notariat* is that *notaires* must (i) obtain the result of a search at a date not earlier than two months before the date of completion covering a thirty-year period of ownership and (ii) register the sale as speedily as possible but in any event not more than sixty days after completion. In such circumstances, many *notaires* in cities and towns and areas where the way of life would not accept a two- or three-month delay before a seller is paid his sale price rely on their professional indemnity cover and pay out proceeds of sale more or less immediately. The requirement of the providers of such cover is that the *notaire* must have obtained a clean search not more than two months before completion which coincides with the profession's own rules. It is pointless to seek logic in such an arrangement but it is essential for a seller, if bereft of suitable advice, always to ask the *notaire* concerned when he will receive his sale price and not be misled into thinking that English methods apply.

The equivalent of a title document is the *expédition* of the *acte de vente* which is a notarially certified copy of that document. It will not be available until the transfer to the buyer has been registered so that it can show the stamp of the *bureau des hypothèques* and the stamp duty and fees paid. This document will normally be prepared automatically on completion of the registration of the transfer but is by no means automatically sent to the buyer. In many cases, it remains in the office of the *notaire* until asked for. This is no great disadvantage unless the new owner wishes to check what he has bought or what rights or liabilities he may have acquired. It is useless as a document of title to prove ownership on any particular day since unlike the English Land Registry Certificate, it proves only that the person shown in it as the buyer bought the land in question on the date of the *acte* but not that he still owns it.

Because of the delay in obtaining an *expédition*, many *notaires* supply buyers on completion with an *attestation d'acquisition* as proof of what they have bought that day. It not only serves to comfort buyers but in some circumstances, it may be necessary to prove ownership in the case of the supply of certain utilities. The document always omits mention of the purchase price since if it is produced to anyone, it might be to persons to whom the French would not wish to disclose how much they had paid for the property.

8

SALES OF LAND 'ON PLAN'

Introduction 69
Vente en l'état futur d'achèvement 70
    The *contrat préliminaire* 70
    Contents of the contract 72
    The deposit 73
    Date of completion of the sale 73
    The *acte de vente* . . . . : 73
    Insurance protection for the buyer 76
Vente à terme 78
    Contents of the contract 79
    Insurance protection 81

Introduction

A sale of land 'on plan' (*vente d'immeubles à construire*) is defined by C.civ.art. 1601-1 as 'a sale by which the seller undertakes to erect a building within a time limit imposed by the contract which may be either a *vente en l'état futur d'achèvement* or a *vente à terme*'. CCH.arts.L.261-22 and R.261-33 apply to all sales of this kind irrespective of the user of the building or the manner in which the purchase price is paid. CCH.arts.L261-10 to L261-19 apply only to buildings or parts of buildings with a residential or a mixed residential and professional user when the purchase price is to be paid by instalments as building progresses. The CCH is the codified result of the Law of 3 January 1967 and the Decree of 22 December 1967 as amended from time to time and most recently by the Loi SRU to which reference is made under the sub-heading 'The *contrat prélimi-naire*' below and in Chapter 3.

As will be readily appreciated, sales *en l'état futur* are nearly always of a part of a building, such as a flat. Such a sale is defined by C.civ.art.1601-3 as one which results in the immediate transfer on completion of the sale by the seller to the buyer of his ownership of the land and of all existing constructions upon it. Additions to the building, which at the time of completion of the sale may have been mere spaces in the air, become the property of the buyer as building progresses. It must be remembered that flats in a building must be owned *en copropriété* (Chapter 15) so that in addition to the flat itself, a buyer acquires a proportion of the common parts of the building in which the flat is situate and of the land itself on which the building stands.

The *vente à terme* is almost exclusively used for the building of individual houses. Sales in such cases, come within the ambit of the CCH.arts.L.231-1 to 231-13 and R.231-1 to 231-14 if the house is to be built in accordance with standard plans supplied by the builder. In the case of a house to be built to the design supplied by the buyer the applicable articles of the CCH are L.232-1 and 2 and R.232-1 to R.323-7. In this type of sale, the seller retains ownership in the land until completion of the construction of the house when it passes to the buyer but with retrospective effect as from the date of completion of the sale. The effect of this provision is dealt with hereafter.

Notwithstanding the difference in the two kinds of sale in the moment of time of the transfer of ownership of the land involved, in the former case the *maîtrise d'ouvrage* remains vested in the seller until the building works are complete. The *maîtrise d'ouvrage* is the right to build on the land on which the construction is to be effected, to obtain planning permission to this end, and to engage builders and experts. This right is effectively the equivalent of absolute ownership of the land in question. The right must not be confused with that of the closely sounding *maitrise d'oeuvre* which is the expertise provided by the professionals in the appropriate field such as architects, engineers, the suppliers of equipment and the builders themselves.

Vente en l'état futur d'achèvement

The contrat préliminaire
The rules laid down by the CCH are *d'ordre public* so that it is not possible to contract out of them. Failure to abide by any of these provisions nullifies the transaction. It is essential, however, to bear in mind that it is not obligatory (although normal practice) to precede completion of such a sale by a contract and one can proceed directly to completion by the execution of the *acte de vente*. The form of contract leading to a sale *en l'état futur*, properly called a *contrat préliminaire*, is often referred to as a *contrat de réservation* because the seller is said to 'reserve' part of a building to be built for the buyer. Indeed, the parties are frequently called '*réservant*' (the developer or 'reserver') on the one hand and '*réservataire*' (buyer or 'reservee') on the other. This is a highly undesirable misnomer liable to create at least in the minds of the non-French a misunderstanding of the significance of the document and the impression that a 'reservation' can be cancelled at will and once the Loi SRU period has passed is not a binding contract.

The CCH indicates that any contract in any form other than that requisite for the *contrat préliminaire* is void but it has been held (Cass.27.10.75) and accepted as established law over a period of years that such a contract is in fact neither a *promesse de vente*, a *compromis de vente* nor a *pacte de préférence* (see Chapters 4, 5, and 6); it is a contract *sui generis*. Since such a contract is specifically not a contract for the sale of land, it cannot be enforced by an order for specific performance. This situation arises by reason of the lack of precision in such contracts as to both the price and the identity of the property to be sold. At best, in addition to the return of his deposit or other moneys paid, a buyer can obtain damages if he has suffered loss by reason of the developer's inability or refusal to complete (Cass.11.6.87).

However, if the relationship is not that of seller and buyer of land, it is nevertheless subject to the ordinary rules of contract law. Whilst a buyer may be unable to obtain the property which he desires to acquire, he nevertheless has a number of remedies of which the mere return of his deposit does not deprive him. Refusal on the part of the developer to complete is *per se* a ground for damages. The developer cannot avoid liability if he fails to keep the buyer fully informed as to the progress of and any important modifications in building works. His silence on such matters is actionable as a departure from the duty of good faith which ought to accompany the carrying into effect of all contractual obligations (C.civ.art.1134). Failure to complete building works by the agreed date will allow a buyer to claim the cost of a hotel and furniture storage charges (Cass.28.7.77) and it has even been held that delay in completing building works with the consequent loss to a buyer of the possibility of entering into a tax advantageous bargain is also actionable (Cass 17.11.93).

Moreover, since a *contrat préliminaire* is not a contract for the sale of land, it would appear on the face of it not necessary to register it under CGI.art.1840-A (see Chapters 4 and 5) but it is generally considered advisable nevertheless to effect this formality once the identity of the building can clearly be established in order to ensure that use is not made by a seller of what is a purely fiscal provision to avoid the contract.

The *contrat préliminaire* provides the background to the right now generally available to repudiate within a short period of time without cause all contracts for the sale of land initially limited to the *contrat préliminaire* if executed ssp. The right first saw light in the Law of 31 December 1989 'to prevent and overcome the difficulties of persons and families overburdened by debt' and later became enshrined in the CCH. It is now elaborated in the Loi SRU and applies to contracts both *authentique* and ssp including the *contrat préliminaire*, still irrespective of whether the party seeking to avoid his contractual obligations is in fact overburdened by debt or not. It also continues to apply notwithstanding that the *contrat préliminaire* does not rank as a contract for the sale of land. In this connection, consideration must be given to the explanation of the effect of *élection de domicile* contained in Chapter 7.

From the point of view of the seller (and indirectly of the buyer), the *contrat préliminaire* has a special significance as a means of testing of the market. Few developers build without recourse to outside sources of finance and the more executed *contrats préliminaires* which can be produced to a bank or other financial establishment, the easier it will be to obtain building finance. The significance to the buyer of the success in this respect of the developer lies in the nature of the guarantee for the completion of the building works which the developer is required by law to give and which is discussed below.

Contents of the contract
The contract must refer to:

1. The area of the property in question, with the number of principal rooms and their position in the building and all such auxiliary areas such as cellars, garages and parking spaces.
2. A full specification (*note technique sommaire*) which must be annexed to the contract giving details of all works to be done and showing the nature and quality of the materials to be used. If the property is a flat, this specification must include details of all common services available to it.
3. The provisional sale price and terms (if any) for its revision.
4. Details of such mortgage finance, if any, as the seller may offer to obtain for the buyer.
5. The earliest date on which the sale may be completed.
6. The reproduction in full of CCH.arts. R261-28 to 31 which read as follows:
    '28. No deposit may exceed 5% of the provisional sale price, if completion of the sale is to take place within a year. This percentage is limited to 2% if completion is to take place within two years and no deposit may be taken if that period is to be exceeded.
    29. The deposit shall be paid to a special account opened in the name of the buyer in a bank or other specially authorized institution or with a *notaire*. Deposits from other buyers of various parts of the same building or the same complex may be grouped together in a single account under the separate names of the buyers.
    30. The seller shall provide the buyer with a draft of the *acte de vente* at least one month before the intended date of completion.
    31. Deposits shall be returned to buyers in full without the deduction of any penalty if (a) the sale is not completed by reason of the default of the seller by the date provided for in the contract (b) the sale price for any reason exceeds by more than 5 per cent the provisional sale price and notwithstanding that this is due to an increase in the layout of the building or improvements in the quality of its finishings (c) any loan to be arranged by the developer referred to in the contract has not been granted or is granted in an amount less than 10% of that mentioned therein (d) any one of the items of equipment mentioned in the specifications is not provided (e) the building or that part of the building the subject matter of the contract suffers a reduction in value of more than 10% by reason of the nature and quality of its construction.'

In any of the above cases the deposit must be returned to the buyer within three months of his request by registered AR post.

The Loi Scrivener (Chapter 3) which makes contracts for the sale of land, if so desired by the buyer, conditional on his obtaining such mortgage finance as he indicates in the contract does not apply to sales *en l'état futur*. This is purely a practical point based on the fact that the buyer cannot make his mortgage application until he knows the final purchase price since the contract price is subject to variation, albeit within certain limits. However, it has become common form for the majority of, if not all, developers to allow buyers to make their *contrats préliminaires* subject to the conditions of the Loi Scrivener. This gesture is, of course, in addition to such offer as the developer may himself make to find mortgage finance for the buyer.

The deposit
The size of the deposit is linked to the intended date of completion of the sale. No deposit may be kept other than with a bank or similar institution or in the account of a *notaire*. Until the time of actual completion, it cannot be dealt with or charged by the developer and is protected from seizure by his creditors. It is a criminal offence for a developer to retain himself any cheque given to him as a deposit. This being so, it would not seem possible for a developer to accept a bank guarantee in lieu of a deposit of cash which would be acceptable in the case of an ordinary *compromis de vente* or *promesse de vente*.

Date of completion of the sale
Whatever the *contrat préliminaire* may say, there are two factors which govern the earliest date upon which completion may take place. These are: (i) the nature of the guarantee which the developer gives for completion of the building works; and (ii) that the developer is the owner of the land on which the building is already or is to be erected and that he has planning permission.

The obligatory guarantee for the completion of building works (*garantie d'achèvement*) is available in two forms and may be a *garantie extrinsèque* or a *garantie intrinsèque*. In neither case does the *contrat préliminaire* normally indicate which obligatory guarantee will be given but pressure should be applied to remedy this omission. If it is a *garantie extrinsèque*, completion of the sale may take place before any building works have commenced but if it is a *garantie intrinsèque*, this cannot take place until the foundations of the building have been completed. Alternatively, the developer may provide a *garantie de remboursement* which covers the repayment of all moneys laid out by the buyer and made available to the seller if the property is not completed in accordance with the terms of the *contrat préliminaire*. If such cover is given, completion may take place in the same way as is the case when a *garantie extrinsèque* is given.

The acte de vente
This document in draft form must be sent to the buyer or his *notaire* at least a month before the date set for completion of the sale in order to enable him to

satisfy himself that the property he is buying corresponds to that which he contracted to buy and must clearly indicate if the amounts said to be due on completion will in fact be due having regard to the state to which building has progressed. It must be said that if the buyer is anxious to complete at an earlier date (which in practice he frequently is), completion may properly take place at a shorter interval but such agreement on the part of the buyer must be express and not implied or in any way equivocal (CA Versailles 14.2.92).

In addition, prior to completion, the buyer should have been given a copy of the *règlement de copropriété* including the *état descriptif* of the *copropriété* in the process of being created (see Chapter 15). This requirement which is not always complied with should be insisted upon since the document sets out (inter alia) the regulations for the management of the block and the method of assessing the service charges. The *acte de vente* should contain the buyer's acknowledgement of the receipt of this document.

The *acte de vente* must contain a description of the property sold and as in the case of the *contrat préliminaire* much of what goes into this document is in pursuance of the requirements of the CCH. In addition to the need solely for tax reasons for the document effecting the sale to be an *acte authentique*, sales *en l'état futur* in any event must be in this form. The *acte* must, in addition to a general description of the part of the building sold, contain references to the 'substance and technical characteristics' of the building (CCH.art.L261-11). These requirements are satisfied by annexing plans and elevations with measurements of the surfaces of all rooms and passages. In the case of a building in a complex comprising other buildings, a plan showing the position of and the number of storeys in each such other building must be supplied. A full indication of all services available to the part of the building bought must also be given.

It must be remembered that not infrequently the price shown in the *contrat préliminaire* is a provisional figure in which case it is possible for the developer to adjust that price as at the date of completion for insertion in the *acte de vente*. This price should then be final but the law allows for revision thereafter to that figure if the buyer so agrees. Any such revisions must be by reference to the National Cost of Building Index BT 01 which is published monthly and cannot exceed 70 per cent of the variation in that Index compared to the figure as at the date when the previous instalment was paid. The circumstances permitting any revision of the price as laid down by the CCH must be set out in full in the *acte de vente*.

Subject to revisions if any, CCH.art.R261-14 fixes how the sale price is paid by stage payments. The *acte* should provide that these are made against architects' certificates. There is no reason why the percentages shown below should not be varied so that payments are made at intermediate building stages so long as the ceilings fixed by law are observed. The *acte de vente* may provide for a penalty not exceeding 1 per cent per month of the sum involved for late payment by the buyer.

The percentage stage payments are:

35% on completion of the foundations
70% when the building is *hors d'eau* (weatherproof)
95% on completion of building works.

The remaining 5 per cent becomes payable on the handing over of the keys (*remise des clefs*) when, if the buyer has no faults to find in the construction of the building, its interior and its services, he takes formal possession. If there is a dispute as to any of these matters, the amount must be *consigné* to a stakeholder whilst the problem is resolved. If a buyer fails to adopt this procedure, the developer is within his rights to refuse to hand over the keys (Cass.13.2.85) which in theory leads ultimately to the loss by the buyer of the property. Buyers are strongly recommended to have a surveyor or similar expert on hand to check progress at least when each stage payment is due and in any event when the keys are handed over. The importance of this cannot be overestimated in connection with the *garantie décennale* described under the following heading which covers *vices cachés* and generally as to deciding what work is obviously defective (*vices apparents*) and how to ensure that it is put right.

In particular, the obtaining by the developer of a *certificat de conformité* which is a planning certificate confirming that the building has been completed in conformity with the planning permission is not sufficient proof that the developer has fulfilled all the terms of his contract. This certificate does not provide proof that the building complies with the plans and *note technique sommaire* which form part of the contract. Thus, many such specifications allow a developer to substitute items of a quality or make equivalent to those in the specifications if he so advises the buyer. This is acceptable within reasonable limits since items may become unobtainable or even may no longer be manufactured. Such limits would, however, be exceeded where, for example, a developer had built a wall which, although acceptable from a planning point of view, was not shown on the contractual plans and which masked the entrance to a block and was adjudged to have depreciated the value of the property and so be liable to the buyer for such loss in value (Cass.20.12.94).

If the failure on the part of the developer is substantial and the property is not completed within the meaning of CCH.art.R261-1, the contract is discharged by reason of the breach of the developer. There have been treated by the Courts as failure on the part of the developer of a substantial nature: (i) the diminution in the agreed area of a room or overall in a flat; (ii) the failure to provide a sun terrace; and (iii) to build otherwise than in accordance with planning permission. In the event of the inability of the developer to remedy such defects, an action in damages lies at the instance of the buyer. Delay in the date of completion of a building also gives rise to a claim for damages unless the contract contains a 'get out' clause (which it frequently will) for reasons additional to the standard force majeure provisions.

Insurance protection for the buyer

The most significant protection for a buyer *en l'état futur* is the insurance which the developer and builders is by law required to provide. It must be remembered that in most cases, the larger part of the purchase price is paid before completion of building works and although stage payments are made only for work certified to have been done, nevertheless, they are a form of credit available to the seller. For this reason, the law obliges the seller to offer to the buyer either a guarantee for the completion of the building works or for the repayment of what the buyer has laid out if the building is never completed. Whilst the two kinds of insurance are exclusive it is possible but unusual for the *acte de vente* to allow substitution of one kind of cover for the other before building is complete.

As has been mentioned above, the kind of cover which the developer will offer is seldom known before the *acte de vente* is available in draft form. This is frequently because the developer himself does not know until his project has been on the market for some time which he can offer, bearing in mind, as will be seen, that *extrinsèque* cover is the more attractive to buyers but usually more difficult for the developer to obtain. As a general rule, a prospective buyer will prefer to have the flat he has chosen completed and available for his occupation rather than have returned to him the money he has uselessly spent on a fruitless exercise.

A *garantie extrinsèque* is, in the words of CHH.art.R261-21, either (i) the opening of a line of credit by a bank or similar financial institution available to the developer or (ii) the acceptance of the liability jointly and severally with the developer, in either case, for the payment of all amounts needed for the completion of building works. The liability of the bank is therefore limitless in the sense that it must provide all such amounts as are necessary to complete the building works but it is a guarantee to provide funds for and not for completion as such of the works. It is also clear that it is for the protection of the buyer and not the developer (Cass.28.10.81).

CCH.art.R261-1 defines the completion of building works as 'when all works have been completed including the installation of all services and equipment necessary for the enjoyment of the property the subject of the sale having regard to its intended user'. There being no clearer definition of the completion of works than is given in this article, it is necessary to rely on the ruling that whether building works had been completed or not should be left to the decision of an independent expert appointed by the Court (CA Paris 7.1.83) and this still remains the standard practice.

However, in the case of a *garantie extrinsèque* it must be noted that the liability of the institution providing the cover comes to an end with the granting of a *déclaration d'achèvement des travaux* (DAT). This is a planning document which together with the *attestation de conformité* confirms that the building has been completed and complies with the terms of the planning permission even if building works have not been completed in accordance with the terms of CCH.art.R261-1 quoted above. This is because cover is given for completion of the building works in conformity with the planning permission and not with the terms of the *contrat préliminaire*. The liability of the guarantor does not therefore extend to the cost of putting right defects or faults in the building discovered after the grant of a DAT. On the other hand, it has been held that the final stage payment may be demanded if the building is completed notwithstanding that a DAT has not yet been obtained (Cass.26.10.88).

A *garantie intrinsèque*, which is the personal guarantee of the developer, may be offered in only limited circumstances. Either (i) the building involved has reached the stage of being weathertight by reason of the completion of its roof and is subject to no mortgage or other charge or (ii) the foundations of the building have been completed and there is available for the completion of the building works from the personal funds of the developer, either in the form of confirmed credits available to him or as a result of already concluded sales, at least 75 per cent of the sale price of the building. The amount of 75 per cent can be reduced to 60 per cent if the personal funds of the developer can cover 30 per cent of the sale price. The availability of credits must be certified by the lending bank and completed sales confirmed by the *notaire* who acted in connection with them. It will be appreciated that a *garantie intrinsèque* is by reason of the conditions which must be fulfilled before it can be given but a guarantee in name only. It has been well described in the words of a leading textbook on the subject as 'a presumption of the probability of an attempt to complete the building' and every effort should be made to obtain a *garantie extrinsèque*.

If a buyer is satisfied with the possibility of the repayment of what he has laid out should the building not be completed, he will be prepared to accept a *garantie de remboursement*. Such repayment is limited to the sale price or such proportion as has been paid over but does not include costs or bank interest or even any penalties due from the developer. Cover of this kind must be provided by a bank or insurance company.

In addition to one or other of the covers described above, the buyer *en l'état futur* enjoys, as do all other owners of property, two statutory rights of action. One is the *garantie décennale* in respect of serious defects *'qui compromettent la solidarité de l'ouvrage ou qui, l'affectant dans l'un de ses éléments constitutifs ou l'un de ses éléments d'équipement, le rendent impropre à sa destination'* (which adversely affect the integrity of the building or which by their effect on one of its constituent components or installations make its intended use impossible). Such defects include a leaking roof, lack of sufficient insulation, defective electrical or sanitary installations, and the malfunctioning of the central heating system. The other is the *garantie biennale* for less important defects such as ill-fitting doors or windows or ill-functioning taps. The former right is provided for by C.civ.art.1792 and becomes statute-barred at the end of a period of ten years by virtue of C.civ.art.2270. The latter right stems from C.civ.art.1792-3 which says *'Les autres éléments d'équipement du bâtiment font l'objet d'un garantie de bon fonctionnement d'une durée minimum de deux ans'* (Accessory items benefit from a two-year guarantee of proper workmanship). It is the prescription periods which give the names of 'ten-year and two-year guarantees' by which these rights of action are known.

The persons who are liable under C.civ.art.1792 are *'tous constructeurs d'un ouvrage'* and the following article deems a *'constructeur'* to include: (i) architects and experts in similar fields; (b) building tradesmen and others under contract to the owner; and (c) all sellers of completed buildings which they have themselves built or caused to be built and all persons acting on their behalf. All such persons are required by law (C.assur.art.L.242-1) to effect insurance cover against these liabilities. Policies of this kind are known as *polices d'assurance dommages-ouvrage*. It is essential that buyers ensure that such a policy has been effected by the appropriate persons. It may not be made subject to any excess and is limitless in amount covered in that it extends to all repairs necessary to repair damage of the kind spoken of in C.civ.art.1792. Details of such policies or failure to effect them must be mentioned in all *actes de vente* to all subsequent buyers since the benefit of such policies is passed on from original to subsequent owners within the ten-year period.

Vente à terme

Sales of this kind are defined by CCH.art.L.261-2 as those 'by which the seller undertakes to deliver a building on its completion and the buyer undertakes to take delivery of it and at that time to pay the price. The passing of the property is effected by the *acte authentique* confirming completion of the building (and such passing) takes effect retroactively to the date of sale.' The effect of this provision is that the document creating a *vente à terme* requires registration at the *bureau des hypothèques* as does the *acte authentique* which confirms the completion of building works. A further and most important effect is that all *droits réels* (Chapter 2), of which the most significant will be mortgages, which have been created by the seller/builder prior to the execution of that *acte* are void as against the buyer unless he chooses to adopt them.

Two different types of contract are recognized by the law as it now stands amended by the Law of 19 December 1990 which applies to all contracts entered into after 1 December 1991 and which are those dealt with below. Such contracts may be for the construction of not more than two individual houses with a residential or a joint residential and professional user and based either on plans submitted to the buyer by the builder or on the buyer's own plans. Both types of contract are subject to the general right for the non-professional buyer to withdraw during the Loi SRU seven-day 'period of reflection'.

A survey carried out in the year 2000 reported that of the 200,000 new houses built in France in that year, over 60 per cent were built to plans supplied by a specialist builder. To undertake oneself a building project in a foreign country even with the help of a bilingual architect is a formidable task and the following exposé of the rules which apply assumes the building of a house on land belonging to the intending occupier by a builder either based on his own plans or on those of the owner. If the arrangement with the builder involves also the sale by him of the land on which the house is to be built, the transaction becomes one of purchase *en l'état futur* the regulations of which have been discussed above and which differ from those for *ventes à terme*.

Contents of the contract

Plans supplied by the builder

C.C.H.arts.L.231-2 and R.231-1 to 4 require that the contract for the building of an individual house contain the following:

1. A detailed description of the land on which the house is to be built and the title of the owner of or of the person entitled to build on that land.
2. Confirmation that the building project conforms to the requirements of the relevant sections of the CCH.
3. The area of the building and its technical characteristics with details of connections to all utilities and the installation of all exterior and interior services, all of which together with other architectural information must be shown on annexed plans and in the *notice descriptive*.
4. The agreed cost of building distinguishing, if needs be, between works to be executed by the builder and those to be carried out by the owner. These latter must be indicated in a special list handwritten and signed by the owner including an indication of his specific liability for such works.
5. Details of the stage payments to be made by the owner.
6. Confirmation that the owner has the right to employ the services of an architect or similar expert in the building field covered by a professional negligence policy at the time of delivery of the completed building.
7. Confirmation that all necessary planning and other consents have been obtained with annexed copies.
8. Details of the methods of financing the building including those of any loans obtained by the owner.
9. The dates of commencement and completion of building works and details of any penalties for late completion.
10. Details of the *assurance dommages-ouvrage* effected by the builder or the owner.
11. Details of the cover obtained by the builder to guarantee completion of the works or for repayment of moneys to the owner in the case of failure to do so.

If the contract is for the building of a single house, it may be in a form in which some of the above items are dealt with as conditions precedent. Thus CCH.art.L.231-4 allows the following to be treated in this manner:

1. The ownership of the land or of rights in the land which entitle the party contracting with the builder to build the house on that land.

2. The obtaining of planning and other permissions subject to provision of the latest date upon which application for such permissions should be lodged.
3. The granting of any loans required for the financing of the building project.
4. The issue of the *dommages-ouvrage* insurance policy and of the cover for completion of the building works.

In the case where a contract contains any of the above conditions, it must give the latest date for their fulfilment. If any condition remains unfulfilled by such date, any deposit paid on signing of the contract becomes repayable.

The contract must give the finally agreed price. It may make provision for variations in this price if the parties so agree on the same basis as variations in the price in the case of sales *en l'état futur*. The price should include the cost of: (i) cover for completion of the building works or for repayment of moneys paid by the owner if they are not completed in accordance with the contract; (ii) preparation of all plans and of the land necessary for completion of the building works; and (iii) all taxes due from the builder (but not the owner) in connection with such works.

A deposit may be required by the builder and this may not exceed 3 per cent of the price calculated in the above manner as shown in the contract. This deposit must be lodged with a bank or other suitable financial institution in the name of the owner. This deposit, in the case of a contract subject to any of the conditions mentioned above, is inalienable and free from the claims of creditors until fulfilment of all such conditions when it becomes a part payment on account of the agreed price. It is returnable to the owner in the case of the non-fulfilment of any of the conditions by the due date or in the event of the cancellation of the contract by the owner within the seven-day cancellation period.

If no such deposit is payable under the terms of the contract, an amount not exceeding 5 per cent of the agreed price is payable on signature of the contract and a similar percentage is payable on the obtaining of planning consent. In such circumstances, CCH.art.R231-8 requires that there is annexed to the contract evidence of the effecting of cover for the completion of the building works. It is absolutely forbidden for the builder to require or accept any payment in money or money's worth prior to the signature of the contract or in advance of the date for stage payments under the contract (the penalty is Euro 19,000 and/or two years' imprisonment).

Stage payments may not exceed:

15% on the commencement of works (to include any deposit)
25% on completion of the foundations
40% on completion of the exterior walls
60% on completion of the roof
75% on completion of interior walls and windows
95% on completion of the installation of plumbing and heating and all carpentry work.

The balance of 5 per cent is payable on the handing over of the completed house subject to any retention for work still to be completed or if the owner is not advised by any expert, not later than eight days from such handing over subject to a similar retention.

The contract may provide for a penalty of 1 per cent per month for late payment of any of these stage payments.

Plans supplied by the owner

In many respects, the form of contract with the builder follows the same requirements as when the builder builds to plans provided by him (*sur catalogue*). However, in certain respects, some of the rules are less severe and the amounts and times of payment of stage payments may be freely agreed between the parties except as to the final payment and advance payments are forbidden.

Insurance protection

The insurance effected by the builder in connection with the completion of building works in accordance with the terms of the building contract is effected with an insurance company or similar institution and provides cover jointly and severally with sub-contractors against any failure on the part of the builder to comply with its terms. A certificate confirming the effecting of this cover must be given to the owner before building work begins. Cover extends from the date when building works commence and finishes when the completed house has been accepted by the new owner or, in the case of non-acceptance, at the expiration of the eight-day period allowed for formal complaints or when the necessary works of rectification have been completed. The cover extends to:

(1) any costs over and above the agreed price necessary to complete the building works including any permitted excess of 5 per cent of the agreed price;
(2) the effect of the builder having obtained a payment in advance or an increase in the agreed price; and
(3) the penalty payable under the contract for any delay exceeding thirty days in completion of the works.

It is the duty of the insurer when advised of any delay in the completion of the works as laid down by the contract or in making good defects after the handing over of the building to give formal notice to the builder. If after notice to the builder, such works have not been completed within fifteen days, the insurers must name a person to carry out such works to whom they make all such payments as may be necessary for the completion of such works.

The rules relating to policies of this nature, as indeed is the case with all French policies, are very strictly interpreted and it is imperative that owners who think that they have a claim should have immediate recourse to the appropriate expert to act on their behalf.

The *constructeur* (which, as has been mentioned above, includes a person who has caused a house to be built) is required (Code des assurances, art.242-1) to effect cover *dommages-ouvrage* for the ten-year period. Mention of the existence of such cover is obligatory in contracts for the building of houses irrespective of who provides the plans and it is important that a check is made to ensure that this cover exists. Failure on the part of the person for whom the house was built to ensure that such cover was effected leads to the possibility of a claim made by a subsequent owner during the next ten years against him and the builder for latent defects in the house.

9

PROPERTY OWNING COMPANIES

Introduction 83
Nature of the French *société* 84
The applicable law 85
Formation of a *société civile* 85
The form of the *statuts* 87
The shareholders 88
Contents of the *statuts* 89
Meetings of shareholders 91
Share transfers 91
Management of a *société civile* 92
Liquidation 93
Fiscal considerations 93
The Companies Registry 94

Introduction

The use of a *société civile* as a vehicle to avoid the impact of French entrenched inheritance rights (*la réserve*) in the case of persons who die domiciled in England is discussed in Chapter 29. There may be other reasons why it is advantageous for those who are domiciled in France as well as those whose domicile is English to make use of the *société civile* as the owner of French land and the object of this chapter is to provide a limited appreciation of the law and procedure applicable to the type of French company most suitably used for property ownership. It is not intended to supply detailed information available from books specializing in French company law.

Whilst it is, of course, possible to make use of a company incorporated in a country other than France as the owner of French property, in the case of property bought for the personal occupation by private individuals and their families, the choice will usually fall best on a company incorporated in that country. In the case of property purchased specifically for the purposes of letting, other considerations primarily of a fiscal nature are called into play which fall outside the scope of this book. In addition and quite apart from the inheritance and tax aspects of the ownership of French land, it is interesting to find that in the light of the evident disadvantages of ownership *en indivision* (Chapter 16), the use of the *société civile* is becoming more and more recognized by French property owners as a suitable vehicle for the joint ownership and the management of family property in various interests with no background thought of the need to indulge in profit-making activities (Me Fernoux (2001) *La Semaine Juridique Notariale et Immobilière*, no 22–23 (1 June).

Nature of the French *société*

An overall requirement of every French company is that it is born of an '*affectio societatis*' or the implicit intention of the intending shareholders to enter on equal terms into a joint venture. It is rarely necessary to apply this test to the intentions of persons forming a company to pursue a common venture but if the lack of such intention can be proved, the company is considered never to have existed.

The word '*société*' has a double meaning in French law in that, on the one hand, it connotes the contract by which two or more persons (*associés*) agree, in the paraphrased words of C.civ.art.1832, to undertake a common enterprise or by the common use of some asset to benefit from the profit they may make or from the savings which may ensue from such use. On the other hand, it is the name given to the entity to which is entrusted that asset which has a legal being of its own, acting in the name of and in the interests of the *associés*. The *société* is a *personne morale* (corporate entity) as opposed to its *associés* who are *personnes physiques* (natural persons).

There are two important distinctions to be made between the French *société* and the company known to English law:

1. All French *sociétés* are either civil or commercial. The definition of a *société civile* is that it is a company which does not indulge in any of the commercial activities contained in the list to be found in C.com.art.632. Activities which can be categorized as civil are, on the other hand, with the exception of agriculture, nowhere defined. The list of *sociétés civiles* is widely drawn, ranging from professional partnerships (*sociétés civiles professionnelles* or SCPs) to companies indulging in intellectual pursuits. Included in the list and probably among the most widely used in its various forms in connection with the ownership of land is the *société civile immobilière* or SCI and the *société civile d'attribution* which is examined in Chapter 10. The *société de pluripropriété* also known as the *société civile d'attribution à temps partagé* is dealt with in Chapter 11.

   In terms readily understandable by the English lawyer, the commercial company is one which 'involves itself in the distribution of wealth with a view to profit'. This is, however, something of an Alice in Wonderland description which can lead to strange anomalies: activities which are civil can, if carried out for the benefit of a commercial company, be deemed to be commercial and vice versa. Thus, it might be thought that the business of letting furnished or unfurnished property was commercial; it is not, since it is specifically excluded as such by the Law of 13 July 1967 which is the foundation of current commercial company law and which designates it as a 'civil' activity.

The business of the hiring *per se* of furniture and household equipment is commercial but the inclusion of furniture and equipment in a flat to create a furnished letting remains a 'civil' transaction. By virtue of C.com.art.632 the purchase of building land for its resale after buildings have been erected on it is specifically a civil business but the purchase of existing buildings with a view to their resale is a commercial activity. The *société civile* is governed by rules laid down in the *Code civil* whilst the *société commerciale* has its own Commercial Code.

2. The *société civile* is an entity separate from its shareholders capable of owning property in its own name. However, it does not provide its shareholders with the protection of limited liability. They are liable for the debts of the *société*, save in the most unusual circumstances, in the proportion in which they hold its shares (C.civ.art.1857). This is normally of no great significance since it involves them in no greater liability than if they were directly the joint owners of the property owned by the SCI and the benefit of limited liability is very seldom the object of the formation of the SCI.

The applicable law

French law applies to all companies whose *siège social* is in France, including its overseas *départements* and territories. The current law of 4 January 1978 as amended by the Law of 17 July 1978 has been in force since 1 July 1978 and applies to all companies incorporated after that date. Companies which were incorporated before that date have been subject to that law from 1 July 1980 or from the date of their registration at the Companies Registry. Registration of *sociétés civiles* formed before 1 July 1978 was not obligatory but has now become so and all unregistered companies must have been registered not later than 1 November 2002. The intended measures of conformity relating to companies in the Treaty of Rome are still unrealized and the only Convention agreed under the Treaty which deals with the mutual recognition of companies has not come into effect since it has not been ratified by all the contracting parties. It was ratified by France in 1969.

Formation of a *société civile*

The basic forms for all *sociétés civiles* are similar but each type has its own special requirements. The rules which follow immediately refer to the formation of an SCI and variations and additional requirements for the *société d'attribution* are set out in the relevant chapters. What is known as the *contrat de société*, or the *statuts* of the company, combines the features of the English memorandum and articles of association.

This document must fulfil certain requirements in addition to the usual conditions relating to the validity of contracts as laid down in C.civ.art.1108. These are:

1. The consent of the parties. Lack of consent is an obvious vice but extends further than the mere failure to give express consent. Consent may be *simulé* or fictitious when it is given in a document which the parties intend should remain secret and which is of a different nature from that which is made public. Thus, consent is *simulé* if parties to the sale of land make use of a company to achieve the sale by the transfer of shares to save stamp duties. Such transactions are, of course, lawful if the object of their use is lawful but notice must be taken of the wide-ranging powers of the French Revenue to apply the doctrine of *répression des abus de droit*. This doctrine of recent years is happily undergoing limitation at the hands of the Courts (of which the French Revenue is inclined to take small notice). It enables the Revenue to garner the fiscal benefits (and penalties) which it alleges it would have been entitled to if the transaction in issue had exhibited its true character.

2. The capacity of the parties. Lack of capacity of any one party renders the company void. Infants may be subscribers to a company notwithstanding that shareholders of an SCI are personally liable to contribute without limit to its debts. The contract is good but formalities in France of a nature not known in English law will subsequently probably be necessary to support its validity. The English, unburdened as they are by the *régime matrimonial*, are taken to have married in the equivalent of *séparation de biens*. There is therefore no problem about spouses individually or jointly being shareholders of an SCI if they were married in England and have an English matrimonial domicile. Companies, whether they are 'civil' or 'commercial' and generally wherever incorporated, can become *associés* of an SCI. In the case of a French 'civil' company, the *gérant* or director usually has power to act on behalf of the SCI. Who will act on behalf of a non-French company will normally depend on the law of the country of its incorporation as evidenced by its articles.

3. The certainty and legality of its objects. The objects for which the SCI is formed must be both clearly stated and be sufficiently explicit. Thus, 'any object which is civil' is considered insufficient. In general terms, the objects clause in the *statuts* of an SCI is less detailed than it is in an English memorandum of association. It is the objects clause which indirectly governs the powers of the *gérant* and is a means of protection for the body of the shareholders, who are liable without limit for the debts of the company, against certain improper acts of the *gérant*.

4. The objects must be lawful. The test of lawfulness is based both on the general wording of C.civ.art.6 ('Private agreements may not contravene the laws relating to public order and good morals') and the rather more abstruse wording of C.civ.art.1128 ('Only commercial activities can be the subject of agreements'). Happily, the Courts have wide powers of appreciation of the application of these articles. If the objects of an SCI are illegal or impossible to attain, the SCI may be declared void but most other irregularities can be cured by means of the appropriate procedures before the Courts.

5. The *cause* for which the company is formed. This is not the same as the objects for the carrying out of which the company is formed. It refers to the reasons which motivated a number of persons to form an association in the shape of a company. Lack or illegality of *cause* can lead to a declaration of invalidity of a company, the objects of which may be lawful but which was formed in pursuance of an agreement between persons which itself was unlawful. Thus companies formed with the sole intention of evading tax or 'money laundering' are void for illegality of *cause* however lawful the objects themselves may be.

The form of the *statuts*

C.civ.art.1835 requires that the *statuts* be in writing. They may be *authentique* or *sous seing privé* but the former is obligatory whenever there is involved an issue of shares for a consideration consisting of land, a leasehold interest for a term of not less than twelve years and generally when the nature of such consideration is such that the transaction requires registration at the *bureau des hypothèques*. It is also considered desirable that the services of a *notaire* be used whenever shareholders of the company are husband and wife or close members of a family but it must be admitted that this is a strictly French view. If there are purely family interests at stake and all that is involved is the formation of the SCI and the purchase of a property by it, this is probably the correct view but if the principal problems are purely commercial, it may well be that the services of an *avocat* (and possibly one who is an ex-*conseil juridique*) are preferable. Subscribers may execute the *statuts* by an attorney.

Every *contrat de société* or set of *statuts* must indicate that proper consideration is provided for the allotment of shares. Such consideration is called an *apport*. An *apport* must have a genuine value. The transfer of an *apport* which is fictitious, for example a copyright which has expired or the equity in an asset which is of negative value, are grounds for a declaration of nullity of the company with the same effect as though it had been wound up by the Court but without prejudice to acts previously done by it.

Apports provided by the subscribers are either cash or its equivalent (*apport en numéraire*) or some asset other than cash (*apport en nature*). Payments *en numéraire*, if they exceed the amount of Euro 40,000 in value, cannot be paid to *notaire* save by means of bank draft drawn on a French bank unless they are paid to his client's account at the *caisse de consignation et de dépôts* on a bank to bank transfer. *Apports en nature* may be and frequently are *immeubles*, including life or reversionary interests or even interests in property sold *en viager*. They can also include shares in other companies and intellectual property rights.

In the case of a contemporaneous formation of an SCI and purchase of property to be owned by it, normally the subscribers will subscribe cash which will be used by the SCI to pay the purchase price of the property. In the case of the formation of an SCI to take over an existing property, the *apport* will be *en nature*.

The shareholders

In the case of a *société civile* there must be at least two shareholders (C.civ.art.1832), called in French *associés* from the notion that each has wished to 'associate' himself with others in the sharing of the benefits and losses of the venture. Save in the case of certain companies formed to carry on professional activities (known as SCPs) such as those of a *notaire*, accountant or doctor, there is no maximum limit of shareholders. C.civ.art.1844 makes provision for the situation which arises when all the shares become united in one holding, for example by reason of the death of a shareholder. In such a case, the company is not dissolved provided that the minimum number of shareholders is restored to two within a year. In default of such action being taken, the company can be wound up on the application of any interested party who, apart from the remaining shareholder, is likely to be a creditor or the Revenue. However, this rule applies only to the situation after the incorporation of a company. Care therefore must be taken on formation when the shares are to be issued jointly *en tontine* (Chapter 16) to ensure that there are two shareholders *ab initio*. This need arises by reason of the legal fiction that neither co-owner *en tontine* owns anything until the death of the first to die when he is then deemed to have been the sole owner from the date of the joint acquisition. Thus, it could be said that there can never have been at any time the requisite minimum of two shareholders. This can be overcome in either of two ways. Either 98 per cent of the shares can be issued jointly *en tontine* and 2 per cent be issued to a third party to be held by him on trust (in the English sense) for the joint holders. Since the shares are personalty, at least in the case of a shareholder who is domiciled in England, he can execute a valid Declaration of Trust in English form in respect of those few shares. Alternatively, the 2 per cent of the shares not issued *en tontine* can be issued to the co-owners of the holding *en tontine* individually in equal amounts.

Care must also be taken in the issue of shares *en indivision* since two different results can follow. If the shares are issued to two persons pro rata their shares in the consideration provided jointly by them, then each co-owner of that consideration acquires the personality of a shareholder in respect of the appropriate number of shares. If the shares themselves are issued *en indivision* or, which is much more probable, become so owned by reason of the death of a shareholder, does the shareholding belong to the *indivision* or to the individual *co-indivisaires*? It seems that the better interpretation of such a situation is that each *co-indivisaire* has the quality of a shareholder although they can only act unanimously (Cass.6.2.80).

A special situation arises in connection with the transfer to an SCI of a property, the consideration for which is the allotment of shares to the transferor who is subject to a PACS (Chapter 21). There appears to be a divergence of opinion as to the effect of such a transaction bearing in mind that prima facie what is owned by the parties to a PACS is deemed to be owned *en indivision*. On the one hand, it is suggested that the result is that both parties acquire the quality of *associé* so that, unless the *statuts* otherwise provide, it is necessary for them to appoint a single representative to exercise their rights on their behalf (C.civ.art.1844). Another view is that the situation depends on the actions of the subscriber. If he informs the other shareholders of the existence of the PACS and the other party to the PACS of his intentions, if the latter accepts that he or she will become a shareholder in the SCI *en indivision*, he or she will acquire the quality of an *associé*. If, on the other hand, the other shareholders have no knowledge of the PACS and the party to that arrangement who is not the subscriber has not been informed by the subscriber what he intends to do (there is no obligation on the latter to inform the former in this manner), it is questionable if the party who is unaware of the subscription of the shares takes on the quality of a shareholder. The latter view appears the more correct if one considers the situation of an SCI composed of members of a profession of which one party to a PACS is not a member or the case of shares acquired other than by subscription, for example, on a death.

Contents of the *statuts*

C.civ.art.1835 requires that every set of *statuts* must contain the following information concerning the company:

1. The name (*dénomination sociale*) of the company. This may be freely chosen provided that its use does not conflict with the rights, such as trade marks or patents, of other companies or persons. Use may not be made of a family name nor pseudonym if this would cause confusion. On the other hand, since SCIs frequently are the owners of a single property, it is not unknown and not incorrect to have the style 'SCI and the address of its property' when it is frequently found that there is another such company with the same style in another part of the country. Both may function with the same name.

2. The *siège social*. This may be looked on as the equivalent of the English Registered Office but is better considered as the place where the company has its effective place of management. It is usually intended that this should be at the premises owned by the company and occupied by the shareholders. In the case of an SCI, it is frequently at the address of the property owned by the company or of the *gérant*. For a period of two years after incorporation, such an address may be used for this purpose notwithstanding any provision to the contrary in any lease of the premises or in the *règlements de copropriété* of a block of flats. There is no equivalent practice such as exists in England for it to be permanently at the offices of a solicitor or accountant. The results of its situation are similar to those of the English Registered Office.

3. The duration of the life of the company. This must be for a determined period which cannot exceed ninety-nine years. Its legal existence can be extended for a further period not exceeding ninety-nine years by a shareholders' resolution passed not later than a year before the date of its legal death.
4. The objects of the company.
5. The capital of the company. No minimum is required in the case of any 'civil' company which is not making a public offer and may be varied if the *statuts* so provide by an appropriate resolution of the shareholders. It is divided into shares each of a fixed nominal value. If the *statuts* so permit, shareholders have the right in contradistinction to the effect of Companies Act 1985, section 162 to 'withdraw' from the company in accordance with the rules laid down in that document. If no such provision exists, this right may be exercised by a shareholder with the consent of all the other shareholders or ultimately for just cause with the consent of the Court. Provided that the *statuts* so provide (but not otherwise) the company may exclude a shareholder by a resolution of the shareholders (Cass.com.13.12.94) for failure, for example, to abide by the rules for the behaviour of an *associé* such as being involved in a business in competition with the company or, if the *statuts* require it, loss of a given nationality or similar qualification. This is in addition to the provisions of C.civ.art.1860 that, in the case of the bankruptcy or situations akin to bankruptcy of a shareholder unless the other shareholders unanimously decide otherwise, he shall cease to be a shareholder and the value of his shares shall be repaid to him.
6. The names of the first shareholders and whether they are subscribing cash (*apport en numéraire*) or some asset other than cash (*apport en nature*).
7. The appointment of the *gérant(s)* although this may be done by subsequent documentation. A *gérant* need not be of French nationality. *Avocats* may not accept this office nor may any *fonctionnaire* (civil servant) unless it is a non-profit-making company in which case *notaires* also may be *gérants* but not otherwise. Suitable as *gérants* if the shareholders are not to exercise this office themselves are usually professionals who manage property such as *administrateurs de biens* or *syndics*.
8. Regulations as to the management of the company, the calling of meetings, voting rights, transfers of shares *inter vivos* and on death, the intent of many of which is easily recognizable by those conversant with English company law. The more important of these are elaborated hereafter.

It is not essential to designate in the *statuts* the manner in which profits (if any) are shared but it is rare not to find such an indication. In default of any such provision, profits are shared and expenses borne in the proportions in which shares are owned. On the other hand, such provisions as the payment of preferential dividends or a limit to a shareholder's liability for his share of the company's debts can be, but rarely are, inserted. On the other hand, a *clause léonine* which deprives a shareholder of all rights to share in profits or exonerates a shareholder from any liability to contribute to the debts of the company is void.

Every shareholder is entitled on demand to an up-to-date copy of the *statuts* to which it is required that there be annexed a current list of the shareholders and of the *gérant(s)*.

Meetings of shareholders

The law makes no general provision for the calling of meetings of the straightforward SCI and these are left to the draftsman of the *statuts*. These will normally provide that meetings are called by the *gérant* and shareholders may require the *gérant* to call a meeting. A notice convening a meeting must be served by registered AR post and give fifteen days' notice but a meeting may be considered validly convened if all the shareholders are present in person or by proxy at that meeting. In the case of the annual general meeting and extraordinary general meetings, information of much the same nature as is required for an English company must be sent to all shareholders save where all the shareholders are themselves *gérants*.

Each shareholder has one vote, shares held *en indivision* requiring a single representative who votes on behalf of the *indivisaires*. If shares are held subject to a life interest, the remainderman has the primary right to vote except in respect of the distribution of profits when the right to vote belongs to the life tenant. A shareholder may appoint a proxy and a corporate shareholder votes by its representative. All decisions may be taken by correspondence with notice of the resolutions being served by AR registered post fifteen days before the date of reception by the shareholders. The *statuts* indicate the time allowed for consideration by shareholders which may not be less than fifteen days.

In the case of the ordinary SCI, the *statuts* themselves may fix the various majorities required to pass resolutions. In the absence of any such requirement, unanimity of votes is required (C.civ.art.1852).

Minutes of meetings must be prepared and kept in a special register. Copies certified by the *gérant* must be circulated to each shareholder.

Share transfers

The normal provision is that all transfers *inter vivos* require the *agrément* (consent) of all the shareholders, following the wording of C.civ.art.1861. That article provides that the *statuts* may indicate what majority less than of all the shareholders is needed or whether the consent of the *gérant* alone will suffice. The *statuts* may also (and frequently do) allow a transfer to another shareholder or his spouse without the need to obtain any *agrément*. Unless the *statuts* otherwise provide, transfers to ascendants and issue of a shareholder do not require any consent. In cases where consent is required but refused, the other shareholders must buy or cause to be bought the shares in question or they must be bought in by the company within a six-month period. If no such purchase takes place within that period, the *agrément* of the other shareholders is deemed to have been granted.

The death of a shareholder does not involve the liquidation of a company unless the *statuts* otherwise provide so that prima facie the company continues with those who inherit a deceased shareholder's shares in his place (C.civ.art.1870). The *statuts* may, and frequently do, make other provisions, allowing, for example, the shares to be freely transferred to a surviving spouse or issue but otherwise only with the consent of the surviving shareholders. In such a case, the situation is not unlike that in England of a beneficiary awaiting the consent of the directors to a transfer to him of shares of a deceased shareholder. Such a person in the case of the refusal to consent to a transfer to him is entitled to a price equivalent to their value if they are bought by a transferee found by the company or if the company buys the shares in.

Management of a *société civile*

The company is managed by one or more *gérants*. Their number and whether they need or not be or may not be shareholders will be dealt with in the *statuts*. There is no statutory age limit. As is said above, they will usually be named in the *statuts* but may be appointed by separate resolution. The appointment of a *gérant* during the life of a company must be by resolution with such a majority vote as is prescribed in the *statuts*, in default of which the majority is a simple majority vote of all the shareholders (C.civ.art.1864-2 and 3). There appears no lawful objection to the co-option of a *gérant* subject to the subsequent ratification of the shareholders. If a *société civile* is without a *gérant* for more than a year, any interested party may petition the Court for the winding up of the company.

The length of time during which a *gérant* holds office is fixed by the *statuts* but if no such term is fixed, he is presumed to hold office for the life of the company (C.civ.art.1846-4). Subject to any provision to the contrary in the *statuts*, the office may be determined at any time by a majority vote of all share-holders. C.civ.art.1851-1 says that any revocation of the appointment of a *gérant* 'without due cause' may give rise to an action for damages. 'Due causes' include as one might expect such acts as the failure to carry out his functions (CA Nancy 2.12.49); embezzlement of the company's funds (CA Aix 13.11.45); or danger-ously imperfect accounting practices (CA Paris 9.4.94).

The task of the *gérant* is to 'undertake all such acts of management as are necessary in the interests of the company' (C.civ.art.1848-1). The extent of the powers of a *gérant* depend solely on what the *statuts* provide. The usual arrange-ment is to place a limit on his powers either as to the nature of the matters where he can without the specific authority of the shareholders bind the company or as to the amount in excess of which such authority must be obtained. In the event of a plurality of *gérants*, each has full power to act on his own but any objection by one to the exercise of his powers by another must if it is to be effective be made before that power has been exercised.

There is no requirement that a *gérant* must be or may not be a shareholder nor any reason why the *statuts* should not forbid a shareholder being a *gérant*.

The acts of a single *gérant* provided that they are within its objects bind the company and any restriction of his powers in the *statuts* does not bind third parties, this being the French equivalent of section 35 of the Companies Act 1985. In the case of more than one *gérant*, since each has individual powers, even the requirement of the *gérants'* joint signatures will not overcome this rule. It follows that acts done by a *gérant* beyond the scope of the company's objects can be avoided (C.civ.art.1849).

The *gérant* is remunerated in any manner and at any time decided upon by the *statuts* or from time to time by the shareholders. Care must be taken to obtain advice as to the tax and social security situation of a remunerated *gérant* which depends on how in fact he is remunerated.

Liquidation

Among other reasons which do not involve its financial situation, a company is wound up when it reaches the end of its stated life unless this is prolonged by resolution of the shareholders at least one year before the end of its life.

It may be wound up voluntarily by a resolution of the shareholders passed by a two-thirds majority or on the application of an interested party if all the shares are held in one hand. The Court may also on the application of any shareholder order the winding up of a company 'for just cause' (C.civ.art.1844-7). The article cites as examples of 'just cause' the failure of a shareholder to carry out his obligations or 'a state of dissension among the shareholders which paralyses the management of the company'.

It is worth adding that as a general rule, the French do not often buy property owned by a company by buying the shares of that company. This seems to stem from an unwillingness to rely on the warranties as to the company's liabilities which in England would be given on such a transaction, bearing in mind the lack of protection of limited liability in the case of an SCI. It is also worth noting that *sociétés civiles* have no method of transferring shares on a simple share transfer of one sheet. The average share transfer will run into pages and probably involve an amendment of the *statuts* since these give the shareholders and holdings at any given time. A *société civile* can, but rarely does, have a share register.

Fiscal considerations

What has been said above is intended to be only a brief resumé of the workings of an SCI. In practice, such a company owning a single property occupied in large measure by its shareholders who are domiciled and resident in England provides a very simple method of ownership allied to the avoidance of French inheritance rules and the mitigation of French inheritance tax. However, its use may give rise to certain UK tax consequences. These are discussed in Chapter 29 and must always be borne in mind.

The Companies Registry

The *Registre de commerce et des sociétés* is the equivalent of the UK Companies Registry and exists in various cities in France. Notification of the formation of the company containing certain information regarding the company must be inserted in a newspaper authorized to publish such insertions in the *département* in which is situate the *siège social*. In addition, a request for registration of the company must be sent to the local Companies Registry accompanied by two copies of the *statuts*, cuttings from the above newspapers and other requisite documents including that relating to the appointment of the *gérant* if made by the *statuts*. Notice must also be given to the local Commercial Court. As in the United Kingdom, the equivalent of the certificate of incorporation marks the date on which the company was incorporated and what is known as an *Extrait Kbis* is issued on request by the Tribunal de Commerce giving all the necessary infor-mation on the company and which serves in much the same way as does the result of an English company search minus any reference to accounts. Depending on whether the consideration for the issue of shares consists only of *apports en numéraire* or *meubles* or only of *immeubles* or a mixture of all three kinds of assets, the *statuts* must also be lodged with the local Collector of Taxes (*la recette*) and the local *bureau des hypothèques* and the appropriate stamp duty (if any) paid.

10

THE *SOCIÉTÉ CIVILE D'ATTRIBUTION*

Introduction 95
   The objects of the SCI 95
Shareholders' obligations 96
Shareholders' rights 96

Introduction

This kind of *société civile* is of interest to buyers of property in France since it is not uncommon for property developers to make use of it to finance the building of blocks of flats rather than to resort to the *ventes en l'état futur* (Chapter 8) or for the renovation of an existing building before selling off the newly created flats in it. The buyer acquires shares in the company in question which carry with them the right to have vested in him as shareholder a particular part of the company's property on a distribution *in specie* on the liquidation of the company.

There may be many reasons why a property developer wishes to proceed in this manner. From a buyer's point of view, it has the same advantage as has the *vente en état futur*, namely that the purchase price of the property to be vested in him is paid by instalments. However, as will be seen from a comparison between the two methods of purchase, there is a difference of some importance from an inheritance point of view. In the case of shares in an *SCI d'attribution*, the buyer has until the liquidation of the company an asset in the form of shares which is not liable to French inheritance rules. Purchases *en l'état futur* vest in the buyer from the date of the *acte de vente* an interest which is land and therefore subject to those rules.

The objects of the SCI
The objects of such a company are the construction and the purchase or renovation of property with a view to the distribution *in specie* on liquidation to its shareholders of either an absolute interest in or a permanent right of occupation of specified parts of its property; and the management of such property until the liquidation of the company. This definition of the objects of such a company which is to be found in CCH.art.L212-1 does not refer to the liquidation of the company as such but puts a term to its existence when 'another organization has taken its place'. This will, of course, normally be the *copropriété* (Chapter 15) which will be formed since the various parts of the building as they become vested in various buyers will of necessity be owned by flat-owners *en copropriété*. The law does not

require that the objects of the company are limited to those referred to above but if it wishes to retain its *transparence fiscale* (Chapter 22), they must be so restricted.

The company may either purchase an existing property or build its own, which will include the purchase of land upon which to build. Basically, the management of the company follows the ordinary rules of the management of a *société civile* but in cases where the company builds its own property rather than disposes of parts of a converted existing property, there are certain additional rules for the protection of the public.

Shareholders' obligations

In addition to those imposed on all shareholders of a *société civile*, they have the special obligations made necessary by the nature of the activity of the company. The total issue price of the shares will be payable by instalments as work progresses and calls must be paid punctually. The company may, if so authorized by its articles, guarantee any loan made to a shareholder to enable him to meet calls on his shares. If repayment of such a loan is not made, the lender may seek a *saisie immobilière* (Chapter 14) on the part of the building due to be vested in the defaulting shareholder.

In the case of calls on partly paid shares, it is open to shareholders to institute proceedings if they consider that the amount claimed from them is more than a quarter higher than it ought to be or that another shareholder has been asked to pay too little by the same proportion. Such an action may be instituted even after the liquidation of the company but before the approval of its final accounts. Such a right becomes statute-barred on the expiration of two years from the date of dissolution or of the complainant ceasing to be a shareholder before liquidation.

In addition, the cost of management of the company and of the maintenance of the building must be met and these are found by way of service charges. To the extent that the situation permits, these are calculated in the same way as are the service charges of a *copropriété*. However, shareholders may apply to the Court for the amendment of these amounts if they consider that their charges are too high by a quarter or those of other shareholders are too low by the same amount and if the Court agrees, it will issue a new basis for the calculation of service charges to take effect thenceforward.

Shareholders' rights

In addition to their usual rights as shareholders of an SCI, shareholders have the right to the exclusive ownership of that part of the property owned by the company allotted to their shares by the *état descriptif de division*. Thus the price they will pay for their shares will be the price which they would pay on the open market for that part of the property. Their right is, however, not a *droit réel* in respect of that part (Chapter 2) but a right against the company to have that part of its property vested in them in due course. Pending such vesting, a shareholder may use that part of the property destined for him (Cass.7.7.82) and may let it but such a letting does not bind the company which may retake possession from a tenant of a shareholder if the latter has been deprived of his right of ownership for any reason. In addition, the right of a shareholder attaching to his shares vis à vis the company is not enforceable against third parties so that a creditor of the company can foreclose on the building and sell it without the shareholder being able to enforce his right to occupation of part.

It is not usual that the various parts of a property are formally vested in the shareholders until the company is dissolved but it is possible for a *retrait anticipé* by a shareholder to be effected. This can only take place if the articles of the company have clearly attributed (as will normally be the case) absolute owner-ship of a part of the building to the shareholder and he has fulfilled all his oblig-ations towards the company such as the payment in full of all calls on his shares. The payment of all outstanding service charges is not a necessity (Cass.3.2.81). Such a vesting of part of a property in a shareholder involves a cancellation of his shares and a proportionate reduction of the capital of the company. The share-holder in question therefore ceases to be a member of the company and becomes in advance of his co-shareholders a *copropriétaire* in his capacity as a direct owner of part of the building vested in him. If that shareholder happens to be the first to adopt this form of vesting of his flat in him, he sets in motion the *syndi-cat de copropriété* and the *règlement de copropriété* begin to apply (Chapter 15). Normally, of course, the vesting in the shareholders of the various parts of the building takes place at one time, that is on liquidation, but the *actes de partage* are seldom all executed by the shareholders on the same day.

11

PLURIPROPRIÉTÉ

Introduction 99
The owning company 100
Share sale offers 100
The *statuts* of the company 100
Management 101
Meetings of the company 101
Disposal of shares 102

Introduction

It is unfortunate that 'time sharing' as a method of ownership has achieved a certain reputation since if adopted in the proper circumstances and subject to the proper safeguards, it can prove a most satisfactory means of avoiding both the effects of the French rules of inheritance and the undesirable results of ownership *en indivision* which are explained in Chapter 16.

Pluripropriété or *multipropriété*, as it is also known, is the description of ownership by more than one person of property on the basis that each owner has the right of occupation of that property during pre-determined periods in any one year. Its advantages lie in that such occupation is achieved by means of share-holdings in a company which itself is the owner of the property. In this way, French inheritance rules do not apply whilst in addition, all the inconveniences of ownership *en indivision* are avoided. All that is needed is adherence to the Articles of the company, most of which are in a form required by statute and which cover comprehensively the management of the company.

The company in question is an elaborated form of an *SCI d'attribution* (Chapter 10), differing from its simple form in that it is intended to remain in being and permit its shareholders the use but not the ownership of its premises. It is not suggested that this method of ownership should be used by more than three or four owners and indeed the contents of this chapter specifically excludes any reference to 'time-sharing' in its commonly accepted form. There are, however, many occasions when potential buyers seek a holiday home in France which in any event they will not occupy for more than a few months in every year but are obliged to invest an amount in its purchase as though they intended its permanent occupation. It is true that during such periods as they are not in occupation the property could be let but this involves a number of complications including the payment of commission and other expenses of such a letting as well as tax on the rent achieved whilst at the same time, it remains subject to French inheritance legislation. The shareholder of a company owning property *en pluripropriété* can freely sell his shares whilst so long as he remains a shareholder, he may without restriction let the property during all or part of the period fixed for his occupancy if he so wishes.

The owning company

The only kind of company permitted by law to carry on the business of *pluripropriété* is the *société civile d'attribution en jouissance à temps partagé*. This type of company was created by the Law of 6 January 1986 ('the Law') which now forms part of CCH as articles L.121-60 to 76. The Law applies in all respects if the property it is to own is situate in France. If the property is outside France, the Law still applies to all the activities of the company other than to the building or acquisition of the property when local law applies. The rights and obligations of shareholders follow those laid down by law generally for *sociétés civiles* subject to the special provisions of the Law. The Law itself follows the provisions of the European Directive 94/47 of 26 October 1994.

Share sale offers

All offers by the company to potential subscribers are required to be in writing and are considered to be the equivalent of sales of rights in the underlying property. Thus the subscriber has the benefit of both the *Loi SRU* 'cooling off' period after accepting an offer as in an ordinary purchase of land and also of the Loi Scrivener conditions if he intends to seek mortgage finance (Chapter 3). Any such offer must contain considerable information about the company and its property such as one would expect to find in a prospectus. It may be assumed that if the object of the formation of the company itself is to enable a small number of persons to own a property which they desire to share in this way, they will already have been advised of and be in agreement over all the statutory requirements and many of the formalities can be avoided. However, as will be seen, much of the information required on an offer to subscribe made by a professional promoter to the public must be made available by a shareholder thereafter on any sale by him of his shares.

The *statuts* of the company

The *statuts* of the company must contain the following information:

1. How the shareholders contribute to the expenses of the company. This will normally be in the proportions in which they own shares in the capital of the company. Assuming that all the shareholders will share equally in the cost of the purchase of the property and will benefit from equal periods of occupation,

they will participate equally in the day-to-day expenses of the property and in any special expenditure voted in general meeting.

2. What action may be taken against shareholders who fail to pay their share of the expenses. This may extend to the forced sale of their shares and such a decision of the shareholders deprives a defaulting shareholder or any tenant of his from occupying the premises.

3. The periods during which each shareholder may occupy the premises. This must appear initially in the *statuts* but may be varied in general meeting. Such an alteration will normally require a majority vote of all the shareholders but clearly in the case of a company formed for the specific purpose envisaged by the chapter, it will be necessary, or at least desirable, to have unanimity of votes.

Since the occupation of each shareholder will normally be of the whole premises, it will not be necessary to annex to the *statuts* an *état descriptif de division* of which parts of the building may be occupied by which shareholder. There must, however, be annexed a set of *règlements* or internal regulations relating to the use of the premises.

Management

The company is managed by one or more *gérants* (art 5 of the Law). The *gérant* is elected in general meeting by an absolute majority of all the shareholders. A similar vote is required for his removal. He alone has powers of management within the objects of the company.

Every company must have a *conseil de surveillance* or Executive Committee. Its members are appointed by the shareholders from among their number and may not include the *gérant* or his spouse or any nominee of the *gérant*. Its task is to assist the *gérant* and any meeting of the company. Its constitution is fixed by the *statuts*.

It is probable that the company will not require a *commissaire aux comptes* or auditor since this is only necessary if it has at least fifty shareholders and a large turnover. However, if such an appointment is not needed the company must appoint a person as *contrôleur de la gestion* who is a suitably qualified 'technician' to audit the books and report to the shareholders (art 18-4 of the Law). He may not be a shareholder.

Meetings of the company

The shareholders must meet at least once in every year in general meeting (art 13-3 of the Law). Meetings are normally convened by the *gérant* but may be requisitioned by shareholders owning not less than 20 per cent of the capital. Any shareholder may during the five days preceding a meeting require production of the company's accounts.

A shareholder has one vote for every share he owns. However, if the matter to be voted on concerns expenses his votes are proportional to his share in those expenses. A shareholder may appoint a proxy who need not be a shareholder. Most resolutions require a simple majority of those present in person or by proxy. For a variation of the *statuts* or of the *règlements* and for the sale of the company's property or for its dissolution the requisite majority is two-thirds of all shareholders. A variation of the periods of occupancy by shareholders requires a two-thirds majority of shareholders present in person or by proxy.

Disposal of shares

As in the case of most *sociétés civiles*, shareholders have the right under C.civ.art.1869 to opt out of the company and sell their shares back to it. The nature of this kind of company, however, makes unavailable the exercise of such a right by shareholders (Cass.2.3.95) but the Court can wind up the company under C.civ.art.1844-7 in the case of disagreement between the shareholders.

As has been said, a shareholder has no interest in the property owned by the company other than the right to occupy it at given times which attaches to the ownership of the shares in addition to the right to receive his share of the property on liquidation. For this reason the Law forbids any reference to a disposal of shares being a disposal of *propriété*, that is full ownership.

Special rules apply to the sale of shares (*cession de parts*) in a company of this kind. Limiting these to cases where both seller and buyer are not engaged in any property dealing business they are:

1. The share transfer must be in writing but may be ssp or *authentique* (art 20-1 of the Law).
2. The *cession de parts* must set out a full description of the rights of occupation attaching to the shares and of the period of occupation.
3. Details must be given of the original notarial document executed on the purchase of the property of the original prospectus issued by the company.
4. An indication whether the shares to be sold are fully paid and if they are only partly paid what remains outstanding and whether that amount has been called or not.

There must be annexed to the contract of sale copies of:

(1) the *Statuts*;
(2) the *Etat descriptif* (if any);
(3) the *Règlements*;
(4) the Schedule of Occupancy;
(5) the latest accounts of the company;
(6) a note of the technical characteristics of the building.

The costs of a purchase of shares in such a company are calculated as though it were a purchase of the underlying property, that is a proportion of the value of the whole property having regard to the period of occupancy granted by the shares sold.

It is clear that in the case of a property owned by such a company with (say) four shareholders where the intention is that each owner will be in occupation of the whole of the premises at pre-determined times, it will be neither convenient nor necessary that the management of the property is conferred on any one of the shareholders. In addition, the company must have a *contrôleur* and whilst he may not be a shareholder, the Law makes no provision for who he should be. There seems no reason why he should not be the same person as the *gérant*. The expenditure of such a company will be *taxe foncière* and *taxe d'habitation* and the costs of day-to-day management such as insurance, cleaning and general upkeep. Each shareholder is individually responsible for any damage he causes to the property during his period of occupation and extraordinary expenses are voted on in general meeting. It would seem, therefore, that the management of the property is simple and can safely be left to a competent *gérant* in the locality of the property who will, by profession, be an *administrateur de biens* or *syndic*.

12

SALES *EN VIAGER*

Introduction 105
Nature of *viager* transactions 106
The consideration 106
The element of chance 107
Viager occupé 107
The *rente viagère* 107
Rights and liabilities of the parties 108
Tax effects 109

Introduction

Transactions *en viager* derive their name from the obsolete French word *viage* meaning 'lifetime'. They are by law sales which must involve some degree of *aléa* or chance. The typical transaction is one in which the seller sells subject to a joint and survivor interest in the property for himself and his spouse and the sale price is paid partly as a lump sum and partly by way of an annuity. If the seller retains possession of the property it is a sale *en viager occupé* but there is no reason why the seller should not give immediate vacant possession when it becomes a *viager libre*. Nor is there any reason why the sale price should not be paid entirely in the form of an annuity with no capital payment (*bouquet*) although this is not usual. In addition, the *cestui que vie* need not be the seller although it is rare that he should not be. The element of *aléa*, the absence of which renders the sale void, lies in the annuity payments which cease on the death of the seller or of his surviving spouse or, indeed, of some other named person. This ensures that it is a matter of chance whether or not the transaction is profitable or not for the purchaser and it has been held that the element of chance is absent if, among other reasons, the property sold provides the buyer with income equal to or in excess of the annuity payments (Cass.5.5.82).

For purely sociological reasons, the French tend to look on sales of this kind as more suitable for elderly property owners who have no children and who want to release the capital tied up in their home without being obliged to leave it. It is, of course, the inbred desire to keep the *patrimoine* in the family, fostered by the existence of the entrenched inheritance rights of children, which tend to make many of the French shy away from such sales although they are far from being uncommon. Indeed, as one leading French textbook has said, 'one does not perpetuate a difficult financial situation simply to featherbed one's heirs'. Be that as it may, for such of the French as do not feel themselves obliged to see all that they own pass on to their children, a sale '*en viager*' enables them to go on living as before and to have capital to spare which they can and do spend as they wish. With this freedom goes the pleasant thought that even if their children may be going without a slice of the *patrimoine*, so is the Collector of Inheritance Tax.

However, sales *en viager* should be viewed in a totally different way by the English domiciled owner of French property. As has been said elsewhere, domicile plays no part in the devolution on death of French land. Chapter 29 deals with the methods which can be adopted to avoid the inroads which French inheritance law can make into the English rule of the freedom of testamentary disposition: the sale *en viager* is one of the recommended methods.

Nature of *viager* transactions

Sales *en viager* are governed by C.civ.arts.1968 to 1983 which are contained in that part of the *Code civil* headed 'Contracts of Chance'. These include insurance contracts (which also have their own Code), gaming contracts and *contrats de rente viagère*. Sales *en viager* are in essence treated from a conveyancing point of view as any other sale of land and all the normal requirements relating both to the contract and to the *acte de vente* apply. The additional requirements deal primarily with the manner in which the sale price is calculated and made payable and the nature of the interest (if any) retained by the seller which governs the rights and obligations of the parties *inter se*.

The consideration

The primary decisions to be made are (i) the proportion of the sale price to be paid by way of *bouquet* (lump sum) and by way of *rente viagère* (annuity payments) and (ii) the life or lives on which the latter are going to be calculated. There are estate agents who specialize in sales of this kind but the seller's *notaire* should also be able to make the necessary calculations. The following may be taken as a typical example.

Mr and Mrs Dupont are aged respectively seventy-two and seventy. They own a flat which they bought twenty-five years ago and which is currently worth Euro 152,000. It has been agreed that the buyer will pay a *bouquet* of Euro 15,200 and the *rente* will be payable monthly in arrears. The following elements go to the calculation of the *rente*: the ages of the sellers coupled with the fact that it is to be a joint and survivor *rente*; the current market return on a flat of the kind involved; whether the sellers will continue to occupy the flat or whether they will give vacant possession to the buyer; the frequency of payments of *rente* and whether in arrears or in advance and whether it will be indexed; whether the *rente* will continue to be paid in full after the death of the first seller to die or will be reduced and if so, by how much. The resultant figure for the *rente*, based on the

ages, value and *bouquet* quoted above and on the basis that the vendors continued to occupy the flat and that the *rente* was to remain payable in full during the
life of the survivor, gives the result of an indexed Euro 930 payable monthly in
arrears. The figures agreed between the parties as the *rente* must be reasonable
having regard to the factors mentioned above. If it is not, it may be adjusted by
the Revenue for tax purposes or be the subject of an action to avoid the whole
transaction instituted by the seller or his successors in title (Cass.12.6.96).

The element of chance

As has been said above, the amount of the sale price and how it is satisfied may
result in it being considered that the necessary *aléa* is absent so that the transaction is void. Among other situations which produce the same result
(C.civ.arts.1974-5) is the unlikely event that the *cestui que vie* is dead at the time
of the transaction or if he was at that time stricken with an illness of which he
died within twenty days of the date of the transaction. In the case of a sale based
on two lives, this rule only applies if the *rente* is *réductible*, that is to say is based
on two separate lives, the second annuity arising only on the death of the first
annuitant to die. If the *rente* is *réversible* or is a true joint and survivor annuity,
the rule does not apply. The twenty-day period runs from the day following the
execution of the sale document.

Viager occupé

The seller who retains occupation of the premises sold does so according to what
is agreed between him and the buyer either as the owner of a *usufruit* (lease for
life) or of a *droit d'usage et d'occupation* (licence to occupy). The distinction
can be significant since a *usufruitier* has the right to let the premises so that the
buyer cannot be certain that he will obtain possession on the death of the relevant annuitant. The person who has a mere *droit d'usage* may only occupy the
premises himself and may not assign or underlet. It is therefore most usual in the
case of sales *en viager occupé* that the seller is allowed only to retain the latter
interest. In any event, it is customary to insert in the *acte de vente* on sales of
this kind that the buyer cannot take possession for a short period of time after
the death of the *cestui que vie* to enable those dealing with his estate to clear the
premises.

The *rente viagère*

Once the sale has been completed, the seller takes on the title of *crédirentier* and
the buyer that of *débirentier*. The due dates payment of the *rente* are known as
arrérages. Annuity payments cease to be due on the death of the only or last
cestui que vie to die. It seems an unnecessary injunction to make in light of the

rule as to the need for *aléa* but C.civ.art.1979 in specific terms requires the *débirentier* to continue to pay the *rente* until the death of the *cestui que vie* '*quelque onéreux qu'ait pu devenir le service de la rente*' (however burdensome payment of the annuity may become). Only agreement between the parties can release the *débirentier* from such liability (Cass.21.5.58) and any *rente* which remains due for payment at his death is a debt in his estate. In the event of the sale of the property by the *débirentier*, he remains as guarantor for the payment of the *rente* by his successor in title unless specifically released therefrom by the *crédirentier*.

In most cases, the *rente* is indexed, the parties being free to choose which index will apply. The most usual index is that of the Cost of Living. In cases where there is no indexation provided for in the *acte de vente*, the Law of 13 July 1963 provides for automatic revision in accordance with a scale fixed by the annual *Loi de finances*. The Law also provides that a *crédirentier* entitled to such an automatic indexation may apply to the Court if that indexation is dispropor-tionately low having regard to the value of the property in question. The increase is limited to 75 per cent of the amount of the *rente* and can as a result of all Lois de finances to date be granted annually although the original Law clearly envis-aged a single revision only.

Only very limited protection is available for the *crédirentier* whose *rente* is unpaid. C.civ.art.1978 says that: 'the mere default in the payment of *rente* when it is due does not give the right to the person entitled to receive it to require the repayment of any capital sum paid or to repossess the premises disposed of by him; he has only the right to seize and sell the goods of his debtor and to require him by agreement or otherwise to provide out of the proceeds of sale a sum suffi-cient to secure the annuity payments'. It is, however, possible and highly desir-able to vary the effect of this article and provide for the revesting of the property in its original owner by means of the inclusion in the *acte de vente* of a clause giving a *privilège de vendeur* (Chapter 14) which then enables the *crédirentier* to foreclose on the property and recover the unpaid amounts. In addition, the *acte* can provide for an automatic re-entry provision in the case of the non-payment of any *rente*.

Annuity payments are basically statute-barred after five years but this relates only where the amounts are fixed and of a clear regularity. Since most such payments are indexed, they are therefore outside this rule and enjoy a thirty-year prescription period.

Rights and liabilities of the parties

The rights and obligations of the *crédirentier* as occupier on the one hand and the *débirentier* as owner on the other hand do not vary much from the standard covenants in a full internal repairing lease. Such liabilities require that the *crédirentier* must:

(1) use the premises *en bon père de famille* which includes liability for all internal repairs and certain external repairs such as soil and water pipes serving the property;

(2) be liable for all damage caused to the property by reason of his negligence;

(3) at all times maintain the permitted user of the premises;

(4) give notice to the *débirentier* of any event which might call into play his liability to effect structural or other repairs for which he is liable and of any encroachment upon the property by unauthorized third parties;

(5) be responsible for all damage by fire unless the same was not due to any default on his part. In this connection, it should be noted that the law does not require him to insure against fire as such; and

(6) pay such annual charges as are his liability to pay in addition to service charges in the case of a flat.

In the case of a *viager libre*, the liability for *taxe foncière* is that of the purchaser. In the case of a *viager occupé* if the seller has retained only a *droit d'occupation*, the liability is that of the purchaser but if the seller has retained a full *usufruit*, it is he who is liable. It is customary to attempt to throw this burden on the purchaser in every case but such arrangement is not binding on the tax authorities. *Taxe d'habitation* is payable by whoever is in actual occupation of the premises on 1 January in every year.

The liabilities of the *débirentier* extend primarily to the repair and maintenance of the structure of the premises. On the other hand, he cannot be compelled to carry out such works. If, however, they are effected by the *crédirentier*, they may be charged to the *débirentier* when the life occupancy falls in if they have increased the value of the premises. The law makes no provision for the rebuilding by either party of any part of the property rendered necessary by reason of its age or of act of God. It follows, therefore, that the *acte de vente* should itself provide in sensible terms what the law fails to provide.

The rights and obligations set out above are substantially the same when the occupier has reserved only a *droit d'occupation* save that in such circumstances, he must provide a guarantor to cover his liabilities and that he is permitted personal occupation only.

Tax effects

The tax rules applicable to sales *en viager* are as follows.

1. *Enregistrement* (stamp duty) on sales. This is calculated at the rate in force at the time of the sale on the value of the *bouquet* plus the capital value of the annuity element.

2. *Plus-values* (capital gains tax). The acquisition price is calculated in the same manner as for the payment of *enregistrement*.

3. The *débirentier* as the maker of the annuity payments is entitled to no special relief in respect of such payments. He is, however, required not later than 1 February in every year to file a return showing all such payments made in the previous year and the identity of the recipient.

   The *crédirentier* as annuitant is entitled to relief in respect of a proportion of each payment provided that such payments arise as a result of a transaction *en viager* for full consideration. The proportion is fixed as at the date of the sale and is as to:

   (a) 70% if the annuitant is aged less than fifty;
   (b) 50% for ages between fifty and fifty-nine;
   (c) 40% for ages sixty to sixty-nine; and
   (d) 30% for ages in excess of sixty-nine.

   If the *rente* is payable on a joint and survivor basis, the percentages are calculated according to the age of the *crédirentier* when he or she first becomes entitled to receive a payment.

4. Wealth tax (ISF). The capital value of a *rente viagère* is an asset in the hands of the *crédirentier* for the purposes of this tax whilst the *débirentier* may deduct such a value from his capital assets for the same purpose.

13

SALES BY AUCTION

Introduction 111
Adjudications volontaires 111
    Pre-auction procedure 111
    Conduct of the sale 112
    Conclusion of sale 114
    Surenchère 114
Adjudication judiciaire 114
    The *saisie immobilière* 114
    Procedure leading to a *saisie* 115
    Pre-auction procedure 115
    Conduct of the auction 117
    Surenchère 117
    Folle enchère 118

Introduction

Sales by auction in France fall into two categories depending on whether the owner has the free choice of this method of sale or whether the sale of his property by auction is forced upon him by an Order of the Court obtained at the instance of his creditors. The sale in the former case is an *adjudication volontaire*. Sales by virtue of an Order of the Court are *adjudications judiciaires*. The law and procedures relating to each type differ in important ways. The former type of auction sale is probably less popular than in England and does not seem to enjoy moments when it is particularly in vogue. They are mainly limited to sales of property in the estates of deceased persons.

Adjudications volontaires

Pre-auction procedure
Essentially, as in England, a sale by auction is subject to all the rules of a sale by private treaty once the price and buyer have been established and exchange of contracts has taken place. It is at that pre-contract period that French and English procedure differ noticeably.

In theory at least, anyone may conduct an auction sale of this kind in France and the services of a *notaire* are not required (Cass.19.5.1847). However, it has always been considered that the *notaire* is the only *officier ministériel* suitable to preside at an auction. This view is now consecrated by the rule that all sale documents which require registration at the *bureau des hypothèques* must be *en forme authentique*. For that reason the profession set up its own '*Marché immobilier des notaires*' which operates in various parts of France to offer property for sale by auction and to conduct sales of this kind.

Any kind of property wherever situate and whatever is its user may be sold at auction including the shares in *sociétés civiles immobilières* and all interests in land including leases. Prior to every sale, a *cahier des charges* must be prepared by the *notaire* dealing with the sale. This document may be compared to English auction particulars and in its essentials should contain, among other information, all that should be found in a French contract for sale by private treaty. It requires the signature of the seller and the *notaire* and its contents binds the ultimate buyer. The costs of the *acte de vente* and ancillary costs fall to be paid by the seller; those of the advertising and conducting the sale are borne by the seller unless the *cahier des charges* follows the common practice of throwing this burden on the buyer and thus increasing the purchase price for stamp duty purposes. Public advertisement of the sale is not required by law and is a matter for the owner. Frequently, the only notice of such sales appears in journals connected with the notarial profession.

The date for payment of the sale price will be shown in the *cahier des charges* as will the manner in which the auction will be effected and whether a *consignation pour enchérir* must be lodged with the *notaire*. It is currently common to require payment of such a *consignation pour enchérir* which is a deposit entitling one to bid. The amount will usually be of a nominal amount and, if required, it will normally be paid in the form of a certified cheque to the *notaire* holding the sale. Its payment is considered to be a token of solvability and that the intending bidder is able to pay if his bid is successful. It will be returned to bidders whose bids are not accepted and used on account of the sale price from the successful bidder.

The reserve price is never shown in the *cahier des charges* but is announced at the opening of the sale if one is fixed. If none is fixed, the opening bid is treated as a basis for the ensuing open discussion of the sale price, the bids being treated as offers by potential buyers which it is open to the seller to reject.

Conduct of the sale
Auctions often take place in the offices of the *notaire* when they must be held '*toutes portes ouvertes*'. They can in fact be held on virtually any premises but the profession was in 1882 and again in 1885 invited not to hold auctions in inns, taverns or restaurants. More recently, in 1953, the local Justices of the Peace were asked to make available to the local *notaire* their Courtrooms for auctions.

Before bidding begins, the *notaire* is required to remind the public of the contents of the *cahier des charges* with particular reference to the effect of a buyer failing to pay the purchase price, if there is any *right of surenchère*, and other matters of importance. He will also call attention to all matters which are not necessarily mentioned in that document, for example the amount of costs involved, the amount, if any, of the reserve (*mise à prix*) and the minimum permitted amount of each bid.

The ordinary rules of capacity govern who may bid at auction. There are certain additions to the list of those who are incapable of bidding; these include the owner's agents, the *notaire* dealing with the sale and acting for the seller. Nor may anyone who is employed in an old persons' home or a home for persons suffering from psychiatric ailments bid at auction for property belonging to any of the inmates of such homes.

There has been held as valid a clause in the *cahier des charges* by virtue of which, if the last bidder fails to pay a fixed part of the price within a certain period of time after the auction, the property is treated as sold to the penultimate bidder (T.civ Beaumes-les-Dames 27.6.53). The practice, which seems a nice variation on the English technique of the 'puffer' (*Gilliat v Gilliat* (1869) LR9 Eq60 and also 39 LJ Ch 142 et seq), seems strange and capable of leading to an arrangement between the seller and a friend who can safely 'bid up' the price in the knowledge that he will never be saddled with the need to buy. It is rarely employed.

Bidding takes place either *à la criée* as in England by bidders calling out their bids or *à l'extinction des feux* in the manner of the now disused English candle auction. By this latter method, three candles are successively lit, each lasting about one minute, the extinction of the smoke of the last candle to go out clearly indicating when bidding is concluded. It is said to be the preferred method of the *notaire* since it relieves him of any accusation of lack of impartiality in his taking of bids.

It is customary for bids to be fixed at the outset at minimum amounts or their multiples. Nods and winks, such as are used by bidders in England, are somewhat piously discouraged to ensure that the *notaire* is not muddled and the *cahier des charges* can restrict the permissible means of bidding.

The extinguishment of the third candle which is the equivalent of the English fall of the hammer does not of itself complete the sale. The *notaire* must formally announce the agreement of the seller to the last bid made. If the *cahier des charges* does not include a reserve price or if the fact that one has been imposed is not announced before bidding begins, as has been said above, bids are only offers which the seller is free to accept or not. It is in fact possible to include in the *cahier des charges* when there is no reserve stipulated a right for the owner to withdraw the property from the sale at any time if the bids never reach a figure which he considers satisfactory.

The law provides a period of imprisonment of fifteen days to three months or a fine running up to Euro 750 for anyone interfering with a person's right to bid freely at auction by any of a number of precisely defined means. If any such behaviour occurs, the *notaire* conducting the auction draws up a *procès-verbal* which he sends to the equivalent of the Crown Prosecution Service.

Conclusion of sale

Since a sale effected at auction follows thereafter essentially the same rules as a sale by private treaty, those relating to registration of the transfer at the Land Registry are similar in both cases. In place of the *acte de vente*, the *notaire* lodges the *cahier des charges* and the *procès-verbal* referred to above. As with any sale of part of a building *en copropriété*, notification of the sale must be made to the *syndic* as soon as possible since it cannot, as with ordinary sales, be made in advance. The Loi Scrivener condition in favour of a purchaser intending to seek mortgage finance does not apply to sales by auction. The right to require cancellation of the sale for *lésion* applies to sales by auction in the same manner as for sales by private treaty, the two-year period running from the date of completion of the auction.

Surenchère

This is a procedure unknown in English law. It has its origins in the provisions of C.civ.art.2185, which gives the right to mortgagees under a registered mortgage to apply for a sale by private treaty by a mortgagor to be reopened. The object of the right is said to be to guarantee mortgagees 'against fraud or surprise' by ensuring that the price obtained for the property by the mortgagor corresponds to its market value. The procedure is also available for use in sales by auction of this kind provided that the *cahier des charges* so announces. The procedure is as follows. Any person may within ten days of the auction give notice that he is willing to make an offer which is at least 10 per cent in excess of the highest bid made at the auction. The auction is then reopened with that increased bid as the opening bid and the sale then proceeds as previously recounted. Unless he is again the highest bidder, the original buyer stands to lose the property since the earlier sale to him is cancelled in favour of another bidder. It is extremely rare to find this right available in this kind of auction, making the result of the original auction subject to the possibility of being reopened and therefore unattractive to the general public.

Adjudication judiciaire

The information given under this heading refers primarily to the procedure involved in the sale by auction itself and other matters which concern the buyers of property sold in this fashion. The situation of the owner of the property sold subject to *adjudication judiciaire* does not strictly fall within the ambit of this chapter and is referred to only in outline. That is the province of the *avocat* and not that of the *notaire*.

The saisie immobilière

Any creditor may seek a foreclosure order for the sale of his debtor's *immeubles* and life interests in such property which are vested in the debtor (C.civ.art.2204).

Article 2 of the Law of 9 July 1991 is both more specific and more restrictive in its contents in that 'the creditor by virtue of any *titre authentique et exécutoire* (defined by article 3 of that Law as including Court Orders, foreign Court Orders and Arbitrators' Awards which have the French Court *exéquateur* and notarial documents) evidencing a money debt due for payment may apply for an Order of foreclosure in respect of the assets of his debtor in the appropriate manner'. In addition, a creditor may seek to foreclose on property in the hands of a third party without the need to await its transfer into the name of his debtor (C.civ.art.2169). Certain property cannot be made the subject of a foreclosure order such as family tombs, shares in *sociétés civiles immobilières*, and a *droit d'usage et d'habitation*. Nor can such an order be made against property owned *en tontine*. A creditor who could have obtained such an order in respect of property before it became owned *en indivision* can obtain the order after an *indivision* has been created. He cannot do so in respect of the undivided share of one co-owner if the *indivision* arose as a matter of law but can do so if it was created by act of parties. A mortgagee can seek to foreclose on the property charged to him and he may seek to obtain the sale of other uncharged property if the mortgaged property is insufficient to repay the secured debt.

A sale so ordered by the Court normally takes place in the local Tribunal de Grande Instance which is always the case of sales following a *surenchère*, a *folle enchère* or where a person under an incapacity is involved. The Court has power on occasions to transfer the sale to take place before a *notaire* chosen by the Court.

Procedure leading to a saisie
The preliminary step to obtaining a *saisie immobilière* authorizing the sale of a property is the service on the debtor of a *commandement* to pay. The requirements as to the contents of such a document are strict. It is served on the debtor by a *huissier* and thereafter must be registered at the Land Registry. It is this registration which sets in motion the foreclosure procedure and in accordance with C.civ.art.2092-3 blocks any dealings with the property in question. On the other hand, if no sale takes place within three years or of any period extended by the Court of registration of the *commandement*, it ceases to have any effect.

Pre-auction procedure
As in the case of the *adjudication volontaire*, a *cahier des charges* is prepared but remains the equivalent only of a draft contract until it has been lodged with the Registrar of the appropriate Court not later than forty days after the registration at the Land Registry of the *commandement* served on the debtor. It must prior to lodgement receive the agreement of all those parties who have an interest in its terms. Thereafter, it becomes a document intended to be binding on those involved in the sale, that is to say the creditor who has foreclosed, all the other

creditors of the owner of the property to be sold, the debtor and the ultimate buyer. It is a contract for the sale of the property and is not a judgment of the Court (Cass.9.6.82).

The *cahier des charges* is prepared and signed by the *avocat* acting for the creditor who has obtained the *saisie*. It recites the title of the creditor giving rise to the order, details of the *commandement* served on the debtor, a description of the property to be sold, the conditions of sale and a *mise à prix* set by the creditor who has obtained the *saisie*. To these statutory conditions should be added all usual provisions peculiar to the sale of the property itself.

The *mise à prix*, which in this type of auction is obligatory, and which is set by the foreclosing creditor, is of interest. In default of any bids, that creditor becomes the owner at the price of that *mise à prix* which may not be less than Euro 1. However, if the property is the principal residence of the debtor, an application may be made to the Court alleging that the amount of the *mise à prix* is manifestly low having regard to the market value of the property and the Court with or without the aid of expert advice will vary the figure if it considers this to be necessary. Such an application must be made not less than three days before the final hearing.

All costs of the procedure are paid by the ultimate buyer and any clause to the contrary in the *cahier des charges* is void. These are taxed by the Court and the amount announced at the opening of the auction.

Not later than eight days after the *cahier des charges* has been lodged with the Court, notice is given to all interested parties, who may make their observations to the Judge, advising them of the date of the hearing of the application for the foreclosure order. CPC.art.697 says: 'The auction should take place after wide publicity thus enabling the largest number of bidders to be present . . . The Judge may limit or increase such advertisement depending on the nature and value of the property to be sold and all other relevant circumstances.' Not more than thirty days nor less than fifteen days before the date of the auction, the *avocat* acting for the creditor must place an announcement in a newspaper circulating in the area in which the property to be sold is situate stating the names and addresses of the parties and their *avocats*, a full description of the property to be sold, the reserve price and the date and time of the auction and the Court where it will take place. A list of suitable newspapers in his *département* taking legal notices is circulated each year by the *Préfet*. During the same period, the *avocat* must cause to be exhibited on the building to be sold, at the entrance of the Court where the auction is to be held and on the 'official' notice board of the *commune* where the property is situate copies of an extract from the notice in those newspapers. The effecting of this multiple advertisement must be attested by the *procès-verbal* of a *huissier*. The Court where the auction is to be held may limit or increase such advertisement including by means of 'bell, trumpet or drum' (CPC.art.700).

Conduct of the auction

The auction takes place at the appropriate Tribunal de Grande Instance and may be presided over by a single Judge. All bids must be made by an *avocat* and the *avocats* for creditor and debtor are present. As bidding commences, three candles are lit one after the other each having a burning time of about one minute. When the last candle goes out, bidding is finished. There is no rule which prevents any other method of taking bids but none has ever been used. An *avocat* may not (evidently) bid for a member of the Court or for the debtor or for anyone who is known to be insolvent. Nor may he bid for himself. Subject to these rules and the general rules as to capacity, anyone may bid through an *avocat*. The spouse of the debtor may bid (CA Toulouse 16.7.1890) provided that he or she is not jointly liable with the debtor or is a person considered by the Court to be *'interposé'*. It is the duty of the *avocat* who bids on behalf of a client to ensure that his client may properly submit bids.

Bidding is over when the third candle is extinguished. If there are no bids during the periods during which the candles are alight, the creditor is deemed to be the buyer at the *mise à prix*. If there are bids during the time that the first candle is lit, the sale must continue until two further candles have burnt out.

The form of judgment confirming the sale to the highest bidder is not a judgment of the Court capable of being appealed against but is rather in the nature of a judicial contract. The judgment of itself vests in the buyer the right to possession of the property. The obligation on the part of the debtor to give physical possession stems from such a judgment so that possession may not be withheld until the price has been paid by the buyer.

The *avocat* acting for the highest bidder must confirm acceptance of his client's purchase within three days of the auction and disclose his power to act, failing which the *avocat* himself is deemed to be the purchaser. However, any buyer may, within twenty-four hours of that declaration, formally declare that he is acting on behalf of a third party. That right is given also to an *avocat* deemed to be the buyer in default of the declaration he ought to have made so that he can escape the burden by so declaring within twenty-four hours of the three days mentioned above.

The successful bidder is provided with suitable documentation in respect of title by the Court. Property in the land as between the buyer and third parties passes to the buyer on registration of the documentation at the Land Registry. This documentation in the form of the *cahier des charges* and the judgment as to the result of the auction is essential to obtain physical possession if the debtor is slow in vacating the premises. The debtor as seller is subject to all the liabilities of an ordinary seller other than in respect of *vices cachés*, specifically excluded in cases of *adjudication judiciaire* by C.civ.art.1645 but he is liable to the buyer for the existence of undisclosed easements and charges.

Surenchère

As has been said above, this procedure is primarily intended for *adjudications judiciaires*. In such cases, the full procedure is as follows. Any person through his *avocat* may make a declaration to the Court that he is prepared to bid not less than 10 per cent more than the final bid made at auction. Such a declaration is irrevocable and other similar offers may be made. Notice of such a declaration must be given within five days of it having been made to the seller, the foreclosing creditor and the buyer at the previous sale. The increased bid may be objected to before the Court but if it is approved by the Court or no objections are raised, a new sale is arranged following the same procedure as for the original sale, the opening bid being that of the *enchérisseur* who either becomes the buyer if no further bids are made or must bid against other bidders if there are any. This procedure happily cannot be repeated since Ossa may not be piled on Pelion by virtue of the dictum that '*enchère sur enchère ne vaut*'.

Folle enchère

This is a procedure available only in *adjudications judiciaires*, again without parallel in English law. If a buyer at auction fails to complete his purchase in accordance with the terms of the *cahier des charges* 'all interested parties', who will normally be the secured creditors of the owner of the property sold at auction but can also be the owner himself, can cause it to be offered again at a further auction. Grounds which can give rise to such a new sale are that the buyer has failed (i) to register his purchase at the Land Registry within the prescribed period, or (ii) to pay the costs for which he is liable within twenty days of the sale, or (iii) to comply with certain requirements of the *cahier des charges* which the Courts have adjudged not to be of a subsidiary nature.

The procedure to be followed depends on whether the Court has issued its *titre d'adjudication* or not. In the former case, the person entitled to receive the sale price serves notice on the defaulting buyer (*fol enchérisseur*) together with his *titre d'adjudication* and a formal order to pay. In the latter event, the seller at auction must obtain from the Court a certificate confirming that the buyer is in default. Not less than five days after completion of one or other of the above formalities, advertisement of a new sale in the same manner as for the original sale takes place, save that in this case the name and address of the defaulting buyer, the sale price obtained at the previous auction and a reserve price must be included. Fifteen days' notice of the holding of the auction must be served on all involved parties. Payment in full of the price and all costs by the buyer in default will cause the second sale to be cancelled provided that he can show that he has not in the meantime substantially altered the premises in question (Cass.16.2.72). Payment of the seller's debt, the cause of the original auction sale, even after a *surenchère* will put an end to the procedure notwithstanding that the debt is paid by the debtor, the owner of the property, with the aid of a loan from the *surenchérisseur* (Cass.15.10.94).

14

CHARGES ON PROPERTY

Introduction 119
Types of mortgages 119
Remedies of a mortgagee 120
Hypothèque conventionnelle 120
   Obtaining a loan 120
Property which can be mortgaged 121
Capacity to mortgage property 122
The execution of mortgages 123
The registration of mortgages 123
Privilèges 124
Transfers of mortgages 125
Release 125
Hypothèque légale 125
Hypothèque judiciaire 126
Le tiers détenteur 127

Introduction

There being no equitable jurisdiction in France, every mortgage is a legal mortgage and there is nothing to be found in the system which simplifies the securing of the relationship between lender and borrower, particularly when it is of a temporary duration, such as the deposit of a Land Certificate. Neither Land Certificate nor Charge Certificate exist and the only way in which the existence of or freedom from a charge on property can be discovered is through the medium of a search. The unsecured creditor is a *créancier chirographaire*.

Types of mortgages

French law recognizes three kinds of mortgages. These are:

1. The *hypothèque conventionnelle* which is created by agreement between the lender and the borrower. This is the usual kind of mortgage which serves to secure house purchase loans or any other kind of indebtedness by one person or company to another.

2. The *hypothèque légal* or mortgage arising by act of law so that it can take effect even in respect of the assets of those under an incapacity. The creation of such a right in favour of a creditor requires registration at the Land Registry against property currently owned by the debtor and takes effect as from the

date upon which it is registered. A creditor may also register such charges as and when the debtor himself becomes the registered proprietor of additional property.

3. The *hypothèque judiciaire* which, save that it constitutes a legal and not an equitable charge, may be seen in large measure as the counterpart of a High Court judgment by virtue of section 195 (1) of the Law of Property Act 1925.

Remedies of a mortgagee

All mortgages of whatever kind provide the mortgagee with two different remedies, namely (i) a *droit de préférence* and (ii) a *droit de suite*. The former is the right for the mortgagee to share in the sale price of the mortgaged property in priority to the mortgagor or to other creditors whose charges rank after his in priority of registration. The latter has two aspects. One is the equivalent of the English power of sale of the mortgaged property in that at such time as the amount secured by the mortgage has become due but remains unpaid, the lender may institute the procedure of a *saisie immobilière* leading to a sale under the control of the Court in the manner described below. The other right given to a mortgagee by the *droit de suite* is, whatever his priority may be, at any time to proceed against the property in the hands of any third party in whom the property has become vested. Such a procedure is described below under the heading *Le tiers détenteur*.

Hypothèque conventionnelle

Obtaining a loan
The rules laid down by the *Loi Scrivener* for the protection of non-professional buyers seeking a loan for the purchase of residential property fall into two groups. Those which deal with the statutory conditions in favour of buyers are covered in Chapter 3. There are, however, also strict regulations imposed on lenders which, in the case of foreigners, apply if (i) the loan contract is designated as subject to French law or (ii) the loan contract is to be subject to a non-French law or is not expressed to be subject to any particular law and the property offered as security is in France and the lending establishment or the residence of the borrower is in France. Every loan offer made to a prospective borrower must be in writing and must as a minimum contain:

(1) the identities of the lender and borrower;
(2) the purpose for which the loan is to be made, the conditions attached to its drawdown and details of its repayment;
(3) the amount of the loan to be granted, its total cost, its *taux effectif global* or APR and any form of indexation applicable;
(4) details of any insurances or guarantors required;

(5) any conditions applicable to a transfer of the loan to a third party;

(6) details of the 'cooling off' period which must be given to the applicant;

(7) details of any costs which the applicant will incur if the offered loan is not made.

The potential lender is required to maintain the conditions contained in his loan offer for a period of thirty days. Failure to comply with these requirements can lead to a fine of up to Euro 3,750 but such failure does not result in any loan made based on such an offer being void (Cass.9.3.99 and 23.3.99).

The person to whom the offer is made may not accept it within a period of ten days of its receipt by him by post excluding the day of delivery. This rule is *d'ordre public* so that an early acceptance invalidates the loan contract (Cass.27.2.01). A subsequent further acceptance outside the ten-day period will not cure the defect of acceptance at too early a date (Cass.30.3.94). Proper acceptance creates the contract for the loan even if the loan moneys have not at that time been made available to the borrower (Cass.27.5.98). The contract is subject to a condition precedent of its being completed within four months unless a longer period is agreed. If this time limit is passed and the loan not completed, the borrower must repay any sums he has been given (this infrequently happens) plus interest and the lender may charge a fee of 75 per cent of the loan not exceeding Euro 150. Any variations of the loan offer as it has been accepted requires a new loan offer subject to the acceptance conditions referred to above. This is not necessary when the original offer was in respect of a loan with a variable rate of interest provided details of these accompanied the offer. Nor is a new offer necessary if all that is in issue is an extension of the period of the loan and of no other condition (Cass.8.10.96). Currently, as a result of the Law of 25 June 1999, variations in a loan offer which are in favour of the borrower may be made by an addendum to the loan offer which allows the borrower a new period of ten days before acceptance.

Property which can be mortgaged

(C.civ.art.2118 says '*Sont seuls susceptibles d'hypothèques* (i) *les biens immobiliers qui sont dans le commerce et leurs accessoires réputés immeubles* (ii) *l'usufruit des mêmes biens et accessoires pendant le temps de sa durée*'. (Only the following may be the subject of a mortgage: (i) immovables which are free of restraint on alienation together with their appurtenances which fall to be treated as immovables; and (ii) life interests in such property but not *droits d'usage* or licences to occupy premises in such property since they are not capable of assignment and their appurtenances for the duration of such interests.) [Translation note: The French expression '*immobiliers qui sont dans le commerce*' is curious and does not, as would appear, limit such property to that which has a commercial use. C.civ.art.2124 says that contractual mortgages may only be created by owners who have unrestricted powers of the alienation of the mortgaged property. A judgment of Cass.29.6.83 confirms that 'dans le commerce' means 'is subject to no restriction on alienability'.] Such property includes *droits réels* (Chapter 2) so that the lessee under a long lease or *bail emphytéotique* can mortgage his interest under that lease. Property which is immovable *par destination* as opposed to that which is immovable *par nature* can be mortgaged when it is part of the former but not when detached from it since it then loses its character of an immovable.

Future interests in land generally cannot be the subject of a mortgage since they cannot be brought within the scope of C.civ.art.2129 which requires that mortgaged property must be fully described as to its nature and situation. However, this is not considered to be an absolute rule and exceptions exist in three cases:

1. If the existing unencumbered property of a borrower is recognized by him as insufficient to provide the necessary security, he may agree to charge future interests as and when they become vested in him (C.civ.art.2130). Such a charge takes effect as from the date of each such vesting but ranks for priority purposes from the date when each is the subject of registration by the lender at the Land Registry.
2. In the event of the value of the property securing a loan becoming insufficient to support that loan by reason of loss or damage, a lender may take a charge on future interests of a borrower as an alternative to calling in the loan (C.civ.art.2131).
3. The owner of rights to build on the land of another may create a mortgage on such buildings whether they are completed or not or even simply still in the plan stage.

Capacity to mortgage property

Only an owner who has full capacity can mortgage his property. Certain difficulties can arise in the case of jointly owned property. If it is owned *en tontine* (Chapter 16) many lenders are not anxious to lend in view of the legal fiction which governs this kind of ownership, namely that it is not until the death of the first co-owner to die that it is known in whose sole ownership the whole property was vested as from the date of purchase. In such circumstances, the best method to adopt is for both co-owners to obtain a single loan on the basis of a joint and several liability, each giving the whole of the jointly owned property subject to his surviving his co-owner as security. In the case of property owned *en indivision*, a mortgage given by a single co-owner is subject to the results of the *partage* or partition of the property. The result of such a partition is that the property is deemed to have belonged *ab initio* to the persons to whom it is attributed and if these do not include the mortgagor, the value of the security is lost. This is not the case if the property is on partition vested in the borrower. However, a mortgage granted by all the co-owners exceptionally retains its value irrespective of in whom the property is vested on partition (C.civ.art.2125).

The execution of mortgages

A mortgage is considered a 'solemn' contract which must be in the form of an *acte authentique* (C.civ.art.2127) which until the Law of 28 December 1966 required also the presence of two witnesses. However, this relates only to the borrower so that a lender, in the unlikely event of there being separate documents for one loan, may execute his document ssp. It is, in fact, customary for a purchase and the loan obtained to finance it to be dealt with in one *acte*. Any power of attorney to execute a mortgage must also be *authentique*.

As to mortgages executed out of France in respect of French property, there is conflict between the provisions of the *Code civil* and a Decree of 4 January 1955 as to the requirements in respect of all documents executed out of France for use in that country. The current situation as to mortgages is covered by a ruling of the French Land Registry that: 'It is recommended that Registrars do not refuse to register mortgages created by any document of whatever kind executed abroad provided that such document has been legalized and deposited in the records of a French Notary or has been recognized by the French Court as enforceable (*rendu exécutoire*) in France and that it is accompanied where necessary by a translation into French.' Me Revillard in *Droit International Privé et Pratique Notariale* (5th edn, Defrénois, 2001) seems to take a view less certain than that quoted above not as to the willingness of the Registrar to accept mortgage documents executed abroad but as to whether they are, if so executed, in accordance with the law. In the absence of any Convention between the United Kingdom and France, she takes the view that the document creating a mortgage over French property should not be executed in the United Kingdom and, if not by the borrower himself before a French *notaire*, then in France by an attorney of the borrower acting under a power in *authentique* form. It cannot be doubted that this is a sure method of proceeding but in any event the view of any *notaire* involved in each specific transaction should be sought.

The registration of mortgages

C.civ.art.2143 provides that as between creditors, as with an English registered charge, priority depends on the date of registration of each charge. The formalities of registration are the task of the *notaire* for the lender who will frequently also act for the buyer.

The *hypothèque conventionnelle* may be registered immediately following the execution of the mortgage document. There is no time limit for such registration save that any mortgage not registered in time will lose priority to a mortgage subsequently registered. There are, however, four cases in which a mortgage cannot be registered. These are:

1. If there has been a previous registration of a disposal (for example, by way of sale or gift) of the property by the borrower to a third party. Such a third party is bound only by mortgages registered prior to the date on which he registered the transaction by which he acquired an interest in the property.
2. If in the case of property included in the estate of a deceased person there has been a prior *acceptation sous bénéfice d'inventaire* (Chapter 34) even if by only one of a number of beneficiaries or there has been a declaration by the Court of a *succession vacante* (Chapter 27).
3. If there has been a prior registration of *commandement de payer* (formal demand for payment of a debt) having the effect of a *saisie immobilière*. Any subsequent registration is without value until such time as the *saisie* is vacated.
4. In the case of prior insolvency proceedings relating to a company or an individual 'who habitually engages in commercial transactions'.

The period for which a mortgage may remain on the register is that terminating with the date for the final repayment of the secured loan plus a further short period which in ordinary circumstances is not more than two years. In any event the period of registration cannot exceed thirty-five years. If the date for repayment is not fixed or has already been reached by the date of registration, the charge may remain on the register for a period not exceeding ten years. It is possible to renew the period of registration before it expires when the original registration retains its priority. Otherwise, registration is automatically vacated.

Privilèges

There is a significant exception to the rule governing the priority of mortgages. This is due to the existence of a number of *privilèges*, some of which affect *immeubles*. The most important of these are the *privilèges de vendeur* and *de prêteur*. The former is in respect of any part of the sale price remaining due from a buyer after completion of the sale. The latter is for moneys due to a lender if they were destined for the purchase of an *immeuble* and the *acte de vente* proves that they were used for that purpose. Such *privilèges* which are 'special' take priority over registered mortgages provided that they are registered according to the rules when they take their priority from the date of the event which gave rise to them. This will normally be the date of the completion of the purchase of the property in issue. Other similar *privilèges* are for the benefit of:

(1) beneficiaries of *immeubles* in an estate;
(2) fees and wages of architects and workmen in respect of the increase in value of a building by reason of the work done by them;
(3) the lender of moneys to pay for such work if supported by an *acte notarié*.

Transfers of mortgages

A mortgagee may freely transfer the benefit of his mortgage to any person of his choice. Such a transfer is unenforceable as against third parties unless it has been noted in the form of a *mention en marge* in the register against the original entry.

Release

The release given by a lender on repayment of his loan is a *mainlevée*. It should be in the form of an *acte authentique*. Who may give a release depends on whether it is given on full or less than full repayment of the secured amount. In the former case, any person entitled to give a receipt for payment may give the formal release. In the latter case, the capacity to give a release depends on the capacity to dispose of the benefit of the secured debt itself. A beneficiary in an estate can execute such a release but it is an act of disposal and can at the instance of creditors deprive that beneficiary of the right to *acceptance sous bénéfice d'inventaire* (Chapter 34).

If the person entitled to give a release cannot or will not provide the necessary document, it will be necessary to seek the aid of the Court under C.civ.art.2159 which will if suitable make the necessary Order. The competent Court is that within the jurisdiction of which the registration of the mortgage has been made. Such an application may be made by any person who has an interest in the property against which the mortgage has been registered who, in addition to the owner himself, may be a subsequent owner or mortgagee. The judgment authorizing the Land Registrar to vacate the mortgage must be in the form of a final judgment.

To obtain and file a *mainlevée* at the *bureau des hypothèques* involves a noticeable, if not large, cost. It is therefore common practice among the French not to remove charges from the register on their repaying loans but let them become automatically vacated in due course of time. Only when they come to sell a property against which a mortgage has been registered but which has been repaid without a formal release having been given, are they obliged to go to the expense of obtaining a *mainlevée*.

Hypothèque légale

The *Code civil* provides a number of circumstances in which this kind of mortgage arising by operation of law may be registered. These include the payment of funeral expenses, the payment of legacies but, more importantly, the recovery of a number of taxes and dues by the fiscal and Customs authorities. Also included is the right of one spouse in certain cases to register a charge against the assets of the other spouse and this is explained in Chapter 20. All that is required is that the appropriate procedure leading to the registration of the mortgage is followed by the creditor, priority being given according to the date of registration. In the case of unpaid tax or any other sum in respect of which this procedure can be operated, the registration of such a mortgage requires the prior service on the debtor of a *commandement* (formal demand to pay) with which the debtor fails to comply. Registration of the unsatisfied *commandement* must be done within ninety days, failing which the procedure must be started afresh. The registration of the *commandement* in due form against property of the debtor blocks dealings of every kind. It is normal that thereafter the procedure leading to a sale by the Court should follow. Appeals against such registration leading to a *saisie immobilière*, which are usually made on the grounds of some procedural defect, are made to the local Tribunal de Grande Instance.

Hypothèque judiciaire

As has been said above, this is a type of charge which flows from all French judgments including the awards of arbitrators given the force of judgments. It can also be used to execute judgments of foreign courts which have been recognized by the Court in France as enforceable in that country.

The procedure to obtain this recognition of a judgment of a non-French Court or *exéquateur* is by way of *ex parte* application to the local Tribunal de Grande Instance supported by evidence that the foreign judgment has been properly obtained in the foreign country. Such an order is needed in all cases where it is sought to execute a foreign judgment on assets or against persons in France but, it should be noted, is not required when the foreign judgment has ruled only on questions of status or capacity. Such a charge may be based on judgments of every kind including judgments by default and whether final or not since it is *conservatoire* only, that is, it is in the nature of a charging order such as would be protected by a notice at the Land Registry in England.

The charge may be visited on all *immeubles* of the judgment debtor including those acquired by him subsequent to any previous registration but it must be registered afresh against each such subsequently acquired property (C.civ.art.2123). Charges registered on several properties, the total value of which exceeds twice the secured debt with interest and costs plus a third of that amount, are considered excessive and the debtor may apply to the Court for the removal from the register of charges on some of the properties (C.civ.art.2161).

Since it may take some time to obtain a judgment on which to base a mortgage of this kind, it is possible to apply to the Court for a provisional charge which will be granted if the creditor can show that the debt prima facie cannot be challenged and its recovery is in peril, for example, where there are outstanding repayments due. The Court may then grant a *hypothèque judicial conservatoire* requiring the creditor to seek a judgment against the debtor within a fixed time limit and stating the time within which the mortgage must be registered of which fifteen days' notice must be given to the debtor and indicating which properties of the debtor are to be subject to the charge. Such a charge remains in force for three years and must be renewed if the judgment on which it will be based has not been obtained within that period. If such a judgment is in favour of the debtor, the *saisie* must be vacated. So long as the charge remains registered, no dealings with the property can take place. If the creditor obtains the judgment he seeks against the debtor, this judgment must be registered within two months when its registration is substituted for the temporary charge with retrospective effect to the date of registration of that temporary charge.

Le tiers déteneur

The right enabling a creditor to take action against a third party who is in possession of property charged to that creditor is by way of *saisie immobilière* described above under *Hypothèque légale*. Failure on the part of that third party to pay all that is due under the mortgage entitles the mortgagor to sell the property. It must be noted that such a procedure does not relieve the original mortgagor of his liability since the recovery of what may be due in this manner is an action against the property and does not release the original mortgagor from his personal liability to the mortgagee.

Although strictly not within the scope of this book, it is convenient to make mention here of the use of the *avis au tiers déteneur* as an extension of the *droit de suite* against assets other than land as means of enforcing payment of debts in a manner akin to a garnishment but unsupported by any Court Order. Suffice it to say that it is frequently used by the tax authorities and by local authorities as a means of recovering unpaid national and local taxes. An *avis au tiers déteneur* is usually served on banks, *notaires*, and employers since these are likely to be holding money for customers, clients and employees and so can be treated as debtors of the person from whom payment is sought. The procedure is for the service of a *commandement* or formal order to pay followed by the service on the third party from whom money is sought of an *avis de tiers déteneur*. This requires payment by that third party of any cash held by him for the benefit of the alleged debtor. Banks can allow a few days' grace but will block accounts and pay over what they have in the debtor's account if the debt is not paid. Notaries will normally reply at once and pay over what they hold. Banks and others will advise those for whom they hold money of the receipt of such a notice but action must be taken at once by the alleged debtor if he does not wish to see his cash disappear without the chance to claim that it is not due to the alleged creditor.

Chapter 7 deals at some length with the payment out of the sale price after completion of a sale and the dangers which can arise by reason of the shortcomings of the French Land Registry search system. Whatever may be the liabilities of the insurers in respect of a *notaire*'s negligence, the *droit de suite* gives the buyer who has not got what he paid for on completion of his purchase a direct right against the property wrongfully sold or mortgaged by his seller after completion.

15

LA COPROPRIÉTÉ

Introduction 129
Definition of *copropriété* 130
Basis for service charges 131
The *règlement de copropriété* 131
Service charges 133
    Calculation of service charges 133
    Payment of service charges 134
Meetings of the *copropriété* 136
    Presence at meetings 137
    Convening meetings 137
The *syndic* 141
The *conseil syndical* 145

Introduction

A very large proportion of French families live in parts of buildings either origi-nally built as blocks of flats or in buildings at one time in single occupation but subsequently converted into flats. It is said that historically this was an arrange-ment which greatly pleased those who governed the country since each such building needed some permanent servant who could organize its security, the enforcement of its internal regulations and its general upkeep and organization but particularly who, by reason of his and his wife's continuous presence, could monitor the comings and goings of the occupants and their visitors. Certainly, for a very long period, the *concierge* was a most trusted and fruitful police informer in addition to keeping each occupant of the block fully au fait with the affairs of all his neighbours. Of recent years, his wages and social security contributions have become a very expensive proportion of the service charges payable by flat-owners so that much use is now made of a non-resident individual or sometimes specialist firm, known as a *gardien*, for the daily upkeep of the block. For those in permanent residence, this may be a welcome reduction of the cost of the service charges. For those who use their flats only for intermittent periods, the absence of a *concierge* can represent serious loss of security.

The current law relating to the *copropriété* stems from the Law of 10 July 1965 as substantially amended by the *Loi SRU* and it is not intended to distinguish between these two sources. A number of *décrets* issued pursuant to both Laws complete the law as it now affects every aspect of the *copropriété*. However, the more recent Law resulted in some of the fundamental documentation used in the management of this type of property becoming out of date and the very many buildings managed in accordance with the older Law have been given until December 2005 to amend this documentation appropriately. It is probable that many of these documents will not be amended by the due date and care will have to be taken when considering their contents.

It must be appreciated that the *copropriété* is not limited to buildings with a residential user only. It can apply to commercial property or to professional users as well as to buildings with mixed users. This chapter deals only with property used for living accommodation or for that purpose and professional purposes which frequently is the case in blocks of flats in France. For the sake of simplicity, the owner of a part of such a building which is owned by all the owners *en copropriété* is referred to as a flat-owner.

Definition of *copropriété*

The status of *copropriété* applies to all buildings or groups of buildings which are divided into *lots* (parcels) each comprising a *partie privative*, that is a flat or office, and a linked *quote-part* (notional share) of the communal parts of the block. All the individual owners of such *lots* together form a *syndicat de copropriété* which is a legal entity managed by its *syndic* and in which the owner of each *lot* has voting rights coupled with the obligation to pay *charges* (service charges) towards the upkeep of the block. The block is managed in accordance with the rules contained in the *règlement de copropriété*. Whilst the technical term to describe this entity used in French textbooks is a *syndicat*, it is in common parlance known as a *copropriété* and the building owned in this manner is the *immeuble*.

The status of *copropriété* can take effect only when a property is fully built (Cass.15.12.66). Until that time, all legal relationships are those which stem from the terms of such contracts as have been entered into on, say, a purchase of a flat *en l'état futur* between purchasing flat-owner and developer (Chapter 8) or on a purchase through an *SCI d'attribution* (Chapter 10) and although the purchaser of such a flat will be the owner before its completion, he has no liability under the rules which govern the *copropriété* until the building of which his flat forms part is fully built.

The flats into which a property is divided each comprise a *partie privative* and a share of the common parts which are indivisible since neither can exist alone (Cass.21.11.72 and 19.1.77). It follows, therefore, from such a rule that certain property cannot be owned *en copropriété* such as that which is owned *en indivision* or where occupation alone but not ownership itself is shared.

The *parties privatives* of a *copropriété* are those in respect of which the owner has the exclusive use. In general terms, this area may be compared to that which would be or be deemed to be included in a flat under an English long lease. The main walls of the building are common parts and interior walls separating one flat from another are party walls. It is not uncommon to find that a flat has the *jouis-sance privatif* (private use) of what is a common part, for example, a garden area or a roof garden or terrace. In the event that the *règlement de copropriété* (known currently as the *règlement*) does not define what is private and what is common or there is any ambiguity, the answer is provided by the law.

Basis for service charges

Les charges payable by flat-owners are based on the proportion which each owns in the common parts of the block as comprised in his *lot*. This proportion expressed in *tantièmes* is always given by tradition as fractions of a thousand or ten thousand and their amounts are shown in the *état descriptif de division* which is a technical document which describes each *lot* by comprehensive reference to its position in the block. The *quote-part* of each *lot* is described in the original and each subsequent *acte de vente* as an integral part of the description of the flat. This fraction has been calculated at a fairly early stage of the development of the block based on such criteria as the quality of the flat itself (ceiling height, its fittings, its aspect), on which floor is the flat (the French flats tend to increase in value the higher in a building they are so that the first floor is not usually considered the best), whether there is a balcony or terrace and the amount of sun it will receive, if there is a separate garage or parking space and private garden and similar advantages.

The proportions of each *quote-part* are unalterable save by unanimous vote of all the flat-owners except in the case where the height of the building is increased when a two-thirds vote of all flat-owners is required. Even the Court cannot vary the *tantièmes* (Cass.6.3.91). These proportions may be and frequently are either general or special. The former relate to expenditure of parts of the block common to all flat-owners; the latter are those which are limited to expenditure in respect of the upkeep of individual blocks in a complex or to cellars or garages used by only certain but not all flat-owners. Not infrequently, a flat will carry with it for this reason *tantièmes* of differing proportions.

The *règlement de copropriété*

No *copropriété* can exist without such a document. It is normally prepared by the *notaire* acting for the developer of the block. It should always be accompanied by the *état descriptif de division* and frequently the two documents are bound together and both are registered at the local *bureau des hypothèques*. On the purchase of a flat *en l'état futur* and on every purchase of a flat in an existing block, it is essential to inspect this document before completion and indeed the *acte de vente* should contain an acknowledgement of its receipt from the vendor. In the event that the vendor has not got his copy which frequently occurs, a copy must be obtained from the *syndic*.

If the document has been amended prior to completion of a sale but these amendments have not been registered at the *bureau des hypothèques* by the date of completion, they are not binding on the purchaser unless he specifically adopts them in the *acte de vente* (Cass.31.1.96). If they are not so adopted by the purchaser and are registered after completion, they do not bind the purchaser even after registration (CA Paris 22.10.97).

In the event of there not being any such document in existence, a purchaser of a flat who has not been advised of this fact by the vendor can obtain the cancellation of the sale to him (CA Paris 4.1.2000). The recent date of this judgment is not without interest since the requirement to have a *règlement* dates back a considerable number of years. It must not be thought that every building which is owned *en copropriété* is a large modern block of flats in a big city or well-known holiday area. The definition of what is a *copropriété* covers every building in more than one ownership and this frequently may mean very few flats in a small building. Although the *syndic* is a recognized profession, his work can be undertaken by anyone without formal qualification and in small blocks is often carried out as a labour of love by one of the flat-owners who is a retired civil servant. In such cases, the strict legal requirements are not always observed and even in larger blocks, the quality of the *syndic* can leave much to be desired.

As has been said above, the most recent legislation makes necessary an overhaul of all *règlements* but stemming doubtless from the number of unqualified *syndics* who manage small blocks many have always been liable to contain errors, usually as to voting rights.

The law requires that the *règlement* may not restrict the rights of any *copropriétaire* in any manner in excess of what is reasonable having regard to the user of the building. Each owner may deal freely with the *partie privative* comprised in his *lot* and freely make use of the common parts of the building provided that his behaviour does not interfere with the rights of other flat-owners or adversely affect the common parts of the building.

It follows, therefore, that it is not possible for any decision taken by the flat-owners lawfully to alter the means of the enjoyment by its owner of a private part of a block or the amenities belonging to it. Nor can exclusive private rights over common parts granted by a *règlement* be varied. Any decision of the flat-owners which purports to limit what activities may be carried on within a private part of a block which are permitted by the *règlement* is void.

Generally speaking, the Courts have sought not to limit work carried out to the interior of the private parts of a block except where such work may adversely affect the rights of other flat-owners or the *destination* of the block. However, it is wise if not obligatory to inform the *syndic* of an intention to do works to a private part of the block if only because this may affect the common parts and require permission. The Courts have, for example, approved the building of an interior staircase between two *lots* owned by the same flat-owner (CA Versailles 29.10.90) and of a mezzanine within a flat (Cass.26.5.93). In the case of works of any significance, a flat-owner should always use the services of an architect or surveyor to avoid any claim against him for damage to any part of the block, be it a common or private part (CA Paris 24.6.98).

The *règlement* will describe the *affectation* (permitted user) of each flat and in general terms these cannot be varied. However, over a period of time, the strict rule to that effect has been relaxed and, for example, garages have been turned into living accommodation and similar transformations have been accepted. From a practical point of view, care must be taken when dealing with any part of a building where this has occurred. Frequently it will be found that all the formalities have not been fully complied with and this has caused confusion in the renumbering of *lots*. Whilst it is usual for flats to be available for both residential and professional use, the latter use is not permitted where the *règlement* limits the user to *habitation bourgeoise* exclusively. This does not apply if the user is *bourgeoise simple* when, as is often the case, the block will house the offices of doctors, dentists, lawyers and other professional people in addition to flats in private occupation.

As to the use of the common parts of the block, there is no reason why the *règlements* should not impose reasonable restrictions on flat-owners. Thus, the areas where cars may be parked, what and where professional and other nameplates may be exhibited, the often disobeyed prohibition of hanging washing from balconies and the limiting of areas (for fire safety purposes) in the common parts where objects may be placed by flat-owners are all acceptable. Any rule which prohibits the keeping of domestic animals (except for ferocious guard dogs) in the block is unlawful and in contradistinction to the rule in the US condominium, it is absolutely forbidden to discriminate against any kind of owner on any ground whatsoever.

Service charges

Calculation of service charges

These fall into two categories, those which result from the cost of the utilities available to all flat-owners and those which cover expenses incurred in the general maintenance and upkeep of the *copropriété*. The older blocks have common central heating and hot water systems. This is not economically desirable in the case of blocks where few of the flat-owners are, as is often the case in the well-known holiday areas, permanent residents since the absentee owners pay for heating and hot water for periods when they are not in occupation. Most flats built after about 1980 enjoy individual systems.

Typical costs of the first kind of expenditure will include cable television where installed, the collection of refuse, the maintenance of the lifts and entryphones, carpeting the common areas, and common central heating and hot water systems where installed. These are borne by each *lot* depending on whether it can benefit from such expenditure or not. Hence, flats on the ground floor do not pay in respect of the lifts nor do garages situate in the basement share in the cost of TV aerials or heating or hot water. Expenditure of the second kind includes the cost of insurance of the building, the fees of the *syndic*, the cost of the *concierge* or *gardien*, the expenses of holding meetings of the *copropriété*, the lighting of the complex and the cost of the maintenance of its gardens in addition to the maintenance of the block including its balconies if these are not included in a *lot* which gives the flat-owner their private use. All these expenses are divided out among the flat-owners according to the fractions in the manner described above. These are normally borne by all flat-owners whether they directly benefit from the expenditure or not and are called '*charges générales*'. It is possible to create '*charges spéciales*' so as to differentiate between blocks in a complex with the result that flat-owners pay a proportion of certain expenditure incurred in respect of their block rather than of the whole complex. It is possible also in limited circumstances to exempt certain *lots* from payment of general service charges if the situation of the *lot* merits it.

All *règlements* registered after 1 January 2003 must by virtue of the *Loi SRU* indicate the *quote-part* of each *lot* with respect to each category of expenditure. As from that date, all *règlements* must give the manner in which these shares, on which the payment of service charges for each owner of a *lot* are based, was calculated. In the case of *règlements* registered before 1 January 2003 which may be in part or in whole not in compliance with the most recent requirements of the law, it is supposed that the *syndic* will be able to supply this information.

Not later than five years after the registration of a *règlement* any flat-owner may apply to the Court for the amendment of that document if he considers that his *quote-part* as shown is 25 per cent in excess of what it should be or that the *quote-part* of any other flat-owner is too low by a similar percentage. The Court may revise the amounts if the application is well founded. A similar right is given to a subsequent purchaser of a *lot* if his application is made not later than two years from the date of registration of the offending document. The time limits and the manner in which they apply are complex and presumably when all *règlements* have been amended by the end of 2005, applications of this kind will become even more unusual than they are now. As the law now stands, it is clear that non-registration of a *règlement* does not preclude the making of such an application (Cass.21.11.2000).

Payment of service charges

The legal requirement that all flat-owners must pay their share of the expenses of the *copropriété* is *d'ordre public* and any provision in the *règlement* negativing that requirement in whole or in part is void. This includes any provision relieving a flat-owner from his share of the cost of *gardiennage* (CA Paris 21.2.96).

The Loi SRU has amended the method for the calculation of annual service charges and their collection. Not later than six months after the end of the *copropriété*'s financial year, a general meeting of the *copropriétaires* must be convened to consider the budget for the ensuing year, which is subject to the approval of a simple majority of votes cast. The budget should cover all expenses likely to be incurred 'for the functioning and administration of the common parts and of the equipment for services used in common' but is not to include the estimated cost of works of a nature to be included in a *décret* to be published in due course. The manner of charging these to *copropriétaires* is to be voted on at a separate meeting.

Payment by flat-owners of the service charges as disclosed by the annual budget is to be made by equal quarterly payments presumably in advance although the new Law docs not say so. If the final accounts for any year show a deficiency in the quarterly amounts paid, that deficiency will be added to the first of the next year's quarterly instalments. It is open to the meeting at which the budget is voted on to alter the periods of payment to take account of the current needs of the *copropriété*.

Flat-owners may also vote that each shall pay a given amount into a *fonds de roulement* (float) to provide funds immediately available in case of emergency. Such payments must be credited to separate accounts in the name of each flat-owner. The general rule is that on a sale of a flat in a block where such a payment has been made, the *syndic* will repay the amount paid by the seller to him and require a similar amount from the buyer. There is no law on this and careful enquiries must be made before completion of every sale to make certain that the *syndic* does not in fact merely change the name of the flat-owner in his books, leaving it to the seller and the buyer to resolve the effect of this between themselves.

Only the *syndic* can take the steps necessary to recover unpaid service charges. He has a variety of methods. If any instalment due in respect of any budget remains unpaid for thirty days after service of a final demand by way of *mise en demeure*, the Tribunal de Grande Instance can, by a process akin to Order XIV proceedings (*en référé*), issue an immediate judgment on which he can proceed to execution. If the flat is let, such a judgment can also 'seize' the rents due to the defaulting flat-owner. It should be remembered that whatever may be the terms of any letting as to the payment of service charges, the flat-owner remains liable to the *syndic* for their payment.

In addition, the *syndic* may take other steps. These may be by way of a direct *saisie* (Chapter 14) or he can register a charge against the property if a *mise en demeure* served on the flat-owner remains unsatisfied and such a charge takes effect from the date of its registration. He can also seize the furnishings in the flat. He also enjoys a *privilège immobilier spécial* which arises on the sale of a *lot*. This enables the *syndic*, if he gives notice to the *notaire* dealing with the sale that he intends to *faire opposition* in respect of the proceeds of sale (Chapter 7), to obtain (i) preference for outstanding unpaid service charges and for certain works for the current and two previous years, or (ii) equality with such charges for similar sums but limited to the two preceding years over any charge which the seller may have created in respect of any part unpaid of the sale price and over any lender of money to the buyer.

All unpaid service charges carry interest at the French 'legal rate' which is fixed by decree each year and which was 4.26 per cent in 2002. The *règlement* may provide that no interest shall be payable but may not vary the rate (Cass.11.6.92). A defaulting flat-owner may also be liable to damages for the loss which he has caused to the *copropriété* by, for example, making it impossible to carry out repairs (CA Paris 24.4.98). Actions for the recovery of unpaid service charges become statute-barred at the end of ten years (Cass.11.5.2000).

It should be noted that whilst the period of time expressed in a *mise en demeure* is not affected, French rules of procedure allow for the extension of time for filing a defence when the service of proceedings is out of the jurisdiction of the French courts. On the other hand, the time which it can take to effect service *par voie de diplomatie* can be unconscionably long and the date of hearing may well have arrived before the writ is served. It would appear that on the whole, *syndics* are loath to sue flat-owners. In the light of the new rules as to quarterly payment of service charges, it may well be advisable to attend the meeting at which the annual budget is agreed and then make payments by direct debit from a bank account in France.

As to the special procedures required by law to be followed on the sale of flats in a block, see Chapter 7.

Meetings of the *copropriété*

French law has adapted the standard manner in which companies are managed by providing that the management of the *copropriété* is in the hands of the flat-owners in general meeting whose decisions are carried out by the *syndic* assisted by the *conseil syndical*. Whilst the general principles which govern the functioning of the *assemblée générale* of a *copropriété* will be readily recognized by the English lawyer, some of the detailed procedure is somewhat individualistic and seemingly complex. Non-French flat-owners must bear in mind that a meeting of flat-owners in France provides a welcome opportunity for argument in public and often a noticeable lack of good neighbourliness. In addition, there is a *syndic* on whose unfortunate head all complaints can be heaped. It is certain that a different atmosphere will prevail at such meetings of a *copropriété* in a large town, where all the flat-owners are permanently in occupation and all of whom speak the language, from that in evidence at meetings of blocks of flats many of whose owners are in occupation for holiday periods only and whose needs and financial outlook are therefore somewhat different from those of the permanent inhabitants. An even more difficult situation arises when the meeting is conducted in a language which a large proportion of voters cannot fully understand, still less since most of what is discussed has a technical background unfamiliar to the non-French flat-owner.

Flat-owners may attend by proxy and those who are not able to be present should take advantage of this right. It is of interest to no one to be absent since the lack of one vote cast may lose a resolution which was for the benefit of all. The proxy appointed need not be a flat-owner in the block but one proxy cannot act for more than three flat-owners unless the resultant votes which he controls do not exceed 5 per cent of the total votes of all flat-owners. It is forbidden to appoint the *syndic*, his spouse or nominees as proxy. It is not unusual for flat-owners to send in blank proxy forms leaving it to the chairman of the meeting to fill in suitable names. This is undesirable since he will probably choose as a proxy whoever will vote in the way in which he wants the vote to go. The choice of a proxy in such a situation by the *syndic* and his spouse invalidates the meeting whatever the circumstances may have been (CA Paris 23.1.98). A proxy may vote only on resolutions which appear on the agenda of the meeting. It is generally considered that it is not possible to appoint a permanent proxy (CA Rouen 14.2.96).

These meetings are the moment to ask questions about service charges and the next year's budget. It pays to ask a suitable local expert to attend so that he can explain to the flat-owner in terms of his own law and procedure what has occurred and can raise questions on behalf of the flat-owner in a form understandable by the French *syndic*.

Presence at meetings
It is evident that every flat-owner has the right to attend and vote at meetings. This rule does not apply in the case of flats owned by the *copropriété* itself when the votes attached to such *lots* may not be exercised at any meeting. Otherwise, any act done which prevents a flat-owner from attending and voting at a meeting invalidates the meeting. All meetings are ordinary meetings except those attended by only certain flat-owners who are those whom the *règlement* designates as liable in respect of certain parts of a block only and who can vote only with respect to the upkeep of those parts.

The votes available to each flat-owner correspond to his *quote-part* of the common parts. In the case where one flat-owner owns more than half the number of such *quote-parts*, his voting rights are reduced to a number equal to the number of votes of all the other flat-owners. Thus, if one flat-owner owns 750/1,000 of the common parts, the remaining flat-owners between them own the balance of 250/1,000. The former can use only 250 votes and total amount cast will be 500. This situation arises frequently after completion of the building of a block of flats when there are a number unsold and still in the hands of the developer.

Convening meetings
At least one meeting of the *copropriété* must be held in every year and it is convened by the *syndic*. Meetings may be requisitioned by the *conseil syndical* or by flat-owners having at least one-quarter of the total votes or less if the *règlement* so

permits. If the *syndic* fails within eight days to convene a meeting when requisitioned, it may be convened by the President of the *conseil syndical* failing which any flat-owner may apply to the Court for power to convene himself or appoint another to convene a meeting. Meetings called by the President of the *conseil syndical* without complying with such formalities are without effect (CA Versailles 9.11.2000).

Notices convening a meeting may be sent to flat-owners by registered AR post or may be delivered by hand by, for example, collection from the *gardien* of the block. At least fifteen days' clear notice of the calling of a meeting must be given except in cases of emergency or if the *règlement* provides for a longer notice. It is the duty of the *syndic* to obtain proof of proper notice having been given by the retention of receipts for letters sent by registered AR post or delivered by hand.

The notice convening a meeting must contain the place, date and time of the meeting and an agenda setting out the resolutions to be proposed at the meeting. Only resolutions appearing in the notice may be voted on and no vote may be taken on any business dealt with under the heading of 'any other business'. Different types of resolution are not given names as in England but depend on the kind of majority needed for their passage. Any kind of resolution may be considered at any meeting of the *copropriété* and the length of notice required is not affected. The agenda must show separately resolutions which call for different majorities as well as those which deal with different subjects and failure to do this renders any decisions taken void.

One or more flat-owners or the *conseil syndical* may not later than six days before the date fixed for the holding of the meeting notify the person who has convened the meeting of additional matters which he or they wish to be added to the agenda and these must be made known to all flat-owners not later than five days before the date of the meeting. It is not within the competence of the convener of the meeting to question the propriety of such additional matters unless they are of too imprecise a nature, are not accompanied by documentation enabling those attending the meeting fully to consider the question raised or are of a nature which 'wholly disrupts' the agenda as originally drawn.

Notices must be accompanied by all such documents as may be necessary and appropriate to enable those entitled to attend meetings to vote with full knowledge of the matters involved. Such documents where appropriate include:

(1) full accounts of the past year;
(2) the budget for the ensuing year;
(3) draft amendments to the *règlement*, *état descriptif de division* and *état des charges* if any alterations to these documents are intended;
(4) basic conditions of any estimates or contracts and the like in connection with any works intended to be carried out to the block;
(5) to authorize the *syndic* to institute legal proceedings;
(6) the report of any *administrateur provisoire* appointed to take the place of the *syndic*.

If the meeting called is the obligatory annual general meeting at which the accounts of the *copropriété* are to be approved, all accounts, contracts, information relating to the supply of utilities and services and the like must be available for the inspection of all flat-owners between the date of the service of the notice convening the meeting and the meeting itself.

Meetings should be held in the *commune* in which the block is situate. It has been held that in the absence of any provision to the contrary in the *règlement*, a meeting held in a neighbouring *commune* and notwithstanding that the place of the meeting had been made available free of charge to the *copropriété* was unlawfully held (CA Paris 11.10.96). It has, however, also been held (Cass.10.6.70) that subject to anything contained in the *règlement*, a majority vote of all the flat-owners may decide to hold meetings wherever they wish.

At every meeting an attendance register must be made available and be signed by every flat-owner or his proxy showing his name and address and the number of votes he is entitled to cast. It must be certified as correct by the chairman of the meeting and retained in a special book. It must be made available to any flat-owner on demand.

The chairman and members of his committee (if any) of each meeting are voted ad hoc at the outset of each meeting, the secretary of the meeting being, subject to any vote to the contrary, the *syndic*. Any meeting at which there is no secretary present is invalidly held.

Minutes are kept of the meeting by the *syndic* and signed by the chairman and his committee. They must record the votes cast for and against each separate resolution with the names of those voting, making mention of any objections raised as to such votes and the names of those who abstain from voting. The result of voting is calculated by comparison between the total number of votes present at the meeting as reflected by the attendance register and the manner in which they were cast and the total number of votes of all flat-owners.

Minutes must be kept in a special register. Whilst the failure of the secretary to sign the minutes does not impugn their validity (CA Paris 14.10.94), the meeting of which the minutes are taken is invalid if they do not mention where required the name and address of all flat-owners who attended (CA Paris 6.5.98). Minutes may be amended on a 'slip rule' basis.

It is open only to flat-owners who voted against a resolution or who were not present at the meeting at which it was passed to seek to contest a resolution. Those who abstain are not within this group unless they accompanied their abstention by suitable comments indicative of opposition. A flat-owner who voted for a resolution which was not passed is treated as having opposed it (Cass.24.1.2001). A purchaser from a vendor who has himself instituted proceedings may take over the proceedings if his right to do so is assigned to him before the hearing of the action. Any action seeking to contest a decision of a meeting of flat-owners must be commenced not later than two months after receipt of the minutes recounting such decision which themselves must be sent to flat-owners not later than two months after the date of the meeting. This period is extended in the event that its last day falls on a Saturday, Sunday, Bank Holiday or when there is a strike, to the next working day. The law imposes no penalty on failure on the part of the *syndic* to comply with his time limit but it is an act of negligence on his part for which he may be sued. If the minutes are not sent to flat-owners within the two-month period, they have ten years in which to question the decisions reached at a meeting as they have if the minutes are sent by ordinary and not by registered post.

As has been said above, resolutions are distinguished by the nature of the majority required for their passing. The references are to the relevant articles of the Law of 10 July 1965 as amended by the Loi SRU. Thus, a resolution will be termed as one requiring a '*majorité de l'article 24*' or of whatever article is apposite. The rules are as follows.

1. Article 24. This is the basic rule that resolutions are, unless another type of majority is required by law, passed by a simple majority of votes cast by flat-owners present in person or by proxy. Such resolutions relate mainly to acts of pure administration, such as the day-to-day upkeep of the block and its facade, the utilities serving it, the authority to the *syndic* to institute legal proceedings and the giving of a release to the *syndic*.

2. Article 25. There are twelve cases enumerated by this article where the majority required to pass a resolution is that of a majority of all flat-owners. The most significant are:
   (a) the delegation to an individual to take decisions which otherwise would require an article 24 vote;
   (b) the appointment and removal of the *syndic* and members of the *conseil syndical*;
   (c) a variation in the method of the division of service charges by reason of a change in the user of a flat;
   (d) to approve works designed to economize fuel consumption the cost of which is capable of being amortized within ten years;
   (e) sales of land belonging to the *copropriété* by reason of local or central government requirements and works made necessary by compliance therewith;
   (f) the authorization of certain flat-owners to carry out at their own expense works which affect the exterior of the block or its common parts;
   (g) the provision of facilities for handicapped persons;
   (h) the approval on a permanent basis of the entry of police into the block and its curtilage.

3. Article 26. A two-thirds majority of all flat-owners is required for:
   (a) all sales or purchases of land other than those referred to under 2(e) above;

(b) the amendment or, if necessary, the creation of a *règlement* insofar as it affects the administration, enjoyment, or user of the common parts of a block;

(c) works involving the transformation of, addition to, or improvement of a block other than those which require only an article 25 majority;

(d) works to ensure the security of entry into a block including decisions as to the hours when entry may be prevented, due regard being had to the users permitted by the *règlement*. Outside such hours, a similar decision may only be made by an absolute majority of all flat-owners if they are provided with means of entry by remote control.

4. A unanimous vote of all flat-owners is required to sell any of the common parts of the block the retention of which is necessary having regard to the *destination* of the block. There is no statutory definition of *destination* but it may be judged from its user as shown in documents, its quality and 'social standing', its surroundings and the area in which it is situate.

The *syndic*

The *syndic* may be defined as the executive officer of the *copropriété*. The office may be held by a private individual or by a company. His precise legal status is not clear but it would seem to be that of a *mandataire* (Chapter 19) of the *copropriété*. The office has been held to be of a non-commercial nature when exercised by a person who is not a *commerçant* (that is to say by a person indulging in commercial activities who has a special status in French law) so that an *avocat* may be appointed a *syndic* (Cass.11.7.88). However, no person may be appointed *syndic* of a *copropriété* if he does not hold a *carte professionnelle* given under the same conditions as for estate agents (Chapter 3) and any appointment made in violation of this requirement is void. However, the non-professional *syndic* of a block in which he himself is a flat-owner is exempt from this requirement whether he is remunerated or not.

The *syndic* is appointed in general meeting by a majority of all the *copropriétaires* whether present or not. His re-appointment requires a similar vote and in the event of such a majority vote not being obtained, the procedure initiated by la Loi SRU is as follows. If the appointment or re-appointment does not receive such a favourable majority vote but is agreed to by not less than one-third of all the *copropriétaires*, the meeting may by a simple majority of the votes of such of the *copropriétaires* present in person or by proxy decide forthwith to pass or to reject the resolution. If the resolution is not then passed by a majority of the votes of all the *copropriétaires* present at the meeting, it can be put to a further general meeting called for a date not more than three months thence when the majority needed to ensure its approval will be a simple majority of the votes of those present or represented at the meeting. If no appointment of a *syndic* is then made, the President of the local Tribunal de Grande Instance may on the application of one or more *copropriétaires* nominate a suitable person to hold office until the ensuing general meeting which the *syndic* so nominated is bound to call.

It may happen that when the building of a block has just been completed, a provisional *syndic* is appointed who is frequently the developer himself or a nominee chosen by him. In such cases, this appointment must be ratified (or not) at the first general meeting which must be held within one year from the creation of the *copropriété* in the same manner as for the ordinary appointment of the *syndic*. When such a confirmation is not made, the procedure for an appointment by the Court may be utilized.

The tenure of office of a *syndic* may not exceed three years but it may be for a term ending with the meeting called to approve the annual accounts so long as the total period does not exceed three years. During the period when the *garantie décennale* (Chapter 8) is in force, the period of office of the *syndic* is limited to one year if he or any of his relatives closer than the fourth degree were directly or indirectly involved in the construction of the building. Renewals of the period of office cannot exceed three or one year as the case may be.

It has for a long time been a common practice for the *syndic* to remain in office after the expiration of his term until either his re-appointment or the appointment of another in his place has been voted. By this method, an interregnum was established and the business of the *copropriété* could proceed. It has, however, been decided that all acts done by a *syndic* during this period are void (Cass.14.10.87) and a *syndic* who nevertheless continues to act on a de facto basis is not entitled to remuneration (CA Paris 25.11.98).

A *syndic* may freely resign his office so long as this does not stem from some misconduct on his part and resignation demands no formalities on his part. Resignation takes immediate effect and requires the appointment of a new *syndic* or the nomination of a provisional administrator which any dissatisfied flat-owner may at any time also ask the Court to appoint in place of the *syndic*.

The main duties of the *syndic* are as follows:

1. To ensure compliance with all the provisions of the *règlement* and to give effect to all decisions reached in meetings of the *copropriétaires*. Thus a decision to carry out certain works to the building requires the *syndic* to obtain tenders and report to the *copropriétaires* who decide which to accept.
2. He is charged with the general administration of the *copropriété*, the payment of service charges, the daily upkeep of the buildings forming the complex, their insurance and security and the negotiation for the provision and cost of all services supplied to it.
3. On his appointment and at least once in every three years, he must submit to a general meeting a resolution designed to deal with all expenditure likely to be incurred within the ensuing three years in the maintenance and renewal of all buildings and their equipment.

4. The establishment and carrying into effect of a suitable programme for the maintenance of the buildings over a period of time with particular reference to all matters of insurance connected with such building.
5. In the case of urgent repairs, he must inform the *copropriétaires* and call an immediate meeting. Failure to do this may render him liable to them for any damage suffered by his default by the *copropriété*.
6. He must create and maintain a *carnet d'entretien* (maintenance record) which must contain the following details:
   (a) the address of the building to which it refers;
   (b) the name and address of the *syndic* in office;
   (c) a list of all policies of insurance effected by the *syndic* with their dates of expiry;
   (d) details of all important works carried out to the building such as the replacement of lifts or of the central heating system or renewal of roofs with the details of the firms carrying out the works;
   (e) details of all *dommages-ouvrage* policies currently in force;
   (f) details of all maintenance contracts currently in force with dates of their determination;
   (g) details of the programme of works to be carried out over a period of years voted in general meeting and any other information relating to the building if so decided in general meeting.
7. To deal with the engagement and dismissal of all personnel subject to the decision of the *copropriétaires* in general meeting as to their number and their type of work.
8. To manage the accounts of the *copropriété* including the collection of a 'float' to cover urgent works and to keep his accounts in accordance with statutory requirements. He must keep up-to-date separate accounts for each flat-owner.
9. Within three months of his appointment, the *syndic* must open a bank account in the name of the *copropriété* into which all moneys belonging to it must be forthwith paid. Failure to open such an account involves automatic revocation of his term of office.

For the information of tenants of flat-owners who have no voice in the affairs of the *copropriété*, the *syndic* must cause to be exhibited in the common parts of the block a précis of the decisions taken by the *copropriétaires* which relate to the maintenance of the building and to works being carried out on it.

The most comprehensive and complex accounting rules are laid down for the manner in which the *syndic* is required to keep his accounts and produce annual accounts and budgets to the flat-owners. These are not covered in this chapter. In the first place, to appreciate these rules, it requires a knowledge of French accounting methods which are wholly different from the English methods and involve the use of technical terms, an understanding of which is best left to the

143

accountant. In the second place, the penalties for failure to comply with these rules are severe and it is the task of the *conseil syndical* to ensure that all is kept in order. The accounts submitted to each flat-owner which show his service charge are usually reasonably simple to follow although they are based on accounts which only the expert can comprehend.

The *syndic* is remunerated by decision of the *copropriétaires* by simple majority in general meeting. There are no fixed rules but usually his fees are agreed at a fixed amount per *lot* for standard management work with supplementary fees for special tasks. His fees are subject to VAT but in the case of a non-professional acting as *syndic* of a block in which he is a flat-owner, the French Revenue does not seek to impose this tax.

Every agreement entered into between the *copropriété* and the *syndic*, his family and relations up to the third degree or with any business of which such persons are owners, shareholders or directors must receive the prior authorization of the flat-owners in general meeting.

It is the *syndic* who institutes or defends proceedings on behalf of the *copropriété* and in such actions he may be joined if it is appropriate by one or more of the flat-owners. In such joint actions, the fact that the claim of one of either the *syndic* or the flat-owner cannot be sustained does not adversely affect the claim of the other. This power does not prevent an individual flat-owner from taking action on his own behalf where appropriate. Such cases are in practice limited to those (i) in defence of their ownership of their *lots*, (ii) to compel compliance with the *règlement*, (iii) in respect of claims against neighbouring *lots*, (iv) claims under the *garantie décennale* in respect of *parties privatives* but not those which deal with rights in respect of the *copropriété* as a whole. The claims by the *syndic* are those which deal with the material welfare of the block including (i) claims under any *garantie décennale* in respect of the common parts of the building, (ii) the enforcement of the rules of the *règlement*, and (iii) the recovery of unpaid service charges.

Actions against the *syndic* are undertaken by the flat-owners in such cases as his mismanagement of the affairs of the *copropriété* or to invalidate meetings or to question the contents or effect of the *règlement*.

Whilst the *syndic* may not generally institute proceedings in the name of the *copropriété* without the prior authority of a resolution of the flat-owners, he does not need any such authority to institute proceedings for the recovery of unpaid service charges and a variety of interlocutory steps in that connection or to defend actions instituted against the *copropriété*. He must, however, give immediate notice of such an event to all flat-owners and place the matter on the agenda of the next general meeting. The power to institute proceedings must be given to the *syndic* personally and cannot be exercised by the *conseil syndical*. The invalid institution of proceedings by a *syndic* without such authority can be validated by a subsequent vote of ratification provided that this is passed before the Court gives judgment.

The *conseil syndical*

Every *copropriété* is required to have a *conseil syndical* (executive committee) the task of which is to help and oversee the *syndic* in the exercise of his functions. Having no status in law, it cannot act on behalf of the *copropriété*. Whilst its creation is obligatory, a general meeting may by a two-thirds majority vote decide to dispense with this requirement, being a decision which can be reversed at a subsequent meeting by a vote of the majority of all the flat-owners. If no candidate presents himself or is considered suitable, this fact must be recorded in the minutes and notified to all flat-owners within one month.

Members of this committee are appointed by a majority vote of all the flat-owners but if none is appointed or there is a decision not to appoint such a committee, the Court on the application of the *syndic* or of one or more flat-owners may either appoint members itself or decide that it is not possible to form such a committee.

Members of the committee must be flat-owners or their spouses or legal representatives and may be private individuals or corporate bodies. The spouse of a flat-owner must hold a power of attorney from the flat-owner to act in this capacity but one alone of a number of co-owners may act as of right. The *syndic*, his issue and ascendants and nominees may not be members of this committee.

The functioning of the Executive Committee is laid down in the *règlement* or in default by a resolution of a general meeting. Elected members appoint their own president and determine their own day-to-day procedures. The duties of the committee are:

1. To advise the *syndic* on all questions concerning the *copropriété* and in particular in connection with all contracts and engagements in value exceeding the limit set by the *copropriété* in general meeting. In any event, the committee can consider any matter which it pleases it to consider.
2. To oversee the workings of the *syndic* by taking note of and obtaining copies of all documentation held by him and by consulting any expert of their choice at the cost of the *copropriété*.
3. If so decided by the *copropriété* it can exercise all the administrative powers in respect of which a simple majority vote only of flat-owners present in person or by proxy is required for their exercise.

With the advent of commonhold tenure in England, those with experience of both the French system of the ownership of flats *en copropriété* and the use of the long lease of a flat with the reversion vested in a single landlord may well not consider that the French system (and therefore the novel English system) has any advantages. From a purely practical point of view, the happiness of a *copropriété* depends both on the quality of its *syndic* whose profession is not looked on with much favour by the average French flat-owner and on the character of the individual flat-owners. The legislature has of recent years through a Commission set up by the French government to make recommendations for the improvement of the law relating to the *copropriété* achieved certain successes. Nevertheless, it contains curiosities and novelties for those who are not French and the English purchaser of a flat in France stands in need of considerable advice before he joins the majority of the French in their guise of *copropriétaires*.

16

JOINT OWNERSHIP OF LAND

Introduction 147
Ownership *en indivision* 147
    The management of property *en indivision* 148
    Management under C.civ.arts.815 et seq (Old Statutory Rules) 149
    Management under C.civ.arts.1873-1 et seq (New Statutory Rules) 150
    Partition under the Old Statutory Rules 151
    Partition under the New Statutory Rules 152
Ownership *en tontine* 154
    History of the *tontine* 154
    Uses of the *tontine* 155
    Disadvantages of the *tontine* 156
    Making use of the *tontine* 156

Introduction

There exist in French law three types of co-ownership. These are ownership *en indivision, en tontine* and *en copropriété*. The third form of co-ownership is when applied to realty, for all practical purposes, limited to the ownership of flats forming parts of a single building and is treated separately in Chapter 15. It must be remembered that in the absence of any trust law in France, the interests of each co-owner are in effect individual legal estates in the land so owned.

Ownership *en indivision*

This type of co-ownership, which is the equivalent of English tenancy in common, was originally designed to provide for the vesting in beneficiaries jointly of assets of a deceased person in which they inherited a *quote-part* or undivided share. In that form it is governed by C.civ.arts.815 to 815-16 coming within that part of the *Code civil* which deals with all the aspects of *successions* or the administration of estates. Professor Souleau writes of this type of *indivision* in disparaging terms. 'It was viewed by the Code Napoléon with disfavour, if not with positive dislike, for its economic inconveniences. A plurality of rights over one set of assets favours neither its dynamic management nor its healthy exploitation, stifling as it does any individual initiative. Hence the framers of the Code applied a studied indifference towards the situation, taking the view that it was not worthy of organization. No rules were promulgated as to the management of assets owned *en indivision* so that any action on the part of the *indivisaires* required the unanimous consent of all' (Armand Colin, *Les Successions* (Paris, 1991)).

The management of property en indivision

If the rules applying to this kind of joint ownership arising by operation of law are considered to be unsuitable in the administration and winding up of estates, they are even less satisfactory when they are called into play by operation of the parties on a joint purchase of property. It was ultimately realized that such a system could not remain alone in force and a wholesale reform was effected by the Law of 31 December 1976 with small further adjustments made by the Laws of 10 June 1978 and 6 July 1987.

These amendments are enshrined in C.civ.arts.1873-1 to 1873-18 and enable owners *en indivision* to side-step the old system. It is unfortunate that recourse to these new articles seems to be had only infrequently and articles 815 et seq still apply to the majority of purchases *en indivision*. It is, however, becoming not uncommon for the French to resort to the use of the *société civile immobilière* to avoid the irritations of this type of ownership. Whatever may be the current propensities of the French, it is clear that English co-owners are frequently advised, or at best are permitted, to make use of this form of joint ownership subject to the old rules contained in the earlier articles. Possibly during the life-time of the original owners, some of whom are married couples with no history of previous marriages, the defects of the system do not manifest themselves but this stands grave risks of ceasing to be the situation on the death of one of the co-owners. The presumption is that unless the document of purchase says otherwise (which it very rarely does), this type of co-ownership is on a 50–50 basis. Examples of the unfortunate results which can flow from a purchase *en indivision* are legion. Two examples will suffice.

Example 1   Mr and Mrs A buy a property *en indivision*. Each has two children by previous marriages and they have one child by their current marriage. On the death of either one of the spouses, a proportion of one half of the property must pass to three children. The residue of that half share remains available for the surviving spouse. The other half share is already vested in the surviving spouse. Thus, there are now four co-owners of the property, two of whom are 'strangers' to the other two.

It is true that in certain cases, a surviving spouse can take a life interest in the whole of his or her deceased spouse's estate (but not if the deceased spouse died intestate and there are children by a previous marriage—Chapter 30) but even if he or she does, the best result which can be obtained is an absolute interest in part of a property and a life interest in the other part of a property with the children as remaindermen in respect of that part. In such circumstances management will be carried on in accordance with unsuitable rules such as those described below. The situation is, of course, made worse if infants are involved and will become progressively more complex as the French rules of entrenched inheritance take effect. It must be added that this method of ownership should never be used for the purchase of a property to be occupied by a number of persons on what is tantamount to a time-sharing basis and a suitable alternative is described in Chapter 11.

Example 2   Mr and Mrs B who were not married at the time of the purchase of their property (but who subsequently married) bought *en indivision* as to one half each but subject to a life interest in each other's half share. This is an unsatisfactory method of purchase designed to ensure that the survivor of a couple (as they then were) *en union libre* (Chapter 21) inherits the maximum amount since neither has any inheritance rights. Mr B died before 1 July 2002 intestate leaving, surviving him, both his parents who were entitled to one half of his share subject to his surviving widow's life interest. She by his death became the absolute owner in possession of the other half share. Neither the widow nor the parents could agree a price at which one side might buy out the other. The matter was decided by the Court which after much delay ordered the sale of the property at auction at a considerable loss.

Management under C.civ.arts.815 et seq (Old Statutory Rules)
The primary rule concerning the management of property under these rules is that all the co-owners must agree to all that is done or should be done to the property. There are, however, certain provisions to be found in articles 815-3 to 815-14 which override this rule. Of these, the most important are:

1. The possibility to appoint one of the co-owners to manage the property as *gérant*. This may be by way of a general or a limited mandate, the latter being, for example, needed for the granting of leases and other acts which are not in the nature of day-to-day administration. If one of the co-owners takes on de facto the work of general management without any formal appointment, he is deemed to have been appointed to that task and to undertake the duties and incur the obligations which this entails. No appointment to undertake acts of a special nature can be implied.
2. A *gérant* is entitled to be remunerated in an amount agreed by all the co-owners or in default of agreement by the Court. He is liable to account annually for all income of and expenditure on the property out of which he may retain his remuneration.
3. Each co-owner has the right to use the property subject only to his respecting its designated use and doing nothing which detracts from the rights of his co-owners. A co-owner, who at any time assumes exclusive use of the property, is liable to make a payment to the *indivision* for such use in an amount agreed between all co-owners or, in default of agreement, by the Court. Such payment (*indemnité*) forms part of the income of the *indivision*.

4. A co-owner who properly expends his own money on improvements (*impenses utiles*) or on the maintenance (*impenses nécessaires*) of the property is entitled to reimbursement and article 815-13 expresses the amount to be so taken as the increase in value achieved by such expenditure at the time of partition or sale of the property. On the other hand, a co-owner who commits waste is liable on the same basis for any loss of value to his co-owners.

5. Until 1976, *co-indivisaires* were not entitled to the income of their share until partition. This rule was then amended so that under article 815-11, each co-owner can require payment annually of his share of the income of the property. Payments of this nature become statute-barred after five years, the intention of the rule evidently being to keep the *gérant* alive to his responsibilities.

6. Any co-owner may ask the Court for an advance on his share in the ultimate partition of the property and subject to there being sufficient funds available, this will normally be granted.

Management under C.civ.arts.1873-1 et seq (New Statutory Rules)
Article 1873-1 specifically authorizes all persons who own property *en indivision*, whether their interests are those of an absolute owner in possession or in remainder or of a life tenant, to enter into agreements regulating the management of their property. Such an agreement must be in writing and must define the property to which it refers, show the interests of each co-owner and comply with Land Registry formalities. In addition, articles 1873-2 to 1873-15 apply when there is no life tenancy involved and articles 1873-16 to 1873-18 further apply when such an interest exists. These provide a complex system permitting agreements to be entered into between both those who enjoy interests of the same nature and those who enjoy different interests in the land. It will be appreciated that both life interests and interests in remainder may well arise by reason of such rights in an estate as are given to surviving spouses (Chapters 27 and 30) but are unlikely to be created on a purchase *en indivision* except rarely for *droits de succession* avoidance purposes.

The articles relating to the modern type of management provide:

1. The co-owners may appoint a *gérant* who, in contrast to the statutory rules, need not himself be a co-owner and who fulfils the twin role of administrator of the property and representative of the body of co-owners vis à vis third parties. The manner of his appointment and removal may be decided on by common consent failing which if (i) he is himself a co-owner, it requires a unanimous decision of the remaining co-owners to remove him, or (ii) if he is not a co-owner, his removal is by such means as are provided for in the agreement or in default of any such provision, by the vote of a majority in number and value in the *indivision*. In any event, a *gérant* may be removed by the Court at the request of any co-owner for such failure properly to exercise his powers as imperils the interests of the co-owners.

2. The powers of the *gérant* are wide but are limited to those which are vested in husbands and wives under the rules relating to *régimes matrimoniaux* in respect of their common property (Chapter 20). There are certain other restrictions which have only a very limited application to realty. Any acts which are beyond the powers of the *gérant* require the authority of a unanimous vote of all the co-owners. The disposal of any land within the *indivision* also requires the unanimous agreement of all co-owners or, if this cannot be obtained, an Order of the Court.
3. More than one *gérant* may be appointed and unless the agreement otherwise provides, their powers are joint and several subject to the right of any one *gérant* to object to any action of his *co-gérant* before it has been completed.
4. The *gérant* may be remunerated in such manner as is provided for in the agreement or in default by the Court.
5. Each co-owner may require production by the *gérant* of all papers relating to his administration and the *gérant* must account annually to the co-owners at which time he must disclose all receipts and provide estimates for expenditure for the ensuing year. Each co-owner is required to contribute to the maintenance and preservation of the property *en indivision* and is entitled to share in its profits in such manner as shall be agreed between them and in default of agreement as under the statutory rules enumerated above.

Partition under the Old Statutory Rules

The distinction between *indivisions* governed by the Old Statutory Rules and those by the New Statutory Rules is of far greater significance than the mere matter of the administration of the jointly owned property. The golden rule propounded by the former system is that contained in the forthright wording of C.civ.art.815: '*nul ne peut être contraint à demeurer dans l'indivision et le partage peut toujours être provoqué, à moins qu'il y ait été sursis par jugement ou convention*' (none can be compelled to remain in tenancy in common and may always require partition subject to any judgment or agreement to the contrary). This means that any one *co-indivisaire* can at any moment seek a partition of the co-ownership property and that a majority of co-owners cannot impose the continuation of the joint ownership against the wishes of the minority. The partition of property *en indivision* is a right given to all individual *co-indivisaires*.

It is open therefore to any one *co-indivisaire*, in the face of the refusal of his fellow *co-indivisaires*, to apply to the Court for an Order forcing the partition of the property so owned. However, in a number of cases, such a distribution of the property may have ensuing economic disadvantages. Thus, agricultural holdings usually need a minimum acreage for satisfactory production and family businesses may suffer from the splitting up of their assets. The Court has therefore been given the power, if so requested by any *co-indivisaire*, to refuse the partition of property held *en indivision* for a period of two years if:

151

(1) in respect of the whole or any part or parts of the relevant property an immediate partition of such assets would cause a depreciation in their value; or

(2) within such a period, one of the *co-indivisaires* is unable (for example, because he has not completed his studies) to take part in the management of an agricultural business forming part of the estate.

In cases which are likely to arise only on the death of a co-owner and which underline the fact that these articles are intended to apply only to the partition of the estates of deceased persons, the Court may also at the request of the persons enumerated below refuse to allow a partition to take place for an initial period of five years and thereafter for further similar periods in respect of:

(1) any agricultural unit the management of which was undertaken by the deceased or his or her spouse;

(2) any property in the nature of a private dwellinghouse or if used for business purposes and so occupied by the deceased at the date of his death;

(3) all items including his tools of trade used by the deceased in connection with his business or profession.

The persons entitled to seek such an Order of the Court are:

(1) if the deceased left issue of which one or more is an infant, by the surviving spouse or by any beneficiary or by the person entitled to act on behalf of any infant; and

(2) if the deceased left issue none of which is an infant, by the surviving spouse provided that he or she was prior to, or by reason of the death of the deceased, became the co-owner with the deceased of any of the above-mentioned assets and in the case of any private dwellinghouse had resided therein at the date of the death of the deceased spouse.

Finally power is given to the Court to effect a partial partition by ordering a distribution of the appropriate share of the co-owner who wishes to be quit of his co-ownership whilst leaving the remainder of the property *en indivision*. In order to achieve such an Order, it is necessary that at least two among the *co-indivisaires* refuse to consent to a partition.

Partition under the New Statutory Rules
Under this system, the co-owners are enabled in considerable measure to make their own arrangements for the future of property held *en indivision* and override the provisions of articles 815 et seq. This may be achieved for one of two periods at the choice of the co-owners.

Period 1   This may be for any length of time not exceeding five years but may be made renewable at its term for a like maximum period either by express or tacit consent. If the agreement is not so renewed, it falls to the ground and the Old

Statutory Rules will thenceforth apply. When such an agreement is in force, partition can only be required for *justes motifs* or good cause for which there appears to be no definition but of which examples would be serious errors of management by a co-owner or a serious misunderstanding between the co-owners.

Period 2   An agreement of this kind may also be entered into for an indeterminate period. This seems at first glance to achieve a situation little better than that which exists under the Old Statutory Rules since partition can be requested at any time. Nevertheless, an agreement for such a period does place somewhat more restraint on the ability of a *co-indivisaire* to seek partition since such a demand is acceptable only if it is not made for reasons *'de mauvaise foi ou à contretemps'*. This is a remarkably imprecise proviso for a draftsman of legislation which provokes the possible translation of 'lack of good faith or for reasons of pique' or as has been suggested by one French lawyer as 'pure animosity'.

As an owner of a recognized form of property, each *co-indivisaire* has prima facie an undoubted right to dispose of or otherwise deal with it. Sales of what in English law are undivided shares in land are rare in France and depending on the method chosen may represent serious legal disadvantages. If what is sold is a determined part of the overall property *en indivision*, the sale of that asset is not void but its effect depends on the future partition of the overall property. It can only become retrospectively valid on partition if that asset is by that transaction specifically distributed to the vendor. If on the other hand, what is sold is a *quote-part* or undivided share in the net global assets of an estate, this is treated as a substitution of the owner of the rights, which the purchaser acquires by virtue of C.civ.art.815-14 'all or some of the rights' in the *quote-part*.

However, there are limits on the disposal by a co-owner of his interest in property held *en indivision*. Prior to the reforms initiated in 1976, such a disposal by a co-owner gave rise to the *retrait successoral* or right of the other co-owners to compel the purchaser to sell back to them the share which he had acquired at the price which he had paid. This was intended to preserve the family unity of the assets and prevent a stranger from becoming a co-owner without the consent of all concerned. This rule has been replaced by a right of pre-emption given to all co-owners. The present rule contained in C.civ.art.815-14 applies to all sales but not to gifts or transfers not for value of undivided shares or if the person intended to acquire the share is already a co-owner. It applies, however, on a sale by the remainderman of an undivided share of his interest to the life tenant who is considered to be a stranger to the *indivision*.

The rigid procedure to be followed depends on whether the sale is to be *à l'amiable* or an agreed transaction or is *par adjudication* following a decision of the Court authorizing a partition of part of the property to one of the *co-indivisaires*. In the case of an ordinary sale, the services of a *huissier* (see Chapter 1) must be used for the service of the documents which are required. When a sale *par adjudication* is involved, it is normal for these to be served by the *avocat* or *notaire* dealing with the case. Failure to follow the prescribed procedure renders void both the intended transactions.

In the case of a sale *à l'amiable*, three stages are involved:

1. The service of notice on the co-owners with rights of pre-emption of the intended sale detailing the sale price, the general conditions of sale and the name, address and profession of the intended purchaser.
2. The acceptance of the terms within one month of the service of the above notice by the recipients, failure to reply to it within one month being treated as a refusal.
3. If the offer is accepted, completion of the sale to the co-owners must take place within two months of the dispatch of the acceptance of the offer by the co-owners.

In the case of a sale *par adjudication*, it is necessary:

(1) to give notice to all the co-owners who enjoy a right of pre-emption not later than one month before the date set by the Court for completion of the intended transfer of the undivided share;
(2) in case any co-owner wishes to be substituted for the purchaser named in the Order of the Court, he must during that period of one month give notice of that wish either to the Court or to the *notaire* dealing with the transaction.

Sales by auction in pursuance of an Order of the Court are described in Chapter 13.

Ownership *en tontine*

History of the tontine

The effect of the joint ownership of property in this manner produces a result akin to that which flows from English joint tenancy, namely ownership of the property automatically passes on the death of one co-owner to the surviving owner(s) until it vests in the ultimate survivor. There the resemblance ceases. The essential elements which must be present in every co-ownership *en tontine* are (i) the conditions to which it must be subject and (ii) the element of *aléa* which must also be present. The application of these elements has been admirably described by Me Pacaud and Me Pujol in a paper read before the 87th *Congrès des Notaires* held at Montpellier in May 1991 thus: 'Each purchaser is the owner of the property purchased subject to the condition precedent of his survival and the condition subsequent of his death. Thus the surviving owner has been the sole owner of the property since the date of purchase and the deceased co-owner is deemed never to have had an interest in the property. C.civ.art.1179 provides that the fulfilment of a condition has effect retrospectively to the date upon which it was imposed. Hence, there is no interest in the property which can form part of the deceased co-owner's estate.' Such a kind of co-ownership requires no intervention by trustees and the comments of Turner LJ in the case of *Oldfield v Preston* [1861] 45 ER 939 highlight the difference between the French *tontine* and the English tontine and its English counterpart of today, joint tenancy. He said 'Neither the investment of the funds (of a tontine), the distribution of the income nor the ultimate division of the capital could be affected (sic) otherwise than by the interposition of trustees.'

The tontine was the brainchild of a Neapolitan banker, Lorenzo Tonti (1630–95) and was widely used in Italy, France and the Netherlands for the purpose of raising state loans. It seems to have made its first appearance in England in 1674 when a proposal to raise funds by the use of a tontine was published by the Corporation of London. The last time it was used by the British government to raise funds was in 1789 by an Act entitled 'An act for raising a certain sum of money by way of Annuities to be attended with the Benefit of Survivorship in Classes', this Act not being repealed until 1887 by the Statute Revision Act of that year. There are still a few hotels and inns which bear the name of The Tontine of which perhaps the most famous is The Tontine Hotel in Peebles built by French prisoners of war between 1806 and 1808 with funds provided by a tontine of 158 subscribers of £25 each. The tontine in English law is now a thing of the past, meriting only a passing reference in *Halsbury's Laws of England* as 'a type of Friendly Society'. It is very much alive in France and its use can be of vital significance.

The French legal history of the *tontine* is unusual. The first reported case on the *tontine* appears to be that heard in the Cour de Cassation on 26 April 1854. This was a Revenue case in which the tax authorities appealed against a decision at first instance that no *droits de succession* were payable on the death of a co-owner *en tontine*. The appeal failed on the grounds that the passing to the surviving co-owner(s) was not by reason of a death but of the terms of the contract creating the *tontine* itself, the death only establishing the date of the passing.

No case dealing with the validity of a purchase *en tontine* seems to have come before the French courts again until 1928 when the Cour de Cassation heard the case of *Epoux Patient-Marty c/ Epoux Chevalier-Marty* on 26 April of that year on appeal from the Toulouse Court of Appeal which confirmed a judgment of the Civil Court at Moissac. This case related to a conveyance under which the purchasers bought *en indivision* but subject to a *clause d'accroissement en tontine*. Not surprisingly, in view of this apparent contradiction, the Court expressed the view that it seemed that neither the *notaire* who drew the document nor the parties who executed it 'understood its effect in law'.

Uses of the tontine
The *tontine* when used in its most simple form is one of the basic methods of avoiding the effect of the rules of entrenched inheritance in contradistinction to ownership *en indivision* by enabling a surviving co-owner to 'inherit' the property free of the rights of any *réservataire*. The use of this type of co-ownership

both in its simple and more complex forms as a method of avoiding the effect of the *réserve* is developed in Chapter 29.

Disadvantages of the tontine

If ownership *en tontine* suffers from any disadvantages they are that co-owners *en indivision* cannot switch into ownership *en tontine* and that it cannot be dissolved except by consent between the co-owners. The former can be circumvented but disagreement between co-owners on, say, a divorce may prove a more serious element but not one which should normally affect a decision to make use of this kind of co-ownership. It is considered that an Order of the Family Division can cure any such problem. It also has the effect of making it difficult to obtain a loan secured on a property which is directly owned *en tontine* since so long as the original co-owners are alive, the property belongs to no one. This can be overcome usually, for example, by the interposition of a company, the shares of which are owned *en tontine* or by fairly simple conveyancing methods and a helpful lender. It also has the result of protecting the property from the creditors of the or one of the co-owners since there is nothing against which a creditor can proceed.

Making use of the tontine

It is thought that now all *notaires* understand the effect of the *pacte tontinnier* or *clause d'accroissement* by which terms the *tontine* is formally known and indeed Me Morin in an article in the *Journal des Notaires*, art 33114 considers that in its present form the clause is the work of an astute *notaire* and that 'so spectacular a result could not be obtained without provoking objections'.

The least valid of such objections would seem to be that it avoids the effect of the *réserve*. It may be that there are French owners who consider that they still owe a duty to preserve the *patrimoine familial* although this is becoming less and less a strongly held view. This cannot be a good reason for the English not to resort to its use in order to preserve the familiar freedom of testamentary disposition. It seems safe, therefore, to disregard the cry of a learned French Professor of Law uttered as late as 1987 that the *tontine* is a 'fraud on the marriage contract' and to prefer the view of Me Revillard, *Droit International Privé et Pratique Notariale* (5th edn, Defrénois, 2001) that it is 'now à la mode'.

Nevertheless, the creation of an ownership *en tontine* requires adherence to certain rules.

1. It must contain a genuine element of *aléa* (chance). Thus, each purchaser must stand an equal chance of survival so that, without being able to lay down any firm guidelines, the respective ages of the co-owners and their states of health are relevant.
2. The purchase must be genuinely for good consideration (*à titre onéreux*) and not in the nature of a gift.

3. It is desirable that the purchase price should be provided equally by each co-owner out of his or her own resources. This is particularly the case when the purchasers are husband and wife. It is for this reason that the share of the price should be furnished to the *notaire* acting for them by each spouse individually and preferably from the separate bank account of each. It has been held that where a husband and wife were buying with the aid of a loan for the repayment for which they both were liable it was not possible to go behind the *acte de vente* which recited this fact and that joint and several liability in respect of the mortgage indicated that each must have provided the balance of the price (CA Aix-en-Provence 13.12.88).

It remains, nevertheless, to consider what a disillusioned *réservataire* can do to upset a *clause d'accroissement* on the death of a co-owner. It is, of course, possible to ask the Court to declare the arrangement void on the grounds that the requirements 1 and 2 above have not been fulfilled. If the purchase has been properly organized, this should not be a viable method of attack. If made with success on the grounds that the *tontine* is void for lack of *aléa*, the property will be deemed to be held *en indivision* and recourse by the heirs can only be had to the deceased co-owner's undivided share of the property. If the *tontine* is upset on the grounds that it was in the nature of a gift from one co-owner to another, what is recoverable is the appropriate share in the value of the property at the date of death of the co-owner.

Generally speaking, any claim against a *pacte tontinnier* which has been properly constructed should fail for it has been held that purchasers *en tontine* may rely on the relevant facts related in the *acte de vente*. It must be admitted that this is prima facie evidence only and the Court may look at other evidence against the arrangement which usually it will be almost impossible to adduce.

Finally, the *clause d'accroissement* can prove to be the touchstone of the quality of advice given on the purchase of property to those who like the English have freedom to dispose on their death of their property as they wish. As has been said, since 1928 the French tax authorities had been concerned that on the death of one co-owner *en tontine*, no French inheritance tax was chargeable but only an amount equivalent to the stamp duty charged on a sale. This was amended by the French Finance Act of 1980 so that thereafter inheritance tax became, subject to certain exceptions, charged on the proportion of value of the property which the deceased co-owner bears to the total number of co-owners. Thus the situation in France is now as it has always been in the United Kingdom but it is still thought of by the French as a fiscal disaster. Hence, despite all the advantages which can accrue to the English from the use of this method of co-ownership, many French advisers will warn against the use of the *tontine* because of its 'tax disadvantages'. To do so when the tax situation is precisely what the English would expect it to be clearly indicates a failure to implement the basic rule that when advising an English person on French law it is essential to know or at least discover ad hoc what is the English law on the subject. Advice not to make use of the *tontine* because of the inheritance tax 'disadvantages' which can ensue should itself, together possibly with the giver of such advice, be treated with much reserve.

It must, however, be appreciated that the use of the *tontine* achieves a specific result, namely that of vesting the co-owned property in the surviving co-owner. It does not remove the property thereafter from the clutches of French succession law so that those entitled to inherit on the death of the survivor as *réservataires* will take. It also may effect a switch of assets from one family to another, if, for example, two spouses who each had children by previous marriages purchase *en tontine*. On the death of one spouse, the totality of the asset vests in the survivor and the children of that deceased spouse have no rights whatsoever on the death of the surviving spouse. There is also the problem that if that surviving spouse wishes to give back to the children of the deceased spouse what they have lost by the use of the *tontine*, those children will pay, as strangers in blood, French inheritance tax at 60 per cent.

17

RESIDENTIAL LEASES

Introduction 159
The extent of the Loi Mermaz 160
    The rent 161
    Lessors' and lessees' obligations 162
    Lessor's obligations 162
    Lessee's statutory obligations 163
    The contents of the lease 164
    Term of the lease 165
    Lessee's notice to quit 166
    Determination during the term of the lease 166
    Lessor's rights at the end of the term 167
    Lessee's rights at the end of the term 168
    Renewal of leases 168
    Re-entry provisions 169
    Seasonal lettings 169
    Furnished lettings 170

Introduction

It is of interest to note that as a result of a survey carried out by the French government in 2001, it was discovered that 45 per cent of the population of France lived in rented accommodation compared to 19 per cent in Great Britain. Landlord and tenant law in France therefore plays a considerable part in the life of the French citizen.

The fundamental law on this subject is to be found in C.civ.arts.1709 to 1778. These articles cover the leasing of properties under what are known in French law as *baux de droit commun* (translatable as basic statutory law and not as common law). However, in certain important respects, this law is overlaid with the effect of special legislation which applies broadly to leases of premises for private occupation. A fair analogy would be to describe the law in England relating to leases as that enacted in Part V of the Law of Property Act 1925 but subject to the effect of various other Acts including and in particular the various Rent Acts when in force.

The extra-*Code civil* rules relating to the leasing of private dwellinghouses apply only to those which are the principal residence of the lessee. This is defined as the place where the lessee resides for at least eight months in every year unless his occupation or some other valid reason requires a shorter period. It follows that a property let for use by the lessee as his secondary residence is subject to the relevant articles of the *Code civil*. It is of course immaterial whether the property is the principal or secondary residence of the lessor. Lettings involving the English as either lessor or lessee are likely to be in the nature of 'holiday lettings'. They are also free of the extra-*Code civil* legislation.

France came much later to the all-embracing legislation envisaged by the English Rent Acts. A measure of protection was afforded by the Law of 1 September 1948 but it was not until 1981 that the then Socialist government produced a nationwide tenant protection measure known as the Loi Quillot after its introducer. Warnings of the effect it would have on the letting market went unheeded but proved correct and this measure was in 1986 amended by the Loi Méhaignerie. Subsequently, this second Law was amended by the Law of 6 July 1989 known as the Loi Mermaz, which, after further amendments by three further Laws and four *décrets* or statutory instruments, currently provides the law which impinges with considerable effect on the letting of the majority of French dwellinghouses for private or for mixed private and professional occupation. The principal objects of the Loi Mermaz are to protect the lessee in possession and only to a limited extent to control rents. It also provides the background to the obligations of both lessor and lessee.

The rules enacted by the Loi Mermaz are *d'ordre public*. It is suggested that whilst normally such a designation makes it impossible for all the parties involved to contract out of their requirements, in this case the rules are solely for the benefit of the party they are intended to protect, namely the lessee. If this is correct, once a lessee has executed his lease and is therefore in a position to know what are his rights and that he can enforce them, he can waive them (Cass.27.10.75). The decision seems strange but in any event, as will be seen, few lessees are likely to take advantage of it.

The extent of the Loi Mermaz

This Law specifically applies only to private dwellinghouses and their appurtenances including those in which the lessee, who must be a private individual, carries on his profession as well as using the demised premises as a principal residence. It is for the Courts to decide if premises are in fact so used (Cass.16.6.99). The Cour de Cassation has also held that a lessee whose lease permits private and professional user must use at least part of the demised premises for his personal occupation to benefit from his rights of renewal described below since such benefits are intended to be basically for the protection of lessees who occupy premises as their home even if a mixed user is permitted to them. It should be remembered that until recently a large number of professional people carried on their profession from home and although this is now less frequent, it was considered necessary that legislation as recent as 1989 provide this special protection.

The Loi Mermaz does not apply to:

(i)   furnished lettings;
(ii)   service tenancies;
(iii)   seasonal or 'holiday' lettings;
(iv)   secondary residences;
(v)   lettings to companies;
(vi)   lettings with a mixed residential and commercial user.

The rent

The rent which may be charged is free of all control if it is in respect of a new letting but not in the case of the renewal of a lease. If a lessor is willing to renew a lease but considers that the rent reserved by the expired lease is too low, he must follow the requirements of article 17 of the Loi Mermaz. He must serve on the lessee not later than six months before the expiration of the lease a notice offering a new lease at the proposed new rent and three examples of rents for comparable premises in the area. Six examples are required for premises in the Paris, Lyon or Marseille areas. The notice must include verbatim article 17 which defines this procedure. The lessee must not later than four months before the lease expires serve a counter-notice either consenting to the new rent or refusing the offer. Failure to reply within this time is deemed to be a refusal. In the case of a disagreement as to the amount of the rent, the matter is referred to the *commission départementale de conciliation*. If either party does not agree the new rent so found, he can apply to the Court which will then fix the rent. In such circumstances, care must be taken to refer the matter to the Court before the expiration of the lease or it will be automatically renewed.

The new rent is payable by instalments over a period of six years if the lease is for that term or otherwise over three years if the term is for three years or the increase is less than 10 per cent. Thus, if the monthly rent of an old lease for three years was Euro 310 and the new rent is agreed at Euro 330, monthly rent will be payable under the new lease as follows:

First year   Euro 310 + 20/3   = Euro 316.66
Second year   Euro 316 + 20/3   = Euro 323.32
Third year   Euro 323.32 + 20/3   = Euro 330

In addition, it is open to the parties to agree either that the lessor or the lessee will carry out certain works to the premises and that such works shall be taken into account by varying upwards or downwards the new rent. It must also be remembered that if the lease contains a rent revision provision, this must be by reference to the Cost of Construction Index which is issued quarterly. Such indexation would apply to any renewed lease and therefore to the figures quoted above.

Although not treated as rent, it is convenient to refer to two other payments for which provision is made in most leases. It is almost inevitable that a lessor will require a deposit to be lodged with him by the lessee to cover possible breaches of covenant. Article 22 of the Loi Mermaz provides that it may not exceed in amount two months' rent. Such a deposit may not be asked if the lessee pays rent more than two months in advance but if a lessee who pays his rent quarterly in advance asks (as he has the right to do) to pay in the future monthly in advance, the lessee may then require payment of a deposit. The deposit must be repaid not later than two months after the lessee has quit the premises and the proportion of the deposit which will be forthcoming will depend on the result of the *état des lieux* or Schedule of Dilapidations. A deposit not repaid in its proper amount or in due time carries interest.

Many lettings are of flats in blocks. The lessee is required by law to pay a proportion of the service charges payable by the lessor. The lessor is allowed to ask for payments on account of this expense at the same time as he is paid rent but once a year these payments must be finalized. The lessor is required a month before asking for this final payment to give his lessee a full account of the figures involved which are themselves available to the lessor in his capacity as *copropriétaire*.

Lessors' and lessees' obligations
In such cases to which the Loi Mermaz does or does not apply, these are substantially those laid down by the relevant articles of the *Code civil*. They also apply to leases subject to the Loi Mermaz to the extent that they are not excluded or modified by it.

Lessor's obligations
These are as follows:

1. That the demised premises if they are the principal residence of the lessee are a *logement décent*. This results from an amendment by the Loi Mermaz to C.civ.art.1719 that premises qualify for that description if they do not present any evident risk which might cause harm to the physical safety or the health of the lessee and which include such fittings as render it fit for use as living accommodation. This does not imply that premises must be 'as new' at the commencement of each letting but they must be fit for the immediate occupation by the lessee. If the premises fail to conform to such a standard, the lessee may require the lessor to take such steps as are necessary to achieve such conformity. If the lessor fails to undertake the necessary works, the lessee may obtain an Order of the Court which sets out the works necessary to achieve such an end and the time within which the work must be completed. Failure on the part of the lessor to comply with such an Order can lead to a reduction in the rent reserved.

2. That the demised premises are in a good state of repair and the household fittings referred to in the lease function properly. Such a definition takes account of the age of a building so that, for example, windows and doors

normally reflecting its age are not considered to be in a bad state of repair (CA Paris 25.2.82).

3. That the demised premises must be free from defects which would adversely affect its use save those to which reference is made in the *état des lieux*.
4. To give quiet enjoyment of the demised premises.
5. To keep the demised premises in a state of repair to enable them to be used for the purpose for which they were leased and to carry out all necessary repairs other than those which are the liability of a lessee.
6. Not refuse permission to the lessee to carry out works to the demised premises so long as these are limited to works of interior reorganization and do not affect the main structure of the building.
7. To provide on demand the lessee with receipts for all payments received, distinguishing between rent, service charges, and other amounts.
8. To permit the lessee to pay his rent monthly if he so requests.

Lessee's statutory obligations
These are as follows:

1. To pay the rent and any service charges payable in accordance with the terms of the lease.
2. To use the demised premises *en bon père de famille*, that is to say to respect the user authorized by the lease and not to cause any annoyance or inconvenience to other occupants of the building or to the neighbourhood.
3. To undertake the repairs to the demised premises (*réparations locatives*) set out in the *décret* of 26 August 1997. This is a long but not exhaustive list of what a lessee is required by law to do. There seems to be no firm legislation or judicial finding on precisely the full extent of this liability. The generally accepted view is that it is for the Court on each occasion to decide whether a repair is *locative* so that it falls on the lessee or not. It will be reasonable to assume that a lessee is liable to keep the demised premises in a good condition, damage caused by force majeure or by the lessor or by the acts of a third party who is not an invitee excepted. The element of 'fair wear and tear' is perhaps less prominent than it is in an English lease.
4. To permit the lessor to enter the demised premises in order to carry out improvement works to the common or private parts of the building and also maintenance works for the benefit of the demised premises.
5. Not to carry out any alterations to the demised premises without the consent of the lessor.
6. To insure against all risks for which a lessee is normally liable such as would be covered by a normal householder's comprehensive policy and to produce evidence of such cover annually.
7. Not to assign or underlet without the written consent of the lessor, such consent to include agreement as to the rent payable by a subtenant. Such a

consent can go further than in England since a lessor may require the joint and several guarantee of lessee and sublessee and to join in the assignment or sublease. An assignment is void as against the lessor if he is not a party to it unless notice of its execution has been served on him by a *huissier*. This requirement stems from the wording of C.civ.art.1689 dealing with the assignment of *droits incorporéals* and mirrors the provisions of section 136 (1) of the Law of Property Act 1925.

8. To permit the lessor and those authorized by him to visit the demised premises with a view to its sale or reletting for periods of not more than two hours on working days.

The contents of the lease

All leases must be in writing but curiously, although either party can insist on adherence to this requirement, it provides no penalty for failure to comply. In any event, a verbal letting agreement is much to the disadvantage of the lessor since, not only will he have difficulty in proving the date of the commencement of the term which, as will be seen from what is said hereafter, can be of considerable importance, but any provisions for rent reviews and the payment of a deposit must be reduced to writing to be enforceable.

All leases must provide the following information:

(1) a full description and address of the lessor;
(2) the date of the commencement of the term;
(3) a full description of the premises, its permitted user and of all fittings and fixtures of which the lessee has the sole use or use in common with others;
(4) the rent and its times of payment and any provisions for its revision;
(5) the amount of any deposit paid.

The following clauses, if contained in a lease, are void. These are those which:

(1) require the payment of rent by direct debit of the lessee's bank account or directly by his employers from his salary or by postdated cheques or promissory notes;
(2) require the lessee to insure only with a company of the lessor's choice;
(3) provide for the payment by the lessee of any sum in respect of damage for which he is liable on a basis estimated in advance by the lessor;
(4) permit the lessor to limit any service provided for by the lease without a corresponding reduction in the rent;
(5) provide for the determination of the lease for the breach by the lessee of any covenant other than for non-payment of rent, service charges, any deposit or the failure to effect a householders' comprehensive policy;
(6) permit the lessor to impose a charge for any failure on the part of the lessee to observe and perform the covenants in the lease or the internal regulations of the building;

(7) permit the lessor in the case of his wishing to sell or relet the premises to visit or cause them to be visited on non-working days or during more than two hours on working days.

It seems clear from some of the information which must be included in a lease and some of the clauses designated that it was supposed by the legislature that most leases will (as in fact will be the case) be leases of flats in blocks *en copropriété*. In such cases the lessor is obliged to provide the lessee with extracts of the *règlements* (Chapter 15) relating to the use of and obligations in respect of the *parties privatives et communes* and certain other information.

It is required that a Schedule of Condition (*état des lieux*) be prepared prior to the handing over of the keys to the lessee and annexed to the lease. This should be organized by the parties at joint cost in the presence of both of them. If one party is recalcitrant, this must be done by a *huissier* also at joint cost when each party will be advised by him of a date to attend not less than seven days ahead. The *état des lieux* should be prepared in two copies of which each should be signed by lessor and lessee and then annexed to the lease. It has been held (Cass.23.5.02) that the statutory requirements are satisfied if only one copy is made and held by the lessor so long as it has been signed by both parties. A lessee fails to have an *état des lieux* prepared at his peril since the presumption under C.civ.art.1731 that the premises were let in a good and tenantable condition cannot be invoked by whichever of the parties to a lease has 'hindered' the making of this Schedule. It is perhaps not unexpected that many lessors easily overlook the making of an *état des lieux* on the grant of a lease but never forget to have made a Schedule of Dilapidations (also called an *état des lieux*) made at the determination of the lease. The costs incurred in the granting of a lease are borne equally by lessor and lessee.

Term of the lease

Every lease to which the Law applies must be for a term of not less than (i) three years if the lessor is a private individual or a *société civile* the shareholders of which are all fairly close members of one family or are owners *en indivision* or (ii) six years if the lessor is a company. The lessee must be a private individual. The distinction is governed by the quality of the parties at the commencement of the term so that the sale of the reversion from one type of lessor to another or an assignment by the lessee to another who is not a private individual has no effect in this respect.

To this rule, which is otherwise absolute, there is an exception. A lease may be entered into for a term of not less than one nor more than three years if the lessor is a private individual or the equivalent as described above and the lease gives a clear reason which would enable the lessor to retake possession 'for professional or family reasons'. The reason must be precise such as that the lessor will wish to live there himself or to house close members of his family. 'Family reasons' has been held (CA Paris 19.2.91) not to be sufficiently precise and 'the need to live in Paris within a two-year period for professional or family reasons' has also been found insufficient to enable a short term to be granted (Cass.14.12.94).

Not later than two months before the date of determination of such a lease, the lessor must confirm to the lessee the happening of the agreed event or put off the date of that event to an agreed date. He can use this facility only once. If the event takes place as arranged, the lessee must quit the premises and if he remains an Order of Possession may be made against him.

If the event referred to in the lease does not happen or if it is not confirmed to him by the lessor, the lessee is then deemed to have a lease for a term of three years from the date of its commencement whatever the term stipulated in the lease may have been.

Lessee's notice to quit
The lessee may give notice to quit at any time during the term by three months' previous written notice served on the lessor either by registered AR post or by a *huissier*. No reason for determination need be given. In certain cases, this notice may be reduced to one month. These are:

(1) if the lessee changes or loses his employment or loses a new employment following on a previous change or loss of employment. This does not apply to the completion of a training course or professional apprenticeship for adults. Nor can a lessee who is a member of a *profession libérale* (learned profession) avail himself of this short form of notice. Resignation is not treated as a loss of employment (CA Paris 30.10.97); negotiated redundancy can, however, be so considered (CA Paris 10.2.98);
(2) if the lessee is aged more than sixty years and the state of his health is such as to justify a change of residence;
(3) if the lessee is in receipt of *revenu minimum d'insertion* (Social Security Income Support).

In such cases, the notice to quit must be served to take effect as closely as possible to the relevant reason justifying its service (Cass.21.7.99) and the notice need not specify the reason permitting short notice to be given which can be proved at a later date (Cass.8.12.99). Such a notice to quit given at too early a date is not bad but takes effect only from the date on which it ought to have been served.

Determination during the term of the lease
The total accidental destruction of the premises comprised in the lease results in the determination of the term by operation of law (C.civ.art.1722). Partial destruction gives rise to a right on the part of the lessee to demand either the determination of the lease or a suitable reduction in the rent.

In the case of the abandonment by the lessee of the premises or his death, the following rules apply. The lease remains in force and its benefit vests in one or other of: (i) the spouse of the lessee; (ii) the issue or the parents or the *concubin notoire* of the lessee who have been living with him for at least a year before he abandoned the premises; (iii) the other party to his PACS (Chapter 21). This right, in the case of the death of the lessee, is subject to the surviving spouse's preferential right to an interest in the premises (Chapter 30). If in either case there are no such persons entitled to have the lease vested in them, it automatically determines.

Lessor's rights at the end of the term
The lessor may give notice to quit, that is, refuse to renew the lease on the grounds that:

1. He intends to live on the premises himself. This right is available to any lessor who is entitled to limit the term of the lease which he grants to three years. The intended occupation can be by the lessor himself or by his spouse, his PACS partner or *concubin notoire* of at least one year's standing, his issue or parents or those of his spouse or of those other persons. His notice need not go into details beyond that he require the premises for the occupation of himself or of those mentioned in the Law. The occupation must be as a principal residence and a lessor who claims vacant possession on these grounds but does not occupy the premises is liable in damages to his lessee (Cass.19.4.2000). But a lessor who gave notice to quit on the grounds that he intended to occupy the premises himself and a subsequent deterioration in his health made it necessary to sell the premises was held to be not so liable (CA Paris 10.2.94).
2. He intends to sell the premises. In such a case, the notice to quit must set out a firm sale price and all the significant conditions of sale. A notice which lacks any of these details is void. The notice must also contain an offer to sell all the premises comprised in the lease. This offer must in accordance with the provisions of *la Loi SRU* (Chapter 3) give the precise area of the premises and also the *quote-part* in the case of a flat but need not have annexed a copy of the *règlements de copropriété*. The identity of a proposed seller need not be disclosed; indeed, it is not necessary that such a person exists at the time of the service of the notice. It is sufficient that the lessor has the intention to sell to enable him to serve such a notice.

Service of such a notice creates in favour of the lessee a right of pre-emption at the price and on the conditions mentioned in the notice. The lessee has then the choice between accepting the offer within the appropriate period or of ceasing to have any interest in the premises. He must exercise this choice within two months of the service on him of the notice to quit. Exercise of the right of pre-emption binds the lessee to sign the *acte de vente* drawn based on the offer to sell subject only to the Loi Scrivener condition if he is seeking mortgage finance (Chapter 3).

The statutory period of two months may be shortened by agreement with the lessee who can also within that period renounce his right of pre-emption. Acceptance by the lessee of the offer has the effect of prolonging the term of the lease (if this is necessary) to the date of completion of the sale. The date for completion is not more than two months from the date on which the lessee accepted the lessor's offer or, if he is seeking mortgage finance, four months from such date. Failure to complete on the due date deprives the lessee of all rights of occupation.

The Law in its original form dealt with the situation which might arise if the lessor, the lessee having decided not to buy, sold to a third party on terms more advantageous to that buyer than those he had offered to the lessee. To eliminate this fraud on the lessee, the Law gave him a right to substitute himself for the ultimate buyer, it being the duty of the *notaire* who acted in the sale to report it to the lessee. This gave rise to certain practical difficulties and the problem was resolved in another manner by the Law of 21 July 1994. This gave to the lessee a second right of pre-emption which arises when the lessor decides to sell to a third party on terms more advantageous than those offered to the lessee. In such circumstances, the lessor or the *notaire* acting in that proposed sale must serve a new notice on the lessee describing all the new terms of that new sale and that notice is deemed to be an offer to sell to the lessee. The lessee has one month in which to accept that offer or it lapses. It follows that any contract which is entered into between the lessor and such a third party must be subject to this additional right of pre-emption.

Lessee's rights at the end of the term
In certain cases, a lessor cannot refuse his lessee's request for the grant of a new lease irrespective of whether he wishes to occupy the premises himself or to sell them. Such cases concern every lessee who is both aged seventy and over and whose income is less than one and a half times SMIC (the minimum salary fixed by law) and who is entitled to retain possession of the premises let to him unless suitable alternative accommodation can be found. This is described in the Law as premises in the same or neighbouring area but in any event not more than five kilometres from the original premises and which correspond as to their facilities and running expenses to those of the premises he is to quit. This rule specifically does not apply when the lessor is either aged over sixty or his income is less than one and a half times SMIC. The relevant age is that at the date of the determination of the lease and income as at the date of the notice to quit. Foreign parties to a lease must produce documentation from their own country equivalent to that which is available in France.

Renewal of leases
As has been said above, if the lessor does not wish to determine the lease, he may make an offer of renewal which should be served on the lessee in the usual

manner not later than six months before the expiration of the term of the lease. It is important to remember that quite apart from the fixing of a rent under any new lease which may be granted, where no properly served notice to quit has been given by either party or an offer to renew made by the lessor, the lease is automatically renewed for three or six years (as the case may be) in accordance with the Law. Any deposit given by a lessee to cover breaches of covenant does not apply to a renewed lease and a fresh deposit must be obtained.

Re-entry provisions

A lease may contain a re-entry provision on non-payment of rent, service charge or deposit or failure to insure. Such a provision, however, takes effect only two months after a *commandement de payer* which must set out precisely the nature of the claim remains unsatisfied. The *commandement* must be served by a *huissier*. Failure on the part of the lessee to pay in due time allows the lessor to issue proceedings for forfeiture. However, not later than two months before the date fixed for hearing, the lessor must serve a notice by a *huissier* on the local Préfet advising him of the action so that he can contact the social departments capable of assisting the lessee. In addition, the Court has wide powers under C.civ.art.1244-1 'in the light of the needs of the debtor and creditor' to make instalment Orders over a period of two years at a low rate of interest in respect of unpaid rent.

Failure within a month on the part of the lessee to comply with the covenant to insure may also result in a *commandement*. This document to be valid must reproduce article 7 of the Law which sets out the statutory obligations of a lessee. A certificate of insurance, even if it covers a period prior to the service of the *commandement*, will not cure the evil if it is produced after the date for compliance given in the *commandement* (CA Agen 2.5.2000).

Finally, there is the overriding right of either party to a lease to apply to the Court under C.civ.art.1741 for a lease to be determined on the grounds that the other party has failed to comply with his obligations. The article leaves it to the discretion of the Court to decide if the matter complained of is of 'a sufficient gravity' to merit the determination of the lease.

Seasonal lettings

These lettings are for periods which extend only for 'the season'. There is no statutory definition of this period, the length of which depends solely on the circumstances which gave rise to the granting of the lease. Thus, the period can be comparatively long, for example, all the summer months or short, such as the time during which certain kinds of game may be shot. It may even be defined by a period of time not normally linked to pleasure as, for example, the length of a university term which can last up to ten months (CA Aix-en-Provence 1.6.86). They must not constitute the principal residence of the occupant (which it is not likely to be the case) but *ex abundante cautela* the document of letting should

169

specifically say so and his principal place of residence should be shown and so described.

Most usually, the period will be the 'summer season' on the coast or the 'ski season' in the Alps. In every case, such lettings are governed by the *Code civil*, the main requirements of which have been enumerated above. It is sensible in all cases to have recourse to a written document and not to organize a letting without the intervention of a qualified person. In such parts of France as lettings can properly be styled '*locations saisonnières*', estate agents specializing in such transactions abound. Most will provide a standard agreement but not all will seek standard commission. It is wise to make careful enquiries. It is essential to have made an *état des lieux* and to ensure that a deposit is taken from the tenant and that the deposit cheque is paid in.

Furnished lettings

The Loi Mermaz expressly excludes furnished lettings from its ambit irrespective of whether the lessor is engaged in the business of letting furnished property or not. The Law of 2 April 1949 defines as a 'professional' for this purpose anyone who 'habitually lets several premises furnished whether or not the letting includes additional services such as the provision of linen, cleaning and meals'. On the other hand, excluded from the definition is 'a person who lets one or more rooms in his own house'.

The Loi SRU, whilst confirming that furnished lettings are not subject to the Loi Mermaz, picks up the provision of that law referred to above that premises let as a principal residence must be a *logement décent* and this requirement applies also to furnished lettings. Subject therefore to this obligation on the part of a lessor and to special requirements in the case of a furnished letting by the professional lessor of more than four furnished premises, the provisions of a lease of furnished premises need not be in writing and within the limits imposed by articles 1708 to 1760 of the *Code civil* may be in such form as is agreed between lessor and lessee. As with seasonal lettings and unlike those subject to the Loi Mermaz, furnished lettings do not require an *état des lieux* but as is said above, it is essential to have one together with an inventory of the contents of the premises prepared on taking possession in the light of the effect of C.civ.art.1731.

Income from the letting of property by persons not resident in France is, with certain exceptions in the case of the letting of part only of the lessor's residence, subject to French income tax. In general terms, all furnished lettings are not subject to TVA unless the letting includes such services as would be provided by a hotel and the lessor is registered at the local Companies Registry in respect of that business activity. Lettings do not attract *taxe professionnelle* if they are lettings of part of the lessor's personal residence which fulfil one of a number of requirements which are not likely to be met with unless the lessor is a professional lessor of furnished premises. The lessor is not liable for *taxe d'habitation* (Chapter 22) if the premises let are not his personal residence and when they are liable to *taxe professionnelle* but if they are used by the lessor as his principal residence when not let, the lessor is so liable. The payment of *taxe foncière* falls on the lessor/owner. Certain *communes* on the coast or in mountain areas may impose a *taxe de séjour* or tourist tax which is trivial in its amount and charged per person per night of occupation. Non-professional lessors are charged to *impôt de solidarité sur la fortune* (wealth tax) in respect of the ownership of property let or intended to be let furnished since only 'professional' assets are so exempt. Professional lessors are exempt if their income from such a source exceeds a certain minimum which currently is Euro 23,000.

18

BUSINESS LEASES

Introduction 173
Term of the lease 174
The rent 174
The contents of the lease 175
    User 175
    The obligations of the parties 177
    Underletting 177
    Assignment 177
Security of tenure 178
Renewal of lease 179
    Règle du plafonnement 179
    Valeur locative 180
    Lessor's refusal to renew 181
Compensation 182
Droit de maintien 183
Droit de repentir 183
Le bail dérogatoire 183

Introduction

Part 2 of the Landlord and Tenant Act 1954 applies to 'any tenancy where the property comprised in the tenancy is or includes premises . . . occupied for the purposes of a business . . .' and 'business' is defined as including 'a trade, profession or employment'. The protection given by that Act was in France originally provided by the *décret* of 30 September 1953 and is now codified in large measure in articles L145-1 to 60 of the *nouveau code de commerce*. The articles of the *décret* 25 to 33, which were not so codified, also remain in force.

    This legislation deals with a narrower range of premises than does the English Act. The lessee must be a *commerçant* or *chef d'entreprise* registered as such at the local *registre de commerce* (Companies Registry). A *commerçant* is a person who regularly carries on a business of a commercial nature for his own account; a *chef d'entreprise* is the manager of such a business. He may also be an *artisan* (self-employed craftsman) registered at the *répertoire des métiers* (Craftsman's Register). The distinction is of interest since the shoemaker and the tailor are usually considered *artisans* and required to appear on the *répertoire des métiers* whilst the butcher and the baker are taken to be *artisans commerçants* and required to register in both places.

Excluded from the ambit of this legislation are all leases with a professional user to which special rules apply. Leases of premises housing co-operative societies such as the French equivalent of friendly societies and those occupied by artists recognized as such by Social Security are also treated as lessees protected by the Law.

Term of the lease

No lease may be granted for a term of less than nine years whether the grant is by written document or is made verbally. Subject to any agreement to the contrary, the lease must contain the right for the lessee to give six months' notice to quit at the end of the third and sixth year. As is to be expected, notice must be served by a *huissier*. The lease may provide for a payment to compensate a lessor for any loss he may suffer from such an early termination of the lease (Cass.21.6.95). Notice once given cannot be retracted save with the consent of the lessor. It is, in fact, not uncommon for leases to be granted on a 3/6/9/year basis.

Notwithstanding the statutory rule, it is lawful for the lessor to retake possession at three-yearly periods if he wishes to carry out certain building works on the premises. Such an event entitles the lessee to be indemnified for his temporary loss of premises and his moving expenses unless the lessor can find him suitable alternative premises.

The rent

There is no statutory restriction on the initial rent which may be charged which is a matter for negotiation between the parties. It is customary to have a rent revision provision and this also is a matter for negotiation. It is not uncommon for the rent to be variable depending partly or wholly on the profits or turnover of the lessee's business and the Cour de Cassation has held such an arrangement to be valid (Cass.2.10.84).

Many business premises form part of a *copropriété*, for example a shop in a parade on the ground floor of a block of flats, in which the lessor is a *copropriétaire*. Even though the lessee will normally not have access to any part of the building of which his premises form part, he will certainly be required to share the lessor's *charges*. Again, this may be freely fixed by the parties and is sometimes agreed at a proportion of the rent or at a fixed amount. It is common in business leases to find the obligation for the lessee to pay '*prestations et taxes*', that is all the services and taxes affecting the demised premises. This will throw onto the lessee a large part of the burden of the lessor's service charges and the taxes involved will include a variety of local taxes such as those for the removal of rubbish and other community taxes.

Most business leases will require the payment of a deposit as in the case of residential leases. The standard figure is six months' rent if rent is payable quarterly in arrears or three months' rent if rent is payable quarterly in advance. The deposit earns interest if it exceeds an amount equal to two rent payments. In the event of the sale of the reversion to the lease, any agreement for the transfer of the deposit to the new reversioner does not bind the lessee who may require its repayment from the original lessor (Cass.18.1.83).

Payment of a premium (*pas de porte*) on the grant of a business lease is lawful. There is no statute to forbid it and it has been specifically approved by the Cour de Cassation (15.2.95). Its precise nature has not been determined as a matter of law and each such payment is open to individual scrutiny by the Courts. Its nature is of importance when considering any rent revision clause and the rent to be fixed on renewal of a lease.

C.comm.art.145-38 provides for the rent of a lease of business premises to be reviewed every three years if the lease does not contain a provision for annual indexation. This provision is *d'ordre public* so that the parties to a lease may not agree to a two-year revision or to no revision at all. Either party may ask for a three-yearly revision. The revised rent will be calculated either by reference to the Cost of Construction Index or to the current rental value of the premises which is governed by a number of local factors. If the rental value has varied by more than 10 per cent, the new rent is limited to that found by the application of the Cost of Construction Index. In the case of disagreement between lessor and lessee, the matter must be referred to the Court.

The contents of the lease

A lease reduced to writing may be by *acte authentique* or may be executed ssp. In any event, it must be executed in two copies. The basic lessor–lessee relationships are those to be found in the relevant articles of the *Code civil* as modified by the Code de commerce. In the case of leases of business premises, there are two situations of particular importance. These relate to the user of and the assignment or subletting of the premises.

User

The lease may prescribe a single user or it may permit any business to be carried on upon the premises. The former type is known as a *bail exclusif*, the latter as a *bail tous commerces*. Not to be confused with the former in the lease containing a *clause d'exclusivité* by which the lessor covenants not to lease any adjoining premises for any business carried on by the lessee. Even without such a covenant on the part of a lessor, it has been held (but not always followed) to be a breach of his covenant in favour of one lessee for quiet enjoyment to let premises in the same building to another tenant for a competitive business.

C.comm.art.145-47 says that 'a lessee may exercise in addition to the user permitted in his lease any use which is ancillary or complementary thereto'. This provision is *d'ordre public*. The Courts have held that 'activities are ancillary (to a permitted user) which have a close connection with it and are complementary if they are necessary for the better carrying out (of such a user)' (CA Paris 27.4.83). There are also a series of other judgments which have held that a library may sell records but not paintings and a pork butcher may sell chickens but a chemist may not undertake laboratory tests. Many judgments have been given on this point, many being contradictory.

A business lessee who wishes to extend or vary his user covenant may do so by resorting to a procedure which is known as *déspécialisation partielle* if it relates to the addition of users which are complementary to that permitted by his lease or *plénière* if the lessee is seeking a wholly new user. Any covenant in a lease of business premises which forbids the lessee to apply for a *déspécialisation* is unlawful (C.com.art.L.145-15). By the same token, a lessor may not plead in opposition to such a request any covenant contained in any lease granted by him to another lessee which protects that lessee from a competitive business being carried on in adjoining premises.

In the case of a *déspécialisation partielle*, the lessee must serve the lessor with a notice indicating what additional users he wishes to exercise. If the lessor is in agreement, he must so indicate within two months of service of the notice on him. Failure to indicate his opposition to such a new user within the two-month period is deemed to be his agreement thereto. In the event of disagreement, it is open to either party to refer the matter to the Court which will reach a decision 'having regard to current commercial practice' (C.com.art.L.145-47).

The *déspécialisation plénière* is based on wholly different issues. Article L.145-48 of the Code commercial permits a change of user to one which is not necessarily complementary to the user permitted in a lease of business premises if the joint effect of 'the economic situation and the need for a rational organiza-tion of distribution' makes this reasonable. The wording is admittedly extraordi-narily vague but some instances of what would be considered within that definition can be given. 'The economic situation' is that of the lessee and may be affected by such things as a loss of clientele by reason of fashion or that local planning events have altered the character of the area. The second part of the defi-nition is even less clear but has been taken to mean that customers now demand a greater concentration of services to be available to them and that this compels the lessee to rationalize his methods of distribution.

The lessee must give notice to the lessor of his wishes and also to such of the creditors as have registered charges against his business who may require certain protection in respect of these liabilities if a change of user is granted. The lessor must reply within three months, failure to do so counting as agreement to the proposed change of user. The lessor may refuse consent for any of the following reasons said to be '*grave et sérieux*':

1. That the overall interests of trade and distribution or the general financial situ-ation do not justify the change of user which would serve only the personal interest of the lessee.

2. That the change of user is incompatible with the user character and situation of the building of which the premises form part.
3. That the proposed new user is forbidden by the *règlement de copropriété* (internal regulations) of the building of which the premises form part.

It is then open to the lessee in the case of a refusal by a lessor to apply to the Court which may either refuse the application or grant it in whole or in part only.

An Order of the Court favourable to the lessee in the case of either kind of *déspécialisation* does not give rise to an immediate increase in rent but may be taken into account on the next three-yearly rent revision.

The change of user on the retirement of a lessee is dealt with under the heading *Assignment* below.

The obligations of the parties

The parties to a lease of business premises have considerable freedom as to their respective repairing liabilities. In the unusual event that these are not dealt with in the lease, the lessee will be liable for day-to-day repairs and what are known as *réparations locatives* (Chapter 17) and the lessor will be liable for *grosses réparations* or repairs to the structure of the building.

Underletting

In distinction from C.civ.art.1717 which permits any underletting by a lessee unless his lease specifically forbids it, C.com.art.L.145-31 forbids the underletting of business premises unless the lease specifically negatives that article or the lessor gives his consent to such underletting. A lease which does not contain such a clause but requires consent for individual underlettings leaves the lessee at the mercy of the lessor who is obliged neither to give his consent nor his motives for a refusal (Cass.com.16.7.62). On every authorized subletting the lessor must join in the underlease. The sublessee under an unauthorized subletting loses such rights as he has against the head lessor in respect of the renewal of his underlease.

On an authorized subletting, the head lessor has the right to increase correspondingly the rent under the head lease if the rent charged by the sublease exceeds the rent under the head lease and the premises let by the head lease are the same as those which are sublet. The rent reserved by a lease of building land cannot be increased if the lessee builds upon it and then sublets those buildings at a higher rent.

Assignment

Code de Commerce, article L.145-16 forbids any provision in whatever form it may take which prevents the free assignment of a lease of business premises. This applies not only to the lease itself but includes the rights of the lessee under it by virtue of the relevant legislation, for example the right to a renewal of a lease or the right to compensation in lieu of renewal (CA Chambéry 7.7.80).

A special rule exists in cases where a lessee wishes to assign his lease on taking retirement or due to ill-health to an assignee who wishes to change the user of the premises. In such a case, such a change of user is permitted by law notwithstanding the user covenant in the lease provided only that the proposed user does not conflict with the user, character and situation of the building of which the premises form part. Consideration of the element of competition from adjoining premises is excluded (CA Paris 16.6.88).

Security of tenure

The lessee who fulfils the qualifications set out in the second paragraph of this chapter enjoys the right to the renewal of his lease of his business premises by virtue of C.comm.art.L.145-8 subject to the right of refusal on the part of the lessor and payment of compensation if there are not sufficient reasons to support such a renewal. In principle, to benefit from the right of renewal, the lessee must be of French nationality unless (i) he fought with the French or allied armies in one of the two World Wars, (ii) he has children who are French nationals, (iii) he is a citizen of a European Union country or of a country with which exists a reciprocal agreement. A non-French company has the nationality of the country in which is situate its principal place of management and business outlets. To enjoy this right, the lessee must be the owner of the business carried on at the premises. It appears that in the case of a franchise or concession, the owner of the franchise or concession may be treated as the owner of the business carried on at the premises (CA Paris 4.10.2000). On the other hand, if the lease is granted to a private individual but the business carried on belongs to a company of which that individual is the majority shareholder, the requirement is not fulfilled.

The lessee must also have carried on business on the premises for at least three years prior to the date of determination of the lease unless in the opinion of the Court he has had sufficient reason to justify a shorter period. It has been held that decisions of the local authority preventing a temporary use of the premises or the refusal of the lessor to allow him to carry out works to the premises are reasons justifying less than a continuous period of trading. The three-year period must be immediately prior to the date of determination so that time prior to the commencement of such a period is of no effect.

A lease in writing is determined only by written notice failing which it continues by tacit agreement. Notice to determine such a lease must be given by the lessor six months prior to the date of expiration accompanied or not as the case may be by an offer of renewal. If the notice offers the renewal of the lease, the parties may negotiate their own terms. If it refuses such a renewal, it must either offer or refuse compensation. If renewal or compensation is refused, the lessor must state his reasons and advise the lessee of his rights to apply to the Court which he must do not later than two years from the date on which the notice takes effect.

On the other hand, the lessee who has not received a notice of determination or of renewal of his lease may himself serve a notice not later than six months (but seemingly not before the beginning of that period in accordance with the judgment in Cass.11.2.87) requiring a renewal of his lease. To such a request, the lessor must reply within three months either accepting or refusing a renewal of the lease with, in the case of a refusal, his reasons. An agreement to renew is deemed to be provisional only and does not bind the lessor if thereafter he discovers sufficient reasons to support a refusal so long as these were not known to him when initially he offered a renewal (Cass.7.12.77). A counter-notice of refusal must inform the lessee of his right to apply to the Court within two years in support of his claim.

Renewal of lease

A new lease normally takes effect from the determination of the previous lease and must be for a period of nine years or longer if the parties so agree. Agreement to renew is not subject to agreeing the rent to be paid under the new lease. The principle of renewal is all that is required (Cass.9.11.81). For this reason if the lessor makes an offer to renew, he should indicate the new rent to avoid delay in it becoming effective.

The terms of the new lease will be substantially those contained in the old lease. However, the new lease is a new letting and so that any guarantor of the rent under the old lease is not automatically guarantor for the new rent. In the same way, if questions of repair arise during the term of the new lease, it is the situation at the date of its grant which is to be considered without reference to the previous period of letting (Cass.11.5.95).

The rent under the new lease may freely be agreed between the parties. Thus, they may agree to submit the matter to an independent expert but in default of agreement, one or other of the following methods of calculation apply. These are that the new rent should either be that according to (i) *the règle du plafonnement* (a capping formula) or (ii) the *valeur locative* (letting value) of the premises.

Règle du plafonnement

This method is used in cases where the new lease is for a term not exceeding nine years or when the expired lease for a term of nine years has been renewed by tacit agreement for a term not exceeding twelve years. The new rent is then fixed by reference to the rise or fall in the quarterly Cost of Construction Index. An exception to this rule occurs when one or more of certain characteristics affecting the demised premises have undergone a notable alteration during the term of the expired lease (Cass.21.6.95 and 2.12.98). These characteristics are those contained in articles 23-1 to 4 of the *décret* of 30 September 1953 and are enumerated under the heading *Valeur locative*. To oust this method of calculating the new rent, the alteration must be 'notable', must relate to the leased premises specifically and must have occurred during the term of the expired lease. If the Court takes the view that one or more such alterations has taken place, the new rent is found by reference to the *valeur locative* of the premises. It is to be noted that such an alteration will be taken into account if in the special circumstances of a lessor exercising his *droit de repentir* it occurs after the expiration of the old lease but before service on the lessee of the lessor's exercise of this right.

This rule is not applied to the lease of buildings built for a single occupation or those occupied solely as offices so that all that is in issue is a comparison with other buildings in the neighbourhood let for similar purposes.

Valeur locative

In utilizing this method of calculating the rent of a new lease, the Court may have regard only to the elements described in the *décret* of 30 September 1953. These are:

(1) the situation of the premises in the building of which it forms part, its area and ease of access to the public;
(2) the significance of the parts of the building designed respectively for the reception of the public and for that part or parts of the building in which the various businesses are carried on;
(3) the state of the upkeep of the building, its age and state of cleanliness and, if appropriate, the extent to which it conforms with local authority requirements;
(4) the nature and state of the facilities in the building and the extent to which the lessee may enjoy them.

Variations in any of these elements will affect the new rent as will a general review of the rent under the previous lease and whether the result of that review seems to have been too high or too low. In effect, a wide variety of matters can be taken into account such as general works carried out by a lessor to embellish the building which result in adding attraction to the demised premises and so increasing the clientele of the lessee.

The *décret* also specifies certain things which on the one hand tend to diminish the *valeur locative* and on the other hand to increase it. Among the former are limitations on the use of the premises, obligations which in the expired lease were those of the lessor but are transferred to the lessee under the new lease and burdens to be borne by the lessee over and above those which are usual. This frequently applies to the proportion of service charges of the building of which the demised premises form part. On the other hand, a term in excess of nine years is considered an advantage for the lessee and worthy of an increase in the *valeur locative* or if the lessor undertakes to bear or share the cost of improvements to the building.

Lessor's refusal to renew

A refusal to renew may be for a number of reasons. The lessor may allege that there are reasons which are *grave et légitime* (good and sufficient) and which may be compared to those set out in section 30(1)(a), (b) and (c) of the Landlord and Tenant Act 1954. Such reasons need not be limited to breaches of covenant by the lessee personally or to the behaviour of the lessee himself and may include acts of violence against the lessor and that the lessee has ceased to carry on his business on the premises. This reason for refusing a renewal of the lease cannot be pleaded unless the lessee has failed to remedy within one month of service on him of a *mise en demeure* the failures on his part referred to in such a notice and on which the lessor's refusal to renew are based. If the refusal of the lessor to renew is judged proper, he is not required to pay compensation to the lessee.

The lessor may also refuse to renew the lease on the grounds that the local authority requires that the premises be partially or totally demolished because they represent a public health hazard or has ordered that the structure of the building of which they form part is in too dangerous a state to be occupied. In such cases, if the Court supports the lessor, no compensation is payable.

Other grounds for refusing a renewal of a lease are:

1. The lessor wishes to retake possession of the premises in order to demolish them and rebuild new premises. In such a case, the lessor is prima facie liable to pay compensation but he can avoid this if he offers to provide the lessee with equivalent premises suitable to his requirements. This offer must be in respect of existing premises. The lessee is then entitled to compensation for his temporary lack of premises, any damage suffered by the goodwill of his business and his costs of moving. If the lessor wishes to obtain vacant possession in order to increase the height of his building, he may do so on payment of compensation to his lessee of not more than three years' rent.

2. In cases where the lessor takes possession intending to rebuild the premises, the lessee has a prior claim on a new lease of the new premises when completed provided that these are for commercial use. The lessor must give notice of this wish to the lessee within three months of leaving his previous premises and the lessor must advise the lessee when the new building is ready for letting and give him the choice of new premises in it. The lessee has three months in which to accept or refuse this offer and in case the terms of a new lease cannot be agreed, they are fixed by the Court.

3. A lessor may refuse to renew the lease of that part of premises used as living accommodation and let with the business premises if he requires them for his own occupation or that of close members of his or his spouse's family. This right is available only if the lessor does not have such accommodation available elsewhere for himself or his family normally living with him. The needs of the lessor in this direction are a matter for the Court which takes into account, for example, his state of health or whether he is about to be deprived

of his existing accommodation. This right is not available to a lessor who has acquired the building for valuable consideration less than six years before the right is exercised.

This right of *reprise* cannot be made use of if in the opinion of the Court the business and living accommodation form a single unit and cannot be reasonably separated or when the lessee can show that such a separation would gravely adversely affect his business. The lessor must occupy the premises which have been vacated by the lessee within six months and remain there for a minimum of six years. If this requirement is not adhered to, the lessee is entitled to suitable compensation. The lessor is also required to offer to make available to the lessee the living accommodation (if any) freed from his occupation by his exercise of this right.

Compensation

The lessor who cannot prove good grounds for his refusal to renew his lessee's lease is required to pay an *indemnité d'éviction* (compensation) equal to the loss the lessee has suffered by this refusal (Cass.7.5.69). The amount of such compensation is based on the market value of the business at the date of the expiration of the lease, the expenses of moving out of old premises and into new premises and the legal costs and expenses payable on the setting up of a similar business.

The valuation of the lessee's business should be made at the nearest possible date to that of his departure from the premises. The *Code commercial* requires that the valuation should be in accordance with normal methods current in the trade. The overall rule is that the Court should take account not only of the value of the business of the lessee but also of the lease itself (Cass.25.4.68). Hence, a high value for the lease by reason of the situation and extent of the premises can offset a low valuation of the business due to its poor trading results and the compensation may relate only to the value of the former asset. It is open to the lessor to prove that the loss suffered by the lessee is less than he claims. This would be the case if the lessee were able to transfer his business with hardly any interruption to premises close by so that he could not have suffered a loss of clientele (Cass.com.30.10.61) or that, for example, a chemist, by reason of the local laws restricting the number of chemists allowed to practise in any town, would not lose business by moving to other premises (Cass.com.21.3.62). As a general rule it is considered that the compensation will be less when the clientele is attached to the personality of the lessee rather than to the situation of his premises.

Certain losses ancillary to a change of premises must also be taken into account. The possibility of redundancy payments to staff, the commercial irritations of moving premises and the loss, if any, of living accommodation which formed part of the original letting are examples of what have been held to be such losses. It has, however, also been held that in certain cases the payment of a premium for a new lease, payments made to staff in lieu of holidays and sums payable in lieu of notice are not losses which can be taken into account.

The lessee is entitled to the proper costs of moving premises and of installing his business in its new premises. He is also entitled to legal and other expenses in connection with the acquisition of his new premises, it being left to the lessor to prove, if such be the case, that his lessee is not intending to take new premises. Capital gains tax payable by the lessee (though it is difficult to see how such a tax can arise in the circumstances unless it refers to the sale of the goodwill of a business which has no premises) is not an allowable expense for inclusion in the calculation of compensation (Cass.11.1.68).

Droit de maintien

A lessee cannot be required to move from his premises until he has received payment of his compensation but he is not required to do so in order to obtain payment. In the case of the sale of the premises by the lessor, this right to remain on the premises until payment of the compensation is enforceable against the purchaser from the lessor.

Droit de repentir

A lessor who has refused to renew a lease of business premises accompanied by an offer of compensation may withdraw that offer and offer instead a straightforward renewal. This right 'of repentance' may be exercised until a date fifteen days after the amount of the compensation has been fixed by the Court. It cannot, however, be exercised unless (i) the lessee is still in occupation of the premises and (ii) has not taken a lease of or bought or built other premises from which to carry on his business (Cass.9.11.81 and 26.1.94). Despite the fact that C.comm.art.L.145-58 joins these two possibilities by the word 'and', it has been held that they are to be treated as alternatives so that if only one is present, the lessor cannot 'repent' of his original offer of compensation (Cass.24.3.81). It is a matter for the Court to decide whether the lessee's behaviour in seeking new premises was proper or merely intended to prevent the lessor from exercising this right. Once exercised and notice given to the lessee, the lessor may not again change his mind. The term of the new lease is deemed to commence on the day when such notice was received by the lessee.

Le bail dérogatoire

It remains to add that it is open to the parties to enter into a lease of business premises which will not entitle the lessee to its renewal. Such a lease cannot be for a term exceeding two years and in practice is often for a term of twenty-three months only. The lease must state in clear terms that the lessee opts out of the protection afforded to him by law (Cass.8.11.72). Such a lease can be granted only once even if its term is for less than two years. At the expiration of such a lease, if the lessee remains in possession of the premises with the consent of the lessor and is a person entitled to the protection available to the lessee of an ordinary lease of business premises, he has the right to the grant of a new lease for the statutory minimum of nine years with all the statutory safeguards.

A *convention d'occupation précaire* under which the licensor may retake possession of premises occupied by the licensee without or at short notice is also free of any statutory control. However, although the precariousness of the occupation arises from the agreement of the parties, it is essential that it is justified by such facts as the small consideration payable by the occupant (Cass.28.2.66) or the impermanence of the use made of the premises by him (Cass.19.2.62). Otherwise, the Court may interpret such an arrangement as an attempt to circumvent the protection available to business tenants.

19

POWERS OF ATTORNEY

Introduction 185
Remuneration of the attorney 186
Duties of the attorney 186
    Accounting to donor 187
Determination of power 187
Enduring powers 188
Duration of powers 189
Copies of powers 189
Execution of powers 190
The Hague Convention 190
Form of power 192
Choice of attorneys 192

Introduction

The equivalent in French law of the Powers of Attorney Act 1971 are C.civ.arts.1984 to 2010. Unfortunately, the Code does not provide for a simple general power such as is to be found in Schedule 1 to the English Act. It is worthwhile noting that the words *mandat* and *procuration* are interchangeable but, whilst perhaps the latter is more commonly used as a description of the document, the donor and donee mentioned in it are called *mandant* and *mandataire* respectively. A power of attorney is also sometimes called a *pouvoir* but this term seems to be more used in current parlance for a proxy to attend company and *copropriété* meetings and the like.

Article 1984 defines the *mandat* or *procuration* as 'a document by which one person gives to another the power to do something on behalf of and in the name of the donor. Acceptance by the donee is required for completion of the contract.' The document which creates a power of attorney may by article 1985 be in any form, that is by *acte authentique* or ssp or even more informally such as by a mere letter. It may also be created verbally but proof of its existence, if so made, must follow the statutory rules for the proof of contracts and agreements. Suffice it to say that word of mouth should never be used as a method of creating a *mandat*. Acceptance may be tacit or result from the mere doing by the attorney of an authorized act. If more than one donee is appointed, article 1995 provides that they are jointly and severally liable to the extent expressed in the *mandat*.

Remuneration of the attorney

Unless otherwise provided for in the power, a donee is not entitled to remuneration. There is a presumption that an attorney who is a member of a profession, the nature of which includes the management of the affairs of others, is entitled to remuneration (Cass.10.2.81) and more specifically when the exercise of his powers is in the course of his normal professional duties (Cass.16.6.98). Notwithstanding these judgments, it is highly desirable that a very carefully drawn special clause akin to an English charging clause should be included in all powers of attorney where the attorney would normally expect to be remunerated. Such a power should be cast in the following terms and if a power which has been drawn by a *notaire* and sent to England for execution lacks such clause, as it probably will, it should be accordingly amended if the attorneys include a qualified person who is other than an employee of a *notaire* (as to which, see below). The suggested clause should read as follows:

'*CONVENIR de tous frais, émoluments et honoraires chargés avec le notaire et tous autres intervenants, procéder au règlement des sommes dues à ce titre après prélèvement de la rémunération du mandataire habituellement pratiquée en la matière suite aux appels de fonds du mandant*' ('TO AGREE the payment of all costs, emoluments and fees charged by the notary and all other persons involved (in the matter) and to pay out of the moneys paid on account by the donor all such sums as may be due subject to the prior payment thereout of the remuneration of the attorney usual in such cases).'

Duties of the attorney

C.civ.arts.1991 to 1997 set out the duties of the donee of the power. He must carry these out in the manner laid down in the power and is liable in damages to the donor for any default. He is required to complete any matter in hand at the date of death of the donor if failure to do so would be prejudicial to the interest of the donor's estate notwithstanding that by provisions of article 2003 the death of the donor revokes the power. He is liable to the donor for all acts which involve a lack of the utmost bona fides towards his donor (*dol*) as well as for acts of mere mismanagement but the burden of care in this respect is less onerous if he is unremunerated than if he receives remuneration. In either case, there is a rebuttable presumption against the donee of failure to act properly, so that if there is an ostensible limitation of such liability in favour of the donee contained in the *mandat* it is for the Court to decide to what extent that presumption has been rebutted. However, the draftsman of documents is presumed fully to have advised all parties to that document for whom he acts and to ensure the validity and efficacy of all documents which he draws (Cass.14.1.97).

Every donee must by article 1993 account to his donor for all sums received by him by virtue of his *mandat* other than those he is expressly authorized to retain even if the same are in fact not due to the donor. A donee is liable to pay interest on sums belonging to his donor of which he has himself made use. In general, he must give a full account of all his acts of management done by virtue of his *mandat*.

Article 1994 holds a donee personally responsible for all acts of any substitute appointed by him if he has not the authority to delegate. If he is so authorized, but appoints a substitute who is known *notoirement* (by common repute) to be unsuitable or insolvent, he is personally liable for the defaults of that substitute. In all cases, the donor may act against any substitute directly.

Article 1997 provides that a donee is not liable in respect of acts done in excess of his powers provided that he has disclosed to the third party the nature and extent of those powers and has not undertaken any personal liability in respect thereof. So far as the donor of a power is concerned, whilst by virtue of article 1998 he is not in general terms liable to third parties in respect of acts done by his attorney in excess of his powers unless he has ratified them, this rule does not apply in cases of a *mandat apparent* or ostensible authority where such third parties had good reason to believe that the attorney was acting within the scope of his powers. The small value of the transaction involved, the 'authority and trustworthiness of a notaire' (Cass.2.10.74) and where a *mandat* has been given by one spouse to another (Cass.11.3.86) have all been held to be circumstances where a third party has reasonable grounds to accept without question the extent of the apparent authority of an attorney. French powers do not contain specific undertakings to ratify.

Accounting to donor
The donor is required to reimburse his donee for all expenses and money laid out by the latter in the execution of his duties and also to pay him his agreed remuneration. Subject to such fault on the part of the donee as may exist, the donor may not withhold such payments merely because the matter in respect of which they were incurred was unsuccessful nor may he make any reduction on the grounds that the amounts involved could have been less. Provided that no impropriety is imputed to the donee, he is entitled to be indemnified for all losses he may have sustained by reason of acts properly done (arts. 1999 and 2000).

Determination of power

A *mandat* is determined under article 2003 by:

1. Its revocation by the donor. The donor may require the donee to return to him the *mandat* which he has given according to whatever was the form in which it was made. Notice of revocation given only to the donee is not binding on third parties who have dealt with the donee in ignorance of that revocation. The donor's remedy lies only against the donee. The giving of a new *mandat*

to a different donee counts as revocation of the previous *mandat* as of the date on which it is notified to the previous donee.

2. Renunciation by the donee of the *mandat*. If such renunciation is 'to the prejudice' of the donor, the latter is entitled to be indemnified by the donee unless the donee can prove that to have continued to act as donee would result in 'considerable prejudice' to him.

3. In the case of 'the natural or civil death or incapacity or *déconfiture* (inability to meet one's financial obligations) of either donor or donee'.

All engagements properly entered by a donee with a third party in bona fide ignorance of the determination of his authority in any of the above circumstances are treated as valid for which the donor remains liable (Cass.8.11.94). In the case of the death of a donee, his estate should notify the donor and make provision in the meantime in the best interests of the donor.

Although articles 1987 and 1988 provide that a power of attorney may be limited in the extent of its powers or may be general in connection with all the affairs of the donor, a power to sell, mortgage or otherwise deal in land in any way whatsoever must be an express power since such transactions are considered specific acts and not acts of general administration. Such a power can nevertheless be included in a power containing powers of a general nature. A *mandat* can be given generally to negotiate loans and the donor need not specify any particular loan but the execution of the loan document requires specific authority (Cass.21.11.95).

Enduring powers

The enduring power, such as may be made in certain European countries such as England, Ireland, and Spain, and in the United States, and the Canadian Provinces of Quebec and British Columbia, does not exist in France. Article 2003 says that a power of attorney is determined by the *tutelle* (the equivalent of the appointment of a Receiver by the Court of Protection) of either the donor or of the donee. However, French private international law says that the proper law of a power of attorney is that chosen by the parties or if none is specified, that most closely connected with its subject. The normal English enduring power will be governed by English law which will be the personal law of the donor. Questions of capacity are in French law answered according to the personal law of the parties, the capacity of the donor of a power being that at the date of the making of the power and not at the date of the carrying out of any of its powers. This being so, the power can in theory be used in France since it is valid according to the laws of England. Obviously, such evidence as is needed to prove that the donee has commenced and continued to have the power to act as attorney will be required. It is certain that in many cases, difficulties will be placed in the way of a donee of such a power. It is advisable in advance to establish what are the reactions of the *notaire* involved to the use of such a power. It is to be hoped that this problem will be remedied by the Hague Convention of 13 January 2000 on the International Protection of Adults. Article 57 of the Convention provides for it to come into force on the first day of the fourth month following the ratification of the Convention by at least three of the contracting parties but it is not yet part of French internal law. For a full resumé of the application of this Convention in France once ratified by that country, see Me. Revillard, *Droit International Privé et Pratique Notariale* (5th edn, Defrénois, 2001). The law in France dealing generally with capacity is to be found in Chapter 24.

Duration of powers

It is probable that the majority of powers of attorney granted by English donors for use in France will be in respect of a single specific event or transaction. These include the purchase, sale and mortgaging of property, the partition of property on death or divorce or for tax reasons, the formation of civil or commercial companies, the transfer of shares, and a variety of financial transactions when it is inconvenient for the donor to come to or remain in France. In the case of the administration of an estate, the power will be general but will also contain specific powers to sell and deal with the assets and each document executed under such a power will need a copy annexed to it. On occasions, a new power limited to the specific transaction will be required.

A further complication is that in practice a power which is more than a few months old (and certainly more than a year old) is frequently deemed unacceptable on the grounds that the donor might have revoked it or have died. There is in French law no procedure such as the Statutory Declaration of non-revocation and although doubtless some *notaires* will accept written confirmation from the donor that his power is still in force, care should be taken to ensure that powers are 'fresh'. This alone can militate against the execution of one power intended to be used over a period of time. It must also be remembered that the *état civil* of the donor might vary, for example by divorce and/or remarriage or the adoption of a *régime matrimonial* over a period and, with a general power in force over a long period, this could give rise to future queries. It is always wise to check with the *notaire* involved.

Copies of powers

The French practice equivalent to that provided by section 3 of the Powers of Attorney Act 1971 is that copies certified by a *notaire* can be treated as originals. This applies not only to a power executed in France since either this will be *authentique* and therefore will be filed in the minutes of the *notaire* before whom it was executed or if it is ssp it can be lodged with a *notaire* to be placed in his records. It can apply also to a power executed abroad since such a power can also be deposited in notarial *minutes* and even if it is not, a certified copy can be made by a *notaire*. As a matter of practice, it must be added that generally in respect of the use of powers of attorney executed out of France much can depend on how helpful or otherwise is the *notaire* involved.

Since the *Code civil* itself does not refer to procedural requirements, it is important to appreciate the different rules which apply to powers executed in France or out of France.

Execution of powers

In the case of powers executed in France, they can in many circumstances be either *authentique* or ssp since only in certain cases need they be in the former style. However, if they are executed ssp, the signature of the donor must be certified and banks do not provide this service in France. The usual method is to go to the local *mairie* or police station since certification is not, as in England, a matter of the personal knowledge of the certifier but of the production of suitable identification. It is essential that unless the donor is permanently resident in France, the power should show a non-French address which presumably will be that which will figure in the document which will be executed by the attorney. On the whole, unless the power is going to be executed before a *notaire* involved in the transaction for which the power is intended to be used, it is often preferable to await the donor's return to England.

The Hague Convention

Execution of the power in England calls into play special procedures. When a power is drawn in France, the average *notaire* will usually suggest that it should be executed before a French Consul which will result in the power being *authentique*. French Consuls are in fact required by French law to 'receive' such documents provided that they are to be used solely in France and only for transactions in land. The sole advantage of the use of a Consul is that the power is *exécutoire* (Chapter 1) but this is not a quality required for a power of attorney. The proper person in England to approach is the notary public and such a document signed in his presence and authenticated by him is treated as *authentique* and acceptable in France without further question provided that the notary public has caused to be affixed by the Foreign and Commonwealth Office the Hague Convention *apostille* certifying his signature. Without this *apostille* the power is valueless in France.

The Hague Convention of 5 October 1961 which abolished the need for the legalization of many kinds of documents of one country for use in another is that which deals with the affixing of the *apostille* referred to above. It will presumably as between countries of the European Union be replaced by the Brussels Convention of 25 May 1987 but so far this has become effective only as between

France, Denmark, Italy, and Belgium. The 1961 Convention lists various types of documents emanating from one country for use in another. As between the United Kingdom (which for the purposes of the Convention includes the Channel Islands, the Isle of Man, and a number of small dependent territories) and France, the following require an *apostille*:

(1) notarized documents;
(2) affidavits and other documents lodged with the Court;
(3) administrative documents other than customs declarations and those directly concerned with commercial transactions;
(4) annuitants' life certificates;
(5) documents ssp ie those which are not *authentique* but which bear certificates of signatures or of the date of execution and the like.

The following are not required to bear an *apostille*:

(1) *actes d'état civil* such as birth, death and marriage certificates;
(2) Judicial Orders and Judgments (including Grants of Representation and Decrees Absolute);
(3) Diplomatic and Consular documents;
(4) Patent Office certificates.

It will be noticed that documents which require an *apostille* include those executed ssp. Hence, in cases where a power in *authentique* form is not obligatory, it is still, at least in theory, necessary to have an *apostille*. In France, banks and lawyers and other professionals and certain other worthies such as members of the clergy do not certify signatures and although this is commonly accepted in England, the signatures of such persons cannot attract an *apostille*. It follows therefore that unless the *notaire* involved in France agrees to forego an *apostille*, the services of a notary public in England would appear to be necessary either to notarize the power if it is to be *authentique* or merely to certify the signature of the parties if it is to be ssp.

In this connection, it must be said that the Foreign and Commonwealth Office appears willing to affix the *apostille* to documents bearing the signature also of a solicitor. This does not, of course, give the character of *authenticité* but it satisfies some *notaires* if the document has been executed ssp and the solicitor is merely certifying a signature. It is submitted, although it must be said that the Legalization Department of the Foreign and Commonwealth Office does not agree, that the *apostille* cannot be given for the signature of a solicitor. The original French wording of the Convention (which the Convention says should prevail) says that it applies to '*les documents d'une autorité ou d'un fonctionnaire relevant d'une jurisdiction de l'état y compris ceux qui émanent du ministère public, d'un greffier ou d'un huissier de justice*' (documents emanating from an official State source or from a civil servant, including those who are public officers . . .). The Legalization Department, relying on the definition in *Halsbury's Laws of England* that a public officer may be said to be one who discharges a duty in the performance of which the public is interested, says that a 'Solicitor . . . holds duties to the Court and in view of the public interest in the administration of justice, may be considered a public official'. Quite apart from the fact that this is a total misconception of what in French law is a *'ministère public'*, he is in the original French but one of the persons included in the overall description of a *fonctionnaire*. A *fonctionnaire* is without question no more nor less than a civil servant and if as a result of the misunderstanding to be found in *Halsbury*, a solicitor is to be held to be a civil servant, then there can be little prospect of that independence of spirit which the solicitor is expected to exhibit and none of that freedom of action for which his profession is known.

Form of power

From a purely practical point of view, there are certain rules which should be borne in mind. It is almost always pointless trying to make use in France of a power drawn according to English law and in the English language. Even if a *notaire* would accept it, it would require translation into French and probably an affidavit of English law to satisfy him of the powers which it vests in the donee. Moreover, to produce a power in English for, say, the purchase of a property, would require the draftsman to have sufficient knowledge of the laws and languages of both countries to be able to produce in English a document which properly expresses all that is needed in French. The answer, therefore, lies simply in the use of a French power of attorney drawn by a suitable person. It is for this reason that the explanations as to the rights and obligations of donor and donee respectively under French law have been given above.

Choice of attorneys

The use of a power given by an English donor for use in France implies the absence of the donor from that country or at least from the place of execution of the document in question. Consideration must be given as to who is going to draw the power and who is or are going to be the attorney/s.

Unless whoever is advising the intending donor is himself familiar with French law and procedure, he will not get much assistance from the *notaire* unversed in international matters, quite apart from the language problem made even greater by the need for each adviser to have a reasonable fluency in the legal language of the other. It cannot be too often stated that in any Anglo–French transaction taking place in France, it is highly desirable to consult a professional in France who is bilingual in the legal language of both countries, expert in the laws of each country and who has practical experience of the procedures in both countries, as the representative of those who advise the donor in England. There is no doubt that the most satisfactory line to adopt is for the power to be drawn in French form by that representative and sent to England for execution.

Clearly that draftsman should be one of the attorneys named to act in France. It is suggested that two other attorneys be appointed to act jointly and severally with him. One should be the donor's solicitor in England so that the contact between him and the donor remains unbroken. Most *notaires* if left to draw their own powers will appoint as sole *mandataire* a member of their own staff. *Notaires* themselves do not act as attorneys. The third donee may, if the expert in France so advises, be one of the members of the staff of the *notaire* acting for the donor but not if that *notaire* is the only *notaire* acting in the transaction. The choice of a third attorney is to provide a 'longstop' if the second attorney in France is unexpectedly unavailable. Without such advice being intended as a reflection on the integrity of the *notaire*, it cannot be desirable that a single attorney is the employee of a sole *notaire* acting for both parties nor is it in the best interest of the donor that such a person be sole attorney even if two *notaires* are involved. In either case, all other considerations apart, this can impose on such a sole attorney a burden which it is unfair to expect him to shoulder.

20

THE *RÉGIME MATRIMONIAL*

Introduction 195
    Creation of a *régime* 195
Le régime de communauté légal 196
Le régime de communauté conventionnelle 197
    Communauté universelle 197
Le régime de la séparation des biens 198
Variation of a *régime* 199

Introduction

As eminent a lawyer as Professor Dicey when referring to the French *régime matrimonial* does so by classing it as 'a marriage contract or settlement' and it may well be thought impertinent to take issue with such a description. It is true that the document which creates a *régime* if the parties to a marriage do not wish to adopt the *régime* provided by law is called a *contrat de mariage*. However, a marriage contract is not a term known to English law and is used by another learned Vinerian Professor of Law, Professor Cheshire, only in the context of contracts prejudicial to the status of marriage. Nor is it safe to describe the *régime matrimonial* as a settlement since in the case of an English marriage settlement, the parties to the marriage have equitable interests only and are not themselves involved in any dealings with the assets of the settlement which are effected by the trustees in accordance with the trusts of the settlement. The parties to a marriage subject to a French *régime* are directly involved with the management of the assets subject to the relevant *régime* and indeed their *régime matrimonial* is an extremely important part of their *état civil*. For these reasons, no attempt is made to translate either *contrat de mariage* or *régime* into English except in the limited circumstances of the *état civil* of an English married couple whose rights and powers in respect of their property have to be explained in French.

Creation of a régime
C.civ.art.1387 in its original form and early nineteenth century translation says that: 'The law does not regulate the conjugal association, as respects property, except in default of special agreements which the married parties may make as they shall judge convenient, provided that they are not contrary to good morals and, moreover, subject to the modifications which follow.' The article further provided that: 'Married persons cannot derogate from the rights resulting from the power of the husband over the persons of his wife and of his children . . .'. It

must be added that the article in its current form now prohibits any derogation from 'the duties and rights which result from marriage and from the rules of parental authority . . .'. The 'modifications' referred to in the article relate to the right for those intending to marry to choose a *régime* but that if they do not exercise such a choice that the *régime* which will apply is that of *communauté légale*. If the couple about to be married do not wish to use the *régime* laid down by law, they must execute a *contrat de mariage* which C.civ.art.1394 stipulates must be by notarial *acte* executed at the same time by the future spouses or their attorneys. After execution of the document, the *notaire* involved must provide free of cost and stamp duty a certificate stating his name and place of residence and the full names, descriptions and residences of the intending spouses. If a *contrat de mariage* has been entered into, the notarial certificate is handed to the Registrar and mention in the marriage certificate is made of the date of the *contrat* and of the *notaire* before whom it was executed. It must also be registered with the local Companies Registry if either party is or subsequently becomes a *commerçant*, that is engages in a commercial activity which requires his registration as such. The object of publicizing the *contrat* is to advise persons dealing with either spouse of the limits of his or her ability to deal with his or her property. Evidence of the nature of a *régime* will always be required by any *notaire* dealing with any transaction in which one or both spouses are engaged by production of a marriage certificate or the notarial certificate referred to above. If the person involved was married out of France, that person must be prepared to satisfy the *notaire* on this point.

    Régimes are *communautaires* or *séparatistes*. The former are either the *régime de communauté légal* which is that which applies automatically to every marriage when the parties do not themselves choose a *régime* or the *régime de communauté conventionnelle* if that is the *régime* chosen by the married couple. The latter are the *régime de séparation de biens* and the *régime de participation aux acquets*.

Le régime de communauté légal

This is the *régime* imposed on all married couples who do not themselves choose a different *régime*. Its full title is the *régime de la communauté de biens réduite aux acquêts*. Its effect and management are covered in C.civ.arts.1401–1440. Assets of all kinds belonging to each spouse at the date of marriage remain the individual property of each as does any property acquired by each during the marriage by way of gift or inheritance. It catches only those assets acquired during marriage with what the husband and wife have themselves earned. An important issue for the French is how the debts of the parties to a marriage are dealt with. In the case of this *régime*, assets acquired in common during marriage are liable for the debts of either spouse incurred during marriage. Those acquired before marriage or in respect of one spouse's individual property are those of that spouse alone. It follows that creditors are interested to know to which of these three sources they may look for payment; hence the significance of the publicizing of the *régime* adopted.

The *régime* comes to an end (i) on the death of one of the spouses, (ii) by divorce or judicial separation, (iii) as the result of a judgment obtained by one spouse on the grounds that that spouse needs protection against 'disorder in the affairs of the other spouse', for example bankruptcy or improper administration of the assets of the *régime*. Complex rules apply to ensure that each spouse obtains his or her due, having regard to all that may have happened to the *régime* assets. The determination of this *régime* frequently follows a divorce by means of a *partage* or partition of the assets. On a death, it is not uncommon (but seldom desirable) to allow the assets to remain *en indivision* (Chapter 16) between the heirs of the deceased spouse and the surviving spouse.

Le régime de communauté conventionnelle

The *régime de communauté* pure and simple, which is prescribed by law for all those who do not choose another *régime*, provides for a minimum situation and it is possible to enlarge its scope by agreement between the parties to the marriage. This can be done by adopting the further *régime de communauté conventionnelle de meubles et acquets*. Persons married under this *régime* are subject to all the rules of the *régime légal* but in addition all assets which are *meubles* such as furniture and furnishings, shares, and the goodwill of a business which were owned by each of the parties to the marriage become jointly owned as do all those which they acquire after marriage by gift *inter vivos* or by inheritance. Excluded from these items are (i) *meubles propres par nature* which are items of a personal character such as clothing and items of a purely family nature but jewellery bought jointly falls into the *régime*, and (ii) any items which have been given to one of the spouses *inter vivos* or by will subject to the condition that they do not form part of the recipient's *régime*.

Communauté universelle

Under this *régime*, prima facie all that the married couple owns at the time of its adoption or thereafter comes to own falls within the *régime*. On the other hand, the spouses can exclude from its effect any particular asset or group of assets owned when the *régime* is adopted or to be caught later by it. For example, all property in France but not elsewhere or all immovables but no movables or vice versa or any combination based on geographical location or type of asset can be made subject to or excluded from the *régime*. Basically, the management of the *régime* and its dissolution follow the rules applicable in the case of the *régime légal*. However, very frequently a special provision is inserted into the *régime* as a result of which the totality of the assets in the *régime* pass to the surviving spouse and are not distributed between the surviving spouse and the heirs of the deceased spouse. This is known as a *clause d'attribution intégrale*. To avoid the heirs of the deceased spouse seeking to limit the effect of this clause to assets other than those acquired during the marriage, a clause is added specifically to deprive them of this *droit de reprise*.

Quite apart from the fact that this *régime* can function so as to ensure that the surviving spouse takes all and that *réservataires* are cut out, there is the added advantage that the assets are transferred to the surviving spouse free of French inheritance tax at maximum stamp duty of 1 per cent. However, there is a very serious limit which can affect the use of this *régime*. C.civ.art.1527 as amended by the Law of 3 December 2001 says that if there are any children who are not children of the marriage to which the *régime* applies, they have the right to recover any excess over and above what the surviving spouse could have received if the *régime* had not taken effect, that is the normal inheritance of a surviving spouse. This normally relates to children of a previous marriage of one of the spouses so that the general rule is that spouses who have been previously married and have children by such marriages do not make use of this *régime*. The existence of such children does not invalidate the *régime* but since children who might benefit from the article cannot renounce their right in advance, many *notaires* are most reluctant to allow their clients to adopt this *régime* if such children do exist.

This *régime* can be of great interest to the English married couple (Chapter 29).

Le régime de la séparation des biens

This is a type of *régime* which normally the parties to a marriage must create by a *contrat de mariage*. It can, however, also arise as a result of a judicial separation, turning a *régime de communauté* into one of *séparation de biens*. In this *régime*, each spouse is and remains the owner of his or her own assets whether owned before marriage or acquired after marriage and by whatever means. Thus, immovables acquired in the name of one spouse, even if financed by the other, are the property of the former (Cass.17.12.91). If an immovable is purchased in the name of both spouses, it belongs to them in the proportions indicated in the *acte de vente*. It cannot subsequently be alleged that these proportions are incorrect; it is only the proportions in which the price was provided which can be questioned in the Courts (C.civ.art.1099-1 and Cass.9.10.91). In the case of movables, proof as to the proportionate ownership of each spouse may be made by production of bills, estate accounts, mention in a *contrat de mariage* or 'by any other means'. In this *régime*, as one would expect, each spouse administers his or her own assets and is responsible for his or her own debts. It is possible to vary the standard terms of this *régime* by including a *société d'acquets* in respect of certain assets acquired during the marriage. Thus a house bought by one can become the property of both as in the *régime légal*.

What may be considered a variation on this type of *régime* is the *régime de la participation aux acquets*. During the marriage, the rights of the spouses are as in *séparation de biens*. However, whilst under the dissolution of that *régime* each spouse takes what are his or her assets, under this enlarged *régime*, each spouse benefits from the *créance de participation* or the increase in the value of the assets belonging to the other spouse. In principle, that benefit is one half of the increase in value of the assets of the other spouse but any other proportion may be agreed in the *contrat de mariage*. Thus, if the husband began the marriage with assets of X and ended the marriage (for example, by death or divorce) with assets of 2X, the wife is entitled to one half of 2X – X, i.e. 1/2X. It will be appreciated that this *régime* in its basic form without a *créance de participation* produces results such as exist between spouses in English law. Indeed, the French consider that English law creates on marriage the 'legal' *régime de séparation de biens* in the same way as French law creates the 'legal' *régime de communauté de biens*. This is quite illogical even if one considers that the result of the Married Woman's Property Act 1882 was to separate the assets of husband and wife and give each control of the assets of each. In French law, a married couple must have a *régime*, be it chosen by them or given to them by law. In English law, the *régime* does not exist so that it can neither be chosen nor given. As has been said elsewhere, the best description for the purposes of a French document that can be given of the property rights *inter se* of English spouses (and then it is not accurate) is that the English marry in the 'English *régime* equivalent to the French *régime* of *séparation de biens* without having entered into any contract prior to their marriage'.

It may be of interest to know that of the European countries, in addition to the United Kingdom, the following have as their 'legal' *régime* that of *séparation de biens*: Austria, the Spanish region of Catalonia/Balearics, Greece, Eire, Liechtenstein, Monaco, the Vatican. Most of the States of the United States have the same rule except Arizona, California, Idaho, Louisiana, Nevada, New Mexico, Puerto Rico, Texas, Washington, and Wisconsin which presumably because of their French or Spanish backgrounds have the *régime de communauté d'acquets*.

Variation of a *régime*

C.civ.art.1397 permits the variation of a *régime* be it *légal* or *conventionnel* either by the substitution of another *régime* or by the alteration of any of the provisions of an existing *régime*. The variation must be made by *acte notarié* and its terms must be *homologué*, that is be approved by the Court. The article says that the variation should be 'in the interests of the family'. Whilst there is no requirement that the variation should be necessary if the family assets are 'in peril' by reason of the liabilities of the spouses under their existing *régime*, it is necessary to satisfy the Court that the interests of the family are in issue. Nevertheless, the mere fact that the variation sought will be to the disadvantage of one or more of the members of the family is not itself a ground for refusal by the Court of the application (Cass.6.1.76). Nor is it necessary for the Court to take into account the views of the children of the marriage (Cass.24.11.93) but it usually does so. As in the case of applications under the Variation of Trusts Act 1958, a variation of a *régime* to gain a tax advantage is an acceptable ground but not if the adoption of the desired variation would produce too significant a disadvantage for the children of the marriage (CA Rouen 3.2.81).

The French Court has jurisdiction in all cases where one or both of the spouses are French notwithstanding that they are domiciled out of France and also in cases of non-French spouses unless they are not domiciled in France. No application may be made until at least two years after the date of the marriage in issue but thereafter, the couple may apply to the Court for further variations at intervals of not less than two years.

The variation becomes effective as between the spouses as from the date of the judgment approving the variation. As between them and third parties, it takes effect three months after the judgment has been noted against their marriage certificate at the relevant *bureau d'état civil* or Register Office of Births, Deaths and Marriages (C.civ.art.1397-6). In default of such a note, the period runs in any case where the spouses in any dealings with third parties declare in the relevant documentation that they have varied their *régime*. If either party to the marriage is a *commerçant*, the application and the judgment must also be filed with the local Companies Registry to be effective as against third parties.

This article also provides that if creditors of either spouse consider that the variation represents a fraudulent avoidance of their rights, they may oppose the application to vary. This is an interesting power born of the fact that, as indicated above, the liabilities of the spouses towards creditors differ depending upon which *régime* governs their marriage. This is a right not to be overlooked since one finds in a leading French journal written primarily for the businessman as the first of the three reasons given for a variation of a *régime* that of avoiding one's creditors.

It is essential to note that where there is a marriage which has an international element, for example, where the parties are or one of them is English, it will almost certainly not be necessary or desirable to resort to the French procedure to change a *régime*. The proper procedure in such cases is to have resort to the Hague Convention of 14 March 1978 and this procedure is explained in Chapter 29.

21

UNION LIBRE

Introduction 201
Proof of *concubinage* 201
Fiscal effect of *concubinage* 202
The ownership of land 202
Financing a purchase of land 204
The *pacte civile de solidarité et du concubinage* 205
Who may enter into a PACS 206
The PACS contract 207
Determination of a PACS 207
Ownership of assets 207
Fiscal consequences of a PACS 208
Other benefits of a PACS 208

Introduction

C.civ.art.518-8 describes *'le concubinage'* which is the legal term for *union libre* or cohabitation as the 'de facto union, between two persons of the same or of different sexes living together as a couple and characterized by a life in common, exhibiting evident signs of stability and continuity'. The extent of stability required for the state of *concubinage* to exist may be judged from the decision of the Courts that it gives one party the right to organize the funeral of the other (CA Douai 7.7.98). Nevertheless, in certain respects the parties *en concubinage* are treated by the law as strangers, for example, in the case of income tax, inheritance tax and gifts tax but not, curiously enough, of *impôt de solidarité sur la fortune* (ISF or wealth tax) when they have always been jointly assessed unless they are married to a person other than that with whom they are *en concubinage*. In other respects, they have achieved certain advantages normally reserved for married couples such as certain Social Security benefits, security of living accommodation occupied by both on the death of the survivor and reductions in the cost of transport.

Proof of *concubinage*

In order to obtain such benefits as may exist in favour of a *concubin*, it is usually necessary to obtain a *certificat de concubinage* from the local *mairie*, the procedure for obtaining which tends to vary from *mairie* to *mairie*. Evidence of living together, such as rent receipts or telephone bills in both names, will be required and frequently two independent witnesses are also needed. The provision of such a certificate is not obligatory and if the local *mairie* refuses to grant one, in some cases Social Security offices may accept a *déclaration sur l'honneur*, again supported by independent witnesses.

Fiscal effect of *concubinage*

From a tax point of view, the effect is most noticeable when inheritance tax (IHT) is in issue. A surviving spouse not only has, as a result of recent legislation, certain substantial rights of inheritance but for IHT purposes enjoys an *abattement* (nil-rate band) currently of Euro 76,000 and pays IHT on a slice basis at comparatively low rates. The *abattement* of a surviving *concubin*, who is a stranger in blood, is Euro 1,500 and the overall single rate of tax is 60 per cent. The same disparity applies to gifts tax.

The ownership of land

The ownership of property gives rise to obvious difficulties in that members of the deceased *concubin*'s family take precedence from an inheritance point of view over the surviving *concubin* in addition to paying the penal rate of IHT on what he or she can inherit. It may be thought preferable in some cases that one alone becomes the sole owner of the property jointly occupied but this is not a solution which recognizes in any way the joint contribution made by both *concubins* to the 'stability and continuity' of their lives together. There are a number of other solutions which need to be considered since whatever the domicile or residence of the couple may be, if the land they own is in France it is subject to French law.

If one *concubin* is already the sole owner of a property, the prime concern of the couple will probably be to secure the right of the survivor of the couple to continue to live in it after the death of the former. This may be achieved to some extent in a number of ways.

1. The owner can make a gift *inter vivos* to the other *concubin* of an absolute interest in the property or can grant him or her a life interest. Neither is desirable since both methods leave it open to the donee to evict the original owner at will.
2. That danger can in theory be overcome by making the gift by means of a legacy in a will and limiting the interest for life to that of a mere licence to occupy. However, such a legacy is subject to the rights in the estate of the testator of the *réservataires* although if the value of the interest exceeds the *quotité disponible* available to those who are not *réservataires* those latter have the option which they may well not exercise of allowing the legacy to stand. It is always possible to cover the IHT liability by assurance.

3. The grant of a licence to occupy the premises owned by one *concubin* alone over a long period of time cannot be considered to be a satisfactory solution. It may well provide the continued right of occupation after the death of the owner but in the light of the wording of C.civ.art.1888, which presupposes a limited length for the use of the object of the licence compatible with the object of the licence, such a grant is open to attack as a means of disguising what is in reality the gift of such a right.
4. The grant by the owner to the other *concubin* of a lease to take effect from the date of his death is bad in law since it constitutes *un pacte sur la succession future* which, unlike the English covenant to make provision for a person by will, is void in French law.

The owner can make available similar rights to the other *concubin* by means of a sale but it must be a genuine sale for full value to avoid the suggestion that the transaction was in effect a gift. As will be readily appreciated, none of these methods provides a satisfactory means of securing the position of a surviving *concubin*.

Other methods are available which involve a joint purchase by the two *concubins*. Thus:

1. The couple can buy *en tontine*. The nature and advantages of this type of co-ownership are discussed in Chapter 16. For the reasons given in that chapter, if the purchase is properly organized, it will usually be considered to be a transaction for full value and therefore not to be a gift in respect of which *réservataires* can make claims. The impact of the French *régime matrimonial de communauté* appears not in the light of a much criticized decision (Cass.11.1.83) to prevent a spouse under such a *régime* from buying property jointly *en tontine* with a co-owner with whom he has an adulterous liaison but this is not a decision which will affect those married in England where the *régime matrimonial* does not exist. The danger of *concubins* buying *en tontine* is that this kind of co-ownership can only be severed by agreement and the severing of the state of *concubinage* is not always the easiest time to sever a *tontine*.
2. If the persons involved have children by whomever that may be, they may not wish to deprive those children of their inheritance rights as would result from a purchase of a property *en tontine*. In such circumstances, it is possible to acquire only joint life interests *en tontine* but for the reversion to be owned by the children.
3. The purchase may be made *en indivision*. Generally, with one important exception, this manner of ownership is not attractive for the *concubin*. The few advantages and the many disadvantages of this kind of ownership are recounted in Chapter 16 and possibly the only practical advantage is that if the *vie en commun* comes to an end, the *indivision* can, if not agreed to between the co-owners, be determined by the Court. It does, however, make possible a method

of ownership which is by no means uncommon, known as an '*achat croisé*'. In such a purchase, each *concubin* purchases the life interest in a one-half share of the property and the reversion of the other one-half share. In the result, on the death of one co-owner, the survivor becomes the absolute owner of a one-half share the life interest in which has fallen in and remains the life tenant of the other half share. In this way, the survivor retains occupation of the property during his or her life. It is said that such an arrangement could possibly but rarely give rise to the complaint by a *réservataire* that it is a sham on the grounds that what in effect took place was that each co-owner bought an absolute interest in a one-half share of the property. Whilst the scheme is designed to ensure the occupation by the surviving *concubin* in the property, it cannot override the power of the beneficiaries of the deceased co-owner to require the breaking of the *indivision* by the Court subject to the payment to the surviving co-owner of the value of his or her interest in the property. Subsequent marriage of the *concubins* does not alter the original situation. An example of the difficulties to which this method can give rise is given in Chapter 16.

4. A possible solution, particularly suitable for the ownership jointly of property by persons who are domiciled in England, takes the property wholly outside the ambit of French law. It involves the purchase of property in the name of a *société civile immobilière* (SCI). This method is fully discussed in Chapter 29 as one of the methods generally available of avoiding French inheritance rules and can be particularly interesting for those domiciled in England and living *en concubinage*.

Financing a purchase of land

If a single loan is sought by both *concubins*, the lender's charge will be imposed on the property as a whole. If two separate loans are obtained, it is the custom of lenders to obtain the guarantee of each co-owner to the loan of the other to avoid the possibility that on a partition of the property it were to be vested wholly in one of the co-owners, when the charge given by the other would become worthless. If separate loans are separately repaid, no problem arises. However, if one co-owner undertakes all of this burden or at least more than his share and assuming that this was not an act of generosity by way of gift, the co-owner who has made the payment stands by subrogation in the shoes of the lender (C.civ.art.1250-1) as is the case if the liability for the loan is joint and several (C.civ.art.1251-3).

If only one *concubin* is the purchaser but both borrow, most lenders will require the joint and several covenant of both but if the liability is several only, the one co-owner who pays his share cannot benefit by subrogation from the lender's rights against the other as would be the case if he had been guarantor of that other part of the loan. If one co-owner stands guarantor for the other and repays a loan for that other, it may be said that such payment is in the nature of a gift (Cass.12.5.82) and the giver of a guarantee in such circumstances should expressly reserve his rights of subrogation which he can always waive at a future date if his repayment is in fact to be taken as a gift.

It is, of course, highly desirable that any borrowing by one *concubin* from another should be recorded in writing with the effect of establishing exactly what was intended between the parties should the situation between the parties cease, for example by death. Possibly even more significant can be the effect of C.civ.arts.1131 and 1133 which read that 'contracts devoid of consideration or based on false or unlawful consideration arc void. Consideration is unlawful when it is prohibited by law, injurious to the public good or to public order.' It has been held (CA Bourges 1.3.88), based on those articles, that a loan by one *concubin* to another may be void when the impulsive and dominating reason for its making was the desire to re-establish *concubinage*.

The provision of finance by one *concubin* to the other may have certain (and possibly unexpected) results. The handing of cash or of a cheque by one to the other or the crediting of the other's bank account are treated as gifts by manual delivery. The payment directly or through the accounts of a *notaire* to the vendor of property to one *concubin* by the other or the repayment of a debt of the other is deemed to be an indirect gift. If an *acte de vente* incorrectly gives the source of the price as that of one *concubin* when in fact it was provided by the other, it is a *donation déguisée*. If the *concubins* marry, C.civ.art.1099-1 will come into play if it is sought to revoke the gift (Chapter 37). If no marriage takes place and the gift is annulled, if it is treated as one of manual delivery, it is the amount paid which must be restituted; if it is treated as a *donation déguisée*, the asset liable to restitution is the property bought with the gift. It is worthwhile noting that the Revenue has the power to enquire into any transaction and seek to ascribe to it its proper character. The ties which bind *concubins* are a happy hunting ground for the Revenue and it must be remembered that *concubins* are strangers in blood and gifts between them are accordingly taxed at a very high rate.

The *pacte civile de solidarité et du concubinage*

Articles 515-1 to 515-7 have by virtue of the Law of 15 November 1999 been inserted in the *Code civil* immediately preceding those which deal with *concubinage*. These rules contain all that is necessary for the creation and functioning of a PACS, the acronym by which the status is widely known. It seems not to have been appreciated by the French citizen that by 1999 no less than seven countries had already passed legislation intended to facilitate marriage between persons of the same sex and at that time at least five further countries had legislation of this kind pending. Other countries had by that time laws which gave rights of inheritance to *concubins* but the PACS does not achieve that.

It may be a matter for reflection that the PACS preceded the Law of 3

December 2001 which gave surviving spouses extended rights of inheritance and considerably modernized other rules of inheritance for the benefit of the family as a unit. The institution of the PACS would seem to have as its object the support of a situation which is in total opposition to marriage. Be that as it may, the PACS, which may be used by persons of any nationality, undoubtedly offers advantages over the state of *concubinage* pure and simple.

The PACS is, according to C.civ.art.515-1, 'a contract concluded between two persons of full age of either different or the same sex to organize their life in common'. This definition may be compared with that of *union libre* which is quoted at the commencement of this chapter underlining the difference between the former which is a legal contract and the latter which arises from a mere de facto situation. There is nowhere defined what is a 'life in common' but it would seem that it requires at least a sharing of a common dwelling place and of the cost of living together.

Who may enter into a PACS

Whilst a PACS may be entered into by persons of the same sex, they may not be ascendants or descendants in the direct line or close relatives of one another. Neither party may be already married or a party to a PACS. No party to a PACS may be under the age of majority as defined by his national law. No person subject to the control of the Court of Protection or its equivalent in any country may enter into a PACS.

The document recording the creation of a PACS must be registered by the Registrar of the local Court within the jurisdiction of which the parties have their common home. It is clear that what is involved is not the domicile of the parties but only their common residence. The explanatory Directive dealing with the registration of a PACS says that the Registrar must verify the address given as one within the jurisdiction of his Court and that residence should be the one where the parties live or intend to live together continuously.

In any event, irrespective of the nationalities of the parties, a residence which qualifies in this manner is sufficient to permit the registration of a PACS. There appears to be no rule that a residence of this kind must be in France since provision exists for the registration of a PACS to be made out of France at French Consulates, in any event when one of the parties is of French nationality. Whether if both parties are of non-French nationality, a common home out of France entitles them to enjoy the benefits of a PACS (as opposed to a residence in France which is not necessarily their sole residence) raises questions of great interest based on the contents of Decrees dealing not with PACS with the powers of French Consuls to take documents in countries other than France, which are discussed in detail by Maître Revillard in *Droit International Privé et Pratique Notariale* (5th edn, Defrénois, 2001). The answer would appear to be that the nationality of the parties to a PACS does not control who may enter into such a contract nor does the fact that their common home in France is not their sole place of residence.

The PACS contract

The law has not provided for any particular form of contract to evidence the entry into a PACS. Hence, it may be either by *acte* ssp or *notarié*. The registration procedure requires the personal appearance of both parties before the Registrar of the appropriate Court with two copies of the executed *acte*. Appearance by an attorney is not possible. They must make a *déclaration sur l'honneur* that they are not prevented by law from entering into a PACS. They will need to produce birth certificates and, if either has been married, appropriate evidence of the determination of that marriage. The parties must also declare as to their appropriate common residence supported, it is suggested, by a certificate from the local *mairie* if it is in France. It seems unlikely that persons will enter into a PACS if they do not have property in France since the advantages of that status would be of little consequence. If, for one reason or another, they are relying on a non-French common residence, it is suggested that they seek the advice of a *notaire* or other suitable adviser in France who has considerable experience of the registration of a PACS rather than of a local French Consul.

It is important to appreciate that a PACS which has not been properly registered remains valid as between the parties but does not bind third parties.

Determination of a PACS

In the ordinary course of events, a PACS may be brought to an end by agreement between the parties. It may also be determined by the unilateral decision of one party by the service of a three-month notice to that effect on the other party. Such an event may in certain circumstances lead to a claim by the 'injured' party. The death or marriage of one party also leads to the determination of a PACS. If one party becomes subject to the Court of Protection or its equivalent, the contract may be determined. In all such cases, notice must be given to the Court which registered the PACS originally since the document has found its way onto the *état civil* registers and must be removed. Although the Code does not say so, presumably marriage between the parties also determines a PACS.

Ownership of assets

The PACS is not intended to be the equivalent of a *régime matrimonial*. The parties are free to agree to any method of ownership of assets during the life of the PACS and how they are to be dealt with on its determination. Subject to any such agreement, C.civ.art.515-7 provides that in the case of disaccord, the Court has power to decide the fate of such assets without prejudice to any damages which one party may be ordered to pay to the other. This will normally be on the basis that the contents of the home will be split into equal shares and all land purchased by the parties during the life of a PACS will be assumed to have been bought *en indivision* in equal shares subject to any other provision contained in the *acte de vente*.

Fiscal consequences of a PACS

It is primarily in the fiscal sphere that the PACS brings reliefs to the parties. These will be available to all those who are subject to French tax and are:

(1) in the case of income tax, the right to be assessed as a married couple in respect of their income earned from the third anniversary of their entry into the PACS onwards;

(2) in respect of ISF, they are assessed jointly;

(3) in the case of inheritance tax and gifts tax, each party to a PACS has a tax-free allowance of Euro 57,000 and pays tax at 40 per cent on the first Euro 15,000 and at 50 per cent on the balance. As *concubins* unlinked by a PACS, the tax-free allowance would be Euro 1,500 and tax at 60 per cent overall. In the case of a house worth Euro 152,500 owned equally by two persons, the surviving party to a PACS would pay French inheritance tax of Euro 8,125 against Euro 44,850 for the surviving *concubin*, whilst a surviving spouse would pay a mere Euro 12.5.

Other benefits of a PACS

The right of a surviving spouse in the case of the death, or the remaining spouse in the case of the disappearance (*abandon de domicile*), of the other spouse who was the lessee of the premises which they jointly occupied to stay in the premises is available to parties to a PACS by virtue of article 14 of the Law of 6 July 1989. This right is available only to a *concubin notoire* (that is, in a stable relationship) who has lived with the lessee for at least one year (TGI Paris 10.2.64).

A party to a PACS who regularly resides in France is treated from a Social Security point of view as the spouse of a person himself entitled to French Social Security benefits. For example, that spouse is entitled to holidays at the same time as the PACS partner. Such persons who are civil servants may invoke their PACS to ensure that they both can be employed in the same place if one is posted to a new place of work.

Although any EU citizen is entitled as of right to a *carte de séjour* (residence permit), one party to a PACS who is not an EU citizen is entitled to have taken into account when applying for a *carte de séjour* the fact that he or she is bound by a PACS to a person who is resident in France. A PACS, however, plays no part in an application for naturalization.

22

LAND AND ITS TAXATION

Introduction 209
Taxes on acquisition 209
Taxe sur la valeur ajoutée 211
Taxes during ownership 212
    Taxe foncière 212
    Taxe d'habitation 213
    Impôt de solidarité sur la fortune 214
    Taxe sur les immeubles détenus par les personnes morales 216
    Transparence fiscale 217
Tax on disposals 218

Introduction

The various taxes the liability for payment of which flows from the ownership of land fall into three groups. These are taxes payable (i) on the acquisition of land, (ii) during the ownership of land, and (iii) on the disposal of land. The rules relating to the payment of income tax or corporation tax are outside the scope of this book and no detailed reference is therefore made to either tax. It is assumed that, where the owner of land is not a private individual, it will be a *société civile* and since shareholders of such companies do not have limited liability and in some cases are directly assessed to tax, payment of tax will virtually always fall on the individual irrespective of whether he is the direct owner or the owner via the medium of a company.

Taxes on acquisition

The principal tax payable on the purchase of property and indeed on virtually any transaction in land is *enregistrement* which may be taken as the equivalent of UK stamp duty. As a French imposition, it describes also *droits de succession et de donation* (inheritance tax and gifts tax) which are dealt with in Chapter 39.

In the case of most transactions relating to land, this tax is combined with the payment of Land Registry fees in what is known as *la formalité fusionnée*. Usually it is charged, as in the United Kingdom, on an ad valorem basis but in some cases is charged as one of a number of *droits fixes*. As in the United Kingdom, *enregistrement* is not charged on items which pass by manual delivery. Where, therefore, a purchase price includes *meubles*, to obtain this benefit, the contract must show such items each separately valued since a global price is not accepted by the French Revenue. The value on which this tax will be charged will normally therefore be the price paid by the buyer exclusive of *meubles*. If the sale contract requires that the sales commission is paid by the buyer and not the seller, that payment is not considered an addition to the price (Cass.com.12.12.95) for *enregistrement* purposes but care is needed in the formulation of this obligation in the contract.

The transactions in land which attract this tax include exchanges and partitions in respect of any *soulte* or price difference. A partition of land such as the break-up of an ownership *en indivision* as the result of a death or a divorce or on a division of property in a *régime matrimonial* where the parties all receive the same value is charged at a maximum of 1 per cent.

The stamp duty payable on a purchase which is currently at 4.89 per cent is made up of three elements. The largest proportion is that of the *droit départemental* payable for the benefit of the *département* in which the property is situate. In addition, there is a proportion for the benefit of the *commune* and finally the State charges 2.5 per cent of the *droit départemental* for the work it does in collecting this tax. Thus on a flat purchased at the price of Euro 300,000 the total stamp duty would be Euro 14,670 made up as follows:

Droit départemental	à 3.6%	Euro 10,800
Taxe communale	à 1.2%	Euro 3,600
Prélèvement d'Etat	à 2.5%	
on Euro 10,000		Euro 270
		Euro 14,670

In this connection, it is worthwhile recalling that the notarial fees alone on a purchase may be taken at 0.825 per cent to which must be added Land Registry fees and small disbursements so that the total *frais de notaire* will be of the order of 7 per cent of value, of which a very large part is stamp duty. This compares with a standard estate agent's sale commission of a minimum of 6 per cent (sometimes ex-TVA and sometimes inclusive of TVA) which includes no disbursements.

The current rate of the *droit départemental* is liable to variation annually by the *conseil général* of each *département* but the maximum rate cannot exceed 3.60 per cent (there are a number of *départements* where it is less) and the minimum cannot be less than 1 per cent. In addition, there are certain transactions which are relieved of *enregistrement* or pay a reduced rate, depending in some cases on the nature of the transaction or of the property dealt with. Of these, the most important is the relief from *enregistrement* in cases where the property in question is within the TVA system, and is exempt from such taxation. Exemptions or reductions are also available in other cases which include agricultural property and property acquired by the equivalent of charitable organizations.

Since all transactions relating to land in France are prima facie subject to the payment of *enregistrement*, if the transaction is effected by an *acte* executed out of France, it must be stamped within a month of the buyer taking possession which normally will be the date of execution. The execution of a document inside France to transfer of land outside that country essentially is liable to be stamped at 4.8 per cent on the basis that the document will be an *acte notarié*. The Anglo-French Double Tax Convention is silent on this point but since a Land Registry transfer is not an *acte notarié* there seems no basis for the payment of this tax.

If a property is transferred to a *société civile immobilière* not liable to corporation tax as consideration for the issue of shares to the transferor (*un apport pure et simple*), no *enregistrement* is payable. Otherwise, the standard rate is 4.8 per cent ad valorem. It is important to note that this freedom from the standard rate of *enregistrement* requires that the shareholder undertakes to continue to hold the shares allotted to him for a period of three years from the date of their allotment. Failure to do so involves the immediate payment of *enregistrement* at 4.8 per cent without the facility to pay by instalments. Such a penalty is not sought if the disposal within that period arises by reason of a death or if the shares are the subject of a gift provided that the donee undertakes in the *acte de donation* to continue to hold the shares to the end of the three-year period.

Taxe sur la valeur ajoutée

This tax which is the equivalent of English VAT and is known in France as TVA is as a general rule charged on the price of land purchased for building purposes. This tax is not, however, charged in respect of land bought by a private individual on which to build a private dwellinghouse not intended to be sold. When property is bought in circumstances in which TVA is payable, it is not also subject to *enregistrement* but only to a Land Registry fee of 0.6 per cent on the ex-TVA price of the property. It follows therefore that land bought for the purpose of building a house for the occupation of the purchaser pays *enregistrement* at the normal rate, being free of TVA.

There are special rules when the property involved is purchased by a person who was not the builder. In such cases, TVA is payable in respect of sales of such buildings or parts of such buildings provided (i) that the sale takes place within five years of the completion of the building and (ii) that there has been no previous sale for value within that period other than to a *marchand de biens* (property dealer). In such a sale, the buyer does not pay *enregistrement* but the seller pays the difference in the TVA paid by the original seller to him and that calculated on the sale price he obtains on the resale. Sales of this kind are advertised as sales 'à frais de notaire réduits'. This highly misleading expression does not mean that the fees of the *notaire* are reduced but that the buyer will avoid payment of about 5 per cent in *enregistrement*.

Taxes during ownership

All property in France is subject to two taxes, one of which, *taxe foncière*, is a tax on the ownership of the land; the other is *taxe d'habitation*, being a tax on the occupation of land which is payable by the person who was the occupier on 1 January in every year.

The value of the property concerned in the case of both taxes is the *valeur cadastrale locative* comparable to the old English rateable value. The rule is that this value is recalculated every six years. The last valuation was made during the years 1970–3 and became effective in 1974 using the year 1970 as the year of reference. An attempt at three-yearly valuations was ultimately abandoned some years ago in favour of a countrywide inflation factor which is announced every year. However, in a further attempt to keep valuations up-to-date, the *cadastre* automatically applies every year to the 1970 values a number of criteria to every property in its area, such as any changes in user, any interior or exterior modifications to a building and any changes in the immediate environment such as the appearance of a local park or the disappearance of a local source of pollution. New buildings are valued on the basis of information required to be supplied by the first owners. The revaluation of old buildings may not exceed by more than 10 per cent their value in the previous year.

The *valeur cadastrale locative*, found as described above, is in the case of the *taxe foncière* reduced by 50 per cent to take account of the cost of maintaining and managing the property including the cost of its insurance and amortization. The *valeur cadastrale locative* in the case of *taxe d'habitation* is not subject to any reduction. On the contrary, the occupier of a principal residence whose *valeur cadastrale locative* exceeds Euro 4,573 pays a 0.2 per cent tax to the State. In the case of a secondary residence, this tax rises to 1.2 per cent for a *valeur cadastrale locative* in the range of Euro 4,573 to 7,622 and to 1.7 per cent in excess of that amount.

Appeals against any valuation so fixed may be made by the owner in the case of *taxe foncière* and the occupier (if not also the owner) in the case of *taxe d'habitation* before the end of the year next following the year in respect of which the appeal is made.

Taxe foncière

This tax falls on all property whether it is land only or buildings. In the case of unbuilt land, a number of exceptions and reductions exist of which the most interesting for the private individual are many types of agricultural land and during varying limited periods land planted with trees of various kinds. It is assessed on the owner. If the property is subject to a life interest, it is the life tenant who is assessed. In the case of *sociétés civiles* which have *transparence fiscale*, such as the *société civile d'attribution* (Chapter 10) or the *société civile de pluripropriété* (Chapter 11), the tax is assessed not on the company but proportionately on each shareholder, but in the case of a *vente à terme* (Chapter 8) it is assessed on the seller until completion of the sale of the property.

In theory it is charged against the owner as at 1 January in every year but by tradition it is apportionable on a sale. Unfortunately, it is by no means uncommon for a sale to remain unnoticed by the local *cadastre* and for demands to continue to be addressed to previous owners of property for more than a year after a sale. It is seldom advisable to allow this inefficiency to be rectified by the buyer but for the seller either to contact the appropriate local *Trésor* himself (by AR registered letter) or to ask the *notaire* who acted for him on the sale to do this on his behalf.

Every demand has a deadline for payment after which a penalty of 10 per cent is charged. Payment can be made by direct debit by a French bank if the owner is content not to question the amount.

Certain property is exempt from this tax, of which the most important is the two-year total relief granted to all new property subject to the right of the local *commune* not to grant this relief in respect of that part of the tax destined for their coffers. The relief, which runs from 1 January in the year next following that in which the building is completed, is claimed by the owner by lodging a declaration giving details of the property within thirty days of its completion. Relief is also available in the case of certain country property and that used for agricultural purposes. Special rules apply to the ownership of unbuilt land.

Relief from this tax is also available to persons in receipt of (French) supplementary benefits, owners of more than seventy-five years of age whose income does not exceed a certain maximum, or aged more than sixty-five years subject to certain other conditions, and is also available to handicapped persons in receipt of Social Security benefits. All these reliefs are available to persons from the United Kingdom who become permanently resident in France and who benefit from the French Social Security system and become liable to French income tax rules.

Taxe d'habitation

This tax is charged in respect of all property which is furnished and used for the purpose of a dwellinghouse. There is no hard and fast rule as to what constitutes furniture for the purposes of this tax. It must be sufficient, even though simple, to afford normal occupation. An overall view must be taken of the premises so that if there are rooms which are without furniture, provided that they are at the disposition of the occupant, the premises as a whole are liable to the tax. Outbuildings, garages, and parking places are considered part of the premises. Caravans and mobile homes are not liable to the tax so long as they retain their means of mobility. There are also exempt among others from this tax property which provides accommodation for students in schools and universities and also the offices of persons liable to pay *taxe professionnelle* if these do not form part of their home. (Such persons are those who, with a number of exceptions, exercise a profession the reward for which does not come in the form of a salary.)

In the case of a principal residence, the tax is subject to an inbuilt reduction to take account of the membership of the occupying family. In addition, local authorities may make reductions of up to 15 per cent in the *valeur cadastrale locative* if they so wish and may also in addition make reductions for occupants of modest means. Other reliefs are similar to those available in respect of *taxe foncière*.

The tax is due from occupiers as at 1 January in every year. There is no method of apportioning this tax and on a sale, unless unusually the contract provides otherwise, the seller will bear the whole of this tax even if he completes his sale on 2 January. To some extent, he is compensated in that on his subsequent purchase, he will have no tax to pay in the same year in respect of his new home. In any event, since the demands appear about nine months in arrears, apportionment would not be easy.

Impôt de solidarité sur la fortune

This tax, currently known as ISF, is a wealth tax. It is due from all persons who are *domiciliés fiscalement* or resident for tax purposes in France on the basis of their worldwide capital. It is a tax calculated on a *foyer* basis so that married couples whatever may be their *régime* are jointly assessed. Also jointly assessed are couples who have entered into a PACS (Chapter 21) and *concubins* of different or the same sex who live together in a stable relationship but not if one party is married to a third party. Subject to any international Convention, if a similar tax is payable in another country, it may in the case of persons subject to French income tax be set off against French ISF which is payable in respect of all assets wherever situate. The Anglo–French Convention is silent on this point.

In the case of persons who are not resident for tax purposes in France, the tax is due only in respect of certain assets situate in France. These do not include investments of a very wide range such as bank deposits, securities of most kinds both registered and bearer and in any currency, sums standing to the credit of shareholders' current accounts in any company which has its registered office or effective place of management in France and assurance policies subscribed with French insurance companies.

The tax catches assets owned as at 1 January in every year. In the case of property which is owned in different interests, for example subject to a life interest or a personal licence to occupy, the tax is due from the life tenant or licensee but the property is valued for the purpose of this tax as though unencumbered by any such interests (Cass.com.20.10.98). Hence, the remainderman is not taxed until his remainder falls in. It is important to note that this rule applies only to that part of the property subject to such interests so that if a property is subject as to a life interest in one quarter, the life tenant is taxed on one-quarter of the value of that interest.

There are exceptions to this method of assessment. If an owner sells or gives to a buyer or donee property reserving to himself a life interest then, assuming that the buyer or donee is not an *héritier présomptif* of the vendor as defined by CGI.art.751, each party is liable for the tax in respect of the value of his respective interest in the property depending on the life expectancy of the seller. In such a case, an *héritier présomptif* is an ascendant or issue or spouse of a buyer or donee. A similar situation arises in cases covered by C.civ.art.767 which deals with the entrenched rights of inheritance of surviving spouses by the creation of a life interest in his or her favour.

Excluded from the assets on which this tax is paid are:

(i)   objets d'art and antiques;
(ii)   jewellery if more than a hundred years old;
(iii)   copyrights, patents, and other intellectual property;
(iv)   the right to a professional retirement pension and to a pension received by way of compensation for personal injuries but not for damage to property.

There are special reliefs for forests and woodlands and for agricultural property let for not less than eighteen years and in a variety of other circumstances.

For the purposes of valuing taxable property the usual rules apply save that in the case of a principal residence occupied on 1 January in the year of assessment, a reduction of 20 per cent in value is made. This reduction is available whether the property is owned by an individual or by a *société civile* which has *transparence fiscale*. In respect of *meubles*, the method of valuation is the same as for *droits de succession*, namely to take them at 5 per cent of the overall value of the taxable assets. This is seldom as advantageous a way of adducing a value as that allowed by the French Revenue as a concession by means of a simplified inventory and a global value which holds good for three years subject to any important change being reported to the tax authorities. Debts due on 1 January of the year of assessment from the taxpayer may be deducted. They are acceptable to the Revenue on the same basis as debts are allowed for *droits de succession* on a death.

The tax, which tends to vary as in the United Kingdom from time to time and over the last few years downwards ostensibly to match inflation, is calculated on a slice basis in the following manner:

Not exceeding Euro 720,000	nil
Euro 720,000 – 1,160,000	0.55%
Euro 1,160,000 – 2,300,000	0.75%
Euro 2,300,000 – 3,600,000	1.00%
Euro 3,600,000 – 6,900,000	1.3%
Euro 6,900,000 – 15,000,000	1.65%
In excess of Euro 15,000,000	1.8%

Net taxable assets of Euro 22,000,000 will on the above scale give ISF of Euro 326,520 or an overall rate of a little under 1.5 per cent.

The following reliefs are available. A reduction of Euro 150 is made for every child under eighteen or who is handicapped living at home. A further similar amount is deducted for every person who is a holder of a *carte d'invalidité*. In the case only of those who are tax resident in France, there is a provision to ensure that the total of income tax and ISF in any one year does not exceed 85 per cent of the income of the taxpayer for the previous year.

Taxe sur les immeubles détenus par les personnes morales

All companies which directly or through others indirectly own one or more *immeubles* or *droits réels* in France are prima facie liable to this annual tax equal to 3 per cent of the value of such property (CGI.arts.990D-G). This imposition has been modified in respect of such companies as have their *siège* in France. The regulations currently governing this tax are set out in the *décret* No 93-819 of 14 May 1993 and an *arrêté* of the same date.

The companies concerned are all those incorporated in France or elsewhere or wheresoever they have their principal place of management provided that they have an entity of their own distinct from their shareholders according to the laws of the country of their incorporation. The Liechtenstein *Stiftung* and *Anstalt* are deemed to be companies for the purposes of this tax. The tax covers companies which own property through the 'interposition of third parties' which is a widely drawn definition but for practical purposes may be considered to catch company A which is a shareholder in company B which owns a property in France. In such a case, it is immaterial how far removed in a chain from the company which owns the property may be the 'offending' company but it is the last one in that chain which bears the tax.

There are a number of significant exemptions from this tax:

1. Companies which own *immeubles* in France, the value of which is less than one-half of the market value of all their French assets. For the purpose of the calculation of this percentage, no account is taken as numerator of this fraction of the assets in the form of *immeubles* of which the company concerned or any interposed company makes use other than in connection with its business of the ownership of *immobilier*.

2. Companies whose *siège* is situate in a country which has concluded with France a Convention which contains a clause providing for mutual assistance in the suppression of tax evasion and fraud. Of the many countries which have concluded such Convention with France, one is the United Kingdom but that territory does not include the Channel Islands or the Isle of Man. To obtain this exemption, it is necessary for the company in question to file annually before 16 May a Return No 2748 showing: (i) the address, description and value as at the previous 1 January of the property owned directly or

by interposed companies; (ii) the identity of its shareholders; and (iii) the number of shares held by each shareholder.

3. Companies which have their effective place of management in France or which by virtue of a Convention concluded with France should benefit in another country from the same tax treatment as companies which have their *siège* in France. Such countries include the United Kingdom (but not the Channel Islands or the Isle of Man) and Switzerland which is an absentee from the list of countries under 2 since Switzerland remains unanxious to provide tax information to France. On the other hand, Luxembourg, Canada, the USA, Denmark, and Belgium do not figure on the list. To benefit from this exemption, the company, if it is not subject to corporation tax, must either fulfil the same conditions as are required in 2 above or must give an undertaking within two months of the acquisition of the property in question to supply such information about the property as the Revenue may require.

4. Companies whose shares are quoted on the Paris Stock Exchange or which are formed with charitable, cultural or philanthropic objects if the ownership of the property is required for the pursuance of such objects.

Failure to make the necessary declarations on time or even at all seldom gives rise to problems if, in the event, the tax is not payable. It is, however, not desirable to omit this formality since ultimately it will be questioned when the property comes to be sold. In fact, thought given to the disclosure of the annual value of a property during its ownership by a company can often be a useful weapon when it comes to dealing with capital gains tax on its sale. The return lodged by the company at the *Centre des impôts des non-résidents*, 9, rue d'Uzès, 75094 Paris Cedex 02 and the application for clearance for capital gains tax are undoubtedly linked together in the files of the French Revenue.

Transparence fiscale

No type of *société civile* provides the shareholders with limited liability so that taxation of all kinds falls to be paid by them. There is, however, a distinction made between the *société civile* which enjoys *transparence fiscale* and those which do not. This tax *régime* by virtue of CGI.art.1655ter. applies to such companies as, despite the fact that they are legal entities separate from their shareholders, are considered not to have a tax existence of their own. In such cases, the shareholders are treated for tax purposes as though they were the direct owners of the proportionate parts of the property owned by the company.

Companies which have *transparence fiscale* are those which are unable by virtue of their objects to exploit the ownership of their property but are obliged to limit its use to occupation by their shareholders whether at a rent or free of any cost, and eventually to distribute that property *in specie* to their shareholders. These companies are *sociétés d'attribution* which must not be confused with other *sociétés civiles immobilières* on the grounds that in most cases it is the shareholders who are liable for the taxation. In both cases, it is the shareholders who pay but where there is *transparence fiscale*, they are assessed directly and where there is not, it is the SCI which is assessed but the shareholders contribute *inter se* to payment. The tax liability in either case includes all taxes such as stamp duties, local taxes and capital gains tax imposed in respect of the property owned by the company.

The tax aspects of the SCI are beyond the scope of this book but, in one respect, the notion of *transparence fiscale* can be of importance to shareholders who are UK tax resident. The occupation by a shareholder of an SCI free of rent is an *avantage en nature* or benefit in kind but is specifically exempt from any tax liability in France on the grounds that it is considered to be occupation by the SCI itself of its own property. Not, however, so in the United Kingdom where, because the Revenue treats the SCI which does not have in France *transparence fiscale* as a company for the purposes of the Income and Corporation Taxes Act 1988, any person who can be held to be a director of that SCI may find himself liable to a Schedule E assessment in respect of the benefit in kind represented by that occupation. This subject is dealt with at some length in the author's article 'Tax trap for owners of French property' in (2002) 146 *Solicitors Journal* no 6, 144.

The use of the SCI as a vehicle for the ownership of French property can be so significant for UK resident taxpayers that this is a question of much importance. Correspondence with the UK Revenue would seem to have elicited the result that if shareholders of an SCI by virtue of its *statuts* are not and cannot be appointed *gérants* and are absolutely debarred from taking any part in the administration of the SCI, they are probably free of this tax liability. There is no reason why properly drawn *statuts* coupled with an intelligent *gérant* should not achieve such freedom but great care must be taken in the drawing of these *statuts* and advice must be taken from English tax experts versed in the problem.

Currently, the Revenue is rethinking its thoughts on this issue, one hopes in favour of the taxpayer.

In the same way, if the acquisition of French property via an SCI is primarily for letting purposes, advice must be sought from competent French tax advisers in France in the form of *avocats* or accountants rather than estate agents who merely manage property. Apart from taxation related to lettings and the 3 per cent tax in the unlikely event that it is payable, it is improbable that an SCI will be faced with any direct or indirect taxation other than that which is to be borne by the private individual.

Tax on disposals

Two systems of capital gains tax apply in France depending on whether the seller is resident in France for tax purposes or not. It is proposed to deal only with the liability insofar as it affects the non-resident seller of land.

The basic rate of capital gains tax (*les plus-values*) for the non-resident is 331/3 per cent. The tax is due on the sale of land or of shares in unquoted companies, the preponderance of whose assets consist of French land. With some exceptions, the non-resident seller is entitled to the same reliefs in respect of this tax as is the resident and these are listed below.

In the case of the private individual, the gross tax is calculated on the difference between the acquisition price adjusted by an inflation percentage (*coefficient d'érosion monétaire*) and the sale price. In the case of the acquisition of a property by way of inheritance, or on the dissolution of a *régime*, the acquisition price is deemed to be its value at the date of death of the person from whom it was inherited or of its entry into the *régime*. This basic calculation may in most cases be adjusted by a number of factors of which the most significant are:

1. The costs of purchase may be added to the purchase price if these can be proved and exceed 10 per cent of the purchase price. If not, a standard 10 per cent is acceptable.
2. The cost of building and repair work may be added to the acquisition price at its cost inclusive of TVA and supported by receipted bills and the inflation factor having regard to the year in which the work was done may be applied. In the absence of such bills, the seller may choose to use a figure of 15 per cent of the acquisition price or rely on the report of an expert whose fees are also treated as an allowable expense. It seems that some local Inspectors will only accept the report of an *expert près les tribunaux*, that is one who is on the Court list of experts, but this is not a statutory requirement. It follows therefore that all bills for work of this nature should be carefully preserved and the temptation to pay free of TVA avoided.
3. The cost of material supplied by the owner multiplied by three since the inflation factor is not applied.
4. Works carried out at the requirement of the local authority.
5. In certain cases, interest on loans for the purchase or repair of second homes, acquired in the case of new properties before 1 January 1997 and in the case of old properties before 1 January 1998. The amounts allowed to be added to the acquisition price vary according to the actual dates of the loans but are not adjusted by application of the inflation factor.

The final recalculated figure of the acquisition price is compared to the sale price and a basic capital gain is thus established. That resultant figure is diminished by 5 per cent per year of ownership after the first two fully completed years so that at the end of twenty-two years' ownership, no tax is payable.

There are other reliefs, most of which are also available to non-residents:

1. If the proceeds of sale are used in the purchase or building of another property within six months of the date of sale but not for works of improvement, the tax

is not payable in full or only proportionately to the amount used for such purposes.
2. A citizen of an EU country being resident out of France is exempt from the tax if:
   (a) he sells a property he owns in France provided that he has been resident for tax purposes in France for at least a year prior to that sale and has had free occupation of the property since its purchase or construction or for a minimum period of three years;
   (b) he sells for the first time a property in France provided that he has been continuously resident for tax purposes in France for at least a year at any time prior to its sale.

In addition, there are the following reliefs:

1. There is a general relief of Euro 915 deductible from any tax found due having regard to the above reliefs.
2. In the case of the first sale of a secondary residence, a relief of Euro 6,100 for a married couple or Euro 4,600 for a single person and Euro 1,525 per child. Thus, a married couple with two grown up children benefits from relief amounting to Euro 9,150.

For the purposes of this tax and indeed for other taxes, the French Revenue has regard to sales of a similar kind in the same neighbourhood within the previous few years. It is generally understood that a difference of 10 per cent in values is usually ignored. Bearing in mind, however, that capital gains tax is essentially at the rate of 33 1/3 per cent for non-residents, and even taking into account where they are appropriate the various reliefs available, it cannot be desirable to attempt to save *enregistrement* of under 5 per cent by paying part of a purchase price other than by lawful means.

Capital gains tax due from non-residents is payable on completion of the sale and it is the task of the *notaire* acting for the seller to account for this to the French Revenue. In order to ascertain what that tax may be, the *notaire* lodges a form 2090 which gives all the relevant figures and reliefs claimed and shows the amount of tax (if any) estimated to be due. Until 31 December 2002, it was the rule that every non-resident must on a sale of his property in France appoint a *représentant fiscal* or tax agent who undertook the liability for any tax found due on further consideration of the file by the Revenue. The period involved is for practical purposes four years after completion of the sale. The form 2090 also sought exemption from the appointment of this tax agent. As from 1 January 2003, the rule has changed. On sales for a consideration of less than Euro 100,000, it will never be necessary to appoint a *représentant fiscal* whilst on sales where the sale price exceeds that amount, such an appointment is obligatory.

The French Revenue alleged that the new procedure would simplify the procedure for the *notaire*, the seller and itself. Since in the past, in the majority of cases, exemption from the appointment of a *représentant fiscal* was obtained whilst many sale prices exceed Euro 100,000, the loser is the non-resident seller. It is essential that the choice of a *représentant fiscal* should not be made by the *notaire* acting for the seller without prior reference to him. The *représentant fiscal* must have formal approval of the Revenue and there are a number of banks and companies which undertake this task. Their average fee is 1 per cent of the sale price but there are also private individuals so approved whose fee may be less.

There is, however, another and more significant reason to be careful in the choice. The *représentant fiscal* will consider each case on its merits to evaluate his risk and in certain cases or even as a general rule may require the deposit of part of the price as cover until the Revenue's claim for additional tax, if any, becomes statute-barred. In cases where the seller has undertaken works, the cost of which can be taken into account in computing taxable gains, but has lost the receipted bills he has paid or has deliberately paid the builder ex-VAT and has no bills to produce, the risk may be greater than that covered by a 1 per cent fee. This should be a matter for negotiation between the *notaire* and the *représentant fiscal* and too many of the former will accept without question whatever is proposed and present it to the non-resident seller as a fait accompli.

There is a further matter to consider which adds strength to the need to file the tax return to obtain exemption from the 3 per cent tax on property discussed under the heading above *Taxe sur les immeubles détenus par les personnes morales*. It must be remembered that the *représentant fiscal* is also liable for this tax if it has not been paid or exemption from it obtained. He is unlikely to assume the leniency of the Revenue when considering what fee to charge.

The following example is typical of what can occur if a non-resident seller is not fully advised. In the 1990s Mr X bought a piece of land for Euro 33,540 and built on it a house for Euro 136,450 making a total of Euro 169,990. Nine years later, the owner sold the house and applying the inflation index to the acquisition price, it was then taken as Euro 190,395. The house was sold for such a sum as taking into account all available reliefs, no capital gains tax was payable and the application for *dispense* so indicated. The *dispense* was refused on the grounds that no bills relating to the building of the house had been submitted. The *notaire* advised the sellers of this refusal but gave no reasons and, without waiting for any reaction from the sellers, immediately contacted a *représentant fiscal* who charged a fee of Euro 2,120 and required a deposit of Euro 30,200 to cover their guarantee. The bills relating to the work were all stage payments supported by architect's certificates but the *notaire* made no reference to this. It is inconceivable that if the seller had appreciated why the *dispense* had been refused, he would not have taken the matter further.

The following is a typical example of the calculation of a capital gains tax liability for a property bought in 1988 by a private individual and sold in 2001.

Sale price Euro 245,000			
Purchase price			Euro 130,000
Costs of purchase (say)			Euro 13,000
Adjusted purchase price			Euro 143,000
Application of inflation factor for appropriate years			
Price & costs Euro 143,000 × 1.27			Euro 181,610
Works to house Euro 9,250 × 1.19	Euro	11,075	
Building materials Euro 2,286 × 3	Euro	6,858	
Loan interest	Euro	7,655	Euro 207,198
Gain			Euro 37,802
Reduction for 12 years' ownership (50%)			Euro 18,901
Net gain			Euro 18.901
Less relief – general	Euro	915	
– married couple	Euro	6,100	Euro 7,015
Taxable gain			Euro 11,886

Care must be taken when the selling owner is a company. In the case of a French company, such as an SCI which has been formed merely to hold the property and allow its shareholders to occupy it free of rent, it is likely to be treated as not being liable to French *impôt sur les sociétés* (corporation tax) in which case it will be treated for capital gains tax purposes as a private individual. If, however, it has indulged in activities such as letting its property which have caused it to become liable to corporation tax, the basic calculation to arrive at a taxable gain will not be between the purchase price and the sale price but between the purchase price diminished by 2 per cent per annum for each full year of ownership, thus increasing the basic tax liability. It seems inevitable that if the company is a UK company it will be treated as one liable to corporation tax and the less advantageous method of calculating the tax utilized. As has been said in Chapter 7, a company not incorporated in France is automatically required to appoint a *représentant fiscal*.

23

CAPACITY

Introduction 223
Infants 224
Adoption 225
    Adoption plénière 225
    Adoption simple 226
Children's capacity to inherit 227
Persons of full age under a disability 227
Capacity in respect of wills 228
Married persons 230

Introduction

For ease of reference this chapter contains the basic rules relating to the capacity of persons involved in a variety of transactions.

As a general rule of French private international law, all questions of capacity are answered by the *loi personnelle* of the person involved. Not only, therefore, is the status and capacity of a person governed by the rules of the law of the country of his nationality when he is in that country but they apply when he is outside that country. In most cases, the capacity of a person of British nationality domiciled in England and Wales will be governed by English law and the French Court will have no jurisdiction. It may be noted that in the case of an infant having both British and French nationality, the French Court will give priority to his French nationality and treat French law as his *loi personnelle*.

It must be remembered that every French person carries with him to be displayed on frequent occasions his *état civil*. It explains what is his legal capacity and immediately advises the *notaire* and others properly interested what his capacity entitles him lawfully to do including the extent to which, if he is married, he can deal with property without the intervention of his spouse. No French *acte* of any significance, and indeed many of very little significance fail to record the parties' *état civil*. A proper appreciation of the part played in French law by the *état civil* can be gleaned from the following quotation from Malinvaud, *Introduction à l'étude de droit* (Editions Litec, 1995): 'For example, when entering into a contract with someone, it is indispensable to ascertain his nationality, his capacity, his marital status, if he is classed as a businessman or as a private individual etc etc and if he represents a company what are his powers . . . When instituting proceedings against a person, it is desirable to know his full name as well as his address at which papers may be served upon him by the *huissier* which also determines which Court has jurisdiction.'

Notice must also be taken of the fact that records kept by the *officier de l'état civil* or Registrar of Births, Deaths and Marriages, of whom there is one in every *commune*, link together these three events so that the ordinary person's *état civil* at any one time is simple to establish.

Infants

The age at which a child attains his majority under French law is eighteen. Under that age, he is represented in law by his parents or by a *tuteur* or guardian. Such a person may be appointed by a notarial will or declaration of the surviving parent, the effects of which are not dissimilar to the appointment of a testamentary guardian under English law. In default of such an appointment, a *tuteur* may be appointed either by a *conseil de famille* which is composed of close members of the infant's family which assists the *juge des tutelles* in arranging certain family situations or by the Court itself.

An infant is automatically *émancipé* or freed from the restrictions of infancy on marriage. *Emancipation* may be granted by the Court on the request of the parents of the child or if he has no parents, of the *conseil de famille*. It releases the child from the authority of his parents but he does not have full capacity in that he cannot marry or enter into a *contrat de mariage* or be adopted without the consent of his parents or of his *conseil de famille*. He can, on the other hand, deal freely with his own estate in that he can sell or make gifts of his own assets save that in respect of commercial transactions, his capacity remains limited.

The infant who is not *émancipé* cannot make a valid will. However, as an important exception to this general rule, an infant aged sixteen may dispose by will of one half of the assets of which he could dispose if he had attained his majority (C.civ.art.904). He may also, with the consent of those whose consent is necessary for his marriage, by his marriage contract, make a gift to his intended spouse (C.civ.arts.1095 and 1398). Gifts made by an infant after marriage to his spouse are valid since marriage has resulted in his *émancipation*. An infant may also lawfully make without the consent of any person small gifts such as birthday and wedding presents and small payments for services rendered.

There are no rules as to the acceptance of a gift by an infant save that the donee, be it of a legacy in a will or made *inter vivos*, must be a person in being. This situation is covered by C.civ.art.906 which provides that it is sufficient if the donee in the case of a gift was conceived at the date of the making of the gift or in the case of a will, at the date of its execution. In both cases, the child must subsequently be born viable.

Special rules apply to the acceptance or renunciation and the retraction of the renunciation by an infant of his interest in an estate. These are included in

Chapter 34 which deals generally with acceptances and renunciations of estates by persons entitled to share in the estate of a deceased person.

It is undoubted French law that in the case of the ownership of French land by an infant of British nationality, it is English law which decides whether dealings with such land are possible (Cass.13.4.32). The proper procedure to adopt is to proceed by way of Application in the Chancery Division under section 53 of the Trustee Act 1925. The Children Act 1989 is not the proper Act to use. Since trusts do not exist in France, in many cases French land will become vested on a death in an infant who by French law takes beneficially whatever his age may be. This is most likely to happen as the result of an inheritance in the French equivalent of tenancy in common if that infant is, for example, one of a class of beneficiaries of French land in an estate, and the sale of such land is not the only incident in which an infant owner could be involved. The French system will recognize the Order of the English Court authorizing a named person to act on behalf of an infant. It will not, save possibly in the most exceptional and urgent cases, be possible to deal with the problem through the *juge des tutelles*.

Adoption

Adoption in France is in two forms. It may be an *adoption plénière* or an *adoption simple*. The former, as in the case in English law, results in the breaking of all ties between the child and its original family. The latter may be thought of almost in the nature of a permanent fostering authorized by the Court since whilst it creates family ties between the adopted child and the adopting parents, it leaves untouched the relationship between that child and its original family.

Adoption plénière

In the case of an *adoption plénière*, the adopted child ceases by virtue of C.civ.arts.356, 357 and 358 to have any relationship with his original family. He takes the name of his adopting parent or, if he is adopted by a married couple, the name of the husband. The adopting parents may ask the Court to change the child's first names. The adopted child has all the rights of a legitimate child of the adopting parents.

As in England, after adoption, there appear on the child's birth certificate only his sex, date and place of birth and his first names and the *état civil* of his adopting parent or parents appears in the place of that of his real parents. It is possible to obtain a copy of the Adoption Order made by the Court but this will not disclose his original parentage except in the sole case of the adoption by one spouse of the child of the other spouse.

This arrangement can lead to difficulties when it is necessary to produce in France to prove *filiation* or parentage the English birth certificate of an English adopted child. The English 'short' certificate does not contain any of the details of the parentage, either original or adopted, of the child.

225

In the case of an *adoption plénière*, the child to be adopted must be less than fifteen years old and if he is aged thirteen or more, his consent must be obtained. The adopting parent must be aged at least twenty-eight except in the case of the adoption by one spouse of a child of the other spouse in which case all that is required is that the couple has been married for at least two years. Normally, the adopting parents must be fifteen years older than the child they adopt or, in the case of adoption by one spouse of the child of the other spouse, the difference is ten years.

In the case of adoptions by English Courts, the situation is covered by C.civ.arts.370-3 to 370-5 which refer to adoptions which take place outside France. These follow the line adopted by the Hague Convention of 5 October 1961 and the subsequent modifying Convention of 19 October 1996 and provide that:

(1) It is the law of the nationality of the adopting parent or, in the case of an adoption by a married couple, of the law which governs the effects of their marriage, which sets the conditions of the adoption.
(2) An adoption Order made outside France has the effect of an *adoption plénière* if it results in a complete and irrevocable break in the previous relationship. Otherwise, the result will be an *adoption simple* which can be converted in France into an *adoption plénière* if the necessary consents are forthcoming.

Adoption simple
The age limits in respect of the adopted child are not enforced in the case of this type of adoption save that if the child is aged thirteen or more, he must consent to the adoption. The age limits regarding the adopters are as for the *adoption plénière*. Adoption confers on the child the surname of the adopter added to that of his original parents but the adopter may both before and after the adoption has taken place ask the Court that his name alone is used. Such an adoption may be revoked at the instance of either adopter (if the child is aged more than fifteen years) or the adopted child or, if the latter is not of full age, of the State. Revocation in the case of a child who is still a minor may also be requested by his original parents or, in default, by any member of his family not more remote than a cousin.

The adopted child, by remaining a member of his original family, conserves all his rights arising from that relationship including those of inheritance. He also has inheritance rights in the estate of his adopting parent but not in respect of the estates of any of the latter's ascendants.

This rule would apply in the following example. Madame Dupont died a widow intestate domiciled in France. She was survived by her three grandchildren, Jean, Marie and Martin who were the children of her deceased brother Paul by his marriage to Claudine. That marriage had been dissolved and Claudine subsequently married again. Some years after that marriage took place, Martin was adopted in England by Claudine and her second husband. The English adoption is treated in France as an *adoption plénière*. By virtue of C.civ.art.356 referred to above an adopted child is treated as ceasing to belong to his former family and becomes part of his adopting family. An exception to that rule is that where the child is adopted by two spouses of which one is the natural parent of the child, this keeps alive that child's inheritance rights in respect of that parent and his or her family. In this case, the three grandchildren would normally take by representation equally between them the share of their deceased father. However, in the light of Martin's adoption, prima facie he ceased to have inheritance rights in his father's family. The exception to the rule referred to above does not apply since the family in which the inheritance lies is that of his natural father and his adopting parents are his mother and a stranger in blood.

Children's capacity to inherit

As from the Law of 3 January 1972, all children are from an inheritance point of view treated on the same basis. The illegitimate child ranks equally with the legitimate child provided that the parentage of the latter has been voluntarily recognized by one or both of the parents or has been established by the Court (C.civ.art.756). The last and shameful distinction between children—that of the *enfant adultérin*, who was a child born to parents one of which at the time of its conception was married to a person who was not the other parent—has now by the Law of 3 December 2001 been abolished. Previously, such a child received less than other children in a parent's estate as a punishment for the sins of that parent. All now are treated alike.

Persons of full age under a disability

French law distinguishes between such persons who are incapable of exercising their rights by reason of some physical or mental disability (*les incapacités d'exercice*) and those who have been deprived of their legal rights by civil or criminal judgment or by law (*les incapacités de jouissance*). In the case of the former, whilst they retain their full rights, they can only exercise them through or with the aid of another. Such another person may be either a *tuteur* or a *curateur*. The procedure is available not only in the case of persons of full age but also of infants who have been *émancipé*.

C.civ.art.490 says that a person whose 'mental faculties are affected by illness or infirmity or are weakened by age or whose bodily functions are affected so as to prevent him from expressing his wishes' may in his own interests be made subject to such systems of protection as are provided either by *la tutelle* or by *la curatelle*. If a person is made subject to either form of protection by the *juge des tutelles* by virtue of C.civ.art.491-2, he retains all his legal rights subject to the power of the Court to vary or annul any engagements entered into by him if thought fit to do so.

A wide variety of persons who may be appointed *tuteur* is available and the Court may decide that the patient has himself the capacity to do certain acts either alone or with the aid of his *tuteur*. Any will made by a testator prior to the appointment of a *tuteur* remains valid unless it can be established that after such an appointment has taken place the reason behind the making of the will has ceased to exist. Prima facie, any will made after the *tutelle* has commenced is void but the Court has a general power under C.civ.art.501 to decide that any particular act done by the patient shall be treated as valid. In the case of a *curatelle* a testator may make a valid will if he is of sound mind. With the consent of the *conseil de famille* gifts *inter vivos* may be made on behalf of the patient to any of his descendants subject to hotchpot or to his spouse.

A person subject to *tutelle* may not enter into a *pacte de solidarité* (Chapter 21). If during the course of the existence of such a *pacte* either party becomes subject to a *tutelle*, the *tuteur*, with the consent of the *conseil de famille*, determines it, failing which the Court itself can put an end to the *pacte*.

Capacity in respect of wills

The *Code civil* states in somewhat stark terms in article 718 that '*Les successions s'ouvrent par la mort naturelle*' and in article 724 that '*Pour succéder, il faut nécessairement exister à l'instant de l'ouverture de la succession*'. The joint effect of these articles is to define who by reason of having survived the deceased is capable of inheriting under his will or in his intestacy. Article 724 continues to point out that 'he who has not been conceived' and 'the child who is not born alive' cannot inherit. A corollary to this is the rule on *commorientes*.

In accordance with the wishes of the majority of *notaires*, by virtue of the Law of 3 December 2001 the archaic rules which theretofore governed the situation in which two persons died in circumstances in which it was impossible to know which died first have been abolished. The previous rules based on the age and sex of the persons produced different results depending on whether the persons involved had reached the age of fifteen or exceeded the age of sixty or were aged between those two limits and whether they were male or female. The new C.civ.art.725-1 says that when two persons of whom one was a potential beneficiary in the estate of the other die as the result of a single event, the order of their deaths is to be established 'by all available means'. If it is not possible so to establish that order, the estate of each is to be administered on the basis that neither had an interest in either.

Old French law at one time made provision for *la mort civile* to be for inheritance purposes the equivalent of physical death. This was abolished in 1854. As a leftover from that concept is the provision in the Penal Code which can, in the case of persons sentenced to long terms of imprisonment under certain conditions, deprive them of the right to dispose of their assets by will (or by gift *inter vivos*). It is pleasing to note that the State has happily also power to restore this right in whole or in part.

Less unusual in its reasoning is the *régime de l'indignité* which has by the recent Law of 2 December 2001 undergone a transformation. Basically, C.civ.arts.726 to 729 now define those who are *indigne* to take in the intestacy or under the will of a deceased person. Such persons are divided into two groups. Article 726 says that persons who have received severe sentences (*peines criminelles*) as principal or accessory to the murder or attempted murder or the manslaughter of the deceased are completely barred from taking any interest in his estate. In this respect, the rule closely follows that of English law save that the effect of insanity of the person committing the crime has no place in the article. By virtue of article 727, the Court may impose a decree of *indignité* in what are considered less serious circumstances, such as in cases similar to those which incur an obligatory *indignité* but where sentences of a lighter character (*peines correctionnelles*) have been imposed. Thus, the giving of false evidence against the deceased in criminal proceedings, the deliberate abstention from preventing the commission of a crime or wrongful act against the person of the deceased or when defamatory evidence has caused the deceased to suffer a *peine criminelle* are examples of acts giving rise to this kind of *indignité*.

The new Law has also provided that:

1. If a testator in the full knowledge of the facts which led to a beneficiary being subject to *l'indignité* wishes to maintain that person's right to share in his estate, he may so declare in his will (the *Code civil* does not require a notarial will) and this overrides the incapacity of *indignité*. Otherwise the Order of the Court is made at the instance of any other beneficiary or in the absence of any such person by the State, within six months of the date of death.
2. Children of a beneficiary excluded from his benefit by reason of his *indignité* are not excluded from any inheritance to which they are entitled directly or by representation but the parent under such a disability cannot enjoy the income from such benefit as the law allows to the parents of infant children.

The following may not benefit under a will:

(1) doctors and chemists who have been involved in the treatment of the last illness of the deceased if the will was made during the course of that illness;
(2) ministers of religion who attended the deceased during his last illness;
(3) the *tuteur* of the deceased so long as the *tutelle* is in force or after its determination until the accounts of the *tuteur* have been approved.

The capacity of certain legatees to accept legacies can be restricted. Thus, religious communities require the authority of the local *Préfecture* or the *Conseil d'Etat* depending on the size of the gift. Certain charities and associations depending on whether they are '*déclarées*' have the power to accept legacies and certain have not. The standard English declaration in wills as to the power of 'the Treasurer or other proper officer' to give receipts for legacies would be meaningless if the charity were French and enquiries should always be made before including such a legacy in a will.

Married persons

The capacity of married persons to acquire and dispose of property is dealt with in Chapter 20 on the *régime matrimonial*.

PART II

INHERITANCE LAW

INHERITANCE LAW

Introduction 233
Source of inheritance law 233
Intestate and testamentary inheritance 235
Executors 236
Types of French wills 236
Agreements to make a will 237
Capacity to inherit 237
Commencement of administration procedure 237
Saisine 238
Acceptance of an estate 238
The réserve 239
Winding up an estate 239

Introduction

There is possibly no branch of French law which is so inimical to the English as that relating to the inheritance of property on death. Its application to assets in France owned by English persons whatever may be their domicile at the date of their death and to all assets wherever situate if their domicile is French is frequently misunderstood. This can lead to much confusion and dismay and often recrimination among beneficiaries who find that they are deprived as a result of the impact of French law of assets which clearly they were intended to inherit. None suffers more noticeably than the surviving spouse even if, of very recent time, his or her position has been ameliorated to a considerable extent. To which assets in the estate of a deceased person French law will apply depends on their situation and the domicile of the deceased at the date of death. The principles of English and French private international law relating to the inheritance to property both provide that the inheritance to *immeubles* or immovables is governed by the *lex situs*, or place where they are situate, whilst inheritance to *meubles* or movables follows the law of the domicile of the deceased owner.

Source of inheritance law

French inheritance law has its foundations in two separate legal systems. On the one hand, Roman law, which flourished in countries maintaining a written system of law, tended to regard the ownership of property as strictly an individual right. This view favoured freedom of testamentary disposition so that a testator might substantially dispose of his property after death in any manner he wished. This freedom was, however, somewhat curtailed by the existence of the *légitime*, under which close relations of a deceased person were entitled to a quarter of what they would have received in an intestacy and which bears a resemblance in concept but not in value to the modern French *réserve*. This rule is said to have stemmed from the notion that a person who did not leave at least a minimum of his estate to his close relatives must have been so lacking in 'pietas' as to be of unsound mind so that his will could on that ground successfully be overturned by those he failed to benefit.

The other system of law which played its part in the creation of modern French inheritance law was based on *droit coutumier* which considered that the owner of property, except in respect of that which he had personally acquired during his lifetime, derived its ownership from his forebears. Thus, property took on the character of a family rather than an individual asset, providing an explanation for the preponderance of intestate over testate succession.

The subsequent development in the rules relating to inheritance effected by the Laws of 17 *nivose an II* and of 4 *germinal an VIII* (8 January 1794 and 25 March 1800) gave an added importance to intestate succession by a further extension of the *réserve* with a consequent diminution of the *quotité disponible* or that part of a person's assets of which he may freely dispose *inter vivos* or by will. However, this did not represent a progression of the *droit coutumier* so much as an application of the political philosophy current at the time of the French Revolution, that property should remain in the family and that freedom of disposition on death should be available in respect of only a very small proportion of a deceased person's estate. These Laws also paid respect to the Revolutionary tenet of equality in all things and, in order to establish such a situation among the heirs of a deceased person, forbade a testator to grant a larger benefit to one *réservataire* than to another.

The *Code civil* in its final form effected a compromise. Ostensibly, it reduced in the eyes of the law the difference in effect between intestate and testate succession. In contrast to the pre-*Code civil* situation, it increased the amount of the *quotité disponible* and at the same time made it possible to give by will unequal benefits to *réservataires* by giving to one *réservataire* but not to others a share in or all of the *quotité disponible* in addition to his share in the *réserve*. It maintained the application of the *réserve* to ascendants and descendants in the direct line. Of no less importance, it gave added protection for those benefiting from the *réserve* against depletion in its value at the date of death not only by gifts made by a deceased in his will but also those made by him *inter vivos*. Since that date, the Law of 26 March 1896 and subsequently the Law of 3 January 1972 have added the illegitimate child and the ascendants and descendants of such a child to the list of *réservataires* (C.civ.arts.757 and 758). They left, however, unchanged the situation of the *enfant adultérin* (that is, a child of parents one of whom was at the time of its conception married to a person who was not the other parent) who was still penalized in many cases by receiving only a reduced share in the deceased parent's estate.

Not until the year 2001 did the legislature enact the Law of 3 December which took effect on 1 July 2002 and which (inter alia) considerably improved the situation of the surviving spouse and remedied the unhappy position of the hapless and innocent *enfant adultérin*. This Law undoubtedly represents a greater awareness of the need to leave behind some of the less attractive features of the inheritance system. The following contemporary comment is significant. 'Curiously enough, notwithstanding that marriage after a spectacular decline in number has not noticeably begun to find favour anew with the younger generation, whilst at the same time the number of divorces is on the increase and the legislature had clearly marked its approval of the unmarried couple by the introduction amid the ensuing outcry of the *pacte civile de solidarité*, it is in respect of the rights of the surviving spouse that the new Law is concerned' (*Répertoire du Notariat, Défrenois* Supplement rapide 19 of 4 December 2001).

Intestate and testamentary inheritance

It is strictly necessary for the lawyer practising English law to abandon any idea that despite recent statutory amendments, French law permits that cherished freedom of testamentary disposition which is accepted as natural in English law. Such inroads into that freedom as can be made in England on behalf of a limited number of disappointed dependants of a deceased person are not only trivial compared to the overall effect of the French system but are at the discretion of the Court depending on the facts of each case. The French rules are rigidly fixed by the *Code civil* and are inviolable as being matters *d'ordre public*.

It is obvious that in a system of law where the ability of a person to dispose of his property on his death is curtailed, the will has played a somewhat less significant role than it has in jurisdictions not subject to that restriction and where the trust exists. The inability in France to control the future devolution of one's property or to take account of the special needs of certain beneficiaries by the use, for example, of the protective trust or of the advantages of the gift of a life interest coupled with a power to resort to capital or to make use of the flexibility of the discretionary trust makes the typical French will a somewhat naked and uninteresting document. Indeed, the legal profession looks on a will as primarily a means by which one spouse can possibly increase the benefits available to the other spouse on his death over and above those which that spouse would take on an intestacy. It is certainly not looked on as a means of ensuring good administration of one's estate or the opportunity to indulge in personal foibles not wholly beyond what English law will support (if they are not too outrageous) as the last wishes of a deceased person. There is certainly no tradition of the well-drawn English will which allows the draftsman, for all but the customary standard clauses, some liberty of style. A 'home made' French will is, therefore, not likely to give rise to the problems of interpretation which can arise in the case of its English counterpart.

Executors

Among the reasons why the Englishman makes a will is that he is thereby enabled to appoint executors whom he trusts to carry into effect faithfully and intelligently the wishes he has expressed in his will. To that end, his choice of executors frequently includes one or more of his professional advisers in addition possibly to a close member of his family. It is true that if he fails to make a will, the law tells him in advance who is most likely to get a grant of letters of administration but it is infrequent that these will include those who are expert in the administration of estates. Executors, such as they are known in English law, do not exist in French law. In effect, the administration of an estate is most frequently effected by the residuary beneficiaries as a group which does not always make either for tranquillity or ease of administration. Nor are there available to assist in the administration of a French estate the wide variety of statutory or express powers which are given to English executors and trustees and which can be so valuable if intelligently exercised within the wide discretion so often available to them. In default of agreement between beneficiaries which is by no means necessarily the order of the day, rigid rules of law apply. Nevertheless, the office of *exécuteur testamentaire* exists but it is of a supervisory nature only with very limited powers and determines a year and a day after the date of death.

Types of French wills

The most usual form of will in France is the *testament olographe* or handwritten will whose disappearance after the death of its maker is by no means unusual. It is in a form which it is the least desirable for the English testator to use if only because its obligatory lack of witnesses represents a constant pitfall for those indoctrinated in this essentially English procedure.

The will which in its form is most closely akin to the English will is the *testament authentique*. This is a will in the form of a notarial document, preserved against loss by the fact that it is held in the records of the *notaire* who drew it and entered at the notarial Register of Wills.

For those who are not anxious to reveal the contents of their wills, there exists the *testament mystique* which is a *testament olographe* put into a sealed envelope and handed in that form to a *notaire* who with certain formalities receives it into his custody. It is a form of will which nowadays is rarely used.

A fourth form of will which is available is the international will created by the Washington Convention of 26 October 1973 and which may be used in France since the Convention came into force in that country on 1 December 1994.

The register of wills is kept at Venelles (Bouches du Rhône) and all wills of every kind, irrespective of the nationality or residence of the testator, which come into the custody of a *notaire* must be registered there. A search of the register is one of the first steps taken by the *notaire* acting in the administration of an estate but it must be admitted that clearly a number of holograph wills are not so registered.

Agreements to make a will

Known in French law as *pactes sur succession future*, they are, with minimal exceptions and unlike their validity in English law, strictly forbidden. This prohibition follows the tenets of Roman law on the subject but they found favour in the Middle Ages as a method of ensuring the retention of the *patrimoine* within the family since a contract was safer than a will. After again becoming suspect, they were permitted if they formed part of a marriage contract but otherwise were void. The Revolution, anxious to maintain equality among heirs, forbade them totally and this ban was maintained by the compilers of the *Code civil*. To them, such an agreement was a bird of prey awaiting the death of the maker of the contract. The liberty of the testator to amend his dispositions (limited though that liberty might be) to the day of his death must be maintained. In the result the Code, as it stands today, prohibits any agreement with certain exceptions dealt with in Chapter 32 whether in respect of one's own estate or in respect of the estate of another 'which has not been opened'. An estate is not 'opened' until the death of the person whose assets are comprised in it.

Capacity to inherit

In order to inherit whether under a will or in an intestacy, a person must in the words of C.civ.art.725 'necessarily be in being at the date of the commencement of the administration'. Whilst there cannot be many cases in which the obstacles foreshadowed by incapacity to inherit from the estate of a deceased person, as elaborated in Chapter 23, are encountered, some of these rules apply also to gifts *inter vivos* where their effect is more likely to be of significance.

Commencement of administration procedure

There is no such procedure under French law such as is required in England to 'prove' a will. Any opposition to the essential validity of a will or its contents requires the institution of proceedings by the person interested in claiming such invalidity. The effect of an English grant is recognized in France, the procedure of obtaining a grant being known as *homologation du testament*. The affixing to an English Grant of Representation for its use in France of the apostille under the Hague Convention of 5 October 1961 is not required. The nearest equivalent in France of a Grant of Representation is the *acte de notoriété* prepared by the *notaire* acting in the estate which annexes the will or recites that none has been found by search in the wills register and certifies the persons accordingly entitled to inherit. It also indicates the domicile and nationality of the deceased in respect of which the remarks made in Chapter 37 should be given careful thought as should the choice of witnesses to that document on whose 'ipse dixit' the *notaire* drawing the *acte* may reasonably rely. In certain circumstances a *certificat de propriété* can be used to prove title of an individual asset and in the case of immovable property, it is necessary to obtain an *attestation immobilière*, the nearest English equivalent of which is the assent. It does not vest title in the person in whose favour it is given in whom title is probably already vested but it forms part of that person's title in the sense that only by its filing at the Land Registry can the beneficiary in question prove title.

Saisine

Since personal representatives as known in English law do not exist, it is necessary to have arrangements for the vesting of the property of a deceased person in the beneficiaries. Certain kinds of beneficiaries have automatic *saisine*. These are, in the case of an intestacy, all the heirs according to law. In the case of a will, the *réservataires*, that is to say those entitled by law to inherit and the *légataires universels* if there are no *réservataires*, have *saisine*. The Latin tag '*solus Deus heredem facere potest, non homo*' (Only God not man can make an heir) reinforces admirably the concept that heirs are primarily thought of as constituted by law (ie in an intestacy) rather than by designation of the deceased.

Acceptance of an estate

French law regards inheritance as a direct continuation of the legal personality of the deceased in the hands of the beneficiaries. English law, on the other hand, looks on inheritance as an acquisition of the assets of the deceased which form an autonomous estate and which do not fall into the possession of the beneficiaries until the distribution of the estate net of all debts and expenses takes place. Hence the beneficiary in an estate governed by French law acquires not only the benefit of his share of the deceased's assets but also the burden of the liabilities of the deceased which existed prior to the date of death of the deceased.

Not surprisingly, French law provides the means for beneficiaries to avoid the problem of the insolvent estate. They have therefore three choices available to them in that they may accept their benefit (i) unreservedly (*acceptation pure et simple*), or (ii) subject to the establishment as to whether it is solvent or insolvent (*acceptation sous bénéfice d'inventaire*), or (iii) they may renounce (*renonciation*). It must cause considerable surprise for the English beneficiary of an estate administered according to French law to discover that he is personally liable for the debts of the deceased and if there is the slightest doubt in the matter, precautions must be taken at the earliest moment. The rules are complex and must be strictly observed.

The *réserve*

Since every estate is administered in both testate and intestate successions with a close eye on the rights of the *réservataires*, a variety of rules exists to ensure that the *réserve* has been correctly ascertained and that no transaction has taken place during the life of the deceased as well as by the terms of his will which might affect the value of this part of the estate. For this reason (and perhaps it is help-ful to have in mind the English rules of hotchpot), it is necessary to have regard to the nature and extent of gifts *inter vivos*. Indeed, the French use only one tech-nical word for gifts made *inter vivos* and those made by will—*libéralités*—and it is also necessary to distinguish between *libéralités* made to spouses and those made to others.

Winding up an estate

Bearing in mind the effect of the *réserve* and the lack of executors with wide powers of administration, there is a strict need for agreement between beneficia-ries if delay and troubles are to be avoided. This is not always easy to ensure when there is a surviving spouse whose rights in certain cases can cause irritation to other beneficiaries. It can be of assistance to know that the accepted rule is that the surviving spouse has by tradition the right of choice of *notaire* to administer the estate but there is no rule as such that any beneficiary cannot be separately advised and on occasions, this is desirable. The rules as to pecuniary and specific legacies are clear and do not usually give rise to difficulties save that payment depends not, as in England, on executors but usually on the residuary beneficia-ries.

The rules which apply on *partage* (distribution) were designed to apply primarily to the joint ownership resulting from the distribution *in specie* to bene-ficiaries of an estate. It is, of course, for this reason, as is explained in Chapter 16, that to buy property *en indivision* is usually so unsatisfactory. The effect of these rules must be taken carefully into account since they will apply in almost every case when an estate includes immovable property and there is more than one beneficiary.

25

DOMICILE AND RESIDENCE

Introduction 241
The significance of domicile 242
Renvoi 243
Droit de prélèvement 244
Residence 245

Introduction

It is not easy to distinguish between the rules of French and English law relating to domicile. In the case of the law of both countries, essentially it is the intentions of the individual concerned which are the paramount issue. The question is to what evidence must one look to support such intentions. When considering the acquisition of a domicile of choice, English law considers that residence in a country for a long period of time raises *per se* no presumption of the acquisition of a domicile of choice in that country. As to intention, English law accepts that a decision never to return to the country of domicile of choice is proof of its abandonment whilst a positive intention to return to the country of domicile of origin at some future date, however remote, will result in that domicile of origin being maintained. In addition, the English courts when considering such intentions have regard to whether or not the deceased has retained any, and if so what, links with the country of his domicile of origin.

The rule as to domicile in French law is that contained in (C.civ.arts.102 et seq which read '*Le domicile de tout français quant à l'exercice de ses droits civils est au lieu où il a son principal établissement*' (the domicile of every Frenchman in relation to the exercise of his civil rights is the place in which he has his principal residence). On the face of it, it seems clear from this and the following articles that the intention of article 102 is that it applies solely to French nationals. However, it is settled law that if French law is that by which a question of domicile is to be determined, the rule applies also to those of nationalities other than French.

In relation to this lack of need in French law to prove the cutting of all ties with one's country of origin, Me. Revillard (*Droit International Privé et Pratique Notariale* (5th edn, Defrénois, 2001) quotes the decision in the case of a French citizen, who left France in 1997 to live in Canada where he married a Canadian woman and continued to live in that country until his death in 2000. The question of his domicile fell to be considered under French law. It had previously been held (Cass.17.7.63) that a person not of French nationality who had entered into a contract to buy property in France with a view to residing there permanently but had died in a hotel in Paris shortly after his arrival whilst awaiting completion of his purchase had acquired a French domicile. In application of that decision, the Court found that the deceased had shed his French domicile and despite the shortness of his residence in Canada had acquired a Canadian domicile of choice. The Court held that the adoption of a domicile of choice arises 'from the existence of a person's genuine residence in another place coupled with the intention of it being his principal residence'.

The prevailing tendency is not to require the abandonment of all intention to return to the country one has left or to one's country of origin in order to show the acquisition of a new domicile. All that is required for that purpose is the effective detachment from one's original social milieu even if links with it are retained. There is no requirement that the new domicile should have been acquired in perpetuity.

The difference in the views taken by French and English law of the acquisition of a domicile of choice as seen by a French lawyer is clearly to be found in the following extract from an Opinion given by the CRIDON of Lyons. It says that if it were wished: 'to prove, according to English law, that the deceased were domiciled in France, one would have not only to rely on the length of his residence in France where (in the case in question) he had virtually all his assets but on all possible evidence of his desire to abandon his English domicile . . . This criterion of domicile in English law, which is one in private international law of the retention of links with the country of domicile of origin, is by the inflexibility of its nature more akin to that of the French concept of nationality than to the criterion of residence which raises questions of internal French law.'

The significance of domicile

It must be admitted that the distinction between the two systems of law can on occasions be narrow but it seems reasonable to say that it is easier to acquire a domicile of choice in France according to French law than to abandon an English domicile of origin according to English law. In practice, this may not cause difficulties in the majority of cases of English persons owning property in France. The majority of such owners remain resident in England and are clearly domiciled in that country at the date of their death. It is only a minority who leave England (usually for reasons of health or on retirement) intending their future life in France to be permanent.

The question of domicile will be of significance to determine the persons who succeed to the deceased's property. In the case of immovable property, no problems can arise since the law of the country in which they are situate applies. In the case of movables, the old rule '*mobilia sequuntur personam*' still applies in French law and prima facie they are deemed to be situate at the place of the last residence of the deceased. However, it may be safely assumed that in the case of English domiciled owners of French movable property, provided that under French law it has not become transformed into immovable property (see Chapter 2), all will pass under English law wherever physically the items may be.

In considering such questions, it cannot be over-emphasized that the French word 'domicile' has two significantly distinct meanings. It means, as a term of strict French law, 'domicile' in the English legal sense. It also means in French legal, civil service and colloquial parlance 'home address'. In France, possibly only the *notaire* with an international law practice recognizes the problem. If this difference is not always borne in mind, confusion can easily follow. For example, the French rule stated above is that the inheritance to movables is governed by the law of the domicile of a deceased. This appears in French as the *'loi du dernier domicile du défunt'*. This clearly means 'domicile' in the English sense. Movables are deemed to be situate at the *'location de l'ouverture de la succession'* of a deceased person which is defined by the Law of 3 December 2001 as the *'dernier domicile du défunt'*. This can only mean 'home address' since it defines, among other things, the locality of the French Court which has jurisdiction over the administration of the estate. Indeed, in the case of the death of a person whose last place of residence was outside France, formalities such as the renunciation by a beneficiary of his interest in that person's estate (Chapter 33) are attended to by the Court in Paris which for that purpose is assumed to be the *'location de l'ouverture de la succession'* since in fact it is out of France.

Domicile can also be in issue if it is necessary to establish whether the English Courts have jurisdiction in connection with the distribution of an estate under the Inheritance (Provision for Family and Dependants) Act 1975 (as amended). In such cases, proof of domicile in accordance with English law can prove difficult. For example, a deceased person whose domicile of origin was English may have lived for many years in France and in the eyes of French law died clearly domiciled in France. The deceased may have made no provision for a person who figures among those entitled to make an application under the English Act. To enable the English Court to have jurisdiction, the applicant must be able to prove that the deceased had retained his domicile of origin. Even if an English domicile can be proved and the application is successful, it is far from clear that an English judgment in favour of the applicant giving him or her the right to any French assets would be enforced by the French Courts particularly if it related to immovable property in that country.

Renvoi

As has been said elsewhere, according to French private international law, the law which governs the devolution of *mobilier* or personalty is that of the domicile of the deceased. It would appear that there is a movement in the *notariat* towards the application of the doctrine of *renvoi* in favour of the law of nationality thus avoiding the use of a system of law which may be unlinked to and at odds with the religious and political concepts of the country of the deceased's origin. Moreover, if a deceased person owned realty in various countries, this results in the application of a number of different laws to assets in one estate so that the interests of the beneficiaries depend solely on the country in which the land is situate.

In the case of France and England, as the law now stands, the doctrine of *renvoi* does not apply to realty in any circumstances but where land is owned in a country where the doctrine is applied, France takes advantage of that doctrine. Thus, Italy applies the laws of the nationality of a deceased person to the devolution of his estate so that the estate of a French national who dies domiciled in Italy owning property in that country is administered wholly according to French law (Cass.3.3.2000).

Droit de prélèvement

The historical background to what has been called 'an exorbitant and anachronistic' rule but which is still in force in France lies in the Middle Ages when nationals of one country were often not permitted to succeed to property in another country unless there existed reciprocal arrangements between countries which usually involved the payment of a fine. The payment of such a fine in France was abolished by the Law of 14 July 1819 but its place was taken by the *droit de prélèvement*. Article 2 of that Law reads: 'In the case of a partition of assets between beneficiaries in an estate, some of whom are foreign and some of whom are French, the latter have a prior claim in respect of assets situate in France equal in value to the assets situate in a foreign country of which they have been deprived by reason of any provision whatsoever resulting from local laws and customs.'

The rule may be applied on any occasion when a French beneficiary considers that he has received less from an estate by reason of the application of a non-French law than he would have received if French law had applied. It is not obligatory to apply the rule but a number of judgments have held that it can be applied even if all the beneficiaries involved are French. The following two examples, one in respect of an intestacy and another where the succession is testate, clearly show the effect of this rule.

Example 1 S G of French nationality died domiciled in England intestate a spinster leaving, surviving her, her father and mother and two brothers. Her estate consisted of personalty only situate in both England and France. English law applied to the devolution of her estate. By virtue of the Administration of Estates Act 1925 section 46(1)(iii), her parents were entitled to the whole of her estate. Under French law, the parents were entitled to a quarter share each, the remaining half devolving on the two brothers in equal shares. The brothers being French were entitled to exercise their *droit de prélèvement* in respect of assets situate in France to the extent of the half share which they had lost by reason of the application of English rules of intestacy.

Example 2 MR of British nationality died domiciled in England leaving surviving his widow and two children, all three of whom were of French nationality. His assets included shares in an SCI in France. His will named his widow as sole beneficiary of his estate. The shares being personalty devolved according to English law so that prima facie all the shares in the SCI passed to the widow. However, the two children were *réservataires* under French law which was the law of their nationality as to two-thirds of those shares. They therefore could claim out of the value of the SCI shares what they had lost by reason of the fact that English law did not recognize their right to part of the value of the shares.

Residence

Residence will normally determine to the tax authorities of which country one is liable to pay income tax and a number of other taxes. In connection with two French taxes of importance, residence is of considerable consequence. In the case of inheritance tax, it is *domicile fiscal* or the residence for tax purposes alone which decides whether those who inherit in his estate are liable to inheritance tax on all the worldwide assets of the deceased or only those situate, or under a Double Tax Convention, deemed to be situate, in France. In the case of capital gains tax, residence plays a large part in determining the amount of tax payable on the disposal of French assets. Wealth tax is payable on worldwide assets in the case of the French resident owner but only on French assets if they are owned by a person not tax resident in France.

It is therefore essential to have at least an outline knowledge of what constitutes *domicile fiscal* in France. It is acquired in the following circumstances.

1. By a person who has his *foyer* or home in the generally accepted sense of the word in France. A *foyer* is the place in which a person or his spouse and children normally live. A person may be regularly absent abroad from that place, for example, on business but it is his *foyer* if his close family continues to live there.
2. By a person who has his principal *lieu de séjour* in France. In this case, the limitation applies to the person himself only and not to his family but it may be a hotel or temporary living accommodation and may be distinct from the place where his family lives. In general terms, it is assumed that a person who spends more than 183 days in any year in France has for the purposes of that year acquired a principal *lieu de séjour* in France.
3. By a person who carries on any professional activity in France unless he can satisfy the Revenue that that activity is purely accessory to his main business.

4. By a person for whom France is the centre of his 'economic interests'. By this is meant the place where a person has the majority of his investments or the principal place of management of his assets or from where he obtains the larger part of his income.

It is clear that to apply for and obtain a *carte de séjour* to which every EU citizen is entitled, and which ought to be obtained after six months' stay in France with the intention of remaining, there is evidence of the intention to become resident for tax purposes in France.

Insofar as inheritance tax is concerned, the Anglo-French Tax Convention of 21 June 1963 applies (it does not apply to gifts *inter vivos*) but it must be remembered that certain of the countries which are favoured by persons ceasing to be resident in the United Kingdom as suitable for banking and investment purposes do not have such Conventions with France. Indeed some, such as Monaco, are considered with sufficient fiscal disfavour by the French to merit close attention by a special office set up by the French tax authorities for that purpose.

26

THE ENGLISH TRUST

Introduction 247
Recognition of trusts 247
Effects of English trusts 248
   As to land 248
   As to personalty 249
Proposed French trust law 250
Fiscal considerations 250
French quasi-trusts 252
   The *substitution fidéicommissaire* 252
   The *charge* 254

Introduction

Not only is the trust unknown in French law but 'it is surrounded by considerable legal and fiscal doubts . . . It is an institution the nature of which is always difficult to grasp, which can only be understood at best imperfectly by reference to and comparison with a system of law with which the French are familiar. Until such a solution has been found, one must be satisfied with answers which are necessarily incomplete and unclear.' That quotation from so distinguished a source as *Memento Lefèbvre 'Patrimoine'* is not a very hopeful beginning to an understanding by the English lawyer, weaned on trust law, of the appreciation of that law by the French. Nevertheless, circumstances frequently arise when it is necessary to have such an understanding since the number of the English who have property in France is very large and those who have interests in trusts is not small. Those who are domiciled or resident in that country stand in need of advice on all fiscal aspects of the ownership of a trust interest whatever the nature or the proper law of the trust assets themselves may be.

Recognition of trusts

The position would be other if the Hague Convention of 1 July 1985 on the Recognition of Trusts had been ratified by France. It has been signed by a considerable number of countries, including the United Kingdom and France, but has been ratified only by some of the signatory countries including the United Kingdom. The Recognition of Trusts Act 1987 is the relevant Act and its Schedule contains a copy of the Convention in full.

    Article 11 of the Convention provides that a trust fund does not form part of the personal assets of a trustee whilst article 12 lays the ground for a trustee to have noted, in the case of land on the register at the *bureau des hypothèques* or any other register such as a share register, the capacity in which he owns French assets and so indicate his fiduciary ownership. Since the Convention has no effect in France, the result merely reinforces the erroneous notion in French law that a trustee under an English or other similar trust who is the owner of French land owns it beneficially.

It is inevitable that French law is obliged despite the non-ratification of the Hague Convention to accept the existence of the trust which it does but on conditions which in most cases make it in practice unrecognizable in France. To be recognized it must be validly constituted according to the laws of the relevant country (which must seldom be a ground for non-recognition) and its terms must not run counter to basic French rules which are *d'ordre public* which inevitably the terms of most trusts do. Thus, (i) any restriction on the inalienability of land in France which may not always be transgressed; (ii) the *fidéicommissaire* rule (described below) of the vesting of property in a person on trust to transfer the same to a beneficiary who is not the parent, child or brother or sister of that person which is likely always to be transgressed; (iii) the organization of trusts which are not in accord with the rules of the *réserve* of the settlor or testator which is almost certain always to be transgressed; or (iv) the impossibility in French law to create interests in favour of persons unborn which is a standard provision of an English trust and also certain to be unlawful in French law all render the normal English trust a problem for the French system.

Effects of English trusts

As to land
Although trustees can own French land in the French equivalent of joint tenancy so that on the death of one trustee his interest in the land passes automatically to the surviving trustees, it is, however, deemed to form part of his personal estate and accordingly to be chargeable to French inheritance tax. If a trustee retires, he must 'sell' his share to the incoming trustee who must pay the notarial fees, stamp duties and other disbursements as though it were a sale for value. There are methods available to avoid this problem but among them it is not usually desirable to make use of a corporate trustee to overcome the difficulty which arises on the death or retirement of a trustee if only for the reasons in respect of capital gains tax given in Chapter 22.

Looked at from the viewpoint of the beneficiary, where the assets involved are land, he comes into direct conflict with the laws of inheritance which limit the ability of a settlor or testator freely to dispose of his assets during his lifetime or on his death if he has living or leaves surviving ascendants or descendants in the direct line. In this connection, it must be remembered that the rules governing the *réserve* apply effectively to gifts *inter vivos* as well as to those made on death since in many cases *réservataires* are entitled at the final reckoning to call back gifts made *inter vivos* by a deceased person in excess of what he is permitted by law to make. Since where French land is subject to a trust, French law applies to its ownership and disposal, any event which eats into the *réserve* is almost certain to be bad. However, the terms of the trust can apply to the *partie disponible*.

As to personalty

Whilst French land in trust ownership gives rise to the problems mentioned above, none usually arises in connection with the ownership or distribution of personalty comprised in a trust fund, whether the settlement was created *inter vivos* or by will, since the law governing those assets will not be French. In such a case, French law will recognize the effect of a trust in accordance with its proper law and the trustees may often freely deal with such assets as are French personalty. Where what is in issue is a will trust, the Hague Convention of 2 October 1973 provides for an international certificate which designates the persons entitled by the appropriate law to administer the personal estate of a deceased person and indicates what are their powers. Thus, English proving executors, can on production of their probate supported in most cases by a *certificat de coutume* or affidavit of English law, call in and sell or distribute French personalty in accordance with the terms of their English will. The Lyons CRIDON has estimated that not more than 2 per cent of trusts which include French assets are created *inter vivos* so that the vast majority are will trusts. The following examples will show the effect of French law in the case of will trusts where the deceased was the owner of French land and personalty.

Example 1 Mrs A of British nationality died domiciled in England and Wales. She was a widow and left one surviving child with whom she was on bad terms and a nephew. Her gift of residue was to a number of charities and she made a settled legacy in favour of her nephew and his family. That settlement consisted of land in England, cash at banks in England and in France and securities in UK and French companies lodged with her bank in France. She appointed separate trustees of that settled legacy. Since she died domiciled in England and Wales, all her personalty passed under the law of her domicile so that all the assets comprised in the settled legacy which were French could be collected in and dealt with by the settled legacy trustees and the terms of the trust declared by the settled legacy could be fully executed.

Example 2 Mr B, originally domiciled in England and Wales, died domiciled in France having by his will in English form left his residuary estate after payment thereout of large legacies, debts, and testamentary and funeral expenses on trust for his three children as to its income until they reached the age of thirty and thereafter as to one-third of the capital to each child. His assets which were worldwide included land in France, shares in various French companies and bank accounts in French banks. He appointed English executors. Since he died domiciled in France, the devolution of both land and personalty was subject to French law. The children were therefore entitled as *réservataires* to three-quarters of the estate. C.civ.art.1004 provides that *réservataires* are absolutely entitled to their share of the *réserve* so that the life interests created by the settled legacy are without effect and each child is entitled to his respective share absolutely free of the life interest notwithstanding that he may have been under the age of thirty at the death of the testator. If all three children were of full age but nevertheless under thirty, they could have agreed that the trusts of the will should be respected but otherwise this could not be done. This difficulty is one which could have been overcome had France ratified the Hague Convention of 1 July 1985.

Proposed French trust law

In 1992 proposals for the establishment of the trust in France were laid before the French Parliament. They did not seek to overrule the effect of the *réserve*. Their fate was certain from the outset since those who desired their introduction looked on the trust as a means of evading taxation and this was a view wholly shared by the French Revenue. The proposals which seem inevitably to have had their birth in Anglo-Saxon trust law but were tinged with an equally evident French outlook are not without academic interest and can be found in an article 'The proposed new Law on Trusts in France' by the author (*The Conveyancer*, November–December, 407).

Fiscal considerations

As to the fiscal effects of the non-French trust on beneficiaries resident for tax purposes in France, the French Revenue, given the difficulty which it has in fully comprehending its nature, treats the trust with the greatest reserve when attempting to apply the rules which relate to tax on trust income, the imposition of *impôt de solidarité sur la fortune* (ISF) and inheritance tax. In the light of that lack of complete understanding of what is and what is not the effect of a trust, the comments appearing below must be treated with very considerable reserve and liable to varied interpretation at any time.

If the beneficiary of an English trust is resident for tax purposes in France, trust income received by him is treated as foreign investment income and taxed accordingly. This general rule applies to the distribution of the '*produits de trust*' but it is not certain precisely what this comprehensive phrase may mean. Is it limited to investment income, that is income received by the trustees from trust investments, or does it include also any distribution of capital gains or indeed distributions of trust capital itself whether made during the life of the trust, for example advancements, or on its termination? There appears to be no judicial decision on the point in issue and to date only Canada and the United States have Tax Conventions with France which deal with trust income separately from other sources of income.

Insofar as income arising in France from assets belonging to an English trust is concerned, a trust, not being a legal entity, cannot qualify for residence or non-residence for French tax purposes under the relevant Convention. English trust law results in there not being an 'owner' in the French sense. The trustees are the 'legal' owners but cannot be considered to be the 'economic' owners of the trust fund since they do not receive beneficially its income. It is considered that the following alternatives are available to the French Revenue. One can consider all the beneficiaries to be the recipients of the trust income which, for example, in the case of a discretionary trust, usually sets an impossible task of identification. Alternatively, one can also consider the trustees taxable as the apparent owners following the old French rule that 'in the case of personalty, possession equals title' against which it must be admitted that they are not the beneficiaries of the income.

The problem is evident insofar as it deals with trust income arising out of France and derived from personalty. It would seem that one way or another, such income is likely to be taxable in France if the recipient is tax resident in that country. The situation regarding realty situate in France is, on the other hand, clear. The owner of such an asset is, as the law now stands, considered the beneficial owner and subject to any provision of any Double Tax Treaty, France considers that it has the right to tax on income arising from such a source, to capital gains tax and to ISF.

If a property is transferred to a settlement, is this a transfer which prima facie ranks for stamp duty as a sale? The view taken by the French Revenue for this purpose alone is that if the settlement is revocable by the settlor, the property has never ceased to be his beneficial property and the transaction is not subject to stamp duty. When the trusts created are irrevocable, since in French law the trust as such is not a legal entity, has there in fact been a transfer to take it out of the ownership of the settlor or does the rule of 'apparent ownership' apply so that the trustee is now the owner or is the transaction in the nature of a gift? It would be interesting, for example, to discover what view the French would take of a settlement which contains a general power of appointment exercisable by the settlor.

It is admitted that unless there are special reasons for such an arrangement, it will be rare that an English trust created *inter vivos* will hold French land. However, trusts involving French land may arise under English wills if, for example, the testator's estate was not subject to the rules of the *réserve* or there was a sufficient *partie disponible* to allow the *réservataires* to be satisfied and still to create a trust over a remaining property. It must be evident that the interplay between French law and English law when trusts are concerned is far from satisfactory. If there is or is to be created an English trust, one or more beneficiaries of which are liable to French income tax, the draftsman treads on shifting sands, and only at his peril will he consider his task properly completed without assistance from suitable advisers who are both well versed in English trust and French and United Kingdom tax law.

French quasi-trusts

Although bereft of the trust as known to English law, there are two procedures available to the French which are very poor relations of the English trust. These are the *substitution fidéicommissaire* and the gift (*inter vivos* or by will) subject to a *charge*. The former, in the days when it was allowed to flourish, had the makings of the strict settlement without the interposition of trustees. The latter is a gift or legacy subject to the condition that the donee or legatee carries out some obligation for the benefit of a third party, himself or even the maker of the gift. It is seldom in the form that one finds in English wills which usually has nothing to do with the subject matter of the gift itself but is frequently the carrying into effect of some foible of the donor. The condition in French law is usually that the recipient passes on the gift to another, that subsequent recipient often being some charitable or quasi-charitable organization not yet in being.

The substitution fidéicommissaire

This has its origins in Roman law with the object of conserving the family fortune within the family. Thus it was possible to provide a scheme of inheritance from generation to generation and it became popular among the great families of France. Not unexpectedly, the system was abolished by the Revolution as inconsistent with its egalitarian principles. The *Code civil* originally forbade it but at the insistence of Napoléon, *substitutions* were reinstated to a limited extent and are still permitted today.

It is not suggested that the *substitution fidéicommissaire* should ever be indulged in by the English and clearly if it were desired that it should, special advice must be sought. The object of referring to it is to suggest that the English trust can be as little appreciated by the French as is the *substitution fidéicommissaire* by the English who must therefore be patient with the French in their doubts of the effects both in civil and in fiscal law of the trust.

C.civ.art.1048 lays down the limits within which the *substitution* may lawfully be used and these encompass a very small family circle. A *substitution* can only be created by a gift *inter vivos* or legacy of assets to one or more of the children of a donor or testator or if he has none, to a brother or sister subject to the obligation that that beneficiary pass on such assets at his death *au premier degré seulement*, that is his children only. Thus, insofar as the original donor/testator is concerned, the ultimate beneficiaries must be grandchildren or nieces or nephews. Few *substitutions* are made by gift *inter vivos* and what follows assumes that they are made by will. There are basic conditions which must be

252

observed and to qualify as a *substitution*, four elements must all be present.

1. The disposition must be legally binding and not merely precatory (Cass.5.6.1899). If it is considered to be in the form of a mere desire, it is void as a *substitution* and in cases of doubt, the Courts tend to lean towards the interpretation of a desire.
2. There must be a double obligation imposed on the first legatee to conserve the assets and to hand them over to the ultimate beneficiary. In certain circumstances, it is possible to impose on a gift a provision forbidding the alienation of the asset given if 'it is temporary and justified for serious and lawful reasons' (C.civ.art.900). Such an obligation alone will not suffice. There must in addition be the obligation to hand over to the ultimate beneficiary the assets which the initial legatee has received under the will of the testator.
3. The provision for such handing over must ensure that it takes place on the death of the initial legatee. In other words, since the assets are vested in him, the *substitution* organizes their disposal in his estate.
4. There must be a double transfer of the property by the testator, that is to say, the testator vests the assets first in the legatee under his will and, on that person's death, in the ultimate beneficiary although notionally, that second vesting is in the estate of the legatee. Thus a legacy 'to A but if he predeceases the testator to B' does not conform to this requirement since no property was ever vested in A.

To ensure that the ultimate beneficiaries are treated equally, the 'gift over' must provide equal shares for all the children in being and to be born of the original legatee. It is obligatory to appoint a *tuteur* whose task is not to administer the assets involved but to oversee their fate. He must organize the preparation of an inventory if the original legatee fails to do so, deal with the sale of *meubles* not specifically required to be kept in their original state and 'control' the use of capital. He is personally liable in respect of his duties to no less an extent than he would be if he were an English trustee. Notice of the restrictions imposed on any assets which are land is given by suitable registration at the Land Registry. If no such registration is effected, which it is one of the duties of the *tuteur* to do, any third party takes free of such restrictions.

It remains to add that generally the *Code civil*, not only by the protection which is afforded by the *réserve* but also by the relaxation of the strict rules which apply to gifts when the *patrimoine* is involved, has shown a special care for the family assets. That the Code in the case of *substitutions* seems to have been particularly severe would seem to stem from the rigidity of the Revolutionary ideals and the Courts, when the validity of a *substitution fidéicommissaire* has been called in question, have endeavoured to find in its favour on the grounds that thereby they are protecting the family fortune when the *Code civil* has in any instance failed to do so.

The charge

The typical manner of creating a *charge* by will is simple. All that is needed is 'I give Blackacre to my friend XYZ *à charge* that he hands it over to the Red Cross Society'. The penalty for not carrying out the terms of a *charge* is that the ultimate beneficiary of the *charge* may sue the donee to ensure the carrying into effect of the terms of the *charge* and to obtain damages for the default. In addition, the maker of a gift *inter vivos* subject to the *charge* and his successors in title and his creditors and also legatees of a share in the donor's estate may seek the revocation of the gift so that it reverts to the donor or his estate (C.civ.art.953 et seq). It is also possible to attach to the gift a penal clause in case of non-fulfilment of the *charge*.

On the assumption that many such gifts are destined ultimately for charity, C.civ.art.900-2 allows an application to be made to the Court for a revision of the terms of *charges* 'if by reason of a change of circumstances their execution has become extremely difficult or extremely burdensome'. Such an application cannot be made during a period of ten years following the death of the disponer or the date of any previous application. The Court has very wide discretion in such an application to which all interested persons must be parties.

27

INTESTATE SUCCESSION

Introduction 255
Order of succession 255
In the absence of a surviving spouse 255
In the presence of a surviving spouse 256
Représentation 257
Droit de retour 258

Introduction

The Law of 3 December 2001 which came into force on 1 July 2002 applies to all deaths after that date. Whilst the major reform to the laws of intestate succession instituted by that Law is in respect of the rights of the surviving spouse, it took the opportunity to make certain other significant changes to the law, not all of which are applicable only to intestacies. The rules as to the order of intestate succession prior to the coming into force of that Law were complex and the order of inheritance was (i) issue, (ii) father, mother, brothers and sisters, (iii) grandparents, (iv) uncles and aunts, and cousins, (v) the surviving spouse. The Law, whilst maintaining overall the degrees of relationship and the order in which they take, has recast the relevant articles 734 to 740 of the *Code civil* which deal with the order of succession as it now stands. No reference is made in this chapter to the law prior to 1 July 2002 except where a comparison between the law then and now is of interest. There are considerable differences in the pre-July 2002 law and in the case of deaths before that date, advice must be sought.

Order of succession

In the absence of a surviving spouse
Article 734 reads as follows: 'In the event of there being no surviving spouse, the persons entitled to succeed are as follows (i) children and issue (ii) the mother and father; brothers and sisters and issue of brothers and sisters (iii) ascendants other than mother and father (v) collaterals other than brothers and sisters and their issue. Each of such categories constitutes an order of the heirs which excludes any which follow it.'

The effect of this article is as follows.

1. Surviving legitimate and natural children take in equal shares *per capita* whether they are children of the last or of a previous marriage of the deceased.

Issue of a pre-deceased child take by representation *per stirpes*. Hence, if there is surviving one child and two grandchildren, the children of a pre-deceased child, the child takes one-half and each grandchild takes one-quarter.

2. In the absence of issue, surviving parents take one-quarter each. If there are surviving brothers or sisters or their issue, such persons take the remaining one-half or three-quarters share (as the case may be). If there are no surviving parents brothers and sisters, or their issue, take all.

3. If only both parents survive the deceased, they each take a one-half share. If only one survives, the share of the pre-deceased parent is taken by the nearest ascendants in his or her line. Thus, in default of issue of the intestate, brothers or sisters or their issue, a single surviving parent takes the whole estate if the deceased parent left no persons entitled to take his or her share.

4. If the intestate left surviving only collateral relations, for example uncles, aunts or cousins, the estate is divided into two parts, one each for the maternal and the paternal line. The share of each line is taken by the surviving relation nearest in degree to the intestate up to the sixth degree. If there are no such relations in one line but there are in the other, the share of that line accrues to the other line.

5. In default of any such persons as are mentioned above, the estate passes as *bona vacantia* to the State.

In the presence of a surviving spouse

The rights of the surviving spouse are dealt with at length in Chapter 30.

The rights of other persons entitled to share in the event that the deceased left a surviving spouse appear in the table set out below adapted from Christian Taithe, *Successions* (19th edn, Delmas, 2002).

Deceased left surviving no spouse but	Interests of other beneficiaries in intestacy
Two children of marriage to the deceased	1/2 share for each child in reversion or 3/8 share for each child in possession
Two children of previous marriage	3/8 share in possession for each child
One child of previous marriage and one of marriage to deceased	As above
Father, mother, two brothers	1/4 share to each
Father and three sisters	1/4 share to each
Mother, two sisters, two children of a deceased brother	1/4 share to each of mother and two sisters, 1/8 share for nephews
Mother, brother, half-brother, uterine sister	1/4 share for mother and 1/4 share for each of brother, half-brother and uterine sister

Father, two brothers	1/4 share for father, 3/8 for each brother
Mother, father, two cousins	1/2 each for mother and father
Father, two children of deceased brother	1/4 for father, 3/8 for each nephew
Mother, cousin	Total estate for mother
Two cousins in maternal line, one cousin in paternal line and children of predeceased cousin in paternal line	1/4 for each cousin in maternal line, 1/2 for cousin in paternal line

Représentation

Section 46(i) of the Administration of Estates Act 1925 says that if the intestate leaves a husband or wife (with or without issue), after making certain provision for that surviving spouse, if the intestate leaves issue, the balance is to be held on statutory trusts for such issue and if the intestate leaves issue but no surviving spouse, the whole of the net estate is to be similar trusts. Section 47(1)(i) defines those statutory trusts as 'in equal shares in more than one, for all or any of the children or child of the intestate living at the death of the intestate . . . and for all or any of the issue . . . of any child of the intestate who predeceases the intestate . . .'.

C.civ.art.741 reads that '*la proximité de parenté s'établit par le nombre de générations; chaque génération s'appelle un degré*' (the proximity of relationship is established by generation each of which is called a degree). Heirs of the same degree are in the same '*ordre*'. C.civ.art.744 explains that '*dans chaque ordre, l'héritier le plus proche exclut l'héritier plus éloigné en degré*' (in each order, the heir nearest (to the deceased) excludes the heir further removed in degree). Thus, if a deceased had two children, one of whom died before the deceased leaving a child who survived the deceased, that child is in the second degree of relationship to the deceased whilst the surviving son is in the first degree. That son, by virtue of C.civ.art.744, would take the whole estate to the detriment of the children of his deceased brother.

The difference between the English and the French rules lies, of course, in the English Act's inclusion of 'issue living at the death of the intestate . . . of any child of the intestate who predeceases the intestate . . .'. The French *Code civil* excludes specifically any such issue. It has been realized that such a situation is not reasonable and had led to the need for the rule of *représentation* or substitution.

This is effected by C.civ.art.751 which reads '*la représentation est une fiction de la loi dont l'effet est de faire entrer les représentants dans les droits du représenté*' (substitution is a legal fiction the effect of which is that the person substituted stands in respect of his rights in the place of the person for whom he is a substitute). In this manner, in the example quoted above the children of the deceased brother will take equally the share which their deceased parent would have taken had he survived his deceased father. The article is cast in somewhat strange language when one considers that an amendment to the article previously quoted might have been more logical. It has, however, been suggested that the reason why substitution of this kind is designated a 'legal fiction' is that whilst the substitute beneficiary inherits in the stead and degree of the deceased beneficiary, he inherits in his own name and not in the name of the deceased beneficiary.

There follow C.civ.arts.752 to 755 which elaborate and limit the fiction of *représentation*, which does not apply to testate successions, it being the choice of the testator whether he wishes to provide a substitution clause in his will or not (Cass.24.11.69). The rule applies in all cases, whether the children of the deceased are in competition with children of a deceased child of the deceased or as between children of a number of children of the deceased who did not survive him, irrespective of the difference in degree (article 752). It does not apply in the case of ascendants, when the nearest in degree to the deceased excludes those further removed (article 752-1). As with issue of the deceased, the rule applies in the same manner to issue of brothers and sisters (article 752-2). When applicable, substitution is *per stirpes* and within each stirps, *per capita* (article 753).

Substitution applies to heirs who predecease the deceased but not to issue of heirs who have renounced their share in an estate (article 754). This rule is, however, limited in its application so that if A has renounced his rights in the estate of his father B and B was a beneficiary in the estate of his father C but predeceased him, A can take in the place of B in the estate of C. Finally, the Law of 3 December 2001 has done away with the rule that the issue of anyone unable to inherit for reasons of *indignité* cannot take by *représentation* and issue may now take in this manner. A person who is *indigne* cannot lay claim to any rights which by law are enjoyed by parents in respect of assets belonging to their children who take by substitution (article 755).

Issue of a beneficiary presumed dead (*déclaré absent*) by Order of the competent Court can take by substitution but those of a beneficiary whose mere disappearance has resulted in an Order of *présomption d'absence* cannot do so. A declaration of presumption of death cannot be made earlier than ten years after a declaration of absence has been made.

Droit de retour

It is a basic principle of French inheritance law that the estate of an intestate is considered to be a homogeneous whole, all of which passes to the lawful heirs irrespective of the source of the assets which compose it. To this general rule, there is an exception known as the *droit de retour*. This right arises in two cases, namely that of *adoptions simples* (C.civ.art.368-1) and where an intestate dies leaving a surviving spouse but without surviving issue or parents (C.civ.art.757-3).

In the case of the death of a person who had been the subject of an *adoption simple* (but not in the case of an *adoption plénière* when the child becomes wholly a child of the adopting family) and who dies without leaving issue surviving, all assets which the adopted child has received from his adopting parents either during their lifetime or as a beneficiary in their estates are returnable to the adopting parents or their issue provided that such assets exist in their original form at the death of the adopted child. They are returned subject to any rights in them which may have been acquired by third parties and to the adopting parents contributing to the debts (if any) of the adopted child. The remaining assets in the estate of the adopted child are divided between the original family of the adopted child and the family which adopted him but without prejudice to such rights as his surviving spouse may have in that estate.

Where in an intestacy a surviving spouse would have taken the whole estate in default of there being surviving issue of parents of the deceased, objects which the deceased had received by way of gift or inheritance from his parents, if they are in the state in which they were originally given, go as to one half to any surviving brothers and sisters of the deceased or their issue who are themselves issue of the parents from whom the gifts originated.

The beneficiary of a *droit de retour* has a right to inherit and is a true *héritier* (Cass.2.7.03). He is a *légataire universel* since he inherits a separate whole. He must therefore have the same capacity to inherit as must have the ordinary beneficiary. It follows that he is liable for the debts of the deceased but only for the proportion which the assets subject to his *droit de retour* bear to the whole estate of the deceased. He can therefore exercise his right to opt for acceptance or for renunciation in respect of that separate part of the estate. He has, remarkably enough, *saisine* and like the State taking *bona vacantia* does not require an *envoi en possession*.

28

LA RÉSERVE

Introduction 261
The *réservataires* 261
Calculation of the *réserve* 263
The surviving spouse 265

Introduction

The background to the institution of the *réserve* is recounted in Chapter 24. It may fairly be said that the French consider that the *réserve* serves two purposes. It protects members of the family against those who are not members of the family by ensuring that at least a proportion of the family assets are reserved for its closest members and also it ensures equality of benefit as between those members. The rules governing the *réserve* cannot be avoided by the French testator and if he tries to do so during his lifetime by one means or another, that which is missing from the *masse de calcul de la réserve* can be called back to complete its value and inequalities between those entitled to share in it can be ironed out. 'One can envisage the suppression of its egalitarian function; its function as the protector of the family must surely be maintained ... Experience shows that within the limited possibilities available to them, parents rarely benefit one child more than another. Why should they make use of such freedom if it were accorded to them? It must therefore be concluded that the *réserve* merits retention in both its functions' (Professor Souleau, *Les Successions* (Armand Colin, 1991)). Admittedly, that is a view expressed before the somewhat liberating effects in favour of the surviving spouse of the Law of 3 December 2001. However, that Law did not find its way onto the statute book with evident ease and whilst it benefits the surviving spouse in cases of intestacies leaves almost unchanged the law as to the *réserve* in cases where there is a will. The last word on the *réserve* should perhaps be that of Ripert and Boulanger in *Traité de droit civil d'après le traité de Planiol* who say: 'It is the law which corrects the mistakes which the deceased has made in the expression of his wishes.'

The *réservataires*

The interests of *réservataires* in the *réserve* in the absence of a surviving spouse, whose rights are dealt with in Chapter 30, are as set out below and follow the provisions of C.civ.art.913.

1. Legitimate, legitimized and natural children
   (a) if there is one child only, one-half of the estate;
   (b) if there are two children, two-thirds of the estate equally between them;
   (c) if there are three or more children, three-quarters of the estate equally between them.
2. Children who have been adopted *plénièrement* are treated on the same footing as legitimate children of the deceased. Children whose adoption is only *simple* are also treated as legitimate children in respect of the estate(s) of their adopting parent(s) but they are not *réservataires* in the estates of ascendants of an adopting parent. Such children maintain also their inheritance rights in respect of their original family.
3. Ascendants
   (a) If there are no descendants, each ascendant has a quarter share of the estate but save in the case of a mother or father, no more remote ascendant takes a share if the deceased left surviving brothers, sisters or their issue.
   (b) If there are surviving issue, ascendants take no share in the *réserve*.

The rules relating to those who are *réservataires* and the method of calculating the *réserve* given below relate to testate inheritance only. That part of his estate which does not form the *réserve* is the *quotité disponible*. The equivalent of the *réservataire* in the case of intestacies is the *héritier* who is defined by the *Code civil*, as in English law by the Administration of Estates Act 1925, in the manner described in Chapter 27. In other words, a testator has in any event a proportion of his estate of which he may freely dispose but its size depends on the members of his family who are *réservataires* and how many there are. In the case of an intestacy, the deceased has by default yielded up his limited powers of disposal to the law and since the result of a French intestacy can be considerably less attractive and more irritating to administer than it is in England, no owner of property in France should fail to make a will (not necessarily a French will) disposing of it. In any event, those entitled to share in the *réserve* are limited to ascendants and issue in the direct line. The net is cast wider in an intestacy.

The rules relating to representation which apply in the case of intestacies have no place in testate successions unless the testator makes substitution provision, but C.civ.art.913-1 defines children as descendants '*en quelque degré que ce soit*'. The initial fractions are calculated by reference to the number of children of the deceased, issue taking by substitution *per stirpes* the share of a predeceased child. In the case of a child renouncing his interests, the initial share is divided among the other children and the *quotité disponible* remains unchanged. Difficulties can arise if a sole beneficiary who is a child renounces when those then entitled to take (parents, for example) are entitled to a different proportion since the share of the former may be larger than that of the latter.

Calculation of the *réserve*

In order to calculate the amount of the *réserve* so as to discover its size, two operations may be necessary. Initially, it is necessary to establish the net value of the estate by taking the gross assets of the deceased and deducting therefrom (i) all interests limited for life, (ii) assets the subject of a gift made by the deceased *inter vivos* subject to a *droit de retour*, that is that if the donee predeceases the donor, the gift is refundable (Chapter 37), (iii) assurances on the life of the deceased written for the benefit of a named beneficiary, and (iv) all allowable debts. In this connection it must be remembered that French inheritance tax is the liability not of the estate but of the beneficiaries (although a will can reverse this liability and make gifts free of that tax). It has, however, been held (Cass.1.12.64) that funeral expenses, and the costs of administration and distribution of an estate, are borne by the estate and are deductible from the assets of the *réserve*.

The law is that the *quotité disponible* relates not only to what the deceased owned at the date of his death but to what he had disposed of during his life. C.civ.art.913 declares that '*les libéralités soit par acte entre vifs soit par testament*' may not exceed certain proportions of a person's assets depending on how many children he has. In addition, C.civ.art.843 requires that 'every heir (in an intestacy) and every beneficiary (under a will) coming to a succession must restore to his co-heirs all he has received from the deceased by donation during life directly or indirectly; he cannot retain such gifts made to him by the deceased unless such gifts have been given to him expressly in addition to and not subject to partition or with a dispensation of restitution'. In the language of English law, gifts may be made subject to hotchpot (*en avancement d'hoirie*) or free of hotchpot (*par préciput et hors part*). The law presumes that gifts made to an 'heir, even beneficiary' are not intended to upset the equality of benefit which each participant has in the *réserve*. Gifts made in pursuance of that presumption are gifts made *en avancement d'hoirie* and must be brought into hotchpot by the donee. To escape that presumption: (i) the document making the gift must clearly state that the gift is intended to be *par préciput et hors part*; (ii) it must be apparent from the nature of the gift, such as a gift which is *déguisée* or a gift which passes by manual delivery; (iii) it is a gift so designated by law such as a gift (inter alia), a gift made by will unless stated to be otherwise (C.civ.art.843); or (iv) be a gift to a descendant in the direct line subject to the reservation of a life interest by the donor (C.civ.art.918). Even so, if the gift made free of hotchpot is found when all the calculations have been made to exceed the *quotité disponible* and there are *co-réservataires* who would thereby suffer, the donee is required to put back the excess into the *réserve*. By a curious rule, a donee who is a *réservataire* who has received a gift subject to hotchpot renounces his benefit in the estate; he is no longer required to bring that gift into hotchpot.

There is a limited number of exceptions to the gifts excluded from this exercise such as birthday or Christmas gifts, gifts made in the context of marriage, payments made by parents for the education and apprenticeship (and honeymoon expenses) of children and premiums in a reasonable amount for life assurance for named beneficiaries.

This exercise, known as the *réunion fictive*, involves discovering which gifts should be brought back to complete the *réserve* and can on occasions prove difficult since it is most likely to be needed when transfers of assets have been made *inter vivos* which the deceased hoped would pass by unnoticed. It is necessary to consider the rules in respect of such gifts set out in Chapter 38 to appreciate the full extent of this *réunion fictive*.

For this purpose, gifts are valued as at the date of death and if any gifts have been disposed of and the price used to acquire other assets, those new assets are so valued.

These calculations completed, it is necessary to pass to the second operation to establish whether the *quotité disponible* has been exceeded and the *réservataires* have been deprived of part of their *réserve*. This calculation, called the *imputation de libéralités*, establishes which gifts impinge on the *réserve* and which can be borne by the *quotité disponible*.

C.civ.art.920 says that 'gifts and legacies (that is all gifts *inter vivos* and by will) which exceed the *quotité disponible* can be reduced to its value at the start of administration of the estate'. Thus, in the case of a *masse de calcul de la réserve* of Euro 1,000,000, the deceased had three children so that the *quotité disponible* is Euro 250,000. The deceased had in fact made gifts *inter vivos* of Euro 350,000. The *quotité disponible* must be reduced by the excess of Euro 100,000. The rule is *d'ordre public* and the donor-testator cannot relieve his donees or legatees of this liability. The amount is recovered, if not repaid voluntarily, by an action *en réduction*.

The requirement that any amount missing from the assets forming the *réserve* should be replaced is, of course, open only to the *réservataires* or their successors in title. Proof of a transaction in an action *en réduction* which is alleged wrongly to have reduced the *réserve* is less strict than that required in many other actions and may be by pure presumption as well as by extraneous evidence (Cass.18.8.1862). It will be appreciated that a typical method of reducing the *réserve* during the lifetime of the testator is by means of *donations déguisées* of a nature discussed in Chapter 38.

The following is an example of the effect of the limit placed on *libéralités inter vivos* on the shares of two children in the estate of one of their parents.

Gross assets of the deceased	Euro 600,000
Less allowable debts	Euro 75,000
Net estate	Euro 525,000
Add value as at date of death of gifts made by the deceased *inter vivos* including *donations déguisées*	Euro 375,000
Notional value	Euro 900,000

Réserve of 1/3rd per child × 2 =	Euro 600,000
Quotité disponible of 1/3rd =	Euro 300,000

The assets available at the date of death amount only to Euro 525,000 whilst the *réserve* of the children exceeds this by Euro 75,000. In such circumstances, the children may require the amount to be brought back into the estate by which the gifts *inter vivos* have exceeded their rightful share. This right belongs solely to the *réservataires* and in the event of any deficiency of the nature which figures above, it is not available to any other legatee or to creditors.

It will be appreciated that different results flow from an action *en réduction* depending on whether the claim is made against one of the *réservataires* or a stranger to the estate. In the latter case, if the claim is successful, the donee will either yield up all or part of the gift made to him or will have to provide an amount in the form of compensation. If the claim is made by the *réservataires* against one of their number who has not renounced his benefits (when he is treated as a stranger to the estate) that *réservataire* may retain his gift provided that he pays over the deficiency to the claimants. He may, if he wishes and unless he has already disposed of it, return the subject matter of the gift (C.civ.art.866) to the donor.

Lest it be thought that the existence of the *réserve* once calculated in accordance with the foregoing rules provides a simple method of establishing the extent of the interests of those entitled to share in it, an appreciation of the contents of Chapter 32 is likely to dispel this idea.

The surviving spouse

It is perhaps too close to the coming into force of the Law of 3 December 2001 in respect of deaths after 1 July 2002 to be able to take a definite view as to the situation of the surviving spouse. He or she has certain inheritance rights which are clearly closely akin to those vested in ascendants and issue as *réservataires* but these only come into play if the deceased left no surviving ascendants or issue and even then, the deceased spouse can deprive his surviving spouse of certain of them. However, these rights in appropriate circumstances are *d'ordre public* and on that basis, the surviving spouse is a *réservataire*. These rights are not dealt with in this chapter but in Chapter 30 which is concerned solely with them.

29

AVOIDING THE *RÉSERVE*

Introduction 267
A company as owner 267
Ownership *en tontine* 269
Sales *en viager* 270
Régime de communauté universelle 270

Introduction

It has been said that Anglo-Saxon law is 'too individualist to admit any restriction on the freedom of a deceased person' such as is imposed by the French *Code civil* and indeed by the laws of many countries which are based on that Code. Such sympathy for a non-French legal system is surprising since it must be admitted that reverence for *le patrimoine* is still a noticeable feature of French life. There is no better moment to observe this than at the completion of the sale of a property in the country which is frequently attended by children and sometimes by other members of the seller's family who watch, not without anxiety, the disappearance from the family *patrimoine* of what should have formed part of their inheritance. The proceeds of sale may well have disappeared by the time that their parents die.

There has certainly been over the years a loosening of the grip of the *réserve* and parents feel less constrained to ensure that all they own passes to their children. Nevertheless, the *réserve* retains its stranglehold as a matter of law and whilst one finds frequent suggestions for the avoidance of *droits de succession* there seems little written about how to avoid the effect of the *réserve*. There are, however, a number of ways in which this can be achieved by the English owner of French property bearing in mind that irrespective of his nationality, domicile or residence, the devolution of immovable property in France will always follow French law.

This chapter sets out in short form some of the methods which are available to the owner of property in France who is not domiciled in that country. None of these methods should be adopted without the comprehensive advice of an expert well qualified to advise in respect of the laws and procedures of both France and the country of domicile of the owner of French property.

A company as owner

The most obvious avoidance tactic for those domiciled in England is to ensure that the assets concerned are of a nature which devolve on death according to

English law. To achieve this, they must be *meubles*. The primary exercise therefore is to turn *immeubles* into *meubles* or to be *ab initio* the owner of only *meubles*. This can be achieved by the use of a company as owner of property which otherwise would have been bought by English domiciled buyers personally but to whom instead the shares of that property owning company are issued.

It is preferable that such a company is a French incorporated company. In no circumstances should the company be what is commonly called 'offshore' which in practice means incorporated in a tax haven country since this gives rise to an annual 3 per cent tax on value (Chapter 22). In any case, what is 'offshore' to the English is not necessarily 'offshore' to the French. Unless there are special reasons to do so, which require the advice of an expert in both UK and French tax, the use of a UK company may well achieve nothing but unnecessary paperwork and possibly unnecessary tax. If, as is most likely to be the case, the choice falls on a French company, it is the *société civile immobilière* or SCI, the workings of which are described in Chapter 9, which will normally best fill the bill.

It is considerably less expensive if the property to be bought is acquired initially in the name of the SCI which is formed contemporaneously with the purchase. SCIs can purchase assets as a company in the course of incorporation. As in England, the purchase price is provided by the cash required to pay for the allotment of the shares. Thus far, there are no problems but it is necessary to consider at the outset whether the property is to be used solely as a residence for the shareholders and close members of their family or primarily or indeed at all for the purposes of letting.

The occupation free of rent by the shareholders and close members of their family of the property owned by the SCI is prima facie an *avantage en nature* or benefit in kind. The French tax rule in this respect is that such occupation is tantamount to occupation by the SCI of its own property and no tax in respect of this occupation is claimed. The situation with respect to UK tax is far less clear. In most cases, when the SCI is used as a *réserve* avoider and for no other purpose, it requires no noticeable management so that it is usual for the shareholders or one of them to be the *gérant* or director/manager. The UK Revenue appears to take the view that in such circumstances, the free occupation of the SCI's premises by the shareholders who are also *gérants* renders them liable to a Schedule E assessment under section 168 of the Income and Corporation Taxes Act 1988. Long correspondence with the Revenue has, it is considered, elicited the view that each case would be dealt with on its merits. On the face of it, if the shareholders were never appointed *gérants* and were wholly debarred from such an appointment thus taking no part whatsoever in the management of the SCI, they would not be treated as shadow directors. It has been impossible to discover a case where such an assessment has in fact been raised even when the shareholders are also the *gérants* but each case merits individual advice in England. There is no reason at all why the Articles of the SCI should not be drawn in a form necessary to avoid this tax liability but since there is no need to achieve this end in France, it is imagined that few, if any, sets of standard articles will have been drawn in this fashion. It is therefore imperative that there be interposed between the purchaser/shareholder and the *notaire* acting for him a suitable adviser with knowledge of both English and French law and tax notwithstanding the possible change of heart on the part of the UK Revenue (see Chapter 220.

Ownership *en tontine*

This method of joint ownership is described in Chapter 16. It represents the simplest method at the time of the purchase of a property of circumventing the *réserve* but is infrequently suggested by a *notaire* to a purchaser. There are still those who counsel strongly against this kind of joint ownership unless they receive in advance a release from such liability as they might incur (they would incur none) from participating in this *réserve*-avoiding scheme. This unhelpful attitude derives partly from a misconception in France as to the French inheritance tax situation compared to that prevailing in England and partly from the residual reluctance to assist issue to forego their rights as *réservataires*. Until comparatively recently the death of an owner *en tontine* gave rise to a very limited tax payment. This rule was amended so that the death of a co-owner gives rise to the payment of inheritance tax on half the value of the jointly owned property which the *notaire*, unaware that that is precisely what happens in England, tells his English clients is a fiscal disadvantage.

It must, however, be borne in mind that the use of the *tontine* whilst successful in its primary object of avoiding the *réserve* achieves another which may be less successful in that it transfers property from one family to another. The share of a property bought by a married couple *en indivision* will on the death of the first joint owner to die end up in the hands of the issue of that marriage and possibly the surviving co-owner. If it is bought *en tontine*, on the death of the first co-owner to die, it will pass to the surviving co-owner in its entirety. If that surviving joint owner has children by a previous marriage or remarries and has further children, those children who are wholly unconnected with the first co-owner to die will also obtain a share in the property. An explanation of how such a result can be avoided is given below.

If a property has ill-advisedly been bought *en indivision*, this gives absolute ownership of the relevant shares in the property to the joint owners. Thus, when they are eventually advised that they should never have bought in this manner, they cannot 'switch' directly into a *tontine* ownership because of the legal fiction which governs this type of ownership and is referred to in Chapter 16. They can, however, as *indivisaires* of the whole property transfer it to an SCI in exchange for an issue of shares which then can be held *en tontine*. This has in addition two advantages. First, there is no inheritance tax payable on the death of the first of (say) two joint shareholders to die. This is because the vesting of the property in the sole name of the surviving joint owner arises from the terms of issue of the shares in the SCI and not from the document of purchase of the property itself. The second advantage is that joint ownership of this kind results in the property bypassing those who may be *réservataires* and rolls it up in its full value in the estate of the surviving joint owner, where the shares can be dealt with under English law and the surviving shareholder can by his or her will make any necessary adjustments.

It is also necessary to appreciate in advance what the tax effect of a share issue *en tontine* will be bearing in mind who will be the beneficiaries in the estate of the surviving joint owner. The interposition of a company will have the effect of totally removing the assets in question not only from the burden of French inheritance law but also from the liability to inheritance tax on the death of the first joint shareholder to die. Inheritance tax will then be payable on the totality of the shares in the estate of the surviving shareholder. Chapter 39 explains how French inheritance tax is calculated and it is desirable to make the comparison between the result of half the shares being in two estates and all the shares being taxable in one estate.

Sales *en viager*

Disposals of property in this manner have been covered in Chapter 12 and should not be overlooked as a means of avoiding the *réserve*. To sell en *viager occupé* is to be able to continue to enjoy the use of one's property but to die owning nothing to be caught by the *réserve*. The *bouquet* which was received on the sale is for the person domiciled in England not subject to French inheritance law nor are the annuity payments which in any event are likely to be spent as they come in. This is a method which is not frequently suggested by French advisers but they look on it primarily as a method of freeing capital whilst retaining occupation of one's home. For the owner not domiciled in France, it can have other attractions.

Régime de communauté universelle

In many cases, the most attractive and the least expensive way in which to avoid French inheritance rules and one which can be used irrespective of the domicile of the owners of property is the use of this *régime*. Its effect and how it can be adopted are discussed in Chapter 20 and, provided that the persons involved have no children by previous marriages, it is frequently the best method to adopt. In the case of married couples whose recourse to the Hague Convention of 14 March 1978 is limited to that permitted by the ownership of land in France, it is probably better to acquire the land they have in mind to buy before adopting this *régime* but the two events can be dealt with more or less simultaneously provided that the *notaire* acting for the buyers is conversant with the Convention procedure.

It is true that the most recent changes in the law have, particularly in cases of intestacy, added to what a surviving spouse can take to the detriment of issue. The law, however, has not suppressed the inheritance rights of issue and ascendants so that so long as immovable property in France remains directly owned by an individual person or by persons *en indivision* or by those who have not adopted the *régime de communauté universelle* the surviving spouse cannot be given the benefits which he or she can be given under English law nor can children be treated on an unequal basis nor can any special arrangements be made for the protection or benefit of any beneficiary.

It cannot be too often repeated that proper and comprehensive advice must be sought before any property in France is bought. It is dangerous to rely on any suggestions made by anyone who is not both fully qualified in the laws of both countries and conversant with the social factors which govern the manner in which their citizens behave.

30

THE SURVIVING SPOUSE

Introduction 273
Capacity to inherit 273
The spouse in intestate successions 274
Rights of the surviving spouse in an intestacy 275
    Application of the rights of the surviving spouse 276
Rights of the surviving spouse in testate successions 278
Donation entre époux 282

Introduction

It cannot be without significance that the rules which apply to the inheritance rights of a surviving spouse in an intestacy are to be found in articles in that part of the *Code civil* dealing with inheritance whilst his or her rights arising by the expressed intention of the deceased spouse by will are to be found in other articles widely separated from the former under the title 'Dispositions between spouses by marriage contract or during marriage'. That the inheritance rights of the surviving spouse should be dealt with in such disparate sections of the *Code civil* seems to underline the view that the framers of the Code looked on intestacy as the fundamental method of inheritance and testamentary dispositions as somewhat of a gloss. In both cases, the extent of the interest of a surviving spouse depends on the relationship of other members of the deceased's family who, in addition to that spouse, survive the deceased. Chapter 28 on *La réserve* mentions the fact that the surviving spouse seems now to have acquired the status of a *réservataire* together with ascendants and descendants in the direct line rather than, as was the case prior to the Law of 3 December 2001, merely a person whose existence reduced the size of the inheritance of those members of the family whose entitlement to inherit is protected by law. The Law has been in force since 1 July 2002 and most commentators appear to have welcomed the surviving spouse into the fold of the *réserve* but it may well be some time before he or she totally sheds the tag of 'quasi-*réservataire*' in that that status strictly arises only when there are no surviving ascendants or descendants. Be that as it may, in the absence of such relatives, the surviving spouse has a right to inherit under an intestacy which cannot be taken away by a disposition elsewhere by the deceased spouse.

Capacity to inherit

In accordance with the general principles of private international law, the law of domicile governs succession to movables; in the case of immovables, it is that of the *lex situs*. However, whilst the classes of those entitled to inherit are established in that manner, whether a person falls within a particular class by reason of his relationship to the deceased is a question to be established by the personal law of those concerned. The relevant law of succession decides whether a person who is (say) the spouse of the deceased is entitled to inherit and fixes his or her share. But the personal law governing the relationship between the deceased and the alleged spouse decides if there was a marriage existing between these persons at the date of death. The rule of French law to be found in the C.civ.art.732 introduced by the new Law is that a spouse capable of taking is one whose marriage to the deceased has not been determined by a decree of divorce or a final decree of judicial separation.

The spouse in intestate successions

The *Code civil* as originally drawn was severe in its terms. A surviving spouse had no rights whatsoever in the estate of a deceased spouse who died intestate where there was left surviving the deceased any relative up to and including the twelfth degree. This ensured that virtually no surviving spouse could ever take. Moreover, when he or she did take, it was considered to be an 'irregular' succession since he or she did not form part of the family of the deceased whose duty was to conserve within itself assets of the family and to ensure that they did not eventually pass into the family of the surviving spouse.

By the nineteenth century, whilst it was still considered to be reasonable to preserve land 'in the family', novel kinds of property primarily in the nature of movables were more frequently acquired by the deceased himself rather than inherited from his family and it became accepted that a deceased person did not necessarily owe to his own descendants that which he had not acquired from his ascendants. The changes wrought over the years in social and economic life brought with them the concept that it was not unreasonable to feel a greater duty towards one's spouse as the person with whom one had shared one's life than towards one's parents whom one might well have forgotten or some distant cousin whom one had never known; or even to rank a surviving spouse as a possible beneficiary last in line immediately before the State, the recipient of inheritance tax.

From this change in outlook came a series of amending Laws. The first, limited though it was in its extent, was the Law of 14 July 1866 which gave a surviving spouse in an intestacy the life interest in intellectual property owned by the deceased spouse. There followed a series of Laws which further ameliorated the situation of the surviving spouse. Initially, these continued to be limited to granting the surviving spouse solely a life interest in the estate. Thus the Law of 29 March 1891 gave the surviving spouse such an interest, the extent of which depended on the relationship of the deceased to other members of his family entitled to benefit. The closer that relationship, the smaller the life interest; the more remote, the larger such an interest available to the surviving spouse. This Law also provided for the payment of maintenance (*créance alimentaire*) to the surviving spouse in case of financial need. This latter provision to which subsequent reference is made is still in force. Not until the Law of 3 December 1930 was the surviving spouse able to qualify for an absolute interest in an intestate estate in certain cases when the deceased left surviving no lawful parent and this situation was further amended in favour of the surviving spouse by the Law of 26 March 1957. By that Law, the surviving spouse took precedence over relatives of the deceased more remote than *collatéraux ordinaires* (for example, uncles, aunts, and cousins). Changes as to who were to be treated as children of the deceased for the purposes of inheriting in an intestacy were made by the Law of 3 January 1972. The law as it now stands is that enacted by the Law of 3 December 2001.

It should be noted that the term 'life interest' which is used generally throughout this book may denote two different kinds of interests known to French law. These are the *usufruit* and the *droit de jouissance viagère*. The former is akin to the English life interest granting rights but imposing obligations; the latter can be explained as a mere personal right to occupy premises for life subject to the assumption of certain limited liabilities. In the context of the administration of estates, the significance of both kinds of interest is that each gives the owner the right to occupy the asset in which the interest exists for his or her life.

Rights of the surviving spouse in an intestacy

The extent of these rights depends upon whom the deceased leaves surviving in addition to the spouse. These are dealt with in the various sections of C.civ.art.757.

1. If the deceased leaves children (or issue by representation) who are children of the marriage of the spouses, the surviving spouse has the choice of a life interest in the whole of the estate or an absolute interest in one-quarter of the estate.
2. If the deceased leaves surviving one or more children (or issue by representation) who are not children of the marriage of the deceased and the surviving spouse, the surviving spouse takes an absolute interest in one-quarter of the estate and has no choice to take a life interest as in 1 above. The reason for this rule is to prevent a second spouse who might be much younger than the deceased 'paralysing' the interests of children of the deceased's previous marriage who may well be of an age with him or her.
3. If the deceased leaves no children (or issue who take by representation), but leaves surviving a father and mother, the surviving spouse takes one half of the estate absolutely. In the event of only one parent surviving the deceased spouse, the surviving spouse takes an absolute interest in three-quarters of the

estate. If the surviving spouse takes three-quarters of the estate of the deceased spouse, and any ascendants of the deceased more remote than a mother or father are in need of financial assistance, they have a prior claim against the estate for a *pension alimentaire* (allowance).

4. In the event of the deceased leaving no issue or parent surviving, the surviving spouse takes the whole of the estate absolutely. This is in contrast to the law previous to 1 July 2002 under which surviving brothers and sisters would have taken an interest to the detriment of the surviving spouse. In addition (C.civ.art.757-3) if the estate of the deceased contains any items *in specie* which the deceased spouse had received from either or both of his parents by way of gift either *inter vivos* or on their death, one half of such items is excluded from the assets in which the surviving spouse has an absolute interest and devolves on the brothers and sisters (or their issue by representation) of the deceased.

Application of the rights of the surviving spouse

The Law makes certain provisions (C.civ.art.758) for cases when the surviving spouse has the option of a life interest or an absolute interest. Somewhat unnecessarily, it would seem, the article provides that until such option has been exercised, the rights which he or she can take on exercise of the option are unassignable. No special method for the exercise of the option is required but if the surviving spouse dies before having exercised the option, he or she is deemed to have chosen a life interest. Any beneficiary entitled by law to inherit may require the surviving spouse to exercise this option and if it is not exercised in writing within three months, the surviving spouse is deemed to have chosen a life interest.

The rules relating to the conversion of a life interest into a *rente viagère* (an annuity) are with minor exceptions the same irrespective of whether such an interest arises in an intestacy or as a result of testamentary dispositions. Either the surviving spouse qua *usufruitier* (life tenant) or any of the *héritiers* in remainder may request such a conversion. Such a right to require the conversion cannot be renounced nor can this right for the benefit of such interests in remainder be negatived by the deceased. An action lies at the instance of a party whose request for such conversion has been refused but becomes barred on final *partage* (distribution) of the estate. The Court may not order the conversion of a life interest in respect of the principal private residence of the deceased or of its contents.

The Law of 3 December 2001 gives the surviving spouse two new and important rights. By C.civ.art.763 when, at the date of death of the deceased, the surviving spouse occupied with the deceased a property as their principal private residence, which belonged either to both or wholly to the deceased, the surviving spouse has a right of free occupation of that property and such of its contents as are included in the deceased spouse's estate for a period of one year. If the property is held under a lease, the rent is payable by the estate. This right is said to be a 'direct incident of marriage' and not a right of inheritance. It is *d'ordre public* and therefore cannot be waived or negatived. In addition, the surviving spouse has a right of occupation of those premises for his or her life together with a similar right of the use of the contents. This right does not permit the letting or other parting with possession of these premises. This right is called a *droit viager au logement* or licence for life to occupy the premises and the other terms on which it is held are those contained in C.civ.arts.627, 631, 634 and 635 which are to be found under the heading 'Rights of use and occupation'. The right may, by agreement between the surviving spouse and the *héritiers* who own the *nue-propriété* (remainder), be exchanged for an annuity or commuted for a capital sum.

There are certain points of significance which must be noted in connection with this *droit viager au logement* to which the following rules apply:

1. The surviving spouse has one year in which to indicate his or her wish to benefit from this right of occupation.
2. As is normal in cases of occupancy of premises by life tenants and the like, either the surviving spouse or any of the legal heirs may require an inventory of the contents to be made and a Schedule of Condition of the premises to be prepared.
3. In the special circumstances that the premises are 'no longer suitable for the needs of the spouse' (C.civ.art.764) they may be let for any use other than commercial or agricultural in order to raise the funds necessary for the provision of other accommodation.
4. The value of the *droit viager au logement* is to be considered part of the interest in the estate to which the surviving spouse is entitled. If the value of this right exceeds the value of his or her total interest, the difference is not refundable to the estate.

Reference has been made above to the *pension alimentaire*, also known as the *créance alimentaire*. The rule previous to the Law of 2001 was to be found in C.civ.art.207-1, namely that the estate of a deceased spouse owed a financial obligation to a surviving spouse who was in need. It was a charge on the estate shared equally by all the legal heirs. It had been suggested that this right, intended to be called a '*droit à maintenance*', should impose on all the beneficiaries the obligation to maintain the surviving spouse in the way of life to which he or she was accustomed. It was, however, realized that this might impose such a burden on some beneficiaries that they would feel obliged to renounce their inheritance (Chapter 33). In the event, the new Law hardly changed the existing provisions.

It did, however, amend another provision for the benefit of the surviving spouse. It had for some time been realized that a surviving spouse when entitled to only a life interest in the deceased spouse's estate might not find this income sufficient for his or her needs. C.civ.art.205 originally provided that in such a case, the estate was liable to pay a *pension alimentaire* or regular income payment to supplement that income. Subsequently, the law came to provide that a surviving spouse might take an absolute interest in one-half or one-quarter of the estate (see above). The right of a surviving spouse to a *pension alimentaire* is now dealt with in C.civ.art.207-1. This payment is charged against the estate as a whole and its amount depends on the amount of the assets of the estate. It is an exception to the rule that beneficiaries who accept an estate are liable for its debts so that a surviving spouse will receive nothing if the estate has no assets and little if its assets are small. The right to claim such a payment must be made within a year of the date of death or at least before the completion of the partition of the assets if this extends beyond that period. It is the needs of the surviving spouse at the date of death of the deceased spouse which govern the granting of a *pension alimentaire* and its amount and not the arising of such a need at a subsequent date. Nor can it subsequently be increased if the need increases since the assets of the estate remain unaltered.

The new Law has not altered the right of a surviving spouse of the owner of certain kinds of business under the Law of 31 December 1989. This is a right to a payment out of the estate of a deceased spouse not exceeding 25 per cent of the assets of the estate to the surviving spouse who has for a period of at least ten years been actively engaged in the business without receiving any salary or share of profits. It is interesting to note that article L123-6 of the *Code de la propriété intellectuelle* confers on the surviving spouse of an author a life interest in the whole of his royalties for the period during which his copyright continues after his death irrespective of who the other surviving beneficiaries may be. This life interest is adversely affected only if it exceeds the *quotité disponible*. The life interest ceases on the remarriage of the surviving spouse.

Rights of the surviving spouse in testate successions

Despite the evident original preference for succession to be governed by the rules of intestacy, there is no suggestion in French law that one spouse should not yield to the very natural wish to benefit the other spouse to an extent greater than the rules of intestacy would allow. Even the most recent amendments made by the Law of 3 December 2001 increasing the rights of the surviving spouse in an intestacy do not seek in any way to deprive a testator of making full use of the rights of disposal of his assets by will accorded by C.civ.art.1094-1.

That article as originally it appeared in the Code of 1804 was more widely drawn than its present form in that it referred only to children and issue, thus including children of marriages previous to that of the deceased and the surviving spouse, and children who were illegitimate. This appeared to the Courts to be too wide in its scope and they interpreted the article to limit children and issue to those of the current marriage, applying the more limited rights of disposal afforded by C.civ.art.913 which takes no account of a surviving spouse. Subsequently, the article became extended in 1972 into its present form so that it now applies 'when a spouse leaves children or issue, whether of the marriage or of a previous marriage and whether legitimate or illegitimate'. However, the opportunity was not then taken to remedy what many considered to be a shameful provision in the Code that *enfants adultérins* should receive less than other children, thus increasing the amount available for the surviving spouse. This and other related provisions of the Code have been repealed by the Law of 3 December 2001. The most important, which cannot apply in an intestacy, is that the deceased can by notarial will but by no other document negative this right. If the residuary estate was insufficient, specific legatees had to share the burden proportionately.

Whilst the right of lifetime occupation by a deceased spouse prima facie applies in all cases where the deceased left a surviving spouse, if the deceased made a *testament authentique* (but not any other kind of will) he may expressly negative this right.

The other group of persons to whom the Code gave special inheritance rights were ascendants. Originally, it gave better rights to a surviving spouse when he or she was in competition solely with the parents or other ascendants of the deceased spouse. The surviving spouse was given three-quarters or a half of the estate absolutely depending on whether there were surviving ascendants in one or both lines plus a life interest in a quarter of the estate. The intention of the framers of the Code was to allow the deceased spouse to give the surviving spouse the means to lead a decent life whilst not wholly depriving his parents of everything. However, the rule was much criticized on the grounds that since the ascendants were likely to predecease the surviving spouse, their reversionary interest had little practical value. The Law of 14 February 1930 changed the situation and allowed the surviving spouse to take the interest to which he or she was entitled in default of *réservataires* plus the reversion to whatever was the entitlement for life available to ascendants. Subsequent amendments have not affected the rights of the surviving spouse until the passage of the Law of 3 December 2001. This has provided a new article 914-1 for the *Code civil* which added the surviving spouse to issue and ascendants thus, as previously suggested but by a different means, adding him or her to the list of *réservataires*. This article now reads 'No gift whether made *inter vivos* or by will may exceed three-quarters of the assets (of the disponer) if the deceased leaves no issue or ascendant but a surviving spouse . . .'. A spouse for the purpose of this article is slightly differently defined from the surviving spouse for intestacy purposes. In the former case, he or she must not have been divorced or be the subject of a decree of judicial separation. In the case of testate succession, there is the additional requirement that there should not have been pending at the date of the deceased's death a petition for either of these remedies. There has also been a significant similar amendment made by that Law to article 916. This, which previously read, 'In default of ascendants or issue, gifts inter vivos or by will can extend to the totality of the assets (of the disponer)', now reads 'In default of ascendants, issue or surviving spouse . . .'.

The rights of inheritance available to a surviving spouse are, in the light of the foregoing, as follows:

1. If there are surviving issue of the deceased, whether by the last or by any previous marriage, the surviving spouse may be given either:
   (a) the ordinary *quotité disponible* the size of which will depend on the number of surviving children, ie one-half if there is one such child, one-third if there are two such children and one-quarter if there are three or more such children in each case absolutely. Such shares are subject to the special rights of children of a previous marriage given under article 1098 of the *Code civil* which are described below; or
   (b) a life interest in three-quarters of the estate with reversion to the children and an absolute interest in one-quarter; or
   (c) a life interest in the whole of the estate with reversion to the children.

   If the share taken by the surviving spouse, whether absolutely or by way of life interest or by a mixture of both, exceeds in value one-half of the estate and the life interest does not encumber the residence of the deceased and surviving spouses at the death of the former and its contents, each child or issue may require that that life interest in respect of his share is converted into a suitably secured annuity. They may also require that an inventory is made of all items subject to such a life interest. This right cannot be negatived by the testator. In addition, children or issue of a previous marriage of the deceased may unless specifically forbidden by the testator in his will so to do elect to require the substitution of a life interest in any part of the estate which the surviving spouse has taken absolutely. This rule stems from the earliest days of the *Code civil* which when there were children of a previous marriage involved was intended to ensure that assets did not pass to another and unrelated family. The original rule has been much relaxed but still remains in its present amended form.

2. If there are no surviving issue of the deceased by any marriage but if there are surviving ascendants, a surviving spouse may be given:
   (a) if there are ascendants in both maternal and paternal lines, one-half of the estate absolutely and one-half in reversion;
   (b) if there are ascendants in one line only, one-half absolutely together with a further quarter absolutely and a quarter in reversion.

In cases where there is a choice of the interests which a surviving spouse may take, the choice is that of the testator. Frequently this choice is expressly left to the surviving spouse subject usually to it being exercised within a limited period from the death of the testator.

Care must be taken to appreciate the effect of this option particularly if French property is disposed of in an English will. Thus, by his will, Mr F, who was survived by his widow and two children, devised and bequeathed all his estate to his wife absolutely. The estate included a house in France. The Lyon

CRIDON advised that such a gift constituted the wife a *légataire universel* and did not confer any right to opt to take in respect of that property any of the alternatives available under C.civ.art.1094-1. In the result, since the house was the sole asset subject to French law, the widow was not entitled to exercise any choice but only to take the greatest in value of the three possibilities referred to in that article. It was not therefore open to the widow to opt, as she had done, to take a life interest in the house unless that was mathematically the correct choice. The option can be exercised by the testator in an English will or the surviving spouse is given the choice. This option if given is personal to the surviving spouse and is considered to be property capable of transmission on death. Thus the heirs of a surviving spouse who dies before exercising the right to choose can exercise it in their parent's place. However, the trustee in bankruptcy of a surviving spouse cannot exercise it on his or her behalf. On the other hand, a creditor of the surviving spouse when there is afoot an action for the reduction of gifts *inter vivos* made by the deceased (see Chapter 38) which would lead to an increase of the *réserve* can oblige the surviving spouse to exercise his or her choice.

The following table compares what can be taken by a surviving spouse in an intestacy and under a will.

Surviving at death of deceased	Maximum share of surviving spouse	
	Will	Intestacy
Issue of marriage of both spouses	Choice of: 1/4 absolutely and 3/4 life interest or life interest in all or 1/2 or 1/3 or 1/4 absolutely depending on number of children	1/4 absolutely or life interest in all
Issue who are not issue of marriage of both spouses	As above	1/4 absolutely
No issue but one or both parents with or without brothers and sisters	All subject to life interest in 1/2 for both parents or 1/4 for one parent	1/2 absolutely if both parents or 3/4 absolutely if one parent
Grandparents	All absolutely	All absolutely
Other relatives up to 6th degree	All absolutely	All absolutely

A number of the rules relating to life interests and other interests which arise in the administration of an estate apply in testate as well as intestate successions. Some have been mentioned above in respect of intestacies but reference should be made to Chapter 36 for a more complete description.

Donation entre époux

Mention is now made in connection with the inheritance rights of the surviving spouse of the use made by the French of the *donation entre époux*. The subject is dealt with at length in Chapter 38 together with gifts *inter vivos* generally but merits a special comment.

It is common in France for provision for a surviving spouse to be made not by will but by means of a notarial *donation entre époux*. The reason for the popularity of the use of this method may well appear obscure to the English practitioner and his client since such a gift takes effect only on the death of the donor and is revocable at any time during the life of the donor. It is responsibly suggested by *notaires* that some 80 per cent of married couples have either on marriage or thereafter executed a *donation entre époux*. The significance of this remarkably high percentage is tempered by the fact that the source of this suggestion (*Le Particulier*, No 950, January 2002) adds that the 'traditional' couple are those 'of a certain age' with only children of that marriage so that the percentage may have been overstated. It has also been suggested that the explanation lies in the fact that the necessary document must be prepared by a *notaire* whilst many wills in France are homemade handwritten holograph wills (Chapter 31) and as such can easily be lost or caused to disappear. On the other hand, the need for the interpretation of wills by the French Court is far less common than in England and the problems involved are simple compared to what from time to time teases an English Judge. Whatever may be the reason for the popularity of the *donation entre époux*, it is subject to special rules which are radically different from those which govern the making of other gifts *inter vivos*. *Code civil*, article 1096-1 says that 'all gifts made by one spouse to another notwithstanding being made *inter vivos* are revocable at any time'. It is said by at least one learned Professor of Law that the reason for this is to protect the donor against ill-considered gifts made by one spouse to the other in an access of passion which he would later regret having made. Roman law held gifts made by one spouse to the other to be without value unless expressly confirmed by a subsequent will, thus indicating that the donor had not acted on a passing whim. The framers of the *Code civil* reversed the situation by making such a gift valid but revocable at the instance of the donor.

There is absolutely no advantage whatsoever in the use of the *donation entre époux* as opposed to a properly drawn will although it is often suggested by the *notaire* as a means of benefiting the surviving spouse. Its terms may on the face of it achieve that result but this may well be better achieved by a French or English will and such a result may also be obtained (and often better obtained for the English) by the use of the appropriate *régime matrimonial* (Chapter 20). To propose its use to anyone other than a French person is an indication that the *notaire* or other adviser who proposes it is ignorant of the interplay of French and English law, very often to the subsequent distress of the survivor of the two *époux*. It is a document into which English husbands and wives, save in the most exceptional circumstances and after the most careful advice, should never enter.

Life assurance can also be a method of benefiting a surviving spouse since, subject to certain exceptions, the policy moneys do not form part of the estate of the deceased assured so that a surviving spouse can take these moneys in addition to his or her entitlement in the estate as such with also certain noticeable inheritance tax advantages (Chapter 39).

31

WILLS

Introduction 285
Types of will 286
Testament olographe 286
Testament authentique 288
Testament mystique 289
The international will 289
Joint wills 290
Revocation 290
Registration of wills 292
Use of non-French wills 292

Introduction

French law tends to regard gifts *inter vivos* (*donations*) and gifts made by will (*testaments*) as two methods of achieving the same result, namely the provision of *libéralités*. What is strange for the English lawyer is that the document which evidences a *donation* requires a greater degree of solemnity than does the standard form of will. The former must be effected by a notarial document; the latter needs but the unwitnessed handwriting of the testator. The reason is said to lie in the existence of the *réserve* or that part of a deceased's estate in respect of which certain members of the family have entrenched inheritance rights whether he died testate or intestate. Gifts made *inter vivos*, which should be reintegrated into the donor's estate in order properly to calculate the size of the *réserve* can easily escape the knowledge of the *réservataires* if not recorded in an unimpeachable form. The consequent appearance before a *notaire* who alone can draw the necessary *acte de donation* is considered to impose on the *notaire* the obligation to advise the donor of his duties towards his family thus leading him 'to reflect and to discourage and foil any efforts in the nature of improper solicitations by a would-be donee. Moreover, the mere fact that he has made known his intentions to a *notaire* is likely to restrain him from making a gift which otherwise would have remained secret' (L and S Leveneur, *Leçons de Droit Civil*, Tome IV, Vol. 2 (Monchrestien, 1999)).

On the other hand, it is not possible to disguise or at best it is extremely difficult to hide gifts made by legacy in a will such as, for example, a legacy acknowledging a non-existent debt and in any event such a legacy will not take effect if it eats into the *réserve*.

Types of will

French wills can be made in four forms:

(1) *olographe*;
(2) *authentique*;
(3) *mystique*;
(4) international.

Most wills made by the French are *olographes*. As has been discussed in Chapter 30, many married couples resort to use of the *donation entre époux*, which is to be discouraged for the English.

Testament olographe

Form of the will. For such a will to be valid in form, it must be written entirely in the hand of the testator and dated and signed by him (C.civ.art.970). There is no rule that the signature of the testator must be 'at the foot thereof' but it must be in a place separate from the body of the will. Witnesses are not required and it is most desirable that there should be none. Article 970 says that such a will 'is valid only if written entirely . . . in the hand of the testator'. It has on several occasions been held that the mere appearance on a will of a signature other than that of the testator, for example a witness, may not of itself render it void but it produces a will which is prima facie void which may well lead to litigation. The use of witnesses should be avoided. In the case of an undated will, the Court has discretion to provide a date if it can do so from intrinsic evidence.

Date of the will. The date inserted in the will may be in the form of an exact date or it may be in the form of a clear indication of the date of execution, for example 'the fiftieth birthday of my wife' or 'two days after Christmas 2000'. Such a will must not only be dated in the hand of the testator but the date must be that of the day on which he executed it. Any other date will according to the strict terms of the *Code civil* invalidate the will. However, a distinction is made by the Courts between a missing or incomplete date in a will and a date which is false. In the first case, a number of decisions have mitigated the strict rule as to the dating of a will. Thus, it has been held (Cass.1.6.94) that it is possible by the production of extrinsic evidence, so long as it does not conflict with such intrinsic evidence as the will itself can provide, to complete an incomplete or missing date. It has also been held (Cass.30.6.92) that if it is possible to prove the continued capacity of the testator until his death and the absence of any document of revocation provided that the period involved is short, a date can be supplied for a will otherwise in default of the provisions of article 970.

The case of a will, the date of which is alleged to be false (by the intention of the testator) or incorrect (by the oversight of the testator), raises an interesting problem. C.civ.art.1328 provides that: 'insofar as third parties are concerned, a document executed *sous seing privé* is deemed to be dated on the day on which it is registered or on the date of death of one of the parties thereto or on the day on which its substantive contents are repeated in any document drawn by an *officier public* such as a list of the assets of a deceased person made on the affixing of seals to his property or in the administration of an estate'. To apply this article to holograph wills would be to deny to the testator the very secrecy which this type of will makes possible. It is generally considered that the terms of article 1328 can be justified only by reference to documents which are wholly different in nature from a will. Hence, it is considered that the date of a holograph will prima facie holds good against all and the burden of proof that this is not correct is on the beneficiary seeking to prove that the date is incorrect. Such proof, in the case of an alleged false date, can be provided from any source. In the case of a mere incorrect date, the rule is different since in such cases, it must be evidence obtained from the will itself, for example, reference to an event subsequent to the incorrect date or sometimes by the nature of the watermark of the paper used.

Loss of the will. It is possible to prove the loss or destruction of a holograph will but the evidence adduced in support of such a claim is strict. The existence at one time of the will must be proved and proof of compliance with C.civ.art.970 must be provided. If it is alleged that the will was in existence at the date of death of the deceased, proof will be less strict than if it is sought to prove the disappearance of a will prior to death. In such a case, it will be necessary to prove the fact that the testator was unaware of the disappearance of the will and in many cases evidence of the persistence of the testator in his wishes said to be contained in his will up to the date of his death will be required. The circumstances of the disappearance of the will must also usually be proved. It is, therefore, desirable to retain a photocopy of an executed will or even execute a number of copies and keep these in some suitable place(s).

Choice of the holograph will. This kind of will can easily be mislaid or be made to disappear and by its very nature is best avoided. There are no attesting witnesses who can provide evidence of its execution if there are doubts as to this formality or if the will is lost. Moreover, attesting witnesses in England are almost always independent persons. In France, it is precisely those who stand to gain or lose who provide the evidence. On the basis that many married couples do not make wills but rely on the *donation entre époux*, there are three reasons why the French make use of this kind of will. First and foremost, it costs nothing. Secondly, it involves the disclosure of its contents to no one. Thirdly, since the law supplants the wishes of the testator in respect of the most significant gifts he may wish to make, in many cases, he lets the law relieve him of the need to make a will at all. However, if he does decide to make a *testa-*

ment olographe, it is the simplest possible document shorn of all technical language, with no reference to trusts or trustees, probably no appointment of executors and save in the most exceptional circumstances in words which require no professional assistance. It is a type of will to be avoided by any English testator who usually is not so concerned about the secrecy of the contents of his will that he does not wish to discuss them with his legal advisers. If, however, he feels impelled to resort to this kind of will, he must have it drafted for him by a lawyer well versed in both the French and English language and in the law of both countries. However, it may be made in any language and any English testator tempted to use such a form of will should deposit it with a *notaire* to ensure that it does not disappear.

Testament authentique

Form of the will.   As the name implies, this kind of will is in the form of an *acte notarié*. Originally, the framers of the *Code civil* deemed this will to be the most solemn of all notarial *actes*. Its execution required the presence of two *notaires* and two witnesses or one of the former and four of the latter. The Law of 25 ventose an XI (15 March 1803) reduced this to two *notaires* or one *notaire* and two witnesses. This has been followed in the current provisions of C.civ.art.971 et seq as a result of the Law of 8 December 1950 save that the use by the *notaire* of a typewriter or computer is now permitted as well as handwriting.

Execution of the will.   Such a will is dictated by the testator to the or one of the *notaires*. The use of the words '*dicté par le testateur*' does not require the *notaire* to take down precisely what the testator says. He may intervene to advise generally and to rephrase wording so as to make it clear but without altering the intent of the testator's wishes. The resultant writing is then read to the testator for his approval. The document must then contain a *mention* (specific reference) that all the requisite formalities have been complied with and the testator then signs the document in the presence of the *notaire(s)* and the witnesses if there is, as is usually the case, only one *notaire* involved. The insertion of the *mention* is essential and if for proper reasons a testator cannot sign, it must specifically refer to this fact and its cause. In the event of (say) the testator being afflicted by a sudden weakness, it will be only the reference in the *mention* of the facts which can provide proof that he approved the terms of his will.

The witnesses must be of French nationality, be able to sign their names and not have been deprived of their civil rights. The witnesses may not be husband and wife nor may beneficiaries or their relatives up to and including the fourth degree be witnesses. Clerks in the office of the *notaire* may not act as witnesses. The document must be in French but a translation can be annexed and it can be read to the testator in that language rather than in French.

A person who is dumb cannot make a *testament authentique* since he cannot answer questions or express intentions save by signs. However, a deaf testator can make such a will since he can read it and then repeat it aloud.

Despite efforts both by the legislature and the *notariat* to popularize this type of will, it is not frequently used. The reasons are not those which would be supported by the average English testator, namely the cost, the need to reveal the contents of a will to a *notaire* and to witnesses with the concomitant 'fear of giving rise to their adverse comments'.

Testament mystique

Requirements for validity of the will.   This type of will which owes its origins to Roman law has been preserved in its present form by C.civ.arts.976 to 980. It is rarely used except perhaps by those who cannot write but do not wish to confide their wishes to a *notaire* or for those who are dumb who would like, in the light of the rule which militates against their use of the *testament authentique*, to express their last wishes in a more solemn form than by *testament olographe*.

Such a will may be written by the testator or for him by another in manuscript or typescript. It must be signed by the testator unless it contains a declaration that the testator cannot write. It must then be sealed in an envelope and handed to a *notaire* in the presence of two witnesses, the testator declaring to the *notaire* that the contents of the envelope are his will and that if it is not written in his own hand that he has personally verified the superscription. The *notaire* writes or causes to be written on the envelope an *acte de suscription* confirming the date and place when it was made, a description of the envelope and of the seal with which it is sealed. This writing is then signed by the testator or the *notaire* and the two witnesses and such a will is void as a *testament mystique* if the writing on the envelope does not indicate by whom the will has been written or fails to relate that the testator has confirmed the writing on the envelope.

It is not obligatory to leave such a will with a *notaire* for safekeeping but it is customary to do this with the *notaire* who prepared the superscription on the envelope. In the event of a *testament mystique* being held to be void for want of any of the necessary formalities, it may well qualify as a *testament olographe* if the formalities indicated above and requisite for such a will have been fulfilled.

The international will

Requirements of the Washington Convention.   This type of will instituted by the Washington Convention of 26 October 1973 was adopted in France on 1 December 1994. It is for such a will that provision is made in sections 27 and 28 of the Administration of Justice Act 1982 which have not yet been brought into force. It is understood from the Principal Probate Registry in London that, until such time as those sections become effective, the Registry will admit to probate all such wills made out of England in a country which has adopted the

Convention provided that the form of such will complies with the requirements of that country. Thus, international wills executed in France in accordance with French procedure under the Convention should, when it is necessary, qualify for an English grant.

A will of this kind must be in writing but not necessarily in that of the testator. The writing may be in any form, that is handwritten or typewritten, and may be in any language. It must be signed or acknowledged, if previously signed by him, by the testator in the presence of a person authorized (*habilité*) by the law of the country of execution to act in connection with international wills and of two witnesses. The person for this purpose in France is the *notaire* and there is no requirement as to the nationality of the witnesses. If the testator is unable to sign himself, he must so indicate to the *notaire* who may accept the signature of a third party on behalf of the testator. The will must be signed 'at the foot or end thereof' and if it contains more than one page, each page other than the final page must be initialled. (This requirement is standard for every document of every kind in France.) It must be dated by the testator and the *notaire* before whom the will is signed must prepare a certificate in the appropriate form which is annexed to the will.

A will of this kind is looked on in France as having the advantages of a *testament mystique* but its complexities make it infrequently used in France or, indeed, in those other countries which have adopted the Washington Convention. Certainly, the impression which its title gives it, of having advantages when a person having the nationality of one country wishes to dispose of property in another country, may appear somewhat illusory.

Joint wills

Joint wills (*testaments conjonctifs*) made by two or more persons in one document are by virtue of C.civ.art.968 void irrespective of whether they dispose of property to a third party or whether they mutually dispose of property to the makers of the will. Article 2 of the Washington Convention specifically maintains this provision with reference to international wills. This rule does not apply to gifts *inter vivos*.

Revocation

The rules apply to all types of wills including international wills and apply to both complete and partial revocation. Revocation may be:

(1) *expresse* when a will or a notarial document contains a specific clause of revocation of a previous will or individual provision in such a will or a situation is created by the testator which de facto makes a will or legacy incapable of being carried into effect (C.civ.art.1035);

(2) *tacite* when a subsequent will without containing a specific revocation clause
  (a) makes provisions which are inconsistent with or contrary to those in a previous will, such earlier provisions are deemed to be revoked (C.civ.art.1036) or
  (b) where the subject matter of a gift has been disposed of by the testator prior to his death even if under a relevant rule of law it had been returned to the testator or the gift was *ab initio* void (C.civ.art.1037).

The rule of English law that marriage subsequent to the execution of a will not expresscd to be made in contemplation of a given marriage revokes a prior will has no counterpart in French law. On the other hand, French law recognizes the intentions of section 18A of the Wills Act 1837 in the case of wills or section 18(2) of the Matrimonial Act 1973 as to the effect of decrees of divorces and of judicial separation though in a slightly different form. The effect of the break-up of a marriage is considered to be revocation by operation of law.

There are also rules relating to the total or partial revocation of wills by the Court after the death of the testator which are beyond the ken of English law. In the following cases, the Court has power to revoke in whole or partially a will where:

(1) a legatee to whom a gift has been made subject to a *charge* (Chapter 26) has not carried into effect the terms of that *charge*;
(2) a legatee is guilty of any of the acts enumerated in C.civ.art.955 as applied to wills by C.civ.art.1046, ie has made an attempt on the life of the testator or been guilty of any crime committed against or has seriously insulted the testator. These are acts which may be committed during the life of the testator but C.civ.art.1047 provides a further cause for revocation, namely that of an act of serious affront to his memory committed after the death of the testator.

In the case of the failure to comply with the terms of a *charge*, the application to the Court is made by the person benefiting from the *charge* and enures for the benefit of his successors in title. In the cases enumerated under (2) above, the application is made by the heirs or those not affected by the alleged offences against the testator. With the exception of a claim based on a serious affront to the memory of the testator which must be made within one year from the date of the cause of action, there is no time limit in respect of other applications to the Court. In general terms, with the exception of gifts subject to a *charge*, a legacy revoked by the Court falls into what English procedure knows as 'residue' or in the case of a joint legacy, to the unoffending legatee unless the testator has provided otherwise.

The *Code civil* makes no provision for the effect of the destruction of a will by the testator himself but a line of cases (Cass.18.7.56 and 12.5.65) have established that such a will is properly revoked if its destruction was effected by or with the knowledge of the testator.

The express total or partial revocation of a will can be cancelled so as to reinstate that which has been revoked in the same manner as was required for the revocation. It is said that the retraction of a tacit revocation requires only the formalities which are required for such a kind of revocation itself but this appears doubtful since such an event is to all intents and purposes the making of a new testamentary disposition and the formalities for the making of such a document would seem necessary.

Unlikely though it is that the situation will arise, it must be presumed that in respect of such of the estate of a testator as is governed by French law (that is, French realty in every case and French realty and all personalty wherever situate in the case of a French domiciled testator) the above rules will apply irrespective of the domicile or residence of any legatee whose legacy it is sought to have revoked by the Court in France.

Registration of wills

A register of wills exists in France. The Basle Convention of 16 May 1972 which is not in force in the United Kingdom but has been ratified by France provides for an international system of the registration of wills. This is organized by each of the contracting countries so that registers in such of the countries as have ratified the Convention are available for inspection by the appropriate authority in all contracting countries. The body in France responsible for such inspection and for the management of the register in France is the *Conseil supérieur du Notariat*. The register is known as the *fichier central des dispositions de dernières volontés* at 13107 Venelles (Bouches du Rhône). The result of every search which must be made by *notaires* at the commencement of the administration of every estate is annexed to the *acte de notoriété*. It is obligatory that all *testaments authentiques* are registered in this manner by the *notaire* before whom they are made. As to other forms of will which come into the hands of a *notaire*, their registration is also obligatory but subject to any objection on the part of the testator.

Use of non-French wills

Apart from the comment in the Washington Convention that international wills may be in any language, there is no requirement as to its intrinsic validity one way or the other as to the language in which it is drawn. A will to be acted on in both England and France may be in either language if the draftsman can be trusted to have it properly vetted by a bilingual lawyer expert in the laws of both countries. In practice, if only one language is used, on the whole English is preferable if only because of the inability of French law to deal with situations which may arise which it is desired to submit to English law. French wills are simple in the extreme since the draftsman cannot create trusts and the law makes virtually every provision for the testator which he might wish to make. The problem also lies in the incompatibility of legal terminology used in the two languages of which none is more frequent or more dangerous than between the French and English terms of art used in wills.

For example, the will prepared by a *notaire* for a testator whose only language was English appointed 'XYZ to be my executor and general devisee (sic) and legatee', clearly the result of resort to a legal dictionary of the wrong kind. Insofar as there was English estate, it was taken to be the appointment of XYZ as executor and residuary beneficiary but since the overriding law of the administration of the estate was French, the description gave rise to endless complications.

Another and most important practical point relates to wills prepared in England for execution in France and vice versa. In this respect, regard must be had to the law in both France and England relating to the essential validity of wills which is in fact the same in both countries. The Hague Convention of 5 October 1961 has been in force in France since 1967 and its terms are embodied in section 1 of the Wills Act 1963. Hence, in both countries, a will is treated as valid in form if it conforms to the internal law of the country (i) in which it was executed, or (ii) in which at the time of its execution or of his death the testator was domiciled or had his habitual residence, or (iii) in a country of which at either time the testator was a national. These rules apply to wills disposing of movables. In the case of *immeubles*, the law of the country in which such assets were situate is added to the list of available laws in respect of the disposal of those assets.

It must be remembered that unless one finds a French *notaire* in England, and since the international will does not exist in England, wills made in England to be valid in France must be *olographe* unless one of the circumstances referred to both in the Wills Act 1963 and the Hague Convention applies. Thus, a French national, domiciled and resident in France, cannot execute in France an English will typed in English form and with attesting witnesses unless it disposes of immovables in England. Whilst it is unlikely that such a situation would arise, the reverse may occur. A French national having executed in England an English will disposing of a house in that country and appointing English executors instructs English solicitors to prepare a codicil to change his executors. They send him a codicil in English form (ie typewritten) to execute in France which he does in the presence of witnesses. This codicil is void since the person executing it fulfilled none of the requirements of the Convention.

Nevertheless, it is frequently asked in the case of English domiciled persons whether it is necessary, as opposed to being desirable, that French property devolve under a separate French will or whether it can as effectively be dealt with in the owner's English will. The answer is that there is no need to have a separate French will but only to ensure that the provisions of the English will comply with French law. French personalty belonging to an English domiciled testator will pass under English law. In the case of land situate in France, whatever may be the terms of a foreign will or trust, French law cannot be overridden. It is considered, however, that that part of French assets not subject to the *réserve* can in all probability be made subject to the terms of the English trust. The answer to this problem therefore lies with the *réservataire* who can agree to the terms of an English trust taking effect rather than the provisions of French law. Since the trustees will have all the usual powers of calling in, conversion, and sale, if it can be established at the outset that such agreement can be obtained, it is frequently preferable to allow the administration in France to be carried out by an attorney of the trustees rather than of the *réservataires*. It is also worthwhile remembering that the method of imposing inheritance tax in France is different from that in the United Kingdom and care must be taken to ensure that the standard reference in an English will to the payment of 'testamentary expenses' will cover, as it does for English inheritance tax, the payment of French *droits de succession* by the estate, if that is what the testator expects to happen and not, as in France, by individual beneficiaries.

French procedure recognizes the effect of a grant of representation and most *notaires* who are in any way familiar with English probate procedure (*homologation de testament*) will be content to work on an office copy of the grant. This document does not need a Hague Convention apostille to be recognized in France. Where one of the *réservataires* is an infant or under some other disability his consent to certain acts done during administration may require an application to the Court under section 53 of the Trustee Act 1925 as explained in Chapter 23.

Whatever the language or the form of a will which disposes of property in more than one country, the draftsman must seek proper advice in respect of both its essential validity and the effect of its contents before such a document is executed by his client.

32

DONATION-PARTAGE AND DONATION DE BIENS À VENIR

Introduction 295
Donation-partage 295
   Historical background 296
   Effects of the gift 297
Donations de biens à venir 298

Introduction

It is not thought likely that either of the arrangements specifically permitted in derogation of the rule against *pactes sur succession future* need figure largely in the English practitioner's knowledge of French law but both are of interest both from a legal and a procedural point of view. Both and in particular the *donation-partage* are in considerable use in France. Moreover, as this book has endeavoured to show, it is an insight into the way of life of a country which assists in understanding its laws and both the *donation-partage* and the *donation de biens à venir* should not be overlooked as part of that exercise.

Donation-partage

It might safely be assumed that the laws of a country whose citizens' ability freely to dispose of their assets by will is as circumscribed as it is in France by the existence of the *réserve* would not provide its practitioners with much trouble in the administration of estates of deceased persons. One of the leading *notaires*, with much experience of probate work, considers that very many administrations lead to hard fought family disputes and that the reason lies precisely with the *réserve*. This is because, whilst there is intended to be equality of inheritance between issue, the rule of the *réserve*, as is explained in Chapter 28, is based on the limitations placed on what proportion of 'gifts whether made *inter vivos* or by will' (C.civ.art.913) an individual may make without impinging on what his issue are entitled to inherit.

It is possible, therefore, lawfully to benefit one child over another only by resort to the *quotité disponible* which is that part of an estate which is not required to answer to the requirements of the *réserve*. Thus, if a testator has three children, three-quarters of his net estate will go equally between them but he may lawfully give if he wishes the remaining one-quarter to any one of those children in addition to his share of the *réserve*. That, of itself, should give rise to no grounds for dispute though it may well cause ill will.

However, there is a fruitful area for dispute among the *réservataires* as to the manner in which the *réserve* itself is calculated. This may occur for two reasons. The first is the need to establish whether the deceased made any gifts *inter vivos* and if he did which should be brought back to form part of the *réserve*. The gift which causes the most obvious problem is the *donation déguisée* which is described in Chapter 38 and is a gift made under the guise of another kind of transaction in the hope that it will not be treated as a gift but as a dealing for value. It is also necessary to consider whether gifts have been made to *réservataires en avancement d'hoirie* or *par préciput* (Chapter 28) and whether any such gifts in fact exceed the share in the *réserve* of the recipient of such a gift.

A further subject which gives rise to disputes is the value to be placed on the assets of a deceased person which, quite apart from the inheritance tax requirements, is obviously an important factor in the calculation of the *réserve*. In the normal course of events, assets are taken at their market value as at the date of death of the deceased so that any beneficiary can object to any valuation until he obtains one which he considers satisfactory for his personal purposes. In addition, when the administration of the estate is complete and ready to be distributed among the beneficiaries, there is frequent difficulty in obtaining agreement among them as to the method of partition. Until this is effected, all the assets remain *en indivision* and if a result cannot even be obtained by the drawing of lots, only the intervention of the Court can solve the problem. For these reasons, it is possible to make *inter vivos* a *donation-partage* which in most cases will avoid these difficulties.

Historical background
The procedure as now known in French law has its foundations in both Roman and Middle Ages customary law. In the former, the father as head of the household could divide *inter vivos* his assets among those who would take on his intestacy provided that each donee received his lawful minimum. No rule as to total equality among donees was imposed. French customary law followed a similar practice which stemmed, however, from a different line of reasoning. In this case, the head of the household abdicated from his position as chief of the joint family ownership of property in favour equally of his presumptive heirs. The framers of the *Code civil* adapted both these procedures as the basis for C.civ.art.1075 '*Les père et mère et autres ascendants peuvent faire entre leurs enfants et descendants la distribution et le partage de leurs biens*'. From this wording is taken the description *partage d'ascendants* by which the *donation-partage* is also currently known. The procedure as originally conceived by the *Code civil* proved unpopular because of the overstrict rules which applied to its use. By a series of amendments to the *Code civil* and finally by the Law of 3 July 1971, the rules were

relaxed and are now cast in a form which is more attractive to those who wish to take advantage of its results.

Effects of the gift

When the inheritance is organized by a *donation-partage*, the value of each item included in the *partage* (contrary to the rule in the case of ordinary gifts) is that at the date of the *partage* provided that by virtue of C.civ.art.1078:

(1) all issue or those who take by substitution living at the date of the death of the donor received *un lot* (a share) in the *donation-partage* and expressly accepted it;
(2) there is no reservation of a life interest involving the payment of a sum of money; and
(3) the donor has not provided for any other date for valuation of the assets.

Thus, on the death of the donor, the parties to the document of *partage* are bound in advance as to values and cannot argue on this score in the administration of the donor's estate. In addition, it is common practice to include in a *donation-partage* a penal clause which enables a beneficiary who wrongfully contests its terms to be deprived of his benefit subject to his receipt of at least his share of the *réserve*. Its use is, therefore, slightly limited but nevertheless can act as a sanction.

As is the case with all gifts *inter vivos*, *donation-partage* is (subject to very limited exceptions) irrevocable and can relate only to assets in the ownership of the donor at the time of the gift (C.civ.art.1076). Since the effect of a *donation-partage* is to vest the property in question in the donees, the warning of the early seventeenth century French jurist Loysel is still not out of place: '*Qui le sien donne avant de mourir, bientost s'appreste moult souffrir*' (He who gives his all before he dies, soon comes to know where sorrow lies). It is, therefore, common to provide in the document of partition one or more of the following protections for the donor:

(1) the reserve of a life interest;
(2) a clause forbidding the sale or charging of the relevant property by the donees without the consent of the donor although in practice it would be impossible for one of a number of co-donees alone to take such action; and frequently
(3) un *droit de retour* so that in the event of the decease of a donee without issue before that of the donor, his share revests in the donor. This enables the donor to redistribute that share among other children if so desired.

It will be realized that the *donation-partage* is a total derogation from the rule as to *pactes sur succession future* in that it organizes the distribution of the assets in an estate of a person still alive. During the lifetime of the *ascendant-donateur*, it produces all the effects of a gift *inter vivos*. Whilst it effects an irrevocable transfer of the assets comprised in the gift to the donees it does not produce the same effect as the 'opening of the succession' of the donor. As between each other, the donees are *co-partagés* in the gift and not in the estate of the donor. On the death of the donor, the donees become *héritiers* when the *donation-partage* takes on the character of the *acte de partage* of the relevant assets. If there are any assets in the estate of the deceased donor not included in the *donation-partage*, they are dealt with in the normal course of administration.

There are also tax advantages which are linked to the *donation-partage* in that they are now treated for *droits de succession* purposes as ordinary gifts (Chapter 38). A kinder interpretation of the use for the *donation-partage* than the need to keep children from fighting over the estate of their parents may be that the older generation wishes to see new blood flowing in the veins of the family business which is parcelled out among the children at a time when the parents also wish to see the increased expenditure of energy and new investment which such a gift may bring. Such a use for the procedure must be very limited compared to its value as a straight distribution in advance of a variety of assets.

Donations de biens à venir

Known also as *l'institution contractuelle* although clearly a *pacte sur succession future*, this kind of gift is expressly exempt from the penalty of invalidity which falls on such contracts. This is because gifts of this kind being those contained in a *contrat de mariage* or gifts made by one spouse to another during marriage are considered to be in the interest of marriage and the family generally. It has something for the English lawyer of the 'feel' of the English marriage settlement in that it can be and is used to enable parents, close members of the family and also strangers in blood (presumably about to be parents-in-law) to provide a source of capital for the about-to-be-married couple and the children to be born of that union.

Gifts of this kind, which fall between a will and a contract, were suppressed by the Revolution as creatures of the feudal system but they were reinstated by the *Code civil* under the innocuous style of *donations de biens à venir*. They are now referred to in C.civ.art.1082 in the following terms: '*Les mères et pères, les autres ascendants, les parents collatéraux des époux et meme les étrangers pourront par contrat de mariage disposer de tout or partie des biens qu'ils laisseront au jour de leur décès tant au profit desdits époux qu'aux profit de enfants à naître de leur mariage dans le cas où le donateur survivrait à l'époux donataire*' (The parents, other ascendants, collateral relatives of the spouses and also strangers in blood may by marriage contract dispose of all or part of the assets to comprise their estates at the date of their death in favour of the said spouses or the children to be born of their union in the event of the donor surviving the donee spouses). The article does not refer specifically to gifts made by one spouse to another during their marriage but C.civ.art.947 excepts from the rules which forbid *pactes sur succession future* gifts of the kind mentioned in Chapter IX of Title 2 of the 3rd Book of the Code which is headed 'Disposals between spouses by marriage contract or during their marriage' so that it is considered that gifts of the latter kind are also not void as being *pactes sur la succession future*. It has been held that unborn children of a future marriage can be direct beneficiaries of such a gift (Cass.10.7.1888) without the interposition of their parents, the future spouses. All such children must be treated on an equal basis and any preference of one over another child is void. Article 1082 quoted above speaks of 'children to be born of their union' thus leaving no room for distinction between them.

Gifts of this kind appear to be a halfway house between a gift and a legacy since the donor remains the owner of the assets until his death as does a testator but the gift itself is irrevocable. The donor may dispose for value of any of the assets caught by the gift and any clause limiting this right is void (Cass.24.2.69). The donee has but a *'spes successionis'* so long as the donor is alive. Thus, if he predeceases the donor, the gift fails. In theory, the right for the donor to dispose of any of the assets only for value but not by way of gift provides a somewhat illusory benefit for the donee since clearly the truth surrounding any such disposal will be difficult to establish.

A gift of such a nature requires capacity which exceeds that needed to make a will since it is irrevocable so that certain persons under an incapacity cannot make such a gift (Chapter 23). However, *'habilis ad nuptas, habilis ad pacta nuptialia'* so that few cases can arise of total incapacity. Although the gift is one of assets not in existence at the date of its making, the donee must have the capacity to receive gifts of existing assets save that if the gift is made in a marriage contract, capacity to be a party to such a contract is sufficient.

33

THE *EXÉCUTEUR TESTAMENTAIRE*

Introduction 301
Powers of *exécuteurs testamentaires* 301
The grant of *saisine* 302
   Completion of duties 302

Introduction

C.civ.art.803 reads '*L'héritier bénéficiaire est chargé d'administrer les biens de
la succession et doit rendre compte de son administration aux créanciers et aux
légataires*'. Thus, it is on the *héritier bénéficiaire*, by which is meant the lawful
heir in an intestacy or the *légataire universel* or *légataire à titre universel* if there
is a will, that is imposed the burden of the administration of the estate and of
accounting for his actions to the creditors and the body of the beneficiaries. This
is a far cry from what is to be found in the Administration of Estates Act 1925 or
the Trustee Act 1925 designed to protect the rights of creditors of a deceased
person and his executors. In an English estate it is a matter of due administration
that the debts of the deceased are paid by the personal representatives before
distribution to the beneficiaries. In France, it is the beneficiaries themselves who
are required by law not only to administer the estate but to account for that administration to creditors.

It is therefore pleasing to note that C.civ.art.804 relieves the *héritier bénéficiaire* from all but *fautes graves* committed by him during the administration.
Whilst this burden cannot be wholly avoided by the appointment of an *exécuteur
testamentaire*, it can to some extent be somewhat eased.

Powers of *exécuteurs testamentaires*

C.civ.art.1025 permits a testator to appoint one or more *exécuteurs testamentaires*. Such a person has no inherent powers to call in and collect the estate assets
although he can be given limited powers in that respect by the testator. The task
of persons so appointed is in general terms that in the words of C.civ.art.1031
they *veilleront à ce que le testament soit exécuté* thus limiting their overall task
to overseeing that the terms of the will are carried into effect.

Their powers are limited to a period of one year and a day from the date of
death of the testator which it is reasonable to assume in very many cases will
elapse before they can complete their duties. They are not entitled to remuneration

but they are entitled to be repaid their expenses by the estate. It is common for the testator to make special provision for their remuneration in the form of what is still called a *diamant*.

Whether their statutory powers are enlarged by the testator or not, it is their duty to see to the affixing of seals to the property of the deceased if there are beneficiaries who are under an incapacity or are absent. They should also together with the main beneficiaries attend the making of the inventory of the assets of the deceased. They may sell *meubles* to raise cash to pay any debts of the deceased if there is not sufficient cash readily available in the estate. As part of the duty of seeing that the terms of the will are carried into effect, they may in the event of any dispute over the validity of the will take such steps as are necessary to support it.

The grant of *saisine*

As will be seen from Chapter 35, *exécuteurs testamentaires* are not included among those who have *saisine* of any of the deceased's assets. If they are given *saisine* by the testator in respect of *meubles* (which includes sums of money), they may then hand over to specific and pecuniary legatees the objects of their legacies and refuse to part with them to those whom they consider not so entitled. This right is limited to the physical handing over of such items and does not extend to the equivalent of a *délivrance des legs*. It is recognized that a testator may also give *saisine* of his *immeubles* to *exécuteurs* so that they may in suitable cases sell such property. This can be an advantage where there are circumstances which would otherwise require an *adjudication judiciaire* or auction sale ordered by the Court.

An *exécuteur testamentaire* to whom *saisine* has not been given cannot require it to be vested in him (C.civ.art.1026) and the beneficiaries can at any time deprive him of *saisine* where he has been given it if they hand over to him such an amount as will enable him to pay legacies comprised of the *mobilier* of which he has *saisine*.

Completion of duties
When the duties of an *exécuteur* are completed or in any event at the end of his statutory period of office of one year and a day, he must account to the beneficiaries. His liability towards them is that of an ordinary *mandataire* (Cass.27.8.1855 and see Chapter 19). If more than one has been appointed, their liability in respect of *mobilier* is joint and several unless the testator has allotted different tasks to each when each is liable in respect of his allotted task only. If he has not completed his duties within the period allotted to him, he may apply to the Court to be named an *administrateur séquestre* which would enable him to continue to retain possession of assets in the estate which were the subject of dispute or litigation.

It is clear that the *exécuteur testamentaire* does not play a large role in the administration of estates in France. This is perhaps not surprising since none of his powers are discretionary and there is no procedure such as the obtaining of probate in which he can play a part. One leading textbook intended primarily for the legal practitioner covers the subject in three-and-a-quarter pages. Another, specifically for use by academics, extends the subject to five-and-a-half pages. It may well be that the law relating to *exécuteurs testamentaires* will in the future evolve as the *Commission de réforme du Code civil* would like. Meanwhile, the comment of Professors L. and S. Leveneur in *Leçons de droit civil*, Tome IV, Vol 2 (Monchrestien, 1999) throws an interesting light on the present situation. They say that, notwithstanding the opposition of the *réservataire*, the Courts have extended the powers of the *exécuteur testamentaire*, since in the absence of *réservataires*, the testator, thus free to exclude any beneficiary he wishes, should also be free to ensure after his death the fulfilment of the terms of his will. Nor is his subsequent comment without interest. 'The Courts have another reason for favouring the intervention of a third party in the administration of estates. It facilitates its winding-up.' This is an event which can take much longer than it does in England.

It is not advisable that English testators who make French wills should appoint *exécuteurs testamentaires* unless there are special reasons to do so and then only after advice from a source which understands the result of such an appointment in French law as compared to English law. It is extremely unlikely that any French lawyer will advise such an appointment of his own volition.

34

THE BENEFICIARY'S ELECTION

Introduction 305
The available options 306
The exercise of the option 307
Acceptation pure et simple 307
Acceptation sous bénéfice d'inventaire 309
Renonciation 309
Revocation of exercised options 310
The effects of international law 310

Introduction

C.civ.art.775 is cast in these terms. *'Nul n'est tenu d'accepter une succession qui lui est échue'* (No one is constrained to accept an inheritance to which he has become entitled). French law distinguishes between a *successible* or a person entitled to inherit who has not exercised his right to accept or renounce his inheritance and a *successeur* who has exercised his right by accepting the benefits given to him in the estate of a deceased person.

It may be asked why it has been thought necessary to provide a potential beneficiary with the right to make such a choice which seems unnecessary to those used to English inheritance law. The answer lies in the French rules of the administration of estates. Unlike the English system, the estate of a deceased person does not maintain any individuality but on the death of the deceased is added to the assets of the beneficiary or beneficiaries in whose personal estates it becomes submerged. From this it follows that the liabilities of the deceased towards his creditors are taken over by the beneficiaries.

It is not a question of a beneficiary inheriting a part of the net estate of the deceased but of inheriting on the one hand his share of the assets and on the other his share of the debts. In other words, if the liabilities exceed the assets, the beneficiary who accepts the estate is liable for the difference.

Such a difference does not run to its entirety since the beneficiaries are not jointly and severally liable. C.civ.arts.870 and 871 provide that *'les cohéritiers contribuent entre eux au paiement des dettes et charges de la succession, chacun dans la proportion de ce qu'il y prend'* (Co-beneficiaries contribute between them to the payment of the debts and expenses of the estate in the proportion in which each takes his share). As will be seen from Chapters 16 and 37, the assets of an estate are held *en indivision* until they are partitioned by agreement or in accordance with an Order of the Court. The liabilities of the deceased are specifically exempt from that *indivision*. In the result, one co-beneficiary is not liable for the share of another co-beneficiary who is unable to pay his share of a debt in the estate.

This system results in the creditors of the beneficiary and those of the deceased ranking *pari passu* to the disadvantage of the latter who may then be in competition with the creditors of a beneficiary burdened with his own personal debts. There is no system in French law for dealing with insolvent estates alone as separate units which results in a total lack of any rules of priority for creditors. Thus, the beneficiary who accepts this burden may pay his own debts and the debts he has inherited in any order he pleases or as pressure from the creditors may compel him to pay them. It is possible for creditors of such a beneficiary to obtain an Order separating the two sources of assets, the procedure and effects of which are outside the scope of this book since they affect the creditors of and not the potential beneficiary in an estate. Nevertheless, as will be seen, the choice available to a beneficiary to accept his benefit outright or subject to certain conditions or completely to renounce it does affect the position of creditors of the estate and the procedures involved take account of their interests.

The available options

In view, therefore, of the burdens as well as the benefits which can fall upon a person named as beneficiary in a French estate, it is small wonder that from time to time it becomes desirable for a *successible* to consider his position when faced with a doubtfully solvent estate. The three options available to him are:

1. *Acceptation pure et simple* (unqualified acceptance). This is the most usual choice confirming the benefits which have been conferred on him which he will make when he is certain that the estate is wholly solvent and his interests are 'good'.
2. *Acceptation sous bénéfice d'inventaire* (qualified acceptance subject to the solvency of the estate). Such a form of contingent acceptance is subject to the result of an investigation to discover if the assets in the estate outweigh the debts.
3. *Renonciation* (renunciation). This option will be chosen if the estate is clearly insolvent. Unusually, it may also be used if the deceased has made to the *successible* a gift *inter vivos* part or all of which can be 'called back' thus reducing his share in the estate. If he renounces, he is free of this obligation and may in the result retain more than he would if he accepted his benefit in the estate. Renunciation can also be made for purely benevolent reasons if, for example, a beneficiary wishes to release his interest in favour of someone who will automatically take in his place.

The rules relating to the exercise of these options are dealt with in detail in the *Code civil* in connection with intestate estates. Whilst there is no reference in the

Code to their being available in estates the distribution of which is governed by a will, they do so apply. They apply, however, only to *légataires universels* or *légataires à titre universel* (Chapter 36) and not to specific or pecuniary legatees since they are not liable for the debts of the estate. It should be realized that in French the word '*héritier*' strictly connotes a person entitled by law to inherit and so is limited essentially to those who take on intestacy. Those who inherit under a will are '*légataires*'. For the purposes of this chapter, the English term 'beneficiary' is used to define both classes and should be taken to mean the person who in French law has the right to exercise the options discussed.

A situation may arise as the result of the terms of a *régime matrimonial* or a *donation entre époux* where the surviving spouse finds him or herself in a situation tantamount to that of a beneficiary in the estate of the deceased spouse. The interest arises, however, not from the operation of law in an intestacy or testamentary disposition but by contract called a *disposition contractuelle*. The surviving spouse is not expected to have been able to know in advance when entering into that *disposition* what the situation would be on the death of the deceased spouse and is therefore given the same protection in such circumstances as any ordinary beneficiary.

The exercise of the option

A beneficiary may not exercise his option before the *ouverture de la succession*. This takes place at the moment of the death of the deceased. The exercise of an option before that date is void as being a *pacte sur succession future* or an agreement *inter vivos* to organize the devolution of assets in certain terms which is unlawful under French law (Chapter 24). From the moment of death, the beneficiary has time to consider whether he wishes to accept outright or subject to *bénéfice d'inventaire*. This is basically three months (see below) but can be extended by the Court. Once the period of deliberation has passed, he may find himself forced to make a decision by a creditor but otherwise his option is not statute-barred for thirty years. However, a beneficiary may not make one choice limited to some only of the assets and another in respect of others. Nor may the choice made be subject to any conditions imposed by the beneficiary. The option of acceptance once exercised cannot be revoked but a renunciation may be retracted and an *acceptation sous bénéfice* may be turned into a full acceptance in certain circumstances.

Acceptation pure et simple

Acceptance of this kind takes effect from the date of death and is, in effect, the renunciation of the other two options available. It requires the completion of no special formality and it may be express or tacit. There is also in certain cases an *acceptation forcée*.

Express acceptance is explained in the words of C.civ.art.778 as being *'expresse ou tacite; elle est expresse quand on prend le titre ou la qualité d'héritier dans un acte authentique ou privé; elle est tacite quand l'héritier fait un acte qui suppose nécessairement son intention d'accepter et qu'il n'aurait droit de faire qu'en sa qualité d'héritier'* (express or tacit; it is express when one adopts the title or quality of beneficiary in any notarial or other document; it is tacit when the heir does any act which of necessity indicates an intention to accept and which he would have the right to do only in his capacity as an heir). Thus, a mere letter or any writing (*acte privé*) will suffice provided that the intention is clear. It has been said that the use of the word 'legatee' as a description of the writer is not a sufficient indication within the meaning of that article since it may only have been used to indicate acceptance of the existence of a will in favour of that person rather than his intention to accept a benefit under it.

Acceptance may also be tacit. For example, to dispose of an asset in the estate clearly means that the disponer considers himself to be the owner. Since it is the intention in this respect which counts, the sale by a beneficiary of an object which he thought was comprised in the estate but which in fact was not amounts to tacit acceptance but to sell an item which the beneficiary thought belonged to himself personally but which in fact belonged to the estate does not amount to tacit acceptance (Cass.17.5.77). Acts of administration such as the grant of a lease or the collection of income are also acts of tacit acceptance but urgent acts of preservation, for example the registration of a mortgage in favour of the estate or the effecting of urgent repair works, do not come within this qualification. Nor does the undertaking of the defence to an action brought by a creditor against the estate amount to tacit acceptance (Cass.13.12.88 and 6.4.94). The line is very thin and a beneficiary who is hesitating whether to accept outright or to accept *sous bénéfice d'inventaire* should not himself indulge in any act concerning the administration of the estate. If necessary, the Court can under C.civ.art.796 authorize the doing of acts including sales by the Court which will not then be treated as tacit acceptance which, if done by a beneficiary without such authority, would so amount. A comparison with the situation of the English executor de son tort is apposite.

There is a third and, it is to be hoped, unusual form of acceptance, namely *acceptation forcée*. This arises in cases of *recel* which is the act of a beneficiary wrongfully extracting assets from an estate with the intention of appropriating them himself. Such a beneficiary is deemed to have accepted the estate *purement et simplement*, thus depriving himself of the other two options available to him. In addition, he cannot benefit from those assets which he has misappropriated once they are returned to the estate. A sole beneficiary cannot commit this offence against himself but it may be committed not only by *héritiers* but by any residuary beneficiary irrespective of whether his interest is absolute or for life only. The offence must have been committed with the intention of creating an imbalance of assets on final partition and not merely with a view to tax evasion

(Cass.4.12.56) which in practice is a not uncommon reason for the disappearance of assets.

Acceptation sous bénéfice d'inventaire

The manner in which this kind of acceptance is effected takes account of two distinct interests. It enables the beneficiary to decide whether he will become liable out of his personal assets for the debts of the deceased. If he opts to become free of that liability, the creditors of the deceased are then compelled to look only to the assets of the estate as their sole security. Hence in the interest of the creditors, the size of the net estate must be established and they must be made aware of the decision of the beneficiary. The decision to accept in this manner is therefore subject to two formal requirements.

Acceptance *sous bénéfice d'inventaire* must be made in the form of a declaration lodged with the Registrar of the Tribunal de Grande Instance of the place of the *ouverture de la succession*. Such a declaration must be made by a beneficiary of full capacity but need not as a matter of law be made by the *tuteur* of an infant or of a person of full age *en tutelle*. In such a case, *acceptation* is deemed to be of this conditional kind until such time as the incapacity in question ceases when thereafter the time limits as to the exercise of the available options apply (Cass.27.3.1888).

The inventory must be prepared in the form of a notarial *acte* and C.civ.art.795 allows three months for the preparation of the inventory and a further forty days for the beneficiary to consider the result and to decide whether to accept or renounce. The Court may accord a further delay in the words of C.civ.art.798 'having regard to all the circumstances'. Even then, further time may be obtained since, by virtue of C.civ.art.800, the beneficiary may still have the inventory prepared with the continued right to accept *purement et simplement* or to renounce provided that he has not already done expressly or tacitly any act tantamount to acceptance or been the subject of any judgment against him in his capacity of a beneficiary who has accepted *purement et simplement*. The reference in this provision to such a judgment is somewhat obscure and the general opinion is that this can only refer to the case of a judgment obtained against the beneficiary in default of appearance or defence. Such a judgment will give the creditor the right to obtain payment of his debt from the beneficiary personally but it has been held (Cass.19.4.1865) that that does not preclude him from accepting *sous bénéfice d'inventaire* in respect of other creditors. The right to accept *sous bénéfice d'inventaire* becomes statute-barred after thirty years.

Renonciation

Renunciation must be effected by means of a declaration filed with the Registrar of the appropriate Court (C.civ.art.784). As with the declaration to accept *sous bénéfice d'inventaire*, this is to mark not only the significance of the situation vis à vis the renouncing beneficiary but to advise creditors of the estate of the possible disappearance of a source of security. Hence any other method of announcing a renunciation is void. However, notwithstanding the article quoted above, a series of cases has established that as between beneficiaries a renunciation which has not followed the requirements of the article may be good *per se* but is not binding on persons other than co-beneficiaries. This formality is not required of the specific legatee since he is not liable for the debts of the deceased. Lack of action for a period of thirty years from the date of death amounts to a tacit renunciation.

Renunciation takes effect retrospectively as from the date of death so that those entitled by representation cannot take. This does not, however, prevent such persons taking if they can do so in their own right (Chapter 27). Renunciation may or may not result in the beneficiary who renounces being required to repay to the estate that which he has received from the deceased *inter vivos*. This depends on whether such payments were made in the form of advancements subject to hotchpot or not as the case may be (Chapter 28). Renunciation results in the disappearance of both the benefits and the obligations arising in the estate in which the renunciation takes effect. It does not, however, destroy family ties and a beneficiary who renounces remains liable for his share of the deceased's funeral expenses (Cass.14.5.92).

Revocation of exercised options

It is not possible to revoke an acceptance *pure et simple*. It is not, however, by the act of acceptance itself that the beneficiary acquires rights and obligations in the estate. It is by the death of the deceased that the beneficiary acquires ownership but until acceptance, it is ownership contingent on his acceptance or subject to his not exercising his right to renounce. It is therefore not correct to say that acceptance *pure et simple* operates retroactively to the date of death.

The option of *acceptation sous bénéfice d'inventaire* can be renounced expressly or tacitly. The result of such an act is that the beneficiary so retracting his option is deemed to have accepted *purement et simplement* and cannot therefore renounce his interest in the estate. The effect of such an act is retroactive to the date of the death of the deceased.

The effects of international law

The exercise of the options described above depends upon the law of the country which governs the administration of the estate. French law recognizes that the devolution of different parts of an estate may be subject to different laws. In view of the basic difference between the English and French systems as to the passing of the ownership in assets on a death, the rule has, however, more academic than practical interest. As to the act of renunciation by a beneficiary in the estate of a domiciled English deceased of an interest in a property situate in France, French rules apply and the declaration must be filed with the appropriate Court in France. This may be done by a suitable donee under a power of attorney in French form executed in England which need not be *authentique* but preferably should be to satisfy the doubts of the majority of *notaires* and *greffiers*. If the deceased did not die domiciled in France, the appropriate Court will be that within the jurisdiction of which is situate the property.

35

SAISINE

Introduction 313
Proof of right to *saisine* 313
Beneficiaries without *saisine* 314

Introduction

The ownership in the assets of a deceased person which in English law vests in his personal representatives, in French law vests in his *héritiers légitimes* or lawful heirs. They have *saisine* by virtue of C.civ.art.724 which reads '*Les héritiers légitimes, les héritiers naturels et le conjoint survivant sont saisis de plein droit des biens, droits et actions du défunt, sous l'obligation d'acquitter toutes les charges de la succession*' (The lawful heirs and the surviving spouse are seised as of right of all property, rights and claims vested in the deceased subject to the obligation to pay all the expenses of the estate). Even then, such vesting by operation of law is subject to its *consolidation* by the unqualified acceptance by each heir of his share in the estate or its negativing by his renunciation of that benefit (Chapter 34). *Saisine* results in the automatic vesting of such ownership without the need for any other formality such as an *envoi en possession* or a *délivrance de legs* which is required in the case of beneficiaries other than those mentioned in the article.

The concept of *saisine* is not difficult to comprehend. What is strange to the English lawyer is that those in whom it is vested are expected to administer the estate in effect as trustees for themselves beneficially but when the administration is completed find themselves as beneficial tenants in common without the interposition of any trustees. Although the atmosphere in which administration takes place in France is different from the manner in which it proceeds in England, one can liken the situation to that of an English estate in which a surviving widow and one child of the deceased are both sole beneficiaries and the two executors. The English system enables them to distinguish between themselves in their capacity as executors and as beneficiaries. The French system can make no distinction since they do not acquire the former capacity.

Proof of right to *saisine*

Proof of the right to *saisine* may be established 'by any means' (C.civ.art.730). This new article, introduced by the Law of 3 December 2001, provides a statutory background to the practice of the preparation of the *acte de notoriété* which for many years has in fact been prepared by *notaires* and which is, from a title point of view, the best equivalent of the English Grant of Representation. This document can, provided that the deceased left no will and his property did not pass by virtue of a *régime matrimonial*, be made by the Registrar of the Court in the *lieu de l'ouverture de la succession*. This choice should not be utilized by the English who should always make use of a *notaire*.

The *acte de notoriété* of which mention has been made in Chapter 25 in connection with questions of domicile sets out proof of death based on a death certificate and recites the *état civil* of the deceased. It relates the existence of any will made by the deceased as a result of a search made at the Wills Registry which is annexed to the *acte* and sets out the devolution of the estate of the deceased based on the contents of such a will or of the intestacy of the deceased. To provide such information in the case of a person who died domiciled in England and Wales, a *notaire* will often need the assistance of a *certificat de coutume* of English law which need not, as is sometimes suggested, be obtained from a lawyer 'accredited' to the French Embassy but by any solicitor or notary public with suitable legal experience and, if possible, a knowledge of French. It also contains the statement by the heirs or their attorney who have requested the *acte* that they are entitled to share in the estate. It must be signed in the presence of two witnesses who can vouch for the facts disclosed in the *acte*. This document does not bind any person shown therein as a beneficiary to accept his benefit. Production of such a document has much the same effect as does production of a Grant of Representation save that in the case of beneficiaries resident abroad, certain assets such as bank balances and shares may not be handed over without proof of the payment of the relevant French inheritance tax.

Beneficiaries without *saisine*

With the exception of the *exécuteur testamentaire* (Chapter 33) to whom *saisine* may be given in certain circumstances, it is necessary to fulfil further formalities if possession of any of the deceased's assets is to be vested in a beneficiary who is not one of those persons mentioned in C.civ.art.724 quoted above. These are either an *envoi en possession* or a *délivrance de legs*. The effect of both may be compared to that of the English assent except that an *envoi en possession* is an Order of the Tribunal de Grande Instance whilst a *délivrance de legs* is obtained by a beneficiary from the *héritiers* usually in the form of a notarial document with the possibility of recourse to the Court if it is initially refused. Such formalities are required in the following circumstances:

1. In the case of *bona vacantia*, the State must always seek an *envoi en possession*.

2. The *légataire universel* or beneficiary of the whole of residue and the *légataire à titre universel* or beneficiary of a portion of residue under a *testament olographe* or *mystique* who is not a lawful heir of the deceased must obtain an *envoi en possession* by proving that the deceased left no *réservataires* (C.civ.art.1008). This formality is not required in the case of a *testament authentique*.

3. If the deceased left *réservataires*, and even if the will in question is *authentique*, legatees of the kind mentioned in 2 above must obtain a *délivrance de legs* (C.civ.art.1004).

4. Individual specific or pecuniary legatees must always obtain a *délivrance de legs* either from the heirs or if there is none from the *légataire universel* who has obtained an *envoi en possession*.

Héritiers who are entitled in that capacity to share in the *réserve* are not required to grant a *délivrance de legs* when it is in an amount which exceeds the *quotité disponible* and so eats into their *réserve*.

36

LEGACIES

Introduction 317
Types of legacies 318
    Conditional legacies 318
Restriction of alienation 319
Penal clauses 319
Lapse 320

Introduction

As in English law, there is no particular formula requisite for the making of a valid legacy. All that is required is that the legatee can be fully identified. Legatees unborn at the time of the execution of a will become identifiable if they are born or at least conceived at the time of the *ouverture de la succession*. In general, the Courts are liberal in their interpretation in doubtful cases. Thus, a legacy to 'one or more charities' with no further description was held to apply to charities functioning in the place in which the deceased lived and as such to be valid (Cass.25.5.60). Similarly, a legacy to 'the charity in the city of Nice for the purposes of the education of deprived children abandoned by their parents' was also held valid (Cass.18.2.86) but a gift to 'a welfare association for the care of unfortunate orphans' was not acceptable to the Court of Appeal in Paris on 29 June 1990. The distinction is admittedly difficult to explain.

Where French law differs from what is good in English law is what follows from the interpretation which the Courts give to (C.civ.art.895 which says that a will 'is a document by which the testator disposes . . . of all or part of his goods . . .'. The conclusion drawn is that therefore the testator must make his dispositions himself and cannot delegate this to another. Hence, a legacy to 'two illegitimate children of ten to twelve years of age being a boy and a girl, living in one of the Homes in the Departement of Gers to be chosen by the Mother Superior of Condom' was held invalid (Cass.12.8.1863) on the grounds that 'the testator must make his own choice of legatees and cannot abandon this to the unfettered choice of a third party who then becomes the real disponer'. Were French law not deaf to the value of the trust and to the uses to which it could be put by executors, many worthy Frenchmen could be usefully engaged in assisting, as they can in England, the deceased testator to choose appropriate recipients of his charity. Possibly, the legacy coupled with a *charge* which is described in Chapter 26 is an approximate answer.

Types of legacies

A legacy may be:

1. A *legs universel* which is the legacy which gives the beneficiary the whole of the testator's estate subject to such deduction as must be made for the *réserve* and specific legacies. It is clearly the English 'residuary estate' but this is a dangerous translation since this implies deductions for legacies and other amounts but not for any disposition so significant but wished on the testator by law as the *réserve*.

   Despite the fact that what the legatee may receive is not the totality of the estate, the possibility that he might receive it if the *réserve* and other legacies did not impinge entitles him to be called the *légataire universel*. If no such depredations exist, he will receive the totality of the estate. This leads to the ability of the testator to name more than one *légataire universel* since if for one reason or another one does not or cannot take, another becomes *legataire universel*. A gift of the *quotité disponible* may be considered to be a *legs universel* for, if the *réservataires* do not take or there is none, the beneficiary under such a legacy will take the whole. Equally, if after making a number of specific legacies, the testator leaves the remainder to a further legatee, that legatee is *ipso facto* a *légataire universel*. A gift of the *nue propriété* (remainder) of all the testator's estate is a *legs universel* since the legatee or his successors will ultimately when the prior life or similar interest falls in become the owner of the totality of the assets.

2. A *legs à titre universel* is a creature of the *Code civil*, which defines it as '*celui par lequel le testateur lègue une quote-part des biens dont la loi lui permet de disposer, telle qu'une moitié, un tiers, ou tous ses immeubles, ou tout son mobilier ou une quotité fixe de tous ses immeubles ou de tout son mobilier*' (a legacy by which the testator bequeaths a share of (that part of) his estate which the law allows him to dispose of such as a half or a third or all his real property or all his personal property or a stipulated share of realty or personalty). Care must be taken to distinguish this kind of legacy from the *legs particulier* since the wording of C.civ.art.1010 quoted above is not easy to follow. Thus a gift of a proportion of property, be it immovables or movables, is a *legs à titre universel* but a gift of all the testator's land in a named place, whilst it may well be a part only of all his land, is a *legs particulier*. The gift of a life interest in property, even if it is of all the property owned by the testator, is always, unlike the gift of the reversion, a *legs à titre universel* since a life tenancy can only be a part of the assets in an estate.

3. A *legs particulier* which is a legacy which is neither of the above kinds, that is a general, specific or pecuniary bequest.

Conditional legacies

A legacy in ordinary terms gives rise to the right to receive it on the death of the testator. A legacy may also be:

(1) *à terme*, the English equivalent of which is the contingent legacy;
(2) *sous condition résolutoire*: this is the English condition subsequent since the legatee becomes in French law entitled to receive the legacy but if the condition is not fulfilled, then it becomes ineffective retroactively;
(3) *sous condition suspensive* which is the equivalent of the English condition precedent which has effects very much in keeping with such English conditions.

Conditions which are illegal or impossible or against public policy are void (C.civ.art.900). Conditions relating to marriage are viewed from what is in the interest of the legatee subject to the condition or his family or his *patrimoine*. Conditions as to remarriage are considered valid (Cass.30.5.27) unless they have been inspired by undesirable motives such as jealousy from the grave. There seems to be no suggestion that such a condition if not accompanied by a gift over is void as it seems to be in English law. A condition imposed by a father on his son that he should not seek a divorce is also valid, in the particular case in which this decision was reached, on the grounds that his son's wife had looked after her father-in-law, the testator, with much kindness (CA Rennes 14.2.72).

Restriction of alienation

Clauses which restrict alienation whilst prima facie repugnant and void are permitted if they are of a temporary nature and can be proved to be in the genuine interest of the beneficiary or even a third person. The rule is to be found in C.civ.art.900-1 which applies also to gifts *inter vivos* and reads as follows: 'Clauses which restrict the alienability of an asset given or bequeathed are valid only if they are temporary and are justified for a significant legitimate reason. Even in such circumstances, a donee or legatee may be authorized by the Court to dispose of it if the interest which justified the clause no longer pertains or an interest of greater importance requires it.'

Penal clauses

A condition not to dispute a will is intended to ensure that legatees respect the wishes of the testator. It is a condition subsequent which will be enforced by the Court on the grounds that it promotes harmony between the beneficiaries, provided that the avoidance of its implementation does not require the fulfilment of any intention which is unlawful or would endanger the *réserve*. It would seem that the French Courts' views are not unintelligent but whether such a clause would permit a beneficiary to take proceedings for the protection of his rights, as would be the case in England, seems doubtful since this would hardly be in the interests of harmonious relations between him and the other beneficiaries.

Lapse

It is obvious that the rules which apply to the revocation of the will itself apply to legacies made by it. There are certain situations which are not brought about by any express or tacit act of the testator, which cause the lapse of a legacy. These are: (i) the death of the legatee before that of the testator. It will be remembered that substitution by law applies only in cases of intestacy and there is no provision in French law equivalent to that contained in section 33 of the Wills Act 1837; (ii) the legatee must be capable in law of taking his legacy at the time of the death of the testator (see Chapter 23); (iii) the loss or destruction of the subject matter of the legacy before the death of the testator. If it is in existence at that time but is subsequently lost or destroyed, the legacy is good and the object has become the property of the legatee. Thus its loss is his personal loss unless, whilst it was in the technical possession of the *héritiers* who had *saisine*, the loss was due to some fault on their part.

The result of a legacy failing to take effect in the absence of any gift over by the testator depends on varying circumstances, so that it will accrue to the *légataire universel* which is the equivalent of the English 'falling into residue' or if it is the gift to a *légataire universel* which lapses, then to those entitled as on intestacy. C.civ.arts.1044 and 1045, however, provide exceptions in the case of legacies made to joint legatees.

Where the will contains a gift of residue (*l'universalité*) to more than one person, for example '*j'institue A et B mes légataires universels*' ('my residuary estate to A and B in equal shares') or jointly of part of residue, for example '*Je lègue à A et B la totalité de mes biens qui constituent la quotité disponible de ma succession*' ('I bequeath to A and B all that part of my estate of which I am by law entitled freely to dispose'), if the share of one co-legatee lapses, his share accrues to the other co-legatee as it would in English law if the gift were in joint tenancy. This is an exception to the general rule that in default of a specific substitution provision, the lapsed share, if of residue, would pass as on intestacy. This is based on the assumption that the testator by making a gift of such a nature had in mind that the legatee who could take should take the lapsed share.

If a testator leaves a legacy of a particular identifiable item to more than one legatee, the effect of lapse in the case of one such legatee depends on the manner in which the legacy is cast. If the legacy is of one item to two persons in which each legatee is to enjoy a pre-determined share, for example 'I bequeath Whiteacre to A and B as to one-half each', lapse in respect of one legatee does not result in the accrual of that share to the other legatee. If, however, the gift is of one item bequeathed to two legatees simpliciter, for example 'I bequeath Blackacre to A and B', on the lapse of that gift in respect of either A or B, the whole will accrue to the other.

It is to be noted that these statutory distinctions, founded largely on Roman law, do not find much favour with the Courts which consider them to be of significance only as a last resort when evidence as to the intentions of the testator cannot be drawn either from the will itself or from any extrinsic source. It is interesting to see that the French attitude as to whether or not a co-legatee is bound to accept an accretion to a gift made to him turns on whether it would involve him in additional *charges* or financial burdens. Since it is within the capability of the testator expressly or impliedly to arrange that such an accretion does not take place, if he has not done so, it must be presumed that he intended that these additional burdens do in fact fall on the legatee to whom his co-legatee's interest accrues. It is interesting to compare this rule with the rule of English law that acceptance of a gift is subject to the burdens which come with it (*Messenger v Andrews* [1828] 4 Russ 478). The accrual in French circumstances occurs as a matter of law but the testator could have ensured that it did not happen. In the English case, the land plus its burdens came directly and deliberately from the giver.

As to the significance of *saisine* with regard to legacies, see Chapter 35.

37

ADMINISTRATION OF AN ESTATE

Introduction 323
Preliminary steps 324
Sealing the property 325
Inventory of contents 325
Bank accounts 326
Documents in an administration 326
    Acte de notoriété après décès 326
    Certificats de propriété et certificats d'hérédité 327
    Envoi en possession 328
    Déclaration de succession 328
    Attestation immobilière 328
Distribution 328
    The beneficiaries' choice 329
    Pétition d'hérédité 330

Introduction

C.civ.art.720 the terms of which were set by the Law of 3 December 2001 is brief: '*Les successions s'ouvrent par la mort*'. This evident statement can be somewhat inadequately translated as meaning that 'death is the precursor of inheritance'. The short article qualifies the relevant death as taking place '*au dernier domicile du défunt*' which must be understood in neutral terms as 'at the place of the last residence of the deceased'. This article has combined and amended the previous articles 110 and 718, the latter referring to the 'natural death' as opposed to 'the death' of the deceased. The Code originally spoke of the 'natural death' and the 'civil death' of the deceased but the latter was abolished by the Law of 31 May 1854.

English probate procedure does not give jurisdiction to issue Grants of Representation on a geographical basis and a grant may be sought in any Registry. That is not the situation in France so that any applications to the Court must be made to the Court of the area in which '*la succession est ouverte*'. This does not mean that the *notaire* dealing with the administration of the estate must operate in that area but that for procedural purposes, the appropriate Court must be chosen. This, for example, governs to which Court one applies for an *envoi en possession* or lodges the renunciation by a beneficiary of his interest in an estate. It is also in that Court that will be heard any contentious matters such as would be heard in the Chancery Division or in the Family Division. The determination of the *lieu de domicile* be it of a French citizen or of a non-French deceased is a matter of French law (Cass.17.11.81). In the case of a deceased person who clearly had a *lieu de domicile* out of France, which is likely to be the case of all English persons who are not resident in France, the Tribunal de Grande Instance deemed to be the Court of the *lieu de domicile* is the Court in Paris.

Preliminary steps

Whilst it is obvious that any lawyer dealing with an administration will require sight of a death certificate, such a document is of 'primordial' significance in France. This arises from the interlinking of births, deaths and marriages in the *état civil* system in France. An English death certificate is acceptable provided it is accompanied by a translation which it is suggested may be made and certified as a true translation by a solicitor (if his French is adequate) since this is a far cheaper method than to use a notary public or a French translator who is *assermenté*. Most *notaires* will accept this.

Most *notaires* will understand that persons who are British and were married in England may safely be assumed to have property rights as between husband and wife equivalent to the French *régime* of *séparation de biens*. Some, in parts of the country where even a limited knowledge of foreign law is not needed, may wish to be comforted by a *certificat de coutume* in respect of any points of English law of which they are ignorant. In this connection it must not be overlooked that since it is the beneficiaries of an estate who are liable to French inheritance tax at varying rates and not the estate itself, it is necessary to explain to the French Revenue in the *déclaration de succession* or inheritance tax account how each beneficiary comes to take an interest and what that interest amounts to. It is desirable to have such evidence of English law available to support such an explanation, for example in the case of a settled legacy.

In the case of a person who has died resident in England leaving property in France, it is necessary to establish the nature of those assets and whether the deceased left a will in France. These are likely to consist of a house or flat and cash at bank. It is unusual for persons who remain domiciled and resident in England to have other assets in France. In the case of persons who live on a permanent basis in France but die leaving assets in the United Kingdom, more extensive enquiries must be made since many have assets, usually in the shape of bank balances and investments, in some third country. In either case, it is highly desirable to contact a qualified person in France who is expert in both English and French law and procedure. It must be borne in mind that in the case of a person who dies resident in England owning a property in France, his only contact with a *notaire* in that country will probably have been on the purchase of that property and that in all probability that *notaire* will not have been of his choice but of the agent for the seller to him. A qualified expert in France of the kind mentioned above will know if that *notaire* is suitable bearing in mind the inevitable interplay of French and English law in which not all *notaires* are well versed.

The situation is not necessarily different if a solicitor becomes aware of the death of a client for whom he holds a will which disposes of property in both the United Kingdom and France and who died resident and possibly also domiciled in France. In many cases, the need for the services of such an expert is essential since in the case of a death of a person domiciled in France owning estate in England, an English Grant will be needed and an affidavit of French law required by the Probate Registry to support the application under NCP Rule 30 for such a Grant.

Sealing the property

Prior to 1986 it was at least in theory obligatory that all property in an estate where the surviving spouse or a beneficiary was absent should be officially sealed. The rule was by no means always enforced. Currently this is now available at the request of among others (i) the surviving spouse and lawful heirs, (ii) any person named as *exécuteur testamentaire*, (iii) certain creditors, (iv) in the case of infant beneficiaries who have no lawfully appointed guardians, the local mayor, chief of the local police or of the *gendarmerie* or anyone who was living with the deceased. An application must be made to the Registrar of the local Court and, if properly made, will be granted unless the Registrar decides that such a procedure is not necessary when he will proceed to have made an inventory of all that is to be found in the house.

The seals, the unauthorized removal of which is a criminal offence dealt with severely, may be lawfully removed by application to the Court in the presence of such of the beneficiaries as choose to attend when an inventory of all the contents is made by one or more *notaires* or *commissaires-priseurs* chosen by the beneficiaries or in default by the Court.

The procedure is cumbersome but experience has shown that in many cases of property both in the country and in towns which has been left unoccupied after a death, contents disappear quickly. Their loss is certainly not covered by insurance unless the non-occupation of the property has been announced to the insurance company and, even then, the claim is difficult to support. This is yet another example of the need to have an attorney in France who can deal with a problem of this kind.

Inventory of contents

As is said in Chapter 39, the value of the contents of a house or flat will in any event not be accepted by the French Revenue at less than 5 per cent of the value of the gross assets of the estate. In any case where the contents are not of such a value or, if the contrary is the case and they include items of considerable value, it is desirable to have an inventory made in the form of a notarial document with the assistance of a *commissaire-priseur*. If there are specific legatees, it is useful. In addition, if there is a surviving spouse who is or becomes entitled to a life interest in such assets, the reversioners can insist on such an inventory being made. In certain cases, an inventory is obligatory as in the case of assets subject to the *régime de communauté* to establish the extent of the liability of the surviving spouse in respect of the debts of the deceased spouse (C.civ.art.1483) or where there is a question as to whether a beneficiary will accept or renounce his interest in an estate.

Bank accounts

A particular difficulty can arise in connection with bank accounts in the name of a deceased person. Usually, the *notaire* involved in the administration of the estate will establish the balance at the date of death and see to the unblocking of the account. Usually all that is needed to that end is the *acte de notoriété* but some banks require the consent of the beneficiaries.

In practice, joint accounts are either '*et*' accounts in that both account holders must sign or '*et/ou*' accounts which allow either account holder to sign. In the case of the latter, which are the more common, it is not the practice of the banks to block accounts on the death of one account holder unless specifically asked to do so. It must, however, be remembered that such accounts are for tax purposes deemed to belong in equal shares to each account holder. Thus, in the case of a husband and wife joint account where the surviving spouse is the sole beneficiary, he or she may freely withdraw more than half the balance at the date of the death of the deceased spouse. If, on the other hand, there are other beneficiaries, any withdrawal in excess of half of that balance eats into what is due to the estate and deprives those other beneficiaries of their share. In cases where the beneficiaries are resident out of France unless they are a surviving spouse or in direct line to the deceased, banks may not pay out amounts in excess of Euro 7,600 without a receipt for paid inheritance tax.

Documents in an administration

A number of documents referred to in this chapter are to be found in the Appendix together with translations or explanations.

Acte de notoriété après décès
There being no equivalent of a Grant of Representation, the important document proving the title of the beneficiaries, the *acte de notoriété* referred to in Chapter 24, has become as a result of the Law of 3 December 2001 a document of considerable importance. Previously, it was a generally accepted way of satisfying all persons of the title of beneficiaries in an estate. Now, by virtue of the new

C.civ.art.730, it has been given statutory value. The article says that 'Proof of entitlement to inherit may be established by any means. Such proof may be by way of an *acte de notoriété* prepared by a *notaire* at the request of one or more of the beneficiaries.'

Among the information given in this document is the domicile (in the English law sense) of the deceased and his nationality both of which may play an important part in assessing the essential validity and contents of any will left by the deceased. It will also set out the names of the persons entitled to take. Much information, if not all except the death itself of the deceased, will in the case of a foreigner be unknown to the *notaire* who is instructed to act who therefore relies on what is told to him. The document requires two witnesses who declare '*avoir parfaitement connu le défunt ci-après nommé et la composition de sa famille*' (that they were well acquainted with the hereinafter named deceased and with the membership of his family). There may be a will registered in France when there is also a will held in England and questions of domicile may come to be of great importance. It is not unknown for such a document to show the deceased's domicile as French whilst the English grant gives a domicile in England and Wales by reason of the different meanings given to the word 'domicile' in each language. Other discrepancies can occur.

In the case of a person dying domiciled in England leaving estate in France, it is unlikely that there will be two persons available in France who can act as witnesses to this document. On the whole, *notaires* are not over-concerned as to who they accept as witnesses and this can lead to problems. In this connection, as in others already referred to, it is highly undesirable to appoint as sole attorney a member of the staff of a *notaire*. Among other dangers is that such an attorney will without full knowledge of the facts act as one of the witnesses and a fellow employee will be the second witness. It is essential to ensure that a suitable attorney as indicated elsewhere is appointed and that he is given all the information needed for a correct completion of the *acte de notoriété*.

The original of this *acte* is retained in the *minutes* of the *notaire* before whom it was made and the *expédition* of that document serves much the same purpose as an original or Office Copy Grant. Plain copies for use in circumstances similar to those where a photocopy of an English grant would suffice can also be obtained.

Certificats de propriété et certificats d'hérédité

The new article referred to above specifically says that the provisions relating to the *acte de notoriété* are without prejudice to the issue of *certificats de propriété ou d'hérédité*. The former is a document attesting the ownership of certain types of assets after a death or a change of ownership. If in the form of an *acte notarial* it is acceptable. If it is issued by the local Court, it is of less value since it is available only if the deceased left no will, made no gifts, had no *contrat de mariage* and is based on information provided by the applicant who must be of

French nationality. The *certificat d'hérédité* which is often issued by the local *mairie* is a positive danger since it is based solely on what the person who asks for the certificate tells the local *fonctionnaire*. In the case of the non-French, it is the blind leading the blind since it is rare that the non-French applicant knows who under French law is entitled to inherit and the resultant certificate is frequently incorrect. It is the bane of the *notaire* but much used by some banks.

Envoi en possession
If it is necessary to obtain an *envoi en possession* (Chapter 35), this is dealt with by an *avocat* instructed by the *notaire* on an *ex parte* application to the local Court. There are no statutory rules on the subject and the Courts follow certain self-imposed rules as to the apparent validity of a will as discussed in Chapter 31 coupled with ensuring that there are no *réservataires* who already have *saisine*.

Déclaration de succession
The contents of this account are discussed in Chapter 38.

Attestation immobilière
Even if it were not desirable to make use of the services of a *notaire* in connection with every administration of an estate in France, it is obligatory to do so when any asset is an *immeuble*. This document is a notarial *acte* which recounts the death of a deceased owner of land and the vesting of it in one or more persons consequent upon that person's death. Once given, it is lodged at the appropriate *bureau des hypothèques* so that the ownership of the property may be changed on the register. It follows that in an estate, property cannot save in the rarest circumstances be sold by executors since without special provisions, it vests in the appropriate beneficiary (see Chapter 33) and can be sold only by him.

Distribution

For the purposes of the following discussion of the distribution of an estate, it is assumed that the deceased is not subject to any French *régime matrimonial*. It is not likely that English couples will have entered into such an arrangement except in the case of the *régime de communauté universelle* in respect of assets situate in France. In such cases, the assets subject to such a *régime* pass directly to the surviving spouse and do not form part of the estate of the deceased spouse.

Since with the exception of specific or pecuniary legacies, all assets in an estate vest in beneficiaries and not in personal representatives, such assets come automatically to be owned *en indivision*. The result is that these assets are subject to the paralysing effect of C.civ.art.815 which has been dealt with more fully in Chapter 16 and this article applies not only to assets inherited in every intestacy as well as by will but also to any asset not purchased *en tontine* by more than one owner. It is true that the legislature has endeavoured to mitigate the rigours of the effect of this article by the introduction of a form of co-ownership in tenancy in common by the introduction of the *indivision conventionnelle* but this does not apply to the distribution of estate assets unless it is agreed to at some subsequent stage.

The beneficiaries' choice

On completion of all the formalities and the ascertainment of the final figure for the net distributable assets and assuming that the deceased has not already dealt with the situation by a *donation-partage* during his lifetime (Chapter 32), the question then arises—*indivision* or *partage*? Chapter 16 on the joint ownership of property explains the circumstances in which it may be necessary to apply to the Court if the beneficiaries cannot agree between themselves to partition the assets to which they are entitled since the basic principle of ownership *en indivision* is that unless the Court has the power to delay a partition, no beneficiary or indeed any owner *en indivision* can be compelled to remain in that unenviable state. If all the beneficiaries are in agreement and all have accepted the estate *purement et simplement* a simple notarial *acte* is all that is required. If the estate has been accepted *sous bénéfice d'inventaire*, the division of the assets must be the subject of a Court Order to prevent them losing the protection of this kind of acceptance.

If an asset in the estate cannot be partitioned without causing a loss in the value of each part taken by each beneficiary or if one or more of the beneficiaries does not wish to take a share, the asset is dealt with by *licitation*. This may take on the character of a sale by which one or more beneficiaries buys out the others by payment of a *soulte* or equality money. If the parties cannot agree, the *licitation* is arranged under the auspices of the Court by means of an auction (Chapter 13) and the sale price is split out among the beneficiaries. If the transaction is between co-owning beneficiaries, the selling parties are covered for the price they will receive by way of *soulte* by the registration of a *privilège* or charge on the property sold at the Land Registry within two months of the transaction. If the sale is to a buyer who was not a co-owner, the ordinary protection for payment of the price is as in a normal sale.

The rules for the ascertainment of the net divisible estate are extremely complex but once it has been established, it is in accordance with C.civ.art.831 'divided into as many equal lots as there are beneficiaries entitled to share in it'. The following article requires that insofar as it is possible, 'each lot should in whole or in part consist of *meubles* or *immeubles*, rights or debts of equal value'. Any inevitable disparity in value is compensated for by the payment of equality money. The lots are made up by one of the beneficiaries, if all can agree on such a choice and in default by an expert chosen by the Court. It is open to any of the beneficiaries to object to the composition of the lots before they are drawn. It is open to a number of beneficiaries including the surviving spouse to claim preferential treatment in the choice of lots comprising agricultural property with a view to the continuance of the business there carried on. Such a claim may also be made in respect of any business of a family nature and also of the residence of the deceased at the time of his death if the claimant was living with the deceased on those premises. It would appear that the powers and discretions given to English executors in respect of appropriation make for the more satisfactory method of winding up the administration of an estate.

The effect in law of a *partage* is that by C.civ.art.883, 'Each co-heir is deemed to have succeeded alone and immediately to all the effects comprised in his lot . . . and never to have had any property in the other assets in the estate . . .'. The covenant for quiet enjoyment which each co-heir is deemed to give to the others relates only to events arising prior to the *partage*.

In addition to the rescission for *lésion* (Chapter 3), a *partage* may be rescinded for (i) violence or behaviour which puts a reasonable person in present fear for his person or his assets or (ii) fraudulent misrepresentation by which one party was induced to enter into the *partage*. An action for rescission on these grounds may be instituted irrespective of the nature of the document putting an end to the *indivision* and whether the *partage* was by agreement between the parties or by Order of the Court. Such an action is statute-barred five years after the date of the partition.

Pétition d'hérédité

Although there is no reference to this action in the *Code civil*, an action may be commenced by any person who is entitled to inherit in an estate but who has in fact been by error or intentionally passed over. In the case of a testate succession, the applicant who will usually be the *légataire universel* will produce a will which had not previously been acted on or in the case of an intestacy, he will have to prove that he is nearer in kinship to the deceased than any person who has in fact taken a benefit in the estate. Such an action is statute-barred in thirty years but it is not certain whether this period runs from the date of death or from when the applicant has asserted his rights.

If the applicant succeeds in his action, the person who has wrongfully received the relevant estate assets must pay them over to the applicant. If the former acted in bad faith in obtaining the assets, he is liable also for waste and for the income from the assets. If he has in the meanwhile sold the assets, he must refund the value of the assets. If he acted originally in good faith and has sold the assets, he is liable only for the sale price if it is less than the market price and nothing if he disposed of it by way of gift.

The situation of the purchaser from the wrongful beneficiary is as follows. In the case of the disposal of *meubles*, the buyer is protected by C.civ.art.2279 which says that 'possession equals title' and the right to reclaim an object as against the holder applies only to objects lost or stolen. As to land, it has been considered that to be able to call back such an asset from a buyer who had good reason to believe that his seller was the true owner would give rise to unreasonable complications (Cass.26.1.1897). The result may be illogical 'but economically and in equity, it is a necessity . . . Error communis facit ius' (Henri Souleau, *Les Successions* (Armand Colin, 1991).

38

GIFTS *INTER VIVOS*

Introduction 331
Donations indirectes 332
Donations simulées 332
Revocation of a gift 333
Gifts between spouses 335
Donations par personne interposée 337
Gifts and marriage 337

Introduction

In two most significant respects the French *donation* differs from the gift made under English law. In the first place, the rules relating to the *réserve* contained in C.civ.arts.913 to 930 apply to '*les libéralités, soit par actes entre vifs, soit par testament*' so that the limitations placed on the maker of gifts during his lifetime are the same as those imposed on his testamentary generosity. There will be a final reckoning at the death of the donor. There is, however, another distinction of importance in that in English law, a perfect gift is irrevocable and if made by deed vests the subject matter of the gift in the donee even if he has not given his specific assent to that event. In French law, whilst C.civ.art.894 announces that '*La donation entre vifs est un acte par lequel le donateur se dépouille actuellement et irrévocablement de la chose donnée en faveur du donateur qui l'accepte*' ('a gift *inter vivos* is an act by which the donor divests himself irrevocably of the thing given in favour of the donee who accepts it'), it also provides circumstances in which a gift may be revoked.

C.civ.art.931 requires that all gifts can only be made by *acte authentique* to mark the solemnity of the event. The *Code civil* also provides for circumstances in which gifts are revocable both by law and also by judgment of the Court. It is wholly in keeping with the philosophy of French law regarding the *patrimoine* that it is suggested that 'the intention of the formalities is to protect the family whilst giving the donor time for reflection and compelling him to listen to the advice of a *notaire* which will discourage or thwart the possibility of undue influence. The mere fact of revealing his intentions to a *notaire* is likely to restrain a donor who might otherwise be prepared to make a secret gift.' It was, in fact, only as late as 1966 that the original requirement of the *Code civil* that an *acte de donation* needed the presence of two *notaires* or one *notaire* and two witnesses, as is still the case for a notarial will, was replaced by the need for only a single *notaire*.

A gift may be, as in English law, set aside if it has been obtained by fraud or undue influence but much store is set in France by the accomplishment of the requisite formalities and failure to abide by them may result in the gift being void. It is also essential, in contrast to English law, that the donee expressly accept the gift. This may be done in accordance with the provisions of C.civ.art.932 by the execution of the *acte de donation* by the donee or may be done subsequently by the donee to whom notice of the gift is given. Until such acceptance has been made, the gift is incomplete and the donor may retract his gift. If between the making of the gift and its acceptance the intended donee dies, the heirs of that donee cannot accept the gift which remains the property of the donor (Cass.18.11.1821).

The exceptions to the rules set out above are gifts by way of marriage contracts to which special rules apply (Chapter 32), *donations indirectes* and *donations déguisées* to which reference is made hereafter. Nor do they apply to gifts by way of manual delivery.

Donations indirectes

There are certain acts which, while not in the nature of direct gifts such as the gratuitous transfer of property, achieve the same result. The effecting of a policy of assurance written for the benefit of a named person can be seen as a gift to that person; the release of a debt is in effect the gift of the amount of the debt to the debtor; and a transfer of an asset where the consideration is less than its full value is a gift of the difference in value from transferor to transferee. In such cases, the formalities of C.civ.art.931 are not required and the document takes the form relevant to the nature of the transaction. Such gifts are intended to be genuine gifts and are subject only to the ordinary rules relating to gifts, for example capacity, lack of undue influence and to those rules which might permit their revocation. A special relaxation applies to such gifts in the form of policies of assurance in that if such a gift is called into question in the calculation of the *réserve*, no reference is made to the capital sum involved but only to such premiums as may appear to be excessive in amount.

Donations simulées

The gifts referred to under this title are 'sham' gifts. Whilst in theory it is possible to envisage a gift of such nature which does not contain an element of legal or fiscal fraud such as a gift to a person to whom one is not married, the making of which would displease one's spouse, the vast majority of such gifts are in fact made with the intention of avoiding some form of taxation or more frequently the effects of the *réserve*. The *donation déguisée* is a gift made in a form which makes it appear to be a transfer for value. The *donation par personne interposée* is a gift the benefit of which is for one person but is made to another who may be considered a bare trustee. The fault lies not in the hiding of the making of the gift but in the deceit as to the true nature of the act. Examples of a *donation déguisée* are the gift of a property effected in the form of a sale; a false acknowledgement of a non-existent debt; or the giving of a receipt for a payment which has not been made.

The arguments as to the validity of a *donation déguisée* are tortuous in the extreme. Since the gift of such a nature with which the English are most likely to come into contact is that made by one spouse to another which is in any event declared void by virtue of C.civ.art.1099, it is not proposed to elaborate these arguments. Suffice it to say that the interpretation by the Courts of the appropriate articles of the *Code civil* has led to the following conclusions. To be treated as a valid gift as between the parties, a *donation déguisée* must (i) present the appearance of a transaction for valuable consideration and (ii) comply with the rules for the making of gifts. The first requirement follows from the view taken by the Courts that if the gift was to be treated as valid notwithstanding that it did not comply with the technical requirements for such a transaction, it must at least comply with those for the transaction under the guise of which it was made. The second requirement stems from the decision that although the transaction can be freed from the rules as to the form of documents effecting gifts, the basic rules must still apply. Thus a *donation déguisée* is subject to all the normal rules as to revocation. In addition, a *donation déguisée* cannot, any more than any other gift, eat into the *réserve*.

It should be noted that in the case of this kind of gift, whilst the donor and donee are limited in the evidence they can produce to support the 'disguising' of the gift by the complex rules of the *Code civil*, all other persons and particularly the heirs of the donor in defence of their *réserve* can seek to prove this 'by all possible means'.

Revocation of a gift

This may occur in a number of circumstances. Some cause the automatic revocation by act of law; others require an application to the Court. It must be noted that revocation has a retrospective effect and the subject matter of the gift becomes again part of the *patrimoine* of the donor. This affects not only donees but also the rights of third parties in the property in question such as mortgagees which are also rendered void by virtue of C.civ.art.963.

Revocation of a gift will occur in the following cases:

1. C.civ.arts.267, 268, 269 and 304 provide for the revocation of gifts in the event of a divorce or judicial separation in terms which vary depending upon the grounds upon which the decree was obtained.
2. C.civ.art.960 revokes all gifts of every kind made at a time when the donor had no children or issue living in the event of a child being subsequently born

to him. A child living at the date of the gift includes a natural child of the donor and a child adopted by *adoption plénière* but it is generally considered not by *adoption simple*. To bring this reason for revocation into play, the child must be born alive after the gift was made even if he was conceived before the date of the gift. There seems to be doubt whether a child adopted after the date of the gift gives rise to revocation. This strange provision seems to be based on the Roman law rule that a gift made by his master to a freed slave was revoked by the subsequent birth of a child to the master. It is a rule which exists in the Civil Codes of a number of other countries. It appears not to please the notarial profession which has for some years sought to have the rule suppressed but there are those who consider it to be for the benefit of issue born subsequent to the date of the gift. Gifts made by future spouses to each other in their *contrat de mariage* and during marriage not unreasonably escape this impending revocation.

3. When a gift is accompanied by an obligation, failure to fulfil that obligation can involve revocation of the gift. This has been referred to in Chapter 26 as a means of creating by a pale imitation of an English trust. Failure to carry out the obligation imposed on the donee is a specific ground for the revocation of a gift by C.civ.art.956. The remedies available are briefly described in Chapter 26. The situation is, of course, somewhat different in the case of a gift *inter vivos* from that in a will since the donor can himself give evidence which can assist the Court in reaching a decision whether to revoke or not. The Court appears to have a very wide discretion and to a large extent takes considerable notice of whether the obligation imposed on the donee was the principal object of the making of the gift.

   Although the article referred to above specifies that revocation must be asked of the Court, there is no reason in law why the reason for such a step should not be included as a condition of the gift so that failure to comply with that condition enables the donor to revoke of his own volition the gift (Cass.14.2.56).

4. The ingratitude of the donee: despite the description of this ground for revocation, the law does not require that the donee evince positive gratitude for his donor. He simply must not commit any of the acts deemed to be ingratitude by C.civ.art.955. Such acts are:
   (a) an attempt on the life of the donor;
   (b) any act of cruelty or of a criminal nature or which is the cause of grave injury to the donor;
   (c) the refusal of financial or similar assistance to the donor of which he may stand in need.

Any action to revoke a gift on these grounds must be instituted within one year of the act of ingratitude or of it coming to the notice of the donor. The donor alone can institute an action for the revocation of his gift but he may forgive it which extinguishes this right. The right cannot be renounced in advance.

Revocation on these grounds cannot be sought by creditors of the donor nor can his heirs institute such proceedings notwithstanding that they may benefit from the revocation of the gift unless the donor had commenced the action prior to his death or if his death occurred within the year commencing with the commission of the act by the donee. It has been held that if the act in question is a criminal act, the period of a year mentioned above runs from the day on which the Criminal Court has established the guilt of the donor (Cass.22.11.77).

In one situation only is it not possible to seek revocation of a gift on the grounds of ingratitude. This is the case of the gift made in consideration of marriage (C.civ.art.959) on the basis that such a gift is for the benefit of the family as a whole, it being the view of the Cour de Cassation that 'the children yet unborn should not be the victims of the donee's ingratitude'.

C.civ.art.1047 provides for the revocation of legacies if the legatee does injury to the memory of the deceased. It is not a specific cause of revocation of a gift but it is thought that it may be included under the heading of ingratitude. Clearly, such a case can only be brought by the heirs of the deceased within the statutory year of his death.

If a gift is revoked on any of the above grounds, the donee must restitute the subject matter of the gift to the donor or its value as at the date of the gift (C.civ.art.958). The donee may, however, retain the intermediate income. The retroactive effect of such revocation specifically does not affect third parties who may have acquired the property or rights over it from the donee and whether for value or not provided that such acquisition occurs before notice of the action to revoke has been registered at the *bureau des hypothèques*.

Gifts between spouses

Roman law counted all gifts from one spouse to another to be void since they might be made 'under the influence of passion'. The rules relating to gifts of this nature are contained in C.civ.arts.1091 to 1100 under the special heading 'Dispositions between spouses either by marriage contract or during the marriage' noticeably separate from the many articles under the general heading of gifts and wills. Whilst such gifts are permitted by the *Code civil*, for the protection of the family of the donor they are limited to the *quotité disponible* and, seemingly for the protection of the donor himself, they are revocable. They may be revocable at the whim of the donor spouse (C.civ.art.1096) or they may be revoked, as has been seen, in certain circumstances when the marriage comes to an end. Whilst the *Code civil* has laid down no rule as to the manner of such a revocation, the Courts insist that it must be either by will or by *acte notarié* even if the gift itself was not evidenced by an *acte authentique*. It will be realized that a letter if written entirely in the hand of the donor and signed and dated by him may well serve as a holograph will. Revocation may also be tacit if it can be inferred from acts on the part of the donor which indicate a clear intention to revoke (Cass.14.12.60). The power to revoke in this manner is personal to the donor and neither his heirs nor his creditors can make use of it. It does not apply to small gifts customarily made between spouses known as *présents d'usage* which generally are outside the rules relating to gifts *inter vivos*.

In addition, the Court can revoke them on the grounds of the donee's ingratitude since these are gifts made during a marriage and not gifts made in consideration of marriage.

Whilst the ingratitude of the donee to the donor cannot be used as a reason for revocation in the case of gifts in consideration of marriage, this rule does not apply to gifts made during the marriage. If such an unusual course is adopted, it will probably be taken by the beneficiaries of the estate of the donor within the statutory year since the donor himself could have effected the revocation himself, had he so wished, by his will or mere notarial act.

It will be recalled that essentially the *donation déguisée* is valid though it may hide an unlawful event. C.civ.art.1099 is categoric in its terms as to gifts of this kind made between spouses: *'Toute donation ou déguisée ou faite à personnes interposées sera nulle'*. That the legislator had in mind the use which could be made of such a gift is evident from the opening sentence of that article which forbids the indirect making of gifts between spouses in amounts which would exceed the *quotité disponible*. Indeed, this is highlighted by a series of judgments of the Cour de Cassation over a period of a hundred years to 30 November 1983, which make clear that any action to confirm the nullity of such gifts can be taken only by the *réservataires* of the donor since it is only the close members of the family that are worthy of protection. Proof of the making of such a gift may not be easy but since it is prima facie unlawful, proof 'by any means' is possible rather than by the provision of the statutory requirements.

A typical case is that of the purchase of an asset by one spouse with funds provided by the other. At some time thereafter, it becomes necessary to decide whether the gift is of the funds provided or of the asset purchased with them. Whilst in the long run it is the intention of the parties which prevails, that intention may not be clear or the parties may be dead when the decision must be made. If the gift is of the funds, it is void and they can be recovered by the donor spouse or his estate. If it is of the asset purchased with those funds, any dealings which the donee spouse may have had with third parties is covered by C.civ.art. 1099-1 which provides that: 'When one spouse purchases property with funds which have been given to him for that purpose by the other, the gift is of the funds and not of the property to which they were applied. In such a case, the rights of the donor or of his heirs are in respect of the funds in the value of the property. If that property has been disposed of, the value in issue is that at the date of its disposal and if another has been acquired in its place, then the value of that new property.'

Donations par personne interposée

Such gifts are also void when made between spouses. Again, it is not the gift itself which is void but when made between spouses lends itself to fraud. Since it may clearly be difficult to ascertain the truth of the transaction, C.civ.art.1099 provides a number of presumptions: 'There shall be deemed to be made to interposed persons, gifts made by one spouse to children of the other spouse by a previous marriage and those made by the donor to a relation of the other spouse of whom that other spouse was at the date of the gift a presumptive heir notwithstanding that that spouse may not have survived that relation.' In addition, the truth of the transaction may be proved 'by all means'.

Gifts and marriage

These are dealt with in Chapter 32 under *Donations de biens à venir.*

39

INHERITANCE AND GIFTS TAX

Introduction 339
Droits de succession 340
    Imposition 340
    Taxable assets 340
    Exempt assets 340
    Life assurance 343
    Personal chattels 343
    Valuation of life interests 344
    Allowable deductions 344
    The *déclaration de succession* 345
    Payment of *droits de succession* 346
    Reliefs 347
    Rates of *droits de succession* 347
    Droits de succession on gifts *inter vivos* 350
Droits de donation 351
    Valuation of assets 351
Reliefs 351
    Exempt assets 352
    Surrender of life interest 352

Introduction

French inheritance tax (*droits de succession*) is payable on the death of every person *domicilié fiscalement* or resident for income tax purposes in France on all his assets wherever situate in the world. In the case of a person who died not resident for tax purposes in France, *droits de succession* are payable in the case of a beneficiary who is not resident in France only in respect of assets situate in France. If the beneficiary was resident in France at the date of the death of the deceased and had been so resident for at least six out of the preceding ten years, the tax is payable in respect of all assets inherited by that beneficiary whether they are situate in or out of France. Non-French unquoted companies, more than 50 per cent of whose assets consist of French land, are considered to be situate in France as to the proportion which such land bears to the company's total assets. In the same manner, land in France owned directly or indirectly by a non-resident through the medium of a company is deemed to be an asset of the deceased taxable in France unless such land was used for commercial, agricul-tural or professional purposes.

France has entered into Tax Conventions with over twenty-five countries which avoid the double payment of inheritance tax. The provisions of the Treaty with the United Kingdom dated 21 June 1963 must be taken into account where relevant. The Convention does not cover gifts tax.

The tax is payable not by the estate as such but by each beneficiary at a rate which depends on his relationship to the deceased. As between *cohéritiers*, that is persons entitled by law to inherit, which in this context includes a surviving spouse, the liability is joint and several but such liability does not extend to *légataires* including *légataires universels* (Chapter 36).

As to the effect of a deceased's *régime matrimonial* on the payment of *droits de succession*, see Chapter 20.

Droits de succession

Imposition

The liability of each individual beneficiary for *droits de succession* stems from the rule of French inheritance law that the estate passes directly to the *héritiers* despite the fact that none is obliged to accept his share and does not, as in English law, pass to the personal representatives of the deceased. In addition, French fiscal law distinguishes between those whom it considers should bear the least burden and those who, because they are further removed in relationship from the deceased, presumably deserve to pay more for the privilege of inheriting. Thus, the *réservataires* who are ascendants and issue in the direct line pay less than brothers or cousins. The surviving spouse, for whom there is no exemption as in the United Kingdom, also benefits from an advantageous rate. In addition to varying rates of tax, groups of beneficiaries enjoy different *abattements* (nil rate bands) which range from Euro 76,000 for spouses to Euro 1,500 for distant relatives and strangers in blood to the deceased.

Taxable assets

Subject to certain exemptions, all assets in the ownership of a deceased person which pass by reason of his death are subject to *droits de succession*. Generally, the rules as to what a deceased person owned at the date of his death are reasonably self-evident but there are certain notable fictions which apply. The most important relates to the ownership of two different interests in the same property to which reference is made below.

In respect of land, the person whose name appears on the *cadastre* as the owner of a property for the purposes of *taxe foncière* and has paid that tax is deemed to be the owner of that property as is the person who is in receipt of income from shares in a company or from the French equivalent of a chose in action or who has dealt with such assets within the year prior to death.

Exempt assets

Certain assets are either free of *droits de succession* or are taxed at a reduced rate.

1. New property acquired between 1 June 1993 and 31 December 1994 which was new when bought or if, bought *en l'état d'achèvement futur*, was completed before 1 July 1994 is subject to an *abattement* of Euro 46,000 per beneficiary provided that it has been in the continuous sole exclusive occupation of the deceased as his principal residence for a period of five years from completion of his purchase or from the date of the completion of its construction, if later.

2. New property built before 31 December 1994 and acquired in its new state between 1 August and 31 December 1995 is subject to an *abattement* of Euro 46,000 per beneficiary if for a period of two years from the date of purchase it has served continuously as the principal residence of the deceased. To obtain this relief, the beneficiary(ies) must undertake to continue to use the property as a dwellinghouse for a period of three years and, if the property is meanwhile sold, to obtain from the subsequent owner a similar undertaking for the balance of that period.

3. Property bought during the period 1 August 1995 to 31 December 1996 if subject to *enregistrement* (that is, not less than five years had elapsed since the completion of its construction so it was outside the TVA period as explained in Chapter 22) is subject to an *abattement* of three-quarters of its value not exceeding Euro 46,000 per beneficiary provided that not later than six months after its purchase it was let for a term of not less than nine years for use as a principal residence to a person who was not a close member of the family of the deceased.

   In the cases mentioned above, introduced by several *Lois de Finances*, the relief applies only on the first death after the acquisition of the property in question and the relief is cumulative with the standard reliefs available to any beneficiary.

4. The value of any property owned by a deceased person at the date of his death is subject to an allowance of 20 per cent of its market value if it was occupied at that date as his principal residence with his spouse or his infant children or their spouses.

5. Subject to certain strict conditions as to the continuation for a period of years of the business concerned, shares in companies and individual businesses carrying on many types of business including agriculture, commercial, handicraft and professional activities are taxed on the basis of one-half of their market value.

6. Forests and woodlands are taxed on one-quarter of their value subject to an undertaking as to their continuing to be exploited for a period of thirty years after the death of the deceased owner.

7. Agricultural land let on a long lease and shares in *groupements agricoles* are taxed on one-quarter of their value if that does not exceed Euro 76,000 and as to one-half in respect of the excess over that value.

8. Historic buildings: listed buildings and their contents are free of *droits de succession* subject to the beneficiaries undertaking with the Ministry in

respect of the upkeep in perpetuity of the buildings and their contents, the rights of access of the public and other pertinent matters.

9. Generally gifts of what would be considered in English law to be of a charitable nature and gifts to the State (CGI.arts.794 and 795) for charitable purposes, legacies to persons wounded in war or by acts of terrorism and sufferers from AIDS. Gifts to certain international charities are also exempt but it is essential to note that the Anglo-French Convention on Inheritance Tax makes no provision for charities. Thus a gift to a UK charity made out of French assets or indeed out of assets situated in the United Kingdom if the deceased died resident in France will carry *droits de succession* at 60 per cent unless avoiding action *inter vivos* is taken.

No tax is as a general rule payable on the cesser of a life interest. However, if such an interest is vested in the deceased at the date of his death whilst the reversion is owned by an *héritier présomptif* defined by CGI.art.751 as an ascendant, issue or spouse of the deceased, the fee simple in possession in the property is presumed to be vested in the deceased. This presumption can be rebutted if the separation of the two interests was created (i) by a marriage contract, (ii) by means of a normal gift made more than three months before the date of death, or (iii) arises by reason of the death of a previous owner. Nor is any tax charged on the passing to the surviving annuitant of a joint and survivor annuity (*rente viagère*) if the survivor is the spouse or an ascendant or issue in the direct line of the deceased annuitant.

Property of which the deceased person was a joint owner *en tontine* (Chapter 16) is subject to special rules. In the case of such property when the joint ownership was created by the document of purchase, inheritance tax is payable on one half of its value on the death of the first co-owner to die at the appropriate rate depending on the relationship between the co-owners. If the property was the principal residence of the co-owners and its value does not exceed Euro 76,000, no tax is charged. This situation relates to all such purchases *en tontine* after 5 September 1979 since before that date the taxation payable on the death of one co-owner was the stamp duty payable on a purchase which would frequently be less than if *droits de succession* were payable.

This has led to many *notaires* advising English clients that the use of the *tontine* carries with it a tax disadvantage, oblivious of the fact that the use of this type of co-ownership can have an advantage for inheritance purposes which far outweighs any financial consideration (Chapter 29) and that the payment of inheritance tax on English property owned in joint tenancy is the normal rule. If the *tontine* is created otherwise than on the purchase of the land, for example on the issue of shares in an SCI which owns the land, no inheritance tax is payable until the death of the ultimate sole owner. This appears to be a tax loophole which for some years has remained unblocked and possibly will so remain.

Life assurance

Whilst what follows takes account of the current law, changes in respect of life assurance are frequent. In the case of life policies which are not written for the benefit of a designated person, the capital sum payable at death or the annuity which commences to be payable from the date of death forms part of the estate of the deceased and is taxable accordingly. On the other hand, such policies if written for the benefit of a person other than the deceased do not form part of the deceased's estate (C.assur.art.L-132-12) since that beneficiary is deemed always to have been the sole person entitled to such policy moneys. Policy moneys therefore are not taken into account when calculating the size of the *réserve* or consequently of the *quotité disponible* nor are the premiums laid out by the deceased taken into account as gifts *inter vivos* for this purpose unless the amounts of any premium paid are obviously inflated. Since this is a means of 'disinheriting' *réservataires*, it is a fruitful source of actions by disappointed children. Nor have creditors of an estate any claim against such policy moneys unless premiums in exaggerated amounts have been paid, for example, large premiums to obtain cover at advanced ages.

It is accepted by the French tax authorities that a life policy written for 'the successors in title of the deceased' for the object of the payment of *droits de succession* may be treated as a policy the proceeds of which do not form part of the estate of the deceased.

However, these seemingly generous rules are subject to certain reservations. In respect of policies effected after 20 November 1991, by virtue of CGI.art.757-8, moneys payable under such a policy are subject to inheritance tax at the rate applicable having regard to the relationship between the deceased and the beneficiary in respect of that proportion of the premiums paid by the deceased after the age of seventy which exceed Euro 30,500. In respect of premiums paid before that age, tax is payable at a flat rate of 20 per cent in excess of the value of Euro 152,500. When more than one policy was effected by the deceased, the calculation is made having regard to all the premiums paid after the age of seventy. If there are a number of designated beneficiaries, this relief of Euro 30,500 is divided among the beneficiaries in proportion to their share in the policy moneys.

As to policies effected after 13 October 1998 or premiums paid after that date in respect of policies then in force, CGI.art.990 imposes a special tax amounting to 20 per cent of the policy moneys payable to each beneficiary in excess of the amount of Euro 152,500. This amount is deducted by the insurance company and paid directly to the tax authorities. It does not apply to life policies under which the policy moneys are payable for the benefit of a handicapped child of the deceased or to group policies for members of a particular occupation.

Personal chattels

As a rough and ready guide, the value of these will be accepted at 5 per cent of the value of the gross estate but the French Revenue may in cases of obviously valuable objects call for a valuation. It must, however, be remembered that, to assist the Revenue in ascertaining if any such objects exist, insurance companies are required by law to report to the tax authorities all policies in excess of Euro 15,000 covering jewellery, objets d'art and antiques generally and to advise such authorities of the death of the holders of such policies. This provision results in the considerable use of bank deposit boxes of which the deceased is seldom the only keyholder.

Valuation of life interests
The French Revenue makes use of an outmoded expectancy of life table to value life interests and reversions. The figures are as follows:

Age of life tenant	Value of life interest	Value of reversion
Under 19	70%	30%
20–29	60%	40%
30–39	50%	50%
40–49	40%	60%
50–59	30%	70%
60–69	20%	80%
Over 70	10%	90%

In the case of a surviving spouse claiming the right to the continued occupation of the property in which he or she lived with the deceased person as their principal residence together with its contents (Chapter 30), the value of that right is to be taken at 60 per cent of the appropriate value of the life interest as shown above. The statutory right to remain in those premises for the first year after the date of death of the deceased spouse is considered to be an incident of the marriage itself and not to form part of an inheritance and hence is not taxable.

Allowable deductions
All debts disclosed as deductions for *droits de succession* purposes must be supported by appropriate written evidence in accordance with *la procédure écrite* (CGI.art.768). Presumptions which are 'sufficiently serious, precise and tending to corroborate' may also be accepted but proof by means of the evidence of a beneficiary is not acceptable. The tax authorities may require the production of certificates from creditors who are bound to supply these if so asked. Until the *Loi de Finances* for 2003, the maximum amount allowed for funeral expenses was Euro 1,000, or little more than the cost of a pauper's burial, and the amount required formal proof. The maximum amount now is Euro 1,500 and no formal proof is required by way of an undertaker's account or otherwise. It is worth noting that funeral expenses amount currently on average to not less than Euro 2,500 to 3,000, of which formalities amount to 10 per cent.

When considering the formalities which in France may be required in support of the existence and the valuation of assets and deductions, it must be remembered that the *déclaration de succession* (inheritance tax account) is made not by executors or administrators whose interest is that of disinterested persons limited to administering the estate in question but by beneficiaries who have a direct personal interest in what is disclosed. In addition, the resultant figure for the net estate plays a part in the choice of the options open to beneficiaries and in particular the surviving spouse and in the calculation of the *réserve*.

The déclaration de succession

Except in cases when there are no assets in an estate or where the sole beneficiaries are in the direct line to the deceased or is the surviving spouse and the gross assets do not exceed Euro 1,500, it is necessary to file a *déclaration de succession*. It may be made in a single copy if the gross value of the estate does not exceed Euro 15,000 but otherwise in duplicate. It should in theory be subscribed by all beneficiaries including any individual among them who is liable to pay *droits de succession* in respect of his benefit by reason, for example, of the relief obtained through application of an *abattement*. More usually, in the case of a person not of French origin where the estate consists only of assets in France, this can be done under a power of attorney given by less than all the beneficiaries or even by English executors provided that those who sign are certain that those on whose behalf they sign are content with the contents of the *déclaration*. This is not a matter which gives rise to difficulties provided that the estate is being dealt with by a *notaire* in tune with English procedure or fully advised in that respect.

In the case of persons dying in France, the account must be lodged within six months of the date of death. In other cases, the time limit is one year. The account is lodged with the deceased's local tax office if he dies tax resident in France. If he died resident elsewhere, it is lodged with the *Centre des impôts de non-résidents*, 9, rue d'Uzès, 75094 Paris Cedex 02. In the case of persons dying resident in Monaco, the account is lodged with the head tax office in Menton, referred to in Chapter 25, this being a special office set up to deal with all those who claim a Monégasque residence but have contact of any kind in France.

The account contains full details of the deceased including his *régime matrimonial* and also a copy of or sufficient extracts from any will he made sufficient to explain the interests of each beneficiary. In the case of the devolution of property by virtue of an English will which is taxable in France, it is sometimes necessary to supply a *certificat de coutume* or affidavit of English law which is most satisfactorily made by an English lawyer with a comprehensive knowledge of French law.

Difficulties which are usually outside the contemplation of the draftsman of an English will can occur when the will is drawn in one or other of the ways designed to take full benefit of the English tax-free band and the draftsman overlooks the fact that trusts do not exist in France. Thus, a will which creates a settled legacy for a surviving spouse and children 'in an amount which is the maximum which can be given without any inheritance tax becoming payable', with a subsequent gift of residue to the surviving spouse with gift over to children in the event of that spouse's failure to survive, creates a considerable puzzle in France if the estate includes property in that country to which no specific allusion is made. Is that property caught by the settled legacy or is it part of residue? In either event, there is the problem that no account has been taken of the children's *réserve* in the house but possibly that can be overcome. The question is, to which gift does the house belong? If it is in residue and the spouse survives, he or she by French law is the owner by reason of the death of the deceased spouse. If it is in the settled legacy, how is the giver of the *certificat de coutume* to explain the legal situation in terms understandable by the French tax authorities?

There are penalties for the late lodgement of a *déclaration de succession*. Interest runs at 0.75 per cent per month on unpaid tax once the six- or twelve-month period (as the case may be) has passed. Complaints that this rate far exceeds the rate given by the Revenue when making a refund has fallen on the deaf ears of the Conseil d'Etat in April 2002 (No 239693) which has said that the Courts have no power to moderate the rate. Failure to file the *déclaration* can also lead to a 10 per cent increase in the tax payable, if the time lag goes beyond the first day of the seventh month following the date when it should have been filed. Failure to file the document within ninety days when formally required to do so by a *mise en demeure* can lead to an increase of the tax of 40 per cent. A request for the remission of interest or increased tax is sometimes granted if there are difficulties linked to the foreign nature of the estate but this is the sole personal decision of the local inspector. A penal 80 per cent increase in tax is possible in cases where there have been 'fraudulent manoeuvres' on the part of the taxpayer.

Payment of droits de succession

As in the United Kingdom, it is normal practice to pay the *droits de succession* shown as due on lodging the *déclaration de succession*. Since there is no equivalent in France of the English Grant of Representation, there is no object in filing an account which does not tell the whole story in order speedily to obtain a Grant to protect the estate's assets. However, there are certain assets which cannot be dealt with, such as bank accounts, unless a receipt for paid tax can be produced. Corrective *déclarations* can be filed as in the United Kingdom.

Droits de succession can be paid by instalments at intervals of not more than six months over a total period of five years. This can be extended to ten years in the case of tax due from beneficiaries who are in the direct line to the deceased or the surviving spouse provided that not less than 50 per cent of the estate consists of non-liquid assets such as land, business assets or unquoted securities. Payment of the tax may also be deferred until the falling in of a reversion. In the case of many business assets, the tax may be both deferred and then paid by instalments.

Reliefs

The *abattements* (tax-free bands) are as follows. They apply to the share of each beneficiary subject as indicated below.

The surviving spouse	Euro 76,000
Ascendants	Euro 46,000
Issue (direct or by substitution) (1)	Euro 46,000
Parties to a PACS	Euro 57,000
Brothers and sisters (2)	Euro 15,000
Handicapped persons (3)	Euro 46,000
Others	Euro 1,500

1. Issue taking by substitution share equally *per stirpes* the overall amount of Euro 46,000. The resultant *abattement* is added to any other *abattement* to which a beneficiary is entitled, for example if he is handicapped.
2. In order to qualify for this *abattement*, a brother or sister must at the date of death of the deceased have been (i) either a bachelor or a spinster, widowed, divorced or judicially separated (ii) aged at least fifty or suffering from a form of illness which prevents him or her from earning a living and must have lived continuously with the deceased for five years prior to his death. The inability to fulfil all these conditions reduces the available *abattement* to Euro 1,500.
3. The conditions applicable to this *abattement* are that the beneficiary must be suffering from a congenital or acquired physical or mental infirmity which prevents him from earning a normal livelihood from the exercise of any occupation or, if he is under the age of eighteen, which prevents him from benefiting from training to bring him to a normal level of proficiency.

In addition to all other reliefs, there are reductions in the amount of tax found to be due from beneficiaries who have three or more children who are alive or who, if then dead, have themselves children at the date of the death of the deceased. The reduction is Euro 610 for the third and further children in the case of an inheritance from a spouse or ascendant or issue and Euro 305 in the case of an inheritance from any other source. Certain other reductions are also available.

Rates of droits de succession

The following rates apply to the share of the relevant beneficiary after deduction from that share of the appropriate *abattement*:

Slice of net estate in Euros	Applicable rate
Surviving spouse	
Not exceeding 7,600	5%
7,600–15,000	10%
15,000–30,000	15%
30,000–520,000	20%
520,000–850,000	30%
850,000–1,700,000	35%
In excess of 1,700,000	40%
Ascendants and issue	
Not exceeding 7,600	5%
7,600–11,400	10%
11,400–15,000	15%
15,000–520,000	20%
520,000–850,000	30%
850,000–1,700,000	35%
In excess of 1,700,000	40%
PACS	
Not exceeding 15,000	40%
In excess of 15,000	50%
Brothers and sisters	
Not exceeding 23,000	35%
In excess of 23,000	45%
Other relatives up to the 4th degree	
All net assets	55%
More distant relatives and strangers in blood	
All net assets	60%

In the following example of the method of calculating *droits de succession*, the deceased died domiciled in England leaving a widow, two children and two grandchildren (the children of a predeceased child) surviving. His net estate in France consisted of a house and contents worth Euro 400,000. In respect of this house, his English will followed the requirements of French law and he left a quarter to his widow and a quarter to each of his children, the children of his predeceased child taking equally by substitution. The contents, being *meubles* and therefore subject to the law of his domicile, could have been bequeathed in any way he wished but in fact followed the gift of the house. Being situate in France both the house and its contents are subject to French *droits de succession*.

Share of the widow	Euro 100,000		
Less *abattement*	76,000		
Taxable balance	24,000		
Tax at 5% on first Euro 7,600	=	Euro 380	
at 10% on next Euro 7,400	=	Euro 740	
at 15% on next Euro 9,000	=	Euro 1,350	Euro 2,470
Less reduction for third child's children			Euro 610
			Euro 1,860
Share of 1st child	Euro 100,000		
Less *abattement*	46,000		
Taxable balance	54,000		
Tax at 5% on first Euro 7,600	=	Euro 380	
at 10% on next Euro 3,800	=	Euro 380	
at 15% on next Euro 3,600	=	Euro 540	
at 20% on next Euro 39,000	=	Euro 7,800	Euro 9,100
Share of 2nd child (as above)			Euro 9,100
Share of 1st grandchild	Euro 50,000		
Less *abattement*	Euro 23,000		
Taxable balance	Euro 27,000		
Tax at 5% on first Euro 7,600	=	Euro 380	
at 10% on next Euro 3,800	=	Euro 380	
at 15% on next Euro 3,600	=	Euro 540	
at 20% on next Euro 12,000	=	Euro 2,400	Euro 3,700
Share of 2nd grandchild			Euro 3,700
Total *droits de succession* (an overall rate of 6.8%)			Euro 27,460

If A had left a life interest in the whole to his widow aged sixty-five, she would have paid tax on the value of that interest calculated at 20 per cent of Euro 400,000 = Euro 80,000 and the children and grandchildren would have paid on the balance of Euro 320,000 as to Euro 106,666 for each child and Euro 53,333 for each grandchild. In such circumstances the tax payable by the widow would have been Euro 200; each child would have paid Euro 10,430 and each grandchild Euro 3,700, making a total of Euro 28,450 which gives an overall rate of 7.1 per cent.

A beneficiary who renounces his interest in an estate is deemed never to have had such an interest. However, the *droits de succession* payable by those who benefit from such a renunciation cannot be less than the renouncing beneficiary would have paid had he not renounced (CGI.art.785). In the case of successive renunciations, the relevant *droits* are those which would have been paid by the first renouncer. A renunciation in favour of a named person gives rise to the payment by the initial beneficiary of *droits de succession* and *droits de donation* in respect of the gift unless the renouncer is a person who would have taken by law on such a renunciation in which case only *droits de succession* are payable.

Droits de succession on gifts inter vivos

Generally, these are not subject to *droits de succession* provided they were made more than ten years before the date of the donor's death and provided that the *actes de donation* have been suitably stamped and have borne the appropriate gifts tax at the time of making. If any gifts have been made by the deceased less than ten years before his death, they must be accounted for in the *déclaration de succession* but the manner in which they are dealt with is different from the manner indicated in Chapter 28 to calculate the *réserve* when gifts have been made *en avancement d'hoirie*. For purely tax purposes, the following rules apply.

(1) the gifts attract the appropriate *abattements* from which are deducted any *abattements* which the donee received at the time when the gift was made;

(2) inheritance tax being imposed on a slice basis, when progressive rates are involved in the calculation of any tax payable, as given above, the value of the gift is taxed at the highest relevant rate;

(3) if any tax deductions are available at that stage, they are reduced by any such deductions from which the donee benefited when the gift was made.

The following example describes the tax liabilities in respect of a gift *en avancement d'hoirie* made in 1992 to a child by a father who subsequently died in March 2002.

Amount of gift	FF 345,000
Abattement then available	FF 300,000
Liable to gifts tax	FF 45,000
Tax at 5%	FF 2,250
Available reduction	FF 4,000
Gifts tax payable by child	NIL

On the death of the father

Interest of child in estate after bringing gift into hotchpot	Euro 76,220
Less gift of FF345,000 =	Euro 52,595
Liable to inheritance tax	Euro 23,625

When the gift was made, the *abattement* of FF300,000 (Euro 45,735) was wholly used up by the child in connection with the payment of gifts tax. The *abattement* in the father's estate was Euro 46,000 so that there was now available the rounded up balance of Euro 265 (ie Euro 46,000–45,735). Of the first slice of taxable gift at 5 per cent, available for assets up to Euro 7,600, only Euro 6,860 was taxed so that there remains available at that rate the difference of Euro 740. The inheritance tax in the father's estate in respect of the child's interest is therefore calculated as follows:

Euro 740 at 5%	Euro 37
Euro 3,800 at 10%	Euro 380
Euro 3,600 at 15%	Euro 540
Euro 15,225 at 20%	Euro 3,045
Total inheritance tax payable	Euro 4,002
Less reduction minus those already used	Euro 877
Inheritance tax payable	Euro 3,125

Droits de donation

Generally, the rules applicable to gifts tax such as rates and reliefs are the same as those which apply to *droits de succession* except that they benefit from certain reliefs depending on the age of the donor. The tax applies both to straightforward gifts and also to *donations-partages* (Chapter 32). The same rules of territoriality apply as in the case of deaths but no distinction is made depending on the country in which the gift is made. A gift of land in France will, therefore, always be liable to French gifts tax. Few Tax Conventions take account of gifts tax as is the case as between the United Kingdom and France. Most of the assets which are free of *droits de succession* are also free of this tax with the notable exception of gifts of businesses. Gifts tax is not payable in respect of assets capable of passing by manual delivery with a few exceptions of which the most common are gifts evidenced by a document subject to *enregistrement*.

Valuation of assets
The rules for the valuation of assets comprised in a gift for this tax follow those for the purposes of *droits de succession* save that (i) the 20 per cent reduction in respect of the value of a principal residence and (ii) the 5 per cent 'one off' method of valuation of the contents of a house are not available. Jewellery, antiques, objets d'art, and the like may be valued at not less than 60 per cent of the value for which they are insured compared to the 100 per cent insurance value for *droits de succession* purposes.

Reliefs

The same reliefs apply as between spouses and ascendants and issue. In the case of a joint gift made by spouses to children or issue, a double *abattement* is available. In addition to any other *abattement*, a gift to a grandchild made after 1 January 2003 carries with it an *abattement* of Euro 30,000. This figure takes account of all gifts made by the same grandparent to the same grandchild within the previous ten years so that if an earlier gift within that period was less than that amount, it can now be topped up to the new maximum. There is no similar relief as between brothers and sisters nor is the standard *abattement* of Euro 1,500 available in default of any other relief. Parties to a PACS benefit from the *abattement* available for *droits de succession* if their PACS has been in force for at least two years.

Gifts made to children of less than eighteen years in amounts which do not exceed Euro 2,700 per annum are free of gifts tax. Transfers of property between ex-spouses are not subject to gifts tax if they are the personal property of one of the parties and take place over a period of less than one year. If the property involved was owned by the spouses *en indivision* and their *régime* is *séparation de biens* (this being a frequent situation with English ex-spouses) or if they were *en communauté*, the transfer from one ex-spouse to the other bears an ad valorem stamp of a maximum of 1 per cent on the net value of the asset transferred.

Relief from the tax due on the making of a gift is also given according to the age of the donor. If the donor is aged less than sixty-five the tax is reduced by 50 per cent and by 30 per cent if the donor is aged between sixty-five and seventy-five. No reduction is made if the donor is above the age of seventy-five. The tax is normally borne by the donee but the payment by the donor of the tax and costs attendant on a gift is not treated as an additional gift. Except in the case of a gift of a business or of unquoted shares, gifts tax is payable on the making of the gift and cannot be deferred or paid by instalments.

Exempt assets
The three kinds of property referred to above under 1, 2 and 3 of the heading Exempt assets for the purposes of *droits de succession* are also exempt from gifts tax in the same circumstances and on the same conditions as those which apply for inheritance tax.

Surrender of life interest
In any case where a donor makes a gift of property subject to the reservation to himself of a life interest therein, it is not unusual to provide that the donor-life tenant can at any time require the reversioner to provide him with an annuity in an appropriate amount in consideration for the release of the life interest. The French Revenue considers this to be an additional gift of the value of the surrendered life interest without any allowance for the capital value of the annuity. If no such provision is included in the original gift, the Revenue will charge the surrender of the life interest to gifts tax if it can show an element of gift in the transaction; otherwise, stamp duty is payable on the capital value of the annuity provided as consideration. A fixed duty of Euro 75 is chargeable in cases of the grant of an annuity to a surviving spouse in exchange for a life interest.

General note		354
A	**Powers of Attorney**	357
	1 Authority to sign a contract	362
	2 Power of Attorney for sale of flat or house	363
	3 Power of Attorney for purchase of flat or house	364
	4 Power of Attorney for adoption of new *régime*	365
	5 Power of Attorney to renounce an interest in an estate	366
	6 Power of Attorney for renunciation of *tontine*	367
	7 Power of Attorney to sell shares in an SCI to a UK company	367
	8 Power of Attorney to purchase shares in an SCI	368
	9 Power of Attorney to form an SCI	369
	10 Power of Attorney to make gift of land	370
	11 Power of Attorney to accept a gift of land	371
	12 Power to partition jointly owned property on divorce donor taking co-owner's share and paying equality money	372
	13 Power to partition jointly owned property on divorce in exchange for equality money	372
	14 Power of Attorney for beneficiary to administer estate	373
	15 Power of Attorney for English Executors to administer French estate	374
B	**Contracts**	375
	1 *Promesse de vente*	375
	2 *Compromis de vente sous conditions suspensives (copropriété)*	378
C	**Certificats de coutume**	388
	1 Declaration of English law for sale/purchase by UK company of French land	388
	2 Declaration of English law on sale by Trustee in Bankruptcy of French property	389
	3 Declaration of English law to obtain *envoi en possession*	390
	4 Declaration as to English intestacy law	391
	5 Declaration of English law as to validity of Will	392
D	**Wills**	393
	1 Holograph Will giving maximum permitted by law to surviving spouse when there are surviving relatives	393
	2 Holograph Will leaving surviving spouse choice of maximum interest in estate when there are surviving *réservataires*	393
	3 Will giving statutory reserve to only child and other half to a stranger	394
	4 International Will	394
E	**Affidavits of French law**	396
	1 Affidavit of French law to lead to an English Grant	396
	2 Affidavit of French law to lead to an English Grant where a beneficiary renounces	397

3 Affidavit of French law to lead to an English Grant of French Will drawn in English 398

F Companies 400

1 Statuts of a *Société Civile Immobilière* 400

2 Minutes of meeting of shareholders to appoint new *gérant* 408

3 Shareholders' agreement to transfer of shares 409

4 Share transfer 409

G MISCELLANEOUS 413

1 Translation of UK birth certificate 413

2 Translation of UK birth certificate (adoption) 414

3 Translation of UK death certificate 414

4 *Acte de notoriété* 415

5 *Prêt à usage* 417

6 Translation of loan offer 419

GENERAL NOTE

It is of the greatest importance that readers appreciate that the Precedents themselves and the accompanying Notes assume that those who use them are conversant with the subject matter of the relevant chapters to which, therefore, no specific reference is made.

French documents are executed in one of two forms. They are either *authentique* (notarial) or they are executed *sous seing privé* ('ssp'). In the case of the former, they will have one of the following opening words.

L'AN DEUX MIL . . . . .
PARDEVANT Maître . . . . .
A COMPARU

followed by the details of the parties (see below) or they may commence with the wording or wording similar to 'Me . . . . . notaire à . . . . . a reçu le présent acte authentique à la requête de [*details of the parties*]. When the document is to be executed ssp it will begin 'Le(s) soussigné(s)' followed by details of the parties.

Details of the parties means a full description of each party citing in full his or her *état civil*. For a married couple this would read as follows:

1. Monsieur [*full name of party*], né le à [*place of birth*], [*occupation*], demeurant à [*home address*] marié avec [*maiden name of spouse*] sous le régime anglais équivalent au régime français de la séparation de biens à défaut de contrat préalable à leur union célébrée le [*date of marriage*] à [*place of marriage*], de nationalité britannique.

2. In the case of a party who is divorced but not remarried, there must be substituted for the words 'marié avec . . . . . . [*place of marriage*]' the words 'divorcé en première noces et non-remarié de Madame XYZ suivant jugement rendu par le High Court of Justice en Angleterre (Family Division) devenu

exécutoire le [*date of Decree Absolute*]'. If the divorce is from a second or third spouse, the word 'première' will need amending appropriately.

3. If a party has been divorced and has remarried, the first formula should be used but after the word 'marié' there should be added the words 'en deuxième noces' or whatever is the proper number depending on how many previous spouses there have been.

4. An unmarried party of either sex is 'célibataire'. A widow is 'veuve non-remariée de [*deceased husband*]' or if she has remarried, as in 1. A widower is 'veuf non-remarié de [*deceased wife*]' or if he has remarried, as in 1.

5. A party who has entered into a PACS should so indicate but it is recommended that the precise form be agreed with the *notaire* involved.

6. If the seller is a company, the wording is as follows: 'Monsieur [*full name, address and occupation*], agissant au nom et pour le compte de la société dénommée [*name of company*] une société de droit anglais en sa qualité de directeur de ladite société et spécialement habilité à l'effet des présentes en vertu d'une résolution des directeurs de ladite société en date du [*date of Board Resolution*]'.

Notarial documents will end with the words 'DONT ACTE' and 'FAIT A', showing also the number of pages and corrections in the document. A document executed ssp will normally use the formula 'FAIT A' and LE [*date of execution*] only.

The precedents which follow are of documents with which the English practitioner will most frequently come into contact. It is not suggested that they should be used for the preparation of documents in England without suitable advice but that they should, together with the notes relating to each document, serve where necessary as a guide to the significance of documents prepared in France for execution by English parties.

The choice of Powers of Attorney reflects in the experience of the author the most usual situations in which such documents are required. The Affidavits of French law are for use in England in foreign domicile Probate applications and do not seek to be exhaustive in their scope. The Affidavits of English law will, of course, be made in England and the examples given are intended to assist those qualified to make them to do so in typical circumstances. It is not possible to provide much in the way of Wills since the law does in most cases for the Testator what the Solicitor does in England and therefore the precedents of Wills can do no more than give the practitioners an idea of what a French Will looks like.

It will be appreciated that these precedents are typical but not inviolable and variations at the whim of the draftsman may occur. In case a document is copied or prepared in England for execution in that country and subsequent use in France, it is worthwhile remembering that a very large left hand margin of not less than two inches should always be given. This is because the originals of most of these documents will come to be bound in a *notaire*'s records and if the margin is less matter will be lost in the binding.

French documents are executed by the parties initialling each page at the foot in the centre and also the box at the end of the document showing how many alterations (if any) have been made and with an ordinary signature on the last page. Black ink is the order of the day for signatures.

It serves no purpose to provide full translations of each precedent since the subject matter refers to procedures which are often not known in English law. However, a short explanation of their contents is given by reference, where it is considered useful, to the opening words of each clause.

Except where the nature of the document makes this necessary, to avoid repetition, the individual precedents omit all opening clauses such as the description of the parties and, in the case of Powers of Attorney, the wording of the appointment of the Attorneys and the standard closing clauses.

It should not be forgotten that French is a language which is very precise about its genders and numbers and has no Law equivalent to the Interpretation Act 1889.

A POWERS OF ATTORNEY

Whether a Power needs to be notarized or whether it can be executed ssp depends to some extent on the nature of the acts which the Attorney will undertake (for example, a Power to execute a mortgage must be notarized) but also to some extent on the whim of the *notaire* in France. The opening parts of the Power (see the General Note) will indicate how it is to be executed. All notarial Powers executed in England will require a Hague Convention apostille. Those executed ssp also need an apostille. It is never necessary to have a Power authenticated by a French Consul whatever may be the instructions of any *notaire*. Conversely, and as a matter of interest, Affidavits for use in England need not be sworn before a British Consul; an Affidavit sworn before a French *notaire* will be accepted in England.

It is desirable that Powers of Attorney executed in England should appoint as Attorneys at least the Donor's adviser in France and due consideration should be given to the suggestions made in the body of this book as to whom should be asked so to act. It is useful that the Donor's Solicitor in England should also be appointed. The addition of a member of the staff of the *notaire* acting for the Donor is a mere 'long stop' appointment in case neither of the other Attorneys is available when a signature is urgently required. Such a person should never be appointed the sole Attorney.

THE APPOINTMENT CLAUSE. This should be in the following form:

'LEQUEL a par ces présentes constitué pour ses mandataires conjointement ou séparément l'un en l'absence de l'autre
[*Name, address and description of First Attorney*]
ET [*Name, address and description of Second Attorney*]
ET tout clerc de l'étude [*address of Notaries*]
A QUI il donne pouvoir pour lui et en son nom:'.

It is not necessary to give more than the full name, address and occupation of each Attorney and a full *état civil* is not required.

THE REMUNERATION CLAUSE. Many Powers drawn in France will not contain such a clause since many Notaries will not draw documents unless they are in receipt of funds in advance and in many cases the right of an Attorney to remuneration is statutory. However, the total fees may on occasion be paid to the Notary acting and out of that amount other professionals may be due for payment or the Notary may be entitled to an Article 4 fee. Such a clause provides specific authority for such payments. A typical clause reads as follows:

'CONVENIR de tous frais, émoluments et honoraires chargés avec le notaire et tous autres intervenants, procéder au règlement des sommes dues à ce titre après prélèvement de la rémunération du mandataire habituellement pratiquée en la matière suite aux appels de fonds du mandant.'

THE GENERAL POWERS CLAUSE. A clause in the following form is to be found in virtually every Power of Attorney:

'AUX EFFETS ci-dessus, passer et signer tous actes, titres et pièces, élire domicile, substituer et généralement faire tout ce qui sera utile et nécessaire.'

Precedents of the following Powers are given below:

1 Authority to sign a contract. There has been included a simple form of authority to sign a contract for the sale or purchase of land. It is sometimes desired to have such a contract signed at a time when it is not convenient or necessary to make use of a full blown Power of Attorney and few French sellers or buyers or their professional advisers will refuse to accept this short form.

2 For the sale of a flat or house. The clauses relate to the following powers:

VENDRE . . . . . This is the overall power to sell. The sale price will normally be paid on completion to the *notaire* acting for the seller (par la comptabilité du notaire) but there is no reason in law why it should not be paid directly to the seller by the buyer (hors vue de notaire). The latter choice must be clearly stated in the Power and should not be made without careful prior advice.

SAVOIR . . . . . There follows a full description of the property to be bought usually down to the very last detail describing the toilets and cupboards.

ETABLIR . . . . . To provide all information relating to the property to be sold including details of all lettings and easements (if any).

OBLIGER . . . . . To provide releases of all mortgages affecting the property, fix the date of vacant possession and of the dates and amounts of payment of the price and to receive the same with interest if any is due, either on completion or otherwise as agreed thereafter or previously.

SIGNER . . . . . To sign all returns for CGT purposes, and appoint a *représentant fiscal*.

A DEFAUT . . . . . To take all necessary steps in default of payment of the sale price or difficulties in obtaining the same ranging from entering into a compromise to obtaining a judgment and executing it.

DE TOUTES . . . . . To give receipts, provide releases, agree to the removal of entries on the Register adversely affecting the property whether in exchange for payment of money or not and to hand over all title documents or bind the Donor to that effect.

3 For the purchase of a house or flat. The clauses relate to the following powers:

ACQUERIR . . . . . This is the overall Power to buy. It is necessary to remember that if the purchase is by more than one person, the joint Power or each individual Power must indicate if the purchase is *en indivision* or *en tontine*.

EMPRUNTER . . . . . If the buyer is obtaining a loan, this power enables the Attorney to agree the terms of the loan and to execute the mortgage which in virtually every case will be included in the *acte de vente*.

OBLIGER . . . . . This authorizes the Attorney to pay the purchase price, carry out any obligations imposed on the buyer, receive the title deeds (which are not always handed over and which are of no value as title documents) and give a good discharge for them.

FAIRE OPERER . . . . . Make all necessary transfers of funds for the purchase.

FAIRE TOUTES . . . . . Make all statutory declarations as to the genuineness of the disclosed price.

APPOSER . . . . . Give the declaration under the Loi Scrivener.

FAIRE OPERER . . . . . Carry out all Land Registry requirements, obtain all releases of charges on the property and undertake all that is necessary to complete the purchase.

FAIRE TOUTES . . . . . Make all necessary declarations as to *état civil* and other matters.

4 For the adoption of the *régime de communauté universel*. The Hague Convention of 14 March 1978 for all practical purposes limits the effects of the adoption of this or any other French *régime* by married couples of British nationality by those who are normally resident in England to land they own in France. In most cases, this is sufficient. However, if one of the spouses is French, or if the couple have their permanent residence in France at the time of adopting a French *régime* or intend that this should be the case in the future, it can extend to all their assets in France or elsewhere. Hence, it is necessary throughout the Power to indicate which of the couple's assets are to be caught, and which are not to be caught, by the *régime* in the light of their residence.

CHANGEMENT DE REGIME MATRIMONIAL . . . . . The clauses which follow set out the rules which will govern the administration of the *régime*. Care must be taken to ensure that the extent of the *régime* is clearly indicated in the clause 'Composition des patrimoines' under sub-clause (a).

5 For the renunciation of an interest in an estate. This is an extremely simple form of Power to enable the Attorney to attend at the appropriate Court and sign the document of renunciation which is prepared by the Court and noted in the Court Registers.

6 For the renunciation of ownership *en tontine*. This is a straightforward Power to turn the joint ownership of property from *en tontine* (joint tenancy) into *en indivision* (tenancy in common). The reverse operation is not possible as a matter of law.

7 For the sale of shares in an SCI to a UK company. This simple Power to sell will presumably be matched by an equally simple Power to buy, that latter

Power being supported by a Certificat de Coutume in the form of Precedent C1 adapted for a purchase of shares by a UK company.

8 For the purchase of shares in an SCI. The wealth of information contained in this Power is made necessary by a similar wealth of information which appears in the *acte de cession* (share transfer) compared to that to be found in an English printed share transfer. The draftsman will require a copy of the *statuts* of the SCI in order to draw the Power. This Precedent assumes that the SCI is for 'jouissance à temps partagé' and the words within ([*DECLARER . . . prix*]) should be omitted if this is not the case.

9 For the formation of an SCI. A straightforward SCI is envisaged. The Power provides for the consideration for the issue of shares to be the transfer of property as in 'FAIRE apport à la société . . .' or for the alternative of the issue of shares to be for cash under the clause 'DEPOSER les fonds . . .'. If the issue is for cash and a purchase of property is intended whilst the company is in the course of incorporation, it will be necessary to insert the clause 'ACQUERIR au nom . . .' and if the company will need to borrow in addition to the allotment moneys, the power 'EMPRUNTER au nom . . .' must be included.

In the event of any shareholding being joint, the alternative power 'SOUSCRIRE tous les parts . . .' should be used if the holding is to be *en tontine*.

The power 'STIPULER que . . .' determines the provisions for the management of the company. The decision whether a shareholder may be a *gérant* must be made at this stage. See the Precedent for the *statuts* of an SCI.

10 and 11 For the making and acceptance of a gift of land. The Power to make the gift must indicate the interest in the land which is given and whether the gift is 'par préciput' or 'en avancement d'hoirie'. The donor gives his Attorney power to disclose all previous gifts made to the same donee and all fiscal information relative to the instant gift. The Power of the recipient of the gift gives power to accept the gift, to submit to such conditions subject to which it is made and to disclose all relevant fiscal information.

12 and 13 For the partition of jointly owned property on divorce. These two Powers deal with the division of jointly owned property following on an Order of the Family Division that one ex-spouse vests in the other his or her share of matrimonial property with or without a compensatory payment (*soulte*). Precedent 13 is for execution by the recipient of the cash payment; Precedent 14 is for the other party to the transaction. In many cases, any money payment will be made in England and if this is the case, the amount of any payment should be shown as 'payable hors vue de notaire'.

14 For the administration of an estate by a beneficiary. The following is a précis of the individual powers given in this Precedent to enable the Attorney(s) in appropriate cases to manage the estate in France of a deceased person. They are chosen from a very large number of powers often cobbled together unthinkingly by the draftsman without reference to the circumstances of individual estates. Precedent 14 has proved sufficient in all cases of the administration of the French estates of persons dying domiciled in England. Each individual power is indicated by its opening words:

REQUERIR toutes . . . . .   To cause to be affixed seals on any property of the deceased or to object thereto; to make inventories, open safes and sealed packages, make all necessary declarations, reserve all rights, execute all documents or absolve the *notaire* from the need therefor, institute or defend proceedings; obtain authority to act without disclosure of their capacity; appoint or oppose the appointment of administrators and choose persons with whom to make deposits of various kinds;

PRENDRE connaissance . . . . .   To obtain all information regarding the estate, to accept or renounce it and make all necessary declarations to that effect;

CONSENTIR ou . . . . .   To agree, contest or compromise *inter vivos* gifts and testamentary dispositions;

REQUERIR toute . . . . .   To obtain all documents of the transmission of title in respect of real property;

FAIRE procéder . . . . .   To deal with the sale of items of personalty and receive the sale price thereof;

VENDRE et . . . . .   To sell by private treaty or auction all real estate at such price and subject to such conditions as is thought fit including the method of payment, to receive the sale price, name stakeholders, and deal with the rights of mortgagees etc;

OBLIGER le . . . . .   To bind the Donors jointly and severally with any other co-owners to observe all legal covenants (e.g. for title and quiet enjoyment) and to provide releases and certificates of clearance (for repaid mortgages);

GERER et . . . . .   To administer the assets in the estate, grant and accept surrenders of leases, require or grant extensions of time, undertake repairs, agree estimates and enter into agreements;

RETIRER de . . . . .   To withdraw from the Post Office letters and packages and receive their contents, encash Postal and Money Orders and redirect mail;

RECEVOIR et . . . . .   To accept or pay moneys in the form of principal, interest or costs which may be due for any reason whatsoever and to demand or agree appropriations, set-offs or mergers;

REQUERIR tous . . . . .   To obtain certificates of ownership and others and of documents attesting the vesting of real property and its registration at the Land Registry;

ACQUITTER tous . . . . .   To pay all inheritance tax, make all declarations, apply for extension of time for payment and to that intent give such undertakings and guarantees to the Trésor, ask for the reduction of any penalties and their repayment, provide certified statements, waive payment of sums due, receive all payments of agreed reductions;

TOUCHER et . . . . . To obtain from banks or other third parties all sums, items, securities and the like forming part of the estate, withdraw sums and give receipts therefor and deposit moneys and securities;

ARRETER tous . . . . . To agree accounts with creditors, debtors, agents and third parties, agree balances and receive or pay the same;

ETABLIR tout . . . . . To agree accounts in 'bénéfice d'inventaire' procedures and make payments to creditors;

PROCEDER à . . . . . To agree estate accounts and make distributions of the estate's assets by agreement or under Order of the Court, appoint experts, pay or receive equality money either at the time of partition or thereafter or in advance, do all things necessary to complete the distribution of the estate including the preparation of further accounts;

FAIRE toutes . . . . . To make all declarations relating to 'état civil' (see the descriptions of the Donors at the beginning of this Power) and other matters;

DE toutes . . . . . To give in respect of all sums paid or received receipts or discharges, acknowledge previous payments, agree to all substitutions with or without guarantees, and give releases and agree to a number of variations relating to mortgaged property and generally deal with moneys and documents as may seem best.

15 For the administration by English executors of French estate. There may be circumstances when it is convenient for the administration of the French estate of a person dying domiciled in England to be effected by the Executors of his English Will. The powers given in Precedent 14 suffice but the details of the Donors should follow the wording in this Precedent.

1   Authority to sign contract

Les soussignés [*details of buyers/sellers*] autorisent par ces présentes [*name, address and occupation of person authorized to sign*] à signer pour eux et en leurs noms un compromis de vente pour l'acquisition/la vente de [*details of property to be bought/sold*] de/à [*name of seller/buyer*] moyennant le prix de Euro [*price in words and figures*] [dont Euro [*value of contents*] meubles meublants] [in case of purchase] avec mention que le prix sera payé sans l'aide d'un prêt/avec l'aide d'un prêt qui ne dépassera pas [*maximum amount of loan*] et à cet effet généralement faire le nécessaire.
FAIT à
Le

2 Power of Attorney for sale of flat or house

PROCURATION
[*HEADING*]
[*DETAILS OF PARTY*]
Ci-après dénommé 'le Constituant'
[*APPOINTMENT CLAUSE*]
VENDRE sous les charges et conditions que les mandataires jugeront convenables à [*name of buyer*], moyennant le prix de [*sale price in figures and words*] (payable hors vue dc notaire) les biens immobiliers ci-après désignés;

SAVOIR: [*description of property from acte de vente to seller*]

ETABLIR la désignation complète et l'origine de la propriété dudit immeuble, faire dresser tout cahier de charge, faire toutes déclarations relatives aux locations, stipuler toutes servitudes;

OBLIGER le Constituant à toutes garanties et au rapport de toutes mainlevées et certificats de radiation, ainsi que de toutes justifications qu'il y aura lieu, fixer l'époque d'entrée en jouissance, convenir du mode et des époques de paiement de prix, le reçevoir en principal et intérêts, soit comptant soit aux termes convenus ou par anticipation;

FAIRE toutes déclarations d'état civil et autres et toutes affirmations préscrites par la loi relatives à la sincérité du prix qui sera stipulé;

SIGNER toute déclaration de plus-value, désigner un représentant fiscal accredité, payer toutes taxes imposées sur la plus-value, signer toute demande de dispense de désignation d'un représentant fiscal accredité;

A DEFAUT de paiement et en cas de difficultés quelconques, exercer toutes les poursuites nécessaires depuis la conciliation jusqu'à l'entière exécution de tous jugements et arrêts par les voies et moyens du droit, en tout état de cause traiter, transiger et compromettre, produire à tous ordres et distribution, toucher le montant de toutes collocations au profit du Constituant;

DE toutes sommes reçues donner quittances et décharges, consentir mentions et subrogations avec ou sans garantie, donner mainlevée avec désistement de tous droits de privilège hypothèque et action résolutoire, consentir à la radiation de toutes inscriptions de privilège de vendeur ou autres avec ou sans constatation de paiement, remettre tous titres et pièces ou obliger le Constituant à leur remise;

[*REMUNERATION CLAUSE*]
[*GENERAL POWERS CLAUSE*]
DONT ACTE
FAIT ET PASSE à
Le

3   Power of Attorney for purchase of flat or house

PROCURATION
[*HEADING*]
[*DETAILS OF PARTY*]
Ci-après dénommé 'le Constituant'
[*APPOINTMENT CLAUSE*]
ACQUERIR (en tontine/en indivision conjointement avec . . . . .) sous les charges et conditions que les mandataires jugeront convenables de [*name of seller*], moyennant le prix de [*purchase price in figures and words*];
SAVOIR [For a flat]:
Dans un ensemble immobilier dénommé [*name of block*] sis sur la commune de . . . . . cadastré section . . . . . numéro [. . .]
LOT NUMERO [. . .]
Un appartement comprenant [*description of flat*]
ET les [. . .]/1.000èmes des parties communes et du sol
[For a house]:
[*description of property from previous acte de vente or contract*]
[EMPRUNTER si besoin est jusqu'à la somme principale de [*amount of loan in figures and words*] des personnes, au taux, pour le temps et sous les conditions que les mandataires aviseront et obliger le Constituant au remboursement du capital et au service des intérêts aux époques et de la manière qui seront convenus et hypothéquer à la sûreté de cet emprunt en principal intérêts et accessoires les biens et droits immobiliers ci-dessus désignés;]
OBLIGER le Constituant au paiement du solde du prix aux époques et de la manière qui seront convenus ainsi qu'à l'exécution des charges qui seront imposées, se faire remettre tous titres et pièces, en donner décharge;
FAIRE opérer conformément à la législation en vigueur tous transferts et mouvements de fonds;
FAIRE toutes affirmations prescrites par la loi relativement à la sincérité du prix;
APPOSER la mention prescrite par l'article 18 de la loi du 13 juillet 1979 et déclarer que pour le financement de l'acquisition ci-dessus le Constituant n'envisage pas de contracter d'autre emprunt que celui dont il est question ci-dessus et que le surplus du prix est assuré des deniers personnels du Constituant;
FAIRE opérer toutes publicités foncières, purges, dénonciations, notifications et offres de paiement, provoquer, faire toutes demandes en mainlevée et exercer toutes actions pour l'exécution du contrat;
FAIRE toutes déclarations d'état civil et autres;
[*REMUNERATION CLAUSE*]
[*GENERAL POWERS CLAUSE*]
DONT ACTE
FAIT ET PASSE à
Le

4   **Power of Attorney for adoption of new *régime***

PROCURATION
[*HEADING*]
[*DETAILS OF PARTY*]
Ci-après dénommé 'les Constituants'
[*APPOINTMENT CLAUSE*]
DECLARER:

– qu'ils sont mariés à [*place of marriage*] le [*date of marriage*]

– qu'ils n'ont pas fait précéder leur union d'un contrat de mariage et qu'ils se sont trouvés soumis au régime anglais équivalent en France au régime de la séparation de biens;

– qu'ils désirent changer de régime matrimonial et adopter pour les biens immeubles et meubles situés en [*country of situation of assets*] à l'exception des immeubles et meubles ci-après indiqués le régime de la communauté tel qu'il est établi ci-après le régime anglais permettant le changement de régime matrimonial par acte notarial dispensé de l'homologation judiciaire.

'CHANGEMENT DE REGIME MATRIMONIAL

Les époux conviennent de changer de régime matrimonial pour les biens immeubles et pour les meubles en [*country of situation of assets*] à l'exception de [*assets not to be included in the new régime*] qui régira leur union de la manière suivante.

Composition des patrimoines

La communauté comprendra:

a) Les biens immeubles situés en France et tous les biens meubles situés en [*country of situation of assets*] à l'exception de ceux ci-dessus indiqués que les époux posséderont au jour de l'acte authentique de changement de régime matrimonial ou qui leur adviendront par la suite à quelque titre que ce soit, notamment par successions, donations ou legs.

b) Les acquêts de biens meubles situés en [*country of situation of assets*], faits par les époux ensemble ou séparément à compter du jour de l'acte authentique de changement de régime matrimonial.

c) Le passif de la communauté comprendra uniquement les dettes afférantes auxdits biens situés en [*country*] ou contractés en vue de l'acquisition et de la conservation ou de l'amélioration desdits biens et, en règle générale, toutes les dettes résultant de leur utilisation.

Administration des biens

Administration conjoints de la communauté:

Les époux ne pourront, l'un sans l'autre, disposer de droits par lesquels est assuré le logement de la famille ni des meubles meublants dont il sera garni. Sous cette réserve:

Chaque époux aura l'administration et la jouissance de ses biens propres et pourra en disposer librement.

Les époux administreront conjointement la communauté conformément à l'article 1503 du *Code civil*. Par suite, les actes d'administration et de disposition des biens communs seront faits sous la signature conjointe des deux époux et ils emporteront de plein droit solidarité des obligations. Toutefois, les actes conservatoires pourront être faits séparément par chaque époux.

Dissolution—Liquidation—Partage

1. Dissolution

La communauté sera dissoute par la survenance de l'une des causes énoncées à l'article 1441 du *Code civil*.

2. Liquidation

La liquidation de la communauté s'effectuera suivant les règles établies aux articles 1467 et suivants du *Code civil*, sous réserve des modifications pouvant résulter des clauses du présent contrat.

3. Partage

a) En cas de dissolution du mariage pour toute autre cause que le décès de l'un des deux époux, le partage de la communauté s'établira par moitié entre eux conformément à l'article 1475 du *Code civil*.

b) En cas de dissolution du mariage par le décès d'un des époux, tous les biens qui composeront la communauté appartiendront en pleine propriété au survivant. Cette stipulation s'appliquera qu'il existe ou non des enfants du mariage et l'époux survivant sera seul tenu d'acquitter toutes les dettes de la communauté.

Les héritiers de l'époux prédécédé ne pourront pas effectuer la reprise des apports et capitaux, tombés dans la communauté du chef de l'auteur, comme le leur permettrait l'article 1525 alinéa 2 du *Code civil*.

Le nouveau régime adopté entrera immédiatement en vigueur dans les relations entre les époux.'

[*REMUNERATION CLAUSE*]

[*GENERAL POWERS CLAUSE*]

DONT ACTE

FAIT ET PASSE à

5   Power of Attorney to renounce an interest in an estate

POUVOIR

Le soussigné,

[*DETAILS OF PARTY*]

Ci-après dénommé 'le Constituant'

[*APPOINTMENT CLAUSE*]

A L'EFFET de se présenter au greffe du tribunal de grande instance qu'il appartiendra pour y déclarer que le Constituant renonce purement et simplement à la succession de [*relationship of donor to deceased*]:

Monsieur/Madame [*name of deceased*], en son vivant [*occupation*], demeurant à [*address of deceased*], né(e) le [*date and place of birth*], [*marital status*], de nationalité britannique

Décédé(e) à son domicile sus indiqué [*or as may be the case*] le [*date of death*]

[*REMUNERATION CLAUSE*]

[*GENERAL POWERS CLAUSE*]

FAIT à

Le

6   Power of Attorney for renunciation of *tontine*

PROCURATION
[*HEADING*]
[*DETAILS OF PARTY*]
Ci-après dénommé 'le Constituant'
[*APPOINTMENT CLAUSE*]
RENONCER purement et simplement conjointement avec son coacquéreur à la clause de tontine, c'est à dire à la double condition résolutoire du prédécès de l'autre et suspensive de sa propre survie, qui avait été stipulée dans l'acte reçu par Me [*name and address of notaire who acted on completion*] le [*date of acte de vente*] contenant vente par [*name of the seller*] des biens immobiliers ci-après désignés:
SAVOIR: [*A full description of the property bought by the donors taken from the acte de vente*]
FAIRE toutes déclarations d'état civil et autres:
[*REMUNERATION CLAUSE*]
[*GENERAL POWERS CLAUSE*]
DONT ACTE
FAIT ET PASSE à

7   Power of Attorney to sell shares in an SCI to a UK company

POUVOIR
Le soussigné,
[*DETAILS OF PARTY*]
Ci-après dénommé 'le Constituant'
[*APPOINTMENT CLAUSE*]
VENDRE à XYZ Limited une société de droit anglais dont le siège social est à [*address of Registered Office*] [*number of shares*] parts de la SCI [*name of company*] dont le siège social est à [*address of Registered Office*] moyennant le prix de Euro [*price in figures and words*] payable comptant
DONNER quittance et décharge de toutes sommes reçues
[*REMUNERATION CLAUSE*]
[*GENERAL POWERS CLAUSE*]
FAIT à
Le

8 Power of Attorney to purchase shares in an SCI

POUVOIR

Le soussigné,

[*DETAILS OF PARTY*]

Ci-après dénommé 'le Constituant'

[*APPOINTMENT CLAUSE*]

ACQUERIR sous les charges et conditions que les mandataires jugeront convenables [*en tontine*] [*en indivision*] de [*name of seller*] moyennant le prix de Euro [*price in figures and words*] [payable hors vue de notaire] [*number of shares*] parts de [*nominal value*] chacune numérotées de [. . .] à [. . .] dans la SCI [*name of company*] ([une société civile d'attribution d'immeubles en jouissance à temps partagé régie par la loi n.86–18 du 6 janvier 1986]) constituée par acte de Maitre [*name of notaire or avocat who incorporated the company*] en date du [*date of statuts*] et immatriculée le [*date of registration*] ayant pour objet [*the main objects of the company*], d'une durée de 99 ans, un capital social de [*authorized capital in figures and words*] divisé en [*number of shares*] parts de [*nominal value*] chacune, et dont le siège social à [*Registered Office*], ([lesdites parts donnant droit à l'attribution en jouissance de l'immeuble social pendant la période de séjour définie aux termes du tableau d'affectation des parts annexé aux statuts chaque associé étant tenu de contribuer proportionnellement aux nombres de ses parts aux appels de fonds nécessité par l'aménagement ou la restauration de l'immeuble social]);

OBLIGER le Constituant au paiement du prix aux époques et de la manière qui seront convenus ainsi qu'à l'exécution des charges qui seront imposées, se faire remettre tous titres et pièces, en donner décharge;

DECLARER avoir connaissance de toutes les conditions de ladite cession de parts pour avoir signé ledit compromis de vente et avoir eu le projet d'acte de cession des parts;

DECLARER avoir reçu un exemplaire des statuts de ladite société, ([du tableau d'affectation des parts du règlement intérieur et de jouissance, une note sommaire sur les caractéristiques de l'immeuble, l'inventaire des équipements et mobilier garnissant l'immeuble social, la situation comptable du cédant, le budget prévisionnel, connaître le montant des charges afférants aux parts cédées pour l'exercice précédant]);

([DECLARER avoir connaissance que l'acquisition des parts sociales confère au cessionnaire seulement la qualité d'associé et non celle de propriétaire de l'immeuble laquelle qualité emporte le droit de jouissance personnel et mobilier exercé par période]);

FAIRE toutes affirmations préscrites par la loi relativement à la sincérité du prix;

FAIRE toutes déclarations d'état civil et autres;

[*REMUNERATION CLAUSE*]

[*GENERAL POWERS CLAUSE*]

DONT ACTE

FAIT ET PASSE à

Le

9   Power of Attorney to form an SCI

POUVOIR
[*HEADING*]
[*DETAILS OF PARTIES*]
Ci-après dénommés 'les Constituants'
[*APPOINTMENT CLAUSE*]
CONSTITUER entre eux une société civile immobilière ayant pour dénomination 'SCI . . . . .', pour objet l'acquisition de tous immeubles bâtis ou non bâtis; l'administration, gestion et exploitation, location par bail ou autrement et vente desdits immeubles et généralement toutes opérations mobilières et immobilières pouvant se rattacher directement ou indirectement à l'objet social pourvu qu'elles ne fassent pas perdre à la société son caractère civil, pour siège social à [*address of Registered Office*] et un capital qui s'élèvera à [*details of capital*] numerotées de [. . .] à [. . .] souscrites en totalité [*or as the case may be*] par les associés;
[when the consideration for the issue of the shares is property]
FAIRE apport à la société les droits immobiliers affranchis de tout passif évalué à Euro [*value in words and figures*] appartenant à [*name of owner*] ci-après désignés:
SAVOIR: [*description of property*]
OR [in the case of the issue being for cash]
DEPOSER les fonds correspondant aux apports en numéraire à un compte joint ouvert au noms des associés auprès de tout établissement de crédit de son choix, faire procéder au virement desdites sommes sur un compte ouvert au nom de la société sur simple justification d'immatriculation de celle-ci au registre du commerce des sociétés;
ACQUERIR au nom et pour le compte de la société en formation sous les charges et conditions que les mandataires jugeront convenables de [*name of seller*] moyennant le prix de [*purchase price in words and figures*] les biens immobiliers ci-après désignés [et moyennant le prix de [*purchase price in words and figures*] les meubles meublants dont l'inventaire a été dressé et sera annexé à l'acte de vente];
EMPRUNTER au nom et pour le compte de la société en formation une somme principale qui ne dépassera pas [*maximum amount of loan*] à [*name of lender*] au taux pour le temps et sous les conditions que les mandataires aviseront et obliger la société au remboursement du capital et au service des intérêts aux époques et de la manière qui seront convenus et hypothéquer à la sûreté de cet emprunt en principal intérêts et accessoires les biens et droits immobiliers ci-dessus désignés:
[SOUSCRIRE au nom de chacun des Constituants [. . .] % des parts de [. . .] Euro dans ladite société] OR
[SOUSCRIRE tous les parts de la société sauf deux aux noms des Constituants et stipuler que ces parts seront en tontine et souscrire au nom de chacun des Constituants une de ces deux parts];
FIXER la durée de cette société à 99 ans;
ETABLIR les statuts de la société en conformité avec les dispositions légales et réglementaires;
STIPULER que les affaires de la société seront gérées et administrées par un ou plusieurs gérants, personnes physiques ou morales [qui ne peut jamais être associé ou le conjoint ou membre de la famille d'un associé ou un de ses préposés] [associés ou non], avec les pouvoirs les plus étendus pour l'accomplissement de tous les actes entrant dans

l'objet social et qui demande l'intérêt social. A cet effet, chacun gérant aura la signature sociale et pourra recevoir et payer toutes sommes, faire tous achats, ventes et marchés pouvant se rapporter à l'objet social, transiger, compromettre, donner tous désistements et mainlevées avec ou sans paiements, exercer et défendre à toutes actions judiciaires, représenter la société à toutes procédures de redressement ou de liquidation judiciaire, souscrire, accepter, endosser, avaliser et acquitter tous effets de commerce;

FAIRE toutes déclarations d'état civil et autres;

STIPULER dans les termes et conditions que les mandataires jugeront convenables toutes conventions relatives aux apports sociaux, aux inventaires, aux prélèvements des associés, au partage des bénéfices et pertes, aux modifications du capital social, aux sommes laissées ou mises en compte courant par les associés dans la société, à la cession par un des associés de ses droits sociaux, à la continuation de la société en cas de perte de tout ou partie du capital social, à sa prorogation, modification, dissolution et à sa liquidation, nommer tous commissaires aux comptes;

DEPOSER les fonds correspondant aux apports de numéraires à un compte joint ouvert au noms des associés auprès de tout établissement de crédit de son choix, faire procéder au virement desdites sommes sur un compte ouvert au nom de la société sur simple justification d'immatriculation de celle-ci au registre du commerce des sociétés;

FAIRE toutes affirmations préscrites par la loi relativement à la sincérité de l'évaluation;

FAIRE opérer toutes publicité foncière, purges, dénonciations, notifications, provoquer et faire toutes mainlevées;

SOUSCRIRE la déclaration de conformité;

PROCEDER à toutes formalités, notamment à la publication de l'acte de société conformément à la loi et à l'inscription au registre du commerce et des sociétés;

DRESSER l'état des actes accomplis pour le compte de la société en formation;

[REMUNERATION CLAUSE]

[GENERAL POWERS CLAUSE]

FAIT à

Le

10   Power of Attorney to make gift of land

PROCURATION

[HEADING]

[DETAILS OF PARTY]

Ci-après dénommé 'le Constituant'

[APPOINTMENT CLAUSE]

FAIRE donation entre vifs [par préciput et hors part] [en avancement d'hoirie] à [details of Donee] le seul enfant et présomptif héritier portant sur la totalité de la [nue-propriété et dont en effet le Constituant se réserve sa vie durant l'usufruit des biens donnés et de sorte que le donataire n'aura la jouissance des biens donnés qu'à compter du décès du Constituant] [pleine propriété des biens ci-après désignés]

SAVOIR: [full description of property to be given as in the acte de vente to the Donor] En conséquence:

ESTIMER les biens donnés à [value of property in words and figures] soit pour [l'usufruit donné] [la pleine propriété donnée];

[CONVENIR que le rapport à faire par le donataire à la succession du Constituant s'effectuera conformément aux règles légales en vigueur au décès de celui-ci;]

FIXER l'époque d'entrée en jouissance du donataire;

FAIRE la donation sous les charges et conditions que le mandataire jugera convenables;

STIPULER qu'à défaut par le donataire d'exécuter les charges et conditions de la présente donation le Constituant pourra comme de droit en faire prononcer la révocation et notamment dans les cas et conditions prévus aux articles 953 et suivants du *Code civil*;

OBLIGER le Constituant à toutes garanties au rapport de toutes justifications et mainlevées et à la remise de tous baux et titres de propriété;

FAIRE toute déclaration d'état civil, de situation hypothécaire et autres, déclarer notamment comme le Constituant le fait ici (i) qu'il est né comme sus-indiqué (ii) qu'il a la libre disposition de ses biens et (iii) que ces biens ne sont pas grevés d'aucune inscription de privilège immobilier spécial ou d'hypothèque conventionnelle, judiciaire ou légale;

REMETTRE tous titres et pièces et en retirer décharge;

FAIRE toute déclaration au point de vue fiscal relativement aux donations antérieures à ce jour que le Constituant a pu faire au donataire susnommé et à la situation familiale dudit Constituant ainsi que toutes évaluations et affirmations requises;

REQUERIR la publicité foncière;

[*REMUNERATION CLAUSE*]

[*GENERAL POWERS CLAUSE*]

DONT ACTE

FAIT ET PASSE à

Le

11   Power of Attorney to accept a gift of land

PROCURATION

[*HEADING*]

[*DETAILS OF PARTY*]

Ci-après dénommé 'le Constituant'

[*APPOINTMENT CLAUSE*]

ACCEPTER la donation entre vifs [par préciput et hors part] [en avancement d'hoirie] que [*details of Donor*] se propose de faire à [*details of Donee*] le seul enfant et présomptif héritier portant sur la totalité de la [nue-propriété et dont en effet le donateur se réserve sa vie durant l'usufruit des biens donnés et de sort que le Constituant n'aura la jouissance des biens donnés qu'à compter du décès du donateur] [pleine propriété des biens ci-après désignés];

SAVOIR: [*Full description of property to be given as in the acte de vente to the Donor*]

En conséquence:

OBLIGER le Constituant à l'exécution des charges et des conditions sous lesquelles ladite donation sera faite;

REQUERIR la formalité de l'enregistrement et de la publicité foncière de tous actes. Lever tous états. Remettre ou se faire remettre tous titres et pièces. En donner ou retirer décharge;

FAIRE toutes déclarations nécessaires au point de vue fiscal et affirmations prescrites par la loi relatives à la sincérité des soultes ainsi que toutes déclarations de l'état civil et autres:

[*REMUNERATION CLAUSE*]
[*GENERAL POWERS CLAUSE*]
DONT ACTE
FAIT ET PASSE à
Le

12 Power to partition jointly owned property on divorce, donor taking co-owner's share and paying equality money

PROCURATION
[*HEADING*]
[*DETAILS OF PARTY*]
Ci-après dénommé 'le Constituant'
[*APPOINTMENT CLAUSE*]
PROCEDER au partage du bien immobilier sous-désigné et l'attribuer au Constituant moyennant le paiement (hors la comptabilité du notaire) d'une soulte de [*amount of payment in words and figures*];

SAVOIR: [*Description of property*]
FIXER la date d'entrée en jouissance;
FAIRE toutes déclarations d'état civil et autres;
S'OBLIGER au rapport de toutes garanties;
[*REMUNERATION CLAUSE*]
[*GENERAL POWERS CLAUSE*]
DONT ACTE
FAIT ET PASSE à

13 Power to partition jointly owned property on divorce in exchange for equality money

PROCURATION
[*HEADING*]
[*DETAILS OF PARTY*]
Ci-après dénommé 'le Constituant'
[*APPOINTMENT CLAUSE*]
PROCEDER au partage du bien immobilier sous-désigné et l'attribuer [*name of person in whom share of property is to be vested*];

SAVOIR: [*Description of property*]
EVALUER ledit bien à la somme de [*value in words and figures*];
FIXER la date d'entrée en jouissance;
FAIRE toutes déclarations d'état civil et autres;
S'OBLIGER au rapport de toutes garanties;
[*REMUNERATION CLAUSE*]
[*GENERAL POWERS CLAUSE*]
DONT ACTE

14   Power of Attorney for beneficiary to administer estate

PROCURATION

[*HEADING*]

[*DETAILS OF PARTY*]

Ci-après dénommé 'le Constituant'

HABILE à se dire et porter héritier dans la succession de [*name, occupation and address of deceased*]

[*APPOINTMENT CLAUSE*]

A L'EFFET de recueillir la succession dudit [*name of deceased, date and place of birth and date and place of death*];

REQUERIR toutes appositions de scellés ou s'y opposer, en demander la levée avec ou sans description, faire procéder à toutes inventaires des biens dépendant de la succession dont il s'agit, rectifications et récoltements; dans le cours de ces opérations faire tous dires, déclarations, réquisitions, protestations et réserves, donner toutes dispenses, introduire tous référés ou y défendre, demander toutes autorisations pour agir sans attributions de qualités, faire nommer tous administrateurs ou s'y opposer à leur nomination, choisir tous gardiens et dépositaires;

PRENDRE connaissance des forces et charges de cette succession, l'accepter purement et simplement ou sous bénéfice d'inventaire ou même y renoncer, faire à cet effet toutes déclarations;

CONSENTIR ou contester l'exécution de tous actes de libéralité, en faire ou accepter la délivrance, demander ou consentir toutes réductions;

REQUERIR toute attestation de transmission de tous droits réels immobiliers;

FAIRE procéder avec ou sans attribution de qualité à la vente des objets mobiliers, en toucher le prix, faire toutes acquisitions;

VENDRE et céder, soit gré à gré, soit par adjudication, toute ou partie des biens ou droits immobiliers dépendant de la succession dont il s'agit aux prix charges et conditions que le mandataire avisera, toucher le prix soit comptant soit aux termes convenus, nommer tous séquestres, faire toutes indications de paiement, consentir toutes délégations aux créanciers inscrits, acquérir tout ou partie de ces biens ou droits, en payer le prix;

OBLIGER le Constituant conjointement et solidairement avec tous covendeurs à toutes garanties ordinaires et de droit et au rapport de toutes justifications et mainlevées et de tout certificat de radiation;

GERER et administrer les biens dépendant de la succession dont il s'agit, passer et résilier tous baux et locations, demander ou consentir toutes prorogations, faire exécuter toutes réparations, arrêter tous devis et conventions;

RETIRER de tous bureaux de poste, de toutes administrations et de toutes entreprises publiques ou privées tous télégrammes, lettres, colis et pacquets recommandés ainsi tous objets avec valeur déclaré, en donner décharge, les ouvrir et recevoir les objets et sommes qu'ils contiennent, toucher le montant de tous mandats postaux, réexpédier le courrier aux mandants en quelques lieux qu'ils se trouvent;

RECEVOIR ou payer toutes sommes en principal, intérêts et accessoires pouvant être dûes à tel titre et pour lequel cause que ce soit, proposer ou accepter toute imputation, compensation ou confusion;

REQUERIR tous certificats de propriété, faire toutes déclarations de non-cumul, requérir toutes attestations de transmission d'immeuble et publications;

ACQUITTER tous droits de mutation, faire toutes déclarations, faire toutes demandes en obtention de délai, prendre à cet effet tous engagements envers le Trésor et constituer à son profit toutes garanties, faire toutes demandes en remise ou en restitution, signer toutes déclarations, certifier tous états, faire toutes renonciations à des créances, toucher le montant de toutes remises ou restitutions;

TOUCHER et recevoir de toutes banques ou de tous tiers quelconques tous sommes valeurs et objets dépendant de la succession dont il s'agit, opérer tous retraits, en donner décharge, faire tous dépôt de sommes et de valeurs;

ARRETER tous comptes avec tous créanciers, débiteurs, dépositaires et tiers quelconques, en fixer les réliquats, les recevoir ou payer;

ETABLIR tous comptes de bénéfices d'inventaire et procéder à toutes distributions entre les créanciers;

PROCEDER à tous comptes, liquidation et partage soit à l'amiable soit judiciairement des biens dépendant de la succession dont il s'agit, nommer et faire nommer des experts, recevoir ou payer tous soultes, soit comptant soit à terme ou par anticipation, et faire tout ce qui pourrait être nécessaire pour l'exécution de partage, procéder à tous comptes complémentaires;

FAIRE toutes déclarations d'état civil et autres;

DE toutes sommes reçues ou payées donner ou retirer quittances ou décharges, reconnaître tous paiements antérieurs, consentir toutes mentions et subrogations avec ou sans garantie, faire mainlevée et consentir la radiation avec désistement de tous droits de privilège, hypothèque, action résolutoire de toutes inscriptions ou saisies oppositions et autres empêchements quelconques, le tout avec ou sans constatation de paiement, consentir ou accepter toutes antériorités et toutes restrictions de privilège ou hypothèques, faire accepter toutes offres et consignations, opérer le retrait de toutes sommes consignées, remettre ou se faire remettre tous titres et pièces, retirer ou donner toutes décharges;

[*REMUNERATION CLAUSE*]

[*GENERAL POWERS CLAUSE*]

DONT ACTE

FAIT ET PASSE à

Le

15   Power of Attorney for English Executors to administer French estate

PROCURATION

[*HEADING*]

[*DETAILS OF PARTIES*] agissant en qualité d'exécuteurs testamentaires de la succession de [*name, address, description and date and place of death of the deceased*] dont le testament en date du [*date of Will*] a fait l'objet d'une ordonnance de Probate de la Haute Cour de Justice siégeant à [*place of Registry from which the Grant issued*] le [*date of Grant*]

Ci-après dénommé 'les Constituants'

[*APPOINTMENT CLAUSE*]

AUXQUELS ils donnent pouvoir de, pour eux et en leurs noms, recueillir ladite succession et en consequence:

[Then as in Power of Attorney 14]

B CONTRACTS

The following two Precedents are of a *Promesse de vente* and a *Compromis de vente*. There are no standard Conditions of Sale such as exist in England but to some extent the relevant Articles of the *Code civil* achieve the same result. One finds, therefore, many standard provisions and on the whole not much derogation from them.

It must be remembered that both kinds of contract are subject to the seven-day 'cooling off' rule. Both Precedents are typically 'notarial' in the sense that they bear the hallmarks of notarial draftsmanship but they are not '*authentique*' so that the rules applying to the payment of deposits are those of the 'contrat ssp'.

All contracts, when the buyer is a 'non-professional' and the property is for private residence purposes, benefit from the Loi Scrivener protection. Many sellers' agents and *notaires* insist that when the protection of the Law is not sought, the buyer makes the declaration to that effect in his handwriting.

In the case of both Precedents, provision is made for each party to be represented by his own *notaire*.

1 *Promesse de vente*

Entre les soussignés:
[*details with full état civil of Vendor*]
    Ci-après dénommé 'Le Promettant'
Et
[*details with full état civil of Purchaser*]
    Ci-après dénommé 'Le Bénéficiaire'
Il a été convenu et arrêté ce qui suit:

PROMESSE DE VENTE

Le Promettant confère au Bénéficiaire la faculté d'acquérir si bon lui semble dans les conditions et délais ci-après indiqués l'immeuble ci-dessous désigné.

En conséquence le Promettant prend l'engagement pour lui et ses héritiers ou représentants, même incapables, de vendre l'immeuble dont s'agit au Bénéficiaire dans les conditions ci-après précisées.

Il s'interdit pendant la durée de la promesse de vente de modifier la situation locative de l'immeuble et de le grever de droits réels quelconques.

Le Bénéficiaire accepte la présente promesse de vente en tant que promesse mais se réserve la faculté d'en demander ou non la réalisation suivant qu'il lui conviendra.

DESIGNATION

[*full description of property taken from Vendor's acte de vente*]
Lesdits biens ci-après dénommés 'L'immeuble'.

L'immeuble appartient au Promettant à la suite des faits et actes ci-après:

[*previous title*]

DELAI DE REALISATION

La promesse de vente est consentie pour une durée qui expirera le [*date of expiry of option*] à [. . .] heures.

Passé ce délai, sans que le Bénéficiaire ait manifesté son intention d'acquérir l'immeuble, la présente promesse sera considerée comme nulle et non avenue sauf les effets du versement de l'indemnité d'immobilisation.

Le Bénéficiaire pourra lever l'option par lettre recommandée avec demande d'avis de réception.

FORME DE LA REALISATION DE LA VENTE

La réalisation de la présente promesse de vente devra être constatée par acte notarié dressé au frais du Bénéficiaire pas plus tard que le [*latest date for completion*] accompagnée du versement de la totalité du prix. Cette acte sera établi par Me [*notaire acting for Vendor*] Notaire associé à [*town of notaire's office*] assisté par Me [*notaire acting for Purchaser*] Notaire à [*town of notaire's office*].

L'entrée en jouissance aura lieu par la prise de possession réelle et effective le jour de la signature de l'acte authentique le Promettant s'obligeant à le rendre libre à cette date.

CONDITIONS DE LA VENTE EVENTUELLE

La vente si elle se réalise aura lieu sous les conditions ordinaires et de droit en pareille matière et notamment sous les conditions suivantes:

1. Le Bénéficiaire prendra l'immeuble dans l'état où il se trouvera le jour de l'entrée en jouissance sans pouvoir exercer aucun recours contre le Promettant pour cause de bon ou mauvais état du sol, du sous-sol ou des bâtiments, vices de toute nature, apparentes ou cachées, erreur dans la désignation ou la contenance, toute différence en plus ou moins, excédat-elle un vingtième, devant faire le profit ou la perte du Bénéficiaire.

2. Le Bénéficiaire profitera des servitudes actives et supportera celles passives à sa risque et péril.

3. Le Bénéficiaire fera son affaire personnelle de la continuation ou de la résiliation de toutes polices d'assurances et de tous contrats d'abonnement auprès des differentes services publics de manière à ne donner lieu à aucun recours contre le Promettant.

CONDITIONS SUSPENSIVES

La présente promesse de vente est consentie sous les conditions suspensives suivantes:

1. Que le certificat d'urbanisme ne fasse pas apparaître de servitudes d'urbanisme et autres limitations administratives au droit de propriété de nature à restreindre le droit de propriété et de jouissance du Bénéficiaire et notamment qu'il ne fasse pas mention d'un projet de voirie emportant élargissement de la rue bordant l'immeuble ou création de voie nouvelle dont l'emprise serait située en tout ou en partie sur l'immeuble.

2. Qu'au cas où les pièces d'urbanisme révèlent que l'immeuble est compris dans une zone à l'intérieur de laquelle existe un droit de préemption, la présente promesse sera prorogée du temps voulu pour purger ce droit mais deviendrait caduque au cas où ce droit de préemption sera exercé.

3. Que l'immeuble ne soit grevé d'aucune inscription hypothécaire tant du chef du Promettant que des précédants propriétaires et dont le montant serait égal ou supérieur au prix de l'immeuble.

Le Promettant s'oblige à effectuer sans délai les formalités nécessaires. Il confère en outre au Bénéficiaire à titre irrévocable tous pouvoirs à cet effet. Par ailleurs, au cas où les pièces d'urbanisme révéleraient des servitudes graves ou autres dispositions de nature à déprécier sensiblement la valeur de l'immeuble, le présente vente pourrait être résolue à l'initiative du Bénéficiaire. Pour notifier sa demande au Promettant, le Bénéficiaire aura un délai de quinze jours à compter de la communication de la note d'urbanisme qui lui sera faite par lettre recommandé avec demande d'accusation de réception.

SITUATION LOCATIVE

Le Promettant déclare que l'immeuble est occupé par lui.

SERVITUDES CONVENTIONNELLES

Le Promettant déclare n'avoir créé aucune servitude et qu'à sa connaissance il n'en existe pas en dehors de celles ci-après rapportées.

[*details of existing easements affecting the property*]
FACULTE DE RETRACTION
EXERCICE DE LA RETRACTION
RESTITUTION DES FONDS VERSES
(As for *compromis de vente*)

PRIX

La vente en cas de réalisation aura lieu moyennant le prix de [*price in words and figures*] qui sera payable comptant au jour de la signature de l'acte authentique sauf à tenir compte de l'indemnité d'immobilisation dont le versement est ci-après constaté.

APPLICATION DE LA LOI DU 13 JUILLET 1979

See page 47.

INDEMNITE D'IMMOBILISATION

En considération de la promesse faite au Bénéficiaire par le Promettant et en contre-partie du préjudice qui peut en résulter pour ce dernier en cas de non-réalisation du fait de l'indisponibilité de l'immeuble pendant la durée de la promesse, le Bénéficiaire verse au Promettant qui le reconnaît la somme de [*10% of the sale price*]. Ce paiement a eu lieu à la comptabilité de Me [*notaire acting for the Vendor*].
Le sort de cette indemnité sera la suivante:

1. Elle s'imputera sur le prix en cas de réalisation de la vente de sorte que l'acquéreur n'aura plus à verser que 2.385.000 francs.

2. Elle sera immédiatement et intégralement remboursée au Bénéficiaire en cas de caducité ou de résolution de promesse pour l'un des motifs indiqués sous le titre Conditions Suspensives.

3. Faute par le Bénéficiaire d'avoir réalisé la promesse de vente dans les délais et aux conditions convenus, elle restera acquise de plein droit au Promettant à titres de dommages-intérêt forfaitement fixés ce qui est expressément accepté par le Bénéficiaire.

NANTISSEMENT

Le montant de l'indemnité d'immobilisation est affecté en nantissement au profit du Bénéficiaire pour lui assurer le remboursement éventuel.

Afin d'assurer l'efficacité du nantissement la somme ci-dessus versée a été remise à . . . . ., comptable en l'office notarial de Me [*notaire acting for the Vendor*], tiers convenu entre les parties dans les termes de l'article 2070 du *Code civil*.

Le tiers convenu agira comme suit:

1. Il versera cette somme au Promettant en cas de réalisation de la présente promesse de vente d'en permettre l'imputation sur le prix de vente.

2. Il restituera cette somme immédiatement et intégralement au Bénéficiaire dans les cas visés au titre 'Indemnité d'Immobilisation'.

3. Il versera cette somme au Promettant dans les conditions du même titre.

Le versement effectué par le tiers convenu dans les conditions qui viennent d'être indiquées emportera décharge de sa mission.

FACULTE DE SUBSTITUTION

Le Bénéficiaire aura la faculté de se substituer toute personne physique ou morale dans les droits résultant à son profit de la présente promesse mais sous réserve que cette substitution n'entraine aucune modification des conditions de la promesse et en particulier dans les délais de réalisation et dans le sort de l'indemnité d'immobilisation.

PUBLICITE FONCIERE

Le Bénéficiaire déclare que les présentes seront publiées à ses frais au bureau des hypothèques par soins de Me [*notaire acting for the Vendor*].

FRAIS

Les frais de l'acte de réalisation seront supportés par le Bénéficiaire.

DOMICILE

Pour l'exécution des présentes les parties font élection de domicile en leur demeures respectives.

FAIT à . . . . . en deux exemplaires

Le

2   *Compromis de vente sous condition suspensive (copropriété)*

Entre les soussignés:

[*details with full état civil of Vendor*]

Laquelle en s'obligeant et en obligeant solidairement ses ayants-droits éventuellement, même mineurs ou incapables, sous la seule garantie de l'éviction.

Ci-après dénommée 'Le Vendeur'.

D'UNE PART—

ET

[*Details with full état civil of Purchaser*]

S'obligeant conjointement et solidairement entre eux, Agissant pour leur compte personnel ou pour le compte de toute personne physique ou morale qu'ils se réservent de se substituer.

Ci-après dénommés 'L'Acquéreur'.

D'AUTRE PART—

IL EST CONVENU CE QUI SUIT:

LE VENDEUR vend par ces présentes, à L'ACQUEREUR, qui accepte, SOUS LES CONDITIONS SUSPENSIVES ci-après:

Les biens désignés ci-après, dénommés 'L'immeuble'.

Que L'ACQUEREUR déclare bien connaître pour les avoir visités en vue des présentes.

DESIGNATION

[*Full description of property taken from Vendor's acte de vente*]

DROIT DE PROPRIETE

Le vendeur déclare qu'il est seul propriétaire de l'immeuble et s'oblige à justifier d'une origine de propriété régulière.

PROPRIETE—JOUISSANCE

L'acquéreur sera propriétaire de l'immeuble vendu à compter seulement du jour de la réalisation de l'acte authentique ci-après prévu, le transfert de propriété étant retardé jusqu'à cette date.

Il en aura la jouissance à compter du même jour par la prise de possession réelle et effective, lesdits biens et droits immobiliers étant libres de toute location ou occupation.

Jusqu'à cette date, le vendeur s'engage à ne conférer aucune servitude, ni créer aucune charge quelconque comme aussi à n'apporter aucune modification ni transformation à l'immeuble vendu.

CHARGES ET CONDITIONS

La vente, si elle se réalise, aura lieu aux conditions suivantes, que l'acquéreur s'oblige à exécuter.

1. De prendre possession de cet immeuble dans l'état où il se trouvera le jour du transfert de propriété, sans garantie pour quelque cause que ce soit, notamment bon ou mauvais état du sol ou du sous-sol, ou des constructions, vices apparents ou cachés, mitoyennetés, et sans garantie de contenance (sauf l'effet des dispositions de la loi CARREZ visée ci-après), le vendeur s'engageant à maintenir l'immeuble dans son état actuel avec tous ses éléments immeuble par destination.

2. De jouir des servitudes actives et supporter celles passives, s'il en existe, sans recours contre le vendeur.

A cet égard, le vendeur déclare qu'à sa connaissance l'immeuble vendu n'est grevé d'aucune servitude, indépendamment des servitudes pouvant résulter de la situation naturelle des lieux, de la loi ou de la réglementation d'urbanisme; et qu'il n'en a personnellement conféré aucune.

3. De supporter les impôts et autres charges de toute nature de l'immeuble vendu, à compter du jour de l'entrée en jouissance, et de rembourser au vendeur les taxe foncière et annexes de l'année en cours, prorata temporis.

4. De continuer ou de résilier, mais à ses frais, toutes polices d'assurance incendie contractées par le vendeur.

5. De faire son affaire personnelle, à compter du jour de l'entrée en jouissance, sans recours contre le vendeur, de l'exécution de tous contrats et abonnements pouvant exister pour le service des eaux, du gaz, de l'électricité et du téléphone, et d'en faire opérer la mutation à son nom et à ses propres frais dans les meilleurs délais.

COPROPRIETE

RÈGLEMENT DE COPROPRIÉTÉ

L'acquéreur sera par le seul fait de la vente subrogé de plein droit, tant activement que passivement, dans les droits et obligations résultant pour le vendeur du règlement de copropriété et de ses éventuels modificatifs.

Le vendeur précise que l'immeuble dont dépendent les lots vendus a fait l'objet: [*full details of this document including name of notaire who prepared it and details of its registration at the local bureau des hypothèques*]

CONTENANCE DE L'IMMEUBLE

La superficie des lots telle qu'elle est indiquée dans la désignation qui précède fait l'objet de la garantie instituée par l'article 46 de la loi du 10 juillet 1965.

SYNDIC

Le vendeur déclare que le syndic de copropriété de l'immeuble dont dépendent les biens et droits immobiliers objets des présentes est:
[*Name and address of syndic*]

APUREMENT DES CHARGES DE LA COPROPRIÉTÉ

Le vendeur s'oblige à obtenir le certificat mentionnant l'apurement des charges de copropriété (article 20 loi du 10 juillet 1965).

TRAVAUX RELATIFS À LA COPROPRIÉTÉ

Le coût de tous travaux décidés à la date de ce jour, exécutés ou non à ce jour, resteront à la charge exclusive du vendeur.

Dans le cas où une assemblée générale des copropriétaires serait convoquée entre la date des présentes et la date de la régularisation authentique prévue ci-après, le vendeur s'oblige à communiquer à l'acquéreur l'avis de convocation à l'assemblée et s'oblige, soit à donner pouvoir à l'acquéreur à l'effet de le représenter à ladite assemblée, soit à participer aux votes, dans le sens que l'acquéreur lui indiquera par écrit.

A défaut, les travaux votés au jour de la vente incomberont au vendeur.

SORT DES VERSEMENTS EFFECTUÉS PAR LE VENDEUR

De convention expresse entre les parties, feront l'objet d'un remboursement par l'acquéreur au vendeur, le jour de la réalisation authentique prévue ci-après, sauf l'effet des dispositions du paragraphe '*Travaux relatifs à la copropriété*' ci-dessus:

L'ensemble, sans exception, des comptes créditeurs du vendeur dans les livres du syndic, y compris ceux relatifs aux provisions spéciales versées en exécution de l'article 35 (modifié) du décret 67-223 du 17 mars 1967, sauf dans le cas où ces provisions correspondent à des travaux dont le coût a été approuvé par l'assemblée.

ASSURANCE INCENDIE

L'ACQUEREUR déclare vouloir résilier tout contrat d'assurance incendie en cours souscrit par le VENDEUR en ce qui concerne l'immeuble vendu.

A cet égard, l'ACQUEREUR mandate par les présentes, pour lui et en son nom, le

VENDEUR qui accepte, à l'effet de résilier toute police en cours, en conformité avec l'article L 121-10 du Code des Assurances à compter de la réalisation authentique prévue ci-après.

Il est toutefois expressément convenu entre les parties que l'indemnité de résiliation éventuellement due restera à la charge exclusive du VENDEUR.

L'ACQUEREUR déclare en conséquence faire son affaire personnelle, à compter du jour de la réalisation authentique prévue ci-après, à ses frais, risques et périls, de la souscription d'une nouvelle police auprès de la compagnie de son choix.

INCENDIE PENDANT LA VALIDITE DU COMPROMIS

Les parties conviennent expressément que si un sinistre par incendie, par catastrophe naturelle, ou toute autre cause de quelque nature que ce soit, frappait totalement ou partiellement l'immeuble vendu, les présentes conventions seront considérées comme nulles et non avenues à compter de la date du sinistre.

BIENS MEUBLES ET OBJETS MOBILIERS

En ce qui concerne les biens meubles et objets mobiliers, l'acquéreur les prendra article par article tels qu'ils figurent ci-dessus, au paragraphe 'DESIGNATION', dans l'état où ils se trouvent, sans pouvoir élever aucune réclamation, demander aucune garantie ou diminution de prix, ni exercer aucun recours ni répétition quelconques contre le vendeur, notamment en raison de mauvais fonctionnement, de mauvais état, défaut d'entretien ou de vétusté.

Le vendeur s'engage, de son côté, à maintenir lesdits biens meubles et objets mobiliers en bon état de fonctionnement et d'usage jusqu'au jour de la signature de l'acte définitif de vente.

AVERTISSEMENT—CHANGEMENT D'AFFECTATION

L'acquéreur reconnaît avoir été informé par le notaire associé soussigné, des dispositions de l'article L 631-7 du Code de la Construction et de l'habitation, relatives à l'affectation des locaux à usage d'habitation à un autre usage, ainsi que des inconvénients pouvant résulter à son encontre de l'inobservation de ces dispositions.

APPLICATION DES LOIS DU 22 JUIN 1982 ET DU 6 JUILLET 1989
(Droit de préemption du locataire)

Il est rappelé que la loi n°82–526 du 22 juin 1982 et celle n°89–562 du 6 juillet 1989 octroient du droit de préemption aux locataires dont le bail entre dans le champ d'application desdites lois, lorsque le propriétaire leur délivre un congé en vue de la vente ou de sa reprise.

A cet égard, le vendeur déclare que l'immeuble vendu n'est pas placé dans le champ d'application de ces textes.

APPLICATION DE LA LOI DU 18 DECEMBRE 1996 (dite loi CARREZ)

La présente vente entre dans le champ d'application de l'article 46 de la loi du 10 juillet 1965 issu de la loi n°96–1107 du 18 septembre 1996 améliorant la protection des acquéreurs de lots de copropriété, et du décret numéro 97–532 du 23 mai 1997 pris pour son application.

APPENDIX

Pour l'application de l'article 46 de la loi du 10 juillet 1965, le vendeur confirme que la superficie du lot vendu répondant aux caractéristiques de ce texte est la suivante:
[*Area of property*]
   1. Le vendeur déclare que le mesurage a été effectué par lui même.

LUTTE CONTRE LE SATURNISME

Le vendeur déclare que l'immeuble objet des présentes n'etre pas dans le champ d'application de l'article L 32.5 du Code de la Santé Publique comme ayant été construit après le 31 décembre 1947.

TERMITES

Le VENDEUR déclare qu'a ce jour et à sa connaissance, l'immeuble n'est pas inclus dans une zone contaminé ou susceptible d'être contaminée par les termites au sens de l'article 3 de la loi n'99-471 du 8 juin 1999, et qu'il n'a pas connaissance de la présence de tels insectes dans l'immeuble.

La présente vente est donc soumise à la condition suspensive que l'immeuble vendu ne soit pas contaminé par les termites, et qu'il en soit justifié par la production d'un état négatif parasitaire ou par un certificat justifiant que l'immeuble vendu n'est pas altué dans une zone contaminée.

PRIX

La vente si elle se réalise, est consentie et acceptée moyennant le prix principal der
[*price*]
Que l'acquéreur s'oblige à payer au vendeur, qui accepte, comptant, le jour de la réalisation authentiques prévue ci-après.

VERSEMENT DE GARANTIE
CLAUSE PENALE

A la garantie des engagements pris par lui, l'acquéreur a remis à l'instant au vendeur, qui le reconnaît, une somme de ONZE MILLE DEUZ CENTS EUROS (11.200.00€).

Cette somme est versée dans la comptabilité de la société notariale sus-nommée.

Ladite somme viendra en compte sur le prix et les frais, lors de la réalisation de l'acte authentique, si elle a lieu, et si la vente se réalise dans le délai ci-après prévu.

Mais au cas où l'acte authentique de réalisation n'aurait pas été dressé par la faute ou du fait de l'acquéreur, dans le délai ci-après prévu, sauf l'effet de toutes conditions suspensives, ladite somme sera acquise définitivement au vendeur, à titre d'indemnité d'immobilisation, et de clause pénale forfaitaire, conformément aux articles 1152 et 1226 et suivants du *Code civil*, et ce HUIT (8) jours après une simple mise en demeure adressée à l'acquéreur, d'avoir à réaliser et restée sans effet par lettre recommandée avec accusé de réception, ce dernier faisant foi, ou par acte extrajudiciaire.

Cette somme s'imputera ou se confondra avec l'indemnité prévue ci-après sous le titre 'CLAUSE PENALE'.

Le notaire sus-nommé, en remettant les sommes dans les conditions ci-dessus prévues, sera bien et valablement déchargé, et à cet effet tous pouvoirs lui sont dès maintenant donnés de façon irrévocable par l'ACQUEREUR.

Il est précisé que la présente clause ne peur être assimilée à une stipulation d'arrhes et n'emporte pas novation. Ainsi chacune des parties aura la possibilité de poursuivre l'autre en exécution de la vente, comme il est dit ci-après sous le title 'REALISATION'.

CONDITIONS SUSPENSIVES

I *Conditions profitant à l'acquéreur:*

La vente est soumise aux conditions suspensives ci-après qui ne profiteront qu'à l'acquéreur, qui pourra y renoncer:

1. Que le certificat d'urbanisme ou la note de renseignements d'urbanisme qui sera délivré ne relève aucune prescription certaine ayant trait à l'alignement, à la destruction ou à l'expropriation de l'immeuble vendu, de nature à restraindra le droit de propriété ou de jouissance.

2. Que l'acquéreur obtienne un ou plusieurs prêts acquisition suivant les modalitées suivantes (application de la loi no 78-596 du 13 juillet 1979)

[Details of intended loan]

3. Que toutes les personnes désignées ci-dessus sous le terme 'Acquéreur' soient encore en vie à la date prévue pour la réalisation authentique des présentes.

4. Que le jour de la signature de l'acte authentique, le vendeur subroge l'acquéreur dans la bénéfice de l'assurance décennale afférente aux constructions objets des présentes et lui justifie de leur bonne conformité.

II *Conditions profitant au vendeur:*

Par dérogation à l'article 1179 de *Code civil*, la perfection de la vente et le transfert de propriété sont subordonnés à la condition de la signature de l'acte authentique, avec le paiement du prix et des frais.

III *Conditions suspensives profitant à toutes les parties:*

La présente vente et en outre soumise aux conditions suspensives ci-après qui profiteront à chacune des parties:

1. Que les parties soient capables au jour prévu pour la réalisation de l'acte authentique.

2. Que l'état hypothécaire qui sera requis préalablement à l'acte authentique ne révèle l'existence d'aucune inscription pour un montant supérieur au prix de vente ni d'aucune publication d'un commandement de saisie.

3. Qu'il n'existe aucun droit légal de préemption ou conventionnel sur l'immeuble objet des présentes, à moins de purge de ce droit avant l'expiration du délai prévu pour la réalisation authentique.

FACULTE DE RETRACTATION DE L'ACQUEREUR

Conformément aux dispositions du premier alinéa de l'article L271.1 du Code de la construction et de l'habitation, dans la rédaction que lui a donnée l'article 72 de la loi n°2000–1208 du 13 décembre 2000, l'acquéreur, non professionnel de l'immobilier, pourra se rétracter, à son seul gré et sans avoir à fournir quelque justification que ce soit quant à sa décision, dans un délai de sept jours à compter du lendemain de la première présentation de la lettre lui notifiant l'acte, si cette notification est effectuée par lettre recommandée avec demande d'avis de réception.

Afin de permettre à l'acquéreur d'exercer, le cas échéant, la faculté de rétractation qui lui est ainsi offerte par le texte précité, une copie du présent acte lui sera notifiée par lettre recommandée avec demande d'avis de réception ou par tout autre moyen présentant des garanties équivalentes pour la détermination de la date de réception ou de remise. Sera notamment considéré comme moyen présentant des garanties équivalentes, la remise d'une copie du présent acte contre signature, par l'acquéreur, d'un accusé de réception daté constatant cette remise.

Dans cette hypothèse, le délai de sept jours courra à compter du lendemain de cette remise.

En cas de rétractation dans le délai précité, les présentes seront caduques et ne pourront recevoir aucune exécution, même partielle.

Pour la notification des présentes, l'acquéreur élit domicile à l'adresse indiquée en tête des présentes.

EXERCICE DE LA RETRACTATION

La faculté de rétractation devra être exercée par l'acquéreur auprès du vendeur dans les mêmes formes que la notification de l'acte, et à l'intérieur du délai précité.

Pour la notification éventuelle de la rétractation, le vendeur élit domicile à l'adresse indiquée en tête des présentes.

RESTITUTION DES FONDS VERSES

En cas de rétractation, le dépositaire des fonds versés par l'acquéreur devra les restituer à ce dernier dans un délai de vingt et un jours à compter du lendemain de la date de rétractation, sur présentation de la copie de la notification de rétractation et de l'avis de réception (première présentation) ou du récépissé du vendeur.

REALISATION

Les présentes, sauf les effets suspensifs, lient les parties définitivement.

La vente sera réalisée par acte authentique à recevoir par le notaire rédacteur du présent compromis avec la participation de Maître [*Purchaser's notaire*], que les parties choisissent à cet effet d'un commun accord, dès la réalisation des conditions suspensives, et AU PLUS TARD LE [*Latest date for completion*].

Cette date n'est pas extinctive mais constitutive du point de départ à partir duquel l'une des parties pourra obliger l'autre à s'exécuter; notamment dès cette date, le vendeur pourra délivrer à l'acquéreur la sommation prévue ci-dessus sous le titre 'VERSEMENT DE GARANTIE'.

A défaut de réalisation avant l'expiration du délai fixé dans ladite sommation, le dépôt de garantie sera définitivement acquis au vendeur et les parties seront dégagées de plein droit de tous autres engagements pris aux présentes, ces dernières devenant nulles et non avenues, à moins que le vendeur ne préfère poursuivre la réalisation de la vente et réclamer tous dommages intérêts auxquels il pourrait avoir droit.

A défaut de réalisation de toutes les conditions suspensives ci-dessus et en cas de non renonciation à qui elles profitent avant la date prévue pour la réalisation de l'acte authentique, vendeur et acquéreur seront déliés de tous engagements sans indemnité de part ni d'autre 48 heures après l'envoi d'une lettre recommandée contenant leur intention d'user du bénéfice de la présente clause. Dans ce cas, le dépôt ci-dessus prévu sera restitué à l'acquéreur.

Le versement du dépôt de garantie prévu ci-dessus ne pourra être considéré comme un versement d'arrhes, et les parties ne pourront en aucun cas se prévaloir des dispositions de l'article 1590 du *Code civil*.

CLAUSE PENALE

Au cas où l'une quelconque des parties, après avoir été mise en demeure, ne régulariserait pas l'acte authentique et ne satisferait pas ainsi aux obligations alors exigibles—sauf l'effet des clauses suspensives prévues ci-dessus—elle devra verser à l'autre partie une somme égale à 10% du prix de la présente vente, à titre de clause pénale, conformément aux dispositions des articles 1152 et 1226 du *Code civil*.

Il est précisé que la présente clause ne peut être assimilée à une stipulation d'arrhes et n'emporte pas novation. Ainsi chacune des parties aura la possibilité de poursuivre l'autre en exécution de la vente, comme il est dit ci-dessus sous le titre 'REALISATION'.

FACULTE DE SUBSTITUTION

La réalisation par acte authentique pourra avoir lieu soit au profit de l'ACQUEREUR, soit au profit de toute personne physique ou morale que ce dernier se réserve de désigner, à la condition que cette substitution n'entraîne pas l'application des dispositions des articles L 312–1 et suivants du code de la consommation.

L'ACQUEREUR sera tenu, solidairement avec la personne substituée ou désignée, de tous les engagements pris envers le VENDEUR aux termes des présentes conventions.

La substitution devra obligatoirement être notifiée au notaire rédacteur des présentes, par lettre recommandée avec demande d'avis de réception:

—Après l'expiration du délai de rétractation réservé à l'acquéreur;

—Au plus tard le [*last date for notification of assignment of contract by Purchaser*].

RÉTRACTATION DU SUBSTITUÉ—MAINTIEN DE L'ENGAGEMENT DE L'ACQUÉREUR PRINCIPAL

Le substitué bénéficiera dans les conditions sus-indiquées, de la faculté de rétractation prévue par la loi 2000–1208 du 13 décembre 2000, s'il remplit les conditions prévues par ladite loi.

Il est toutefois expressément convenu qu'en cas de rétractation du substitué, l'acquéreur aux présentes, n'ayant pas utilisé la faculté de rétractation, sera tenu sans réserve (sauf l'effet des clauses suspensives) à l'exécution des présentes conventions.

FRAIS

L'acquéreur paiera tous les frais, droits et émoluments des présentes et de l'acte de vente, savoir:

1. *En ce qui concerne la vente*

Montant des frais, évalués par provision, en fonction des tarifs à ce jour, et de la destination de l'immeuble:

[*costs and disbursements of purchase*]

2. *En ce qui concerne la mise en place des prêts*

Les frais relatifs à la mise en place du ou des prêts, et des constitutions de garanties son évalués par provision à environ à:

[*costs and disbursements of loan*]

En cas de non réalisation du fait de l'acquéreur et si le dépôt de garantie est acquis au vendeur, il sera dû à la société notariale sus-nommée pour les présentes et toutes démarches et débours, à forfait, une somme égale à UN POUR CENT (1%) du prix stipulé.

ENREGISTREMENT

A la demande expresse des soussignés, les présentes ne seront pas enregistrées, mais si cette formalité devenait nécessaire, les droits simples seraient supportés par l'acquéreur, mais les pénalités et intérêts de retard, le cas échéant, seraient supportés par celles des parties qui auront rendu cette formalité nécessaire et ce pour quelque cause que ce soit.

PLUS-VALUE

Les parties reconnaissent avoir connaissance des dispositions fiscales concernant les plus-values et déclarent agir en toute connaissance de cause.

ETAT—CAPACITE

Les contractants confirment l'exactitude des indications les concernant respectivement telles qu'elles figurent ci-dessus.

Ils déclarent en outre qu'ils ne font l'objet d'aucune mesure ou procédure susceptible de restreindre leur capacité ou de mettre obstacle à la libre disposition de leurs biens.

L'acquéreur précise en outre:

—Qu'il déclare réaliser la présente acquisition à titre personnel.

—Qu'il n'est pas engagé dans le cadre d'un pacte civil de solidarité conclu dans les conditions prévues par la loi n°99 944 du 15 novembre 1999.

ELECTION DE DOMICILE

Pour l'exécution des présentes et de leurs suites, chacune des parties élit domicile en sa demeure sus-indiquée.

AFFIRMATION DE SINCERITE

Les parties déclarent sous les peines édictées par la loi que le prix stipulé aux présentes n'est modifié ni contredit par aucune contre-lettre contenant une augmentation du prix.

POUVOIRS

Du consentement de tous les intéressés, les présentes conventions ont été établies en un seul exemplaire qui demeurera entre les mains d'un des notaires associés de la société notariale sus-nommée dans l'intérêt commun des parties.

Les parties se donnent réciproquement tous pouvoirs à l'effet de déposer, si besoin est, les présentes conventions aux minutes de la société notariale sus-nommée, avec tous pouvoirs de reconnaître et réitérer les écritures, mentions et signatures, qu'elles déclarent dés à présent expressément reconnaitre et réitérer, et pour faire procéder aux formalités de publicité foncière.

Ce dépôt ne pourra être effectué, savoir:

SI LE REQUERANT EST LE VENDEUR, qu'après consignation dans la comptabilité de la société notariale sus-nommée des frais, droits et émoluments de l'acte de dépôt;

SI LE REQUERANT EST L'ACQUEREUR, qu'après consignation dans la comptabilité de la société notariale sus-nommée des frais, droits et émoluments de l'acte de dépôt, et du prix, ou de la partie du prix stipulée payable comptant.

Les parties confèrent expressément au présent mandant un caractère irrévocable.

FAIT [*number of original copies*]

Ainsi qu'il est dit ci-dessus,

A

Le

C. CERTIFICATS DE COUTUME

A leading textbook on French Private International Law says that in the light of the most recent decisions of the Cour de Cassation, 'the *notaire* should know the rules of French International Law and when these indicate that a foreign law applies, he should so advise the parties and seek the information himself'. It may be obtained 'by any means' but usually is provided by the parties themselves by means of a 'certificat de coutume' or Affidavit of Foreign Law. In the case of English law, this will be made by a Solicitor or by Counsel. The examples which follow give some indication of the circumstances in which such a Certificat is required.

1   Declaration of English law for sale/purchase by UK company of French land

CERTIFICAT DE COUTUME

Je soussigné [*name of Declarant*] demeurant à [*address*] Solicitor de la Cour Supreme en Angleterre [or other suitable qualification]
VU:
Une copie conforme du Certificat de Constitution de la société de droit anglais [*name on incorporation*] Limited en date [*date of incorporation*] et du Certificat de Changement de Désignation Sociale en date du [*date of change of name*] au nom de [*new name*] Limited
Une copie conforme de l'acte de constitution et des statuts de ladite société
Les registres concernant ladite société qu'elle est tenue de garder
Une copie conforme du procès-verbal d'une réunion du Conseil d'administration de ladite société tenue le [*date of Board Meeting*] dont une copie certifiée conforme avec traduction demeurent annexées aux présentes
Les lois et coutumes anglaises en matières de sociétés
ET ATTENDU:
1. Que le Certificat de Constitution sus-visé fait foi en droit anglais de la constitution sous forme de société à responsabilité limitée par actions de [*name on incorporation*] Limited et que le Certificat de Changement de Dénomination Sociale fait foi de la dénomination sociale actuelle de la société de [*new name*] Limited.
2. Que toute société de droit anglais est constituée pour une durée illimitée sauf dissolution volontaire ou forcée et une verification des registres tenus par le Greffier des Sociétés révèle qu'il n'y a aucune inscription tendant à une telle dissolution.
3. Que le siège social de ladite société est sis à [*Registered Office*], le capital de ladite société est de £[*authorized capital*] divisé en [*number of shares*] actions de £[*nominal value*] chacune et que [*names of Directors*] sont les administrateurs.
4. Que l'acte constitutif de ladite société qui n'a subi aucune modification depuis son adoption fait sauf le changement de dénomination sociale apparaître que les objets pour lesquels ladite société a été constituée comprennent l'acquisition ou vente ou par tout autre moyen l'aliénation en totalité ou en partie de tous biens mobiliers et immobiliers de sorte que rien n'empêche en droit anglais que ladite société [vende] [acquiert] un immeuble en France.

5. Que les statuts de ladite société font apparaître qu'elle est gérée par un Conseil d'administration dont le nombre sera déterminé par les associés de ladite société en assemblée générale qu'une telle détermination n'a jamais été faite à défaut de laquelle il sera composé d'un maximum illimité et d'un minimum d'un seul administrateur et que le Conseil d'administration est actuellement composé des personnes visées sous la rubrique 3 ci-dessus.

6. Que les pouvoirs du Conseil d'administration de la société sous réserve des modifications créés par les Articles of Association sont ceux visés aux Articles du Table A qui fait partie du décret SI 1985/805 (modifié ensuite par le décret SI 1985/1502) qui a modifié les articles des parties I et II du Table A du Companies Act 1948 réputés reproduits aux statuts en vertu de l'article 1 des Articles of Association qui font partie desdits statuts.

7. Qu'en vertu de l'Article 70 dudit Table A également réputé reproduit aux statuts de la société le Conseil d'administration a tous les pouvoirs pour engager la société et à une réunion du Conseil tenu le [date of Board Meeting] a résolu de [vendre] [acquérir] le bien immobilier [description of property] moyennant le prix de [sale/purchase price].

8. Que selon la loi anglaise sur les sociétés de 1985 la copie conforme du procès-verbal de ladite réunion signée par un membre du Conseil d'administration de ladite société doit être reçu comme faisant foi de son contenu.

CERTIFIE ET ATTESTE:

[Name of company] Limited est une société de droit anglais régulièrement constituée et toujours en existence ayant les siège social capital objets et administrateurs ci-dessus visés ayant valablement délibéré de [vendre] [acquérir] ledit bien immobilier et d'autoriser [name of Attorney] à signer au nom de ladite société un acte de vente et généralement faire tout ce qui sera utile ou nécessaire.

EN FOI DE QUOI je délivre le présent certificat de coutume pour servir et valoir ce que de droit.

Le

2   Declaration of English law on sale by Trustee in Bankruptcy of French property

CERTIFICAT DE COUTUME

Je soussigné [name of Declarant] demeurant à [address] Solicitor de la Cour Supreme en Angleterre [or other suitable qualification]

VU:

Une copie conforme ci-annexée du jugement déclaratif de faillite prononcé le [date of Order] par le Tribunal [Court making the Order] qui a déclaré en faillite [name of bankrupt owner]. Une copie conforme ci-annexée du certificat de M le Secrétaire d'Etat de confirmation de la désignation par ledit Tribunal de [name, address and occupation of Trustee in Bankruptcy] syndic de la faillite dudit [name of Bankrupt] à compter du [date of effect of Order]. Les lois et coutumes anglaises en matières de la faillite.

ET ATTENDU:

Qu'en droit anglais un jugement déclaratif de faillite entraine la cession automatique de la propriété de tous les biens meubles et immeubles appartenant à la personne contre qui a été prononcé un tel jugement à la personne qui a été nommé syndic en sa faillite de sorte que seul le syndic a la capacité de vendre ses biens et de donner quittance pour le prix de vente.

CERTIFIE ET ATTESTE:

Que [*name of Trustee in Bankruptcy*] a été régulièrement nommé syndic de la faillite de [*name of Bankrupt*] qui a été déclaré en faillite par un jugement déclaratif de faillite prononcé le [*date of Receiving Order*] par le tribunal de [*Court making the Order*] et qu'en conséquence il est la seule personne en droit anglais qui a la capacité de vendre à [*name of buyer*] les biens immobiliers plus amplement désignés dans sa procuration en date du [*date of Power of Attorney*] et de donner quittance pour le prix de vente de [*sale price*].

EN FOI DE QUOI je délivre le présent certificat de coutume pour servir et valoir ce que de droit.

Le

3   Declaration of English law to obtain *envoi en possession*

CERTIFICAT DE COUTUME

Je soussigné [*name of Declarant*] demeurant à [*address*] Solicitor de la Cour Supreme en Angleterre [or other suitable qualification]

CERTIFIE ET ATTESTE ce qui suit:

1. [*Name and address of deceased*] est décédé le [*date and place of death and nationality and domicile*].

2. Son testament est en date du [*date of Will*] dont une copie certifiée conforme par moi-même demeure annexée à ce certificat. Par article 1 de son testament le de cujus a désigné [*names of Executors*] pour etre exécuteurs testamentaires.

3. Une ordonnance du Grant of Probate en date du [*date of Probate*] dont une copie certi-fiée conforme par les Solicitors chargés de régler la succession demeure annexée à ce certificat a été délivrée par le Principal Probate Registry of the Family Division de la Haut Cour de Justice en Angleterre ce qui atteste la validité dudit testament et la nomination comme exécuteurs testamentaires desdits [*names of Executors*].

4. Par article 4 de son testament le de cujus a légué tous ses biens immobiliers et le surplus de ses biens mobiliers à son épouse [*name of surviving widow*] sous condition qu'elle soit toujours en vie 28 jours après son décès. Son épouse est toujours vivante de sorte que tous les autres articles de son testament qui ne devaient entrer en vigueur que si son épouse ne lui avait pas survecu pendant au moins 28 jours sont sans objet.

5. La succession en France comprend un bien immobilier à savoir [*description of the property*].

6. Le de cujus a laissé un seul héritier réservataire de ses biens immobiliers en France à savoir son fils [*name of son*] qui a renoncé à la succession de son père de sorte que l'arti-cle 4 de son testament joue sur la totalité de ses biens en France.

7. La loi applicable à l'étendue des pouvoirs des exécuteurs testamentaires est la loi anglaise. Ils ont la saisine de tous les biens meubles et immeubles de la succession y compris le pouvoir d'effectuer l'envoi en possession.

8. [*Names of Executors*] en tant qu'exécuteurs testamentaires du de cujus ont donc tous les pouvoirs nécessaires pour envoyer ladite [*name of surviving widow*] en possession dudit bien immobilier situé en France et généralement de faire le nécessaire.

EN FOI DE QUOI j'ai délivré le présent certificat de coutume.

Le

4   Declaration as to English intestacy law

CERTIFICAT DE COUTUME

Je soussigné [*name of Declarant*] demeurant à [*address*] Solicitor de la Cour Supreme en Angleterre [or other suitable qualification]

VU:

Le décès de Monsieur [*name of deceased and date and place of death*] domicilié en Angleterre sans aucune disposition de dernières volontés laissant lui survivant son épouse et deux enfants légitimes

L'acte de décès avec traduction du défunt qui demeure annexé à ce certificat

La survie de l'épouse de 28 jours après le décès du défunt

Les lois et coutumes anglaises en matière de successions

ET ATTENDU:

1. Que la succession dudit défunt consiste entièrement en mobilier en Angleterre et en France de sorte que la loi anglaise seule régit sa succession.

2. Que le défunt était propriétaire de [*number of shares*] parts de [*nominal value*] chacune entièrement libérées dans le capital de SARL ABC une société de droit français qui représentent 40% du capital de la société. Suite d'un arrêt du [*date of judgment*] de la Cour d'Appel de Montpellier 1° Chambre Section B il avait droit au jour de son décès au paiement de 40% de la somme maximale de [*amount of judgment*]. Cette somme représente approximativement l'équivalent de £60,000.

3. Que la succession du défunt en Angleterre ne dépasse pas le montant de £25.000 de sorte que la valeur net de sa succession ne dépasse pas le montant de £100.000.

4. Que selon Article 33-1 de la Loi anglaise sur les successions (The Administration of Estates Act 1925) modifié par une série de Statutory Instruments (Décrets) dont le dernier est numéro 2906 de 1993 à la date du décès dudit défunt quand un conjoint est en concours avec un ou plusieurs enfants, ce conjoint recueille en priorité la somme de £125.000 net de tous frais et droits de succession avec intérêt au taux de 7% du jour du décès et les meubles meublants et effets personnels du défunt. Si la succession dépasse cette valeur, le conjoint suvivant recueille l'usufruit de la moitié de l'excédant et les enfants la nue-propriété.

5. Que selon l'article 1-1 du Law Reform (Succession) Act 1995 pour être capable de succéder, son conjoint doit survivre le défunt par 28 jours.

CERTIFIE ET ATTESTE:

Que le défunt est décédé domicilié en Angleterre que sa succession est composée entière-ment de mobilier qui ne dépasse pas la somme de £125.000 et que selon la loi successo-rale qui régit sa succession en Angleterre et en France qui est la loi anglaise son épouse survivante recueille la totalité de sa succession à l'exclusion de toute autre personne.

EN FOI DE QUOI je délivre le présent certificat de coutume pour servir et valoir ce que de droit.

Le

5   Declaration of English law as to validity of Will

CERTIFICAT DE COUTUME

Je soussigné [*name of Declarant*] demeurant à [*address*] Solicitor de la Cour Supreme en Angleterre [or other suitable qualification]

CERTIFIE ET ATTESTE ce qui suit:

1. [*Name of deceased*] domicilié à [*address in France*] est décédé le [*date of death*] à [*place of death in France*].

2. Selon l'article 1 de la Convention de la Haye du 5 octobre 1961 qui est en vigueur en France un testament est considéré comme valable quant à la forme si celle-ci répond à la loi interne du lieu où le testateur a disposé ou du lieu de la nationalité du testateur.

3. Son testament est en date du [*date of Will*] dont une copie certifiée conforme par moi-même avec une traduction faite par moi-même demeurent annexées à ce certificat. Il est établi en Angleterre en la forme anglaise, c'est à dire en présence de deux témoins et signatures concomitantes du testateur et les deux témoins selon les conditions requises par l'article 9 du Wills Act 1837 modifié par l'article 17 de l'Administration of Justice Act 1982. En plus, il était de nationalité britannique.

4. Le testament de [*name of deceased*] est donc valable en France.

EN FOI DE QUOI je délivre le présent certificat de coutume pour servir et valoir ce que de droit.

Le

D. WILLS

It is not possible nor of any value to provide a series of precedents of Wills. In the first place, it will rarely be necessary for an English Testator to make a French Will and in many cases the law itself makes the necessary provisions. Nor is there any object in giving a Precedent of a 'testament mystique' which is only a holograph Will in a sealed envelope and virtually never used or a 'testament authentique' which in its contents is the same as a 'testament olographe' save that its terms are likely to be expressed with more elegance since it is the *notaire* who translates the wishes of the Testator into words.

1   Holograph Will giving maximum permitted by law to surviving spouse when there are surviving relatives

Je soussignée [*name, address and occupation of Testator*] révoque toutes dispositions antérieures aux présentes en ce qui concerne ma succession en France.

1. Je lègue à mon époux/se la pleine propriété de tous les biens meubles et immeubles qui composeront ma succession en France au jour de mon décès sans exception ni réserve.

2. Si la réduction de ce legs à mon époux/se est demandée, je lègue à mon époux/se en toute propriété un quart et en usufruit trois quarts de ma succession en France au jour de mon décès. Pour les biens dont mon époux/se aura l'usufruit, je le/la dispense de faire emploi et de fournir caution et de faire dresser inventaire. Si l'un de mes enfants vient à mourir avant moi sa part reviendra à ses enfants suivant les règles de la représentation et à défaut de descendants, la part du légataire décédé accroîtra aux survivants.

Fait et écrit et daté entièrement de ma main à [*place and date of execution*].

2   Holograph Will leaving surviving spouse choice of maximum interest in estate when there are surviving *réservataires*

Je soussignée [*name, address and occupation of Testator*] révoque toutes dispositions antérieures aux présentes en ce qui concerne ma succession en France.

Je lègue à mon époux/se à son choix à être exercé dans les [*number*] mois après mon décès soit de la pleine propriété la quotité disponible la plus large permise par la loi en faveur d'un étranger et le cas échéant de la nue-propriété de la fraction constituant la réserve des ascendants soit de l'usufruit de l'universalité de tous les biens qui composeront ma succession soit de la pleine propriété d'un quart et à son gré d'un ou de trois autres quarts de l'universalité de tous les même biens.

Ce choix appartiendra exclusivement à mon époux/se et au cas où il/elle décède avant d'avoir exercée son option, il/elle sera considéré(e) avoir opté pour l'usufruit universel.

Fait et écrit et daté entièrement de ma main à [*place and date of execution*].

3 Will giving statutory reserve to only child and other half to a stranger

Ceci est mon testament:

Je soussigné [*name, address and occupation of Testator*] prends les dispositions suivantes.

Je révoque tout testament antérieur.

Je nomme pour exécuteurs testamentaires [*names, addresses and occupations*] avec faculté d'agir avec ou sans solidarité et la faculté pour chacun de se faire remplacer par une personne de son choix dans les pouvoirs résultants du présent testament.

Mes exécuteurs auront la saisine de tous les biens meubles pendant le délai légal d'un an et un jour à compter du jour de mon décès et auront le choix de notaire pour régler ma succession. Ils seront rémunerés des honoraires qui leur seront dus.

Je désire être [incinéré et les cendres . . . . .] [enterré dans le cimetière de la commune où je serai domicilié au jour de mon décès.]

Je lègue à mon fils [*name*] la moitié de l'universalité des biens qui composeront ma succession. Au cas où il viendra à décéder avant moi, sa part sera recueillie par ses descendants selon les règles de la dévolution légale et de la représentation. A défaut de descendant, sa part accroîtrait à la moitié léguée à [*name of legatee of the other half*].

Je lègue à . . . . . l'autre moitié de l'universalité des biens qui composeront ma succession. Au cas où il viendrait à décéder avant moi, sa part profitera à ses héritiers.

Fait écrit et daté en entier de ma main à [*place and date of execution*].

[*Signature*]

4 International Will

Je, soussigné [*name, address and full état civil of Testator*], déclare faire mon testament de la façon suivante:

Je désigne . . . . . pour exécuteurs testamentaires avec les pouvoirs les plus étendus en ce qui concerne le mobilier.

J'institue pour mes légataires universels par égale part entre eux pour moitié chacun [*names and addresses of residuary legatees*].

Avec précision qu'en cas de prédécès de l'un d'entre eux, la part du prémourant accroîtra à celle du survivant.

Je lègue à titre particulier net de tous frais et droits savoir [*names and addresses of specific and pecuniary legatees*].

Je révoque tous testament et codicilles antérieurs.

Signé et daté le . . . . . à . . . . .

[*Signature of Testator and signatures of two witnesses*]

ATTESTATION

(délivrée en vertu de la Convention de Washington du 26 octobre 1973, ratifiée t entrée en vigueur le 1er décembre 1994 en France)

LA SOUSSIGNEE [*name of notaire*], notaire à [*town*], personne habilitée à instrumenter en matière de testament international.

ATTESTE

Que le [*date and place*], [*the Testator*] s'est présenté au notaire accompagné de ses témoins et a déclaré que le document ci-joint est son testament et qu'il en connaît le contenu.

E. AFFIDAVITS OF FRENCH LAW

NCP Rule 19 requires that in foreign domicile cases, the Probate Registry will ask for an Affidavit from a suitably qualified person as to the law in the country of the domicile of the deceased to establish who is entitled to a Grant in accordance with Rule 30. Each case can present widely varying circumstances and it is desirable to submit the Affidavit in draft form to the Registry before it is sworn. The Registry is extremely helpful in difficult cases.

1   Affidavit of French law to lead to an English Grant

IN THE HIGH COURT OF JUSTICE
FAMILY DIVISION
THE . . . . . PROBATE REGISTRY
IN the Estate of . . . . . ABC . . . . . deceased
I, [*Name and address of Deponent*], [*professional qualification such as Solicitor*], make oath and say as follows:
1. I am conversant with the laws of France having for upwards of [. . .] years advised on and been involved in many cases of persons who have died domiciled both in France and in England and Wales both testate and intestate who have made Wills in a form valid according to the laws of France and whose estates are subject to the laws of that country.
2. ABC ('the deceased') died domiciled in France a widower leaving surviving him only his three lawful children DEF, GHI and JKL. By his Will dated the . . . . . day of . . . . . Two thousand . . . . . he disposed of the whole of his estate which did not include immovable property in England or Wales to his said children.
3. The said Will is in my opinion valid according to the laws of France since that country is a signatory to the 1961 Hague Convention on the formal validity of Wills which came into force in France on the 19th November 1967. In accordance with that Convention, the deceased who was a British subject could make a Will recognized by French law as valid as to its form if the same was validly executed in accordance with the laws of England and the same appears to be so validly executed.
4. Since the deceased died domiciled in France, French laws of succession apply to his estate. Article 913 of the French Civil Code reads (in translation) 'No disposition whether made *inter vivos* or by Will may exceed one half of the assets of the disponer if he leaves surviving him one child; one-third, if he leaves two children; one-quarter, if he leaves three or more children and so that no distinction shall be made between legitimate and illegitimate children save in the case provided for by Article 915.' The provisions of this Article are d'ordre public and therefore cannot be varied by the disponer nor can any variation made be declared valid by the Court.
5. The terms of the said Will of the deceased therefore wholly accord with the relevant provisions of the French Civil Code.
6. Article 1004 of the French Civil Code reads (in translation) as follows: 'When on the death of a testator, there are heirs who are by law entitled to a share of his estate, there shall by virtue of such death become vested in such heirs all the assets comprised in the estate . . . . .' The said children of the deceased are heirs within the meaning of that Article. Ownership of such assets includes the power to exercise all the rights vested in the

deceased at his death. No Order of the French Court is required to confirm who are these heirs nor to vest this ownership (la saisine) jointly in them and such proof of the rights of such persons as may be required by third parties depends entirely upon an acte de notoriété après décès prepared by the Notary instructed by them.

7. It follows therefore that the administration of the estate of the deceased in accordance with the law of his domicile at the date of his death is vested solely in the three said children of the deceased irrespective of whoever may have been named as Executors in the said Will and they are the persons entitled to a Grant of Probate under the provisions of NCP Rule 30 (1) (b).

SWORN etc.

2   Affidavit of French law to lead to an English Grant where a beneficiary renounces

IN THE HIGH COURT OF JUSTICE
FAMILY DIVISION
THE . . . . . PROBATE REGISTRY
IN the Estate of ABC deceased
I, [*name and address of Deponent*], [professional qualification such as Solicitor], make oath and say as follows:

1. I am conversant with the laws of France having for upwards of [. . .] years advised on and been involved in many cases of persons who have died domiciled both in France and in England and Wales both testate and intestate who have made Wills in a form valid according to the laws of France and whose estates are subject to the laws of that country.

2. ABC ('the deceased') died domiciled in France intestate leaving surviving her lawful husband and a lawful sister of the whole blood.

3. Since the deceased died domiciled in France, French laws of succession as they were at the date of death of the deceased prior to the 1st July 2002 applied to her estate. Article 765 of the French Civil Code then read in translation 'If the deceased left no persons within the degrees entitled by law to succeed or if he left only collateral relations other than brothers and sisters or their issue his estate vests absolutely in his surviving spouse.' Article 767 of the said Code read in translation 'The surviving spouse who is not entitled to succeed absolutely to the whole of the (deceased's) estate . . . . . is entitled to a life interest in one half of the estate if the deceased left surviving brothers or sisters. . . . .'

4. Articles 784 and 785 of the said Code read in translation 'renunciation of an inheritance . . . . . can only be made to the Registrar of the Court in the place in which the administration of the estate takes place and is recorded in a register kept for that sole purpose. A person entitled to an interest in an estate who renounces such interest is presumed never to have been entitled thereto.'

5. The said sister of the deceased duly renounced her interest to which she was entitled in the estate of the said deceased by notice to the Registrar of the Tribunal de Grande Instance at . . . . . and the same was recorded in the appropriate register on the . . . . . day of . . . . . 1995. There is now produced and shown to me marked ' . . . . . ' a certified copy of an extract from such register recording such renunciation as aforesaid. Hence, in accordance with the said Article 785 she is deemed never to have had an interest in the estate of the said deceased and therefore by virtue of the said Article 765 the surviving spouse of the deceased is the only person entitled to the estate of the said deceased.

6. Article 724 of the said Code provides that all the rights and powers of a deceased person vest in (among other persons who are entitled to succeed to the estate) a surviving spouse subject only to payment of all liabilities and expenses of the estate and no Order of the Court is required to confirm who are these such persons nor to vest this ownership in them.

7. It follows therefore that the administration of the estate of the said deceased is in accordance with the law of her domicile at the date of her death vested solely in her lawful husband.

SWORN etc.

3 Affidavit of French law to lead to an English Grant of French Will drawn in English

IN THE HIGH COURT OF JUSTICE
FAMILY DIVISION
THE . . . . . PROBATE REGISTRY
IN the Estate of ABC deceased
I, [*name and address of Deponent*], [professional qualification such as Solicitor], make oath and say as follows:

1. I am conversant with the laws of France having for upwards of [. . .] years advised on and been involved in many cases of persons who have died domiciled both in France and in England and Wales both testate and intestate who have made Wills in a form valid according to the laws of France and whose estates are subject to the laws of that country.

2. ABC ('the deceased') died domiciled in France without parent or issue surviving him.

3. The deceased executed a holograph Will dated the . . . . . The said Will is in my opinion valid according to the laws of France since it is written entirely in the hand of and is signed and dated by the deceased. This accords with the requirements of Article 970 of the French *Code civil* which reads (in translation) 'A holograph Will shall not be valid unless it is written entirely in and signed and dated by the hand of the Testator and no other formality is required.'

4. The said Will which, save for the date of execution, is written entirely in English has clearly been drafted by a person other than the deceased and that person had a very limited knowledge of the English language and far less knowledge of English law than she thought she had. The result is that the draftsman has used a form of English wording which is in part a literal translation from French and in part is mock legal English.

5. The phrase 'I appoint DEF as my Executor and general devissee [sic] and legatee. He will have to deliver to . . . . .' is a translation of 'Je nomme pour exécuteur testamentaire DEF et je l'institue pour mon légataire universel à charge par lui de . . . . .'.

6. Given that the concept of a trust is unknown in French law, the making of a legacy to a named person 'à charge de . . . . .' creates an obligation in favour of the person whose name follows these words to pay over the legacy and is the best equivalent available to a French Testator of the creation of an English bare trust. In such a case, the 'légataire universel' or residuary beneficiary is entitled to benefit from the assets comprised in the estate of the testator subject to his handing over to the person named as the recipient such of those assets as are subject to the 'charge'. If the 'légataire universel' fails to comply with this requirement, by virtue of the joint effect of Articles 954 and 1046 of the French

Code civil, he may be deprived of his own benefit under the terms of the Testator's Will. He nevertheless inherits as though he were a beneficial owner whose benefit is liable to defeasance and not as a fiduciary owner.

7. Since the said deceased died without parent or issue surviving him, there are no 'héritiers réservataires' (ie persons who according to the laws of France have inheritance rights in his real or personal estate) and he could therefore lawfully dispose freely of his estate in any manner he may have wished.

8. The Will of the deceased is a holograph Will and therefore the said DEF, being a 'légataire universel' but not an 'héritier réservataire' or person who is entitled to inherit by law, is required by Article 1008 of the *Code civil* to obtain an Order of 'envoi en possession'. This is not an Order confirming his benefit under the said Will but confirming the validity of the said Will and such an Order was obtained from the Tribunal de Grande Instance at on the [*date of envoi en possession*].

9. The appointment of the said DEF as 'executor' takes effect only as an appointment as 'exécuteur testamentaire' in accordance with French law. He had in that capacity no property vested in him nor did he have any administrative powers of any consequence. As Article 1031 of the French *Code civil* says an Executor merely 'oversees the carrying into effect of the terms of the Will'. In any event, even if it were said that a person appointed an 'exécuteur testamentaire' is 'an executor therein named' referred to in section (3)(a)(i) or (ii) of the Non-Contentious Probate Rules, the appointment of the said DEF to that office lapsed on the first anniversary of the death of the said deceased and the duties and powers of an 'exécuteur testamentaire' can never be such as to 'constitute him executor according to the tenor of the Will'.

10. Article 724 of the French *Code civil* reads (in translation) 'There vests by operation of law in the lawful heirs (of a deceased) . . . . . all the estate, interests and rights of the deceased subject only to the discharge of any liabilities in respect thereof.' Thus, in this case, the said DEF in his capacity as 'legataire universel' is entitled as from the date of death of the deceased to the benefit of the whole of the estate of the deceased without the intervention of any further formality.

11. It follows, therefore, that the said Will having been confirmed as valid by the said Order of 'envoi en possession', the said DEF is the only person who fulfils the requirements of Rule 30 (1) (b) of the Non-Contentious Probate Rules as the person entitled to apply for an English Grant of Representation.

SWORN etc.

F. COMPANIES

The Precedent for the *Statuts* of an SCI is in standard form. Care must be taken with the clauses relating to capital, how it is provided, to whom issued and, if it is held jointly, in what manner. Alternatives are provided for who is to manage the company and a decision should not be reached in this respect without expert advice. No difficulties should arise in connection with the other Precedents.

1   Statuts of a *Société Civile Immobilière*

L'AN,
Le,
EN L'OFFICE NOTARIAL CI-APRES DENOMME,

Maître
A reçu le présent acte authentique entre les parties ci-après identifiées.

STATUTS DE SOCIETE CIVILE
IDENTIFICATION DES ASSOCIES
PRESENCE—REPRESENTATION
[*Details of Subscribers*]

ETAT-CAPACITE

Chaque associé confirme l'exactitude des indications le concernant respectivement, telles qu'elles figurent ci-dessus.
Il déclare en outre n'avoir fait l'objet d'aucune condamnation ou mesure entraînant l'interdiction de contrôler, diriger ou administrer une société. Lesquels ont établi ainsi qu'il suit les statuts d'une société civile présentant les caractéristiques suivantes:

PREMIERE PARTIE
STATUTS

ARTICLE 1—FORME

La société est de forme civile régie par le titre IX du livre III du *Code civil*, modifié par la loi du 4 janvier 1978 et le décret du 3 juillet 1978.

ARTICLE 2—DENOMINATION

La dénomination de la société est [*name of company*].
La dénomination sociale doit figurer sur tous documents émanant de la société destinés aux tiers, précédée ou suivie des mots 'société civile', puis de l'indication du capital social, du siège social, de son numéro d'identification au SIREN, de l'indication du siège du tribunal du greffe où elle est immatriculée à titre principal.

ARTICLE 3—SIEGE SOCIAL

Le siège social est fixé à [*Registered Office*].
Il peut être transféré partout ailleurs sur décision collective des associés de nature extraordinaire.

La société sera immatriculée au registre du commerce et des sociétés de [*relevant town*].

ARTICLE 4—OBJET SOCIAL

La société a pour objet:
– l'acquisition, soit en pleine propriété, soit en jouissance, soit sous toutes autres modalités, de tous immeubles bâtis ou non bâtis;
– la réalisation de tous travaux de construction, amélioration, agrandissement et rénovation des immeubles;
– l'administration, la gestion et l'exploitation desdits immeubles nus par bail;
– l'emprunt de toute personne ou établissement financier en une ou plusieurs fois, de toute somme en principal en vue de l'acquisition des biens immobiliers entrant dans l'objet social. La société peut notamment constituer tout privilège ou hypothèque portant sur les immeubles sociaux, dès lors que ces actes ou opérations, ne portent pas atteinte à la nature civile de cet objet.
– Et, plus généralement, toutes opérations, de toute nature qu'elles soient, se rattachant directement ou indirectement à cet objet, et susceptibles d'en favoriser la réalisation.

ARTICLE 5—DUREE

La durée de la société est de 99 ans à compter de son immatriculation au registre du commerce et des sociétés.

ARTICLE 6—APPORTS

[Les associés font apport à la société, savoir:
Mr ABC, de la somme de Euro 50.000 en espèces, ci: Euro 50.000
Mme ABC, de la somme de Euro 50.000 en espèces, ci: Euro 50.000
Total des apports: Euro 100.000]
[or]
Il n'est fait aucun apport en numéraire
Mr ABC fait apport à la société de la moitié indivise du bien ci-après désigné. Lequel apport évalué à Euro 50.000 est fait à titre pur et simple.
Mme ABC fait apport à la société de la moitié indivise du bien ci-après désigné. Lequel apport évalué à Euro 50.000 est fait à titre pur et simple.

DESIGNATION DE L'APPORT

[*description of property as in acte de vente on purchase by subscribers*]
Libération des apports en numéraire:
Les sommes dues devront être versées dans les quinze jours de la demande qui sera notifiée, sous pli recommandé avec demande d'avis de réception, par la gérance.
Tout versement tardif sera générateur d'intérêts au taux légal.

ARTICLE 7—CAPITAL SOCIAL

Le capital social s'élève à la somme de Euro 100.000 montant des apports ci-dessus effectués. Il est divisé en 1.000 parts sociales de Euro 100 chacune, numérotées de 1 a 1.000 et attribuées aux associés dans la proportion et en rémunération de leurs apports respectifs, savoir:

[if the Subscribers take individually:]
Monsieur ABC à concurrence de 500 parts numérotées de 1 à 500
Madame ABC à concurrence de 500 parts numérotées de 501 à 1.000
[or if the Subscribers take en tontine:
Monsieur et Madame ABC conviennent par la présente convention de mettre 998 parts sociales qu'ils viennent de souscrire en tontine à titre de pacte aléatoire au profit de celui d'entre eux qui survivra à l'autre sans que les héritiers et représentants du prédécédé puissent prétendre à aucun droit sur lesdits biens.

ARTICLE 8—PARTS SOCIALES

Titre:
La propriété des parts sociales résulte seulement des statuts, des actes les modifiant, des cessions et mutations ultérieures, qui seraient régulièrement consentis, constatées et publiées.
Tout associé peut, après toute modification statutaire, demander la délivrance d'une copie certifiée conforme des statuts en vigueur au jour de la demande. A ce document est annexée la liste mise à jour des associés, des gérants et, le cas échéant, des autres organismes sociaux.
Les parts sociales ne sont pas négociables.

Droits attachés aux parts:
Chaque part donne droit, dans la répartition des bénéfices, des réserves et du boni de liquidation, à une fraction proportionnelle au nombre de parts existantes.
Chaque part donne également droit de participer aux assemblées générales des associés et d'y voter.

Usufruit:
Si une part sociale est grevée d'usufruit, le droit de vote appartient à l'usufruitier pour les décisions prises lors des assemblées générales ordinaires et au nu-propriétaire pour celles prises en assemblée générale extraordinaire.

Indivisibilité des parts:
Chaque part sociale est indivisible à l'égard de la société. Les propriétaires indivis d'une ou plusieurs parts sociales sont représentés auprès de la société dans les diverses manifestations de la vie sociale par un MANDATAIRE unique choisi parmi les indivisaires ou les associés. En cas de désaccord, le MANDATAIRE est désigné en justice, à la demande du plus diligent des indivisaires.

ARTICLE 9—MUTATION ENTRE VIFS

Opposabilité:
Toute mutation entre vifs de parts sociales doit être constatée par acte authentique ou sous seing privé.
Elle n'est opposable à la société qu'après la signification ou l'acceptation prévue à l'article 1690 du *Code civil*.

Domaine de l'agrément:
Toutes opérations, notamment toutes cessions, échanges, apports à société d'éléments isolés, attributions en suite de liquidation d'une communauté de biens du vivant des époux

ou ex-époux, donations, ayant pour but ou pour conséquence le transfert d'un droit quelconque de propriété sur une ou plusieurs parts sociales entre toutes personnes physiques ou morales à l'exception de celles qui seraient visées à l'alinéa qui suit, sont soumises à l'agrément de la société.

Organe compétent:
L'agrément est de la compétence de la collectivité des associés se prononçant par décision ordinaire.

Procédure d'agrément:
Le CEDANT notifie le projet de cession avec la demande d'agrément par acte d'huissier de justice ou par lettre recommandée avec demande d'avis de réception, à la société et à chacun de ses associés, en indiquant les nom, prénom, domicile et profession du futur CESSIONNAIRE ainsi que le délai dans lequel la cession projetée doit être régularisée.
La collectivité des associés statue dans le mois de la notification, sur la totalité des parts faisant l'objet du projet de cession.
En cas d'agrément d'un ou de plusieurs CESSIONNAIRES, avis en est immédiatement donné au CEDANT par lettre recommandée avec accusé de réception.

Procédure de non-agrément:
Préalablement à un refus d'agrément, les associés disposent d'un delai d'un mois pour se porter ACQUEREUR et si plusieurs d'entre eux manifestent cette volonté, ils sont réputés ACQUEREURS à proportion du nombre de parts qu'ils détenaient antérieurement.
Si aucun associé ne se porte ACQUEREUR, la société peut faire acquérir les parts par un tiers agréé par la gérance. La société peut également procéder au rachat des parts en vue de leur annulation.
La gérance notifie au CEDANT, par lettre recommandée avec demande d'avis de réception, le nom du ou des ACQUEREURS proposés, associés ou tiers, ou l'offre de rachat de la société, ainsi que le prix offert.
En cas de contestation sur le prix, celui-ci est fixé conformément aux dispositions de l'article 1843-4 du *Code civil*.
Toutefois, le CEDANT peut décider de conserver ses parts lors même que le prix adopté par les experts serait égal à celui moyennant lequel devait avoir lieu la cession projetée.
Si aucune offre d'achat n'est faite au CEDANT dans un délai de six mois à compter du jour de la notification par lui faite à la société de son projet de cession, l'agrément est réputé acquis à moins que les autres associés ne décident dans le même délai, la dissolution anticipée de la société.
Dans ce dernier cas, le CEDANT peut rendre cette décision caduque en faisant connaître qu'il renonce à la cession dans le délai d'un mois à compter de ladite décision.

ARTICLE 10—DECES
DISPARITION D'UNE PERSONNE MORALE ASSOCIEE

Les héritiers, légataires, dévolutaires d'une personne morale associée, doivent justifier de leurs qualités et demander leur agrément, s'il y a lieu, selon ce qui est dit à l'article 9.
Les héritiers, légataires ou dévolutaires qui ne deviennent pas associés n'ont droit qu'à la valeur des parts sociales de leur auteur. Cette valeur doit être payée par les nouveaux titulaires des parts ou par la société elle-même, si celle-ci les a rachetées en vue de leur annulation.

De même, sous quelque prétexte que ce soit, ils ne peuvent requérir l'apposition de scellés sur les biens et documents de la société, ni s'immiscer en aucune manière dans les actes de son administration.

ARTICLE 11—RETRAIT D'ASSOCIE

Tout associé peut se retirer totalement ou partiellement de la société sur l'accord de tous les autres associés.
Il peut aussi intervenir pour juste motif ou décision de justice.

ARTICLE 12—RECOURS À L'EXPERTISE

En cas de recours à l'expertise et à défaut d'accord entre les parties, les frais et honoraires sont respectivement supportés par moitié par les anciens et nouveaux titulaires des parts sociales, mais solidairement entre eux à l'égard de l'expert. La répartition entre chacun d'eux a lieu au prorata du nombre de pars anciennement ou nouvellement détenues.
En cas de retrait, le retrayant supporte seul la charge de l'expertise éventuelle.

ARTICLE 13—GERANCE

Nomination:
La gérance est assurée par un ou plusieurs gérants, personnes physiques ou morales [qui ne sont pas associé ou le conjoint ou membre de la famille d'un associé ou un de ses préposés] [associés ou non], avec les pouvoirs les plus étendus pour l'accomplissement de tous les actes entrant dans l'objet social et qui demande l'intérêt social. A cet effet, chacun gérant aura la signature sociale et pourra recevoir et payer toutes sommes, faire tous achats, ventes et marchés pouvant se rapporter à l'objet social, transiger, compromettre, donner tous désistements et mainlevées avec ou sans paiements, exercer et défendre à toutes actions judiciaires, représenter la société à toutes procédures de redressement ou de liquidation judiciaire, souscrire, accepter, endosser, avaliser et acquitter tous effets de commerce,
Cette nomination résulte d'une décision collective ordinaire des associés.
La durée des fonctions de la gérance est indéterminée.

Première nomination:
La gérance de la société sera exercée sans limitation de durée par: [*name of first gérant*].
Les 'cogérants' déclarent accepter les fonctions qui viennent de leur être conférées.
Le décès de l'un des co-gérants entraînera le transfert de la gérance au survivant.

Pouvoirs—Rapports avec les tiers:
Dans les rapports avec les tiers, le gérant ou chacun des gérants engage la société par les actes entrant dans l'objet social. L'opposition formée par un gérant aux actes d'un autre gérant est sans effet à l'égard des tiers, à moins qu'il ne soit établi qu'ils en ont eu connaissance.

Pouvoirs—Rapports avec les associés:
Dans les rapports avec les associés, le gérant peut accomplir tous les actes entrant dans l'objet social que demande l'intérêt social.
S'il y a plusieurs gérants, ils exercent séparément ces pouvoirs, sauf le droit qui appartient à chacun de s'opposer à une opération avant qu'elle ne soit conclue.

Rémunération:

La gérance [n'a droit à aucune rémunération] [a droit à une rémunération dont le montant et les conditions seront arrêtées par l'assemblée générale des associés] et au remboursement de ses frais de représentation et de déplacement sur justification.

Révocation:

Un gérant est révocable par décision de justice pour cause légitime.

Il est également révocable par décision unanime des autres associés.

Décidée sans juste motif, la révocation peut donner lieu à dommages et intérêts.

Le gérant révoqué peut se retirer de la société à la condition d'en présenter la demande dans les quinze jours de la décision de révocation.

A moins qu'il ne demande la reprise en nature du bien qu'il avait apporté, le gérant révoqué a droit au remboursement de la valeur de ses parts fixée, à défaut d'accord amiable, conformément à l'article 1843–4 du *Code civil*.

ARTICLE 14—DECISIONS COLLECTIVES

Forme:

Les décisions collectives sont prises en assemblée, par voie de consultation écrite ou constatées dans un acte revêtu de la signature de tous les associés.

Décisions extraordinaires:

Sont de nature extraordinaire toutes les décisions emportant modification directe ou indirecte des statuts, ainsi que celles dont les présents statuts exigent expressément qu'elles revêtent une tell nature.

Décisions ordinaires:

Sont de nature ordinaire toutes décisions collectives qui ne sont pas dans le champ d'application des décisions de nature extraordinaire.

Composition:

Tous les associés ont le droit d'assister aux assemblées et chacun d'eux peut s'y faire représenter par un autre associé. Chaque associé dispose d'un nombre de voix égal à celui des parts sociales dont il est titulaire.

Convocation:

Sauf lorsque tous les associés sont gérants, les assemblées sont convoquées par la gérance ou sur la demande d'un de plusieurs associés représentant la moitié au moins de toutes les parts sociales.

Les convocations doivent être adressées par lettre recommandée au moins quinze jours avant la date de réunion. Celles-ci indiquent le lieu de réunion, ainsi que l'ordre du jour, de telle sorte que le contenu et la portée des questions qui y seront inscrites apparaissent clairement sans qu'il y ait lieu de se reporter à d'autres documents.

Les convocations peuvent aussi être verbales et sans délai si tous les associés sont présents ou représentés.

Consultations écrites:

En cas de consultation écrite, le texte des résolutions proposées ainsi que les documents nécessaires à l'information des associés sont adressés à chacun d'eux par lettre recommandée avec demande d'avis de réception.

Chaque associé dispose pour émettre son vote par écrit du délai fixé par la gérance; ce délai ne peut être inférieur à quinze jours à compter de la date de réception de ces documents.

Le vote résulte de l'apposition au pied de chaque résolution, de la main de chaque associé, des mots 'adopté' ou 'rejeté', étant entendu qu'à défaut d'une telle mention, l'associé est réputé s'être abstenu.

Procès-verbaux:

Les procès-verbaux des décisions collectives sont établis et signés par tous les associés conformément aux dispositions de l'article 44 du décret n° 78–704 du juillet 1978, sur un registre spécial tenu conformément aux dispositions de l'article 45 de ce décret, les décisions résultant du consentement exprimé dans un acte étant mentionnées à leur date, avec indication de la forme, de la nature, de l'objet et des signataires de l'acte. Ce dernier lui-même, s'il est sous seing privé, ou sa copie authentique s'il est notarié, est conservé par la société de manière à permettre sa consultation, en même temps que le registre des délibérations. Les copies ou extraits des procès-verbaux des délibérations des associés sont valablement certifiés conformes par un seul gérant et, en cas de liquidation, par un seul liquidateur.

ARTICLE 15—EXERCICE SOCIAL

L'exercice social s'étend du 1er janvier au 31 décembre de chaque année. Exceptionnellement, le premier exercice social qui commencera lors de l'immatriculation de la présente société au registre du commerce et des sociétés prendra fin le 31 décembre de la même année.

ARTICLE 16—COMPTABILITE—COMPTES ANNUELS—BENEFICES

Les comptes sociaux sont tenus conformément au Plan comptable national.

Les bénéfices nets sont constitués par les produits nets de l'exercice, sous déduction des frais généraux et autres charges, en ce compris toutes provisions et amortissements.

Le bénéfice distribuable est constitué par le bénéfice net de l'exercice, diminué des pertes antérieures et augmenté des reports BENEFICIAIRES.

ARTICLE 17—AFFECTATION DU RESULTAT—REPARTITION

Par décision collective, les associés—après approbation des comptes de l'exercice écoulé et constatation de l'existence d'un bénéfice distribuable—procèdent à toutes distributions, reports à nouveau, inscriptions à tous comptes de réserves dont ils fixent l'affectation et l'emploi.

Ils peuvent également décider la distribution de toutes réserves.

Les modalités de la mise en paiement sont fixées par la décision de répartition ou, à défaut, par la gérance.

Les pertes, s'il en existe, sont, au gré des associés, compensées avec les réserves existantes ou reportées à nouveau.

ARTICLE 18—DISSOLUTION

La société prend fin par l'expiration du temps pour lequel elle a été contractée.

La collectivité des associés peut, à toute époque, prononcer la dissolution anticipée de la société.

Cette décision doit être prise à la majorité des voix dont dispose l'ensemble des associés et à l'unanimité s'il n'y a que deux associés.

La société n'est dissoute par aucun événement susceptible d'affecter l'un de ses associés, et notamment:

Le décès, l'incapacité, le redressement ou la liquidation judiciaire d'un associé personne physique.

La dissolution, la liquidation, le redressement ou la liquidation judiciaire d'un associé personne morale.

La société n'est pas non plus dissoute par la révocation d'un gérant, qu'il soit associé ou non.

ARTICLE 19—LIQUIDATION

La dissolution de la société entraîne sa liquidation hormis les cas de fusion ou de scission. Elle n'a d'effet à l'égard des tiers qu'après sa publication.

La personnalité morale de la société subsiste pour les besoins de la liquidation jusqu'à la publication de la clôture de celle-ci.

La société est liquidée par la gérance en exercice lors de la survenance de la dissolution, à moins que les associés ne décident la nomination d'un ou plusieurs liquidateurs associés ou non.

Cette nomination met fin aux pouvoirs de la gérance et entraîne la révocation des pouvoirs qui ont pu être conférés à tous mandataires.

Les associés fixent les pouvoirs des liquidateurs; à défaut ceux-ci ont tous pouvoirs pour terminer les affaires en cours lors de la survenance de la dissolution, réaliser les éléments d'actif, en bloc ou par élément, à l'amiable ou aux enchères, recevoir le prix, donner quittance, régler le passif, transiger, compromettre, agir en justice, se désister, acquiescer, et généralement faire ce qui est nécessaire pour mener à bonne fin les opérations de liquidation.

Après extinction du passif, les liquidateurs font approuver les comptes définitifs de liquidation par les associés qui constatent la clôture des opérations de liquidation; comptes et décision font l'objet d'une publication.

L'actif net subsistant est réparti entre les associés dans les conditions précisées supra à l'article 8. Les liquidateurs disposent de tous pouvoirs à l'effet d'opérer les répartitions nécessaires.

ARTICLE 20—ATTRIBUTION DE JURIDICTION

Toutes les contestations qui peuvent s'élever pendant le cours de la société ou de sa liquidation, soit entre les associés au sujet des affaires sociales, soit entre les associés et la société, sont soumises aux tribunaux compétents du lieu du siège social.

ARTICLE 21—FRAIS

Les frais, droits et honoraires des présentes, de leurs suites et conséquences, seront supportés par la société, portés en frais généraux dès le premier exercice social et en tous cas, avant toute distribution de bénéfice.

En attendant l'immatriculation de la société, ils seront avancés par les associés ou l'un d'entre eux.

Le remboursement de cette avance interviendra au plus tard dans les deux mois de ce jour.

DEUXIEME PARTIE
FORMALITES—FISCALITE

Enregistrement:
Conformément aux dispositions de l'article 635–1, 1er et 5ème du CGI, le présent acte sera soumis à la formalité de l'enregistrement dans le mois de sa date.
Les apports faits à la société étant uniquement constitués de numéraire, seul le droit fixe sera perçu.

POUVOIRS POUR ENGAGER LA SOCIETE

Les associés confèrent à [*person dealing with registration of company*], avec faculté d'agir ensemble ou séparément, le mandat de prendre les engagements suivants pour le compte de la société avant son immatriculation au registre du commerce et des sociétés:
Faire toutes déclarations d'existence et toutes formalités;
Faire ouvrir tous comptes courants et dépôts bancaires ou postaux au nom de la société en formation et les faire fonctionner sur la seule signature d'un MANDATAIRE;
Conclure avec toute personne des contrats entrant dans l'objet social.
Aux effets ci-dessus, passer et signer tous actes et pièces, élire domicile, substituer et généralement faire le nécessaire.

ETAT DES ACTES ACCOMPLIS POUR LE COMPTE DE LA SOCIETE EN FORMATION

Néant.
DONT ACTE

2   Minutes of meeting of shareholders to appoint new *gérant*

SOCIETE CIVILE IMMOBILIERE
SCI '. . . . .'
PROCES-VERBAL D'ASSEMBLEE GENERALE EXTRAORDINAIRE L'AN DEUX MIL . . . . .
Le
A [. . .] heures
Les associés de la SCI '. . . . .' régulièrement convoqués, se sont réunis en assemblée sur l'ordre du jour suivant:
1. Décision de nomination d'un nouveau gérant suite à la démission de l'ancien gérant Mr . . . . .
Tous les associés sont présents savoir:
[*Names of the shareholders present*]
Soit au total les associés propriétaires de la totalité des parts. La séance est présidée par [*name of Chairman*] susnommé, qualifié et domicilié, associé
L'assemblée étant composée des associés propriétaires de toutes les parts sociales, elle peut donc valablement délibérer sur la question de la compétence d'une assemblée générale extraordinaire mise à l'ordre du jour.
2. S'agissant de la décision de nomination d'un gérant Monsieur [*name of Chairman*] expose la démission du gérant Mr [*retiring gerant*] et demande la nomination d'un

nouveau gérant de la société. L'assemblée générale des associés nomme à l'unanimité Mr [*new gerant*] en qualité de gérant de la société pour [une durée indéterminée] [pour la durée de [. . .] ans]. L'ordre du jour étant épuisé et personne ne demandant plus la parole, le Président déclare la séance levée à [. . .] heures. De tout de ce que dessus, le nouveau gérant a dressé le présent procès-verbal, signé par tous les associés, pour servir et valoir ce que de droit.

3   Shareholders' agreement to transfer of shares

SOCIETE CIVILE IMMOBILIERE
[*Name of the Company*]
Au capital de Euro [. . .]
Siège social: [*Registered Office*]
Nous, les soussignés, [*details of all the shareholders*] étant les associés propriétaires de toutes les parts sociales de la SCI [*name of company*] donnent notre agrément à la cession de [*number of shares to be transferred*] parts sociales d'une valeur nominale de Euro [. . .] par [*name of transferor*] au profit de [*name and address of transferee*] moyennant le prix de Euro [*sale price of shares*].
FAIT à
le . . . . . 200..

4   Share transfer

CESSION DE PARTS SOCIALES

ENTRE LES SOUSSIGNES
    Ci-après dénommé 'Le Cédant'
    [*Name and full état civil of Transferee*]
    Ci-après dénommé 'Le Cessionnaire'
    Le Cédant a préalablement à la cession des parts faisant l'objet des présentes exposé ce qui suit:

EXPOSE

Constitution de la société
    La société a été constituée aux termes d'un acte reçu par Maître [*name of notary*], notaire à [*town*] le [*date of formation of company*] enregistrée le [*date and place of registration*]
    Caractéristiques de la société
    La société dénommée 'SCI [*name of company*]' dont les parts sont présentement cédées présente les caractéristiques suivantes:
    Dénomination: SCI [*name of company*]
    Forme: société civile immobilière
    Objet: l'acquisition soit en pleine propriété, soit en jouissance, soit sous toutes autres modalités de tous immeubles bâtis ou non bâtis et tous meubles
    Siege social: [*Registered Office*]
    Durée: 99 ans à partir de son immatriculation

Capital social: [*Details of authorized capital*]

Cession des parts: L'agrément des cessions de parts sociales entre vifs obéit aux dispositions légales et/ou aux dispositions statutaires en son article [*relevant article*]

Exercice social: L'exercice social commence le 1er janvier et se termine le 31 décembre de chaque année

Répartition actuelle du capital social

Le capital social de la société est actuellement réparti entre les associés comme suit: [*Details of shareholdings*]

Ceci exposé il est passé ainsi qu'il suit à la cession de parts de la société civile immobilière [*name of company*] convenu directement entre les parties.

CESSION DES PARTS

Le Cédant cède par les présentes au Cessionnaire qui accepte sous les garanties ordinaires et de droit [*number of shares transferred*] parts qu'il possède dans la société ci-dessus visée.

Au moyen de la présente cession le Cédant subroge le Cessionnaire dans tous les droits et actions envers la société émettrice attachés aux parts cédées.

ORIGINE DE PROPRIETE

Le Cédant est titulaire des parts cédées.

TRANSFER DE PROPRIETE ET JOUISSANCE

Le Cessionnaire aura la propriété des parts cédées à compter de ce jour et jouirira de toutes les prérogatives et assumera toutes les obligations attachées à sa qualité d'associé conformément à la loi et aux statuts.

Il participera ou contribuera aux résultats sociaux à proportion des droits attachés aux parts cédées à compter de ce jour.

PRIX

La présente cession est consentie et acceptée moyennant le prix de [*sale price*] lequel prix a été payé comptant par le Cessionnaire au Cédant qui le reconnaît et lui en consent quittance.

DONT QUITTANCE
GARANTIE DE PASSIF

Le prix visé ci-dessus a été fixé en considération du bilan établi par la société émettrice des parts cédées à la date de la cession, le Cédant garantissant la situation active et passive de la société.

AGREMENT

Le Cédant a justifié de l'agrément accordé à la présente cession de parts en présentant au Cessionnaire la lettre originale émanant de la société émettrice des parts le lui notifiant.

OPPOSABILITE A LA SOCIETE

En vue de l'opposabilité de la cession à la société la partie la plus diligente fera signifier le présent acte de cession à la société par acte d'huissier de justice.

En tant que besoin tous pouvoirs sont donnés à cet effet au porteur d'une copie authentique, étant entendu que les frais et honoraires de la signification seront à la charge du Cessionnaire.

DECLARATIONS

Le Cédant et le Cessionnaire déclarent:

Que leurs date et lieu de naissance et leur situation matrimonial sont bien tels qu'ils figurent en tête des présentes;

Qu'ils disposent de pleine capacité civile;

De son côté, le Cédant déclare:

Que les parts cédées sont libres de tout nantissement saisie ou autre mesure pouvant faire obstacle à la cession anéantir ou réduire les droits du Cessionnaire;

Que la société n'a assujettie à aucune procédure collective résultant de la loi du 25 janvier 1985;

Que la société n'a jamais effectué d'opérations commerciales de nature à assujettir la société à l'impôt sur les sociétés.

FORMALITES
ENREGISTREMENT

Le présent acte sera registré à la recette des impôts de [*relevant Tax Office*].

Le Cédant déclare que les parts cédées représentent des apports en numéraire et en conséquence le Cessionnaire sollicite l'application de l'article 726 du Code Général des Impôts sur le prix de cession des parts.

GREFFE DU TRIBUNAL DE COMMERCE

Deux expéditions des présentes seront déposées au Greffe du tribunal de Commerce en annexe au Registre de Commerce et des Sociétés de [*relevant town*] conformément à l'article 52 du décret numéro 78-704 du 3 juillet 1978 en vue de son opposibilité aux tiers.

SIGNIFICATION

Le Cessionnaire fera signifier par acte d'huissier et à ses frais la cession des parts au gérant de la société SCI . . . . . conformément à l'article 1690 du *Code civil*.

TITRES

Les titres des parts cédées ainsi que ceux concernant la société ont été remis dès avant ce jour au Cessionnaire qui le reconnaît pour qu'il soit à même de solliciter tous conseils de practiciens et d'apprécier l'étendue de ses obligations et de celles de la société.

FRAIS

Les droits frais et honoraires des présentes et ceux qui en seront la suite et la conséquence seront supportés par le Cessionnaire qui s'oblige à les acquitter.

MENTION

Mention des présentes est consenti partout où besoin sera.

ELECTION DE DOMICILE

Pour l'exécution des présentes les soussignés font élection de domicile en leur demeure respective.

TELLES SONT LES CONVENTIONS DES PARTIES

FAIT à

Le

En autant d'exemplaires que de parties, dont un pour l'enregistrement.

G. MISCELLANEOUS

It has been thought worthwhile including translations into French of English Birth and Death Certificates. It is unreasonably expensive to have them translated in France and a Solicitor's certificate as to the correctness of the translation will normally be accepted.

The *acte de notoriété* is among the most important documents in the administration of an estate and is the nearest equivalent to an English Grant of Representation.

The *prêt à usage* is an agreement under which a person undertakes to return to its owner a thing, which may be realty or personalty, when he no longer requires it. It may not provide for any money payment but may impose rules as to the use of the thing lent.

It can usefully be used for informal lettings such as the occupation of trust premises by a beneficiary.

The Loan Offer is standard and it is useful to have an English translation.

1   Translation of UK birth certificate

COPIE CERTIFIÉE D'UNE DÉCLARATION DE NAISSANCE

Fait au bureau général de l'état civil   N° de demande
Quartier
Naissance dans la commune de . . . . . dans le . . . . . de . . . . .
Numéro:
 1. Lieu et date de naissance:
 2. Nom:
 3. Sexe:
 4. Prénom et nom de famille du père:
 5. Prénom, nom de famille et nom de jeune fille de la mère:
 6. Profession du père:
 7. Signature, signalement et domicile du déclarant:
 8. Date de déclaration:
 9. Signature de l'officier de l'état civil:
10. Nom ajouté après déclaration: nul.
Certifiée copie exacte d'une inscription dans la copie certifiée conforme d'un registre de naissances dans le quartier mentionné ci-dessus.
Fait au bureau générale de l'état civil avec apposition de son cachet officiel le . . . . .
L.S.
Certifiée traduction exacte

2   Translation of UK birth certificate (adoption)

COPIE CERTIFIÉE D'UNE INSCRIPTION DANS LES REGISTRES D'ACTES DE L'ÉTAT CIVIL

Fait au bureau général de l'état civil   N° de demande
1. Numéro d'inscription:
2. Date et pays de naissance:
3. Prénom et nom de famille de l'enfant:
4. Sexe de l'enfant:
5. Prénom et nom de famille, adresse et occupation de/des parent(s) adoptif(s):
6. Date de jugement d'adoption et le Tribunal qui l'a rendu:
7. Date d'inscription:
8. Signature de l'officier de l'état civil:
9. Nom ajouté après déclaration:
Certifiée copie exacte d'une inscription dans le registre des enfants adoptés.
Fait au bureau général de l'état civil avec apposition de son cachet officiel le . . . . .
L.S.
Certifiée traduction exacte

3   Translation of UK death certificate

COPIE CERTIFIÉE D'UNE DÉCLARATION DE DÉCÈS

Fait au bureau général de l'état civil   N° d'inscription
Lieu d'inscription
Arrondissement
Région administrative
1. Lieu et date de décès:
2. Prénom et nom de famille:
3. Sexe:
4. Nom de jeune fille:
5. Date et lieu de naissance:
6. Profession et domicile:
7. (a) Nom et adresse de déclarant:
    (b) Qualification:
    (c) Domicile:
8. Cause de décès:
Certifié par
9. Je certifie sur l'honneur que les détails ci-dessus sont exacts pour autant que je sache
(Signature du déclarant)
10. Date d'inscription:
11. Signature de l'officier d'état civil:
Certifiée copie conforme
Officier d'état civil principal
Date: . . . . .
Certifiée traduction exacte

4   *Acte de notoriété*

L'AN . . . . .
Le . . . . .
EN L'OFFICE NOTARIAL CI-APRES DENOMME,
Maître [*name of Notary*]
A reçu le présent acte authentique sur le témoignage de:

IDENTITE DES TEMOINS

Madame [*name of witness*] demeurant à [*address*]
De nationalité [*nationality*]
Née à [*date and place of birth*]
Epouse de [*name of spouse*]
Et Monsieur [*name of witness*] demeurant à [*address*]
De nationalité [*nationality*]
Né à [*date and place of birth*]
Epoux de [*name of spouse*]

ACTE DE NOTORIETE

Les témoins sus-nommés déclarent, par les présentes, avoir parfaitement connu le défunt ci-après nommé et la composition de sa famille; ils attestent pour vérité, comme étant de notoriété publique, les faits ci-après énoncés et la dévolution de sa succession.

DECES ET DEVOLUTION DE LA SUCCESSION

Monsieur [*name of deceased*] en son vivant retraité, demeurant à [*address of deceased*] célibataire,
Né à [*date and place of birth*]
De nationalité [*nationality*]
Est décédé à [*place and date of death*]
On ne lui connait aucune autre disposition de dernières volontés que celles résultant de son testament olographe en date [*date of Will*] ouvert, décrit et déposé au rang des minutes de Maître [*Notary holding Will*] notaire suivant procès-verbal en date du [*date of acknow-ledgement of safe custody of Will*]
   Il n'a laissé ni enfant légitime, naturel ou adoptif, ni descendant d'eux, ni frère, ni ascendant dans les lignes paternelle ou maternelle.
   <u>Par suite, le défunt a laissé pour recueillir sa succession, en vertu du testament sus-énoncé:</u>
Monsieur [*name of Residuary Beneficiary*] demeurant à [*address of Residuary Beneficiary*]
Né à [*date and place of birth*]
Epoux en uniques noces de Madame [*Name of spouse*]
De nationalité [*nationality*]
Résidant [*country of residence*]
LEGATAIRE UNIVERSEL à charge de délivrer divers legs particuliers

ANNEXE

Aux présentes est demeuré annexé, après mention:
– Un extrait de l'acte de décès du défunt;
– Une lettre du fichier central des dispositions de dernières volontés à VENELLES, inter-
rogé par les soins du Notaire soussigné aprés le décès, indiquant qu'aucune autre disposition de dernières volontés du défunt n'a été mentionnée sur ce fichier.

MENTION

Conformément aux dispositions de l'article 69, paragraphe 4, du décret n. 55–1350 du 14
octobre 1955, le Notaire soussigné a informé les ayants droit à la succession dont il s'agit,
de l'obligation qui leur est imposée par l'article 29 du décret n. 55–22 du 4 janvier 1955,
de faire constater dans une attestation notariée la transmission ou constitution par décès à
leur profit des droits réels immobiliers pouvant dépendre de cette succession et lesdits
ayants droit ont chargé le Notaire soussigné d'établir cette attestation, si elle est nécessaire,
dans le délai prévu par la loi.

DONT ACTE

Le [*date in words*] à [*time in words*], est décédé [*date and place of death*] [*name of
deceased*] né à [*place of birth*] le [*date of birth*] retraité, fils de [*parents of deceased*],
Célibataire.
Dressé le [*date in words*] à [*time in words*], sur la déclaration de [*name*], âgé [*age*] de ans,
Employé des Pompes Funèbres domicilié [*undertaker's address*], qui, . . . lecture faite et
invité à lire l'acte, a signé avec Nous, [*name*], Rédacteur Chef, Officier de l'Etat-civil par
délégation du Maire de [. . . . .].

DEPARTEMENT	MAIRIE DE	REPUBLIQUE
[*Département*]	[*Town*]	FRANCAISE

COPIE certifiée CONFORME
selon le procédé de traitement informatisé

LE MAIRE,
P. Le Maire,
L'Agent communal
délégué

Fichier Central des Dispositions
de Dernières Volontés
13107 Venelles Cedex—Tel.: 04 42 54 90 80—Fax: 04 42 54 90 90

Annexé à un acte reçu aux minutes de
OFFICE NOTARIAL

COMPTE RENDU D INTERROGATION   NUMERO: [. . .]

NOM: [*surname*]

PRENOMS: [*first names*]   SEXE:

NE LA: [*date of birth*]

CONJOINT: [*name of spouse*]   DATE DE DECES: [*date of death*]

        AUCUNE INSCRIPTION AU FICHIER EN DATE DU: [*date of search*]

Rédigé sur trois pages.

Contenant

Fait et passé aux lieu et date sus-indiqués.

La lecture du présent acte a été donnée aux parties et les signatures de celles-ci sur ledit acte ont été recueillies par:

clerc de la Société Civile Professionnelle sus-énoncée, habilité à cet effet et assermenté par actes déposés aux minutes de ladite Société.

Lequel clerc habilité a également signé le même jour.

Le notaire a lui-même signé le même jour.

5   Prêt à usage

Entre les soussignés:

[*name, address and occupation of Licensor*]

(désigné ci-après 'le Prêteur')

et

[*name, address and occupation of Licensee*]

(désigné ci-après 'le Preneur')

il est convenu ce qui suit:

PRET A USAGE

Le Prêteur prête à titre de prêt à usage ou commodat à titre gratuit conformément aux articles 1875 et suivants du *Code civil* au Preneur qui accepte les biens ci-après désignés.

DESIGNATION

Les lots de copropriété ci-après désignés dépendant d'un ensemble immobilier situé à [*town and département*] dénommé [*name of block*] cadastré section [*cadastral description*].

SAVOIR

LE LOT NUMERO [*number*]

Un appartement situé au deuxième étage du bâtiment A portant le numéro . . . au plan comprenant: hall d'entrée avec placard, salle de séjour avec balcon, cuisine, une chambre avec placard, salle de bains et WC

Avec les [*share*] des parties communes générales
Et les [*share*] des parties communes spéciales au bâtiment A

LE LOT NUMERO [*number*]

Une cave située au rez-de-chaussée du bâtiment A portant le numéro 15 au plan
Avec les [*share*] des parties communales générales
Et les [*share*] des parties communales spéciales au bâtiment A

LE LOT NUMERO [*number*]

Un garage situé au deuxième sous-sol portant le numéro 39 au plan
Avec les [*share*] des parties communes générales
Et les [*share*] des parties communales spéciales aux garages

LE LOT QUATRE [*number*]

Un emplacement à usage de parking extérieur pour voiture automobile portant le numéro
3 au plan
Avec les [*share*] des parties communales générales
Et les [*share*] des parties communes spéciales aux parkings

USAGE

Le Preneur s'oblige expressément à n'utiliser les biens prêtés qu'à l'usage pour son habitation personnelle et celles des membres de sa famille.

DUREE

Le présent prêt est conféré à titre personnel au Preneur pour la durée de sa vie. Il s'éteindra à son décès et ne se transmettra pas à ses héritiers conformément aux dispositions du deuxième alinéa de l'article 1879. Le Preneur aura la jouissance des biens prêtés à compter de ce même jour.

CONDITIONS

Le présent prêt est fait sous les conditions ordinaires et de droit en pareille matière et, en outre, aux conditions suivantes que le Preneur sera tenu d'exécuter à peine de tous dommages-intérêts et même de résiliation du prêt si bon semble au Prêteur:
—le Preneur veillera en bon père de famille à la garde et à la conservation des biens prêtés;
—il s'opposera à tous empiétements et usurpations et, le cas échéant, en préviendra le Prêteur afin qu'il puisse agir directement;
—il se servira personnellement des biens prêtés et ne pourra les confier à des préposés et ne devra les utiliser que pour l'usage ci-dessus défini;
—il fera à ses frais toutes les réparations qui sont dès maintenant indispensables et toutes celles qui deviendront nécessaires au cours du prêt y compris les grosses réparations telles qu'elles sont définies à l'article 606 du *Code civil* de sorte que dans le cas où la valeur des biens prêtés se trouverait diminuée par suite d'incendie ou autre cause, le Preneur devra tenir compte de cette diminution de valeur au Prêteur; à cette fin éventuelle,

le Preneur sera tenu de s'assurer à son nom et au nom du Prêteur contre toute risque de son occupation exigée par le Prêteur par une assurance suffisante contractée auprès d'une compagnie d'assurance notoirement solvable. Il devra justifier de cette assurance et du paiement des primes à toutes réquisitions du Prêteur par production de la police et des quittances;

—il paiera pendant toute la durée du prêt les impôts de toute nature grevant les biens prêtés.

FRAIS

Les frais des présentes et de leurs suites seront supportés et acquittés par le Preneur qui s'y oblige.

DOMICILE

Pour l'exécution des présentes et de leurs suites les parties font élection de domicile en leurs demeures respectives.

Fait en deux exemplaires à

le

Le Prêteur   Le Preneur

. . . .

6   Translation of loan offer

Subject to the provisions of Law No. 79.596 of the 13th July 1979 and Décret No. 80.473 of the 28th June 1980

Date

Name and address of Lender:

Name and address of Borrower:

Drawdown of the loan is subject to the prior acceptance of this Offer by the Lender.

The loan will be in the amount of Euro . . . . . and will be made in one instalment by the transfer of that amount to the account of Me . . . . ., notaire associé of . . . . .

The purpose of the loan is in connection with the purchase of . . . . . , France.

The loan will be repaid on a date [. . .] years from drawdown or on earlier sale and may be repaid (without any penalty but) with the payment of all interest due to the date of such repayment on any date prior thereto either in full or in amounts of not less than Euro [. . .] subject to three months' prior notice in writing to the Lender.

Until repayment of the loan, it shall bear interest on the amount of the loan from time to time outstanding at the rate of [. . .]%. Such interest shall be paid by the Borrower to the Lender every [. . .] months in arrear, the first of such payments to be made [. . .] months from the date on which the loan is drawn down.

The loan will be secured in its full amount by a legal mortgage to be prepared by Me . . . . .
contemporaneously with the conveyance to the Borrower of the said property.

The Borrower will effect comprehensive household cover on the property in an amount of
not less than Euro [. . .] and provide the Lender with suitable evidence of this cover. The
Borrower will also effect life and accident cover in such amount as the Lender may reason-
bly require and will, in any event, provide such personal guarantees in support of the loan
as may be reasonably required.

No charge is made in connection with the granting of the loan. The estimated cost of the
mortgage document is Euro [. . .].

The estimated total cost of the loan is Euro [. . .] and the 'taux effectif global' is Euro [. . .].
This offer remains open for a period of 30 days from the date hereof and may be accepted
at any time after but not before 10 days from the date hereof.

GLOSSARY

Many of the words and expressions in this Glossary are already explained in the body of the text. They may be mentioned only once and then in a chapter dealing with a subject in which the reader is not at that particular moment interested. They may appear in different chapters in more than one context. In order to minimize cross-referencing in the text, this Glossary is intended to be in the nature of a secondary index indicating the pages on which a particular word or phrase occurs in its most explicit context with the exception of such words as *acte* or *notaire* which recur frequently. Where the explanation of a word or phrase itself contains a French phrase, an explanation of what appears in French will also appear in this Glossary.

This Glossary may also include words or phrases which do not appear in the text but an understanding of which may be useful to the reader.

abandon de domicile   the quitting of leased premises which results in the automatic determination of the lease unless there remain in occupation the spouse of the lessor, close members of his family or a person with whom the lessee has entered into a PACS.
. . . .**167**

abattement   the tax-free band for *droits de succession* and *droits de donation* the extent of which depends on the relationship of deceased to beneficiary or donor to donee.
. . . .**347**

abus de droit   strictly the exercise by a person of a lawful right in an unlawful manner with the intention of causing damage to another. It has come to be used by the French Revenue to mean tax evasion.
. . . .**86**

acceptation pure et simple   the unqualified acceptance of an interest in the estate of a deceased person.
. . . .**238, 305**

acceptation sous bénéfice d'inventaire   the acceptance of an interest in the estate of a deceased person subject to the solvency of the estate.
. . . .**238, 305**

achat croisé   a method of purchase sometimes adopted by unmarried couples under which they buy *en indivision* in equal shares the share of each being subject to the life interest of the other.
. . . .**204**

acte authentique   a document drawn by an *officier public*, which *fait foi* until its contents are disproved by *inscription de faux*. The *notaire* does not have the monopoly of drawing *actes authentiques* which include such documents as birth, death and marriage certificates, Court judgments and certain documents prepared by the *huissier*. When drawn by a *notaire*, they are called *actes notariés*.
. . . . .passim

acte de cession   a document of transfer such as of shares which is normally ssp or of assignment of a lease or chose in action such as a debt or copyrights which will more frequently be *authentique* but not normally used to describe a sale of land.
. . . .**91**

acte de notoriété   the document prepared by a *notaire* in the estate of a deceased person which contains a copy of the will (if any), lists the beneficiaries and gives other necessary information about the deceased such as his date and place of birth, domicile and nationality and which from a title point of view performs a function similar to an English Grant of Representation.
. . . .**3, 21, 314, 326**

acte de partage   deed of partition executed on the partitioning of property held *en indivision* usually on the completion of the administration of an estate when it is also known as a *partage successoral* either by agreement between the beneficiaries or consequent on an Order of the Court. A *acte de partage de communauté* partitions assets which are subject to a *régime matrimonial*. An *acte de partage d'ascendant* is an alternative description of a *donation-partage*.
. . . .**151, 295, 329**

acte de vente   document transferring land or an interest in land on a sale for value. It is not used, for example, for a sale of shares.
. . . .**4**

actif   in an estate, the gross assets of a deceased person. In a balance sheet, the assets side.

action en réduction   an action instituted by one or more *réservataires* to reintegrate into the *réserve* amounts which it is alleged have been wrongly disposed of *inter vivos* by a deceased person.
. . . .**264**

actionnaire   shareholder of a company other than a *société civile*.

adoption   may be *plénière* or full with results similar to an English adoption or *simple* when the adopted child becomes part of the adopting family whilst retaining legal links including certain inheritance rights with his birth family.
. . . .**225**

adjudication judiciaire   public auction of property by Order of the Court.
. . . .**111, 114**

adjudication volontaire   public auction of property by order of the owner.
. . . .**111**

administrateur   an *administrateur de biens* is a term which is fairly loosely used as a generic description to indicate a managing agent who manages property such as a *gérant* or a *syndic*. An *administrateur judiciaire* is a person nominated by the Court to administer assets in an estate or in a bankruptcy when the need arises. An *administrateur séquestre* is appointed by the Court to hold property which is the subject of litigation. An *administrateur provisoire* acts in the absence of a *syndic* of a *copropriété*.

agent immobilier   estate agent who deals with every aspect of the sale, purchase, letting and management of land and who seems to be outnumbered in France only by the chemist. In all his transactions, he is controlled by the Loi Hoguet. His rates of commission considerably exceed those in England. Many consider that they act for both seller and buyer instead of acting clearly in the sole interests of the seller, their client, which since buyers are seldom independently advised can be a matter for concern.
. . . .**28, 30**

agios   bank charges.

agrément à l'amiable   agreement (usually for a sale) by private treaty.

à la criée   method of bidding at public auction. Also known as *à l'extinction des feux* from the fact that auctions are candle auctions such as used to be the practice in England.

. . . .**113**

aléa   chance: contracts which are *aléatoire* are contracts which must contain an element of chance such as gaming contracts and sales *en viager* and which are not unlawful but void if that element of chance is not present.

. . . .**105**

amiante   asbestos, the presence of which in certain blocks of flats is subject to stringent regulations and the disclosure of which is obligatory by a buyer in a contract for sale of land.

. . . .**45**

apport   consideration for the allotment of shares in a company. If *en numéraire*, the consideration is cash; if *en nature*, it is other than cash.

. . . .**87**

apostille   the legalization certificate provided under the Hague Convention of 5 October 1961 by the Foreign and Commonwealth Office in the case of certain documents executed in the United Kingdom for use in France and other foreign countries.

. . . .**190**

arrérages   payments due in respect of an annuity or pension.

. . . .**107**

arrhes   in its most simple terms, *arrhes* is a deposit asked for on account by a seller of goods when the total price is not paid with the order. In the case of a contract for the sale of land, it is the deposit paid by the buyer on account of the sale price which if the buyer defaults is retained by the seller but if the seller defaults is refundable in twice its amount to the buyer.

. . . .**36**

artisan   a self-employed craftsman who is registered on the Register or Index of Craftsmen. Depending on his craft or calling, he may also be an *artisan-commerçant*.

. . . .**173**

assemblée générale   general meeting of a company or *copropriété* which may be annual or extraordinary in circumstances similar to those in English law.

. . . . **91, 136**

associé   a shareholder of a *société civile*.

. . . .**88**

assurance dommages-ouvrage   obligatory insurance for a period of ten years covering defective workmanship which must be effected by all owners or sellers of buildings in respect of which building works are carried out.

. . . .**78**

à titre onéreux   a transaction for valuable consideration ie the opposite of a gift.

attestation d'acquisition   a notarial certificate confirming the purchase of a property to enable the purchaser to satisfy utilities and other third parties that he is the owner of the property pending completion of the registration of the transfer to him which takes a matter of months. It is not often needed but serves as a document of comfort for the non-French buyer. Some *notaires* provide such a certificate on completion as a matter of course.

. . . .**67**

attestation immobilière   the notarial document which confirms to the Land Registry passage of the ownership of property belonging to a deceased person to a beneficiary in

his estate. Such ownership in almost every case vests automatically by reason of the death of which this document is mere confirmation but is necessary to complete the title from a Land Registry point of view. It is convenient but incorrect to equate it to an assent.
. . . . **42, 238**

authenticité   the legal quality attaching to an *acte authentique*.
. . . . **1**

avancement   a payment made *inter vivos* to a potential *réservataire* which may be *d'hoirie* or *préciputaire et hors part*. The former is subject to hotchpot and the latter is not.
. . . . **263**

avantage en nature   emolument or benefit in kind received from a company.
. . . . **268**

avant-contrat   this is the somewhat misleading term applied to contracts usually, but by no means always, for the sale of land which precede an *acte notarié* which is required to complete the transaction the subject matter of the contract. The term results from the fact that that subsequent document is called by the French 'the contract' so perforce that which has previously been entered into by the parties is an *avant-contrat*.
. . . . **26**

avenant   a deed of variation.

avocat   the equivalent of the barrister or the solicitor who specializes in litigation and who also deals with general legal matters not within the province of the *notaire*. This distinction becomes quite clear in practice when one attempts to obtain advice from the wrong lawyer.
. . . . **9**

avoir   a credit with a third party eg when faulty goods are returned to a seller. Also *avoir fiscal*, a tax credit in respect of dividends.

avoué   an *officier ministériel* who has the monopoly of the right to *postuler* ie to draft pleadings and organize procedure before the Court of Appeal in civil cases (but not in connection with agricultural tenancies or Employment Tribunal or Social Security appeals). He is not allowed to *plaider* ie plead in Court which is the task of the *avocat*.
. . . . **9**

ayant droit   successor in title.

bail à construction   a building lease for a term of not less than eighteen nor more than ninety-nine years resembling the Victorian ground lease, the user of the building (usually a block of flats) when erected by the lessee being limited to the letting of its various parts.
. . . . **17**

bail dérogatoire   a lease of business premises the term of which may not exceed two years which by agreement between lessor and lessee does not provide any security of tenure or compensation.
. . . . **183**

bail de droit commun   a lease not subject to any Law providing security of tenure or other protection for the lessee but is substantially subject only to the provisions of the *Code civil*.
. . . . **159**

bail emphytéotique   a lease for a term of eighteen to ninety-nine years usually of agricultural land the terms of which are designed to encourage the lessee to increase the value of the land.

. 17

bail à réhabilitation a lease for a term of a minimum of twelve years granted only to the equivalent of a Housing Association (HLM) under which the lessee undertakes to refurbish a property and let at much reduced rents.

. 17

bâtonnier chairman of the local Bar Council.

. 9

biens goods, property, assets, chattels.

. . . . .passim

bornes boundary markers. Also roadside milestones.
bornage the exercise of fixing boundaries between two privately owned properties.
bouquet the capital sum (if any) paid on a sale *en viager*.

. 105

Bureau des hypothèques the French Land Registry. The Chief and local Land Registrars are known as *Conservateurs* and Land Registry fees are called the *salaire du Conservateur*.

. . . . .20, 21

cadastre the Land Registry Index Map with a note of the owners of each plot. The updating of the system is now more or less complete so that references to plots (*lots*) are to the numbers on the *cadastre renové*. Descriptions of property are by reference to a *lieudit* or named place, a section and a lot number. Thus, '*lieudit Saint Pons, commune de Beausite (Loir et Cher) Section A Number 291*'.

. . . . .20, 21

cahier des charges generally a separate list of conditions to which a contract is subject. Particularly, conditions of sale for a public auction.

. 112

Caisse Centrale de Garantie the equivalent for the notarial profession of the Solicitors' Indemnity Fund.

. 8

Caisse des dépôts et de consignation this quasi-bank with branches in various cities throughout France was founded in April 1816 and is where *notaires* are required to bank clients' account money. It is not a clearing bank and transfers of money to it from outside France, which appear to pass through Paris, can take longer than they should. It does not pay interest on money which it holds which is why *notaires* do not themselves pay interest on clients' money held in their clients' account. It is, however, possible, if the *notaire* concerned is willing to arrange it, for large sums of money such as deposits pending completion of sales to be invested short term so that the income earned is available to the client.

. . . . .7, 61, 87

carnet d'entretien this record which must be kept by every *syndic* of a *copropriété* shows the state of the block of flats, all important works carried out and to be carried out to it, insurance policies, standing contracts and other useful information relating to the management of the block.

. 143

carte de séjour residence permit to which all EU citizens are entitled and which must be obtained after six months' residence in France. The holder of such a *carte* must operate a resident bank account and will find it difficult successfully to hold that he does not have a *domicile fiscal* in France.
. . . .**246**

carte professionnelle without this card issued by the local *Préfecture* no person may engage in the business of an estate agent in France or in respect of dealings in property situate in France. It can, in suitable circumstances, be issued to any EU citizen.
. . . .**27**

certificat de concubinage this certificate may be issued by the local *mairie* to those living *en concubinage* who have not entered into a PACS.
. . . .**201**

certificat de conformité a planning certificate issued on completion of building works to confirm that they are in accordance with the planning permission which authorized them.
. . . .**75**

certificat de coutume the equivalent of an affidavit of foreign law.
. . . .**201**

certificat d'hérédité a low grade certificate issued by the *mairie* of the place where a person died indicating who are his lawful heirs. Accepted by some banks but otherwise of little value and unlikely to be issued in the case of a person who died out of France.
. . . .**327**

certificat de propriété a certificate (usually *notarié*) proving a change of ownership, usually on a death, of a shareholder or annuitant.
. . . .**238, 327**

cession de parts share transfer.
. . . .**91**

Chambre des Notaires the equivalent of a local Law Society save that each has full and independent disciplinary and regulatory powers.
. . . .**7**

charges in the case of a *copropriété* these are the service charges. The *charges locatives* are the taxes paid by or services supplied by a lessor the cost of which he may lawfully recover from his lessee. The phrase *à charge de* indicates the obligation of a beneficiary or donee imposed by a testator or donor to make certain payments or vest property for the benefit of or in another.
. . . .**131, 133, 254**

chef d'entreprise a technical term of significance in connection with leases of business premises indicating a person who is an employer but not necessarily the owner of a business in respect of which he has the powers to employ staff.
. . . .**173**

chose thing, property, assets. More or less interchangeable with *biens*.

chose jugé *res judicata*.

clause (a) *d'attribution intégrale*: the right for a beneficiary in an estate to seek an Order of the Court awarding him in a partition certain types of property held *en indivision* when their sale by auction in order to partition the proceeds of sale would result in a loss of value; **329**

(b) *léonine*: an unfair or oppressive condition; **90**

(c) *pénale*: a penal clause; **37**

(d) *résolutoire*: a clause permitting one party to a contract to rescind for the breach of the other party **65**

coefficient d'érosion monétaire   capital gains tax inflation factor.
. . . .**219**

commandement   an order, usually served by a *huissier*, with which the failure to comply will lead to proceedings and in particular to a *saisie*.
. . . .**126**

commerçant   a person who routinely engages in commercial transactions and who has a special status in French law. The list of commercial activities is limitless. An infant cannot be a *commerçant* and certain professions are forbidden to foreigners eg stockbroker, insurance agent, banker. A foreigner must have a *carte de commerçant étranger* to carry on business in France unless he is an EU citizen or is from Andorra, Monaco, Algeria.
. . . .**173**

commissaire aux comptes   a company auditor.

commissaire-priseur   an *officier ministériel* authorized to value items other than land for probate, insurance and similar purposes and to conduct auction sales of such items.

comourants   commorientes.
. . . .**228**

commune   the smallest administrative authority in France to which the French are greatly attached. There are more than 35,000 of them in the country and they enjoy a large measure of decentralization as a result of the Law of 2 May 1982. They play an essential role in matters affecting the local police, political and professional elections, local public services, highways and transport and planning.
. . . .**20**

compromis de vente   bilateral contract for the sale of land.
. . . .**31**

concierge   porter of a block of flats usually living in with his or her spouse.
. . . .**129**

concubinage   see *PACS* and *union libre*.

conditions suspensives   conditions precedent.
. . . .**46**

conjoint   spouse but virtually never used except when speaking of surviving spouse as *conjoint survivant*.

conseil juridique   a defunct profession now amalgamated with the *avocat*. The *conseil juridique* could not plead and tended to specialize in commercial and financial cases. Many *avocats* deliberately mention that they are ex-*conseils juridiques* to indicate a breadth of practical legal knowledge.
. . . .**9**

conseil de famille   a body of four to six persons whose task is to assist the *tuteur* of a person under an incapacity. Its members are chosen by the *juge des tutelles* and are close members of the family of the person *en tutelle*.
. . . .**224**

conseil supérieur du notariat   the governing body of the *notariat*.
. . . .**7, 67**

conseil de surveillance   the executive committee of an *SCI d'attribution en jouissance à temps partagé*.
. . . .**101**

conseil syndical   the executive committee of a *co-propriété* whose members are chosen from among the flat-owners.
. . . . **145**

contentieux   litigation. *Service du Contentieux* is the Legal Department of businesses and government departments.
constat   report made by a *huissier*.
. . . . **10**

contrat de mariage   the contract by which about to be married couples choose their *régime*. If they wish to adopt the *régime légal*, they are said to marry *sans contrat*.
. . . . **1, 195**

contrat préliminaire   also known as *contrat de réservation*, is the form of contract required by law to be used for a *vente en l'état futur d'achèvement*.
. . . . **31, 33, 70, 71**

contrôleur de la gestion   auditor of an *SCI d'attribution en jouissance à temps partagé*.
. . . . **103**

convention d'indivision   agreement between co-owners *en indivision* for the management of the jointly owned property overriding the basic rules laid down by the *Code civil* in the case of *indivision* arising by operation of law on a death or on a purchase.
. . . . **150**

convention d'occupation précaire   a licence to use business premises which enjoys no statutory protection for the licensee.
. . . . **184**

copropriété   the form of ownership which is obligatory in respect of any building, parts of which are in more than one ownership.
. . . . **19, 130**

créance de participation   the right of one spouse to benefit from an increase in the value of the assets achieved by the other spouse in a *régime matrimonial* which includes *participation aux acquets*.
. . . . **199**

créancier chirographaire   unsecured creditor.
. . . . **119**

créancier hypothécaire   a creditor whose debt is secured by a charge; a mortgagee.
. . . . **120**

créancier privilégé   a creditor whose debt benefits from a *privilège* giving preferential rights of repayment depending on the nature of the debt.
. . . . **124**

crédirentier   seller of property *en viager*.
. . . . **107**

CRIDON (Centre de recherche d'information et de documentation notariale)   high level advisory service run by specialist *notaires* available only to *notaires*.
. . . . **6**

curatelle   the system of protection afforded to a person who is not an infant and whose incapacity is not sufficient to warrant his being placed *en tutelle*. His affairs are managed by a *curateur*.
. . . . **227**

DAT (déclaration d'achèvement des travaux de construction)   This is the declaration which must be provided by every builder within thirty days of completing the construction on which he was engaged. It marks the beginning of the five-year period during which French value added tax applies to the building to the exclusion of *enregistrement*. This is the period during which '*frais de notaire réduits*' are charged.

....**76**

débirentier   purchaser of property *en viager*.

....**107**

déclaration de succession   French inheritance tax account.

....**345**

de cujus   the deceased.

....passim

dédit   as near as may be the equivalent of the straightforward English deposit paid on a purchase of land.

....**36**

décret   this is best described as a Statutory Instrument.

....passim

DIA (déclaration d'intention d'aliéner)   this declaration must be served on the local *mairie* giving the details of an intended sale of a property in case the *commune* has a right of compulsory purchase. The latter has two months in which to reply, silence indicating that either no such right exists or it is not intended to exercise it.

....**48**

déconfiture   inability to meet one's debts.

....**188**

démembrement de propriété   the division of an absolute interest in property into a life interest and an interest in remainder.

....**16**

dénomination sociale   the name of a company.

....**89**

déspécialisation   the procedure by which a lessee of business premises seeks a variation or extension of his user covenant.

....**176**

destination   user of premises.

....**42**

dispense   see *représentant fiscal*.
dol   fraud, misrepresentation.

....**45**

domicile   has the double meaning of domicile in the English legal sense and in current French language that of one's place of residence.

....**241**

domicile fiscal   residence for tax purposes.

....**245**

donation   gift.

....**295, 331**

donation déguisée   a gift made to resemble a transfer for value usually with the intention of defeating the rights of the *réservataires*.

....**332**

donation entre époux   a gift by one spouse to another.
. . . .**282**

droit au bail   the right of the lessee of business premises to the renewal of his lease.
. . . .**178**

droit de maintien   the right of a lessee of business premises to remain in occupation until he has received compensation on the non-renewal of his lease.
. . . .**183**

droit départemental   that part of *enregistrement* payable on land transactions which is claimed by the *département* in which the property is situate.
. . . .**210**

droit de passage   right of way.
. . . .**16**

droit personnel   right *in personam.*
. . . .**17**

droit de préférence   the preferential right of a registered mortgagee of land or of the holder of a *saisie* on land.
. . . .**120**

droit de prélèvement   the right of a French citizen to receive a compensatory benefit in the estate of a deceased person when he considers that by reason of the application of foreign law in respect of foreign assets he has been deprived of his full share.
. . . .**244**

droit de repentir   the right of the lessor of business premises who has offered compensation in lieu of the renewal of the lease to withdraw that offer and grant a new lease.
. . . .**183**

droit de reprise   the right of the lessor of business premises to retake possession at the expiry of a lease in order to occupy the premises himself.
. . . .**181**

droit de retour   the provision often inserted in a *donation-partage* that in the event of the decease of a donee without issue before the donor, his share revests in the donor. Also the right of ascendants in certain cases to inherit assets which they have given to issue who have predeceased them without leaving surviving issue and in the case of the death of children the subject of *adoptions simples.*
. . . .**258**

droits d'enregistrement   taxes due in respect of a variety of events such as sales, exchanges, transfers of assets, formation of companies, including inheritance and gifts tax.
. . . .**209**

droit réel   right *in rem.*
. . . .**16**

droits de donation   gifts tax.
. . . .**351**

droits de succession   inheritance tax.
. . . .**340**

droits fixes   fixed stamp duties.
. . . .**209**

élection de domicile address for service of documents frequently inserted in *actes*.
. . . .**65**

émancipation the vesting in an infant of rights prior to his obtaining his majority.
. . . .**224**

émolument scale fees charged by *notaires* and other *officiers publics et ministériels*.
. . . .**6**

en bon père de famille the standard internal repairing liability of a lessee is to keep the demised premises in a state as though it were his child. There does not seem to be any formal description of what that may mean but it would be wise to assume that every judge treats his children in a proper manner.
. . . .**42, 57**

enchérir to bid at auction.
. . . .**112, 118**

en indivision tenancy in common.
. . . .**147**

en brevet a notarial document not retained in the records of the *notaire* but handed to the person on whose instructions it was drawn, eg a Power of Attorney.
. . . .**3**

en concurrence when more than one notary is engaged in the same matter acting for different parties they are said to be *en concurrence*.
. . . .**49**

en minute a notarial document the original of which remains in the records of the *notaire*. Known as 'minute' because traditionally it was written in small characters as opposed to copies of such documents called 'grosses' (compare the English 'engross-ment') because they were written in capital letters.
. . . .**3**

enregistrement the formality of recording an *acte* on the appropriate register (usually at the Land Registry) coupled with the payment of the appropriate tax.
. . . .**21**

en tontine joint tenancy. Also known as *pacte tontinier* or *clause d'accroissement*.
. . . .**88, 154**

envoi en possession Order of the Court vesting in the *légataires universels* who do not have *saisine* assets comprised in their legacies.
. . . .**314**

état civil an individual's civil status ie details of birth, death, marriage(s), *régime*, nationality etc.
. . . .**21, 64**

état descriptif de division that part of the *règlement de copropriété* which lists the *tantièmes* in respect of each flat.
. . . .**96**

état hypothécaire Land Registry search.
. . . .**22**

exécuteur testamentaire a person nominated by a testator to oversee the administration of his estate for a period of one year but without any of the powers or discretions of an English executor.
. . . .**236, 301**

exécutoire enforceable as in the case of a judgment or of an *acte authentique* which creates a right in favour of one of the parties.
. . . .**2**

exéquateur Order of the Court authorizing the enforcement in France of a foreign judgment.
. . . .**115, 126**

expédition a notarially certified copy of an *acte authentique*.
. . . .**3, 67**

extrait Kbis company search.
. . . .**94**

fait foi the concept that the contents of an *acte authentique* are correct rebuttable only by a successful *inscription de faux* at the instance of a person claiming the contrary.
. . . .**2**

fiche parcellaire Land Registry property register.
. . . .**21**

fiche personnelle Land Registry proprietorship register.
. . . .**21**

filiation parentage.
. . . .**23**

folle enchère procedure under which a property is re-submitted to auction if a buyer at a previous auction fails to complete his purchase.
. . . .**118**

fonctionnaire French civil servant.
fonds de roulement a float maintained by a *syndic* of a *copropriété*.
. . . .**135**

formalité unique the system uniting payment of *enregistrement* and Land Registry formalities previously dealt with separately. See *enregistrement*.
. . . .**21**

foyer 'hearth and home'.
frais d'acte the scale fees charged by a *notaire* in respect of the preparation of an *acte notarié*.
. . . .**49**

frais de notaire charges of the *notaire* in relation to a transaction including all disbursements. They are said to be '*réduits*' in cases where no *enregistrement* is payable.
. . . .**7, 41**

gage lien, security.
. . . .**19**

garantie d'achèvement guarantee for the proper completion of building works.
. . . .**76**

garantie décennale ten-year cover for building defects required by law to be given by the builder.
. . . .**75, 77**

garantie extrinsèque guarantee for completion of building works on a sale *en l'état futur* provided by a bank or similar institution.
. . . .**73, 76**

garantie intrinsèque guarantee for completion of building works on a sale *en l'état futur* provided by the developer himself if he can fulfil certain conditions.
. . . .**73, 77**

garantie de remboursement insurance policy for repayment to the purchaser of all sums paid by him in a sale *en état futur* on failure of the developer to complete the building.
. . . .**77**

Garde des Sceaux the French equivalent of the Lord Chancellor in his judicial capacity.
. . . .**1**

gardien a *concierge* who does not live on the premises.
. . . .**129**

gérant generally an agent managing the affairs and property of another. Specifically the manager (director) of an SCI.
. . . .**92**

habitation bourgeoise exclusive/simple description of the user of flats in a block as either solely residential or for mixed professional and residential use.
. . . .**133**

héritier lawful heir strictly in an intestacy but also used to indicate those who benefit under a will.
. . . .**passim**

HLM (habitation à loyer modéré) low cost housing.
. . . .**17**

hoirie an old-fashioned term for the estate of a deceased person.
. . . .**263**

homologation confirmatory Court Order eg *homologation de modification de régime* is the Court's confirmation of a change of *régime matrimonial. Homologation du testament* (which is a procedure which does not exist in France) is the French translation of an English Grant of Representation (probate).
. . . .**294**

honoraires professional fees chargeable by agreement.
. . . .**6, 7**

hors d'eau watertight (of a building).
. . . .**75**

huissier *officier ministériel* whose work includes that of bailiff and process server as well as provider of *constats*.
. . . .**2, 10**

hypothèque (a) *conventionnelle* by agreement between parties; **119**
(b) *légale* arising by operation of law; **119**
(c) *judiciaire* based on an Order of the Court. **120**

immeubles immovables.
. . . .**passim**

impenses expenses incurred in the conservation and improvement of a property.
. . . .**150**

incapacité legal incapacity.
. . . .**223**

indemnité d'éviction   compensation payable by the lessor of business premises on his refusal to renew a lease.
. . . .**182**

indemnité d'immobilisation   sum payable by a purchaser under a *promesse de vente* ie option money.
. . . .**36, 51**

inscription de faux   the crime of falsification by a *notaire* or other *officier public* of any fact in an *acte authentique*.
. . . .**2**

ISF (Impôt de Solidarité sur la Fortune)   wealth tax.
. . . .**214**

jouissance à temps partagé   time-sharing.
. . . .**19**

jouissance privative   the exclusive use by a flat-owner of an otherwise common part of a block.
. . . .**130**

légataire à titre universel   a legatee of a share in the estate of a testator.
. . . .**317**

légataire particulier   specific or pecuniary legacy.
. . . .**317**

légataire universel   residuary legatee.
. . . .**318**

legs   legacy of any kind.
. . . .**317**

lésion   the right of a vendor to apply to the Court for recission of a sale based on the claim that the sale price was only five-twelfths or less of the proper value. This can also apply to a *partage* but not to a sale *en viager* or other *contrat aléatoire*.
. . . .**34**

libéralités   a general expression for gifts whether *inter vivos* or by will.
. . . .**331**

lieu de séjour   a fiscal expression for one of the criteria which fixes residence for tax purposes in France. Presence in France for more than 183 days a year assumes the acquisition of French *lieu de séjour*.
. . . .**245**

Loi de Finances   French Finance Act.
. . . .**passim**

Loi Hoguet   law regulating estate agents' practices.
. . . .**27**

Loi Mermaz   the current rent restrictions law.
. . . .**160**

Loi Scrivener   law governing house purchase loans.
. . . .**34, 47, 51, 56**

Loi SRU   law covering a multiplicity of matters including the seven-day cooling off period in respect of all land purchases.
. . . .**28, 31, 47, 51, 57**

lotissement   the French equivalent of an English housing estate in large measure governed by *copropriété* rules.
. . . .**33**

lot   basically a plot of land but also used to describe the divisions of blocks of flats *en copropriété*.
. . . .**20, 21, 130**

mainlevée   document of release on repayment of mortgage or other charge.
. . . .**125**

mairie   local town hall or municipal offices.
. . . .**passim**

mandat   generally an authority to act on behalf of another person. A Power of Attorney. Also a Post Office money order.
. . . .**185**

mandataire   an agent or attorney under a *mandat*.
. . . .**4, 7, 185**

mandat de vente   authority required by the Loi Hoguet without which no estate agent may act in the sale of property in France or receive commission.
. . . .**28**

maître d'oeuvre   the person or company directing and overseeing building construction works.
. . . .**70**

maître de l'ouvrage   the person or company on whose account building works are effected.
. . . .**70**

marchand de biens   a dealer in property for his own account.
. . . .**27**

mention   traditional words such as 'Bon pour . . .', 'Vu et lu' etc, the use of which in most cases has no basis in law and is totally unnecessary.
. . . .**37**

mention en marge   notes relating to transactions on a *fiche* at the Land Registry.
. . . .**125**

meubles meublants   furniture and contents of a house or flat.
. . . .**62**

mise à prix   reserve price at an auction.
. . . .**113, 116**

mise en demeure   formal notice in respect of almost anything, usually to rectify a failure to comply with some lawful obligation.
. . . .**36**

moyens de contraint   a euphemism for the various types of deposit in contracts in the sale of land.
. . . .**36**

multipropriété   see *pluripropriété*.

notariat   the official body of French *notaires*.

note technique sommaire   specifications for property built *en état futur d'achèvement* or *à terme*.

. . . .**72**

notoire   well known, notorious (but not pejoratively). Hence *notoriété* as in *acte de notoriété* which sets out facts of common repute.

nue propriété   the interest in property in remainder expectant on the determination of a prior interest.

. . . .**16**

officier ministériel   members of certain professions including *notaires*, *huissiers*, *avoués*, *avocats* practising before the Conseil d'Etat and the Cour de Cassation, all of whom are under the control of the French Ministry of Justice and have the right to nominate a successor on vacating their office.

. . . .**2, 9, 10**

officier public   certain *officiers ministériels* are also *officiers publics* as are also those entitled to carry out public functions such as celebration of marriages (*le maire*), issuing *actes d'état civil* (Registrar of Births, Deaths and Marriages) and the preparation of *actes authentiques* (*notaires*).

. . . .**1, 2**

offre d'achat/de vente   unilateral offer to buy/sell.

. . . .**33**

opposition   normal notification of objection to the making of a payment eg by the *syndic* of a *copropriété* to a *notaire* not to pay the seller his proceeds of sale until unpaid service charges have been paid. Also *faire opposition* in the case of a cheque is to impose a stop which can only be done in very limited circumstances.

. . . .**64, 135**

ordre public   public policy making it impossible to contract out of any obligation which is *d'ordre public*.

. . . .**passim**

ordonnance   any order emanating from a judicial source. It has also a wide variety of meanings in constitutional law.

. . . .**passim**

ouverture de la succession   the death of a deceased person giving rise to the administration of his estate.

. . . .**323**

PACS   acronym for *pactes civils de solidarité et du concubinage*. Pronounced pax and now in the form of a verb 'pacser', to enter into a PACS.

. . . .**89, 201**

pacte de préférence   agreement to give first refusal.

. . . .**31, 55**

pacte de préemption   pre-emption agreement.

. . . .**31, 55**

pacte sur succession future   covenant to make testamentary dispositions.

. . . .**237**

pacte tontinier   see *en tontine*.

participation aux acquets in the appropriate *régime matrimonial* it is the difference between the assets brought into the *régime* and those on its dissolution ie those acquired by each spouse during marriage.
....**199**

pas de porte premium payable on grant of lease.
....**175**

passif liabilities in an estate. In a balance sheet the liabilities side.
parties communales common parts of the building owned *en copropriété*.
....**131**

parties privatives parts of a building owned *en copropriété* of which the owner has exclusive use.
....**130**

patrimoine the family assets.
....**19**

pension alimentaire
....**278**

personne morale company or corporate body.
....**84**

personne physique private individual.
....**84**

pleine propriété absolute ownership in possession of land.
....**16**

pluripropriété time sharing ownership through share holding in SCI which owns the property.
....**99**

plus-value capital gains tax.
....**218**

pouvoir Power of Attorney or any authority to an agent.
....**185**

Préciputaire see *avancement*. **27**
Préfecture offices of the *Préfet* of any French *département*.
préscription acquisitive ownership by adverse possession.
....**18**

privilège a type of charge which gives the creditor rights of preference in respect of the assets of his debtor. Also in respect of unpaid sale price and service charges.
....**22, 124, 135**

procès-verbal of a meeting, the minutes. Of a motoring or parking offence etc, the ticket.
....**65**

procuration Power of Attorney.
....**185**

promesse de vente option agreement for the purchase of land used in parts of France as a straightforward contract instead of the *compromis de vente*.
....**22, 30, 51**

publicité foncière registration of a transaction at the Land Registry.
....**20**

quote-part   share of the common parts of a *copropriété* attaching to a flat which governs the amount of service charge payable.
. . . .**20, 131**

quotité disponible
. . . .**262**

reçevoir un acte   the authentication of a document by a *notaire*.
. . . .**64**

régime matrimonial   contract chosen by married couples prior to their wedding or in default imposed on them by law which governs their property rights *inter se*.
. . . .**23**

Registre de commerce et des sociétés   Companies' Registry.
. . . .**94**

règle du plafonnement   the calculation in certain specified circumstances of the rent under a renewed lease of business premises.
. . . .**179**

règlement de copropriété   internal regulations for management of a block of flats.
. . . .**131**

réiteration de vente   the *acte authentique* executed at completion of the sale of land. The sale having been 'made' by the *avant-contrat* it is 'reiterated' by the *acte de vente* mainly for fiscal reasons.
. . . .**59**

remise des clés   the handing over of the keys on completion of a sale or of building works, eg a new flat.
. . . .**75**

renonciation   renunciation usually of a benefit under a will or intestacy.
. . . .**238, 309**

rente viagère   annuity.
. . . .**106**

réparations   structural repairs (*grosses*) are normally borne by the lessor and *réparations locatives* by the lessee in accordance with the list set out in the Decree of 30 December 1982.
. . . .**163**

Représentant Fiscal Accredité   such a person or, more usually, a company is appointed on the sale of property (i) by a seller who being a private individual is not resident for tax purposes in France, or (ii) by a company not incorporated in France, irrespective of the amount of the sale price to guarantee the payment of capital gains tax. The buyer if he is resident in France may act as such an *agent* but as may be imagined seldom does.
. . . .**63, 220**

réprésentation   the right for issue to stand in the place of deceased parents in an intestacy.
. . . .**257**

réservataire   a beneficiary entitled to share in the *réserve* in the estate of a deceased.
. . . .**261**

réserve   that part of the estate of a deceased person in which ascendants and descendants and to a certain extent surviving spouses have entrenched inheritance rights.
. . . .**261**

réunion fictive the method of calculating the *réserve* to take into account *inter vivos* gifts made by the deceased.
....**264**

SAFER *Les Sociétés d'Aménagement Foncier et d'Etablissement Rural.* Local agricultural committees which are designed to control the market in agricultural land.
....**16, 48**

saisie charging order in respect of assets generally which may be *conservatoire* or *arrêt* ie which either blocks dealing with the asset or enables the holder of the *saisie* to sell it.
....**115**

saisie immobilière a *saisie* in respect of land.
....**114**

saisine ownership of assets in the deceased's estate which is either vested automatically in a beneficiary or requires certain formalities depending upon the nature of his inheritance.
....**313**

SCI (Société Civile Immobilière) a type of French civil company whose objects are limited to dealings related to property.
....**83**

SCI d'attribution an SCI the shares of which entitle the holders on liquidation to ownership of a specified part of the company's property eg a flat in a block.
....**32, 95**

SCI d'attribution en jouissance à temps partagé an SCI which it is obligatory to use in the case of time-sharing activities.
....**99**

SCP (Société Civile Professionnelle) the equivalent of an English professional partnership.

séparation de biens one of the *régimes matrimoniaux* the effect of which is that each spouse is the sole owner of his or her own property. The French consider that the English marry in the equivalent of this *régime*.
....**198**

siège social a company's registered office.
....**89**

société civil a French form of company whose objects are limited to 'civil' objects as opposed to those which are 'commercial' such as those of the *Société Anonyme* or *Société à Responsabilité Limitée*. The distinction is not that between the UK public and private company.
....**83**

soulte equality money on a partition.
....**329**

ssp (sous seing privé) documents which are not *authentiques* are said to be executed in this manner.
....passim

statuts the Memorandum and Articles of a company.
....**89**

substitution fidéicommissaire an imitation trust with very limited possibilities, infrequently used.
....**252**

sur catalogue   a new house built according to plans provided by the builder and not by the owner is said to be built *sur catalogue*.

. . . .**81**

surenchère   the ability to reopen a public auction of land by an offer within ten days to over-bid by at least 10 per cent the previous closing bid.

. . . .**114, 117**

syndic   the manager of a *copropriété*.

. . . .**141**

syndicat de copropriété   the legal entity formed by the *copropriétaires* or all the owners of flats in a block.

. . . .**141**

tantièmes   the fraction in which the *quote-part* of the common parts of a *copropriété* attributed to each flat is expressed. The denominator is usually thousands or ten thousands.

. . . .**131**

taxe foncière   an annual tax on the ownership of land payable by the owner.

. . . .**20, 62**

taxe d'habitation   an annual tax payable in respect of the occupation of land payable by the person in occupation on 1 January in any year.

. . . .**62**

termites   the eradication of termites and other wood-eating insects is an obligation of the occupier of a building or part of a building in any *département* in which there is a prefectoral order to that effect. This must be referred to in any contract for the sale of relevant property.

. . . .**46**

testament authentique   a will in notarial form.

. . . .**2, 288**

testament international   a will executed in accordance with the provisions of the Washington Convention of 26 October 1973 (in force in France since 1 December 1994) or the provisions of sections 27 and 28 of the Administration of Justice Act 1982 which are based on the Convention but are not yet in force in the United Kingdom.

. . . .**289**

testament mystique   a will which will usually be a *testament olographe* handed to a *notaire* in a sealed envelope accompanied by certain formalities.

. . . .**289**

testament olographe   a type of will written, signed and dated entirely in the handwriting of the testator.

. . . .**286**

tiers déteneur   a person who holds assets for another person who is alleged to be a debtor may be required to part with those assets to a creditor on service upon him by a *huissier* of a *sommation* or Order to make such payment. It is a garnishee procedure shorn of any need for a prior judgment or Order of the Court.

. . . .**127**

titre exécutoire   an *acte* based on which the equivalent of a writ of execution can be obtained. These include the judgments of French Courts and of foreign Courts in respect of which an *exéquateur* has been obtained, a notarial document which creates

an obligation on the part of one of the parties and certain Orders issued by the Social Security Department.
. . . .**127**

transparence fiscale   the fiscal fiction applicable to certain kinds of SCIs that the company does not have in matters of direct taxation a personality distinct from its shareholders.
. . . .**217**

Trésor Public   the department which manages public finance to which, among other taxes, *taxe foncière* and *taxe d'habitation* are paid.

Tutelle   the equivalent of Court of Protection Receivership.
. . . .**227**

TVA (taxe sur la valeur ajoutée)   British VAT. HT = hors taxe = ex-VAT. TTC = toutes taxes comprises = inclusive of VAT.
. . . .**29**

union libre   this is a more socially acceptable description of *concubinage* or the living together of two persons as though they are married but are not.
. . . .**201**

usucaption   see *prescription acquisitive.*

usufruit   a *droit réel* or 'legal estate' in land entitling the owner of such right to use land in the ownership of another or to enjoy the income from it. In the absence of the trust in French law it is difficult to give an accurate explanation comprehensible to the English lawyer but *usufruit* in land may safely be taken as a life interest in real property provided that it is remembered that it has none of the attributes of the English life interest except possibly those of such an interest under a strict settlement.
. . . . **16, 107**

valeur locative   in the case of such property as is subject to the 1948 Law governing rents, it is the maximum rent which may be charged calculated in accordance with that Law as amended from 1 July 1960. In the more usual case of the lease of business premises, it is the rent fixed by the Court in default of agreement between the parties on the renewal of such a lease.
. . . .**180**

vente aléatoire   a sale such as a sale *en viager* where the element of chance eg the life of an individual is in issue.
. . . .**34**

vente à réméré   a now rarely used type of sale where the seller reserves the right to repurchase the property he has sold within five years on payment of the original sale price and costs or any other formula as to the price which may be agreed between the parties.
. . . . **31, 56**

vente d'immeuble à construire   a sale which is either *à terme* or *en état futur d'achèvement.*
. . . . **19, 31, 69**

vente à terme   a sale by virtue of which the seller undertakes to deliver a property when it has been built, the seller remaining the owner of the land until such delivery has been effected.
. . . . **19, 31, 70**

vente en état futur d'achèvement a sale under which the seller, who remains *maître d'ouvrage* until completion of the building works, sells a property yet to be constructed (usually a flat in a block) and title to the land in question passes to the buyer on exchange of contracts as does thereafter title to the accretions to the building as construction work proceeds.

. . . .**19, 31, 69, 70**

viager libre a sale *en viager* when the buyer is given vacant possession.

. . . .**19, 105**

viager occupé a sale *en viager* when possession is retained by the seller and/or another person chosen by the seller.

. . . .**19, 105**

vices apparents apparent defects.

. . . .**75**

vices cachés latent defects.

. . . .**43, 75**

INDEX

abroad, documents executed 3–4
acceptance
  auctions 117
  beneficiaries 306–10
  children 224–5
  express 308
  forcée 307, 308–9
  gifts 224, 332, 371–2
  inheritance law 238–9
  mortgages 121
  powers of attorney 185
  pure et simple 307–10
  qualified 306
  retroactive 310
  saisine 313
  solvency of the estate, subject to 306
  sous bénéfice d'inventaire 309–10
  tacit 308
  unqualified 306
  wills 229–30
accessoires, droits 16
accounts 135, 139, 143–4, 345–6
achat croisé 204
acte authentique
  completion 59
  gifts 331, 335
  Land Registry 22
  mortgages 123, 125
  notaires 1–3, 33
  plan, sales on 74
  powers of attorney 185, 190–1
acte de vente
  auctions 112
  completion 59–60, 63–7
  expédition 67
  Land Registry 65–6
  plan, sales on 73–4, 78
adjudication judiciaire 111, 114–18
adjudications, titre de 118
adjudication volontaire 111–14
administrateur séquestre 302
administration of estates 323–30
  administrateur séquestre 302
  assets, enquiries as to 324
  auctions 329
  avocats 328
  bad faith 330
  bank accounts 326
  beneficiaries 305–11, 373
    accounting to 301
    distribution 328–30

commencement of 237–8
commissaire-priseur 326
court
  applications to 325, 328, 329
  choice of 323
coutume, certificats de 324
creditors 301, 325
criminal offences 325
death 323
death certificates 324
distribution 328–30
documents 326–7
domicile 311, 323–5, 327
donation-partage 295–8, 329
due execution 301
English law 301, 303, 310–11, 323–6, 328, 330
envoi en possession 323–4, 328
état civil 324
exécuteur testamentaire 301–3, 325
  completion of duties 302–3
  expenses 302
  liability 302
  powers of 301–3
executors 330, 34–5, 374–5
expenses 302
experts 324–5
fraudulent misrepresentation 330
grants of representation 237–8, 323, 325, 326
hérédité, certificats de 327–8
hérédité, petition de 330–1
homologation du testament 237–8
immeubles 329
immobilière, attestation 328
indivision, ownership *en* 147, 328–30
infants 325
inheritance law 236–8
inheritance tax 324, 326
insurance 325
intestacy 328, 330
inventory of contents 325–6
joint bank accounts 326
Land Registry 329
légataire universel 330
lésion 330
lictation 329
matrimonial, régime 328
meubles 302, 325–6, 329, 330
notaires 1, 323–8
notoriété après décès, acte de 326–7

INDEX

administration of estates (*cont.*):
powers of attorney 327, 373–4
preliminary steps 324–5
proof of entitlement 326–7
proper law 310–11
propriété, certificats de 327–8
régime de communauté, universelle 328
régime de séparation de biens 324
renunciation 323
rescission of *partage* 330
saisine, grant of 302–3, 313
sealing the property 325
succession, déclaration de 328
surviving spouse 326
tontine, ownership *en* 328
wills 293–4, 301, 324–5, 327
winding up 303
adoption 224–7, 259, 262, 334, 412–13
adultery, children born in 234–5, 279
advancements 310
adverse possession 18
advertisements 112, 116
affidavits 355
French law 395–8
grants, leading to 395–8
precedents 395–8
renunciation 396–7
will drawn in English, French 397–8
age of majority 225
agricultural property 16–17, 151–2, 212–13, 215, 341
aléa 154, 156–7
alienation, restrictions on 319
alimentaire, pension 277–8
animals, keeping in flats 1, 33
annuities 105, 106–10, 276, 277
apostille 4, 190–1
apportionment 62, 214
apports 87–8
architects 133
arrhes 36–7
artisans 173
asbestos 45–6
assignment
business leases 177–8
contracts 49
pacte de préférence 56
promesse de vente 52
réméré, sale *à* 57
residential leases 163–5
standard conditions 49
associés 88–9
attestation d'acquisition 67
attestation immobilière 238, 328
attorney, powers of *see* **powers of attorney**
auctions 111–18
acceptance 117

acte de vente 112
adjudication judiciaire 111, 114–18
adjudication volontaire 111–14
advertisements 112, 116
avocat 9, 117–18
cahier des charges 112–18
cancellation 114
capacity 113
conclusion of sale 114
conduct of the sale 112–13, 117
creditors 114–16, 118
criminal offences 113
deposits 112
documents 117
folle enchère 118
foreclosure 115–16, 118
Land Registry 117
location 112
mortgages 114
notaires 111–12
notice 116
pre-auction procedure 111–12
price, failure to pay the 113
registration 112
reserve 112, 113
saisie immobilière 114–15
saisine 302
surenchère 114, 117–18
titre d'adjudication 118
auditors 101
authentiques, testaments 236, 286, 288–9, 292, 315
avocat 9, 117–18, 328
avoué 9

bail à réhabilitation 17
bail dérogatoire 183–4
bail emphytéotique 17
bail exclusif 175
bail tous commerce 175
bankruptcy, trustees in 389–90
banks
accounts 326
administration of estates 326
completion 61
notaires 326
surviving spouse 326
tiers détenteur 127–8
transfers 61
Basle Convention on the Establishment of a Scheme of Registration of Wills 1972 292
bâtonnier 9
beneficiaries
acceptation
express 308
forcée 307, 308–9

444

beneficiaries (*cont.*):
  pure et simple 307–10
  qualified 306
  retroactive 310
  solvency of the estate, subject to 306
  sous bénéfice d'inventaire 309–10
  tacit 308
  unqualified 306
  accounting to 301
  administration of estates 301, 305–11, 328–30
  advancements 310
  authorization 308
  capacity 309
  creditors 309
  dead, presumed 258
  debts 305–6, 309
  declarations 309–10
  disposition contractuelle 307
  distribution 328–30
  donation entre époux 307
  election 305–11
  English law 305
  exercise of the option 307
  héritiers 301, 307
  hotchpot 310
  indivision, ownership *en* 147–8, 305–6
  infants 309
  insolvency 306
  international law 310–11
  intestacy 307
  joint and several liability 305–6
  misappropriation 308–9
  notaires 309
  ouverture de la succession 307
  pacte sur succession future 307
  qualified acceptance 306
  recel 308
  régime matrimonial 307
  renunciation 306, 307, 309–10
  revocation of exercised options 310
  saisine 313, 314–15
  surviving spouse 307
  tax evasion 308
  time limits 307
  unqualified acceptance 306
  vesting 147–8
  wills 307
biennale, garantie 77–8
biens à venir, donations de 298–9
birth certificates 23, 412–13
bona vacantia 314
Brussels Convention 1968 17
Brussels Convention abolishing the Legalization of Documents in the Member States of the European Communities 1987 190–1

building contracts 10
building leases 17
business leases 173–84
  artisan 173
  assignment 177–8
  bail dérogatoire 183–4
  bail exclusif 175
  bail tous commerce 175
  business, meaning of 173
  capital gains tax 183
  change of use 176, 178
  chef d'entreprise 173
  commerçant 173
  Companies Registry 173
  compensation
    capital gains tax 183
    demolish and rebuild, lessor to 181
    early termination 174, 178
    renew, refusal to 181–3
    right to remain on premises until receipt of 183
    valuation of losses for refusal to renew 182–3
  competition, restrictions on 175
  concessions 178
  contents of 175–8
  convention d'occupation précaire 184
  copropriété 174, 177
  covenants 175–6
    breaches of 181
    déspécialisation partielle 176–7
    déspécialisation plénière 176–7, 178
    extension or variation of 176–7
    notice of additional users 176
    quiet enjoyment, for 175
    renewal, refusal for breach of 181
  Craftsmen's Register *see* répertoire des métiers 173
  demolition 181
  deposits 174–5
  execution of 175
  franchises 178
  housing co-operatives 174
  improvements 180
  loss of premises for works, indemnity for 174
  maintien, droit de 183
  mixed use 182
  notice of determination 178–9
  notice to quit 174
  obligations of the parties 177
  possession for works 174
  précaire, convention d'occupation 184
  premiums, payment of 175
  professional user 174
  quiet enjoyment, covenants of 175
  rebuilding, demolition and 181

business leases (*cont.*):
  renewal 178–83
    bail dérogatoire 183–4
    compensation 182–3
    covenant, breaches of 181
    demolition 181
    mixed use, premises with 181–2
    refusal of 178–83
    rent 179–80
    repairs 179–80
    valuation of loss for refusal 182–3
    withdrawal of refusal 183
  rent 174–5
    calculation of 175, 179–80
    capping 179–80
    improvements, value of 180
    letting value 180
    renewal, following 179
    review of 175, 180
    sub-letting, increase following 177
  repair 177, 179
  repentir, droit de 183
  sale 175
  security of tenure 178–9
  service charges 174, 180
  sub-leases 177
  tax 183
  term of 174, 180
  use 174–8, 181–2, 184
  works 174

cadastre 20–1, 40, 340
cahier des charges 112–18
caisse de garantie 8
capacity 223–30, 237 *see also* **infants**
  auctions 113
  beneficiaries 309
  biens à venir, donations de 299
  compromis de vente 41–2
  curateurs, appointment of 227–8
  disability, persons of full age under a 227–8
  domicile 223
  dual nationality 223
  état civil 223
  governing law 223
  married persons 230
  mental disabilities 227–8
  mortgages 122–3
  nationality 223
  notaire 223
  powers of attorney 188
  prisoners 228–9
  Société Civile Immobilière 86
  surviving spouse 273–4
  tuteurs, appointment of 227–8
  wills 228–30
capital gains tax 217, 218–19

business leases 183
  compensation 183
  completion 63
  non-residents from 220–2
  notaires 220
  rate of 218–22
  représentation fiscal, need for 221
  residence 245
  returns 221
  secondary residences 220
  viager, sales *en* 109
carte professionnelle 27–8
cash, purchase in 62
certificat de concubinage 201–2
certificat de conformité 75
certificat de coutume 314, 324, 388–92
certificat de propriété 238, 327–8
certificat d'hérédité 327–8
Chancery Division, applications to 225
change of use 176–8
charges 62, 119–28 *see also* **mortgages,**
     service charges
  English trusts 252, 254
  gifts *inter vivos* 252, 254
  immeubles 20
  legacies 321
  sale *à réméré* 56
  standard conditions 47
  wills 254, 291
charges, cahier des 112–18
charging clauses 186
charities 229–30, 254, 317, 342
chef d'entreprise 173
cheques 61
children
  acceptance of interests in estates 224–5
  adoption 225–7
    age limits 226
    English adopted children 225–6
    état civil 225
    gifts 334
    inheritance law 226–7
    intestacy 259
    parentage, proof of 225
    plénière 225–7, 262
    precedents 412–13
    simple 225–7, 259, 262
  adultery, born in 234–5, 279
  age of majority 224
  beneficiaries 309
  British nationality, of 225
  Chancery Division, applications to the 225
  concubinage 203
  conseil de famille 224
  curatelles 227–8
  donation-partage 295–6, 298
  English law 224–5

children (*cont.*):
  gifts 224, 333–4, 335, 338
  governing law 225
  huissier 224
  illegitimacy 227
  inheritance law 225, 226–7, 234–5
  inheritance tax 343, 346–50
  intestate succession 255–7
  life assurance 343
  marriage, *émancipation* on 224
  régime matrimonial 198, 200
  Registrar of Births, Deaths and Marriages 224
  renunciation or retraction of interests 224–5
  réserve 262, 265, 267, 346
  surviving spouse 275–6, 278–9
  tuteurs, appointment of 224
  wealth tax 352
  wills 224
civil status *see état civil*
client money 7, 28
codicils 293
cohabitation *see concubinage*
cohéritiers 340
commerçant 173
commerces, bail tous 175
commercial property 130, 133
commissaire-priseur 326
commission 28, 29, 49, 63, 210
commonhold 19, 145
commorientes 228
communautaire, régime 196
communauté légale 196
communauté universelle, régime de 270–1
companies
  Companies Registry 94, 173, 196
  corporate trustees 248
  documents 339
  inheritance law 339, 341
  offshore 268
  precedents 399–411
  réserve 267–9
  tax 216–17
compensation *see* **damages**
competition, restrictions on 175
completion 59–67
  acte de vente 59–60, 63–7
  additions 65
  after 66–7
  apportionment of outgoings 62
  attendance at 59–60
  attestation d'acquisition 67
  attorneys, representation by 61
  bank transfers 61
  buyers 61–3
  capital gains tax 63

cash 62
cheques 61
commission 63
completion statements 62
corrections 65
damages in lieu of 65–6
date for 49, 60, 73–4
definition 76
delay 75
delivery 65
domicile, élection de 65
encumbrances 66
English law 59–62, 64, 66 7
estate agents, commission of 63
état civil, details of 64
failure to complete 65–6
flats 62, 63–4
frais de notaire 62
huissiers 65
insurance 62, 67, 81
interpreters 64
keys, handing over the 65
Land Registry 65–6
loans 59
location 59–60
marriage, place of 64
meubles 62–3
mortgages 65, 66
notaire 59–65
Notice to Complete 65
plan, sales on 70, 73–6, 81
powers of attorney 61
recevoir l'acte 64
searches 66–7
sellers 63–4
stamp duties 67
standard conditions 49
tax 62, 63
title documents 67
compromis de vente 31, 35–6, 39–49
  acte authentique 39–40
  avoidance of 40
  cadastre 40
  capacity 41–2
  contracts 39–49
  death or incapacity of party 41–2
  deposits 41
  description 40
  drafting 39–40
  easements 41
  exchange of letters 39
  flats 40
  identity of the property sold 40
  Land Registry 39–40
  mistake 30
  negligence 40
  notaire 39–41

compromis de vente (*cont.*):
  plans 40
  price 41
  promesse de vente, comparison with 39–40,
    51–3
  quiet enjoyment 43
  root of title 40
  rural property 40
  sale of land 31, 35–6, 39–49
  seller's obligations 42–9
  value 41
  writing, in 39
compulsory purchase 48
concession immobilière 17
concessions 178
concierge 129, 134
concubinage 201–8
  achat croisé 204
  certificat de concubinage 201–2
  children 203
  definition 201
  domicile 204
  English law 203–4
  financing a purchase of land 204–5
  fiscal effect of 201–2
  funerals, organization of 201
  gifts, *inter vivos* 202
  guarantees 204–5
  indivision, ownership *en* 203–4
  inheritance law 202–5
  inheritance tax 202
  joint purchase 203
  licences 203
  life interests 204
  matrimonial de communauté, régime
    203
  notaire 205
  ownership of land 202–4
  pacte civile de solidarité (PACS) 205–8
  proof of 201–2
  réservataires 202, 204
  sale to other partner, transfer by genuine
    203
  Société civile immobilière 204
  subrogation 204
  tax 201–2, 214
  tontine, ownership *en* 203
  wealth tax 201
  wills, legacies in 202
conditions *see also* **standard conditions**
  cahier des charges 112–18
  mortgages 34, 120–1
  plan, sales on 79–80
  promesse de vente 52
  residential leases 165
  sale of land 34, 36–7
  tontine 154–5

conflict of interests 6
conflict of laws 17, 248
conformité, certificats de 75
conseil de famille 224
Conseil supérieur du notariat 7–8, 292
conseil syndical 145–6
constat 10
constructeurs 78, 82
consuls 190
contents *see* **meubles**
contracts
  assignment 49
  biens à venir, donations de 298
  building 10
  classes 30–1
  compromis de vente 39–49
  conditional 34, 36–7
  disposition contractuelle 307
  English law 26
  estate agents 29, 30, 37
  gaming 106
  latent defects 43–5
  mortgages 34
  notaires 8, 30–4
  pacte civile de solidarité 207
  pacte de préférence 55–6
  penalty clauses 36
  plan, sales on 69–82
  precedents 376–97
  préliminaire 31, 69–78
  printed 37
  promesse de vente 51–3
  régime matrimonial 196, 198
  registration 71
  sale *à réméré* 56–7
  sale of land 25–37
  signatures 37
  Société civile immobilière 84
  sous seing privé 32–3
  translations 37
convention l'occupation précaire 184
conventionnelle, régime de communauté 196,
    197–8, 199
'cooling off' period 100
co-ownership 147–58 *see also* **copropriété,**
    indivision, tontine
co-partage 298
copropriété 19, 63–4, 69, 95–7
  accounts 139, 143–4
  animals, keeping 133
  architects 133
  business leases 174, 177
  change of use 177
  commercial property 130, 133
  common parts 130–1, 133, 141
  commonhold 145
  concierge 129

copropriété (*cont.*):
  conseil syndical 145–6
  definition 130–1
  discrimination 133
  documentation 129–33
  exclusive use of parts 130–1
  executive committee 145–6
  gardien 129, 134, 138
  lots 130, 133
  maintenance 1 43
  meetings 134–41
    accounts 139
    convening 137–41
    location of 139
    minutes 139
    notices 138
    presence at 137
    proxy, attendance by 137
    resolutions 138–41
    voting 137–41
  parties privatives 130–1, 133
  permitted use 133
  plan, sales on 74
  precedents 379–86
  private parts of property 130–1
  professional use 133
  règlement de 74, 130–4, 165
    adoption of 132
    cancellation due to lack of 132
    registration of 131–2
    service charges 134
  residential leases 165
  restrictions 133
  sale of land 19
  service charges 129–31, 133–6, 144, 162, 174
  share sales 19
  société civile d'attribution 95–7
  syndicat de copropriété 130, 132, 136–46
    accounts 143–4
    actions against 144
    appointment of 141–2
    definition 141
    duties of 142–3
    litigation, conduct of 144
    provisional 142
    remuneration 144
    tenure of office 142
  surveyors 133
  use 133, 177
  works 132–3
corporation tax 211, 222
copyright 278
corporéals, droits 19
costs 7, 43, 49
coutume, certificats de 314, 324, 388–92
covenants
  breaches of 162, 181

business leases 175–8, 181
deposits 162
déspécialisation partielle 176–7
déspécialisation plénière 176–7, 178
extension or variation of 176–7
health hazards 45–6
notice of additional users 176
pactes sur la succession future 297–9, 307
quiet enjoyment, for 42–3, 175
renewal, refusal for breach of 181
residential leases 162
Craftsmen's Register *see répertoire des métiers*
creditors
  administration of estates 301, 325
  auctions 114–16, 118
  beneficiaries 309
  inheritance law 344
  régime matrimonial 200
  tontine 156
crédirentier 107–10
criminal offences 113, 325
croisé, achat 204
curatelles 227–8
customary law 296

damages
  business leases 174, 178, 181–3
  capital gains tax 183
  completion 65–6
  demolish and rebuild, for 181
  early termination 174, 178
  Land Registry 21–2
  latent defects 44
  notaires 8
  powers of attorney 186
  promesse de vente 43
  quiet enjoyment 43
  renew, refusal to 181–3
  right to remain on premises until receipt of 183
  sales on plan 71, 75
  service charges 136
  Société civile immobilière 92
  valuation of losses for refusal to renew 182–3
death certificates 23, 324, 414
débirentier 107–10
debts *see also* **creditors**
  beneficiaries 305–6, 309
  gifts 332
  patrimoine, le 19
  régime matrimonial 196–7
  release of 332
  tiers détenteur, le 127–8
décennale, garantie 77

déclarations d'achèvement des travaux 76–7
déclarations de succession 345–6, 351
déclarations sur l'honneur 207
dédit 36
deeds 20
déguisées, donations 296, 332–3, 335
delivery
  completion 65
  definition 42
  délivrance de legs 314–15
  gifts 332
  information 42
  manual 332, 351
  plan, sales on 74
  wealth tax 351
demolition 181
départemental, droit 210
deposits
  arrhes 36–7
  auctions 112
  avocats 33
  business leases 174–5
  compromis de vente 41
  covenants, breach of 162
  English law 36
  estate agents 28, 33, 34
  liens 28
  notaires 28, 33–4, 41
  promesse de vente 51
  residential leases 162
  sale of land 33, 36
  sales on plan 33, 71–3, 80
  standard conditions 49
dérogatoire, bail 183–4
déspécialisation partielle 176–7
déspécialisation plénière 176–7, 178
destruction 166, 287, 291, 320
development land 211
directors 86
disability, persons of full age under a
  227–8
disabled persons 216, 347
disposition contractuelle 307
discipline 9
discrimination 133
divorce 156, 197, 274, 279, 291, 333,
  372
domicile 241–5
  abandonment of 241–2
  administration of estates 311, 323–5, 327
  capacity 223
  choice, of 65, 71, 241–2
  companies 339
  completion 65
  concubinage 204
  English law of 241–5
  English trusts 249–50

home address 243
immeubles 242, 243
inheritance law 233
Inheritance (Provision for Family and
  Dependants) Act 1975 243
inheritance tax 339, 348
intention 241–2
jurisdiction 243
meubles 242–3
nationality 241–2
notaires 3, 243
origin, of 241, 243
pacte civile de solidarité 206, 208
plan, sales on 71
prélèvement, droit de 244–5
proof of 243
régime matrimonial 200
renvoi 243–4
saisine 314
significance of 242–3
Société civile immobilière 86
surviving spouse 273–4
tax 214
viager, sales *en* 106
wills 292
donation, droit de see **gifts tax**
donation entre époux 282–3, 286, 287,
  307
donation-partage 295–8
  administration of estates 295–8, 329
  children 295–6, 298
  co-partages 297–8
  customary law 296
  effects of the gift 297–8
  future, pactes sur la succession 297
  héritiers 298
  historical background 296–7
  life interests 297
  procedure 296–7
  réserve 295–7
  retour, droit de 297
  substitution 297
  tax 298
  valuation 297
  wealth tax 351
donations de biens à venir 298–9
donations déguisées 296, 332–3, 335
donations indirectes 332
donations par personne interposée 331
donations simulées 332–3
double tax 211, 214
  English trusts 251
  inheritance tax 339–40, 342
  residence 245
  UK–France Double Tax Convention 340,
  342
  wealth tax 351

droit accessoire 16
droit coutumier 234
droit de jouissance viagère 275
droit de maintien 183
droit de préférence 120
droit de prélèvement 244–5
droit de repentir 183
droit de retour 258–9, 297
droit de suite 120
droit départemental 210
droit personnel 15
droits principaux 16
droit réel 15, 17, 67, 216
droit viager au logement 277
dual nationality 223
duress 35

easements 16, 41–3, 47
emphytéotique, bail 17
encumbrances 42–3, 66
enforcement of judgments 9, 19, 126
English trusts 247–54
  certificates 249
  charge, gifts subject to a 252, 254
  charity, gifts *inter vivos* to 254
  conflict of laws 248
  corporate trustee 248
  domicile 249–50
  double tax 251
  effect of 248–50
  Hague Convention on the Recognition of
    Trusts 1985 247–8
  income tax 252
  inheritance law 248–50
  inheritance tax 248, 250
  inter vivos gifts 252, 254
  land, trusts of 248–9
  personalty 249–50
  proposed law on 250
  quasi-trusts 252–4
  recognition of 247–8
  registration 248
  réserve 248–51
  residence 251
  settlements, transfer to 251
  Société civile immobilière 88
  stamp duty 251
  strict settlements 252
  substitution fidéicommissaire 252–3
  tax 250–2
  trustees 248–9
  wealth tax 250
  wills 294
envoi en possession 314, 323–4, 328, 390
époux, donation entre 282–3, 286, 287, 307
estate agents 27–9
  carte professionnelle 27–8

  choice of 36
  client money 28
  commission 28, 29, 49, 52, 63
  completion 63
  contracts 29, 30, 37
  deposits 28, 33, 34
  European Union, citizens of 27
  fines 27–8
  fraud 29
  French language, knowledge of 27
  liability of 29
  mandat de vente 28, 29, 30
  notaires 29–30
  price 41
  qualification to act 27–8
  remuneration 29
  standard conditions 49
  translations 37
estates, administration of *see* **administration**
  of estates
état civil
  administration of estates 324
  adoption 225
  birth certificates 23
  capacity 223
  completion 64
  death certificates 23
  immeubles 22–3
  Land Registry 21
  personal details 22–3
  powers of attorney 189
  régimes matrimoniaux 23, 195
  role of 223–4
European Union, citizens of 27
exclusion clauses 44–5
exécuteur testamentaire 301–3
executors
  administration of estates 330, 374–5
  inheritance tax 345
  powers of attorney 374
  precedents 374
  saisine 313
  wills 236
expédition 3, 67
expenses
  administration of estates 302
  exécuteur testamentaire 302
  funeral 344
  inheritance tax 344
  pluripropriété 100–2
  powers of attorney 187
  réserve 263, 294
  residential leases 165
  service charges 133–5
  wills 294
experts 44–6, 324–5
extrinsèque, garantie 73, 76–7

famille, conseil de 224
faux, inscription de 2
fees
  avocat 9
  Land Registry 20, 21, 209–10
  notaires 6–7, 30, 210
  réméré, sale à 57
  tax 209–10
fidéicommissaire, substitution 252–3
fines 2–3, 27–8, 121
fixtures and fittings 15, 162–3
flats 129–46 *see also* **copropriété**
  completion 62, 63–4
  compromis de vente 40
  description 40
  measurement 40
  notaires 63–4
  plans, sales on 69
  price 63–4
  residential leases 162
  sale of land 19, 32, 135
  service charges 63–4, 135
  société civile d'attribution 95–6
  standard conditions 49
  works to be carried out, voting on 62
folle enchère 118
foncière, publicité 20
foncière, taxe 212–13, 214
fonctionnaire 192
foreclosure 115–16, 118
Foreign and Commonwealth Office Legalization Department 191–2
forests 215, 341
forfeiture 169, 291
frais de notaire 62
franchises 178
fraud
  administration of estates 330
  estate agents 29
  gifts 332, 337
  inheritance tax 346
  misrepresentation 330
  sale of land 35
funerals 201, 344
furnished lettings 170–1
furnished property 213–14
furniture and contents of houses *see* **meubles**
futur d'achèvement, vente en l'état 19, 68–78

gaming contracts 106
Garde des Sceaux 2
gardien 129, 134, 138
gérants 90, 92–3, 101, 149–51, 218, 268
gifts
  acceptance 224, 332, 371–2
  acte authentique 331, 335
  adoption 334

biens à venir, donations de 298–9
  charges 252, 254
  charities 254
  children 224, 333–4, 335, 338
  concubinage 202
  consideration 333
  death 332
  debts, release of 332
  déguisées, donations 332–3, 335
  delivery, manual 332
  divorce 333
  donations par personne interposée 332
  English law 331–2
  English trusts 252, 254
  époux, donation entre 307
  formalities 333
  fraud 332, 337
  indirectes, donations 332
  ingratitude of the donee 334–5, 336
  inheritance tax 350–1
  inter vivos 202, 252, 254, 331–7, 350–1
  irrevocable 331
  judicial separation 333
  land, of 370–1
  life assurance 332
  marriage 307, 332–8
  notaires 331
  obligations, accompanied by 334
  pacte civile de solidarité 208
  patrimoine 331, 333
  powers of attorney 370–2
  precedent 370–2
  réserve 263–5, 296, 331, 332–3, 335–6
  restitution 335
  revocation 333–6
  setting aside 332
  shams 332–3
  simulées, donations 332–3
  spouses, to 307, 332–7
  tax 208, 209
    avoidance 332–3
  undue influence 332
  wills 285, 331, 335–6
glossary 419–40
grants of representation
  administration of estates (English) 237–8, 323, 325, 326
  inheritance law 237–8
  inheritance tax 346
  precedents, affidavits of French law leading to 395–8
guarantees 73, 75–8, 204–5

habitation, taxe d' 212, 213–14
Hague Convention abolishing the Requirement of Legislation for Foreign Public Documents 1961 190, 293–4

Hague Convention on the International Protection of Adults 2000 189
Hague Convention on the Law Applicable to Matrimonial Property Regimes 1978 270
Hague Convention on the Recognition of Trusts 1985 247–8
health 45–6
hérédité, certificats de 327–8
hérédité, petition de 330–1
héritiers
   beneficiaries 301, 307
   cohéritiers 340
   donation-partage 297–8
   exécuteur testamentaire 301
   inheritance law 340
   inheritance tax 340, 342
   legacies 321
   légitimes 313, 314–15
   liability 301
   présomptif 215, 342
   réserve 262
   saisine 313, 314–15
   surviving spouse 276–7
   tax 215
historic buildings 341–2
holiday lettings 160
holograph wills 287–8, 336
homologation du testament 237–8
honneur, déclaration sur l' 207
hotchpot 263, 310
housing co-operatives 174
huissiers 10, 165, 168, 224
hypothèque conventionnelle 20, 119–21, 123–4
hypothèque judiciaire 120, 126–7
hypothèque légale 119–20, 125–7

identity documents *see état civil*
illegitimacy 227
immeubles 13–23
   administration of estates 329
   agricultural property 16
   charges 20
   conversion of 14–16
   definition 14
   devolution on death of 293
   domicile 242, 243
   droits personnels 15, 17–18
   easements 16
   English law 13, 15
   état civil 22–3
   inheritance law 233
   interests in property 16
   Land Registry system 20–2
   life interests 16
   meubles 13–16

   nature of 13–16
   notaires 2
   ownership 18
   patrimoine, le 19
   personam, rights *in* 15, 17–18
   pipes 14
   planning 16
   plants 14
   promesse de vente 52
   régime matrimonial 271
   rem, rights *in* 16–18
   réserve 268
   rights over land 16
   saisie 114–16
   saisine 302
   sales of land 19–20, 25, 34
   surviving spouse 273–4
   tax on company ownership 216–17
   trees 14
   usufruit 16
immovables *see immeubles*
improvements 150, 180
income tax 170, 208, 252
incorporéals, droits 19
indemnité d'immobilisation 51, 53
indemnity insurance 8
Index Map 40
indexation 108
indignité, régime de 229
indivision, **ownership** *en* 147–54
   administration of estates 147, 328–30
   agricultural property 151–2
   beneficiaries 305–6
      assets of deceased vested jointly in 147–8
   concubinage 203–4
   conventionnelle 329
   death of co-owner 152
   documentation 151
   English law 147
   exclusive use, payment for 149
   gérant
      appointment of one co-owner as 149–51
      removal 150
      remuneration 149, 151
   improvements 150
   income 150
   Land Registry 150
   life interests 148–50
   limits on disposal 153
   maintenance 151
   management 147–51
   partition under old statutory rules 151–4
   pre-emption rights 153
   régime matrimonial 271
   réserve 296
   residential leases 165
   sale 153–4

indivision, **ownership** *en (cont.):*
  Société civile immobilière 148
  spouses 151
  tenants in common 147
  use 149
  wealth tax 352
infants *see* **children**
ingratitude 334–5, 336
inheritance law 233–9 *see also réserve,* **wills**
  acceptance of an estate 238–9
  administration of estates 236, 324, 326
    commencement of 237–8
    English grants 237–8
  adoption 226–7
  adultery, children born in 234–5
  attestation immobilière 238
  capacity to inherit 237
  certificat de propriété 238
  children 225–7
  concubinage 202
  distribution 239
  domicile 233
  English law 235–8
  family assets 234
  freedom of testamentary disposition 233–5
  homologation du testament 237–8
  immeubles 233
  insolvency 238–9
  intestacy 234, 235–6
  Land Registry 238
  légitime 234
  lex situs 233
  meubles 233
  notaire 237–8
  pacte civile de solidarité 208
  partage 239
  relatives 234
  renunciation 238–9
  residence 245–6
  Roman law 233–4
  saisine 238
  Société civile immobilière 94
  sources of 233–5
  surviving spouse 233, 235, 239
  tax 215
  tontine 155–7
  viager, sales *en* 106, 270
  wills 285
  winding up an estate 230
Inheritance (Provision for Family and
    Dependants) Act 1975 243
inheritance tax 209, 270, 339–51
  accounts 345–6
  agricultural land 341
  ascendants 340, 342, 348
  assets, taxable 340
  businesses 341

cadastre 340
charities 342
children 343, 346, 347–50
cohéritiers 340
companies 339, 341
concubinage 202
creditors 344
déclaration de succession 345–6, 351
deductions 344–5
disabled persons 347
domicile 339, 348
double tax conventions 339–40
English law 340, 342, 345–6, 348
English trusts 248, 250
executors 345
exempt assets 340–2
forests 341
fraud 346
funeral expenses 344
gifts *inter vivos* 350–1
grandchildren 349
grant of representation 346
héritiers 340
  présomptif 342
historic buildings 341–2
imposition 340
instalments 346–7
interest 346
life assurance 343
life interests 349
  cesser of 342
  valuation of 344
meubles 348
new property 341
nil rate bands 340–1, 344, 347–50
notaires 342, 345
ownership 340
pacte civile de solidarité 348
payment of 346–7
penalties for late lodgement 346
personal chattels 343–4
powers of attorney 345
principal residence 341
rates of 347–9
régime matrimonial 198, 345
relatives 348
reliefs 347
réméré, sale *à* 57
renunciation 349
réserve 263, 294, 296, 345, 346
réservataires 340
residence 339
siblings 347, 348
Société civile immobilière 94, 342
stamp duty 232
substitution 347
surviving spouse 340, 344, 346–9

inheritance tax (*cont.*):
  tontine, ownership *en* 157–8, 269–70, 342
  UK–France Double Tax Convention 340,
    342
  valuation 344, 345
  vesting 342
  wealth tax 351–2
  wills 345–6
  woodlands 341
inscription de faux 2
insects 46
insolvency 124, 238–9, 306
insurance
  administration of estates 325
  avocat 9
  builders 4–5
  children 343
  completion 62, 67, 81
  gifts 332
  indemnity 8
  inheritance tax 343
  life 281, 332, 343
  new builds 4–5
  notaires 4–5, 8
  plan, sales on 76–8, 81–2
  réserve 343
  residential leases 169
  searches 67
  service charges 134
  tax 212
intellectual property 15, 274, 278
interpreters 64
intestate succession 255–9
  adoption 259
  beneficiaries 307
  children 255–7
  collateral relations 256–7
  dead, beneficiaries presumed 258
  English law 235, 257
  exécuteur testamentaire 301
  grandchildren 256
  héritier bénéficiaire 301
  inheritance law 234, 235–6
  legacies 320
  order of 255–9
  parents 256
  precedents 390
  régime matrimonial 270–1
  representation 257–8
  réserve 234, 239, 261–2
  retour, droit de 258–9
  siblings and their issue 256
  substitution 257–8
  surviving spouse 255, 257, 259, 273–9,
    282
  trusts, held on statutory 257
  wills 229

intrinsèque, garantie 73, 77
inventory of contents 325–6

joint and several liability 305–6
joint bank accounts 326
joint ownership of land 147–58 *see also*
  copropriété, indivision, tontine
jouissance à temps partagé 19–20
jouissance viagère, droit de 275
judgments, enforcement of 9, 126
judiciaire, adjudication 111, 114–18
judicial separation 197, 198, 274, 279, 291,
  333
jurisdiction 2, 17, 200, 206, 243

keys, handing over the 65, 75, 165

Land Registry scheme 20–2
  acte authentique 22
  acte de vente 65–6
  administration of estates 329
  attestation immobilière 328
  auctions 117
  cadastre 20–1, 40
  completion 65–6
  compromis de vente 39–40
  damages 21–2
  état civil 21
  fees 20, 21, 209–10
  immeubles 20–2
  indivision, ownership *en* 150
  inheritance law 238
  mortgages 22, 128
  ownership 20
  pacte de préférence 56
  plan, sales on 78
  plots 20
  privilège de vendeur 22
  promesse de vente 22, 52
  Property Register 21
  Proprietorship Register 21
  publicité foncière 20
  réméré, sale à 57
  searches 22, 66
  sous seing privé 22
  tax 20, 22, 209–10
  time limits 22
  transfers of land 21
  voluntary registration 22
language 27, 37, 192–3, 290, 292–4, 355
latent defects
  contracts 43–5
  damages 44
  exclusion clauses 44–5
  experts 44
  good faith 44
  liability 43–5

latent defects (*cont.*):
  notaire 45
  sales on plan 45, 75
  sellers 43–5
  surveys 45
  use 43–4
lead 46
leases *see also* **business leases, residential**
  leases
  agricultural land 17
  building 17
  concession immobilière 17
  droits réels 17
  life, for 107
  long 17
  meubles 15
  pacte de préférence 55
  rent 17
  Société civile immobilière 218
  surviving spouse 276–7
  tax 218
  viager, sales *en* 107
legacies 317–21
  alienation, restriction on 319
  charges 321
  charities 317
  concubinage 202
  conditional 318–19
  délivrance de legs 314–15
  destruction 320
  English law 317, 319
  formalities 317
  héritiers 321
  intestacy 320
  lapse 320–1
  légataire à titre universel 318
  légataire particulier 318
  légataire universel 301, 307, 315, 318, 330
  loss of subject of 320
  marriage 319
  penal clauses 319
  public policy 319
  réserve 318, 319
  residuary estate 318, 320
  revocation 320
  saisine 320–1
  sous condition résolutoire 319
  substitution 320
  terme, à 319
  types of 317–18
  wills 317–21
legal profession 1–10 *see also* **notary**
légal, régime de communauté 196–7,
  199
lésion 330
licences 107, 203, 214, 277
lictation 329

liens 28
life assurance 281, 332, 343
life interests
  cesser of 342
  concubinage 204
  donation-partage 297
  inheritance tax 342, 344, 349
  immeubles 16
  indivision, ownership *en* 148–50
  leases 107
  licences 277
  preservation of 34
  sale of land 34
  surrender of 352
  surviving spouse 274–7, 279–82
  tax 212–15
  valuation 344
  viager, sales *en* 107
  wealth tax 352
liquidation 93, 95
local authorities 48
lodgings 170–1

mainlevée 125
maintenance 143, 151, 212, 275, 277–8
maintien, droit de 183
mandat de vente 28, 29, 30, 185–8, 193
map, Land Registry index 40
marriage *see also* *matrimonial, régime,*
  surviving spouse
  biens à venir, donations de 298–9
  capacity 230
  children 224
  completion 64
  divorce 333
  donation entre époux 307
  émancipation on 224
  English law 298
  existence of 283
  gifts 307, 332–8
  indivision, ownership *en* 151
  judicial separation 333
  legacies 319
  place of 64
  Société civile immobilière 86, 87
  tontine 269
  wealth tax 351–2
  wills 291
mental disabilities 227–8
meubles
  administration of estates 302, 325–6, 329,
    330
  completion 62–3
  conversion 14–16
  definition 14–15
  domicile 242–3
  droit réel 15

meubles (*cont.*):
  fixtures and fittings 15
  immeubles 13–16
  in rem rights 15
  inheritance law 233
  inheritance tax 348
  intellectual property 15
  inventory of contents 325–6
  leases 15
  moorings 15
  réserve 268
  saisine 302
  sale of land 25
  sales of shares, tax treatments of 15–16
  surviving spouse 273–4
  tax 209–10
minors *see* **children**
misappropriation 308–9
misrepresentation 330
maîtrise d'oeuvre 70
maîtrise d'ouvrage 70
mixed use, premises with 69, 181–2
mobile homes 213–14
money
  completion in cash 61
  laundering 87
  patrimoine, le 19
moorings 15
mort civile, la 228–9
mortgages 119–28
  abroad, documents executed 123
  acceptance 121
  acte authentique 123, 125
  attorneys, power of 123
  auctions 114
  avocat 9
  capacity 122–3
  completion 65, 66
  conditions 34, 120–1
  contracts conditional on 34
  co-owners 122–3
  declarations 47
  deeds 20
  demand to pay 126
  enforcement of foreign judgments 126
  English law 20–2
  equitable 120
  execution of 123
  fines 121
  Hague Convention 1978 270–1
  hypothèque conventionnelle 20, 119–21, 123–4
  hypothèque judiciaire 120, 126–7
  hypothèque légale 119–20, 125–7
  insolvency 124
  Land Registry 22, 128
  legal 20, 119–20

  loans 121
  mainlevée 125
  mortgages 20, 123
  notaire 20, 123
  plan, sales on 72–3, 78
  pluripropriété 100
  préférence, droit de 120
  priority 123–4
  privilèges 124
  promesse de vente 53
  property which can be mortgaged 121–2
  registration of 9, 119–20, 123–6
  release 125
  rem, rights *in* 17
  remedies 120
  réméré, sale à 56–7
  saisie immobilière 127
  sale of land 34
  standard conditions 47
  suite, droit de 120
  third parties 127
  tiers détenteur, le 127–8
  tax 127
  time limits 121, 127
  transfer of 125
  types of 119–20
movables *see* **meubles**
moyens de contrainte 36
mystique, testament 236, 286, 289, 290, 315

nationality
  capacity 223
  children 225
  dual 223
  domicile 241–2
  pacte civile de solidarité 206–7
negligence 4–5, 8–9, 40, 66
notaires 1–8
  actes authentiques 1–3, 33
  administration of estates 1, 323–8
  advice, provision of 4
  appointment 1–2
  auctions 111–12
  bank accounts 326
  beneficiaries 309
  capacity 223
  capital gains tax, accounting for 221
  choice of 6, 29–30
  client money 7
  compensation fund 8
  completion 59–65
  compromis de vente 39–41
  compulsory purchase 48
  concubinage 205
  conflicts of interest 6
  Conseil Supérieur 7–8

notaires (*cont.*):
  contract 33–4
    claims in 8
    classes in 30–1
    time limits 33–4
  costs 7
  CRIDON (*Centre de recherche,*
    d'information et de documentation
    notarial) 6
  deposits 28, 33–4, 41
  discipline 7
  domicile 3, 243
  encumbrances 66
  English law 2–8
  enquiries 66
  estate agents 29–30
  expédition 3
  fees 6–7, 30, 210
  fines 2, 3
  flats 40
  frais de notaire 62
  Garde des Sceaux, appointment by 2
  gifts 331
  Hague Convention apostille 4
  immovable property 2
  inheritance law 237–8
  inheritance tax 342, 345
  inscription de faux 2
  insurance 4–5, 8
  jurisdiction 2
  latent defects 45
  negligence 4–5, 8, 66
  negotiations 30
  offers 33–4
  officier ministériel, as 2
  officier public, as 2
  outrages against 2
  pacte civile de solidarité 207
  plan, sales on 73–4
  powers of attorney 186, 187, 189–93
  recevoir un acte 64
  régime matrimonial 196, 270–1
  remuneration 6–7
  role of 1–6
  saisine 314
  sale of land 6–7, 29–31, 33–6
  sale of property 2
  searches 66–7
  self-regulation 7–8
  Société civile immobilière 87, 269
  standard conditions 49
  surviving spouse 282
  tax 210, 220
  testament authentique 2–3
  tontine 156–7, 269, 342
  tort, claims in 8
  warnings, providing 4

wills 228, 236–7, 285, 288–90, 292–4
Notary Public 191
notice to quit 166, 167–9, 174
notoriété après décès, acte de 326–7, 413–16

offers 31, 55–8
officier ministériel 2
officier public 2
offshore companies 268
options
  beneficiaries 310
  pacte de préférence 55–6
  promesse de vente 51–3
  revocation of exercised 310
  sale of land 30–1
  surviving spouse 275–6, 280–1
ouverture de la succession 307

PACS (*pacte civile de solidarité*) 205–8
  concubinage 201–2
  contract 207
  déclaration sur l'honneur 207
  definition 206
  determination of a 207
  domicile 206, 208
  gifts tax 208
  income tax 208
  inheritance tax 208, 348
  jurisdiction 206
  nationality of parties 206–7
  notaire 207
  ownership of assets 207–8
  persons who may enter into 206–7
  registration 206–7
  same sex relationships 205–6
  social security 208
  Société civile immobilière 89
  succession 205–6, 208
  tax 208, 351–2
  wealth tax 351–2
pacte de préférence 31, 55–6
pactes sur la succession future 297–9, 307
parentage, proof of 225
partage see donation-partage
partage, réscission of 330
parties privatives 130–1, 133
patrimoine, le 19, 267, 331, 333
penal clauses 319
penalty clauses 36–7
pension alimentaire 277–8
personnels, droits 15, 17–18
petition d'hérédité 330–1
pipes 14
planning 16, 47, 75, 76
plan, sales on 69–82
  acte authentique 74
  acte de vente 73–4, 78

INDEX

plan, sales on (*cont.*):
breach of contract by developer 75
builders, plans supplied by 79–81
buyers, insurance for 76–8
certificat de conformité 75
completion 70
  date of 73–4
  definition 76
  delay in 75
  insurance 81
conditions 79–80
constructeurs 78, 81–2
contrat préliminaire 69–78
  contents of 72–3
  registration 71
contracts 69–82
damages 71, 75
defects 75, 77–8
definition 69
delivery 78
deposits 33, 71–3, 80
domicile, élection de 71
droits réels 78
elevations 74
finance 71–2
flats 69
good faith 71
guarantees 73, 75–7
insurance 76–8, 81–2
keys, handing over the 75
Land Registry 78
latent defects 45, 75
maîtrise d'oeuvre 70
maîtrise d'ouvrage 70
mixed residential and business use 69
mortgages 72–3, 78
notaire 73–4
owners, plans supplied by 81–2
passing of property 78
penalties 74, 81
planning 75, 76
price 71, 74, 80
registration 71, 78
règlement de copropriété 74
repayments 77
réservant 70
réservataire 70
residential use 69
sale of land 19, 32, 69–82
service charges 74
services, indication of 74
specific performance 71
specifications 72, 75
stage payments 74–6, 80–1
standard plans 70
surveyors 75
tax 74

time limits 69
transfer, time of 70
vente à terme 69–70, 78–81
vente en l'état futur d'achèvement 69–78
plants 14
plénière, adoption 225–7, 262
pluripropriété 99–103
auditors 101
cooling off 100
Executive Committee 101
expenses 100–2
gérants 101
inheritance 100
management 101
meetings 101–2
mortgages 100
owning companies 100
sale of land 19–20
shares
  disposal of 102–3
  sale offers 100
shareholders 100–2
Société civile d'attribution 99, 100
statuts 100–1
tax 99–100
powers of attorney 185–93
abroad, executed 190
acceptance 185
accounting to donors 187
acte authentique 185, 190–1
administration of estates 327, 373–4
adoption 365–6
authority 187
Brussels Convention abolishing the Legalization of Documents in the Member States of the European Communities 1987 190–1
capacity 188
charging clause 186
choice of attorney 192–3
completion 61
copies of 189–90
damages 186
death 188
definition 185
determination of power 187–8
disclosure 187
divorce 372
duration of powers 189
duties of the attorney 186–7
enduring power 188–9
English law 186, 189–94
état civil 189
execution of powers 190
expenses 187
Foreign and Commonwealth Office Legalization Department 191–2

powers of attorney (*cont.*):
form of power 192
French Consuls 190
gift of land 370–2
Hague Convention apostille 1961 190–1
Hague Convention on the International
    Protection of Adults 2000 189
inheritance tax 345
mandat 185–8, 193
mortgages 123
notaires 186, 187, 189–93
Notary Public 191
partition on divorce 372
precedent 355–75
    administration of estate by beneficiary
        373–4
    administration of estate by English
        executors 374–5
    adoption of new *régime* 365–6
    gift of land 370–2
    partition on divorce 372
    purchase of flat or house 364
    renouncing an interest in an estate 366–7
    sale of flat or house 363
    Société civile immobilière, formation of
        369–70
    Société civile immobilière, purchase of
        shares in 368
    Société civile immobilière, sale of shares
        of 367
    tontine, renunciation of 367
procuration 185
remedies 187–8
remuneration of attorney 186, 187
renunciation 188, 366–7
revocation of 187–8, 189
sale 363
Société civile immobilière 87, 367–70
solicitors 193
substitutes 187
tontine 367
translations 192–3
precedents
administration of estates
    beneficiary, by 373–4
    English executors 374
    power of attorney 373–4
adoption 412–13
affidavits 355
    French law 396–9
    grants, leading to English 396–9
    renunciation 397–8
    will drawn in English, French 398–9
birth certificates, translation of UK 413–14
companies 400–12
contracts 375–95
copropriété 378–87

coutume, certificats de 388–92
death certificate, translation of UK 414–15
declaration of English law
    envoi en possession, obtaining 390
    intestacy law in England 391
    sale/purchase by UK company of French
        land 388–9
    sale of French property by trustee in
        bankruptcy 389–90
    wills, validity of 392
details of parties 354–5
divorce
    partition 372
    power of attorney 372
envoi en possession, obtaining 390
execution 355–6
executors
    administration of estates by English
        374
    power of attorney 374
form of 354–5
gifts
    acceptance of 371–2
    land, of 370–1
    power of attorney 370–2
grant of representation
    affidavit of French law leading to 396–7
    French will drawn in English 398–9
    renunciation 397–8
intestacy law, declaration of English 391
land
    declaration of English law for
        sale/purchase by UK company 388–9
    gift of 370–1
    power of attorney 370–1
loan offers, transfer of 419–20
notarial documents 355
notoriété, acte de 415–18
partition on divorce 372
powers of attorney 355–74
    administration of estate by beneficiary
        373–4
    administration of estate by English
        executors 374
    adoption of new regime 365–6
    gift of land 370–2
    partition on divorce 372
    purchase of flat or house 364
    renouncing an interest 366–7
    sale of flat or house 363
    Société civile immobilière, formation of
        369–70
    Société civile immobilière, purchase of
        shares in 368
    Société civile immobilière, sale of shares
        of 367
    tontine, renunciation of 367

precedents (*cont.*):
  purchase of flat or house, power of attorney
    for 364
  renunciation
    affidavit of French law 396–7
    grant of representation 396–7
    power of attorney 366
    tontine, renunciation of 367
  sale of flat or house, power of attorney for
    363
  shareholders' meetings, minutes of 408–9
  shares, transfer of 409–12
  Société civile immobilière 400–412
    formation of 369–70
    gérant, shareholders' meeting to appoint
      new 407–8
    power of attorney 367–70
    purchase of shares in 368
    sale of shares to UK company 367
    shareholders' meetings, minutes of 408–9
    statuts 400–8
    transfer of shares 409–12
  standard conditions 46–9
  suspensive, compromis de vente sous
    condition 378–87
  tontine, renunciation of 367
  translations 355
  trustee in bankruptcy, sale of French
    property by 388–9
  usage, prêt à 417–19
  vente, promesse de 375–8
  wills 355, 393–5
    affidavits of French law 398–9
    declarations of English law as to validity
      of 392
    English, French wills drawn in 398–9
    grants of representation 398–9
    holograph 393
    international 394–5
    réserve 394
pre-emption rights 48, 153, 167–8
préférence, droit de 120
premiums 175
préscription 18, 43
price
  auctions 113
  compromis de vente 41
  estate agents 41
  flats 63–4
  plan, sales on 71, 74, 80
  promesse de vente 43, 52
  réméré, sale *à* 56–7
  standard conditions 48
  tontine 157
  'under the table' transactions 41
Principal Probate Registry 289–90
prisoners 228–9

privilège immobilier spécial 135–6
privilège de vendeur 22
probate 294
procuration 185
professionnel de l'immobilier 52–3
promesse de vente
  acte de vente 53
  assignment 52
  compromis de vente 39–40, 51–3
  conditions 52
  contracts 51–3
  deposits 51
  English law 51
  estate agents, commission of 52
  exercise of the option 52–3
  form of 51–2
  immeuble 52
  indemnité d'immobilisation 51, 53
  Land Registry 22, 52
  mortgages 53
  options 51–3
  penalties 52
  precedent 376–9
  price 52
  sale of land 51–3
property owning companies *see société civile*
  d'attribution, Société civile immobilière
Property Register 21
Proprietorship Register 21
publicité foncière 20

quasi-trusts 252–4
quiet enjoyment, covenant for 42–3, 175
quit, notice to 174
quotité disponible 262–4, 295, 335–6, 343

real property *see immeubles*
rebuilding 109, 181
recel 308
recevoir un acte 64
réduction, **action** *en* 264–5
réel, droit 15, 17, 78, 216
re-entry 169
régime matrimonial 195–200
  administration of estates 328
  assets 196–9
  beneficiaries 307
  children 198–200
  commercial activity, engaging in 196–200
  communauté conventionnelle 196, 197–8,
    199
  communauté légale 196–7, 199
  communauté universelle 197–8, 270–1
  Companies Registry—registration with 196
  concubinage 203
  contrat de mariage 196–8
  creation of a 195–6
  creditors 200

régime matrimonial (cont.):
  death 197
  debts 196–7
  divorce 197
  domicile 200
  English law 23, 195, 199
  état civil 23, 195
  exclusions from 197–8
  family, interests of the 199–200
  Hague Convention of 14 March 1978
    199–200
  immeubles 271
  indivision, ownership *en* 271
  inheritance tax 198, 345
  intestacy 270–1
  judicial separation 197–8
  jurisdiction 200
  notaire 196, 270–1
  participation aux acquêts 199
  saisine 314
  séparation de biens 198–9, 324
  settlements 195
  surviving spouse 197–8, 283
  tax 200, 210
  termination of 197
  trusts 195
  variation of a 199–200
Registrar of Births, Deaths and Marriages
  224
registration *see also* **Land Registry**
  auctions 112
  contracts 71
  English trusts 248
  mortgages 9, 119–20, 123–6
  pacte civile de solidarité 206–7
  plan, sales on 71, 78
  Société civile immobilière 87
  wills 292, 327
rem, **rights in** 16–18
  bail emphytéotique 17
  bail à réhabilitation 17
  Brussels Convention of 27 September 1968
    17
  conflict of laws 17
  droits accessoires 16
  droits principaux 16
  English law 17–18
  exclusive jurisdiction 17
  immeubles 16–18
  meubles 15
  mortgages 17
  personam, rights *in* 17–18
  recovery of land, rights of 16–17
remboursement, garantie de 73, 77
***réméré*, sale à** 56–7
remuneration
  attorneys 188

avocats 9
copropriété, syndic de 144
estate agents 29
gérants 93, 149, 151
notaires 6–7
powers of attorney 188
renovation 95
rent 17, 161–3, 174–5, 179–80
renunciation
  affidavit of French law 397–8
  beneficiaries by 306, 307, 309–10
  children 224–5
  inheritance law 238–9
  inheritance tax 349
  precedent
    affidavit of French law 397–8
    grant of representation 397–8
    power of attorney 366
    tontine, renunciation of 367
  réserve 262, 263
  saisine 313
  sale of land 32–3
renvoi 243–4
repairs 136, 162–3, 177, 179–80
repentir, droit de 183
répertoire des métiers 173
représentant fiscal accredité 63, 220–2
rescission of *partage* 330
réserve 238, 239, 261–5
  adoption 262
  ascendants 262, 265, 340
  avoiding the 267–71
  calculation of 262, 263–5, 296, 345,
    346
  children 262, 265, 267, 346
  companies as owners, to avoid 267–9
  concubinage 202, 204
  donation déguisée 296
  donation-partage 295–7
  English domicile, avoidance by people with
    an 267–71
  English law 263, 267
  English trusts 248–51
  exceptions 263–4
  exécuteur testamentaire 303
  expenses 263, 294
  gérants 268
  gifts 263–5, 296, 331–3, 335–6
  héritier 262
  hotchpot 263
  immeubles 268
  indivision, ownership *en* 296
  inheritance tax 263, 294, 296, 345, 346
  intestacy 234, 239, 261–2
  legacies 318, 319
  life assurance 343
  meubles 268

réserve (*cont.*):
occupation rent free of property owned by
    SCIs 268
offshore companies 268
patrimoine, la 267
plan, sales on 70
purpose of 261
quotité disponible 262–4, 295, 335–6,
    343
réduction, action *en* 264–5
régime de communauté universelle 270–1
renunciation 262, 263
representation, rules relating to 262
réservataires 70, 202, 204, 234–5, 239,
    261–5, 294, 315, 340
restoration 263
réunion fictive 264
saisine 315
Société civile immobilière 268–9
substitution 262
surviving spouse 261, 265, 273, 279
tax 268
tax havens 268
tontine, ownership *en* 269–70
valuation 263–4, 296
viager, sales *en* 270
wills 234, 262, 285, 294
residence 245–6
capital gains tax 245
double tax 245
English trusts 251
income tax 245–6, 251
inheritance tax 245–6, 339, 341
principal 341
wealth tax 245
residential leases 159–71
abandonment 167
assignment 163–5
contents of the lease 164–5
contracting out 160
copropriété 165
death of lessee 167
defects 163
deposits for breaches of covenant 162
destruction of the premises 166
determination during the term of the lease
    166–7, 169
English law 159, 163
expenses incurred in granting 165
family reasons, taking possession for 165–6
fittings, function of 162–3
flats 162
forfeiture 169
furnished lettings 170–1
holiday lettings 160
huissier 165, 168
income tax 170

indivision, ownership *en* 165
insurance 169
keys, handing over the 165
lessees' obligations 162–4
lessors' obligations and rights 162–3
lodgings 170–1
notice to quit 166, 167–9
pre-emption rights 167–8
principal residence 159–60, 162, 169–70
professional use 160
re-entry 169
renewal 161, 168–9
rent 161–3
    consent to 161
    control 160
    increase 161
    instalments 161
repair 162–3
sale 167–8
Schedule of Conditions 165
seasonal lettings 169–70, 171
service charges 162
service of notice to quit 167–8
Société civile immobilière 165
sub-tenancies 163–4
suitable alternative accommodation 168
tax 170–1
tenant protection 160
term of the lease 165–6
    increasing the 168
    lessee's rights at the end of the 168
    lessor's rights at the end of the 167–8
tourist tax 171
residuary legatees 318, 320, 330
restitution 335
réunion fictive 264
Roman law 233–4
royalties 278
rural property 40

saisie 114–15, 127
saisine 313–15
acceptance 313
beneficiaries, who have 313, 314–15
bona vacantia 314
certificats de coutume 314
death, proof of 314
délivrance de legs 314–15
domicile 314
English law, comparison with 313–14
envoi en possession 314
exécuteur testamentaire 302
héritiers légitimes 313, 314–15
immeubles 302
inheritance law 238
legacies 315, 320–1
légataire universel 315

saisine (*cont.*):
  meubles 302
  proof of right to 313–14
  renunciation by a beneficiary 313
  réservataires 315
  vesting 313
  wills 314, 315
sale *à rémeré* 56–7
sale of land 25–37 *see also* **auctions,**
  compromis de vente, copropriété, estate
  agents, plan, sales on, promesse de
  vente
  arrhes, les 36–7
  business leases 175
  buyers, statutory protection for 31–4
  cancellation 32, 33–4
  commonhold 19
  completion 59–67
  contracts for the 25–32
    classes of 30–1
    common to all, matters 35–7
    conditional 34, 36–7
    English law 26
    huissiers 10
    mortgages, conditional on grant of 34
    penalty clauses 36
    printed 37
    signatures, *mention* added to 37
    sous seing privé 32–3
    translations 37
  copropriété, en 19
  dedit 36
  definition 25
  deposits 33, 36
  duress 35
  English law 26
  en l'état futur d'achèvement 19, 31
  flats 19, 32, 135
  fraud 35
  immeubles 19–20, 25, 34
  indivision, ownership *en* 153–4
  inspections 32
  jouissance à temps partagé 19–20
  life interests, preservation of 34
  meubles 25
  mortgages 34
  moyens de contrainte 36
  negotiation of sales 26–7
  notaire 2, 6–7, 29–31, 33–6
  offers 31, 57–8
  options 30–1
  pacte de préférence 31, 55–6
  penalty clauses 36–7
  plan, sales on 19, 32, 69–82
  powers of attorney 363
  precedents 363
  pre-contracts 26, 32

  promesse de vente 51–3
  proof 26, 35–6
  rémeré, sale *à* 56–7
  renunciation, right of 32–3
  service charges 135
  Société civile d'attribution 19
  surveys 32, 36
  types of 19–20
  'unmaking' of 34–5
  valuation 32, 36
  viager, en 19
  writing, evidenced in 25–6
same sex relationships 205–6
schedule of condition 165
SCIs *see Société civile immobilière*
sealing the property 325
searches 22, 66–7, 292, 314
seasonal lettings 169–70, 171
security of tenure 178–9
seizure 19, 135
sellers
  health hazards, covenants as to 45–6
  information, to provide 42
  latent defects 43–5
  obligations of 41–9
  quiet enjoyment 42–3
  standard conditions 46–9
séquestre, administrateur 302
service 10, 136, 167–8
settlements 195, 251
shams 332–3
shares
  allotment of 87–8
  built, property yet to be 19
  copropriété, en 19
  disposal 102–3
  meubles 15–16
  offers 100
  pluripropriété 100–3
  precedents 407–11
  sales 15–16, 19, 100
  shareholders 96–7, 100–2, 218, 268
    death of 92
    gérants 268
    meetings 91, 407–8
    minutes of meetings 408–9
    names of 90
    Société civile immobilière 85, 87–92,
      218
    tax 218
    transparence fiscale 218
    UK resident 218
  Société civile d'attribution 96–7, 218
  Société civile immobilière 85, 87–92, 218
siège social 89
signatures 37, 42, 286, 290
social security 208

Société civile d'attribution 95–7
  copropriété 95–7
  flats, financing the building of 95–6
  instalments 95
  liquidation 95
  management 96
  objects of 95–6
  pluripropriété 99, 100
  renovation 95
  shareholders 96–7, 218
  tax 212, 217–18
  transparence fiscale 217–18
Société civile immobilière 83–94
  applicable law 85
  apports 87–8
  associés 88–9
  attorneys 87
  capacity of parties 86
  capital 90
  cause for which company is formed 87
  civil 84–6
  commercial 84–7
  Companies Registry 94
  concubinage 204
  consent 86
  contents of the *statuts* 89–91
  contracts 84
  contrat de société 85
  corporation tax 211
  damages 92
  definition 84
  directors 86
  domicile, matrimonial 86
  duration of the company 90
  EC law 85
  English law 85–6, 94, 268–9
  English trusts 88
  families 87
  form of the *statuts* 87–8
  formation of 85–7, 94, 369–70
  gérants 218
    appointment of 90, 92, 407–8
    management of 92
    remuneration 93
    réserve 268
    role of 92–3
    shareholders, as 268
  illegality 87
  incorporation 85
  indivision, share ownership *en* 148
  inheritance tax 94, 342
  invalidity, declarations of 87
  liquidation 93
  letting purposes, for 218
  list of 84
  management of 92–3
  meetings of shareholders 91

money laundering 87
name of the company 89
nature of 84–5
notaires 87, 269
notification of formation of 94
objects 86, 90
pacte civile de solidarité 89
powers of attorney 367–70
precedents 400–12
  formation of 369–70
  gérant, shareholders' meeting to appoint
    new 408–9
  power of attorney 367–70
  purchase of shares in 368
  sale of shares to UK company 367
  shareholders' meetings, minutes of
    408–9
  statuts 400–8
  transfer of shares 409–12
profits, share of 90–1
purchase of property contemporaneous with
  formation of 87
registered office 89–90
registration 87
réserve 268–9
residential leases 165
sale of land 19
shareholders 85, 87–9
  death of 92
  gérants, as 268
  meetings of 91, 408–9
  names of 90
  transparence fiscale 218
  UK resident 218
shares
  allotment of 87–8
  transfer of 91–2, 367, 408–9
siège social 89
spouses 86, 87
statuts 399–407
tax 93–4, 211, 213, 217–18, 222
  avoidance 94
  corporation 211
  English 268–9
  evasion 85, 87
  inheritance 94
  réserve 268
  transparence fiscale 217–18
  transfer 88–9
  writing, *statuts* in 87
sous seing privé, **documents** 22, 32–3
specific performance 71
specifications 72, 75
spouses *see* **marriage**, *régime matrimonial*,
  surviving spouse
stamp duties 209–11
  English trusts 251

INDEX

stamp duties (*cont.*):
  inheritance tax 232
  réméré, sale *à* 57
  viager, sales *en* 109
standard conditions
  assignment of contracts 49
  buyers, for the benefit of 47–8
  charges 47
  completion date 49
  compulsory purchase 48
  conditions, meaning of 46–9
  costs 49
  deposits 49
  easements 47
  enquiries 47
  estate agents, commission of 49
  flats 49
  loans 47
  local authorities 48
  mortgages 47
  notaire 49
  planning 47
  pre-emption rights 48
  price 48
  SAFER 48
  sellers 46–9
  title, root of 47
  vacant possession, date of 49
strict settlements 252
subrogation 204
substitution
  donation-partage 297
  inheritance tax 347
  intestate succession 257–8
  legacies 320
  powers of attorney 187
  réserve 262
substitution fidéicommissaire 252–3
sub-tenancies 163–4, 177
succession *see* **inheritance law, intestate succession, wills**
succession, déclaration de 328, 345–6, 351
succession, droits de see **inheritance tax**
suitable alternative accommodation 168
surenchère 114, 117–18
surveyors 75, 133
surveys 32, 36, 45
surviving spouse 273–83
  absolute interests 275–6, 278, 280–1
  administration of estates 326
  adultery, children born in 279
  annuities 276, 277
  application of the rights of 276–8
  ascendants 275–6, 279–81
  bank accounts 326
  beneficiaries 307
  businesses, ownership of 278

capacity to inherit 273–4
children 275–6, 278–9
conversion 276
copyright 278
distribution 276
divorce 274, 279
domicile 273–4
donation entre époux 282–3
gifts *inter vivos* 282
governing law 274
héritiers 276–7
immeubles 273–4
inheritance law 233, 235, 239
inheritance tax 340, 344, 346–9
intellectual property 274, 278
intestacy 255, 257, 259, 273–9, 282
jouissance viagère, droit de 275
judicial separation 274, 279
leases 276–7
licence for life 277
life assurance 281
life interests 274–7, 279–82
maintenance 275, 277–8
marriage, existence of a 274
meubles 273–4
notaires 282
occupation, right of 276–7, 279
options 275–6, 280–1
parents 275–6, 279–81
partage 276
pension alimentaire 277–8
régime matrimonial 197–8, 283
relatives 274–5
réserve, la 261, 265, 273, 279
royalties 278
siblings 276
testate succession 278–82
usufruit 275–6
viager au logement, droit de 277
syndicat de copropriété 130, 132, 136–46

tax 209–22 *see also* **capital gains tax, double tax, inheritance tax, wealth tax**
  acquisition, on 209–11
  agricultural land 212–13, 215
  apportionment 214
  avoidance 94, 332–3
  beneficiaries 308
  business leases 183
  commission 210
  companies 216–17
  completion 62, 63
  concubinage 201–2, 214
  corporation tax 211, 222
  declarations 217
  development land 211
  disabled persons 216

tax (*cont.*):
 disposals, on 218–22
 domicile 214
 donation-partage 298
 droit départemental 210
 droits réels 216
 English law 268
 English trusts 250–2
 enregistrement 209–11
 evasion 26–7, 85, 87, 133–5, 216–17, 308
 exemptions 213–14
 foncière, taxe 212–13, 214
 forest 215
 furnished property 213–14
 gifts 208–9, 332–3
 habitation taxe d' 212, 213–14
 havens 268
 héritier présomptif 215
 immeubles détenus par les personnes
  morales, taxe sur les 216–17
 income tax 170, 208, 252
 inheritance, entrenched rights of 215
 insurance 212
 Land Registry 20, 22, 209–10
 land, unbuilt 212–13
 leases 218
 licences 214
 life interests 212–13, 214–15
 maintenance 212
 management 212, 217
 meubles 209–10
 mobile homes 213–14
 mortgages 127
 notaires 210
 occupation 212
 ownership, during 212–18
 pacte civile de solidarité 208
 partition of land 210
 planning 47
 plan, sales on 74
 pluripropriété 99–100
 rateable value 212
 régime matrimonial 200, 210
 reliefs 215–16
 représentant fiscal accredité 63, 220–2
 réserve 268
 residence 245–6, 251
 residential leases 170–1
 shareholders, UK 218
 Société civile d'attribution 213, 217–18
 Société civile immobilière 85, 87, 93–4, 211,
  213, 217–18, 222, 268–9
 stamp duty 57, 67, 109, 209–11, 232,
  251
 tax returns 221
 tiers déteneur 127–8
 time limits 213

 tourist 171
 transparence fiscale 217–18
 'under the table' transactions 26–7
 valuation 210, 212, 215
 VAT (*taxe sur la valeur ajoutée*) 211
 viager, sales *en* 109–10
 woodland 215
tenants in common 147
termites 46
testament, authentique 236, 266, 268–9, 292,
  315
testament, homologation du 237–8
testamentaire, exécuteur 301–3
tiers déteneur 127–8
time limits
 beneficiaries 307
 extension of 136
 Land Registry 22
 mortgages 121, 127
 plan, sales on 69
 service 136
 service charges, actions for unpaid 136
 tax 213
time-shares *see* ***pluripropriété***
title documents 67
titre d'adjudication 118
tontine*, ownership *en 154–8
 administration of estates 328
 aléa 154, 156–7
 chance, element of 154, 156–7
 concubinage 203
 conditions 154–5
 creditors 156
 death of co-owner 157, 269
 disadvantages 156
 divorce 156
 history of 154–5
 indivision, ownership *en* 156–7, 269
 inheritance, rules of entrenched 155–7
 inheritance tax 157–8, 269–70, 342
 joint tenancies 154–8
 loans 156
 marriage 269
 notaires 156–7, 269, 342
 precedent 367
 price 157
 release from liability, obtaining 269
 renunciation 367
 réserve 269–70
 survivorship 154–5, 158, 269–70
 use 155–8
 validity of 155
tourist tax 171
translations 37, 192–3, 355, 413–15
transparence fiscale 217–18
trees 14
trustees in bankruptcy 389–90

trusts *see* **English trusts**
tuteurs 224, 227–9, 254

'under the table' transactions 26–7, 41
undue influence 332
union libre see concubinage
unmarried partners *see concubinage*
use
  business leases 174–8, 181–2, 184
  copropriété 133, 177
  change of 176–8
  exclusive, payment for 149
  indivision, ownership *en* 149
  latent defects 43–4
  mixed 69, 181–2
  permitted 133
  prêt à usage 416–18
  professional 130–4, 160, 165, 174
  residential 69
  tontine 155–8
usufruit 16, 275–6
utilities 133

vacant possession 49
valuation
  business leases 182–3
  compensation 182–3
  compromis de vente 41
  donation-partage 297
  inheritance tax 344, 345
  life interests 344
  réserve 263–4, 296
  sale of land 32, 36
  tax 210, 212, 215
  wealth tax 351
VAT 211
vendeur, privilège de 22
venir, donations de biens à 298–9
vente, acte de see acte de vente
vente, compromis de see compromis de vente
vente, mandat de 28, 29, 30
vente, promesse de see promesse de vente
vente, terme à 69–70, 78–81
viager, **sales** *en* 105–10
  annuities 105, 106–10
  bouquet 106–7
  capital gains tax 109
  capital, release of 105
  chance, contracts of 105–10
  consideration 106–7
  créditrentier 107–10
  débitrentier 107–10
  domicile 106
  gaming contracts 106
  indexation 108
  inheritance rights, entrenched 105–6
  inheritance tax 106, 270

  insurance contracts 106
  joint and survivor interest, sale subject to
    105–10
  lease for life 107
  libre 105
  licence to occupy 107
  lump sum *see bouquet*
  nature of transactions 106
  occupé 105, 107
  parties, rights and liabilities of 108–9
  rebuilding 109
  réserve 270
  sale of land 19
  stamp duty 109
  tax 109–10
  wealth tax 110
vices cachés see also **latent defects**

warranties 42
Washington Convention on International
    Wills 1973 289–90, 292
wealth tax 214–16, 351–2
  age of donor 352
  ascendants 351
  children 352
  concubinage 201
  delivery, manual 351
  donations-partages 351
  double tax conventions 351
  English trusts 250
  exemptions 352
  grandparents 351
  indivision, ownership *en* 352
  inheritance tax 351–2
  instalments 352
  life interest, surrender of 352
  nil rate band 351
  pacte civile de solidarité 351–2
  séparation de biens 352
  siblings 351
  spouses 351–2
  rates 351
  reliefs 351–2
  residence 245
  valuation 351
  viager, sales *en* 110
wills 285–94
  accept legacies, capacity to 229–30
  administration of estates 293–4, 301, 324–5,
    327
  affidavits of French law 398–9
  agreements to make 237
  authentique 236, 286, 288–9, 292,
    315
  Basle Convention on the Establishment of a
    Scheme of Registration of Wills 1972
    292

wills (*cont.*):
  beneficiaries 307
  biens à venir, donations de 298
  capacity 228–30
  charges 254, 291
  charities and associations, acceptance by 229–30
  children 224
  codicils 293
  commorientes 228
  concubinage 202
  Conseil supérieur du Notariat 292
  date of 286–7
  deaf testators 289
  declarations of English law as to validity of 391
  destruction 287, 291
  dispute, conditions not to 319
  divorce 291
  domicile 292
  donation entre époux 282–3, 286, 287
  drafting 235–6, 288, 292–3
  dumb, persons who are 288–9
  English, French wills drawn in 398–9
  English law 230, 285, 291–4
  English trusts 294
  exclusions 229
  exécuteur testamentaire 301
  execution of 288–9, 293
  executors 236
  expenses 294
  forfeiture 291
  forms of 286, 288
  formalities 288
  freedom of testamentary disposition 235
  gifts *inter vivos* 285, 331, 335–6
  grants of representation 398–9
  Hague Convention abolishing the Requirement of Legislation for Foreign Public Documents 1961 293–4
  handwritten 236, 285, 287–90, 293, 315
  holograph wills 287–8, 336, 392
  immeubles 293
  indignité, régime de l' 229
  inheritance rights, entrenched 285
  inheritance tax 345–6
  international 236, 286, 289–90, 393–4
  intestacy 229
  joint wills 290
  judicial separation 291
  language 290, 292–4
  legacies 301, 307, 317–21
  légataire à titre universel 301, 307
  légataire universel 301, 307

  loss of 287
  marriage 291
  medical treatment, persons involved in 229–30
  ministers of religion 229
  mort civile, la 228–9
  mystique 236, 286, 289, 290, 315
  non-French wills 292–4
  notaires 228, 236–7, 285, 288–90, 292–4
  precedents 355, 392–4
    affidavits of French law 397–8
    declarations of English law as to validity of 391
    English, French wills drawn in 397–8
    grants of representation 397–8
    holograph 392
    international 393–4
    réserve 393
  Principal Probate Registry in London 289–90
  prisoners 228–9
  probate procedure, English 294
  proving a 237, 286–7
  purpose of 235
  register of 236–7
  registration of 292, 327
  réserve, la 234, 262, 285, 294, 393
  revocation 290–2
    expresse 290
    partial 291–2
    tacite 291–2
    total 291–2
  saisine 314, 315
  searches 292, 314
  signatures 286, 290
  substitution fidéicommissaire 252–3
  tuteurs, exclusion of 229
  types of 236–7, 286
  validity, requirements for 289, 293–4
  Washington Convention on International Wills 1973 289–90, 292
  witnesses 286, 287–90, 327
  writing, in 290
winding up 230, 303
witnesses
  acte de notoriété après décès 327
  wills 286, 287–90, 327
woodlands 215, 341
works
  business leases 174
  copropriété 132–3
  flats 62
  possession, for 174
  voting on 62